EA

birkhauser
basel

EVENTS

EA

events: situating the temporary

E V
E N
T S

E V E N T S

herman verkerk/event– architectuur

EA

birkhäuser basel

E V E N T S

herman verkerk/event-architectuur

EA

birkhäuser basel

EA

events: situating the temporary

E

V E

N T S

Material

white perforated board

Material
cork
foam

industrial felt

Material

Material

foam

fiber fabrics

Material

Material

wood panels

marmoleum

Material

mirror tile

Material

wood

Material

fluorescent tube light

Material

bubble wrap

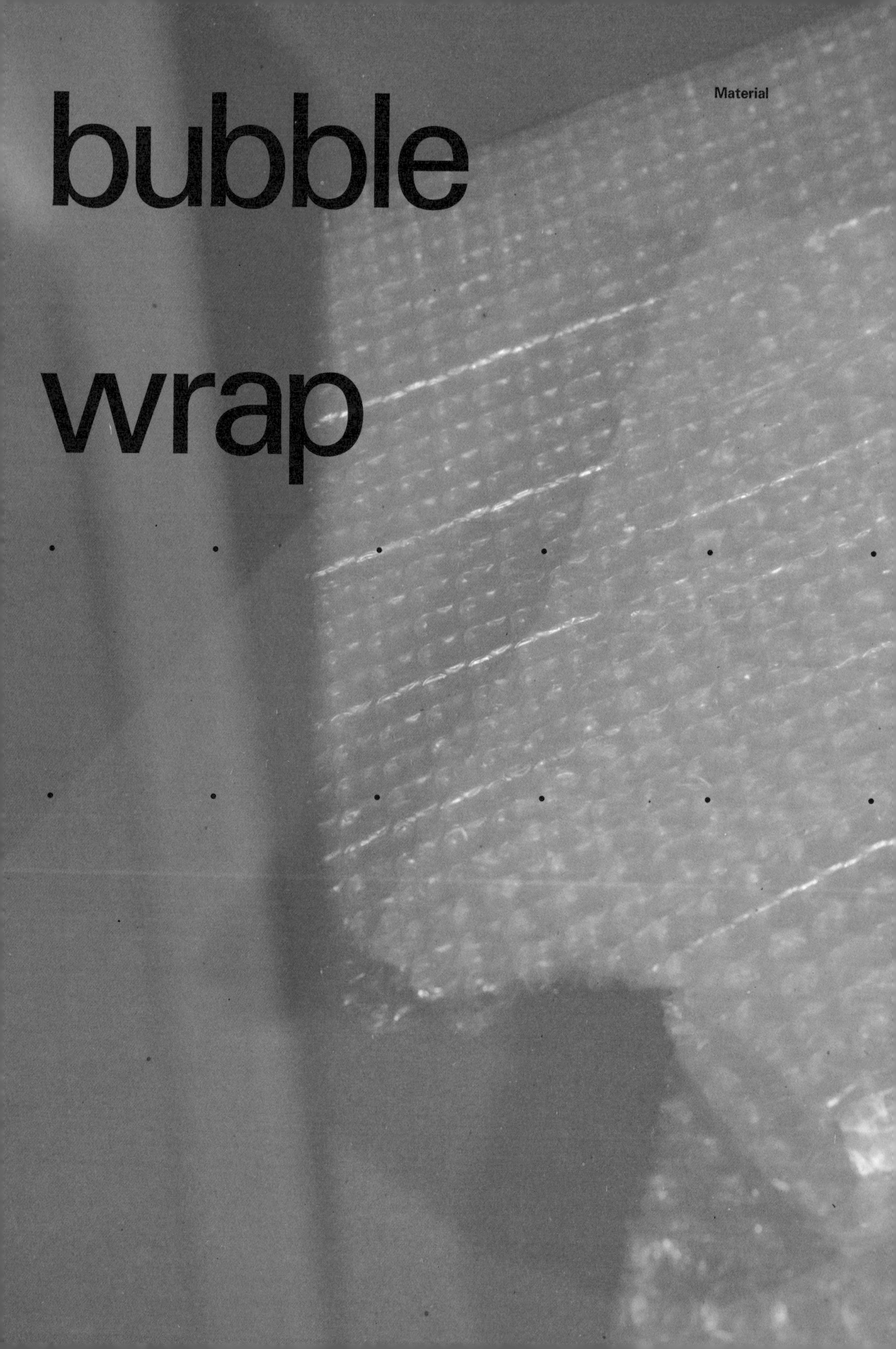

Material

stucanet

For GB

0

events: situating the temporary – preface

Design interventions by EventArchitectuur 1990–2015

Wouldn't it be nice to have a voice-over starting to speak to you, now that you have opened this book? A calming voice, speaking English with a posh accent, that would grab your attention and guide you through the episodes of this coincidently enormously corpulent book. Like a manifestation of memory, almost like a prompter, it would create the impression that there was always a hypertext, a reason, an anecdote, logic, or inspiration that triggered the production of the content of this book, hovering over and commenting on the different shifts and stages that have shaped a body of work that defies any singular interpretation. A voice that would be soothing and understanding, and understandable, one that would be humane and could make sense of the string of fragments that are laid out in front of you. It would explain why this book is dedicated to the temporary, and how it attempts to find a place for temporary constructions in contemporary history.

He knew he was living in the here and now. But he also had a wild imagination. Not that the things around him would change into other substances, or that he would see ghosts. But he liked that the spatial and material qualities of his surroundings could make him act in a specific way. To squeeze, stroke, and feel pressure on his skin. He liked being manipulated by materials and structures, and made up all kinds of rules with which to interact with the material world. To play games with white and gray tiles, zigzag between the white striping on the road.

Basically, the voice-over would tell you that the book seeks to demonstrate the qualities of the temporary in architecture. That it is actually part of the development of cultural production, which is sometimes associated with different disciplines, like art, design, or performance. And it seeks to show how the temporary might be the place where contemporary architecture is linked to creative and form-finding new realities (proposals, utopias, dystopias, and fantasies).

O

He had an interest in how ideas came into being, how associations came about, and how to implement these into existing surroundings. It was a juvenile recklessness where the surroundings would be interpreted as décors for actions, reenacting episodes from historical and contemporary examples in the literary genres that have developed over time, like travelers' tales, science fiction, detective stories, and epics, but also formats from TV series and cartoons.

Events: Situating the Temporary
Page 26

In this staging, he felt a love for the existing, the things he found when he temporarily undertook something somewhere. His childhood memories of locations that had been appropriated and transformed to play games and perform reenactments triggered his fantasy and imagination. His interpretation of the existing was a form of fabrication, of weaving together elements to create the new.

So with the temporary as a guiding principle, the voice-over would continue, the book proposes a connection between the development of a body of work over twenty-five years, infused with a certain vibe that was in the air during any (arbitrary) five-year period. The voice-over would explain that the natural and straightforward connection with the zeitgeist led to the development of a method that could continue over time, yet always in a different form. The qualities of the temporary were researched in each of these five-year periods, connecting the temporary to the narrative, the staging, the critical, the experiential, and the merging.

It would speak of research trajectories that were all deeply concerned to promote improvisation, with the underlying motivation to act as an incentivizer and catalyzer, to make a proposition, not the product; always envisaging rewriting a play while using the same fixed setting: the existing fabric.

These stages formed an interesting list:
The two conifers standing close together in the backyard forming an entrance.
The place underneath the table.
The daybed as an island.
The backrest of the daybed used to display the crochet needles for spool knitting.
In bed, underneath the sheets, a library.
The windows of the linen cupboard and the internal windows in the house used as mirrors.
In mother's bed, listening to the radio.
The bath and the frosted mirror.
The foul smell of the adolescent brother's den.

The crazy whim of the sister's decision to sleep in the attic, where you could only crawl.
The rhythm of the click-clack of the Bakelite light switch.
The pale yellow curtains that the light still shines through at ten o'clock in the evening.
The swing in the opening of the shed's door.
Dad's shed, with its detailed classification of tools and materials.
Outside, the forest, with the asylum and the bunkers from the war; the pergola with roses and the mirroring pond, the big water, the channels, the city, the underworld along the canals.

The voice-over would talk about the temporary not being supposed to belong to architecture, because transformation would be immanent and this ephemerality was at variance with the qualities of architecture. But if we admit that, eventually, transformation is permanent, the voice-over would ponder, ephemerality could also be one of architecture's qualities. Its time-based aspect would be emphasized.

While spending five years in architectural education, he became fascinated with the analytical approach. Comparing constructions, structures, patterns, and programs, the stories of coming into being, the narrative of the constructions themselves, whether measuring and copying plans and sections, or rescaling and remodeling them into new guises and constellations. Urban design and landscape architecture helped one to understand how to build toolboxes for design; not to design in detail, but to design a system or structure, in which variations and subplots could have their place. And because of the closeness of the analytical to the transformational, analysis provided a shortcut from the physical nature of architecture, art, and design into other fields, such as dance, film, theater, and music, where storytelling and narrative, the symbolic and the suggestive, were alive on a more immaterial level. Anything could become a composition, a choreography, a score.

The voice-over would continue to talk about the five distinct episodes that manifested themselves during EventArchitectuur's twenty-five years of practice; periods that were all driven by one question concerning the discipline of architecture, which had undergone so many developments in such a short time. The question was reformulated several times, each time in a different way, depending on the spirit of the time. The question was whether architecture could be seen as a cultural phenomenon and, if it could, how it would express this cultural agenda in the here and now, from 1990 to 2015. The arbitrary five-year periods make sense, first of all, in the development of the work of EventArchitectuur. Of course, the development of

0

EventArchitectuur is not an isolated entity, but reflects the spirit of the time. This permanent interaction and cross-fertilization between context and work should give the reader the chance to relive a certain period, and perhaps to elaborate on the "as found" aspect; not in the literal, physical sense, but in the sense of mind-sets, politics, and other works and reflections on these episodes. In this way, the works acquire an essayistic quality, not only with regard to the specific topics, but also to capturing the ingredients that make up the time and place.

Events: Situating the Temporary
Page 28

1990–1995 The first research period investigated the question by exploring the tools with which architecture defines spaces and events without actually being materialized.

The Narrative
He noticed how the notations and communications (2D and 3D drawings, 3D animation, models, and photographs and movies of the model) of architecture could evoke whole worlds of experience and create scenarios like settings and stagings of ordinary life, without actually being built. And he saw how this "paper architecture" could address issues about the cultural and social role of architecture, as well as program social urgencies.

1995–2000 The second take on the question investigated the relationship between architecture and time-based events.

The Temporary
Once he had been asked to design a fashion show, and had introduced a spatial and time-based quality to the medium. He was asked to do it again, this time also directing the show. This led to a keen interest in temporary constructions of reality, almost like a 3D sketchbook, giving contours and outlines, hints for interpretation, redefining the value of the ephemeral. Together with a respected designer, he developed a way to create these fleeting moments from frugal materials and everyday objects.

2000–2005 The third take on the question delved into the relation between architecture and the great outdoors. The focus was on the "as found," going outside and starting over.

The Critical
Walking in the fields of Friesland, he found the freedom and expansive liberty to experience space and time. And he found a craving for improvisation, using the "as found" and the 1:1 model as a method for critically countering the digitized perfection of architectural production. He reconnected with a good friend and architect with a similar craving, and

they traveled through the Dutch landscape while making projects together.

2005–2010 The fourth take on the question addressed how architecture deals with low and high culture, how luxury and comfort are being redefined by new technologies and economics.

The Experiential
Definitions of luxury and comfort, two elements previously ignored, started to fascinate him. He came across some interesting clients who redefined the qualities of luxury and comfort in a way that made him see how high and low culture shared a common interest in the experiential. He found a perfect ally to develop models for this experiential design.

2010–2015 The fifth take on the question relates the generic to the specific, the contemplative to the spectacle, the cultural to the commercial.

The Convergence
In the wake and at the height of the financial crisis, reorganization of production processes became paramount, especially in a field where huge spaces were supposed to be (re-)used and transformed into biennial venues and temporary museums. He started to look at modular design as a way to tackle this challenge. He and his ally used prefabrication and toolbox design, and connected these to on-site improvisations and finishings. With three new allies, he experimented with the convergence between a museum and a retail space.

To place the work of EventArchitectuur in the midst of the conversations, reflections, and analyses of its own work and that of other makers, other tendencies, and reflections on the time frames of the rhythm of five-year cultural shifts, the voice-over would state that it gives this book the quality of an open narrative exhibition model, a display where the temporary constellations become permanent in their interactive and interrelating existence as propositions. To see how the demands and agenda from the cultural field and individual fascinations and references overlap, and to read the qualities and specifics of what Giedion called *Space, Time and Architecture*, and Tschumi rephrased as *Space, Event, Movement*.

One thing that would be paramount while introducing the content of the book, the voice-over would stress, is how all of these efforts were a matter of teamwork: the assembling of people and means for the creation of a fleeting moment of clarity or suspense. By showing how layered and detailed things are, not measured by the longevity or brevity of their existence. By showing how, in compressing and concentrating material and mental energy, one could physically experience certain bundles of knowledge at a specific moment in time and in a specific place.

So why did he come to make these temporary architectural constructions?

Dostoyevsky: "Why do we have a mind if not to get our own way?"

Gratitude and honor to Bernard Tschumi, who taught that there is no possibility of bringing together the logic and systems of use and space. They are meant to have a discrepancy, a disjunction, as he calls it. And to Andrei Tarkovsky, who taught how to plan things down to the finest detail and to "construct" the eloquence of a fleeting moment. Who delved into his own childhood for images and stories and connected these to the myths and stories of our times. And finally to Guus Beumer, who taught the important lesson inspired by the John Cassavetes movie, *Love Streams*: that it is not only love that streams; life itself streams, and it makes no sense to try to capture or fix a certain truth. We thrive on temporary moments of insight.

significance and intention

The discourse on the role of the temporary in architecture as a place for creative production, research, and in-depth study is still quite young. Moreover, the discourse, if it exists at all, mainly takes place within separate disciplines, like design, the arts, sociology, philosophy, and architecture. EventArchitectuur would like to use its experience and quest for affinities within these disciplines to come to a fruitful exchange of knowledge in this hybrid field of practice. Cross-sectorial collaboration and research is actually the key to understanding its possibilities and effects.

This publication is an excellent chance to reflect on the practice from a theoretical angle with curators and theorists, and also to give a voice to former collaborators and professionals that have worked together with EventArchitectuur over the course of many years. It is this common interest that EventArchitectuur wishes to share with its readers, giving insights into the transformations of the temporary in architecture through their way of thinking and working over a twenty-five-year practice.

0

Events: Situating the Temporary
Page 32

bernard
tschumi

seeking for architecture

A conversation with Bernard Tschumi

Klaske Havik, Véronique Patteeuw, Herman Verkerk

When speaking of architecture and events, of temporality and of experimentation at the borders of the discipline, the name of architect Bernard Tschumi immediately comes to mind. Exploring architectural experience and representation since the early 1970s, through texts as well as – in a later stage – built projects, Tschumi has inspired many architects and authors. His work, in that sense, has provided a basis for the investigations and projects in this publication. In December 2015, we met with Tschumi in Amsterdam to discuss his take on the very themes of this book: narrative, critical models, temporary architecture, experience, and the role of the architect within a culture of convergence.

1. Narrative

H/P/V: The narrative is an important method in your architectural work, particularly in your teaching and in some theoretical projects, such as *The Manhattan Transcripts* (1976–1981). Narrative is a term closely tied to literature and other forms of storytelling, such as cinema. It can be defined as the way a story unfolds in space and time. Narrative is thus both spatial and temporal. Narrative, as a tool for architectural design, can indeed structure a sequence of actions in various ways. You stated that "the unfolding of events in a literary context inevitably suggested parallels to the unfolding of events in architecture."[1] In your work, particularly in *The Manhattan Transcripts*, narrative is taken as a tool to investigate the relation between spaces, movements, and events. It explicitly departs from an action: an action taking place in a particular space that causes the narrative to unfold, and thereby changes the way spaces "behave" or are perceived. This tool worked in an investigative sense: it allowed space, time, and action (or rather space, movement, and event) to be brought together, and showed their interactivity. Hence narrative, in this case, was a tool for exploration. How would you look back on the narrative as a tool for exploration?

1 Bernard Tschumi, "Spaces and Events," *Architecture and Disjunction* (Cambridge, MA: The MIT Press, 1994), 146.

O

Events: Situating the Temporary
Page 34

T: I would be very careful with the word "narrative." I don't believe that architecture tells stories. Many architects have argued that you could tell stories with architecture. That was never my goal; my intention was rather to see how whatever happens in a space is intricately related to the space itself. My quest has been to examine the nature of the interaction, of that relationship between "space" and "event." And, as you said correctly, it happens in time. Hence, we are dealing with sequences, since time unfolds in space. And as soon as you acknowledge this, it forces you to look at other areas of knowledge that use time as a way to document things that happen. Of course, literature and film are among the primary ones. The key issue was to investigate things that happen in space. I first wondered whether we should simply catalogue what is normally thought of as the standard use of spatial sequences. This seemed interesting, but predictable. Instead, I felt I had to go into things that were not normally documented in a typical architectural way. In other words, addressing space and what happens in it – and, at the same time, movement and space.

Retrospectively, I realize that when I started with *The Manhattan Transcripts*, I had no idea where I was going. By the time I had finished the first episode, I began to understand that it led to a kind of coherence. By the time I was at the fourth episode, I knew exactly what I was doing. So *The Manhattan Transcripts*, as a work, was simultaneously an exploration and a research, which at the beginning was totally intuitive and at the end very precise. It had become an argument, and its structure of four episodes was essentially a part of that. There could not have been a fifth episode.

In *The Manhattan Transcripts*, I used narrative in the sense of giving a thread to the story. That thread becomes more tenuous in the third episode, "The Fall": the argument there is about space and the movement of the body, either horizontally or vertically, and nothing else. Then, the last episode becomes a series of moments that are totally disconnected. The drawings in that episode are tools for exploring the nature of different types of movement, their interaction or collision with spaces or spatial types. This extends until the moment when space and movement become interchangeable, when space and movement coincide. You don't know which is which. In the work of an architect, there are plenty of times when space and movement are indistinguishable: "Is it the ramp that shapes the movement or the movement that shapes the ramp?" I am still applying this to my current projects.

H/P/V: To what extent was it important that *The Manhattan Transcripts* were related to New York? Was it New York that gave the method, or was it an exploration of certain themes that were applied to the context of the city of New York?

T: After all these years, New York still continues to fascinate me. The project derived from my immediate presence there, my very subjective fascination for the city. I used four different archetypes for each of the four pieces: the park, the street, the tower, and the block. I intentionally did this as a way of anchoring the project in existing urban categories, thereby framing it. Within that framework, the logic of the investigation could be pushed to an extreme.

Especially for the first two episodes, I was spending a lot of time in Central Park, or walking up and down 42nd Street. I was aware of my bodily perception and documenting it. I still have the Polaroid shots of every small moment encountered along the street. But, as I said, by the third episode, I felt I knew what I was doing and, amusingly, the block that I used in the final episode isn't real, but rather is an architectural fiction. It is based in New York, but derived from a photograph – a fragment of a New York block. I have often argued that much of our knowledge about architectural history and precedents is essentially photographic, presented as a series of two-dimensional images. Frames are important throughout the *Transcripts*, but especially for that final episode. The whole episode is drawn from inside out, rather than outside in. You never see what the block looks like from the outside.

At that time, I was also making the *Screenplays*, based on excerpts from films. I found extraordinary film books from the Strand, a secondhand bookstore in New York. You could dissect films like *Psycho*, *The Maltese Falcon*, or *Frankenstein*, frame by frame. I would select some of those frames and rearrange them. This made me realize that architecture, literature, and film have something in common – the ability to be combined and recombined. The ideas of combination and permutation fascinated me. Take, for example, a short chapter in a book by Roland Barthes called *Sade, Fourier, Loyola* (1971). Barthes talks of the *Marquis de Sade* as the master of permutation because he describes every possible sexual, incestuous, and religious permutation he can think of. At one moment, Barthes says that all creation is about permutation.

H/P/V: We are moving naturally from the narrative as a tool of investigation toward the narrative as an experimental design tool. When looking back at some of your work, we were interested in the moments when you've used stories or fragments of literary texts in your teaching at the AA as a kind of generator for design.

0

Many of the stories used in these exercises raised questions of program, and of the possible conflicts between spaces and their use: "pole vaulting in the chapel, bicycling in the laundromat, sky diving in the elevator shaft..."[2] Here, rather than using narrative as a structuring mechanism, it seems that the imaginative power of fiction is at stake. It seems that confronting spaces with fictional programs derived from literary stories, while using stories as a base for architectural projects, also allowed the irrational, the madness, the "folie" to enter.

Events: Situating the Temporary
Page 36

2
Ibid.,145.

T: Let's start with bouncing against literary texts, which indeed offer a variety of different structures and potentials. Through working in this way, I began to realize that architectural programs are rarely determined from so-called functional needs, but rather mostly for social and cultural reasons. I asked myself, why don't I start with culture itself? So I began to look for short stories as a point of departure for teaching. First, at the AA, my students and I did three or four sessions experimenting with texts by Jorge Luis Borges, Italo Calvino, Hermann Hesse, and James Joyce. At Princeton, I used a text by Edgar Allan Poe. Each of the stories came with different characters. Sometimes they had a direct correlation with architectural themes, and sometimes they did not. The more interesting ones, frankly, were those without such correlations. Joyce is pretty impenetrable, so you have to translate it in some way. That's where architecture came in, with its own logic. You have to find out where the logic of words and the logic of buildings have something to do with one another, as well as where they differ.

Spatial sequences have always existed, for example, in religious architecture, or ancient Egyptian temples. They provide a narrative of sorts. But when we arrive at the more contemporary situation of having complete social, cultural, and political fragmentation, with no correlation between cause and effect, then architecture becomes quite a challenge.

H/P/V: Is the narrative as tool related to the specific time frame of the 1970s? Was it related to semiology at that moment of investigation in literature; to the idea of deconstruction of the text in order to reconstruct a new architecture?

T: I was not really into semiology. Similarly, the word "deconstruction" has been so overused, and mostly misused, while it had more to do with what I would call questioning and dismantling. The whole history of architecture is filled with clichés. So you try to dismantle it, hoping to find something else. What interested me in Derrida's deconstruction was its questioning of some of these preconceived ideas.

But you are right about the fact that there was a time when the critic was just as much a writer, philosopher, or historian. Think of Barthes or Foucault. Different disciplines were essentially merging, and yet used to question conventional literary values. There was the same questioning in film – for example, in Jean-Luc Godard as a critic addressing the issue of montage – or in art, with Robert Smithson's writings constituting an important part of his art. Inevitably, the same type of questioning had to happen in architecture. The seventies were probably a time that was substantially more "investigative" than the one we are in today.

2. Critical models

H/P/V: A lot of your work is driven by a critical attitude to the superficial mainstream architecture, as well as the all-too-theoretical "academization," focused on linguistics and semiotics in an extremely abstract way.[3] Your written work can be seen as a constant questioning of conventions. The *Advertisements for Architecture* (1976–1978) is a well-known example of your early work in which you take a critical stance toward ways architecture was looked upon. We also think of texts such as "Architecture and Transgression" and "Violence of Architecture." Can we see these (theoretical) projects as attempts to develop critical models early in your career?

T: As a practicing architect who actually builds, I face such conventions again and again. Let me give you an example. I'm currently working on a project that raises this fundamental question of conventions and received ideas. The people who wrote the program and who will use the future building are correctly obsessed with the idea that teaching and research have to interact with one another. In my own way, I agree one hundred percent, and will develop that program in order to bring the two together architecturally, in order to encourage that interaction. But then, curiously, there is a moment when the client body forgets it all, and all they want to see are images, renderings; all they want to know is what the facade will look like. And by a strange metamorphosis, they become totally and subjectively image-oriented without prioritizing what they wanted and needed at the beginning. This happens again and again in architecture. What we, as architects, have done, or perhaps the media, is to brainwash society to somehow believe that what architecture looks like is more important than what it does.

Now, to get back to text as a critical model, Susan Sontag once said, "I write in order to find out what I think." Generally, the texts I write start with a commission: someone asks me to write a text or an article. These texts are extremely important for me. They

3
"If most of architecture has become surface, applied decoration, superficiality, paper architecture... how can architecture remain a means by which society explores new territories, develops new knowledge?" See Bernard Tschumi, "Six Concepts," *Architecture and Disjunction* (Cambridge, MA: The MIT Press, 1994), 236–237.

Events: Situating the Temporary
Page 38

allow me to take a certain distance vis-à-vis my design work, while simultaneously informing it.

H/P/V: Most often in the case of a text there is no client, no deadline, no budget. Is the text therefore giving you another kind of opportunity, a space where you can be more free, where you can reflect more freely on what you are doing?

T: There are two types of texts. If I write while I'm working on an architectural project, I will use the medium of the text in order to better understand some of the issues I am dealing with in the project. But the earlier texts that you are referring to, like those in *Architecture and Disjunction*, were more remote or removed from actual projects. I was not building at that time. Only in the pieces on the Parc de la Villette, the text and the architecture were closely intermingled; you could say they were both text and project, simultaneously. But La Villette is a complex story, because I was really learning about architecture at the same time. I had never designed a project that was intended to be built before, with all the technical, legal, or political constraints.

H/P/V: We spoke of texts forming a critical distance to your work, and texts as critical models or reactions to something. On the other hand, architectural projects can also work critically toward society and toward the profession. Do you need to be aggressive or provocative to be critical?

T: I recently had a client who asked me whether I would ever do or design things with a secret intent. I told him, "No, I would possibly have an evil intent, but in all honesty I would have to tell the client." If you write about theory, your only responsibility is toward theory. If you build, you have many responsibilities toward others, and you are not working entirely for yourself anymore. To design and build something critically is possible, but the very fact that it is built means that it not only needs to be legally approved by others, but also becomes part of other people's personal experiences.

H/P/V: Couldn't the power of the critical model be that it has this ability to convince people of a certain statement? In that sense, the project of the Parc de la Villette can be seen as a critique of the idea of pre-programming or pre-defining people's actions and movements.

T: The Parc de la Villette involved an amazing set of circumstances. What made it possible is that very few people in that process had any idea of what they were doing. And that's probably an advantage for the architect.

3. The Temporary

H/P/V: Parc de la Villette, Paris (1982–1998), is a prominent example of your aim for architecture to create conditions for events, conditions for different and unexpected uses. In creating a system of planes, lines and dots, you have conceived a complex layering of meeting points between these layers, thereby opening the park to unforeseen, unprogrammed events. This means that it deliberately gives a role to time and temporality.

T: We recently published a book on La Villette with original competition drawings in which the concept is explained sequentially. In a way, La Villette comes directly out of *The Manhattan Transcripts*. It uses similar devices, including the superposition of multiple systems that have nothing to do with traditional landscape design. Even the points (the *folies*) come from other experiments, such as *Joyce's Garden*. It is indeed very much about time; you are absolutely correct. I recently discovered incredible early drawings where we measured not only the time to go from A to B, but also the time you would stay inside each *folie*, depending on what you were doing. The time factor was clearly spelled out.

H/P/V: Did you study how it worked afterward? Did you observe how people used it?

T: Yes, I've been there many times since we designed it. But I have to say that I haven't documented it in the way it should be documented.

H/P/V: Do people in the park use the *folies* in a completely different way than you imagined? Were rituals established, even?

T: From day one onwards. The first phase had just been completed. The park was not yet open to the public, but the machines had gone. I went there by myself on a Saturday, and I heard this huge noise of birds, like in the Hitchcock movie. Suddenly the birds had arrived, where there had been no birds before. The birds were the first visitors. Before the park opened, we imagined all kinds of different activities that might happen, and do you know what? Among the thousands of people, there were twelve older men playing *pétanque*. I had never, ever thought of that. But that was all part of the unexpected that we had hoped for. The improvised rituals were quite extraordinary: drummers from a variety of ethnic groups started to come, performing all along the cinematic promenade, each occupying one segment of the sequence of gardens spontaneously. There was also a place where someone was selling pot.

O

Events: Situating the Temporary
Page 40

My argument was that, historically, much of nature is a human fabrication. So I made the park, as the plane of reference, absolutely flat. We used the technology of soccer fields. I knew that people would come and play with a soccer ball, but I never thought there would be organized teams with cleats. They destroyed the grass and were kicked out. You know, there were these kinds of "emergences," together with summer film festivals, when the park was filled with deck chairs. Or hundreds of political photographs hung along the covered galleries for an entire week.

H/P/V: You seem to provide conditions for uncertainty to happen.

T: That's right – and it's really important. But under no circumstances do I design actual events. I try to design the conditions for events. That's very, very different.

H/P/V: To what extent do you allow such uncertainty or chance in a design process? In other words, do you search for chance in the outcome, or also within the process of design itself?

T: The best example is, again, the Parc de la Villette. I used the random idea of Duchamp's loose threads for *3 Standard Stoppages* for the curvilinear cinematic promenade. Once you have established the dimensions of the regular point grid, it never changes. But with the random curve, you cannot resist changing it afterward, according to new functional or technical constraints. So you realize that something that is arbitrary or random is more fragile, impermanent, because you or others can always change it, while other decisions that seem to involve rigid, authoritarian decision-making are actually more generative in the long run.

H/P/V: But you could try to trigger the use of the architecture in motion?

T: Exactly. And that's the most interesting kind.

H/P/V: This might be at stake at the Video Pavilion in Groningen. With its oblique floor, the pavilion is about instability; it forces people to move. Was that specifically to "disturb" the visitor of the pavilion?

T: You can read it as a critical model, as something that challenges what we expect of architecture. The pavilion was originally meant to show music videos. It has now been twenty-five years since we first built it. Video screen technology was not as luminous then as today, and we knew that the videos would be mostly seen at night. I intentionally wanted people to not quite keep their balance as they would go up the tilted floor, because I was aware that the video images would be reflected on the glazing. It was hard to distinguish between reality and its reflection; everything was a game of inversions. The pavilion was initially supposed to be enclosed and opaque. But we intentionally made it the opposite, using a lot of transparent glass. Structurally, the walls and the roof are entirely made out of glass, including the beams and the vertical supports. We wanted to give the place a public and urban presence.

H/P/V: Last October, a celebration took place in Groningen on the occasion of the Video Pavilion's twenty-five years of existence. You were there, and your tilted glass pavilion is still standing, while it was intended as a temporary project. How did you look upon this project when revisiting it after twenty-five years?

T: Indeed, the pavilion was meant to be temporary. We were given a lot of freedom as architects, most likely because it was to be temporary. What is amazing is how people in Groningen have adopted it. It's incredibly well maintained; it's even cleaner than when it was new. And there are many art installations in it that are really great.

H/P/V: Can we relate these two themes: the critical model and the temporary? Does the temporary allow you to be more critical?

T: No question about that! You know, if an architect builds anything that stands there for less than a year, it sometimes doesn't need a building permit; many questions are not going to be asked. So the temporary facilities can allow you to do unexpected things. It's like street theater: if I design a conventional theater in the middle of a town, and millions of euros are needed to build it, I will be under constant scrutiny. If I improvise something cheap and temporary, less so.

H/P/V: Did you do more temporary projects?

T: Relatively few, except in the very early days. The constructions – the so-called 20th-Century Follies – that started in New York in the late seventies were all temporary pavilions. There are plenty of funny stories. I built the first two projects with my own hands, with plywood, nails, and a hammer. They were part of what the art scene then called "site-specific installations." One was even built in the Netherlands, in Middelburg. And then there were some that were indeed for Kassel, at *documenta*. In the latter case, I started out with a photograph from the Kassel town hall, which was then being cut up and reassembled to generate a series of constructions. Each of these installations was an exploration; they were not about use. They were investigations from an architectural viewpoint. In a way, they were a built counterpoint to *The Manhattan Transcripts*, which were intended to remain on paper. The 20th-Century Follies were all meant to be built in materials, space, and time.

H/P/V: They were made slightly earlier than the period in which you were working on the La Villette competition, right?

Events: Situating the Temporary
Page 42

T: Definitely earlier. The first one was built in 1979. But they were not sculptures. I ironically called them "follies." It is very likely that I used the word *folie* (with one "l," as in French) at La Villette because I had already worked on these 20th-Century Follies.

H/P/V: The last question on temporary architecture is about exhibition as a specific kind of temporal architecture. For instance, did you yourself design the exhibition about your work in the Centre Pompidou?

T: Yes. The five themes in the exhibition correspond to the five chapters in my book, *Red is Not a Color*, as well as in the Pompidou catalogue. There was one constraint: the 1,100-square-meter exhibition space of the Centre Pompidou had only one wall. The other walls are glass, so we had to construct our own walls, display the work horizontally on tables, or suspend it. Suspension was not allowed. We tested a number of different concepts. We designed many variations of the exhibition, each with a different logic.

4. Experience

H/P/V: Especially in the museum world, we find more and more demands for entertainment and spectacle for the masses, experiences imposed by architectural operations guiding visitors. This requires a different attitude for the architect. We have the impression you do not so much propose to the visitor an immersion in a new world, but rather push him into an active role in an unstable environment.

T: Leading the visitor is a very risky issue. Thirty-five years later, the people who run the Parc de La Villette say, "People always get lost!" and "Can't we add a wayfinding system?" Then they hire graphic designers to do signage. But it never works. The park has a completely different logic.

H/P/V: Creating a human experience can be done in different ways. In your work, movement and sequence are crucial. For example, at the Acropolis Museum in Athens (2001–2009), the aspects of movement and sequence are important conceptual tools enhancing the architectural experience.

T: The photographs do not even begin to show it! I knew I wanted to have the Parthenon Frieze on the top floor, in full view of the Parthenon. The question steering the design thus became how to get there. The design involves the superposition of three different parts. It was based on the constraints of the site itself, taking into account the fact that the existing archaeological ruins, the city grid, and the Parthenon each have their own orientation. I rotated the glass gallery on top so that it would be oriented exactly east-west, like the Parthenon. This operation gives it a certain independence in relation to the other two layers. The device of superimposition that I have used in a number of projects was certainly important here. However, it was the result of the constraints of the site, as I read them. That was my conceptual interpretation.

We were one of the very few of the fifteen competitors who restored the continuity of the frieze and its narrative. For me, that was really very important – and it provided a link between my early work and more recent work. In a way, the frieze and the thirty-two-foot-long, or eleven-meter, drawing of *The Manhattan Transcripts* represent the same way of thinking. It was only when I did the Acropolis Museum project that I discovered this parallel.

H/P/V: The schemes and drawings for the building show the interest you have long had in cinematographic elements. Would it be fair to say that this cinematographic interest provides a practical tool to steer the experiential sequences a building might offer its visitors?

T: The *Alexander Nevsky* notation by Eisenstein had an enormous influence on my early work. But I had never seen the film. Only when I finally saw it while working on the Acropolis Museum did I discover that, unbelievably, Eisenstein had used the Parthenon Frieze as his script for the battle sequence in *Alexander Nevsky*. That blew my mind. Then I did some research. I knew the famous text that Eisenstein had written about architecture and montage, and that he was in Athens around 1936 or 1937.

So I first saw Eisenstein's notation around 1976. This drawing triggered the second episode of *The Manhattan Transcripts* ("The Street"). I was already experimenting with tripartite notations. When I started to do the eleven-meter-long drawing, it became challenging. You can only look at the drawing by using your body, by walking. The Parthenon Frieze is exactly the same. One hundred sixty meters long, it has to be experienced not only

O

in space, but also in time, through movement. This is precisely what Eisenstein was about. Cinema is about movement, even if the screen itself does not move. Architecture is also about movement, even if the structure is rarely made to move.

H/P/V: Despite your interest in architectural experience, you have not frequently discussed the questions of perception brought forward by phenomenological inquiries driven by the work of Merleau-Ponty, and introduced in the architectural field by people such as Steven Holl, Alberto Pérez-Gómez, and Juhani Pallasmaa.

Events: Situating the Temporary
Page 44

T: That's correct. I am not interested in atmosphere. Atmosphere is a theatrical device. That's why I would not call myself a phenomenologist: I am interested in experience – in material, tactility, touch, and smell – but I draw a line when I'm supposed to create specific emotions deliberately. I'm very cautious about that. For example, I am rather critical of the way that, in Daniel Libeskind's Jewish Museum in Berlin, you are supposed to cry, to feel certain ways when you enter specific spaces.

We should distinguish concept, percept, and affect from one another. Architecture is made up of all three. I am aware of specific affects when I use certain materials. For instance, when we did the two concert halls – one in which the inner envelope is concrete and the outer one is steel (in Rouen), and the other one in which the inner hall is wood and the outer one is translucent polycarbonate (in Limoges) – the material selection was totally self-conscious. I knew that the difference in materials would generate differences in perception, and perhaps cause people to feel different emotions. But I would certainly object to trying to manipulate the visitor's psyche.

This may go back to Georges Bataille and the relation between the pyramid of reason (concepts) and the labyrinth of senses (emotion or experience).

H/P/V: So it's always a question of not resolving the paradox you have often discussed – the paradox between architecture as "a product of the mind, a conceptual and immaterial discipline," and architecture as a "sensual experience of space, a spatial practice" – but rather bringing these irreconcilables together.

T: Absolutely. This applies both to the texts I wrote before I started to design anything and to what I do in design today.

H/P/V: Could you compare it to work of Bertolt Brecht? Where you would have experience as an immersed situation, but you could also have an experience as a construction, so you would be aware of the story, or something that is being told, but as in being told in a sort of objective way?

T: A problem with Bertolt Brecht is that you have the choir, which tells you what to think. Architecturally, I couldn't do that. I am not going to put signs on my built projects trying to explain their concepts. I get back to "the concept of dog doesn't bark," as Spinoza famously said. The one doesn't have to imply the other. It's assumed that anyone should be able to read the work on different levels. However, "defamiliarization" is something else. Clearly, both La Villette and the Groningen Video Pavilion were also about "defamiliarization," as was Le Fresnoy, the cultural center in Tourcoing.

H/P/V: When discussing open-endedness, chance, and indeterminacy, some architects would almost do nothing, but you deal with it in a more specific architectural way, using an explicit language. Is the open-endedness of your architecture related to a formally powerful gesture, or maybe to some sort of "signature"?

T: Yes. Again, I'm nervous about the word "formal." Of course, form is part of the job. Concepts and their materialization work together, whether it's through contradiction or reinforcement. The tension between the underlying concept and the experience of architecture is something that interests me in project after project. First of all, it has different outcomes. Secondly, different people will read the relationship differently. But I do use certain concepts, strategies, and devices that reappear in a number of projects, from superposition to programmatic interaction, to movement vectors and envelopes, to contextual differentiation, and so on. But I make sure that they never read as style or "form."

5. Convergence Culture

H/P/V: In an interview with Enrique Walker, you stated something very interesting in reference to the notion of *détournement* by the Situationists: first, they wanted to critique the spectacle, but then they made a spectacle themselves. This played out in the seventies, when the spectacle and the critical seemed to converge. We could draw a parallel with the present. Today's convergence culture is coming to a climax: we think of all kinds of strategies to meet the client's demands, or demands of society. However, the questions clients pose to us may also become more limiting, for instance, the aspect of fear and safety is increasingly entering architectural projects. How should architects respond to that? Do you change your way of working, or do you adapt your vocabulary to find new words, new definitions for certain

Events: Situating the Temporary
Page 46

architectural questions? For example, you introduced the notion of the envelope before, and in a later stage your work focused on context and concept. Could we say this is a conscious act, let's say, to communicate differently in a different period, or to actualize the work?

T: Let me give you an example. We have all been going through a creatively perverse period in which one-liners are common practice, in which the word "icon" became the norm; every building had to be "iconic." Iconicity, the instantly recognizable image, and architecture as logo have pervaded everybody's attitude. This occasionally includes me, despite my very strong resistance. And it means a huge reduction in architectural intelligence, as we have seen in the past ten to fifteen years. For some reason, if we try to give it a start date, I'd suggest that the beginning of the era of iconic architecture does not begin with Bilbao, but rather with 9/11.

H/P/V: Because of the destruction of an icon?

T: No, because of the quest for the new icon. The Yamasaki Twin Towers were, at "core," anti-iconic. When first built, they were hated by both critics and architects. It was said that the very fact that they were identical twins was denying the unity or "oneness" of great architecture. I always thought they were beautiful and I loved them. Because they were an identical double, they were negating the uniqueness of icons. Their nearly silent architectural expression made their pairing even more powerful. By the time the Twin Towers were destroyed in 2001, society had changed. After the society of the spectacle, we have now become the society of the image. Society is now committed to turning objects into images. This goes far beyond the architectural scene. And I believe it is something that will eventually have to be addressed by architects far more critically than they do today.

H/P/V: How do you position yourself as an architect, knowing that this is happening?

T: I keep doing my work. Or, more precisely, and returning to your earlier question about "how to communicate in a different period, or actualize the work": I consider what I do as a lifelong investigation into what architecture is. The issues evolve: space and event, program superposition, vectors and envelopes, concept and context, and so forth. Once an issue has been explored, it often leads to the next one. And concepts bounce between built buildings and theoretical texts. They both feed one another.

H/P/V: If the 1970s were all about criticality, there was a recent period in which criticality seemed almost absent. Now we see in the work of our students and young offices that there is a lot of interest in what happened in the seventies and eighties, and in the kind of work that you were involved with. Do you notice this?

T: I'm sort of aware, and I don't know what I feel about it. But the point is that some of the current excesses need to be questioned seriously, in particular, the rather meaningless icons that everyone seems to be striving for. I wish there would be ideas instead of icons. Whether they are built or not doesn't matter. I always say, a concept by Ledoux is not the same as a concept by Boullée. But they are equally important, even if one was built and the other one wasn't. So I feel there still is a lot of room today for intelligent critical investigation.

Now, I'm going back full circle to your starting point of looking at other fields, other areas of interest that have always been constants in culture. You know, not only in architecture, but also in film or science, people tend to look at things that happen elsewhere, outside of other disciplines. While this is extremely important, you also have to ask yourself whether Hans Hollein's statement, "Everything is architecture," makes any sense. If everything is architecture, then so is this glass of water and so is this pencil. And then you're nowhere, right? So there is a moment when architecture must have a concept, refer to a certain materiality, or to a specific use.

H/P/V: Returning to the seventies, and knowing you were, at that time, very much a European based in the United States, how do you position yourself, between European postmodernism and American postmodernism, between Aldo Rossi and Robert Venturi?

T: I would need to think about it retrospectively. At the time, I couldn't care less. The two postmodernisms were absolutely non-existent. Now, this is interesting: at that time, there was no father figure to look for, and no father to kill. Neither Rossi nor Venturi were father figures. I felt equally critical of both, and of what they represented. But maybe I'm talking about my own perception. People often forget that I graduated from architecture school in early 1969, but decided to engage in my first building project only in 1982. That's over twelve years. During those twelve years, I actively rejected anything that was based on received ideas of what architecture was supposed to be. I wanted to start from scratch. So, for me, there was no Venturi, no Rossi, none of that. I had some heroes in the twentieth-century avant-garde, but most of them were not architects. That's important: they were not necessarily architects.

H/P/V: Eisenstein, for instance?

T: Yes, that's a good example. But there are also artists and literary figures, like Marcel Duchamp, James Joyce, and Antonin Artaud, up to the so-called "poststructuralist" scene. Ultimately, it was about trying to reconstruct something, to eventually arrive at what I would call "architecture."

1

2

3

4

5

1	literary bonds	1990
2	lib that moment!	1995
3	mirrors, models, shacks & yards	2000
4	immersed in the amazing maze	2005
5	merging matters	2010

1

1 literary bonds: architecture and the narrative

1990

1995

1

literary bonds

1

The Narrative

Before the physical structure, architecture was a narrative tool for reading landscapes and making sense of complex environments, full of chaos, danger, and intrigue. Architecture was defined by the linear procession, the dramatic vista, the crescendo of the gathering, and the allegory of the repeating path. Plato's allegory of the cave was not only a metaphor for the relationship between the merely observable and the real – it also positioned collectively inhabited space as the projection screen for the unfolding of myth.

The projects in this chapter are not built in concrete or steel, yet they are realized in communicative media. As the Internet and virtual reality arose, they provided architecture with a new apparatus to construct dreams. And like the dreams of the somnolent, these imaginaries were layered and nonlinear, both figurative and literal. They are postmodern, not in the formal sense of collage, but rather in the symbolic and interlinking sense of the hypertext. The model, the measured drawing, and the render were the tools for telling stories. In these scenarios, architecture was not merely the stage but the event itself.

1990: Tim Berners-Lee at CERN builds the first web browser, and the first website is published.
1991: The Soviet Union dissolves and the Cold War ends.
1992: Kunsthal Rotterdam opens to the public.
1993: The European Union is established through the Maastricht Treaty.
1994: Penguin Books releases the first electronic novel on two floppy disks.
1995: *Toy Story*, the first feature-length computer-animated film, is released.

Johannes Schwartz
Paashoop, 2003
Page 57

johannes schwartz

Johannes Schwartz
Paashoop, 2003
Page 59

1 ernie mellegers: cockaigne–

Events: Situating the Temporary
Page 60

This is not a straightforward essay (i.e., story-defining and interpreting the narrative in architecture). It is an exploration meandering from subject to characteristic to detail, and a personal one at that. Along the way, some phenomena, ideas, terms, and details, such as markers, decoration, layout, organization, life, private and public, circulation, themes, symbolism, character, space, and events, will be addressed, while others will be passed over. The goal is to provide enough connections and context to get into the story of what architecture communicates: the narrative that is to be recognized in any construction.

fragmented lecture on architectural narrative

0001a markers – 1
photo: E.J. Mellegers, 2010

Menhir de Men Marz (Brignogan-Plages, 4500–2500 BCE)
With this miraculous sable stone, not dug in, as usual, but in balance on the ground, the sixth-century figure of Saint Pol de Léon is said to have marked the edge of the "tidal" no-man's-land (i.e., this is how far inland he allowed the sea).

0001a markers – 2
photo: E.J. Mellegers, 2010

Cairn de Barnénez (Presqu'île de Kernéléhen, from 5000/4000 BCE)
One does not need legends to grasp the metaphysical meaning of the carefully chosen locations of (megalithic) prehistoric monuments. What André Malraux dubbed – in the (later) style of Alberto Uderzo and René Goscinny – the *Parthénon des Bretons* is an exceptionally large tumulus with eleven burial chambers (dolmen) at an

impressive location on a peninsula overlooking a bay, the sea, and a river.

0001a markers – 3
photo: E.J. Mellegers, 2012

Vlieter monument (Afsluitdijk, Willem Dudok, 1933)
The tower marks the spot where Cornelis Lely's dyke was closed in 1932. While climbing the stairs, a virtually continuous view of the now appeased IJsselmeer, the former Zuiderzee, is offered, while the untamed Waddenzee on the other side of the dyke is only visible from the top platform.

English archeologist Francis Pryor researched (partly by speculation but based on his experience with prehistoric monuments) the ritual acknowledgment of the difference between negotiable and non-negotiable; inhabitable and non-inhabitable, land and sea, wet and dry; the transition of one to another as where the prehistoric metaphysical starts – the beyond where the gods and ghosts exist. Offerings were made and borders marked. Pryor identified it with the concept of liminality – the geographical border between physical and metaphysical – defining the threshold.[1]

1
See Francis Pryor, *Seahenge, New Discoveries in Prehistoric Britain* (London and New York: HarperCollins, 2001).

0001b markers – 1
photo: E.J. Mellegers, 2013

Unité d'Habitation (Firminy, Le Corbusier with André Wogenscky & Fernand Gardien, 1959–1967)
In the same vein, and with almost prehistoric aesthetics, the first stone for the last of Le Corbusier's phenomenal apartment buildings illustrates both the entrance into another space as well as symbolically indicates one of the important design principles defining that space: the daily cycle of the sun. *Posed on May 21, 1965, by Le Corbusier and mayor/initiator Eugène Claudius Petit.*

0002 tattooed – 1
photo: E.J. Mellegers, 2013

Unité d'Habitation (Firminy, Le Corbusier with André Wogenscky & Fernand Gardien, 1959–1967)
On the level of the actual apartment, the pragmatic implications of this principle are carved out, etched, or tattooed on the elevation on ground level, next to the entrance – *in a less abstract fashion.*

0002 tattooed – 2
photo: E.J. Mellegers, 1998

Bedieningshuis (Merwedebrug, Rijkswaterstaat, 1960–1961)
A tile mosaic mirrors the stream of automobiles that pass over the bridge. The postwar nation was reconstructing and celebrating each step towards modernity in a fitting imagery – *retro-futurism* – that its carrier, the architecture, only vaguely hints at.

0002 tattooed – 3
photo: E.J. Mellegers, 2008

Hong Kong facade (sauna near New Mandarin Plaza Shopping Centre, Kowloon, 2008)
The architecture is only the bearer of the message, the meaning (the story); it is not the messenger. But, not unlike Robert Venturi and Denise Scott-Brown's decorated shed, it is literally covered, or tattooed, with

screaming hardcore commercial signs, but still retains its shape.

0002 tattooed – 4
Marcello Nizzoli's photomontage was first published in *Quadrante*; see Ada Francesca Marciano, *Giuseppe Terragni, opera completa 1925–1943* (Rome: Officina Edizioni, 1987), 94.

Casa del Fascio (Como, Giuseppe Terragni, 1933–1936)
The anti-bureaucratic local party's headquarters should, in the words of the architect, present "no hindrance, no barrier, no obstacle between Fascist leaders and the people." Therefore, Benito Mussolini's concept of fascism as "a house of glass into which all can look" was literally taken as a guideline. The building was also contextually rooted in the surrounding public space, even extending well into the building during ceremonies through a row of eighteen doors at ground level. The representative marble also facilitated a possible use of the Casa del Fascio as billboard, as Marcello Nizzoli's photomontage suggests.[2]

2
Giuseppe Terragni, "La Construzione della Casa del Fascio di Como," *Quadrante* 35/36 (October 1936), cited in Richard A. Etlin, *Modernism in Italian Architecture 1890–1940* (Cambridge, MA: The MIT Press, 1991), 439ff.

0002 tattooed – 5
photo: E.M. van Ojen Het Nieuwe Instituut, Rotterdam/archief TENT

Coöperatie De Volharding (The Hague, Ir. J.W.E. Buys & Joan B. Lürsen, 1927–1928)
The use of the building as an advertising column was literally one of the demands made by the workers' co-op. Participation supplied the possibility of good dental care, reasonable prices in its own shop – thus, the positive results needed to be advertised to stimulate growth and advocate the idea, also at night. This resulted in an expressionist light spectacle that the functionalist architectural faction condemned as too decorative.

0002 integrated – 6
photo: E.J. Mellegers, 2012

Österreichische Postsparkasse (Vienna, Otto Wagner, 1903–1912)
A building that surprised the world. Everything was new, maybe not all the materials themselves, but surely the way Wagner applied them, while breaking free from architectural history. He headed for a new, contemporary monumentality. The iron bolts and aluminum caps may not structurally keep the cladding of the facade in place, but they provide a new language hinting at a pure representation of the underlying principles of the specific architecture.

0002 integrated – 7
photo: E.J. Mellegers, 2012

Kärntner Bar, a.k.a. American Bar (Vienna, Adolf Loos, 1908–1909)
As a precursor to De Volharding – or J.J.P. Oud's *De Unie* (Rotterdam, 1924–1925), for that matter – Loos's café-facade integrates a modern commercial and functional theme with atmospheric statement into an integral aesthetic comprehensive unity. A new message is incorporated, a new type of elevation born.

0002 integrated – 8
photo: E.J. Mellegers, 2010

Mosse-Haus (Berlin, Erich Mendelsohn with Richard Neutra, 1901–1903 & 1921–1923; renovated in 1995)
Rudolf Mosse's early 1900s publishing and printing headquarters was literally a center of the Spartacist uprising in 1919, and was severely damaged. Mendelsohn's reconstruction provided extra floors, a new entrance, and an extra layer that incorporated the change of time organically – without aesthetic compromises or tricks – while leaving the story intact. The actual addition is also related to the building's direct spatial context by its dynamic answer to the movement of traffic in the street. In spite of more damage, reconstruction, and a now quiet street, it still has a strong presence.

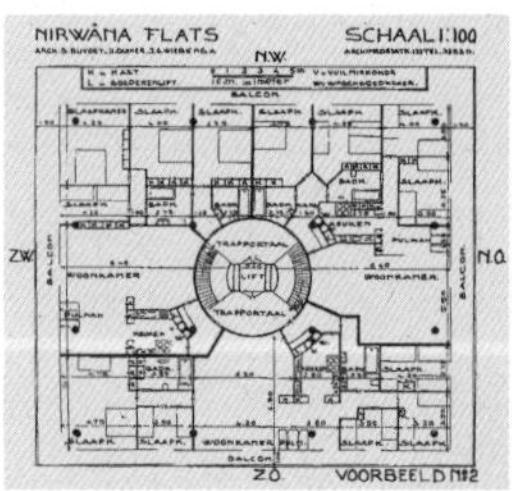

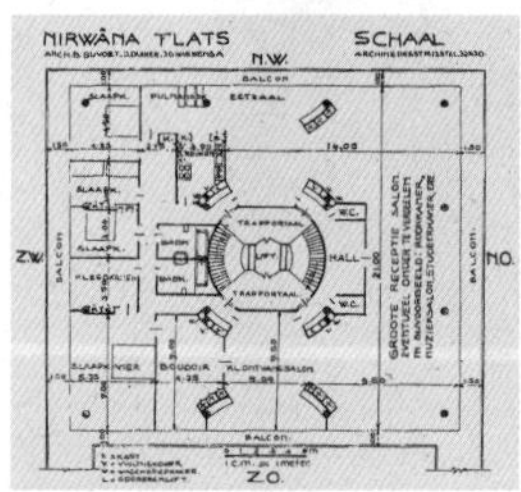

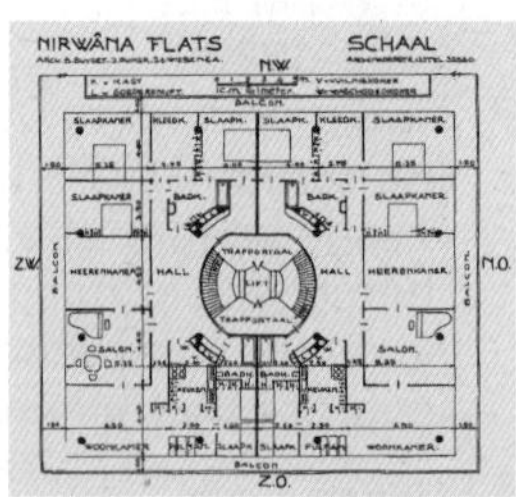

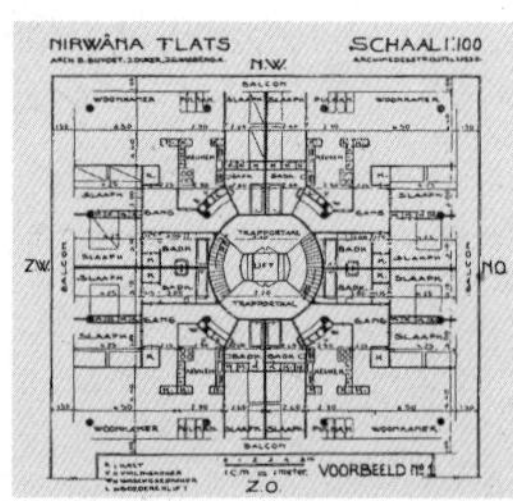

0003a floor plan, organization, life – 1 to 4
published in J. Luthman, "Bij de Nirwânaflats van Irs Bijvoet,

Nirwâna apartment/hotel (The Hague, Jan Duiker, Jan Gerko Wiebenga & Bernard Bijvoet, 1925–1930)
The domestic liberation through a (reinforced concrete) skeleton frame: all of a sudden, anything seemed possible. Floors could each offer a different and

Duiker en Wiebinga," *Bouwkundig Weekblad en Architectura* 48 (1927): 306–310.

alternative arrangement, tell a different story, facilitate a different way and organization of life. That is how it was sold – different suggestions for the arrangement of Nirwâna with two, three, four, or one huge communal apartment per floor, with Edward Bellamy's kitchen-less apartment as a distant ideal (for communal living). Science fiction, utopist, and visionary design found themselves in the same time slot.

0003b layout, organization, life – 1 to 2
photos:
E.J. Mellegers, 2008

1. Escalator system and elevated walkway systems (Hong Kong, from 1970s) & 2. Atrium (Hong Kong, Royal Garden Hotel, 2008)

The only north-side or up-down hill pedestrian thoroughfare on Hong Kong's side is the escalator system. It is part of a fairly recent push for pedestrian infrastructure and integrating developments in the hyper-dense fabric. Connected to the elevated bridges and walkways – even those in Kowloon – it links the new urban hotspots and provides much needed new ground. The city literally started to have two floors – for example, with shop windows on the first floor – with the ground floor's immediate vicinity either becoming less corporate, financial but still commercial, or abandoned. The elevated network itself grows freely and autonomously, connecting to the private interior spaces, such as lobbies of office buildings and malls, that are publicly accessible – or not – thus blurring the distinction between inside and outside, public and commercial, private and communal.[3]

3
See also Leslie Lu, "The Asian Arcades Project: Progressive Porosity," *Perspecta* 3 (2005): 86, 89–91.

0003c circulation, wandering – 1
published in:
G. Richou, “La Piste en Spirale du Palais-Sport à Paris,” *La Nature. Revue des Sciences et de leurs applications aux art et à l’industrie* 24, no. 1189 (1896): 225.

Palais des Sports (Paris, 1895)

The former panorama building just off the Champs-Élysées provided just about the perfect setting for a spectacular bicycling school – a new phenomenon. The bicycle was still special and, to a certain extent, still elitist enough to provide leisure while biking up and down the ramp decorated with a painted countryside (by MM. Rubé and Moissin) while friends looked on and enjoyed a drink. On the ground floor there was a bike storage, repair, and a showroom – a bastion of modern (mechanized) life.

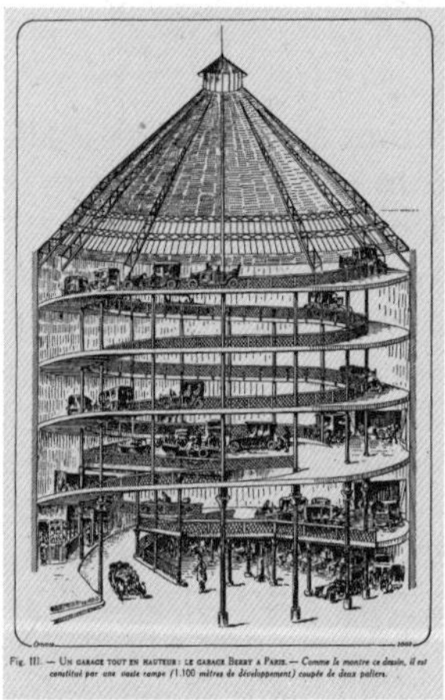

0003c circulation, wandering – 2 to 3
2. published in ‘Un Garage tout en Hauteur: Le Garage Berry à Paris’ from Paul Meyan, “Les Garages Modernes,” *Omnia Revue Pratique de l’Automobile,* nouvelle série 17, no. 26 (1922): 90.
3. photo: E.J. Mellegers

Garage Berry (Paris, 1913) & Garage Rue Lebouteux 13 (Paris)

Just before the First World War, the Palais des Sport was converted into a garage – one of the many in the Champs-Élysées area, the heartland of European car industry and automobilism. The automobile literally took over the bicycle’s infrastructure – physical, organizational, and in events – and penetrated architecture. The ramps provided its route in.[4]

4
Ernie Mellegers, *Turning Circle: Le Corbusier and the Parisian Parking Garage* (paper delivered at the 64th annual Society of Architectural History meeting, New Orleans, April 16, 2011).

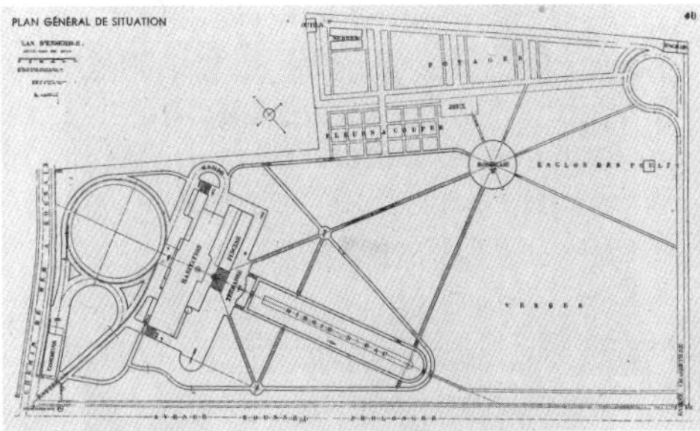

0003c circulation, wandering – 4 to 5
4. plan: Robert Mallet-Stevens (arch.), published in: "La Maison de M. C. à Croix," *L'Architecture d'aujourd'hui* 3, no. 8 (1932).
5. photo: E.J. Mellegers, ca. 1995

Villa Cavrois (Croix, Robert Mallet-Stevens, 1929–1932)

This penetration, in first instance the arrival protocol by car, quickly becomes an important characteristic element of any modernist and modern architecture. The automobile is the modern fetish and *the* indication that one is modern. To loosely quote Le Corbusier: one cannot drive a car and still sleep in a handcrafted Breton bed.

Robert Mallet-Stevens carefully choreographs this arrival in the design for the enormous Villa Cavrois in the North of France. From the entrance gate, the driveway leads to the concrete canopy above the main entrance. From this point, the driver either follows a full circle to a position ready to pick up his passengers whenever they appear again, finds his way to the garage, or returns to the main gate. All these routes and options are strictly calculated and laid out, based on the car's turning radius and the view of the architecture though the car windows.[5]

5
Ernie Mellegers, "Hoe de gemechaniseerde mens arriveert," *Platvorm*, no. 44 (2001): 38–45.

0003c circulation, wandering – 6
published in: Richard Vieille, e.o., *Banville* 1925–1991 (Paris: France Construction et Nationale-Nederlanden/Immobilier, 1991): 58.

Hill Climb (Paris, Garage de Banville, Saturday, February 26, 1927)

Mallet-Stevens's solution, however elegant and well calculated, still left the car and the driver in the cold. That is, one still had to get out of the car and into the architecture on foot. The parking of the automobile in its stable – the garage – remained a sort of afterthought in the protocol. A particular event in a Parisian parking garage provided an illustration for more radical solutions. The Garage de Banville, a 17th arrondissement bastion of *automobilisme* with an extended program, celebrated its official opening with a hill climb, a race along its ramp (600 meters, with seventeen corners) from bottom to top floor.[6]

6
Ernie Mellegers, "Het parkeerseizoen of the day the automobile came to town," in *Parkeren op Niveau: De parkeergarage als ontwerpopgave*, eds. Floortje Louter and Ed van Savooyen (Bussum: Uitgeverij Thoth, 2005), 239–240.

0003c circulation, wandering – 7a to 7b
back of Banville bill from Richard Vieille, e.o., *Banville* 1925–1991 (Paris: France Construction et Nationale-Nederlanden/Immobilier, 1991): 38–39.

Garage de Banville (Paris, Henri Decaux & Henri Terrisse, 1925–1929)

The hill climb was organized by Robert Benoist, the sales manager of the garage and a grand prix racer. His presence, as a motorsport personality, was part of the master plan that made the Banville garage a magnet for *automobilistes*, just as were the regular functions such as garage, workshop, individual parking boxes, showrooms, waiting room for chauffeurs, etc. However, what made the Banville special were the extra annuities like the (small) indoor and outdoor golf courses on the roof, the restaurant, the bar, the salons and dressing rooms, the indoor tennis courts, table tennis on the top floor, and the gymnasium – all in a building designed for automobile circulation; an apartment building for the car.[7]

7
Ibid.

0003c circulation, discovery – 8 to 9
photos:
E.J. Mellegers, 2008

Villa Savoye, a.k.a. Les Heures Claires (Poissy, Le Corbusier & Pierre Jeanneret, 1928–1931)

It only took Le Corbusier to add things up. He

experimented with bringing the car into the domestic building, both apartment buildings and detached houses, but failed to find the proper solution, yet. However, the Parisian parking garage, with its automobile circulation system, provided the protocol – among others – for the Villa Savoye solution. Point of departure for this design was the thirty-kilometer drive by automobile that connected the clients to Paris.[8] So, the ideal was to get out of the car within the building, at the front door in the apex of the turning circle that shapes the route. After descending and entering, the pedestrian virtually becomes an automobile himself while ascending the ramps to the different floors, experiencing the *promenade architecturale* that ends at the frame, shaped as a car window on the roof terrace.[9]

8
Le Corbusier, *Oeuvre Complète de 1929–1934* (Zürich: Ed. Girsberger, 1935), 24.

9
Ernie Mellegers, *9079U2: Le Corbusier en de Auto* (Rotterdam: Les Editions Finistère, 1992).

0003c circulation, interaction – 10
photo: E.J. Mellegers, ca. 1997

Grands Magasins de la Samaritaine (Paris, Frantz & Francis Jourdain, 1905)
Le Corbusier's Villa Savoye solution was related to the École des Beaux-Arts concepts of *marché* and *composition*. Therefore, it was certainly akin to Charles Garnier's Parisian Opera (1861–1874) with its circulation from ramped (carriage) entrance via the grand stairs to the main hall. Those stairs were an important place to parade for the new middle class, hence also the elaborate examples in department stores such as La Samaritaine.

0003c circulation, education – 11
photo: Anne Karine Lemstra, 2007

Notre-Dame de Laon (Laon, 1155–1235)

Whatever may be, the automobile penetrating the building or the Beaux-Arts *marché* were all preceded by the medieval Romanesque and Gothic cathedrals and churches that were solely designed to underline and illustrate gospel and liturgy, and – sometimes – accommodate and service masses of pilgrims.
True storytelling machines.

0003d narrative system – 1 to 1a
1. Ted Benoit in *Corbu vu Par* (Brussels: Pierre Mardaga Ed., 1987), 69.
1a. Le Corbusier, *Oeuvre Complète de 1929–1934* (Zürich: Ed. Girsberger, 1935), 56.

Appartement de M. de Beistegui (Paris, Le Corbusier, 1929–1932)

The amount of technical gadgets and meters of electrical wiring in the de Beistegui penthouse often provoke comparison with the modern house in Jacques Tati's *Mon Oncle* (1958). However, the moving hedges and periscopic projections did not only serve surrealist-inspired parties, but also illustrate Le Corbusier's view of the city as a car ride (i.e., a series of landmarks with space to play with in between).

0003d narrative system – 2
Bartolomeo Del Bene, *Civitas Veri sive Morum* (Paris, 1609), printed by Ambroise and Jérôme Drouart – engraver unknown.[10]

Civitas Veri (City of Truth, Bartolomeo Del Bene, 1565/1609)

A Counter-Reformation poem with integrated illustrations, introducing a utopian city with an organization that educates – starting at the gates (each dedicated to a sense).

10
Reproduced in Virgilio Vercelloni, *La Cité idéale en Occident* (Paris: Éditions du Félin, 1996), 79.

0003d narrative system – 3a to 3b
photos:
E.J. Mellegers, ca. 1993

Stourhead (Wiltshire, Henry & Richard Colt Hoare, 1735–1783)

Taking inspiration from the *Italienesc* paintings of Poussin, and even more importantly, Claude Lorrain, the Hoares laid out a narrative in their landscape garden. Starting by improving on an already dramatic setting, they installed scenes that were engaging by themselves, but also interacted as the backdrop for others, and thus formed a whole; a narrative system.

photos:
E.J. Mellegers, ca. 1997

0003d narrative system – Vaux-le-Vicomte 4a to 4b, Versailles 4c

Vaux-le-Vicomte (Melun, André Le Nôtre, Louis Le Vau, Charles Le Brun, 1641–1661) & Versailles (from 1661)

Vaux is a "secular baroque," that is, the idea of all disciplines joining in to celebrate one singular entity,

whether it is the king or his superintendent, Nicolas Fouquet. In any case, and according to legend, the young King Louis XIV became jealous of Fouquet's estate and imprisoned him. The truth is that he was already aware and weary of Fouquet's machinations for power before the infamous soirée on August 17, 1661. In any case, Vaux-le-Vicomte is what Versailles was not, in the end: an elegant and intelligent design that focused on the universe, along the main axis, but held all the surprises and excitement that an exploration of a formal geometric garden could hold – thanks to the genius of André le Nôtre. Except for Saturdays, there is always one element missing, though: the people. Luckily, Versailles always provides this.

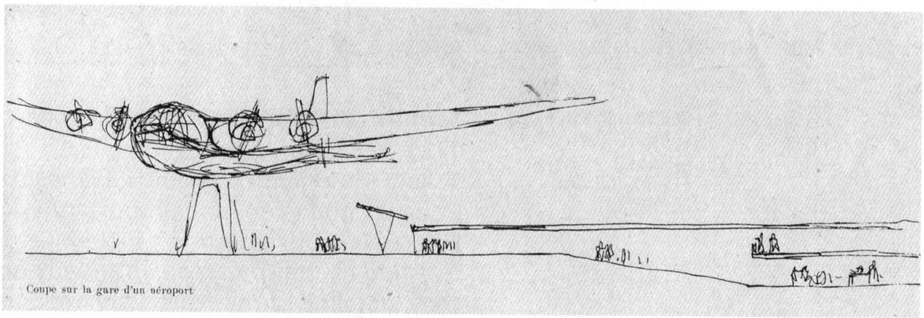

0003d narrative system – 5
Le Corbusier, *Oeuvre Complète de 1938–1946* (Zürich: Ed. Girsberger, 1946): 190.

Architecture and modern airports (Le Corbusier, 1946)
True to form, Le Corbusier wiggled himself into the reconstruction of France after the Second World War. This also meant getting involved with the idea of the modern airport; two-dimensioned architecture, as he dubbed it. He proposed a very modest architecture for the terminals so that the naked airport would be dressed up and identified by the airplanes on the platform themselves, in all their mechanical beauty – his favorite being the Lockheed Constellation.

0004 parlante – 1
Étienne-Louis Boullée, "'A Newton' Projet de cénotaphe, élévation perspective" (1784), Paris, Bibliothèque Nationale, Cabinet des estampes (Ha 57 pl. 6).[11]

Projet de Cénotaphe "à Newton" (Étienne-Louis Boullée, 1784)

Boullée's *genre terrible* is focused on anxiety, terror, and other sublime emotions provoked though scale, strong geometrical shapes, serenity, and the use of light to signify the divine. Monumentality as expression of the Enlightenment works only as long as these ideas are represented in the works themselves. If not, the result is "dead," empty, and gigantic shapes.

11
Reproduced in Annie Jacques, Jean-Pierre Mouilleseaux, Anne-Maria Garcia, and Frédéric Morvan, *Les Architectes de la Liberté 1789–1799* (Paris: École nationale supérieure des Beaux-Arts, 1989), 4.

0004 parlante – 2
photo: E.J. Mellegers, 2012

Saline Royale gate (Arc-et-Senans, Claude-Nicolas Ledoux, 1775–1778)

In one view, Ledoux shows what Arc-et-Senans is about: neoclassicist architectural ideals, shown by the columns and other details; the expression of the character of the building, visible within the entrance as a salt cave; control, shown by the always present director's house; and clear-cut and undiluted geometrical shapes, visible in the clean brickwork and hard edges.

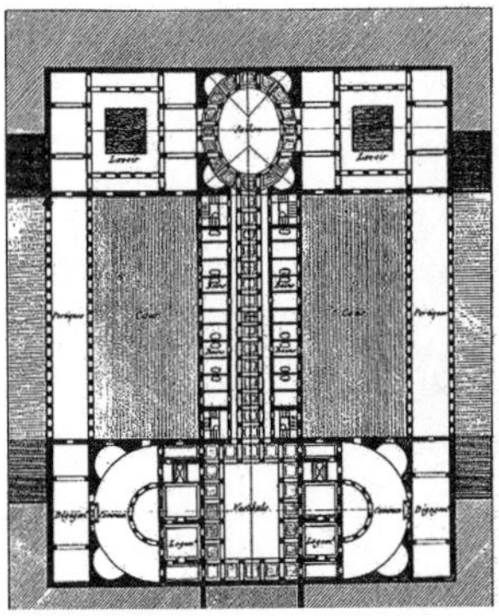

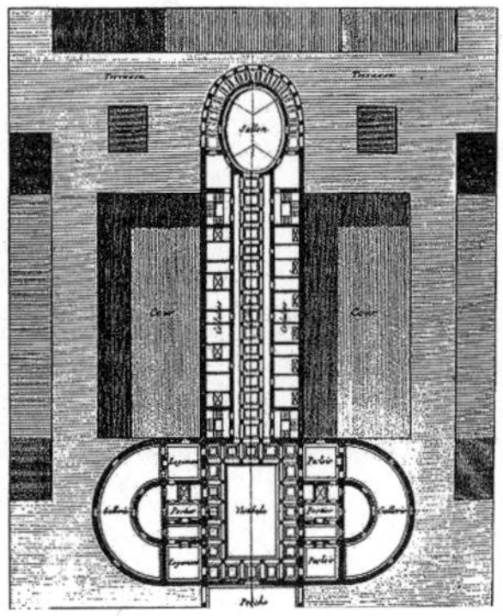

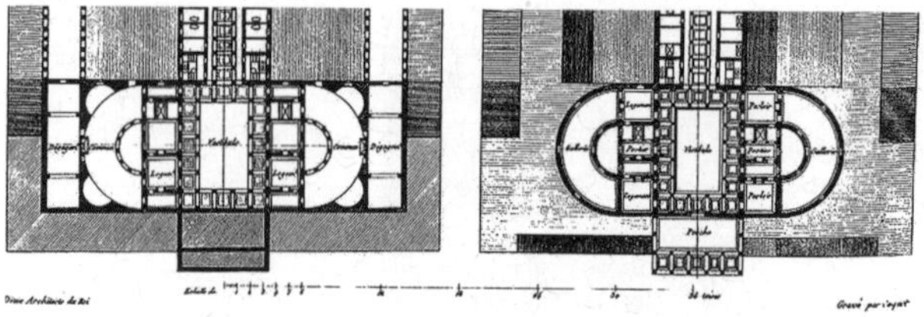

0004 parlante – 3
Oikéma, ou Maison de la passion (Chaux, Claude-Nicolas Ledoux, 1785–1804)[12]

Oikéma (Chaux, Claude-Nicolas Ledoux, 1785–1804)
To get it out of your system would be a way to describe the Oikéma. In Ledoux's ideal city of Chaux, this was where youth could indulge in libertine "action," but only when young and only here – discretely. Ledoux concentrates on functional differentiation, with each building catering to a specific function that should reflect in its design – more than *caractère... architecture parlante*.

12 Published in Claude-Nicolas Ledoux, *L'architecture considérée sous le rapport de l'art, des moeurs et de la législation. Tome 1* (1804) – Bibliothèque nationale de France, département Réserve des livres rares, RES-V-42.

0005 anthropo-morphic – 1
photo: Anne Karine Lemstra, 2007

A Symphony of Lights (Hong Kong, Tourist Board, since 2004)
Every night at 20:00, with good weather, a fourteen-minute laser show, with music and sometimes pyrotechnics, celebrates the (new and older) architectural achievement of Hong Kong. Best seen from the Tsim Sha Tsui "Avenue of Stars," it specifically highlights the buildings on the Hong Kong side. What is more interesting than this touristy event itself is the introduction of the individual buildings, at the start, like the players or main characters in a play.

Château Branlant (Saint Lunaire, Jeanne Devidal, possibly from 1955)

0005 anthropo-morphic – 2
photo: E.J. Mellegers, ca. 1987

In a bourgeois neighborhood close to the coast, Jeanne Devidal started extending her *pavilion* with anything she could find: crates, shoes, tins, buckets, whatever. There was no push for something attractive, as in other instances like these. By the 1980s, the neighbors started to worry about the value of their property, and cars with tourists started to divert into the small street. After an accident in 1990, she was hospitalized and did not return. The house was torn down the year after, but Jeanne lived on until 2008. She worked on it every day for about thirty-five years, but her motivation remained an enigma. Somehow she seemed to have protection, maybe from as high up as General de Gaulle.

0005 anthropo-morphic – 3
Casa Malaparte "Casa come me," still from La Pelle (Liliana Cavani, 1981); screenshot by Anna Battista.

Casa Malaparte "Casa come me," still from *La Pelle* (Liliana Cavani, 1981) (Capri, Curzio Malaparte & Adalberto Libera, from 1937–1957)
A famous anecdote has Curzio Malaparte stating to German General Erwin Rommel, when visiting his house on Capri, that he bought the house but designed the landscape. Obviously, nothing could be further from the truth. Of course, the location was carefully chosen based on natural beauty, reclusiveness, and economics, but also for its connection to the *Odyssey*. The house, like himself, holds other keys to his personality; maybe more than is evident from his book or his public persona.

0005 anthro-pomorphic, identity, confirmation – 4
photo: Hans Werlemann (copyright OMA)

House at Floirac (Floirac, OMA, 1998)
Built on architectural principles, coincidence, and fate, the house could also be seen as an ultimate stance of the middle class – bourgeois life. Why else would the elevator room regulate the access to the wine cellar?

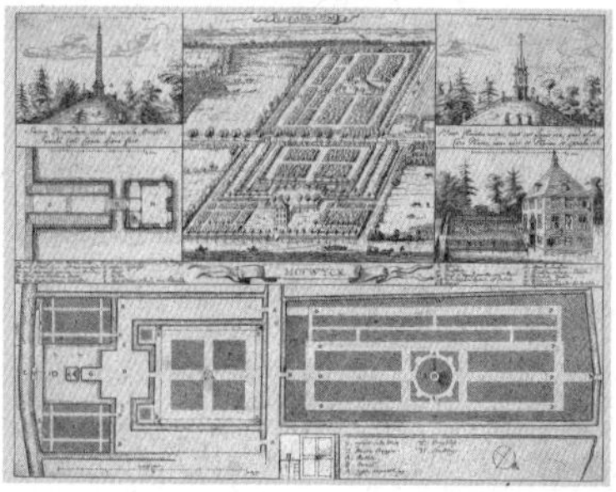

0005 anthropo-morphic – 5
"VitaluliumHofwijck," printer's proof with handwritten additions by Constantijn Huygens, 1653). collection: Huygensmuseum Hofwijck[13]

Hofwijck (Voorburg, Constantijn Huygens, 1639–1642)
The size of the small house that Constantijn Huygens had built as a hideout – within short distance of the busy court life he was part of – indicates that it really was about the garden. He points out in a poem he later writes about the estate that the garden was anthropomorphic – in a strictly literary sense. His proportions and physical characteristics were mirrored in the layout, based on Vitruvius. But, this is the easy layer. The garden offers his whole life, including aging.

13
Reproduced in Ad Leerintveld, ed., *'t Liefste Pad.Hofwijcks tuin in oude luister hersteld* (The Hague: Valerius Pers, 2005) VIII, copyright Huygensmuseum Hofwijck, Voorburg.

0006 identity, confirmation – 2
published in "Algemene beschrijving van een flatgebouw met 224 flats...," brochure, Haags Gemeente-archief, Df180.

Cofamilie (The Hague, Mart J. Stam, 1932)
The name is short for "cooperative family" but it is not hinting at a socialist utopia. Cofamilie would have been the grandest of apartment/hotels, a building type particularly popular in The Hague. Apart from the building itself, the cooperative part was aimed at collectively buying supplies, food, services and, in this case, maintaining a small fleet of eight automobiles for the use of the inhabitants of the 224 flats. One for all and all for one – securing a middle-class lifestyle.

0007a symbolism – 1
photo: E.J. Mellegers, ca. 1995

Monticello (Charlottesville, Virginia, Thomas Jefferson, from 1767)

Jefferson's plantation took its first appearance from the Palladian idea. It is the second and bigger incarnation, started in 1796, that incorporated first-hand experience with these European examples. It was more authentic, with its absolute strive for the image of a gentlemen's hideout on the edge of the wilderness, as witnessed in the clever manipulation of windows of the different floor levels to enhance the illusion of a small, one-story pavilion.

0007a symbolism, education, discovery – 2
steel engraving: "University of Virginia, Charlottesville, 1831, William Goodacre, draughtsman, and Fenner Sears & Co., engraver/printer. A color version was published by H. L. Hinton & Simpkin and Marshal. collection: E.J. Mellegers

University of Virginia (Charlottesville, Virginia, Thomas Jefferson, from 1819)

As Jaquelin Robertson suggested, Jefferson's university is a last effort of the Enlightenment; an urban system with a layout for the educated; an ideal(listic) design for immediate and realistic use. Two ribbons of student rooms, the inner incorporating faculty pavilions, flank the central rectangular lawn and form a U-shape with the rotunda on one end of the lawn. This central rotunda, a pantheon, is not a church but a library – a place of learning. The open end of the U-shape offers an open view to nature, the wilderness, the sublime.[14]

14
Jaquelin T. Robertson, "The House as the City," in *New Classicism: Omnibus Volume*, eds. Andreas Papadakis and Harriet Watson (New York: Rizzoli, 1990), 229ff.

0007b monument – 1
postcard: "Verdun convie la France à commemorer sa Victoire," Héliogravure Martin-Colardelle, Verdun. collection: E.J. Mellegers

Monument à la Victoire et aux Soldats de Verdun (Verdun, Leon Chesnay, inaugurated in 1929)
In 1915, in the soggy trenches, surrounded by the desolate, moonlike landscape of the North-French front line, subaltern A. Gillespie reflects on a monument by which later this strange, new First World War can be commemorated. He envisions a monumental tarmac road, a "sacred" commemorative route, covering the no-man's-land along the hundreds of miles of the front.

0007b monument – 2
photo: E.J. Mellegers, 1988

Peugeot 202 (Oradour-sur-Glane, 1988)
Automobilism and the car make the horrors of this century tangible.[15] Memories of the Second World War, in many ways a continuation of the Great War, illustrate this phenomenon. The destroyed French town of Oradour-sur-Glane, consolidated as monument, is a chilling example. It is especially the car wrecks of the murdered inhabitants that, walking through the ruins of this town – annihilated on June 10, 1944, by SS troops – make the dimension of the disaster palpable. Modern man has more affinity with the tortured steel, the rust, the smell of escaping oil and rot that surrounds abandoned cars than with the rows of neatly kept crosses in huge stretches of well-mowed lawn of a war cemetery, only impressive by its numbers. Gillespie's idea touches the right "esprit."[16]

15
See also Modris Eksteins, *Rites of Spring: The Great War and the Birth of the Modern Age* (Boston: A Peter Davison Book/Houghton Mifflin Company, 1989).

16
Ernie Mellegers, "Souviens-Toi!: The Art of Remembrance (1989–2001)," *Decorum* 10, no. 1 (2002): 44–47.

0008a topographical nostalgia – 1
photo: E.J. Mellegers, 2014

Bauhaus studio building (Dessau, Walter Gropius & Adolf Meyer, 1925–1926)
Spend the night like a *Bauhäusler* in the *Prellerhaus*; the strange attractions of topographical nostalgia. Sometimes knowing that something happened in a particular spot is enough.

0008b suggested story (unauthentic) – 1
photo: E.J. Mellegers, 2015

Jiangsu Road (Shanghai, 2015)
Architecture offering the suggestion of a story, the suggestions of an evolution through time, although it is pretty obvious that this is not the case.

0008c themed – 1
photo: Anne Karine Lemstra, ca. 1999

Auto-Hal Éts. Bainier (Saigon, ca. 1927)
André Citroën took great care of the architecture of his extensive network of dealerships. He was one of the first to dictate a corporate style, or better, a corporate

atmosphere with some room for interpretation – locally. In any case, the spaces should be luxurious but restrained, like a jewelry box, not overpowering the exhibited automobiles. The showroom was to be an experience where, sometimes, only the seed of a future sale was to be planted. His showroom in Deauville, for example, boasted comfortable sofas so that (future) clientele could take a break on their walk from *Les Planches* on the beach and the nearby grand hotels to the horserace track, more inland. Or, near Place de l'Europe, one could see all Citroën models in one big exposition center.

0008c themed – 2
photo: E.J. Mellegers, 1998

Cité de l'Europe (Coquelles-Calais, Paul Andreu and team, 1993–1995)

The Chunnel, or Eurotunnel, was a nineteenth-century vision that finally became true in 1994, when service through the tunnel started. The themed shopping mall was, among others, meant to accentuate what was actually a bit of a subterranean non-event: a ride of about thirty minutes in the dark. The design used the actual shape of the tunnel and translated it into a sign, a *duck* maybe, to stay close to Robert Venturi and Denise Scott-Brown's Las Vegas research. Also, its food court was to be a sampler of European cuisine, in order to illustrate the new, tighter, and quick connection that the old continent was establishing. It was therefore located within the parameters of the *Camp du Drap d'Or* where, in 1520, the English and French kings Henry VIII and François I met in an attempt to establish peace in Europe. In France, every decision is reasoned.[17]

17 Ernie Mellegers, "Cité de l'Europe in Coquelles," *De Architect* 6 (September 1998): 18–23.

0008c themed – 3
photo:
E.J. Mellegers,
ca. 1998

MP3 bunker, Les Landes (Jersey, Atlantic Wall, from 1941)
The Nazis contribution to modern architecture is obviously stealthy but present. This observation tower is one of in total nine such towers planned on the island. Three were built and served to scout the sea. The view is guided, horizontal, not unlike that from Le Corbusier's *fenêtre en longueur*, and of course there is a link with the postwar aesthetics of brutalism. The tower even has defensive, or maybe aggressive, anthropomorphic connotations when seen as a clenched fist.

0008c themed – 4
postcard: "253 Deauville – Plage Fleurie – Les Nouveaux Bains – L' Atrium"
photo: Simon, Addo Architecte, Compagnie Alsacienne des Arts Photomécaniques.
collection:
E.J. Mellegers

Les Nouveaux Bains – L'Atrium, a.k.a. Les Bains Pompéiens (Deauville, Charles Adda, 1921–1922)
The extended dwelling (i.e., leisure time in the seaside resorts on the Atlantic coast) resulted in a free-for-all architecture that suited its clientele. That is, as long as it combined a longing for surprise, amusement – in short, *nouveautés* with recognizable *grandeur* – for old and new money. The Roman baths were an obvious choice, also connected to the ongoing popularity of Caesars Palace in Las Vegas.

0008c themed – 5
published in Régis Gignoux, "Les Routes de L' Automobile," *L' Illustration* 83, no. 4309 (October 1925): 350.

The road, the automobile circuit, measured up by "points d'Essence" (*L'Illustration*, October 1925)

The service station was, with the big parking garage, the most visual and earliest manifestation of automotive architecture. The design of the most interesting ones took its cue from speed-reading – through the windscreen of a moving car – and the iconography of *automobilisme* itself. It explains the amused assessment that this "poste de ravitaillement" along the road from Paris to Deauville "pleasantly imitated the shape of a gas canister."[18] The signal was clearly readable for the passengers of this Voisin 10CV C7.

18 Régis Gignoux, "Les Routes de L' Automobile," *L' Illustration* 83, no. 4309 (October 1925): 350 (my translation).

0008c themed – 6
photo: E.J. Mellegers, 2015

Kiosk (Shanghai, 2015)

The obvious translation of function into form is not limited to automotive architecture. The purpose of this small building, and the goods for sale, also leave little doubt.

0008c themed – 7
photo: E.J. Mellegers, ca. 1997

Service station (near Andel)

Industrial designer Walter Dorwin Teague prudently

established a connection between service stations and ancient temples when he was designing for Texaco in the 1930s. But, would it not be more an oasis, or in this case, "heaven's gate"?[19]

19
Ernie Mellegers, "Don't bother, I'll take drive through at the wayside market," *Stedebouw & Ruimtelijke Ordening*, no.1 (2002): 18–23.

0009 mechanical – 1
photo: copyright Neurdein/Roger-Voillet, Hollandse Hoogte

Rue de l'Avenir (Paris, Blot, Schmidt & Silsbee, 1900)
The *trottoir roulant* may have been the actual climax of the 1900 Exposition Universelle in Paris. Finally, the infrastructure itself was moving, and the slowest link in the traffic chain, the pedestrian, could fully concentrate on the attractions along the three-kilometer circuit while travelling at twice the normal walking pace.

0009 mechanical – 2
postcard, HLM editions
collection: E.J. Mellegers

Pont Roulant (Saint Malo – Saint Servan, Alexandre Leroyer, 1873–1923)
The mechanization of pedestrian movement – so, moving the road – became an attraction with the Industrial Revolution, especially by the end of the nineteenth century, when speed started picking up and mass started to accumulate, daily, in urban streets. The *pont roulant* was suitable for short harbor crossings where there was no room for a bridge high enough not to hinder sailing boats, and with such a large tidal difference that a ferry would be useless at low tide.

0009 mechanical – 3
postcard
collection:
E.J. Mellegers

Pont Transbordeur (Marseille, Ferdinand Arnodin, 1905)
The *pont transbordeur, ingénieur* Arnodin's patent, offered another complex combination of ferry and bridge. Although a joined invention of a Spanish-Basque engineer, it thrived best in France where the public enjoyed such complexity. In short, it consisted of a gondola suspended at "street level" from a trolley going back and forth over the high bridge deck. The true attraction, though, was its even more delicate construction, compared to the sturdy Eiffel Tower, its "evaporating" mass, and its role as a framing device when looking at city, harbor, or open water.

0009 mechanical – 4
photo: Getty Images, photo by Sovfoto/Contributor (Collection Universal Images Group)

Monument to the Third International (St. Petersburg, Vladimir Tatlin, 1919–1920)
Tatlin supplies this moving game with a symbolic meaning in the proposed headquarters of the Comintern. The speed with which the cube, pyramid, cylinder, and hemisphere rotated – or not – within the double helix is linked to their individual program. The interesting pointlessness sensed in the other mechanical pedestrian tools is gone.

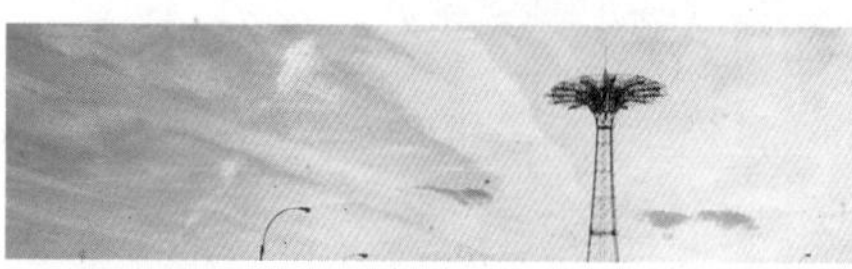

0009 mechanical – 5
photo: Olga Limarenko, 1999

Parachute Jump (Coney Island, Brooklyn, NY, 1939–1941)
Providing a pointless and perfectly safe parachute jump, just as amusement, this attraction further missed the point. Now it is only about the action itself, and there is virtually no interaction with daily life and environment. It is, however, a technical masterpiece and a distinct shape – shown first at the 1939 New York World's Fair.

0010 classicism – 1
photo: E.J. Mellegers, 2006

Altes Museum (Berlin, Karl Friedrich Schinkel, 1822–1830)
For the Berlin Lustgarden, Schinkel came up with a prototype for a new building type, that of the museum, as well an icon of classicism. No dull imitation nor reconstruction, but a clever and practical combination of the layout of the Pantheon flanked by the floor plans of two temples. All this disguised as an antique backdrop providing the aspiring Kingdom of Prussia with heritage and (mythological) origins.

0010 classicism – 2
photo: E.J. Mellegers, 2016

Villa Pignatelli (Naples, Piero Valente, 1826 and later)
Initiated by Anglo-Italian Sir Ferdinand Dalberg-Acton,

the neoclassicist villa offered a direct connection with the origins of "everything" antiquity in the days that Naples was the cultural heartland of Europe. The Pompeii room offers an extra reminder close by, also a great conversation piece.

0010 classicism – 3
photo: Getty Images, photo by ullstein bild/Contributor (Collection ullstein bild)

Elvis, Graceland & Phantom V (1960)
Classicism is an invention, it is what we decide it to be, it is what we reach consensus on, as far as considering it the core of our values. We can trace the classic triangular tympanum all to the same roots, but to understand its meaning, context matters. For Thomas Jefferson, it was a reference to the ideals of the Enlightenment; for Elvis, it might have been a reference to the big mansions, the plantations that he knew while growing up. However, the one on the car connects to another story as well, another time.

0011 blank space – 1
photo: Anne Karine Lemstra, 2015

Trade fair (Guangzhou, 2015)
Generic, global spaces (i.e., non-places) offer no story and need to be explained through signage, wayfinding, and the like. They are so impersonal that any relation, connection, or interpretation is impossible. They offer a nice sensual break, though, especially when traveling.

0012 space – 1
photo: E.J. Mellegers, 2009

Eiffel Tower (Paris, Gustave Eiffel, 1889)
This is where modern architecture took off, through this marriage of the purely functional focus and state-of-the-art construction knowledge of the engineer with the poetics of the architect, while constructing a tower that had no exact purpose. If it does one thing, it is to illustrate the new modernist idea of continuous space that becomes apparent when one climbs up and senses the relation with the wide-open space through the minimalistic iron lacework.

0012 space – 2
photo: Anne Karine Lemstra, 2011

Vostok 1 (Musée de l'Air, Le Bourget, 1961)
Yuri Gagarin used a Vostok 3KA on his first manned flight in space, on April 12, 1961. The implications of spatial design are maybe nowhere more extreme than in a spacecraft or submarine. Only fairly recently are the benefits of architectural design, and what it can imply, recognized in the design of such vehicles.

0012 fleece [skin] – 3
photo: E.J. Mellegers, 2014

Bauhaus facade (Dessau, Walter Gropius & Adolf Meyer, 1925–1926)

The iconography of the window and the glass facade is complicated. There is a long tradition in using the sexual implications of this transparent border between inside and outside, private and public, in painting and other arts. In architecture, there is the (in)famous *transparency*, either literal or phenomenal. However, the everyday workings are just as interesting – why this feeling of privacy and security, despite everybody seeing you?

0012 space – 4
photo: E.J. Mellegers, 1999

Stairs, director's house (Arc-et-Senans, Claude-Nicolas Ledoux, 1775–1778)
Was it an advance on the disappearance of the church service during the French Revolution, a tentative attempt to build a community, or just plain pragmatic use of space? In any case, the double function of the stairs in the director's house of the Saline Royale is too intriguing to not ask for an answer, but the attention Ledoux gave to the direction of the natural light provides a clue.

0013 events – 1 to 2
photos:
E.J. Mellegers, 2014

Scaffolding (Hong Kong, 2014)
Temporary construction is vital for all construction. No building happens without scaffolding, and sometimes this scaffolding is a building in its own right – and seems to do the trick.

0013 events – 3
published in:
Humberto Mezzadri, "Mies no Weissenhof / Mies at Weissenhof," *ARQTEXTO* 13 (2nd semester 2008): 28.

Pavillon de l'Esprit Nouveau (Paris, Le Corbusier & Pierre Jeanneret, 1925)
The pavilion represented a section of a more permanent solution (i.e., the Immeubles-Villas, a predecessor of the Unité d'Habitation).

0013 events – 4
published in:
Le Corbusier, *Oeuvre Complète de 1910–1929* (Zürich: Ed. Girsberger, 1937), 174.

Pavillon Nestlé (Paris, Le Corbusier & Pierre Jeanneret, 1927–1928)
This pavilion was more of a commercial billboard combined with a commercial space and a presentation area that could travel (i.e., could be taken down and built up again). Again, a building that communicated an urgent message.

0013 events – 5
published in:
Le Corbusier, Des Canons, Des Munitions? Merci! Des Logis... (Paris: Ed. De L'Architecture d'Aujourd'hui, 1938), 36.

Le Pavillon des Temps Nouveaux (Paris, Le Corbusier & Pierre Jeanneret, 1936–1937)
A built book with the carefully planned circulation providing the sequence of chapters – actually, a tent.

0013 events – 8
(uncredited photo in Catherine Rossi, *Architecture at the Disco: Radicals, Rhythms and the 1970s Avant-Garde* (2014).[20]

Space Electronics vegetable garden, Mondial Festival, 1971 (Florence, Gruppo 1999, 1971)
The rebellious architectural radicals of the late 1960s found another stage (i.e., outlet for their interventions): the disco. Space Electronics even held a vegetable garden in 1971.

20
See https://spaceelectronic.wordpress.com/2014/06/04/article-architecture-at-the-disco.

0013 events – 9
photo: copyright Pierre-Antoine Demachy/Roger-Voillet/Hollandse Hoogte

Festival of the Supreme Being / Fête de l'Etre suprême au Champ de Mars (Pierre-Antoine Demachy, 1794)
As Spiro Kostof analyzed, the only legitimization for the street is public space – the city could not do without the latter.[21] The fundamental value of the street is political. The street provides society with structure; it serves as stage for public meetings. Robespierre was the first to exploit this stage, to forge unity and support – many revolutions and dictators followed suit.

21
See also Spiro Kostof, *The City Assembled: The Elements of Urban Form through History* (London: Thames and Hudson, 1992), 195ff.

0013 events – 10 to 11
photos:
E.J. Mellegers, 2008

Streetscape & Avenue of Stars (Hong Kong, 2008)
The street holds the truth; it is where a society represents itself to itself. It is where values and heroes are introduced and celebrated – the late Bruce Lee, for example.

To be continued, extended, and elaborated... at some point, in the near future.

1

Events: Situating the Temporary
Page 94

project 1

1990

Literary Bonds
Page 95

Villa Karamazow
Project: Book
Year: 1990
Data: page 628

Villa
Karamazow
Page 97

project 1

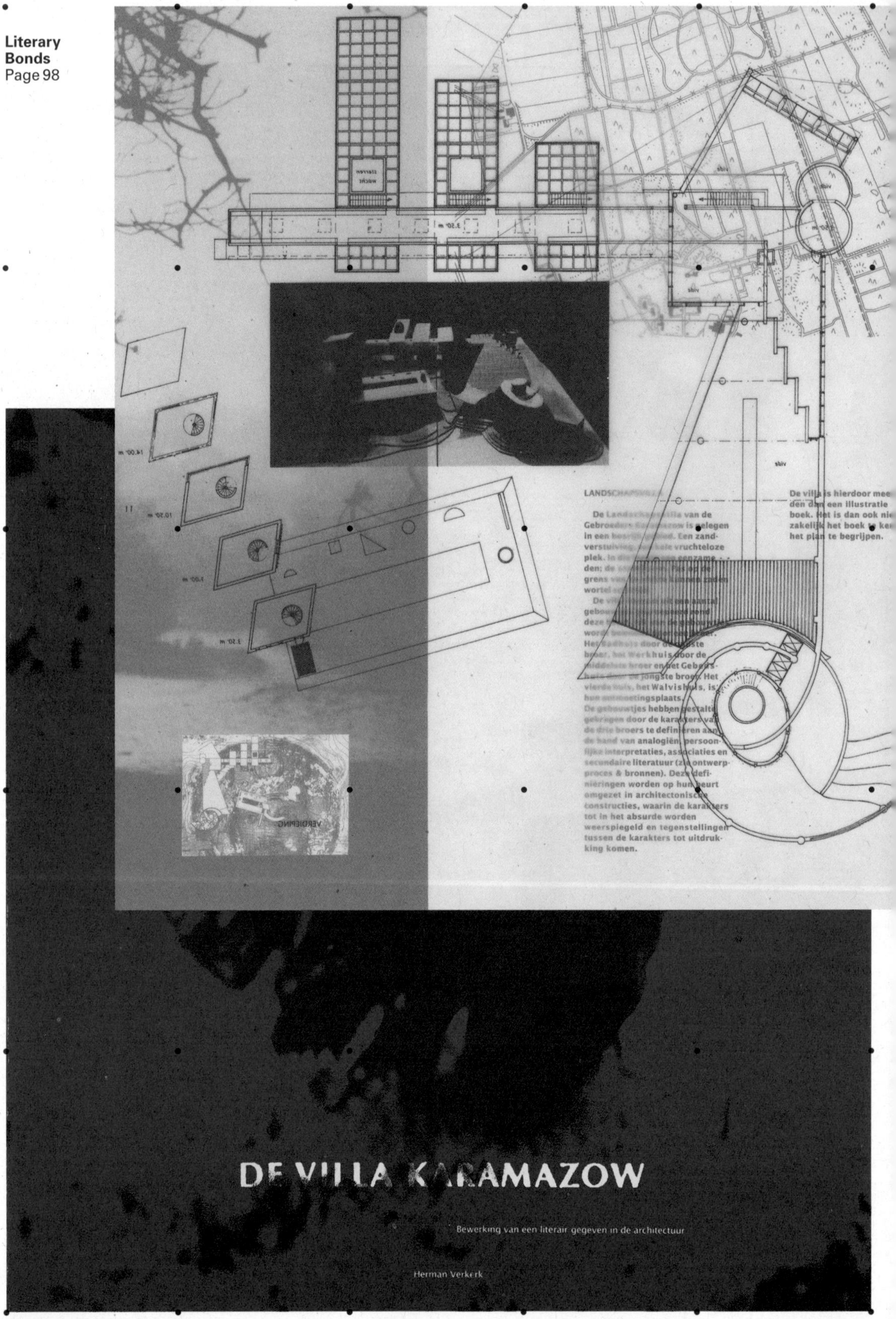
DE VILLA KARAMAZOW
Bewerking van een literair gegeven in de architectuur
Herman Verkerk

Villa Karamazow
Page 99

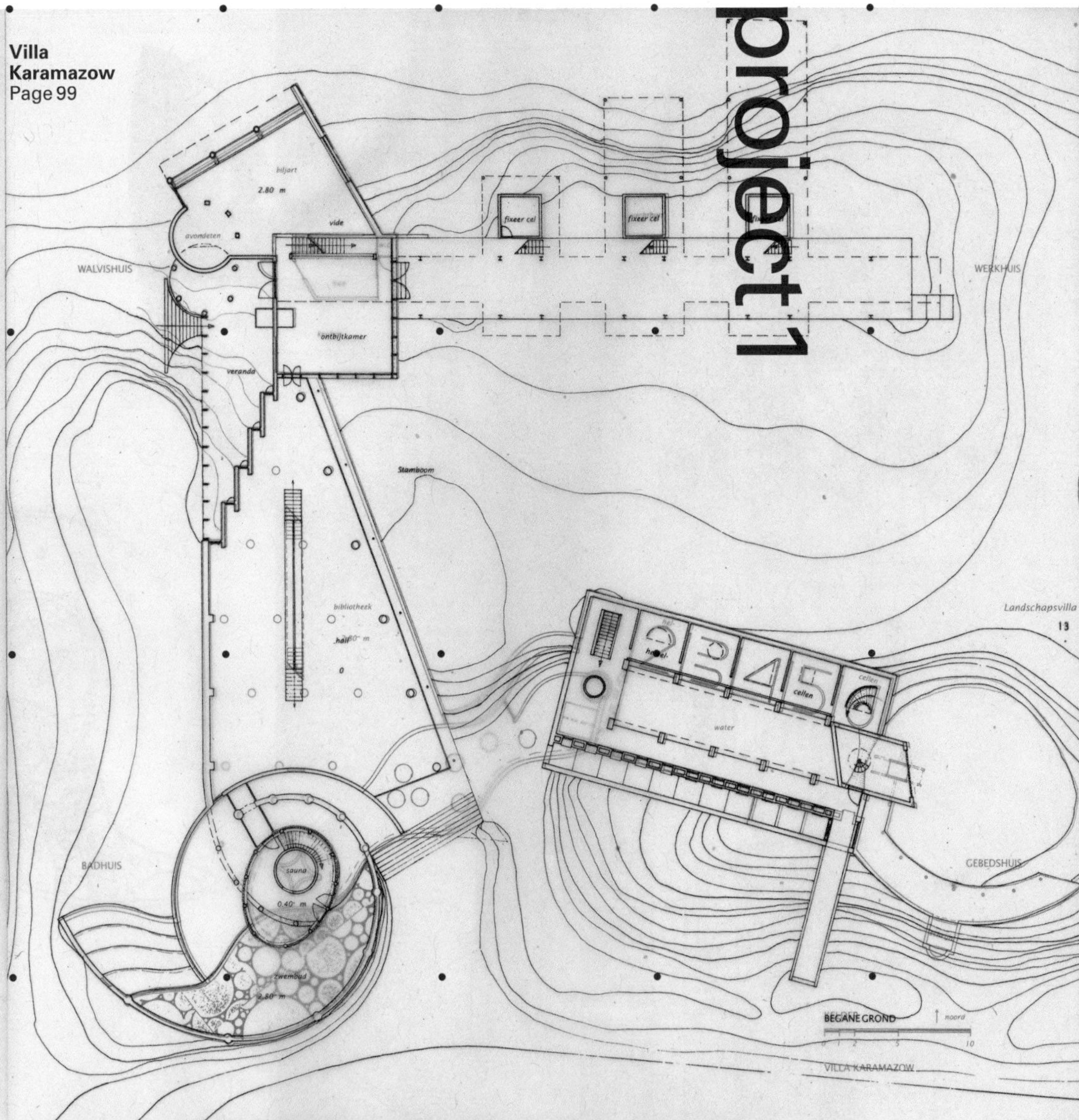

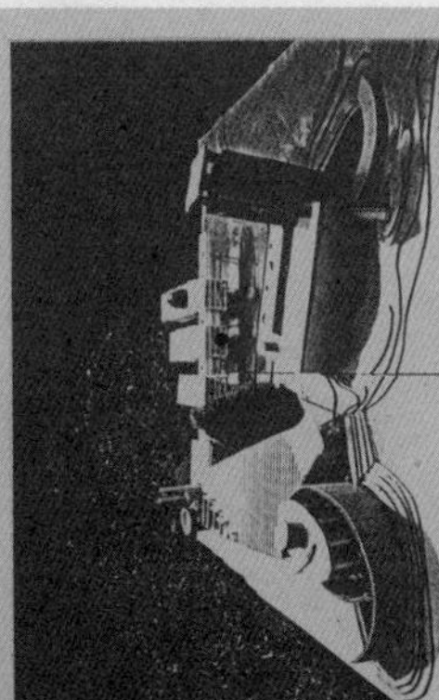

videostills 'De Villa Karamazow' (5 min.)

Literary Bonds
Page 100

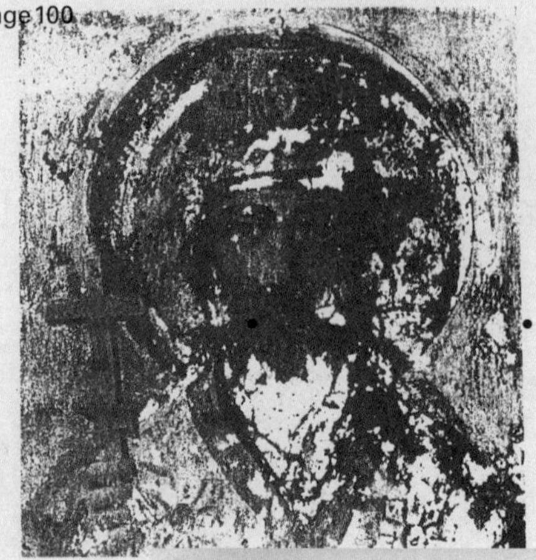

Through one he breathes the air;

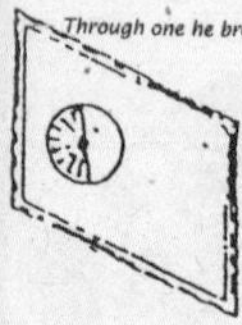

Through one hears music of the spheres;

Through one the eternal vine flourishes that he may recieve the grapes;

Gebedshuis
18

HET GEBEDS

De jongs
vrome jong
vloed door
in een russi
gebouwtje
wordt een
neerd, gein
Progress' va
van Terragn
spaanse en
tocht langs
wereld, om
stad waar d
eeuwige lev

Het gebo
gesloten kl
tectonische
betekenisd
Doorloop
langs de tw
trede een n
gebrandsch
het spiegel
houten kol
schoorstee
punt), de m
helcellen, w
seerde beg
zes hemelc
in het dak
je uiteindel

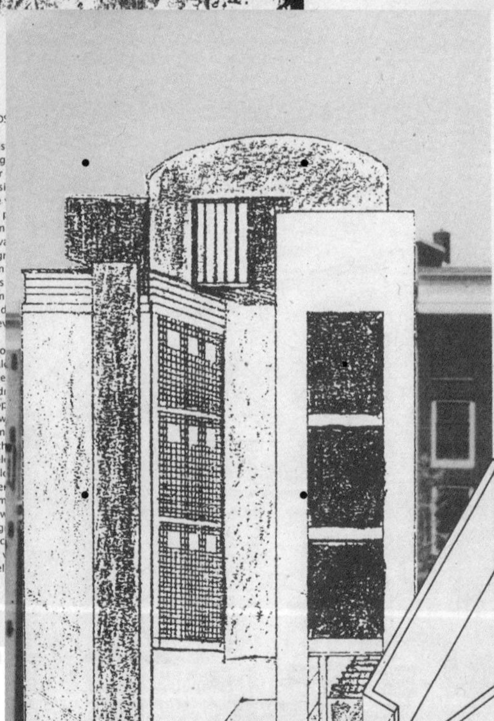

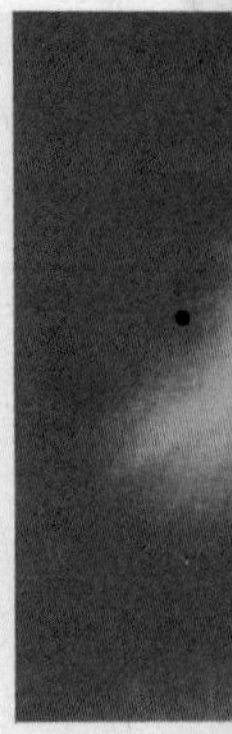

begane grond 0

kelder -4

Ter illustratie een aanta
ten, die deel zijn van dat
historische en actuele fei
stellingen en interpretati
oude binnenstad van Am
- een steegje, dat ooit
volume doorsneed, word
introduceerd.
- de kolommen, die he
dragen, zijn een verwijzi
aloude bouwen op palen
- de gevel, die de rooil
houdt de stedelijke wand
water in stand.
- het stapelen van ruim
komend uit het, sinds ee
de, ruimtegebrek.

DE KELDER EN BEGANE G

In de kelder en op de b
zijn ruimtes met een bes
Hier kan men genieten v
ken, film, dans en muzie
trap dient tegelijkertijd a
voor het bekijken van vi
De w.c.'s zijn geplaatst ir
kamer, die zich tot in he
lijkt uit te strekken.

project 1

bovenaanzicht kelder

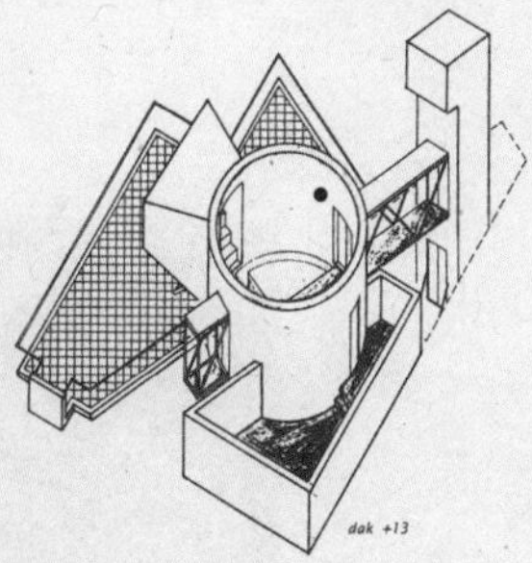

dak +13

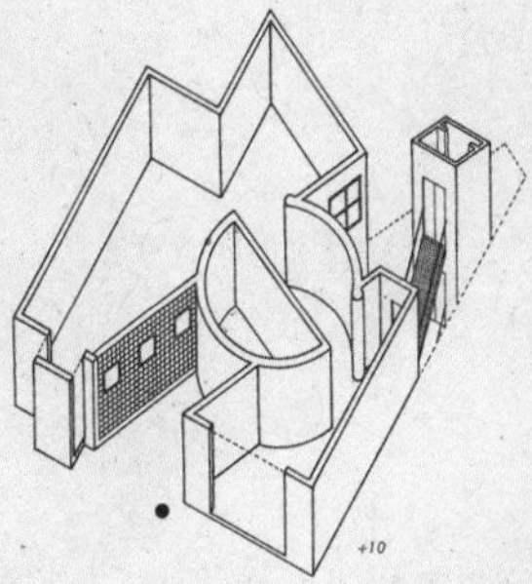

+10

DE WONINGEN

Drie woningen zijn ingeklemd tussen gemeenschappelijk te gebruiken ruimten op de begane grond/ kelder en het dak. Binnen de woning heeft elke ruimte een andere lichtintensiteit.

Bij binnenkomst treft men een uitwaaierende ruimte met een groot venster op de Amstel (eventuele keuken). Vervolgens verbindt een cilinder, zonder licht, de entree met een toelopende ruimte. Deze krijgt strijklicht van een erker aan de straatzijde (eventuele werkruimte). De zijgevel van deze ruimte wordt gevormd door een wand van glazen bouwstenen. Tenslotte ligt er aan de achterzijde, grenzend aan het binnenhofje, een vertrek met een melkglazen raam (eventuele slaapruimte).

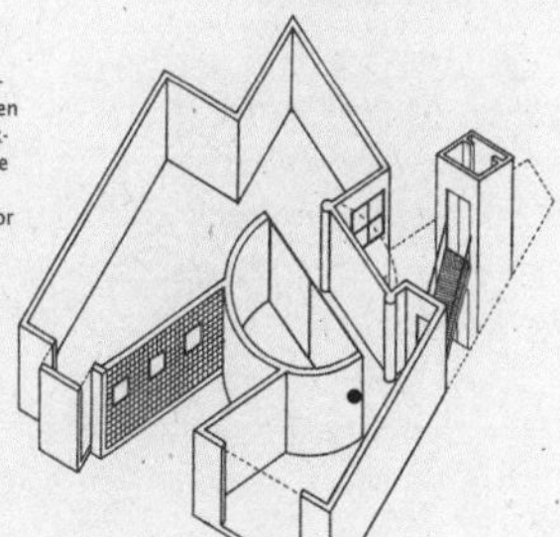

+7

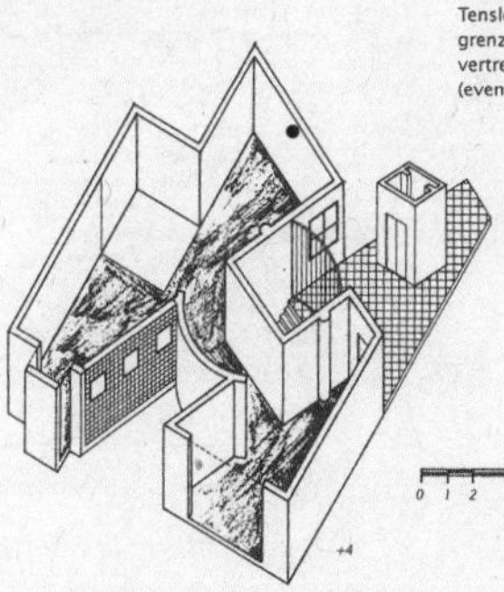

+4

HET DAK

Het dak bestaat uit de cilinder, die nu voor een deel gevuld is met water. Hierover bevindt zich een draaiend bruggetje. Komt het bruggetje bij de opening in de cilinder, aan de kant van de lift, dan kun je je laten meevoeren naar een besloten dakterras, een boven de villa zwevend nisje, of een tribune, die ook toegang geeft tot een 'open' dakterras.

Aangezien het bruggetje niet te bedienen is -het heeft een tijdklok- zul je daar bij aankomst en vertrek rekening mee moeten houden.

DE CILINDER

De cilinder, die buiten de onderdelen zowel in horizontale als verticale zin samenbindt, blijkt binnen op elk niveau anders. Zij raakt niet de grond, maar wordt gedragen door vier kolommen, die langzaam in de cilindervorm oplossen. Tussen deze kolommen bevindt zich een monumentale trap. Deze komt uit op een plateau waar de daadwerkelijke verbinding tussen de lagen van het huis is; de lift.

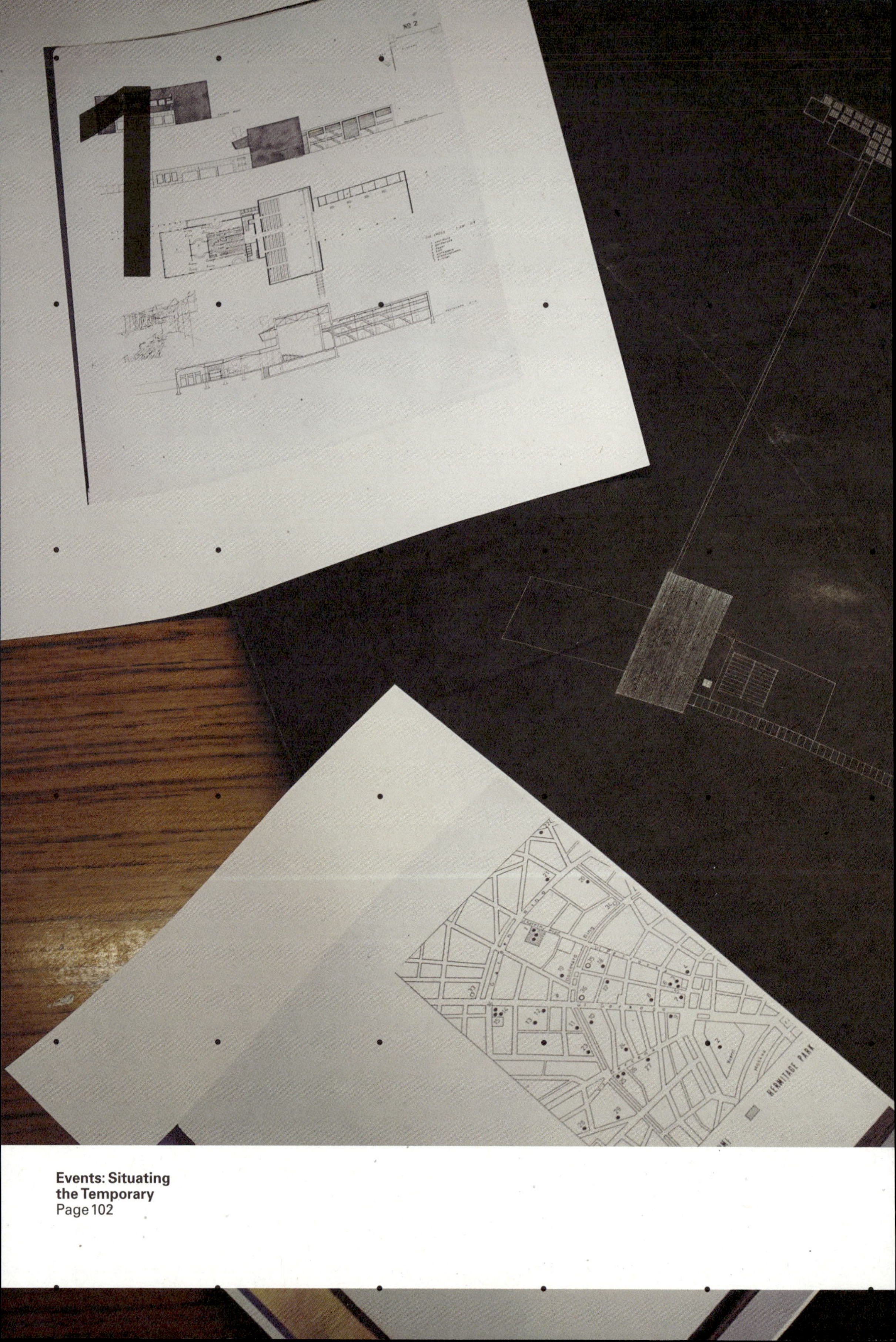

Events: Situating the Temporary
Page 102

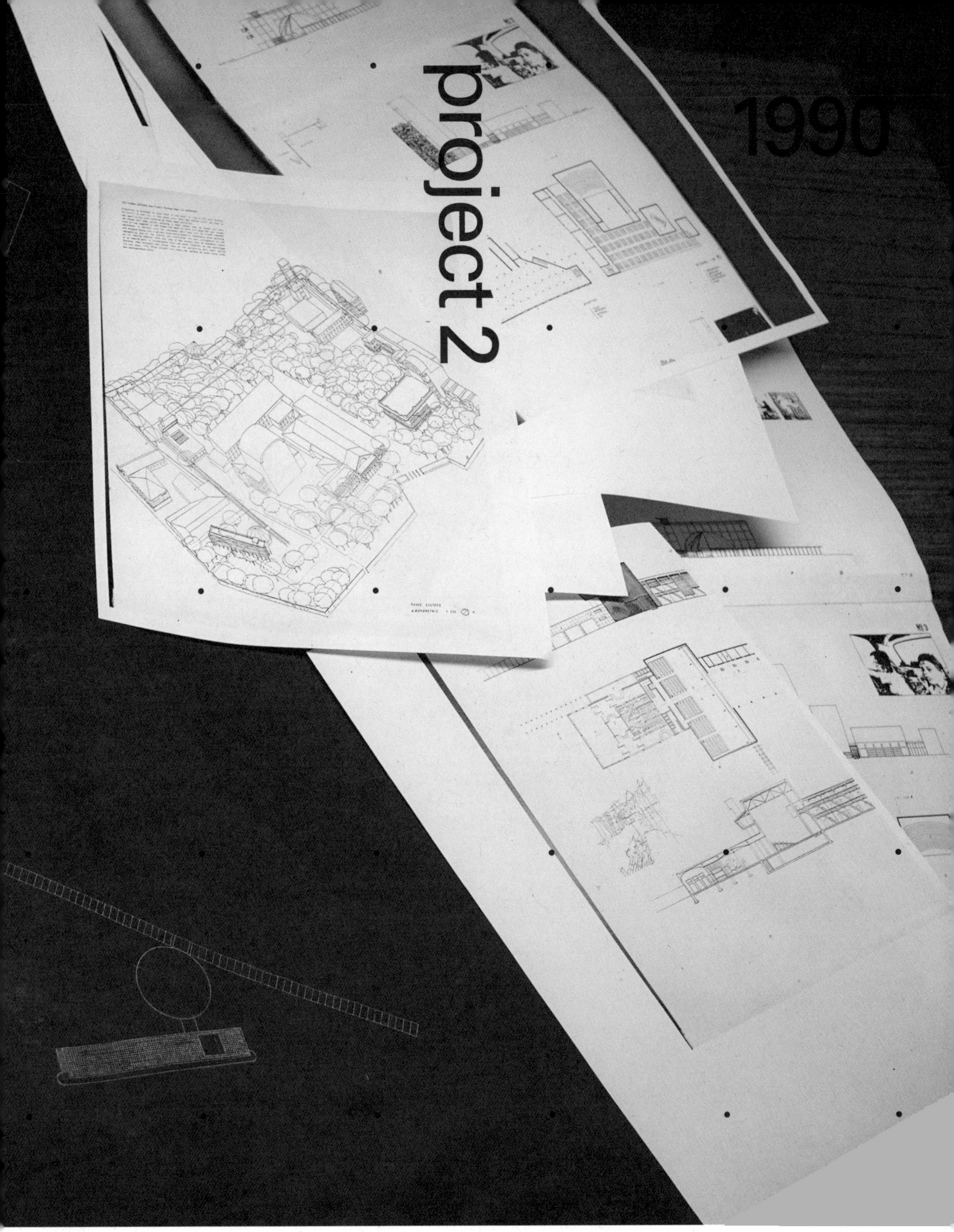

Literary Bonds
Page 103

Three Sisters
Project: Competition
Year: 1990
Data: page 629

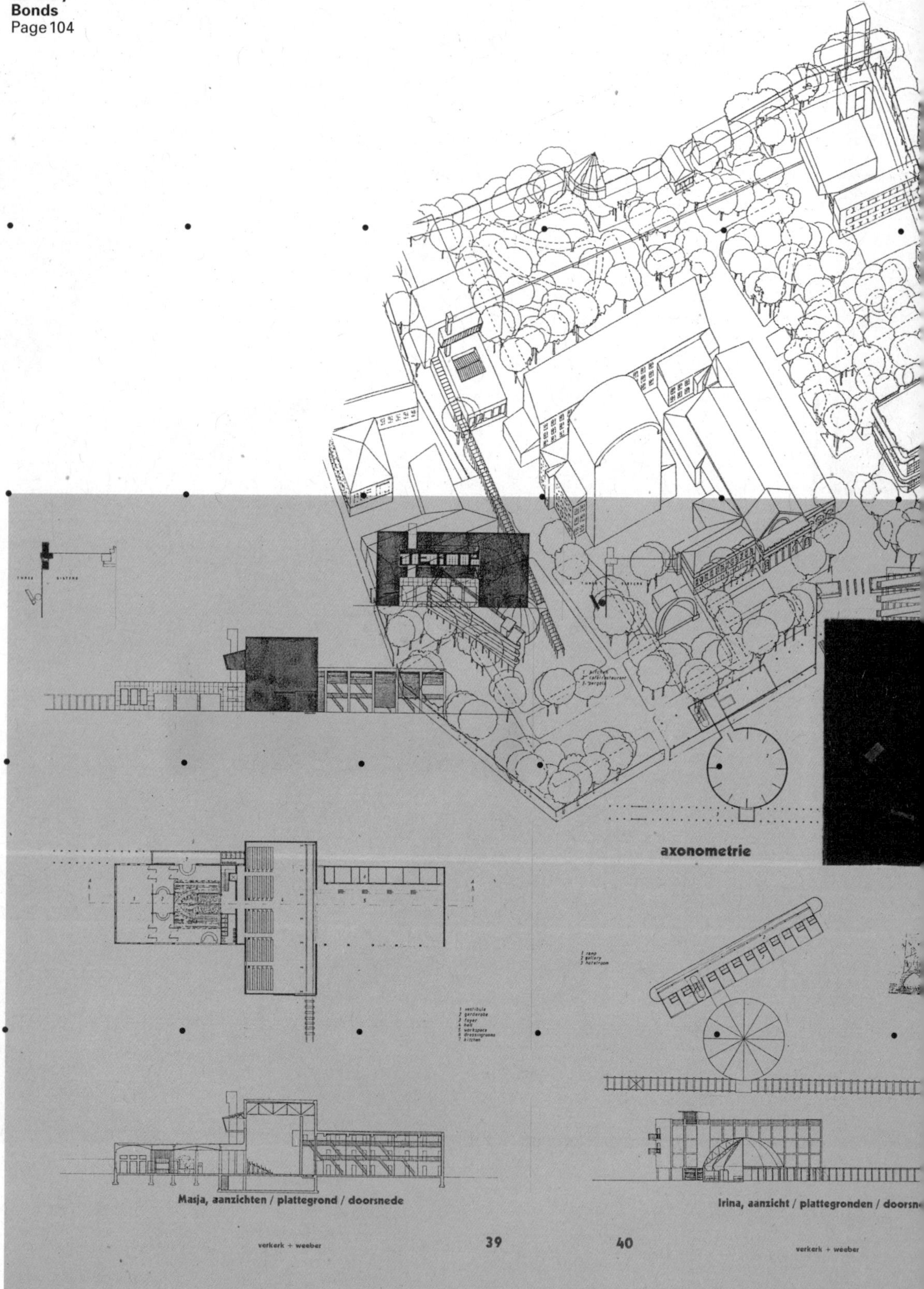
axonometrie
Masja, aanzichten / plattegrond / doorsnede
verkerk + weeber
39
40
Irina, aanzicht / plattegronden / doorsn
verkerk + weeber

project 2

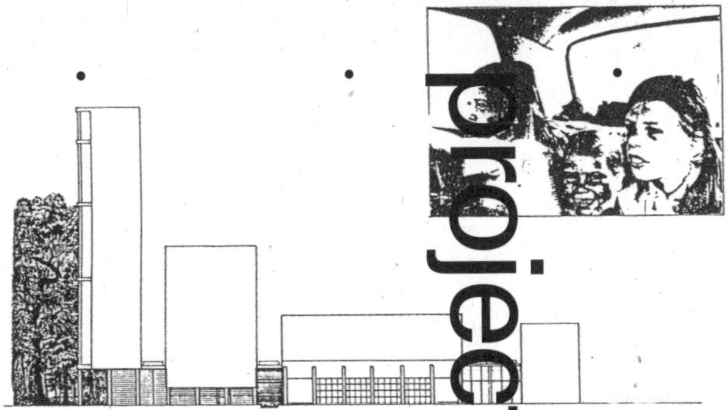

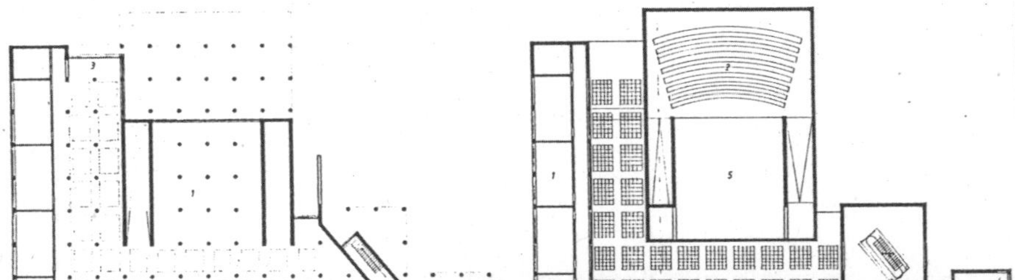

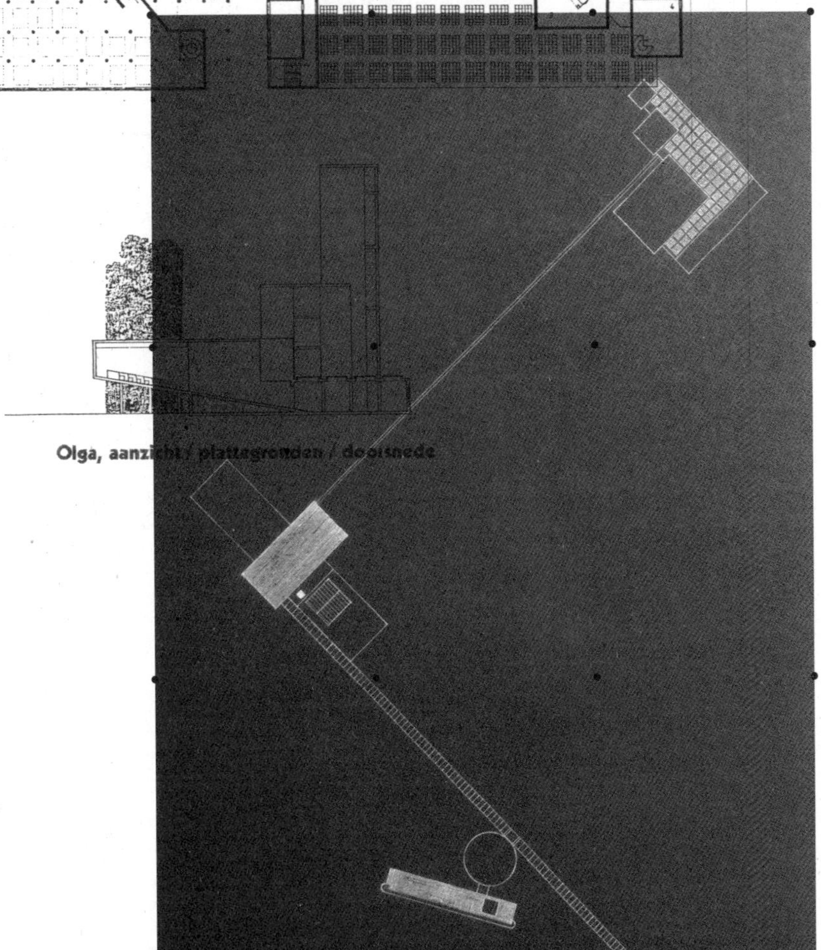

Olga, aanzicht / plattegronden / doorsnede

1

Events: Situating the Temporary
Page 106

edzard mik: speculations on literature and architecture

In their early work, EventArchitectuur drew inspiration from literature. Later on, architecture itself – the history of architecture – became their source of inspiration.
That may look like something of a volte-face, but the difference is less than it seems. Literature is a collection of stories, and architectural history, likewise, is nothing but a story, told using the vocabulary that makes architecture into architecture: the architectural elements. That story, as Rem Koolhaas showed with his *Elements of Architecture* exhibition during the Venice Architecture Biennale in 2014, is in danger of being erased by modernity. Architectural elements like the facade, ceiling, roof, door, window, and stair are afforded fewer and fewer opportunities to speak; technology has usurped their functions. Seen in this light, EventArchitectuur's decision to turn once more to architectural history can be construed as a critical move. Whereas architecture seems increasingly condemned to silence, EventArchitectuur allows it to speak. The fact that this often involves temporary structures only accentuates the critique. Architecture is summoned time and again, only to disappear just as easily.

There are architects who draw inspiration from literature. Conversely, there are also writers who appropriate their ideas from architecture.
Architecture lends itself to being charged with symbolism. So many human aspirations come together in architecture that symbolism is intrinsic to it; it fairly fizzes with it. As a writer, you don't have to try very hard; you can set to work immediately.

1

A construction pit that remains a construction pit stands for longing and impotence (Andrei Platonov, *The Foundation Pit*), an inaccessible castle for the impossibility of "solving" life (Franz Kafka, *The Castle*), transparency for its opposite, mendacity (H. M. van den Brink, *Heart of Glass*), a tower for pride (the Bible), a cell for solipsism (Vladimir Nabokov, *Invitation to a Beheading*), a bedroom for our most intimate interior world (Franz Kafka, *The Metamorphosis*), et cetera.

Literary Bonds Page 108

Not just architecture, but also its creator, the architect, is now and then deployed in literature. This usually happens in order to chronicle the conflict between ambition and morality. The architect is a vehicle for addressing a universal theme: that of immorality or, somewhat more subtly, the impossibility of morality.

An architect is perfect for this role. His or her work is, by definition, a balancing act. On the one hand, it is the exponent of individual ambition; on the other, its realization depends on economic, political, and social forces. Society is always involved, and so also morality.

This is not to say that the deployment of an architect as protagonist is always a success from a literary viewpoint. The symbolism is so compelling, and so obvious, that the scope for the emergence of a literary experience is not infrequently lost in the reading. That one thing stands for something else, and in doing so invests it with meaning, is essential to the operation of literature. But if it is too obtrusive, it can crush or smother that literary effect.

In our thinking, we use spatial structures. Thought and space are inextricably linked; they imply one another. The same is true of stories and space, for what are stories but mental structures used to organize events and connect them in a meaningful way? Writers unfold a novel as a space; readers move through a novel as through a space. That space can assume all manner of forms: ramified, labyrinthine, linear, spiral, or cyclical. For every novel it is possible to find a spatial equivalent, just as every spatial organization embodies a novel. Similarly, the impression a novel creates, the experience it generates, comes across as a space. Through the alchemy of characters, plot, style, and sentence rhythm, a literary text can oppress or create latitude, be restrictive or offer panoramic views, tempt us down all kinds of twisting paths, or offer a clear overview – no different from a painting, a film, or a piece of music. There are also thoughts that open up a space, thoughts that transform or divide a space, thoughts that close off a space...

When the space we are in changes, literature changes, too. In the nineteenth century – the century in which the novel blossomed in

Europe – that space was characterized by stratification and distance. More so than today, it was of vital importance whether you were socially or physically close to, or at a distance from, one another. There was a crucial difference between proximity, in a living room or home, and distance, between houses, villages, cities, and countries; between those who were inside, in a salon, and those who ventured outside; between citizen and farmer, director and worker; between admirer and admired; between yourself and the people you encountered while strolling along the street; between from where you had come and to where you were going. That stratification and distance determined nineteenth-century architecture, but it was also reflected in that century's novels. It lent them their content and structure, their language and spatial quality, their foundations and rationale. Likewise, they caused the novel to flourish, for as if framed in the salon, from the sanctuary of the armchair, the bourgeoisie longed to break out of the stratification, to bridge distances and set foot in places where no one had ever been before.

Since then, the space in which we find ourselves has undergone a breathtaking metamorphosis. Distance and stratification have become relative, space has simultaneously been broken open and shrunk, first by train, car, airplane and telephone, and later by the Internet and GSM. It was technology, much more than open, transparent architecture, that perfected the modernist ideal: we can be everywhere at once, and are continuously in one another's vicinity. There is nothing we can keep hidden anymore, secrets can no longer exist; it is as if we are all crammed together on a stage and incessantly spying on and shouting at one another.

If space is completely open, the classic novel has lost its rationale. There is no room anymore for longing, everything is within reach and accessible, there are no distances to bridge, no walls to raze, no secrets to disclose, and no uncharted regions to explore. So small has the space become that everyone interferes with everyone else and feels obligated to make an impact on one another.

This in turn defines the contours of the literary space, which is nowadays one of reciprocal monologues, of characters who talk to, but do not understand, one another, of unbridgeable proximity, of deadlock and immobility in a world of unprecedented possibilities and hypermobility, of emptiness in the absence of longing or, for the last, incurable romantic, of longing for longing. The one who creates that space, the writer, is no longer what he once was. He doesn't investigate anymore, he no longer delves, but grants himself the right to speak and makes his presence felt, just like the characters in his novels.

No wonder that the space in which literature is enacted has started to look more and more like a stage, and the writer like an actor playing the role of writer.

1

Literary Bonds
Page 110

In the past, you would write something like: "Rolf walked to the window and saw her approaching through the rain. At the front door she folded her umbrella, tidied her hair, looked hesitantly about her, and rang the bell."
But what if there is no window, but a glass wall instead? In that case, Rolf would be standing there in full view, and be just as visible to her as she to him. Glass walls, lifts, escalators, air-conditioning, as well as the Internet and the mobile network, mean that some events can no longer be described and have been replaced by other events. Instead of the slow, theatrical, metaphysical disappearance of a character who ascends the stair, it is a sudden disappearance or appearance as they enter or exit the lift. Instead of the private hesitation in front of a door, a visible and thus self-conscious approach from a distance, they are observed from behind a glass wall or sliding door. Instead of the opening of a window and the hailing of an acquaintance in the street, it is the fishing of a mobile phone out of a trouser pocket and the act of calling them. Secrets, double lives, bungled appointments, getting lost in a city, untraceable addresses, vanished lives? As a writer, you need to be endlessly inventive to make such marvelous lapses, which literature has always gratefully exploited, still sound plausible.

What a space has to say to you is determined by the way architectural elements have been deployed. They speak to you as you enter; you feel inspired to adopt an attitude, play a social role. It is no different for the character in a story. The writer knows that his character behaves differently in a corridor than in a salon, differently in a classroom than in a square, differently in a waiting room than on a stair. Those spaces are no mere decor, they affect the way characters behave and provide meaning. What characters do, or fail to do, is always connected with the implicit codes of a space.
This is why the decline of the architectural element, as raised by Koolhaas in Venice, inevitably has consequences for the way stories are told. Modern characters, characters of the present day, find themselves in spaces that are less specific, less differentiated, less meaningful. Even the intimacy of one's own home or one's own room means less when it is undermined from within by the endlessly expanding spaces contained by the television, the computer, and the smartphone.
If the space does not express much, it doesn't matter all that much, either, and as a writer you are forced to keep descriptions to a minimum and to focus on action and dialogue, or monologue. And indeed, this is what strikes you when comparing a contemporary novel with one from the nineteenth century: the interminable descriptions have vanished; it's all action and dialogue, or monologue.

There will come a time when words like “window,” “door,” “stair,” and “ceiling” can no longer be used, or at best nostalgically. Or with a sliding, ambiguous meaning; in other words, purely poetically.

You could also imagine a literature that can no longer borrow anything from spaces and has broken free from them altogether. A literature that consists of nothing but fragments of images and ideas, a poetic literature.

1

Events: Situating the Temporary
Page 112

project 14

1993

Swimming poollibrary
Project: Video
Duration: Very short-term, 30 minutes
Year: 1993
Data: page 633

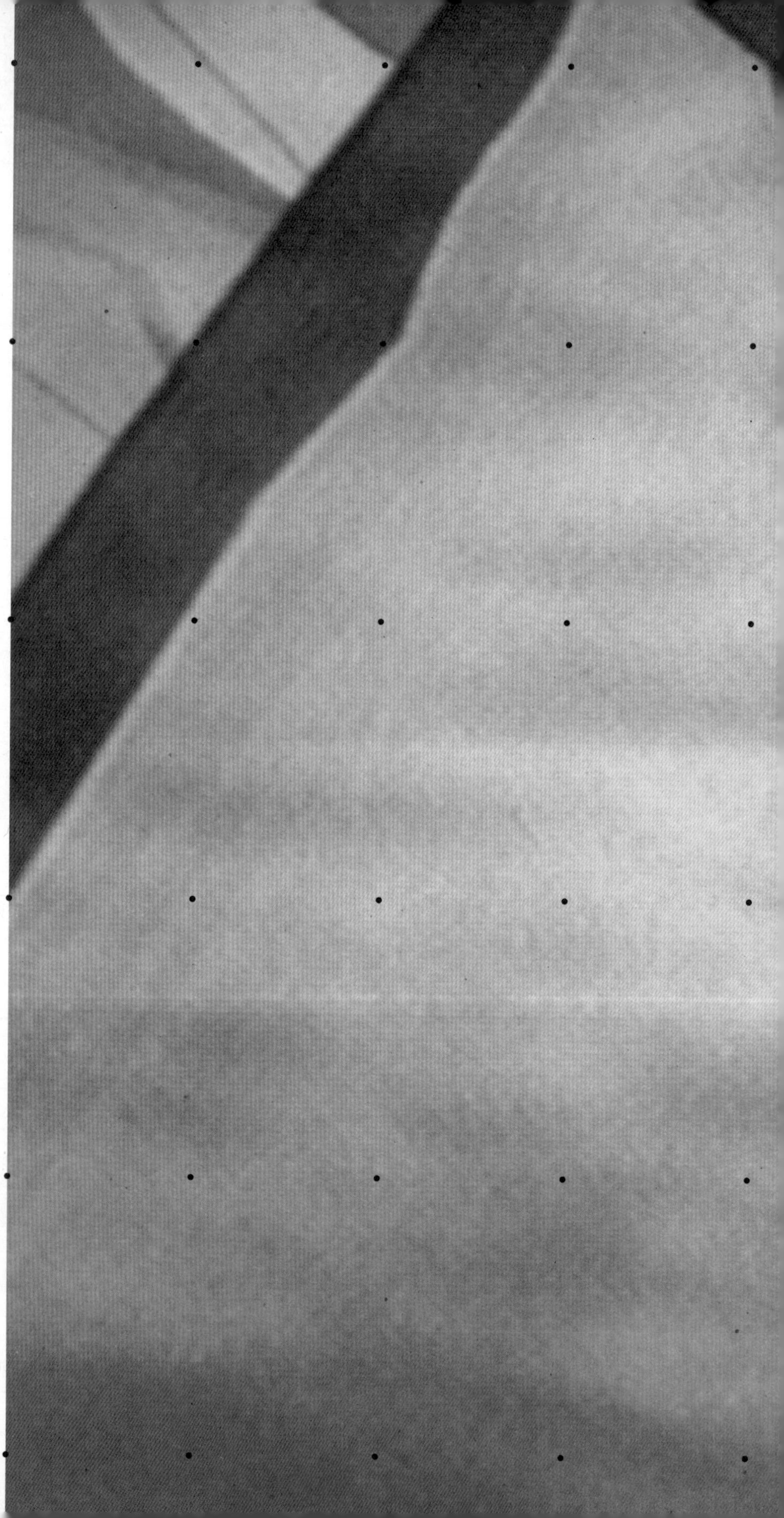

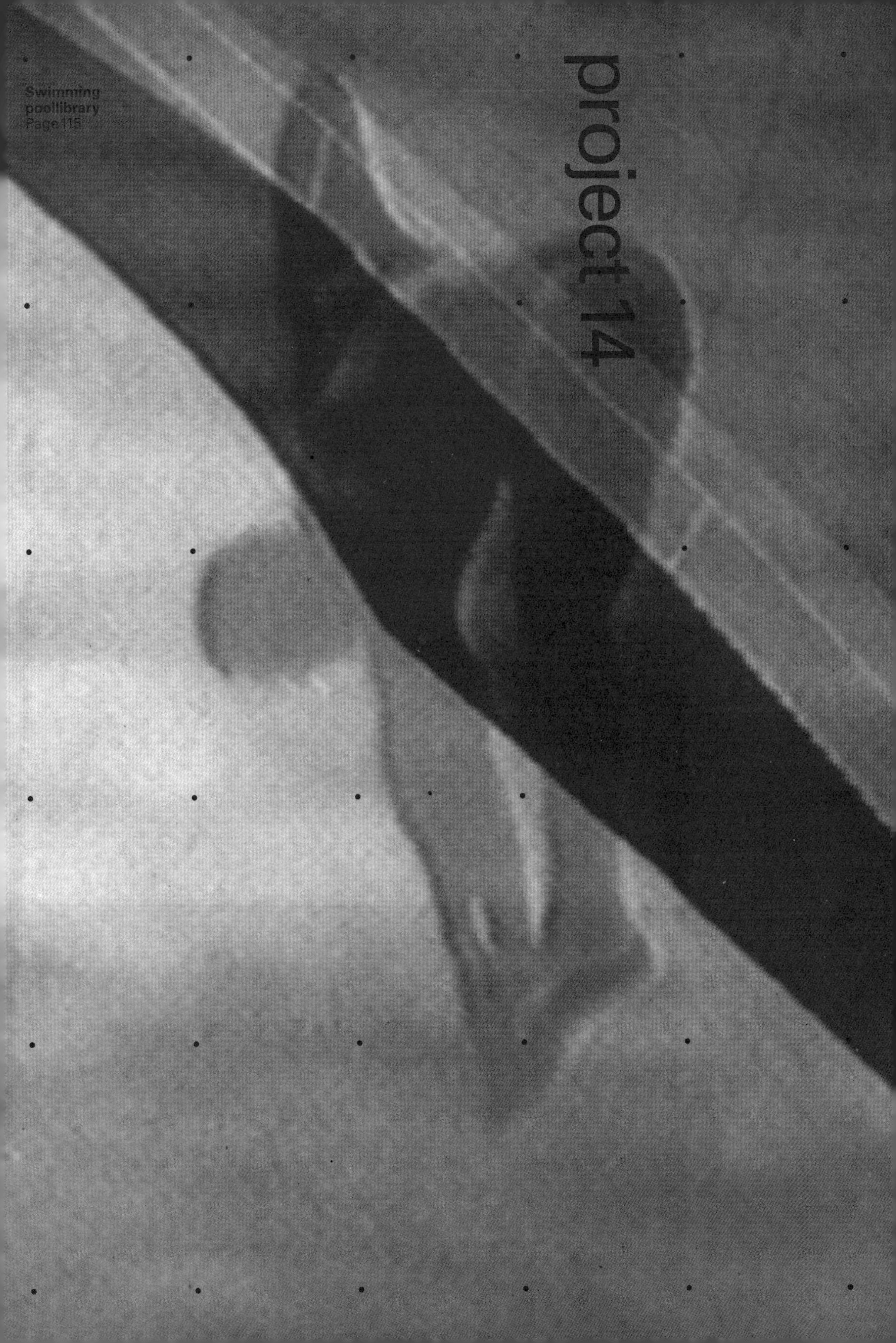
Swimming
poollibrary
Page 115
project 14

Swimming poollibrary
Page 117

project 14

project 14

project 14

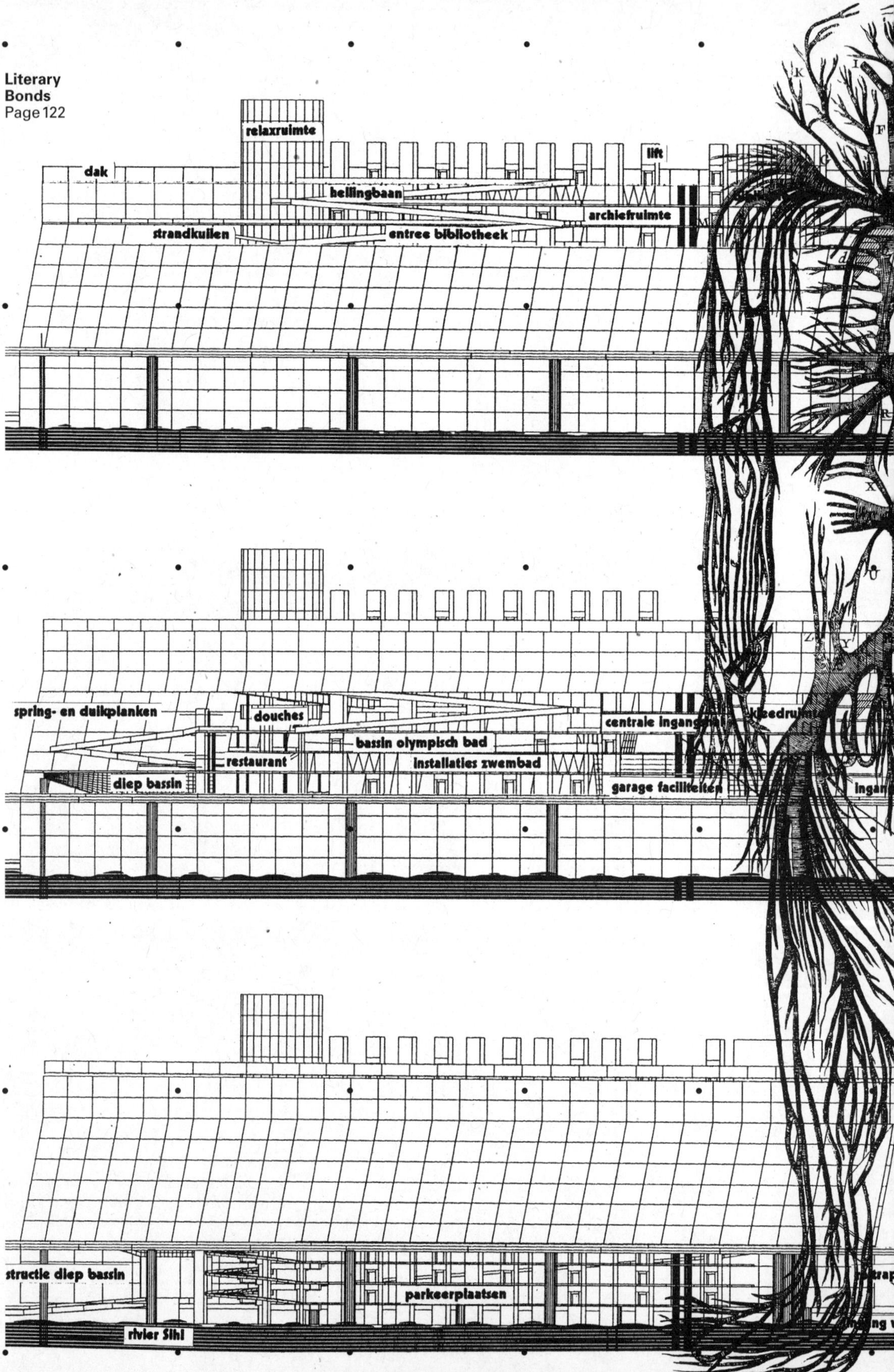
relaxruimte
dak
lift
hellingbaan
archiefruimte
strandkuilen
entree bibliotheek
spring- en duikplanken
douches
centrale ingang
bassin olympisch bad
restaurant
installaties zwembad
diep bassin
garage faciliteiten
structie diep bassin
parkeerplaatsen
rivier Sihl

project 14

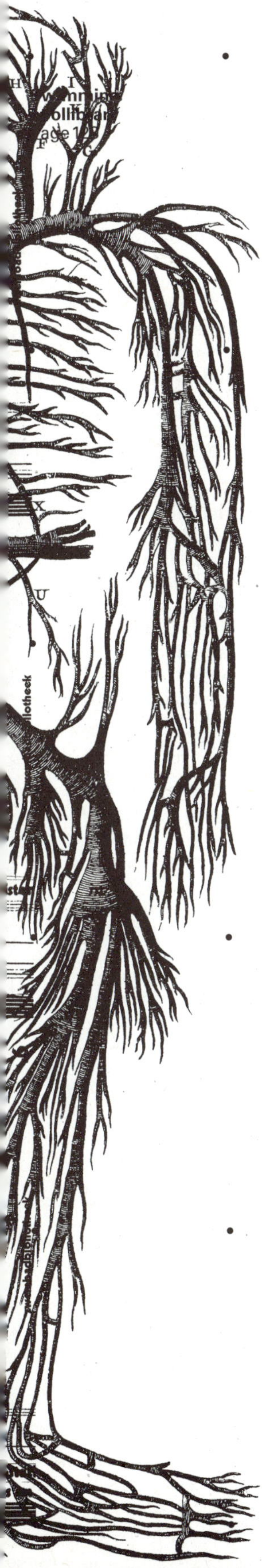

Events: Situating the Temporary
Page 124

cabinet

Cabinet of curiosities

Philipp Teufel

The sixteenth-century cabinets of curiosities presented the world in the lord's own parlor. The macrocosm was displayed in the collector's microcosm. The different types of nineteenth-century museums of the kind with which we are still familiar today have their roots in these microcosms. These archives of the whimsical, these atlases of things through which visitors can stroll, have retained their fascination right up until the present day.

Museum Wormianum is one of the best-known historical cabinets of curiosities, and has been reconstructed a large number of times. However, these reconstructions have never been able to match the fascination of the original. This collection belonging to a professor of medicine, Ole Worm, was not a showcase like the princely chambers of art and cabinets of curiosities, but a place of research. Before his death, Worm published a four-volume work with many illustrations. This work elevated him to the ranks of one of the major sources of inspiration for the European museums, which resulted from the earlier chambers of art and cabinets of curiosities.

The phenomenon that is the cabinet of curiosities is presently experiencing yet another boom, with a large number of current museum projects rediscovering their potential. Even with Europe's largest cultural project, the Humboldt Forum in Berlin, which is scheduled to open its doors in 2019, there is a direct connection with the Renaissance chambers of art and cabinets of curiosities. The Berlin museums had their genesis in Berlin's City Palace. At the beginning of the nineteenth century, the palace's chamber of art and cabinet of curiosities were transferred to scientific collections at universities.

The collections were democratized, catalogued, ordered, archived, preserved, and later passed on to various present-day museums. Or, as the historian Horst Bredekamp puts it in sensory terms, "My personal starting point is always the chamber of art located in the palace, which – in this respect Berlin is a special case – up to the mid-19th century, gave birth, so to speak, to all kinds of different museums."[1]

The fact that the term "cabinet of curiosities" is currently on everybody's lips is, perhaps, heralding a new era in the museum business. However, this is not a step backwards but, to paraphrase Walter Benjamin, "long-reverberating thunder."[2] Many museums are now once again getting away from those smooth, white, sterile, sometimes even aseptic forms of presentation. Away from those unchanging curatorial concepts and systems of organization. Away from media overkill. The principle of the cabinet of curiosities once again allows people to stand and gawk; it enjoys the advantage of surprise. The new cabinets of curiosities bring together things and subjects that would never otherwise encounter one another. And it is true that this does discomfit the minds of some curators, designers, and visitors, because it takes more effort to both devise such concepts and be on their receiving ends.

Daniel Spoerri and Marie-Louise von Plessen rediscovered, breathed new life into, and developed the concept of the cabinet of curiosities in their own particular way for their exhibition *Musée Sentimental de Paris*, in 1977.

1
Horst Bredekamp, "Franz Kugler and the Concept of World Art History," http://bgc-apps.rubensteintech.com/blogs/event-test/files/2010/01/HUPpapers1.pdf, 25.

2
The original reads, "In the fields with which we are concerned, knowledge comes only like lightning. The text is the long roll of thunder that follows." See Walter Benjamin, *Arcades Project*, trans. Howard Eiland and Kevin McLaughlin (Cambridge, MA: Konvolut N, 1999), 456.

Events: Situating the Temporary
Page 125

# of curiosities

The new cabinet of curiosities as a curatorial concept and guiding principle is successful not only because it evokes associations and works with powerful images, but also because it is poetic and imagination-driven. This transforms the contemporary cabinet of curiosities into a new "super-museum" that opens up the eyes of its curators, designers, and visitors, finally providing them with more opportunities to dream, make associations, and resurrect their own memories.

These new cabinets of curiosities are now taking their places in museums and flagship stores, and at triennials and expos. At Museum Folkwang in Essen, for example, the two Cuban artists known as Los Carpinteros have implemented this kind of super-museum that can be interpreted as both a sculpture in its own right and a kind of exhibition architecture. This new cabinet of curiosities is a giant helmet (as indicated by the title of the work, *Helm/Helmet/Yelmo*), one in which visitors can walk around and, at the same time, an outsize display case that people can enter like a room in a museum.

The situation at Mmuseumm in New York City is completely different. This contemporary take on the cabinet of curiosities also incorporates the curatorial idea of the historical cabinet of curiosities. Using contemporary items, it explains the complexity of the world we live in – all this inside the space that used to be occupied by an elevator shaft.

The flagship store for the Louis Vuitton brand on London's Bond Street is the best example of how the principle of the cabinet of curiosities can be conveyed in the context of a luxury brand. This cabinet of branded curiosities contains an assortment of products for connoisseurs, collectors, and tourists in search of something special and unique. The idiosyncrasy of the goods and the perfect way that they are presented means that the customer experience includes both the product's exclusiveness and the uniqueness of the brand environment. In summer 2015, Swarovski opened sixteen cabinets of curiosities with its Crystal Worlds in Wattens, where visitors are offered a holistic spatial experience.

Although it may seem dead and forgotten, the cabinets of curiosities concept is now more alive than ever, in our midst and utterly up-to-the-minute, both as a curatorial archetype and as the guiding principle for design.

Tapestries? Tapestries!

The compelling suggestion of a dream world

Koen Kleijn

The Burgundian duke Charles the Bold lost his life in the Battle of Nancy, on January 5, 1477. His army was cut to ribbons by a company of Swiss and German troops; the survivors took to their heels, and so the entire inventory of Charles's court fell into the hands of the enemy. It was quite a bounty: standards, insignia, gold and silver plate, crystal goblets, precious stones in sumptuous settings, clocks, candlesticks, mirrors, reliquaries, chalices, crosses, book bindings, ceremonial robes, armor, paintings, costumes, tapestries, et cetera. A major part of the spoils are still held in Swiss museums.

During the course of the fourteenth century, the Dukes of Burgundy had greatly expanded their ancestral territory, centered on Dijon. They achieved this in part through tactical marriages, but more especially by force of arms; wedged between France, Germany, and Switzerland, they provoked conflicts on all sides. The greatest gains were to be made in the north. In 1369, they became lords and masters of Flanders, then the economic powerhouse of Europe, and gradually increased their possessions in the Low Countries until, under Charles the Bold, all seventeen provinces were in Burgundian hands.

Flanders became their most important territory. Charles married in Bruges, and what was left of his body after the Battle of Nancy was buried there. Yet the Burgundians did not have a permanent castle in Flanders, or a palace of their own. The court traveled. The duke was in a permanent state of war, and therefore also permanently on the road. The ducal household was a "portable grandeur," a mobile palace, a traveling theater, fully equipped for public display wherever it happened to find itself. When Charles occupied a local castle for a few days, or set up camp somewhere, all those peripatetic

tapestries!

treasures were used to furnish a temporary court.

The tapestries played an exceptionally important role in this. Nowadays, given their size and fragility, most of them hang somewhat forlornly in museums, but in Charles's time they were the most expensive works of art, far more important than permanent wall paintings, which were in fact often painted in imitation of the tapestries. Charles the Bold owned several series, depicting the lives of great exemplars like Alexander, Caesar, and Achilles.

In 1472, the city of Bruges presented him with an eleven-piece series depicting the Trojan War. Each carpet was 475 centimeters high and 950 centimeters long; together they formed a frieze of almost 100 meters. Gold and silver threads had been worked into the weave so that in the evenings, by torchlight, they glinted brightly.

They enabled the duke to transform any courtroom in his dukedom and any army tent in the field into a palace room, with what the historian Johan Huizinga called "the compelling suggestion of a dream world," a well-considered spectacle of dynastic pretensions and chivalric codes.[1] He could present himself as an invincible strategist, or conversely, as a wise and reasonable judge, as the political situation dictated. The artists in his retinue designed all manner of ephemeral works: table decorations in sugar, theatrical costumes, wine fountains, masks for the *morisca*, spectacularly decorated platters, and architectural structures such as spectator stands, rostrums, and canopies.

And that was just the material side of things. Inside that temporary court, power and the social order were meticulously choreographed, quite literally: gestures and movements were precisely stage-managed according to relative status. Who should enter first, and who next? Who should sit beside whom?

Thus the duke moved around his temporary palaces in a dream world, a symbolic pageant in which chivalric ideals took shape. The gruesome reality of the battlefield, where Charles had earned his dashing nickname, was a long way away.

tapestries?

1
See Johan Huizinga, *The Autumn of the Middle Ages*, trans. Rodney J. Payton and Ulrich Mammitzsch (Chicago: University of Chicago Press, 1996). First published in 1921 as the second Dutch edition.

2

lib that moment!

2 the ephemerality of an event 1995

and the permanence of a pavilion 2000

2

lib that moment!

2

The Temporary

Even as architecture became material, its relationship with time would remain complex. Whereas a building often promises "forever," the event is confidently finite, although elastic in its temporal boundaries. What could architecture create in the moment, and how would it harness contemporary networks and technologies to achieve that? The flow – not the being, but the becoming – emerges from the provisional, the ephemeral, the play of light and sound and air.

Yet the fragility of the space, the temporality of the architectural installation, would inversely demand more meaning, more communication, achieved through the theater of the event. The fashion show offered a paradigm, an apogee of sensorial intensity that would die and be reborn again and again. Inflatable, metallic, projected, recorded, and streamed. The permanence of stone broken down into the space of a breath, a reflection at the speed of light, the vectors of bits and bytes.

1996: The first large-scale live broadcast is streamed online.
1997: Paul Rudolph and Aldo Rossi pass away.
1998: Apple launches the iMac.
1999: The first season of *Big Brother* debuts.
2000: The dot-com bubble reaches its peak and the stock market falls.

Johannes Schwartz, Winkel, 2007
Page 133

johannes schwartz

2

Events: Situating the Temporary
Page 134

project 60

1999

Lib That Moment!
Page 135

Doors of Perception 5: Play
Project: Temporary interior
Duration: Short-term, 3 days
Year: 1999
Data: page 638

project 60

3

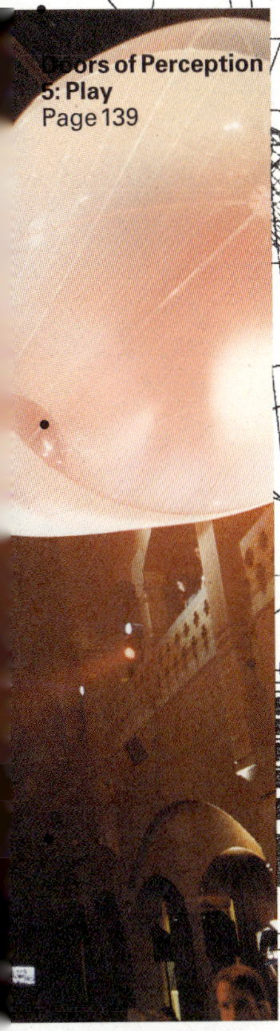

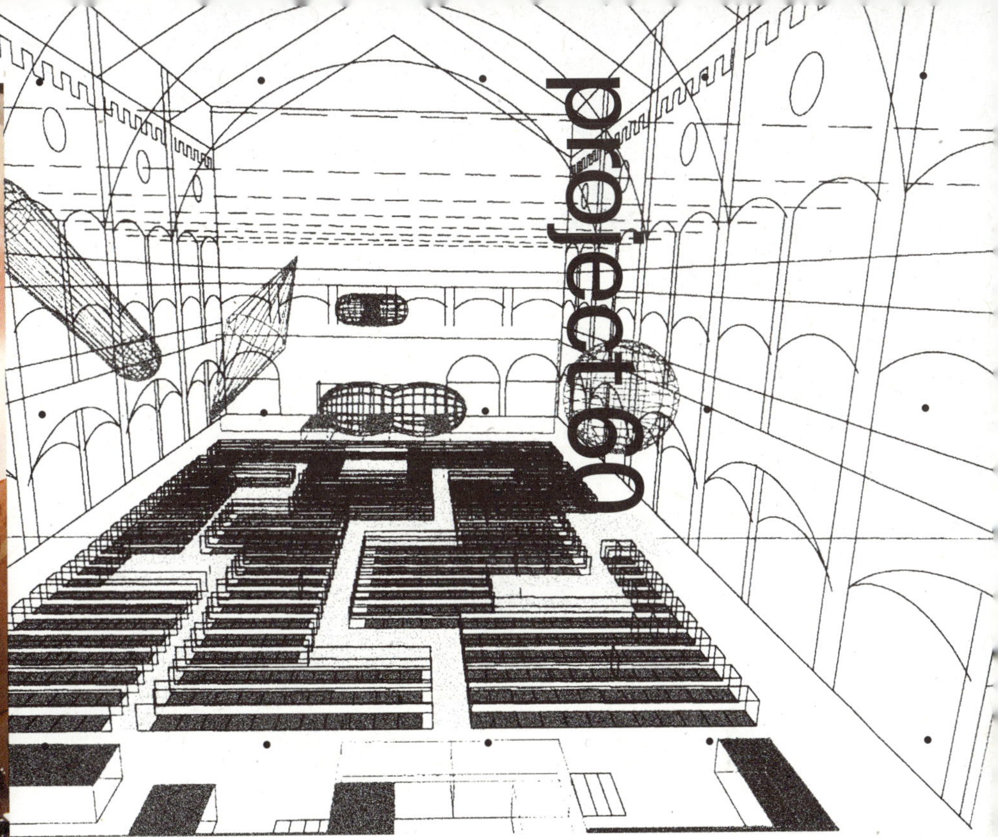
project60

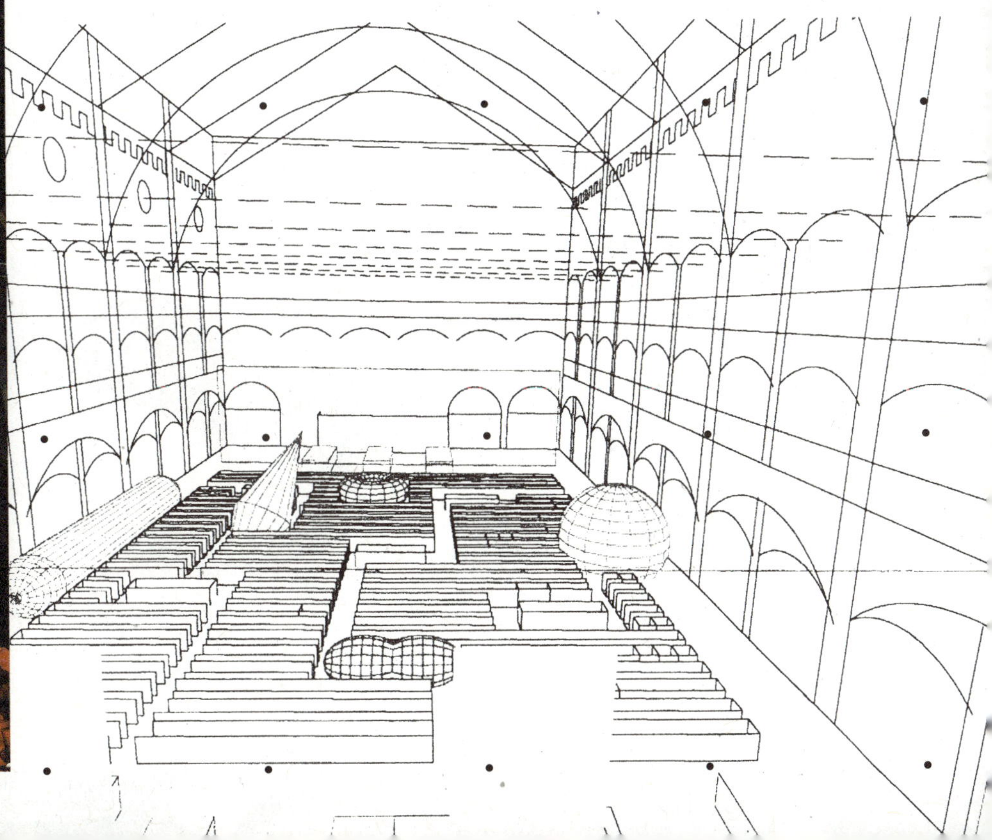

2

Events: Situating the Temporary
Page 140

Lib That Moment!
Page 141

Fashion Shows
Project: Fashion Show
Duration: Very short-term, 20 minutes
Year: 1989–2008
Data: Amsterdam, page 630 / Paris, page 633

15. Fashion Show,
orson + bodil
Paris, March 1994

project 15, 16, 25

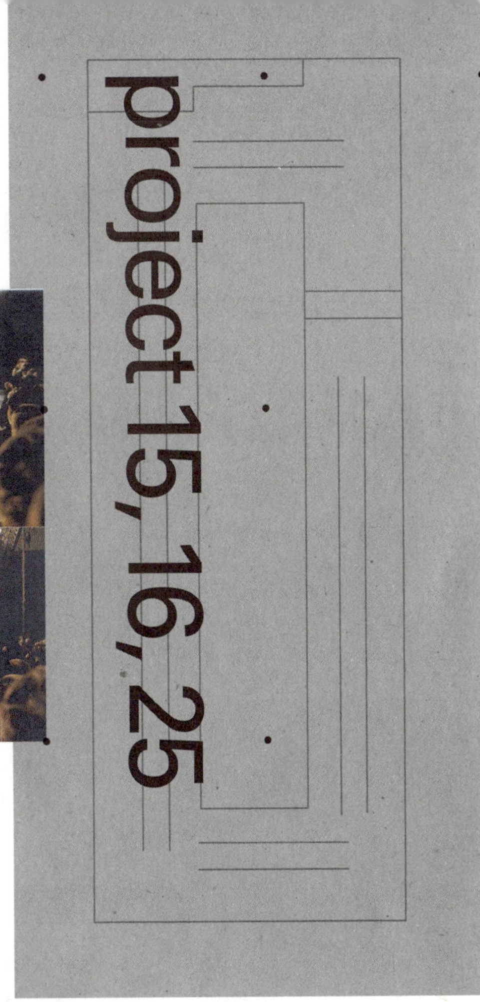

16. Fashion Show,
orson + bodil
Paris, October 1994

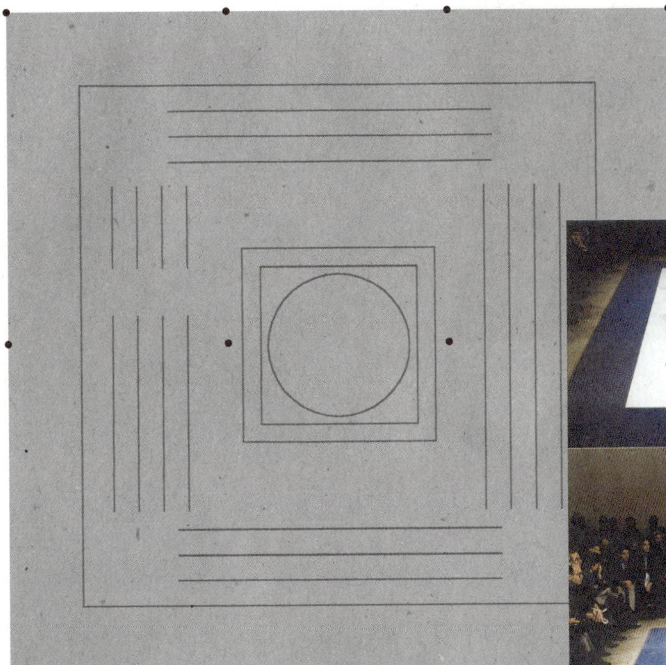

25. Fashion Show,
orson + bodil
Paris, March 1995

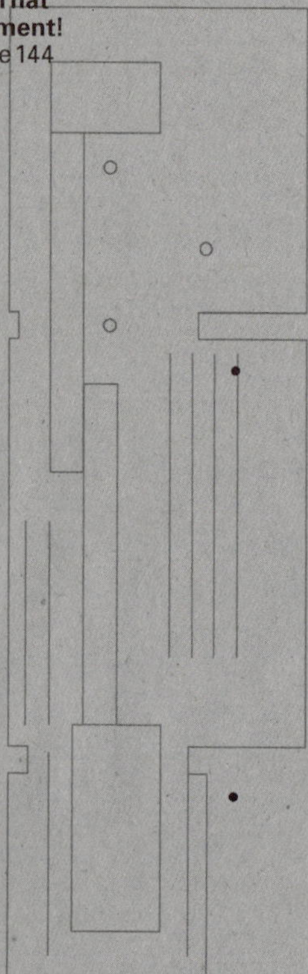

17. Fashion Show,
SO by alexander
van slobbe
Paris, July 1994

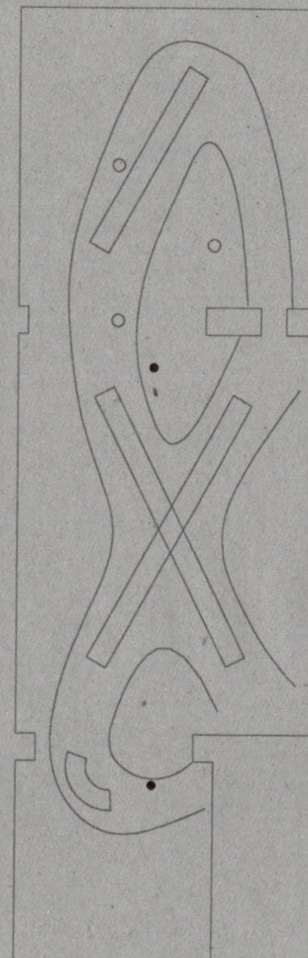

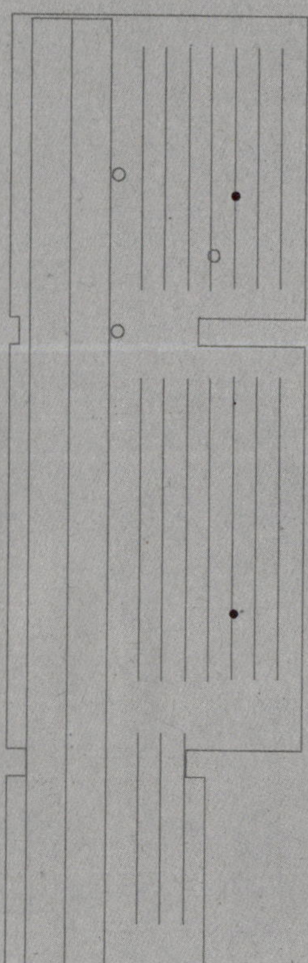

33. Fashion Show,
SO by alexander
van slobbe
Paris, January 1996

project 17, 26, 27, 33, 34

26. Fashion Show, SO by alexander van slobbe Paris, January 1995

27. Fashion Show, SO by alexander van slobbe Paris, July 1995

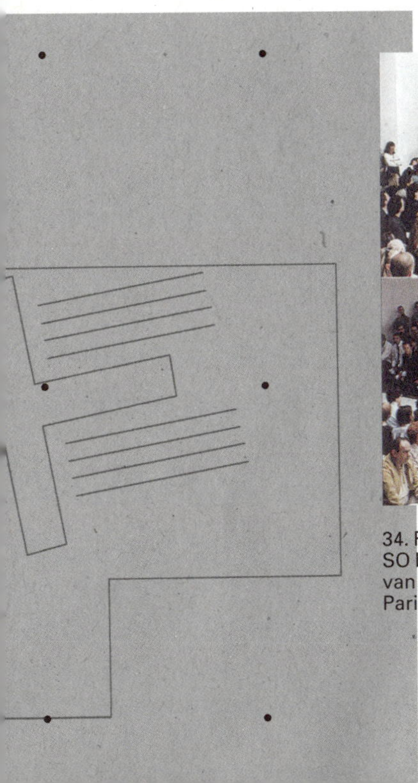

34. Fashion Show, SO by alexander van slobbe Paris, July 1996

Lib That Moment!
Page 146

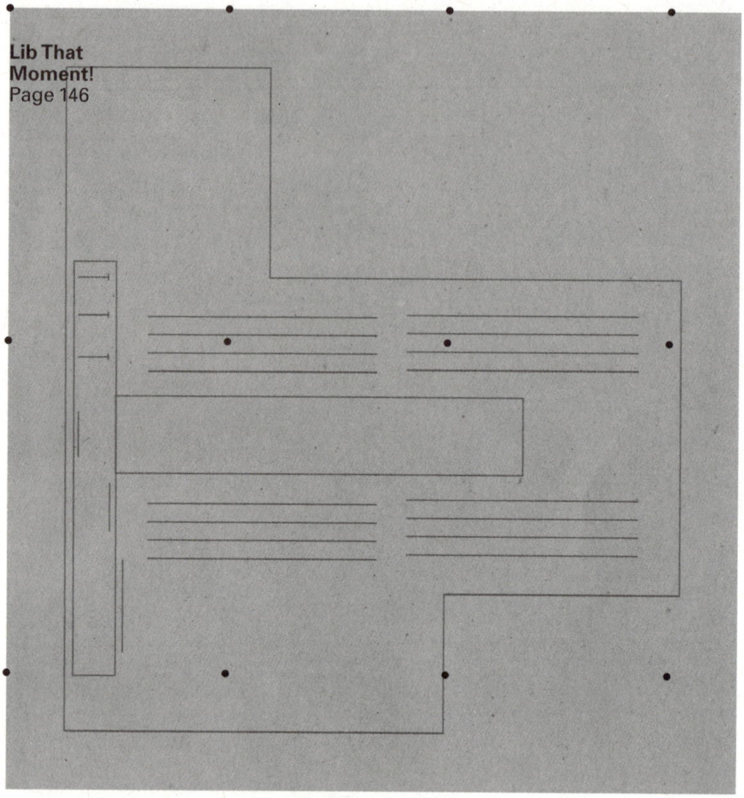

42. Fashion Show,
SO by alexander
van slobbe
Paris, January 1997

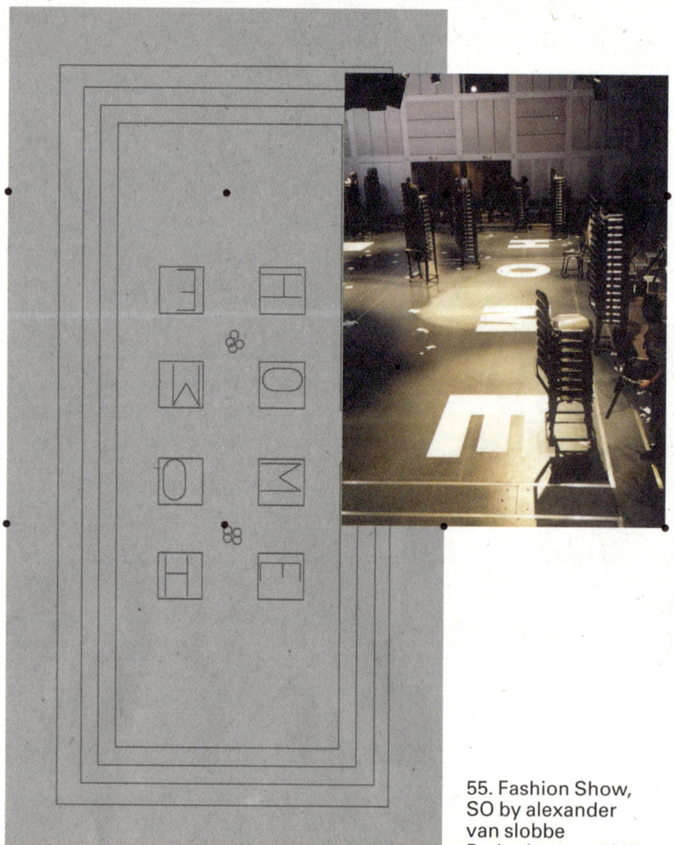

55. Fashion Show,
SO by alexander
van slobbe
Paris, January 1998

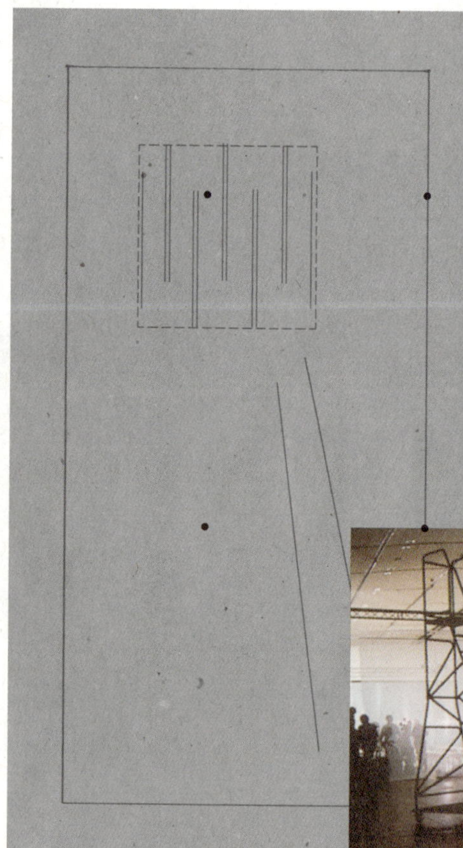

project 42, 43, 55, 56

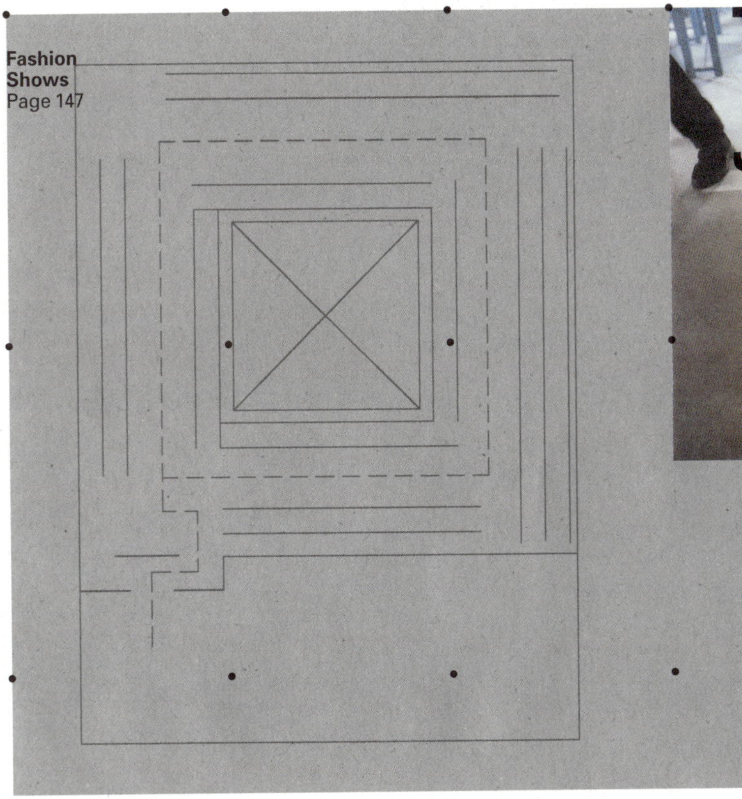

43. Fashion Show,
SO by alexander
van slobbe
Paris, July 1997

56. Fashion Show,
SO by alexander
van slobbe
Paris, July 1998

Lib That Moment!
Page 148

66. Fashion Show,
SO by alexander
van slobbe
Paris, January 1999

74. Fashion Show,
SO by alexander
van slobbe
Paris, July 2000

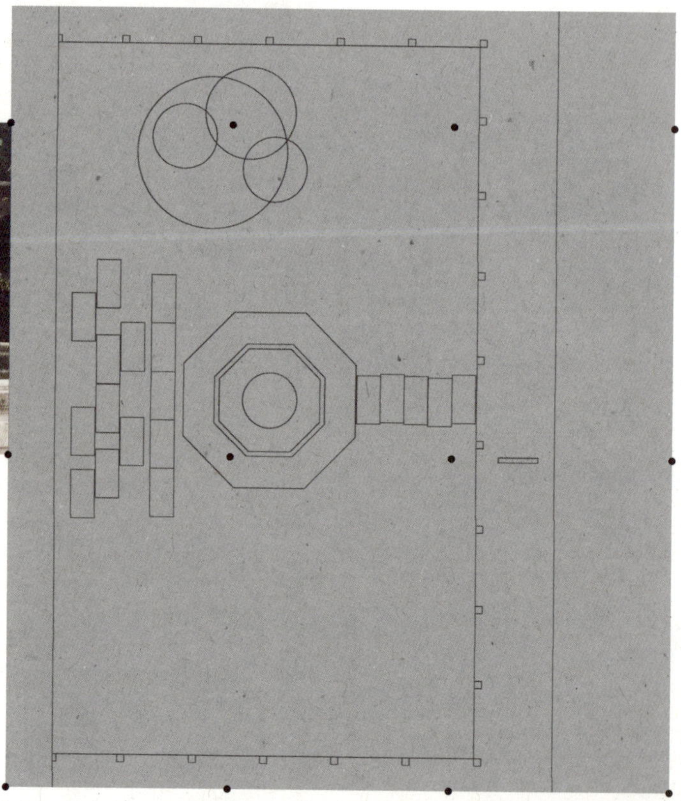

project 66, 67, 74, 80

67. Fashion Show,
SO by alexander
van slobbe
Paris, July 1999

80. Fashion Show,
SO by alexander
van slobbe
Paris, January 2001

project 73, 81

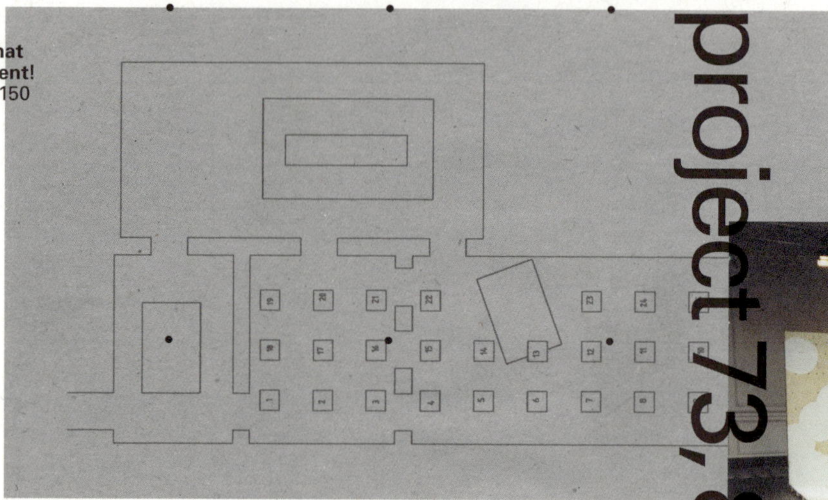

73. Fashion Show,
SO by alexander
van slobbe
Paris, January 2000

81. Fashion Show,
SO by alexander
van slobbe
Paris, July 2001

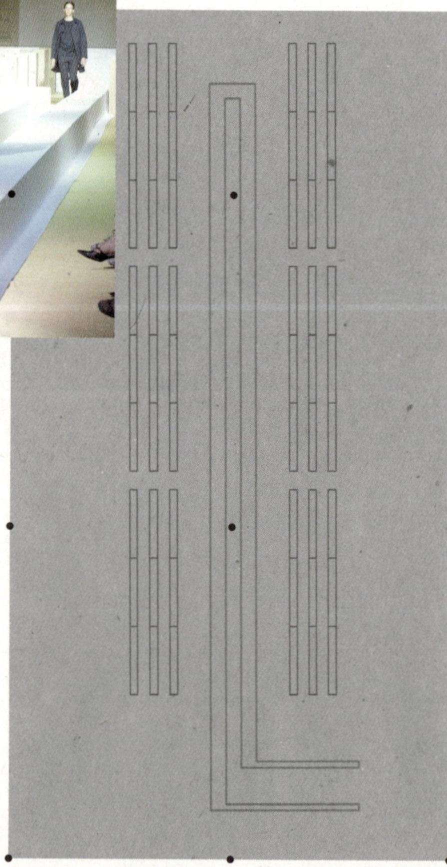

project 4, 160

4. Fashion Show,
orson + bodil and
Lilian Driessen
Amsterdam, 1989

160. Fashion Show,
orson + bodil and
Francisco van Benthum
Amsterdam, 2008

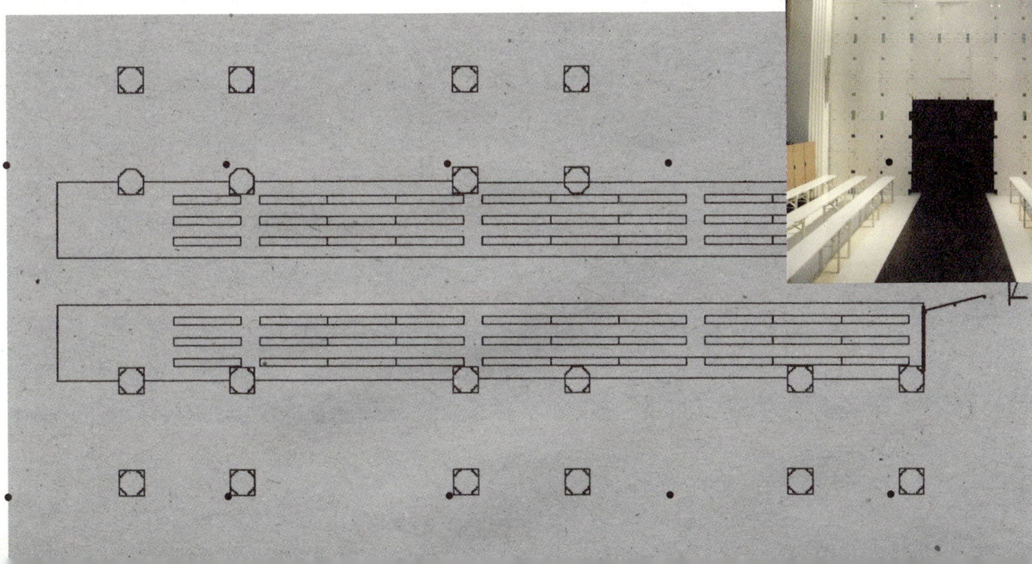

2

Events: Situating the Temporary

Page 152

jorinde seijdel: loose, empty, and light

Identity and affinity in EventArchitectuur

The design studio headed by Herman Verkerk always looks for the essence of each new commission. It approaches this task not from the perspective of a fixed identity that it imposes from without, or places at the service of the client, as is often the case in traditional design practice, but from the viewpoint of (a quest for) "affinity." EventArchitectuur's designs include presentation models for fashion and for art, seemingly antithetical domains in which, however, "display" and "identity" play a significant role. Is it possible to play with the dominant presentation models and identities of fashion and art without deploying a fixed presentation model or personal identity?

"To pass freely through open doors, it is necessary to respect the fact that they have solid frames. This principle, by which the old professor had always lived, is simply a requisite of the sense of reality. But if there is a sense of reality, and no one will doubt that it has its justification for existing, then there must also be something we can call a sense of possibility. Whoever has it does not say, for instance: Here this or that has happened, will happen, must happen; but he invents: Here this or that might, could, or ought to happen. If he is told that something is the way it is, he will think: Well, it could probably just as well be otherwise. So the sense of possibility could be defined outright as the ability to conceive of everything there might be just as well, and to attach no more importance to what is than to what is not."[1]

1 Robert Musil, *The Man Without Qualities*, trans. Burton Pike and Sophie Wilkins (New York: Alfred A. Knopf, 1995), chapter 4.

Architecture that wants to start all over again

Anyone considering Herman Verkerk's studio, EventArchitectuur, finds her- or himself confronted with a remarkably "loose" and immaterial oeuvre made up of a heterogeneous collection of concepts, semi-applied and semi-autonomous designs, and temporary and permanent installations. The design studio is mainly concerned with contemporary forms of presentation and communication, such as fashion shows, events, exhibitions, magazines, and shop interiors, for which it develops bespoke models or supports, architectural and conceptual structures, the elaboration and completion of which is left to the client and the public.

The means employed are usually "light" in the sense of being non- or only minimally material: smell, light, time, music, text, photography, film...

In the Netherlands, EventArchitectuur has designed exhibitions for the Centraal Museum in Utrecht, De Vleeshal in Middelburg, the Stedelijk Museum in Amsterdam, and the NAi (now Het Nieuwe Instituut) in Rotterdam, and devised presentations for fashion shows and shops, in particular for Alexander van Slobbe's SO and orson + bodil labels. It has also launched publications like *Forum* magazine and, together with Rianne Makkink, *SLOOM* (www.sloom.org).

In addition, the studio collaborates with many other individuals, including Maarten Theuwkens (artist/designer), Guus Beumer (curator/publicist), Hermen Maat (artist), Laura Weeber (architect), Bart Guldemond (designer), Joke Robaard (artist), Erik Blits (architect), Erik Wong (graphic designer), Richard Cameron (DJ), Ruud Pouwels (lighting designer), Eddy de Clercq (DJ), and Jop van Bennekom (graphic designer).

The specific nature or orientation of the studio is not immediately apparent from this summary. Unless it is that EventArchitectuur expressly taps into a wide range of disciplines and domains, and operates within both specifically museological contexts and the arena of fashion and design. A number of the designs appear to be primarily supporting and facilitating structures. For example, for the opening of the Rem Koolhaas/OMA archives at the NAi in Rotterdam (*Start*, 2004), EventArchitectuur collaborated with Bart Guldemond to design a "depot" consisting of rudimentary doorless cupboards containing box files, which visitors could browse through. And for *MARK*, an exhibition of Dutch graphic design (Stedelijk Museum, 2004), EventArchitectuur teamed up with Paul Kuipers to design another archive-like setting, this time constructed entirely from rough timber pallets and mirrors. For an exhibition about the art of painting in De Vleeshal in Middelburg, *We'll slide down the Surface of Things* (2002), Verkerk installed "white cube-inspired" spaces as supports for the paintings.

In addition, there are less "applied" designs, at least from a traditional point of view.

In De Vleeshal in 2001, Verkerk staged an installation oriented towards shopping and fashion of transparent but empty displays, *Higher Truth no. 5*. For the *Waterproof* exhibition in Fort Asperen (2001), EventArchitectuur's contribution consisted of equipping visitors with a survival belt complete with a flashlight, a fleece blanket, and a map of the fort.

To what extent does EventArchitectuur's practice reveal an overarching design ideology or a recognizable signature? A substantial part of Verkerk's "architecture" does seem to indicate a strong predilection for accentuating the formal vocabulary and idiom of the archive and the exhibition; for the cupboard, the pedestal, the depot, and the "display." And, in the context of fashion and "show," for the catwalk, the clothing rack, and the display case.

To a degree, of course, this is intrinsic to the design of presentation models in general, but precisely by emphasizing and "designing" the formal and conceptual foundations of these models, EventArchitectuur appears to be seeking a new engagement with content and the public. The firm allows the design and architecture to be largely determined by the given context and discipline, which are constantly changing. In that sense, there is no question of an "established" style. We are also dealing with an "architecture that wants to start again," as Verkerk himself puts it; with an architecture that is consciously determined to eschew a readily recognizable, unambiguous identity. This reflects the decidedly complex desire to be identity-free in a world – of art, fashion, design, and media – that is strongly tied to brand, image, and identity. So, an architecture that desires to begin from scratch. But with what? And does this constitute a utopian or, on the contrary, a critical attitude?

Identity

In the discourse of modern art, "identity" in the sense of "individuality" or "personality" is related to the industrialization that began in the eighteenth century and the emergence, in the nineteenth century, of the artist as autonomous subject; as a creative individual and maker of artworks that are unique, authentic, and original. The "special" identity of the artist and his/her work was often enlisted against the leveling effect of the burgeoning culture of reproduction and the social alienation attributed to the Industrial Revolution. At least art could still ensure authenticity and individuality in the cultural industry of the new middle-class society, so the reasoning went (though a paradoxical consequence was the division between art and everyday reality that this generated). At the same time, the unique identity of one work of art vis-à-vis another grew in importance: as an evaluative, selective, and classifying factor in both the history and economy of art.

It is this defining identity-thinking, this thinking in terms of entities, that the postmodernism of recent decades in art, culture, and science challenged in favor of a more differentiated way of thinking. This did not, however, imply the disappearance of "identity" as a defining term within cultural discourse. Yet the new focus on "small" individual stories and personal freedom of choice meant that identity was increasingly construed as a temporary or relative condition. Switching from one identity to another became decisive, based on the assumption that there

2

Lib That Moment!
Page 156

was no longer any center, or any overriding meta-identity. In art, this new interpretation of identity was mirrored by the simultaneous existence of many movements and approaches, by an "anything goes" attitude. In short, by the ever-increasing economic and cultural turnover rate of identities.

The postmodern "death of the author" may have signaled the death of the romantic image of the artist, but it also signaled the birth of the artist (or designer) as entrepreneur, star, VIP, or brand. In general, the postmodernist, liberating notion of identity has become increasingly associated with a pragmatic and utilitarian market mentality in recent years. If identity is switchable, it is clearly also interchangeable and makeable, and thus marketable and (re)producible. Identity is now strongly geared towards image, brand, lifestyle, label, and the like, and is viewed less and less as a natural phenomenon or historically evolved condition, and more and more as an artificial construct used to market and promote people and things.

The exchange of codes that has been taking place recently between art, fashion, design, and even architecture, has only made the notion (and understanding) of identity even more complex: the abandonment of individual identity boosts the rise of global and ephemeral identities. Identity is increasingly a matter of instant recognition and visibility, attributes that now largely determine the success and impact of art, fashion, and design, as well as architecture, as if they were positive qualities. A lack of identity in products or people is associated with a lack of charisma, communication, or relevance, and thus also with a lack of marketability. A person or product regarded as lacking an identity, or with an identity that has lost its appeal or doesn't seem to be working, hires a firm or a consultant for a "total makeover." Identity is increasingly about the "outside," about the shell or "skin" around an empty core.

The primacy of identity is simultaneously its crisis. In the social and political dynamic of present-day Western society, cultural identities are just as easily abandoned as reanimated. There is a nostalgic and repressive side to the current quest and desire for identity, which lends identity a disciplinary and corrective effect. The new thinking on identity is still based on demarcation and closure.

Affinity

"I'm not interested in trading on a personal signature," Verkerk says. "I'm looking for connection." This is another statement that signals EventArchitectuur's refusal to be part of the ubiquitous quest for identity and recognizability. You might once again wonder whether this is the futile dream of a naive architect or, conversely, a subversive and artistic move that has its eye on an alternative space: "connection," which is to say, solidarity,

rapport, or affinity. Connection, in the sense of affinity, also implies correspondence; in other words, similarity, analogy, common ground, consensus...
All terms that are more or less at odds with the connotations of identity, in which the emphasis is on difference and singularity. Although an identity can be shared as a commodity, in essence it is and remains a notion that comes about as a result of showcasing those characteristics of something that are unique, or at least different with regard to something else. It seems inevitable that, in the course of producing identity, a process of substantive reduction should occur. And whereas identity is ascribed or produced, affinity is something that has to be sought or found, or that must be recognized. In chemical terms, "affinity" means a tendency to form compounds, which further underscores the point that this is about mutual attraction, or a projective relationship.
How can affinity be a driving force, or an alternative to identity for a design studio? The affinity with other disciplines and domains, which underpins EventArchitectuur's practice, would seem to be impossible unless the studio also subjects its own discipline, architecture, to critical evaluation. The *SLOOM* actions and publications are an attempt to do just that; an attempt to return to the basic ingredients of architecture – light, mass, location, program, et cetera – free from commercialism, strategies, and branding. For *SLOOM 2*, for example, inspired by improvised barns and other farm buildings, the studio decamped to the Frisian countryside to investigate the aesthetic of non-professional construction. *SLOOM 3* took place in Berlin, and used interviews to focus on the position of small firms and organizations in the cultural sector within the dominant market economy.
The *SLOOM* projects are about going back to basics and rebuilding one's practice from a self-imposed *tabula rasa* and slowness, and by means of a process of bricolage.
This rediscovery of an affinity with the basis of architecture, and of the common ground shared with other domains, is not, however, purely the result of a search for correspondence. EventArchitectuur's search for affinities also derives from a more critical interest, from an apparent tension and antithesis, as in the fashion projects with SO and orson + bodil.
"Architecture longs to be fluid, to be able to transform itself and relocate, to appear and disappear. Fashion longs for a place of its own, to settle down, to have a support and the possibility of moving within itself, to feel a space between the form and the support," Verkerk has said.[2]
It is always about a process of identification, but one based not on a surrender to fixed identities, but rather on a search for critical affinities. Identity is partly constituted by what does

2
Herman Verkerk, "Stollen and Stromen" (lecture for Architectura & Amicitia, Mode Geland/Landed Fashion Biennale, Antwerp, 2001).

not belong to it, by that which cannot be part of it, and so is no longer drawn upon. It is precisely that "not" with which EventArchitectuur often seems to attempt rapprochement. The concept of mimesis plays a role here, as a type of affinity that occurs between things and between people and things. "Mimesis refers to certain patterns of similarity or resemblance. It has to do with copying, but a specific form of copying that implies a critical moment."[3]

Lib That Moment! Page 158

3 Hilde Heynen, *Architecture and Modernity: A Critique* (Cambridge, MA: The MIT Press, 1999), 6.

Loose, empty, and light

The presentation models EventArchitectuur designs for fashion or art are, as previously stated, often archive-like structures in which the emphasis is on the dynamics and the logic of the act of displaying and showing. Yet they are not neutral or objective spaces, but rather installations or "depots" in which specific materials, lighting, and routing are used to create a context for the public in the form of a special time-space – one in which the focus is not purely on what is being displayed, but also the way the public relates to it, and which also queries what exhibiting/display actually is, as if to discourage a too facile consumption of the contents. The exhibition models function explicitly as conceptual constructs, and thus also as cultural metaphors. They also function as a kind of dynamic interface between public and content, content and reality. The sense of impermanence they convey, often because of their low-tech character or their loose and flexible installation format, means that they are experienced as propositions rather than as definitive statements.

According to EventArchitectuur, "[The studio] defines space as a three-dimensional organization of light, sound, and movement. Architecture in this definition becomes the temporary stopping of certain processes (matter) to organize other processes (time). Designing, then, is to make this moment/snapshot of space that can last five minutes, but also fifteen years, depending on the assignment."

Start, the exhibition of Rem Koolhaas's archives in the NAi, was arranged as an "open depot" in which the public could actually look up information, and the spatial design was such as to render the transition between the depot as storage space and the presentation of the archival material "fuzzy" or ambiguous. In the design and staging of the fashion show "and, and, and no.1" for Alexander van Slobbe's SO (Hôtel Saint James, Paris, 2000), EventArchitectuur played with the formal boundary between "front" and "back." For this fashion show, visitors were admitted to a dressing room where twenty-four fully attired models waited their turn to be photographed. Visitors were allowed to finger the clothing. Each model stood on a small, numbered platform and kept moving, one platform at a time, in the direction of the space reserved for photographers, where there was a mini-catwalk. Here, the models were each photographed in turn, after which they took their place again at the back of the queue in the dressing room. For a fashion exhibition featuring work by orson + bodil in the Centraal Museum in Utrecht (2000), the display consisted of rows of changing cubicles, open only from above, which had been boarded up to form archive boxes. The garments were inside these cubicles – to see them, you had to kick a hole in the cubicle walls.

In the way they subvert traditional hierarchies, these interactive, but also reflective, presentation models behave like playful deconstructions, laying bare the hidden premises of the museum space and/or the domain of fashion. One could also do as Verkerk does, and call them "1:1 models of a supposedly better world." The putative neutrality of the archive, of the institutional presentation, is called into question, not from any negative critique, but rather from an engaged affinity. These are models that lay claim to an institutional void. But if this is about "architecture that wants to start from scratch," that "from scratch" necessarily begins in a void, whereby the emptiness of the void should not be construed as a shortcoming, but as a positive quality, as a space that is unoccupied or unwritten, with all the possibilities that implies. Architecture, in other words, that wants to start again from the recognition of an emptiness into which every identity disappears.

The challenge facing such a practice is to continue to be loose, empty, and light within the definition, fullness, and weight of current reality. EventArchitectuur must keep on inventing itself.

2

Events: Situating the Contemporary

beatriz colomina: pavilions of the future

"The architects of the Renaissance established ways of going about things which perhaps we unconsciously follow: for example, between the idea sketchily stated and the commission for the permanent building came the stage-architecture of the court masque; the architectural settings and decorations for the birthday of the prince, for the wedding of a ducal daughter, for the entry of a Pope into a city state; these events were used as opportunities for the realization of the new style; the new sort of space; the new weight of decoration; made real perhaps for a single day... the transient enjoyably consumed, creating the taste for the permanent."[1]

Alison and Peter Smithson saw the tradition of temporary theatrical structures as a centuries-old practice in architecture that plays a crucial role in stimulating the evolution of ideas and tastes.
As in the Renaissance, their *House of the Future*, commissioned by the *Daily Mail* as a pavilion for the 1956 Ideal Home Show in London, was staged architecture, a shimmering masque, which does not make the proposal less provocative, but more so: "Like all exhibitions, they live a life of say four weeks in reality, then they go on and on forever. Like the Barcelona Pavilion before it was reconstructed."[2]
The temporary turns out to be permanent.
The German Pavilion that Mies van der Rohe constructed for the 1929 Barcelona International Exhibition – and dismantled at the closing of the event – became an architectural legend, dramatically redefining the ambitions of architects worldwide. The pavilion can be the architect's strongest weapon. In fact, many of the most extreme and influential proposals in the history of modern architecture were made in the context of temporary exhibitions, including: Bruno Taut's Glashaus, the pavilion for the glass industry in the 1914 Werkbund Exhibition in Cologne; Le Corbusier and Pierre Jeanneret's L'Esprit Nouveau Pavilion in Paris (1925); Konstantin Melnikov's Market in Moscow (1924) and USSR Pavilion in Paris (1925); Mies and Lilly Reich's Silk Exhibition, Berlin (1927); the Glass Room in Stuttgart (1927) and, of course, the Barcelona Pavilion (1929); Le Corbusier and Pierre Jeanneret's Nestlé Pavilion in

1 Alison and Peter Smithson, "Staging the Possible," in *Italian Thoughts*, eds. Alison and Peter Smithson (Sweden: A&P Smithson, 1993).

2 Beatriz Colomina, "Friends of the Future: A Conversation with Peter Smithson," *October* 94 (Fall 2000): 24.

Ludwig Mies van der Rohe, Barcelona Pavilion (German Pavilion at the Barcelona International Exhibition), Barcelona, 1929. photo: Wikimedia Commons/Rith

2

Lib That Moment!
Page 162

Paris (1928); Walter Gropius's Werkbund Exhibition in Paris (1930); Alvar Aalto's Finnish Pavilion at the World Exposition, Paris (1937), and his Finnish Pavilion in the 1939 New York World's Fair; Le Corbusier and Iannis Xenakis's Philips Pavilion in Brussels (1958); Buckminster Fuller's Geodesic Dome for the American Exhibition in Moscow (1959) and his US Pavilion for the Expo '67 in Montreal; Eero Saarinen and Charles and Ray Eames's IBM Pavilion for the 1964 New York World's Fair; the Pepsi Pavilion for the Expo '70 in Osaka by E.A.T. Experiments in Art and Technology; Coop Himmelb(l)au's *The Cloud*,[3] a prototype for future living, designed for *documenta 5* (1972); and Aldo Rossi's Il Teatro del Mondo, a temporary theater built for the Venice Architecture Biennale of 1979, to recall the floating theaters of Venice in the eighteenth century, popular during carnivals. No matter how temporal and site-specific, pavilions are often brought back to life. At the end of the Biennale, Il Teatro del Mondo crossed the Adriatic to Dubrovnik, where it was dismantled. Its ephemeral existence and its very transience was its *raison d'être*. Nevertheless, like many temporary pavilions, the structure was reconstructed in 2004 by Germano Celant as one of the installations for the exhibition of the European Capital of Culture in Genoa. The tradition of the pavilion as the site for architectural experimentation continues into the turn of the century: mythical projects like Diller+Scofidio's Blur Building in Yverdon-les-Bains, Switzerland, a media pavilion for Swiss Expo 2002 (now destroyed), and the series of pavilions that spring up every year at the Serpentine in London being cases in point.

In this tradition, the Smithsons saw their *House of the Future* as a site of innovation. As always, they positioned their work in a genealogy of "three generations," each building upon and transforming the vision of the previous one. In particular, they saw their exhibition building as the inheritor of a twentieth-century tradition, a third-generation work extending the strategies of Le Corbusier's Pavilion of 1925 (from the first generation) and the exhibition design of the Eameses (from the second generation): "The *House of the Future*… 'staged' as an exhibition house, confronted the changes that domestic machines, the emergent consumerism, the anticipated technology of the nineteen eighties; as two generations earlier the Pavilion de l'Esprit Nouveau had confronted the use of the products and the technology which it assumed would soon be generally available."[4]

The Smithsons' pavilion echoes the way Le Corbusier constructed a model apartment and filled it with everyday objects to present his vision of modern living – with the difference that the Smithsons would

3
The Cloud was a mobile inflatable sphere containing a core of technical elements providing for physical and psychological pleasure. The pneumatic house could be stored in a container, transported on a truck, and assembled in ninety-seven minutes.

4
Alison and Peter Smithson, "Staging the Possible," 20.

Alison and Peter Smithson, *House of the Future*, London, 1958. published in: "Alison + Peter Smithson: The Shift," *Architectural Monographs* 7 (Academy Editions, London): 29.

display and draw from the "transient materials" of an ever-changing market. Found objects, perfected types like the Thonet chair or the generic wineglass, give way to imagined disposable objects and food packaging. More importantly, it could be argued that they moved from displaying the object as such to displaying the image of the object, as exemplified in the glossy ads they collected; the shining fantasy world of consumer goods. The *House of the Future* was itself just an advertisement, a seductive image. Perhaps this was even its most accomplished mission. As Reyner Banham put it at the time, the *House of the Future* was successful in producing a "powerful and memorable visual image."[5]

5
Reyner Banham, "Things to Come: Architecture and Industry Look into the Future," *Design* (July 1956): 28.

6
Alison and Peter Smithson, "Staging the Possible," 18.

From Charles and Ray Eames, the Smithsons had learned how to transform the images on display into the architecture itself: "The exhibition material becoming itself the means of spatial organization."[6] This was already evident in their 1963 exhibition with Nigel Henderson and Eduardo Paolozzi, *Parallel of Life and Art*, where an architecture of images was inserted into a traditional room, creating a room inside a room. And it would continue when the same team assembled *Patio and Pavilion* in 1956, essentially another room within a room, like the *House of the Future*, except that now the inside walls of the outer room (the patio) were lined in aluminum, making the visitor – endlessly reflected on the walls – part of the exhibit.
The space was filled with archaic found objects treated as images, laid out like a large "walk-through" painting in the patio, or viewed from behind the wires that replaced the missing wall of the pavilion to keep visitors out, or looked up at through the translucent corrugated plastic roof of the pavilion, which had the effect of an almost photographic vision. The *House of the Future*, on the other hand, was a display case that, like the objects it displayed, was pure image. Both the house and the objects inside were treated as images, and they combined to produce one single, smooth image, a glossy ad that could be placed alongside any other ad, participating in the flow of popular imagery – intense images that dominate for a moment only to be quickly replaced.

The house itself was as expendable as the objects within it. The *House of the Future* was like a futuristic prototype of a car, which will no doubt leave soon after it arrives. The tradition of the experimental pavilion is first and foremost about the construction of an image – a striking image exposed to a mass audience through popular exhibitions, which then gain further exposure in newspapers, magazines, films, television, and now, the Internet. Modern architecture is all about the mass-media image. That's what makes it modern, rather than

2

Lib That Moment!
Page 164

Le Corbusier and Pierre Jeanneret, Pavillon de l'Esprit Nouveau, L'Exposition internationale des arts décoratifs et industriels modernes, Paris, 1925. published in: Humberto Mezzadri, "Mies no Weissenhof/ Mies at Weissenhof," *ARQTEXTO* 13 (2nd semester 2008): 28.

the usual story about functionalism, new materials, and new technologies. In fact, modern architecture, as Banham pointed out, is not very functional at all. And the technologies? Who can forget the images of Le Corbusier's houses under construction, exposing the bricks before they were carefully covered over with plaster and paint, to give the impression that the houses were actually made of concrete? Or the walls of the Barcelona Pavilion, which were in the end load-bearing, even if Mies claimed that it was there, in the pavilion, that he first realized the independence of wall from supporting structure (let alone the fact that the principle had been announced five years earlier by Le Corbusier, and that the practice was long in place in American steel-frame structures). And Alison and Peter Smithson's curving *House of the Future*, which was not made of plastic at all: it was a simulation, a full-scale mock-up in plywood, plaster, and emulsion paint; traditional materials collaborating to produce the effect of a continuous molded plastic surface.

Even when modern architecture was permanent, it retained the mentality of the pavilion: conveying a lightweight, transitional feeling, even when built of heavy materials. If Le Corbusier's pilotis created an image of an architecture walking on stilts, here today but perhaps gone tomorrow, with Archigram's Ron Herron we get whole urban formations on the move in his project Walking City; and with Archigram's Instant City, a whole city arrives and leaves in a single day. The logic of exhibition and the temporary pavilion, in particular, has organized an entire century of architectural innovation. Indeed, most of the influential houses of the twentieth century were literally produced for exhibitions. Take Mies van der Rohe's Concrete and Brick Country Houses in the Berlin Art Exhibitions of 1923 and 1924, for example – the projects that established his reputation as one of the leaders of modern architecture. The houses that he was building at the time were very conservative, but the exhibition acted as a site for an experimental architecture. With the display of experimental models and drawings, a crucial transition occurs: both the language that architects use among themselves and the experimental structures built for a wider public are exposed. An instance of the former is the extraordinarily influential De Stijl exhibition in the Galerie de L'Effort Moderne in Paris (1923), where Van Doesburg and Van Eesteren's innovative models of houses were shown; models whose effect is still evident today.

An instance of the latter is Le Corbusier's Pavillon de l'Esprit Nouveau, a unit of his proposed Immeubles-Villas built for the Paris Exposition des Arts Décoratifs in 1925. The first exhibition was in what would now be understood as a commercial gallery, with an audience of cognoscenti, the second in a huge public fair. Pavilions

Ludwig Mies van der Rohe and Lilly Reich, Velvet and Silk Café at the Women's fashion exhibition, Berlin, 1927. published in: Christiane Lange, *Ludwig Mies van der Rohe. Architektur für die Seidenindustrie* (Berlin: Nicolaische Verlagsbuchhandlung, 2011), 75.

Bruno Taut, Glashaus, pavilion for the German Glass Industry, Werkbund Exhibition, Cologne, 1914. published in: Manfred Speidel and Bruno Taut, *Natur und Fantasie 1880–1938* (Berlin: Ernst & Sohn Verlag für Architektur und technische Wissenschaften, 1995), 129.

are public statements of radical propositions that were first incubated in drawings and models for a smaller audience, in anticipation of eventually redefining the future of public space.

With the Pavillon de l'Esprit Nouveau, the house itself became an exhibit; that is, the space of the exhibition and the exhibit were one and the same. The apartment, which was meant to be suspended high up, looking out over a new, modernized Paris, was plopped in the middle of a park like some kind of spaceship from the future. The exhibition organizers were so worried about this pavilion that they built a twenty-foot-high fence to hide it. Le Corbusier had filled the model house with all the furnishings and works of art he considered appropriate for modern life. Visitors could walk through it, imagining a new lifestyle, only separated from the fantasy by thin ropes. Le Corbusier even exhibited his plans for the city within the structure of the pavilion. Indeed, the domestic house became the site for his whole architectural philosophy.

At the Berlin Building Exposition of 1931 – dedicated to the theme of "The Dwelling in Our Time" – full-scale models of houses and apartments were built within another building. Upon entering the large exhibition hall, visitors were confronted with houses by the Luckhardt brothers, Hugo Häring, Ludwig Mies van der Rohe, and Lilly Reich, which occupied the center of the space. All around the periphery was a continuous strip of model apartments and rooms by Walter Gropius, Ludwig Hilberseimer, Marcel Breuer, Otto Haesler, Karl Voelker, and Wassily Kandinsky. Additionally, a materials exhibition designed by Reich was installed on a balcony that ringed the space.

The work of Mies van der Rohe and Reich provides particularly good examples of the way that designers use exhibitions to produce experimental work. At the Berlin Building Exhibition, they both constructed houses in the main hall, tied together by a wall that extended from the heart of Mies's house into the heart of Reich's. Reminiscent of the Brick Country House walls sliding out into infinity, this umbilical cord may be a clue about the two architects' enigmatic partnership. Once again, Mies was able to achieve one of his most radical spaces in the context of an exhibition. Likewise, the exhibition allowed Reich to build a house for the first and only time in her career. Reich's house is very stark. It uses sensuous fabrics, textures, and colors to define spaces in ways she had already experimented with in her exhibition design.[7] In fact, both Mies and Reich repeatedly stretched the concept of exhibition into that of the house. When the German Glass Industry commissioned a display of their products for the Die Wohnung Exhibition in Stuttgart, they turned their "Glass Hall" display into a house; a

7
For more about Lilly Reich's work, see Matilda McQuaid, *Lilly Reich: Designer and Architect* (New York: The Museum of Modern Art, 1996). See also Sonja Guenther, *Lilly Reich 1885–1947: Innenarchitektin, Designerin, Ausstellungsgestalterin* (Stuttgart: Deutsche Verlags-Anstalt, 1988).

2

flowing space subdivided into dining room, living room, and work room by freestanding glass walls. The illusion of a ceiling was produced by strips of stretched fabric; the floors were covered with white, gray, and black linoleum areas that produced a sense of movement by not quite coinciding with the rooms; the walls were of etched, clear, and gray opaque glass; the chairs were covered in white chamois and black cowhide; and the bench table was in rosewood.[8] Even a sense of the outside was produced by placing plants and a sculpture of a woman by Georg Kolbe on the other side of one of the glass walls. This strategy anticipates the Barcelona Pavilion, Mies's most famous project.
When commissioned to build the German pavilion for the 1929 International Exhibition in Barcelona, Mies asked the Ministry of Foreign Affairs what was to be exhibited. "Nothing will be exhibited," he was told, "the pavilion itself will be the exhibit."[9] It was precisely in the absence of a traditional client or program that Mies was able to take his work to new limits, and one of the most influential buildings of the century emerged. Once again, Mies and Reich, who collaborated on the project, had taken the opportunity to experiment in the context of a temporal exhibition. The flowing space of the pavilion, defined by the strategic placement of sensuous materials, continued the investigations started with the Velvet and Silk Café, a collaborative work of Reich and Mies for the Exposition de la Mode in Berlin (1927), where draperies in black, orange, and red velvet, and black and yellow silk, hung from metal rods to form the space.

Eventually, the experiment would fall into different hands: in the 1985 Milan Triennale, OMA constructed its Body Building House, a Barcelona Pavilion "bent" to fit the curve of their allotted site within the exhibition building: "By then, phobic about the duty to reveal, we decided to embody our resistance in an exhibit about exhibition. At the time, a clone of Mies's pavilion was being built in Barcelona. How fundamentally did it differ from Disney? In the name of higher authenticity, we researched the true history of the pavilion after the closing of the 1929 World's Fair and collected whatever archaeological remnants it had left across Europe on its return journey. Like a Pompeian villa, these fragments were reassembled as far as possible to suggest the former whole, but with one inevitable inaccuracy: since our 'site' was curved, the pavilion had to be 'bent.'"[10] OMA's "true history" of the pavilion is actually a fantasy intended as a homage to the pavilion, but also to modern architecture, under attack in those years as lifeless, empty, and puritanical. "It has always been our conviction that modern architecture is a hedonistic movement, that its abstraction, rigour and severity are

8
Franz Schulze, *Mies van der Rohe, A Critical Biography* (Chicago and London: University of Chicago Press, 1985), 141–142. See also McQuaid, *Lilly Reich: Designer and Architect*, 25.

9
Julius Posener, "Los primeros anos: De Schinkel a De Stijl," *Mies van der Rohe, A&V Monografías de Arquitectura y Vivienda* 6 (1986): 33.

10
Rem Koolhaas and Bruce Mau, *S,M,L,XL* (New York: The Monacelli Press, 1995), 49.

in fact plots to create the most provocative settings for the experiment that is modern life."[11]

In the Body Building House, the Barcelona Pavilion is inhabited by gymnasts, bodybuilders, and exercise equipment in a suprematist explosion of projected images, lighting effects, and lasers. Mies's minimalist statement is engorged with activities. The references multiply. The project alludes to the tradition of the Body Building House in modern architecture: from Marcel Breuer's room for Piscator in Berlin; to Gropius's gym in his apartment for the Berlin Exhibition; to Richard Docker's gym; to the thousand-meter running track that Le Corbusier proposed for the roof of his Immeubles-Villas; to Richard Neutra's Lovell House; and even to the transformation in the 1960s of Mies's Villa Tugendhat in Brno into a children's gym by communist bureaucrats. OMA takes modern architecture's dream of a healthy body to a new level. Experimentation in exhibitions always becomes collective in the end. Architects pick up on others' ideas, work on them, and then the results themselves are responded to in future exhibitions. This is what architectural discourse is.

The rebuilding of the Barcelona Pavilion is itself an important part of the story of the pavilion. While many of Mies's buildings have been destroyed, the temporary exhibition pavilion had become such a central monument in architectural culture that it was reconstructed in 1987 on the original exhibition site as a kind of simulacrum. The same thing happened to Le Corbusier's L'Esprit Nouveau Pavilion. Since 1977, a replica sits in a park in Bologna, exemplifying ninety-year-old principles. As Peter Smithson wrote: "To visit it is to be reminded that an architect always needs to have his pots and pans and his view of nature ready, in case he is asked."[12]

To some extent, the reconstructions interfere with the discourse. Many exhibition experiments gain more force by disappearing. They inhabit the spaces of publication, of memory, of fantasy. The lack of a specific client or site gives them a permanent role. Since they have not been pinned down, they remain open to speculation. Reconstruction fixes them, if not finishes them. The full force of the pavilion is always the possibility that it will leave as abruptly as it arrived, reorganizing ambitions and calling for new connections between what were previously felt to be utopian fantasies and what are now plausible built realities. A permanent pavilion is not a pavilion anymore. The real sign that a building is a pavilion is that it leaves – it flies away, or at least promises to do so. The encounter with an object that is about to leave is fundamentally different. The thought that you might not be able to return to it makes the experience elusive, even romantic.

Exhibition pavilions in the twentieth century acted as sites for the incubation of new forms of architecture that

11
OMA: Office for Metropolitan Architecture, "La Casa Palestra," *AA Files* 13 (1986): 8.

12
Peter Smithson, *ILAUD Yearbook*, (Urbino, 1981).

Konstantin Melnikov, Novo Sukharevsky Market, Moscow, 1925. published in: Selim O. Khan-Magomedov, *Konstantin Melnikov* (Moscow, 2007), 77.

2

Lib That Moment!
Page 168

were sometimes so shockingly original, so new, that they were not even recognized as architecture at all. Think again of Mies van der Rohe's Barcelona Pavilion, widely understood as the most influential building of the twentieth century. It was, in fact, seen by "nobody." Despite its prominent location in the layout of the 1929 Barcelona International Exhibition, even journalists sent by professional architectural magazines passed it over entirely, unable to detect its significance. Naive visitors and local journalists provided the only testimony to its existence. They commented on the "mysterious" effect, "because a person standing in front of one of these glass walls sees himself reflected as if by a mirror, but if he moves behind them, he then sees the exterior perfectly. Not all the visitors notice this curious particularity whose cause remains ignored."[13] It is necessary to go back to these kinds of statements to understand the surprise that a glass building produced in 1929, something that a generation accustomed to Hilton international hotels may have difficulty imagining.
It was only in the 1950s, in the aftermath of the 1947 Mies exhibition at the Museum of Modern Art, curated by Philip Johnson, that the pavilion burst into every architectural publication.[14] As glass architecture became dominant, the pavilion was hailed as the most beautiful building of the century, exemplifying the cult of transparency. A building that was known only through magazine images – it was dismantled at the closing of the exhibition in Barcelona and its fragments misplaced during its return trip to Germany – became the most significant monument of modern architecture.
What is crucial about the Barcelona Pavilion is that it was both real (a 1:1 construction that existed for a time) and an image (a media construction). Before its reconstruction in 1989, all we knew about it were the photographs. It lived in the photographs. If temporary buildings like the Barcelona Pavilion had their full force as images, then some images have the full force of buildings.
Pavilions make dreams seem real, and reality seem dreamlike. The lingering memory of the Barcelona Pavilion is of a simple, solid object producing a complexity of space, movement, and reflected light. But the exact nature of the solid is elusive. It is the unique role of a pavilion to fuse image and structure in this way. The pavilion is the key instrument for negotiating the relationship between image and physical structure.

Etymologically, "pavilion" comes from *papillon*, the French for butterfly; the sides of an open, lightweight nomadic tent were associated with the wings of a butterfly. The pavilion, classically a royal tent in a park, is that which arrives, fluttering in from an unknown place; a pure image in flight hovering for a moment,

13
A local journalist from Barcelona reviewing the pavilion. Quoted in Josep Quetglas, "Fear of Glass: The Barcelona Pavilion," in *Revisions 2*, ed. Beatriz Colomina (New York: Princeton Architectural Press, 1988), 130.

14
For the reception of the Barcelona Pavilion, see Juan Pablo Bonta, *Architecture and its Interpretation: A Study of Expressive Systems in Architecture* (New York: Rizzoli International, 1979), 131–174.

touching down and standing there with its image fully exposed, before fluttering away again, leaving everything changed in its wake.

2

Events: Situating the Temporary
Page 170

project 9, 35, 53, 62, 70, 71

1992

2000

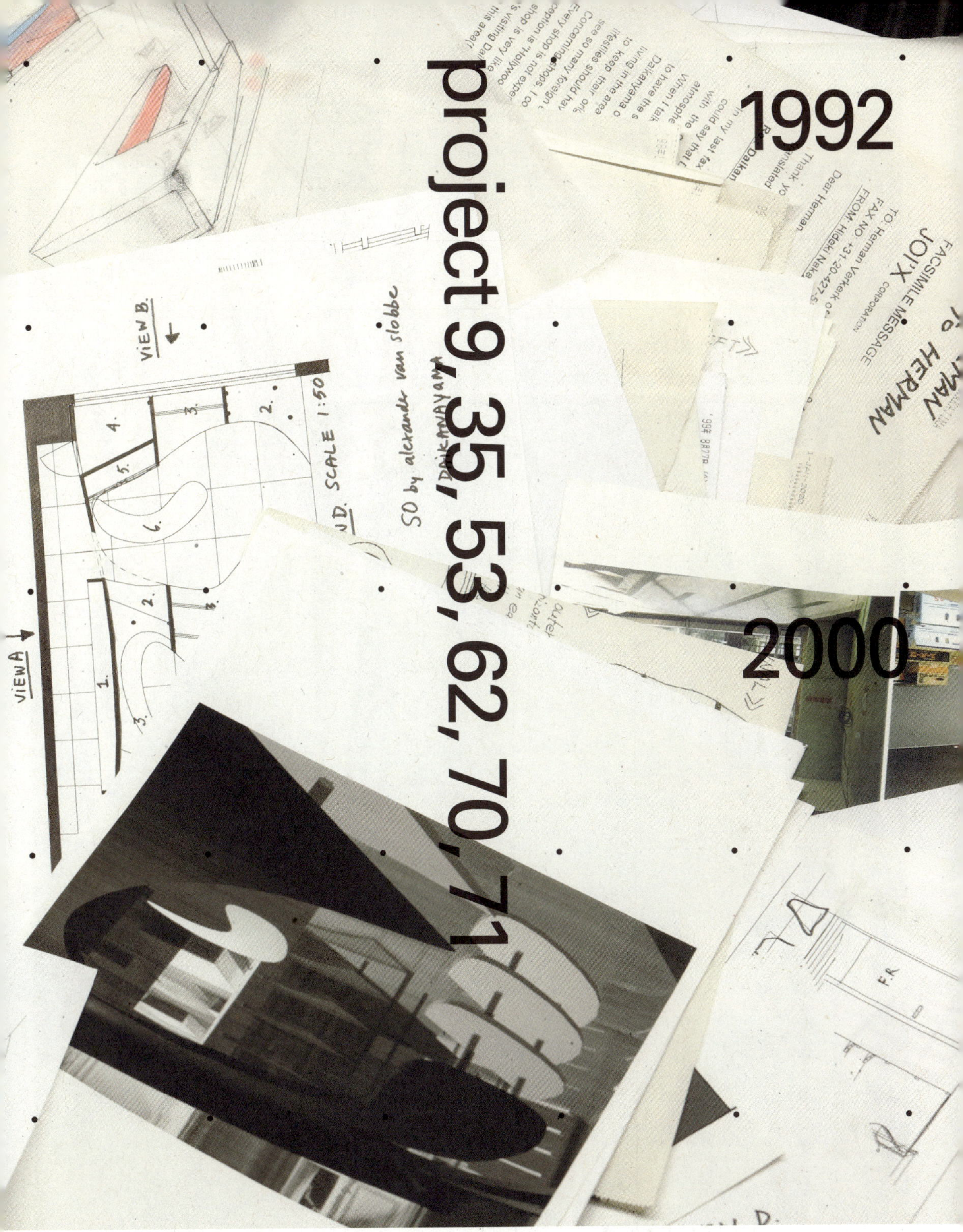

Lib That Moment!
Page 171

Fashion Stores & Showrooms
Project: Interior
Year: 1992–2000
Data: page 631

Lib That Moment!
Page 172

Booth, TiPi,
Paris, 1992

project 9

orson + bodil
10 years,
Centraal Museum,
Utrecht, 2000

project 71

Lib That Moment!
Page 176

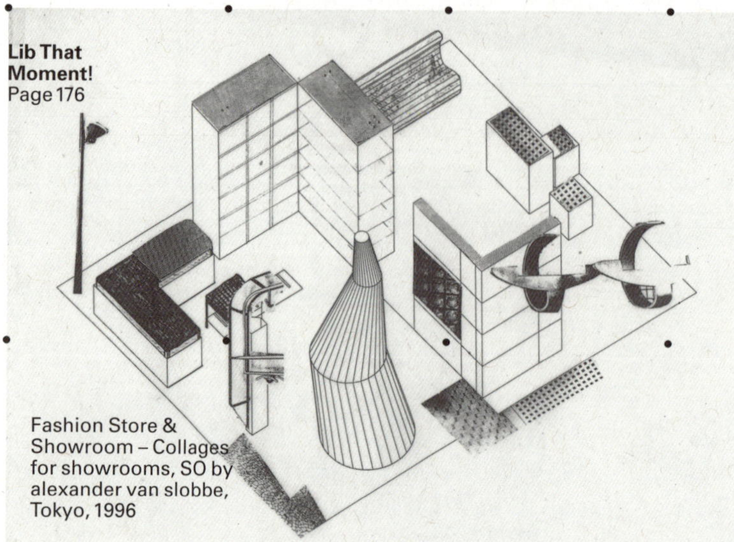

Fashion Store & Showroom – Collages for showrooms, SO by alexander van slobbe, Tokyo, 1996

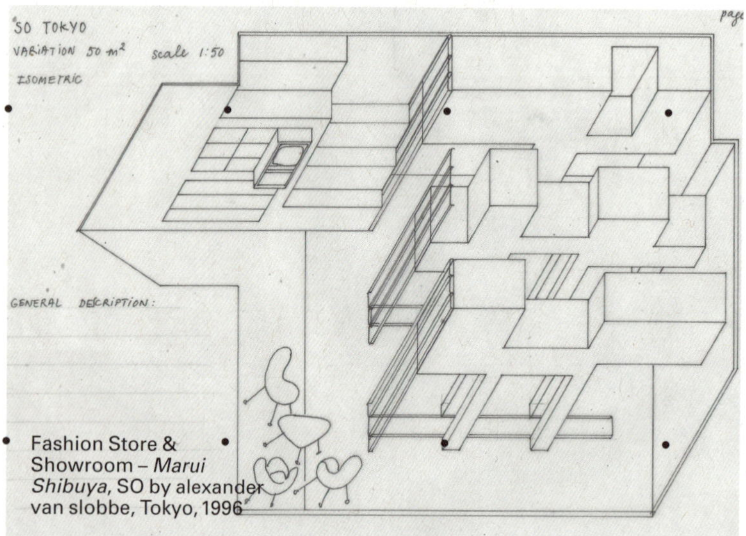

Fashion Store & Showroom – *Marui Shibuya*, SO by alexander van slobbe, Tokyo, 1996

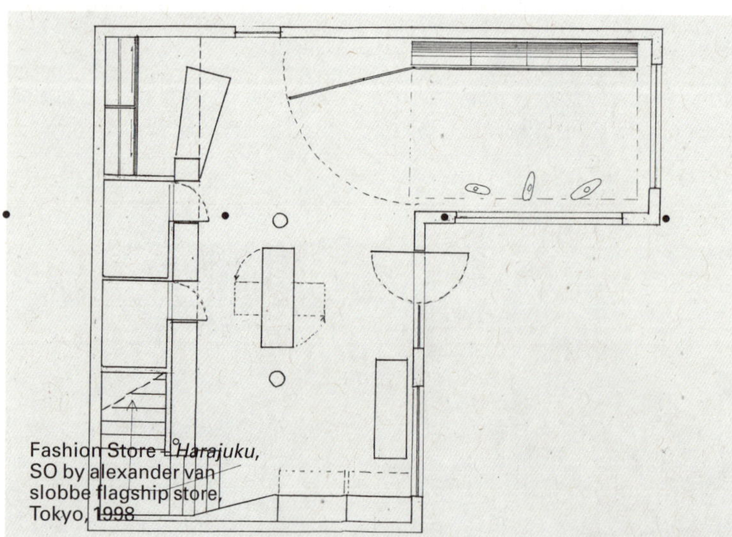

Fashion Store – *Harajuku*, SO by alexander van slobbe flagship store, Tokyo, 1998

project 35, 53

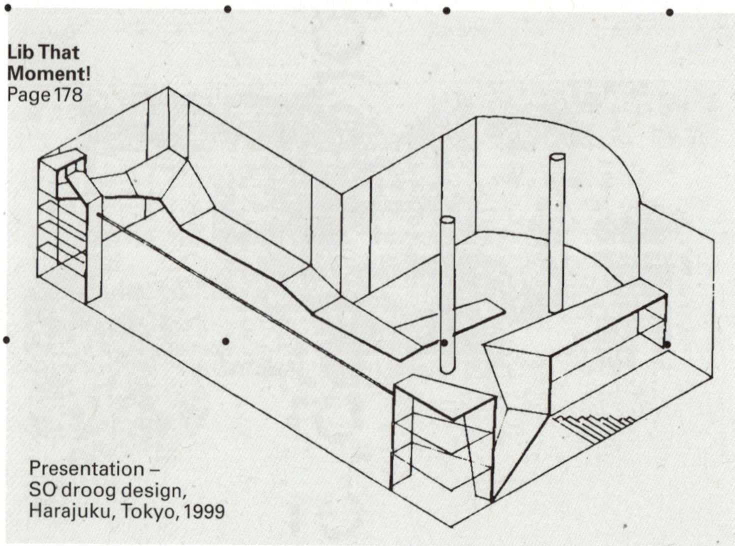

Presentation –
SO droog design,
Harajuku, Tokyo, 1999

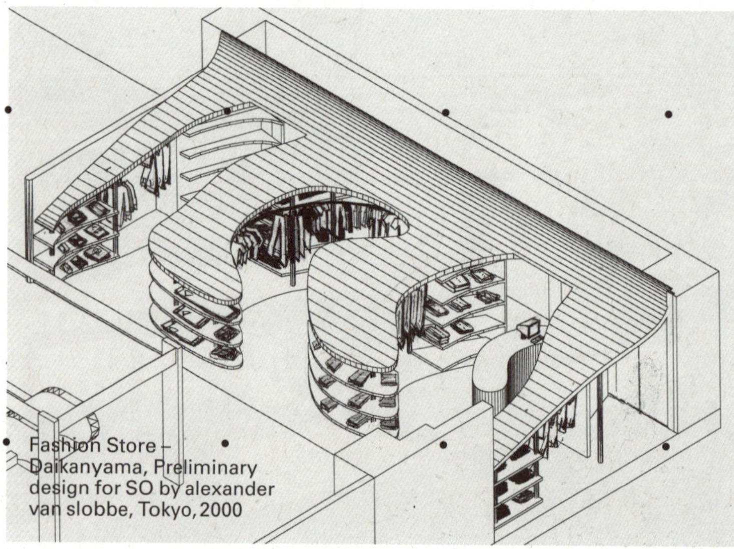

Fashion Store –
Daikanyama, Preliminary
design for SO by alexander
van slobbe, Tokyo, 2000

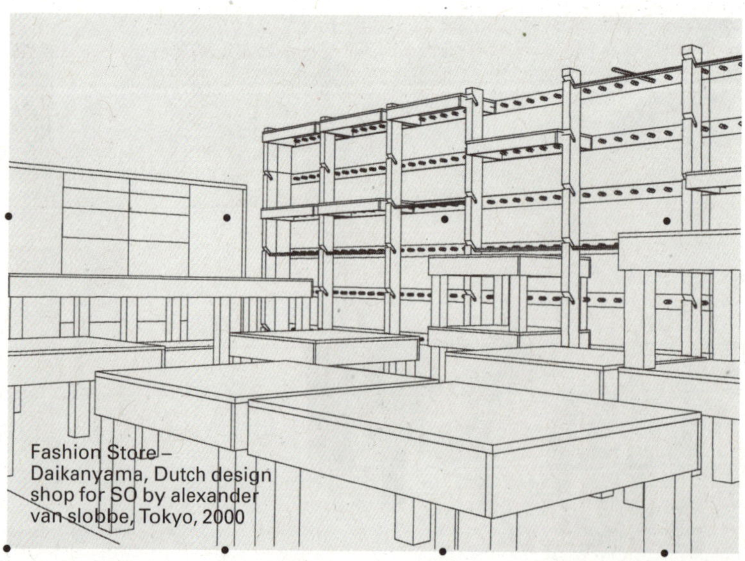

Fashion Store –
Daikanyama, Dutch design
shop for SO by alexander
van slobbe, Tokyo, 2000

project 62 70

Fluorescent tube lamp

Eva Stricker

Most recent buildings are not equipped with fluorescent lamps any longer, but with much more efficient light-emitting diodes (LEDs). The still slightly higher costs, meanwhile, amortize within a few years. The fluorescent tube thus represents an almost outdated technology, just like the bulb-shaped filament lamp, which is practically a collector's item nowadays. Its prohibition caused a lot of agitated reactions in the media. People really seem to miss the beauty of its shape and its characteristic warm, candle-like light. One is tempted to ask if the fluorescent tube lamp also has potential to evoke such nostalgic emotions. And, if so, what are the characteristic features that will make us cherish it?

Its immediate sensory impressions are probably not the decisive factor. The quality of its light seems neither pleasant nor flattering. Somehow it manages to be matte and sallow, while at the same time glaring. Also, the characteristic strobe-effect and "brrrm-clack-click" sound whenever the lamp is turned on does not seem particularly appealing. It even underlines the sobering character of the light it announces. Imagine a tube light at the end of its life cycle, flickering, buzzing, trying vainly to ignite completely – is there a better picture for desolation and decay?

The filament lamp instantly creates more positive associations. It seems like the logical and worthy successor of traded light sources in the era of electrification. Like a lantern, the glass bulb protects the delicate filament, which keeps alive the picture of a glowing candlewick. Its functional manner seems direct, immediate, comprehensible. It determines the warm and homey color of its light.

A fluorescent tube, in contrast, works according to a rather opaque chain reaction. The activated gas filling of the tube produces radiation, which in turn triggers the fluorescent substance with which the glass tube is coated. The composition of this substance determines the color of the light, which adds an almost alchemical touch to the whole process. Due to the coating, the tube is non-transparent, spreading non-directional, intense but diffuse light without a visible origin.

According to its character, the fluorescent tube has changed and enriched our repertoire in lighting design. The bulb might represent the sparkling center of a classical luminaire, a visible and carefully designed source of light, which is attached to a room as decorative object, or even center.

The fluorescent tube, however, appears more like a standardized construction element, which is part of the building and follows or even underlines the rhythm of its construction. Its longish form and repetitive quality do not emphasize one certain point as source of light. The lamp as object seems to be less important than the light it produces. Due to their intense, glaring light, fluorescent tubes are often used for indirect lighting, covered with a shield or hidden in a niche while the lamp remains invisible.

Maybe one could even argue that the light itself is turned into a building material, when tube lamps create "luminous" elements by illuminating backlit materials, or when their light is used as refining finish of a surface with the help of hidden light-bands along walls or ceilings.

Whenever the tube lamp itself is exposed as visible source of light, it looks somehow naked. It represents a reduced, raw, "industrial" form of aesthetics – a reminiscence of its original purpose as simple, cheap, and effective illumination of industrial workplaces, warehouses, or car parks. Like other strictly standardized low-cost mass products, it regularly attracts the attention of artists and graphic designers looking for ready-mades. It appears as an absolutely functional, technical, quasi-design-free industrial product, and therefore virtually invites one to explore its aesthetic qualities and their limits without bias.

As an inexpensive staple, however, the fluorescent lamp will soon be forced out of the market. LED lamps are about to take over, and will soon determine design options according to their own specific technical characteristics – not only in high-end artistic applications, but also in everyday life.

Nevertheless, the attraction of the elegant, slim, linear form of the fluorescent lamp will persist; the fascination of the evenly glaring tube, of geometrized, tangible light. The laser sword among standard lamps, so to speak.

fluorescent

lamp

tube

2

Events: Situating the Temporary
Page 182

project 63

1999

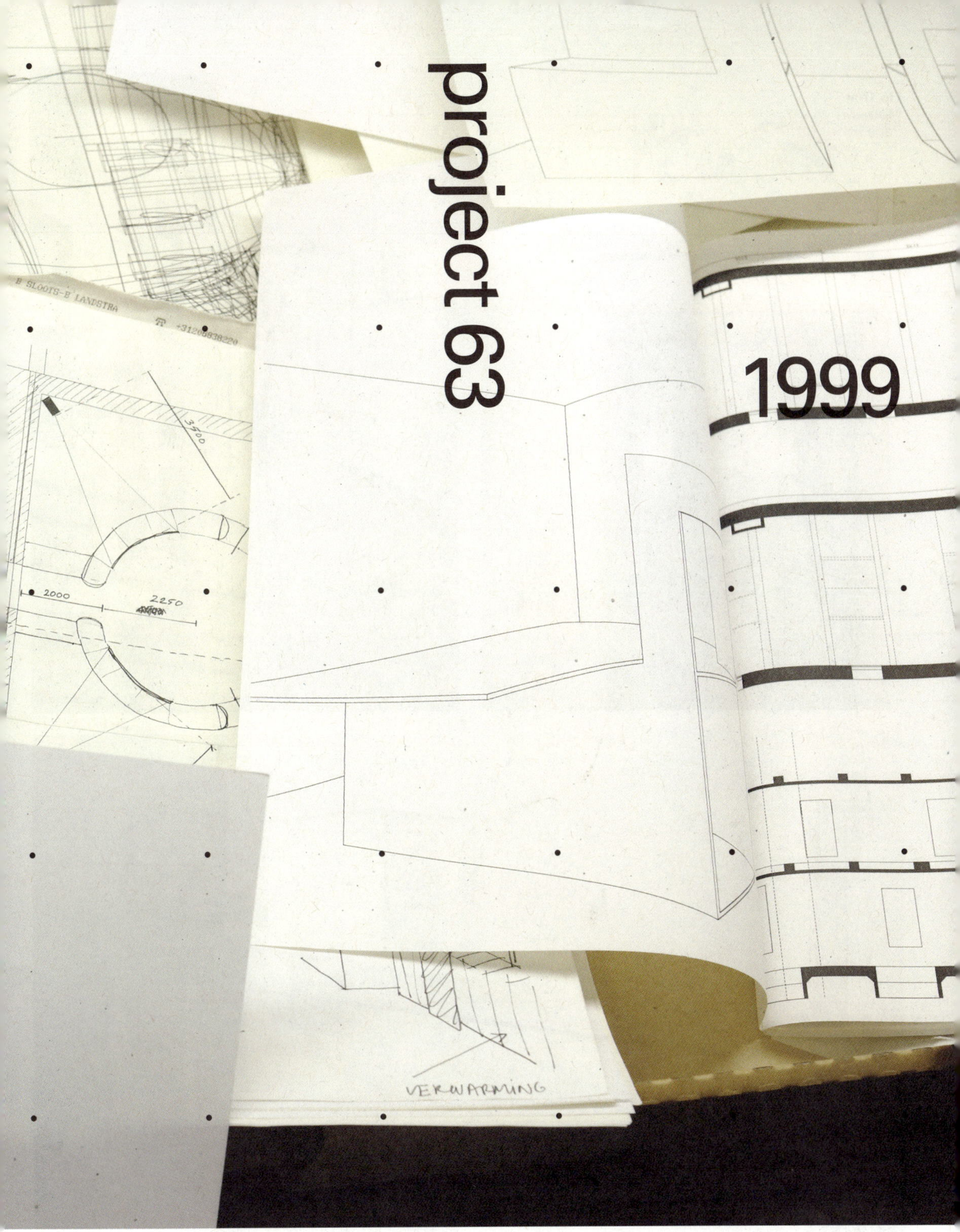

Lib That Moment!
Page 183

AEX Amsterdam EXposé
Project: Exhibition
Duration: Medium-term, 2 months
Year: 1999
Data: page 640

Lib That Moment!
Page 184

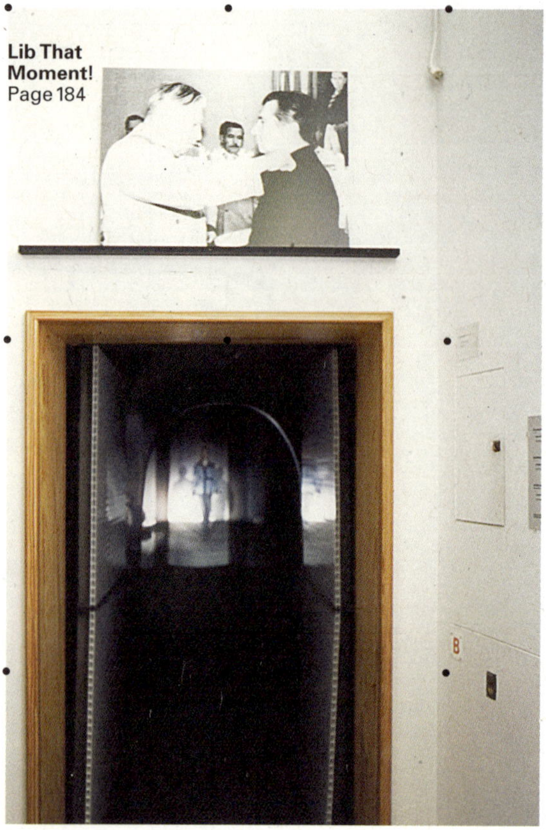

project 63

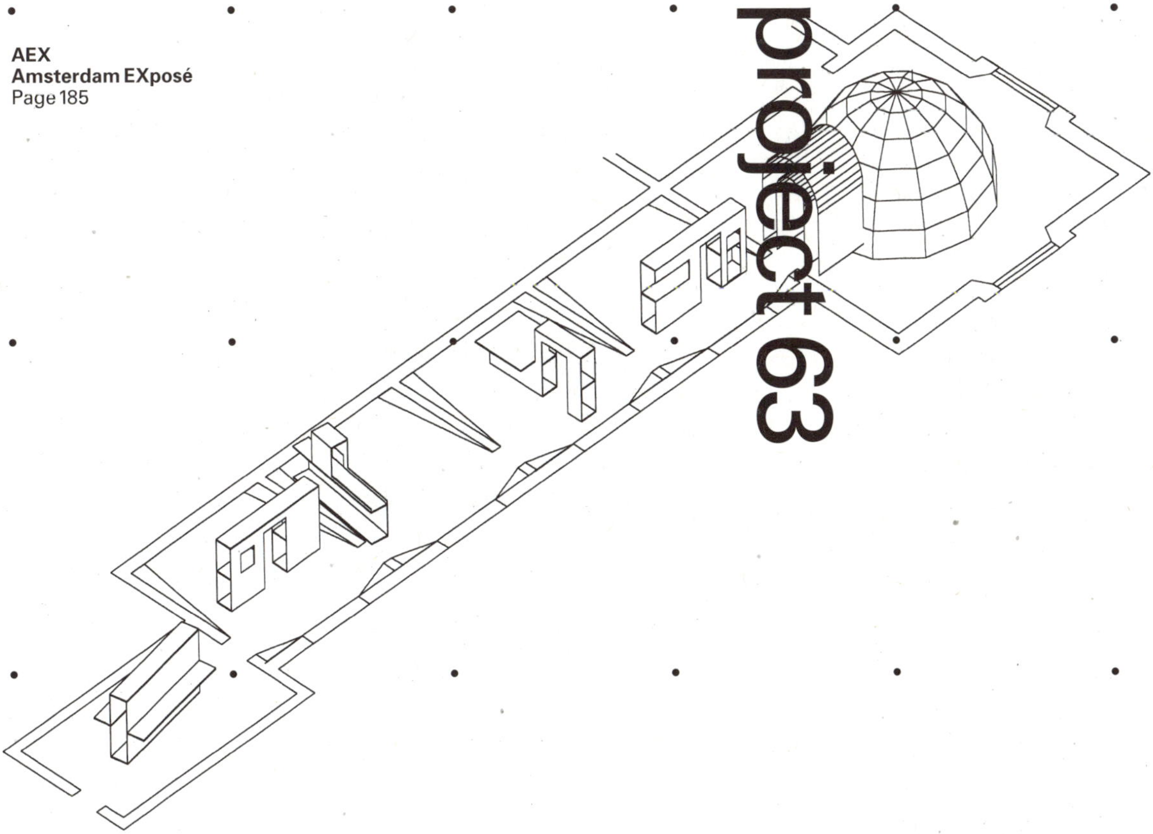

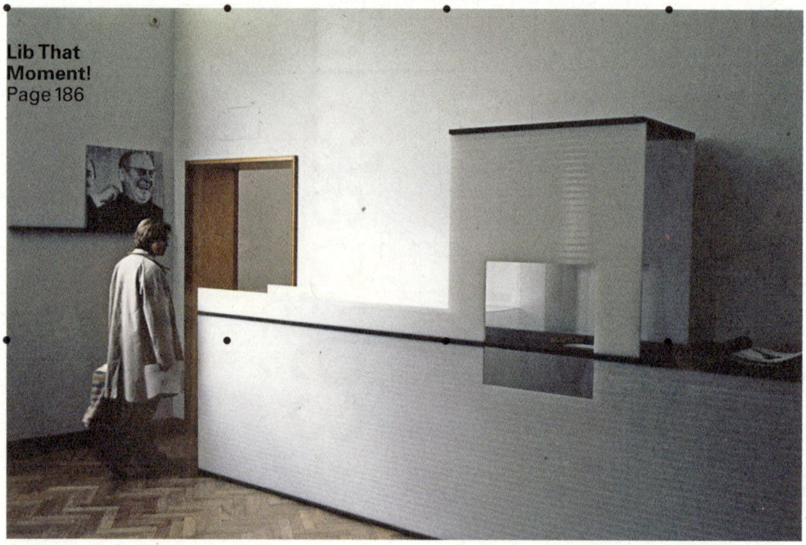
Lib That
Moment!
Page 186

project 63

2

Events: Situating the Temporary
Page 188

Lib That Moment!
Page 189

Breitnerstraat, Rotterdam
Project: Performance
Duration: Very short-term, 2 hours
Year: 1996
Data: page 637

File Edit Convert View Help
TellusVision Viewer ZOOM = 0.9
File Edit Convert View Help

project 38

Beste Breitnerstraatbewoners,

Morgen, 10 september 1996, van 9:00 uur tot 12:00 uur zal de Breitnerstraat worden vereeuwigd op foto's door de Gemeentewerken Rotterdam, in het kader van het Optitheek project van Rotterdam Festivals. De Optitheek is een informatiesysteem waarin van elke straat in de gemeente Rotterdam foto's zijn opgeslagen die je met behulp van een computer kunt bekijken. Van Euromast tot Maasvlakte, van Kralingen tot Lijnbaan, alle plekken in de stad zijn te bezichtigen en vormen zo een tweede digitale versie van de stad Rotterdam. Een soort schaduwstad.

Het is echter geen levende stad. Optitheek Live! probeert hier wat aan te doen. Bijvoorbeeld door U van te voren te informeren dat de foto's gemaakt gaan worden zodat U bewust 'vereeuwigd' kunt worden met Uw straat. Bovendien zal Herman Verkerk een kleine happening organiseren die reageert op het Optitheek systeem en die ingaat op het werk van de schilder Breitner. Hij heeft hiervoor een aantal borden gemaakt waarop afbeeldingen en teksten geplaatst kunnen worden (o.a. schilderijen van Breitner). Door deze afbeeldingen in de voortuinen te plaatsen of in handen van voorbijgangers/vrijwilligers zullen ze ook onderdeel gaan worden van de 'panorama'foto's.

Wij vragen U of het mogelijk is voor een ogenblik zo'n bord in Uw voortuin te mogen plaatsen en natuurlijk of U zin heeft morgen op de foto te komen.

Bij voorbaat hartelijk dank,

Met vriendelijke groeten,

Herman Verkerk
namens Optitheek Live!

(P.S. U heeft zich misschien allemaal wel eens afgevraagd wie die Breitner was die zijn naam heeft gegeven aan deze straat.
Het was een schilder die leefde aan het eind van de vorige eeuw en met zijn schildersezel de straat op ging om het dagelijkse leven in de stad vast te leggen. Vaak had hij naast zijn schildersezel ook een fotocamera bij zich en hij gebruikte de foto's die hij daarmee maakte als hulpmiddel bij het vervaardigen van de stadsgezichten.)

Breitnerstraat Live!
De straat op!
Een project van Herman Verkerk voor Rotterdam Festivals

Proloog
01. Aankomst/ 02. Brei[illegible]atbewoonster met demonstratiebord uit raam; Enter!/ 03. Voorbijgan[illegible]ers gro[illegible]ten elkaar

Entree Breitnerstraa[illegible]
04. Entree Breitner[illegible]traat/ [illegible]. Bouwwerkzaamheden; zwart-wit afbeeldingen van schilderijen va[illegible] a. [illegible]sneeuwde bouwput van de winkelgalerij in de Raadhuisstraat 1898 b.Heiwerk aan de Van Diemenstraat (bij het IJ) 1897 c.Heiwerk aan de V[illegible]menstraat 1897) Breitner heeft de ontwikkeling van een plek in d[illegible] sta[illegible] v[illegible]tgelegd, eerst met de camera dan met penseel.

De knik in de Breitner[illegible]aat 1
06. Koffietijd (1)/ 07. [illegible] deze mensen hier?/ 08. Maken tentoonstellingsborden/ 09. Plaats[illegible]n bord[illegible]/ 10. Koffietijd (2)/ 11. Plaatsen borden/ 12. Openbare Galerij. [illegible]ordkart[illegible]nnen straten als hulpmiddel voor een episode in de geschiedenis d[illegible] de [illegible]chitectuur niet kon bijbenen; de Russische Revolutie. De bourgeoisie gevel[illegible] worden verstopt achter straatdecors die de nieuwe klassenloze maa[illegible]presenteren en waar de 'nieuwe' mens doorheen kon marchere[illegible]. Agip[illegible]p.

De Knik in de Breitnerstraat 2
13. Demonstratie! De s[illegible]at op m[illegible] leuzen en symbooltjes geleend van het internet vocabulaire ui[illegible] de c[illegible]put[illegible] die daar een verborgen achterliggende wereld suggereren Eer[illegible] bo[illegible] P[illegible]h!/ 14. Demonstratie! Tweede bord Click here!/ 15. Demon[illegible] de bord Dump!/ 16. Demo op straat (drie personen, bewegen[illegible]/ 17. Demo op straat (drie personen, staand)/ 18. Exit! (bewegend)/ [illegible]taand)

De Knik in de Breit[illegible]erstr[illegible]t 3
20. Demo! Met bewoner[illegible])/ 21. Demo! Met bewoners (staand)/ 22. Demo! + voorbijganger/ 23. Demo! Met echtpaar, vrouw en kind/ 24. Demo! Bewoners kijken toe

Intermezzo
25. Schuilen bij het autootje dat de foto's maakt

Een Dialoog in de Breitnerstraat
26. Ontmoeting/ 27. A biedt B sigaar aan/ 28. A houdt monoloog/ 29. A en B in gesprek/ 30. Einde

Hotel Breitner
31. In gesprek met de monteur/ 32. Met hoteldame voor het hotel

De Bewoners 1 (bruidsluier)
33. Jongetje voor zijn huis/ 34. Vrouw en kind voor hun huis

De Garages in de Breitnerstraat
36. De garage gevel is een bord met een naam of een plaatje; click here!
37. De vrijwilligers nemen afscheid

De Bewoners 2
38. Vrouw met demonstratiebord/ 39. Vrouw voor haar huis

Met dank aan: Monica Adams, Rianne Makkink, Klaar Plattel, Ludolf Boelens van Frank Data, Maarten Sprenger van Rotterdam Festivals, John Oud en Kees-Jan Kokke van Gemeentewerken Rotterdam, Mevrouw Markies voor de heerlijke koffie met cake, en de overige Breitnerstraatbewoners.

EXIT!

2

Events: Situating the Temporary
Page 192

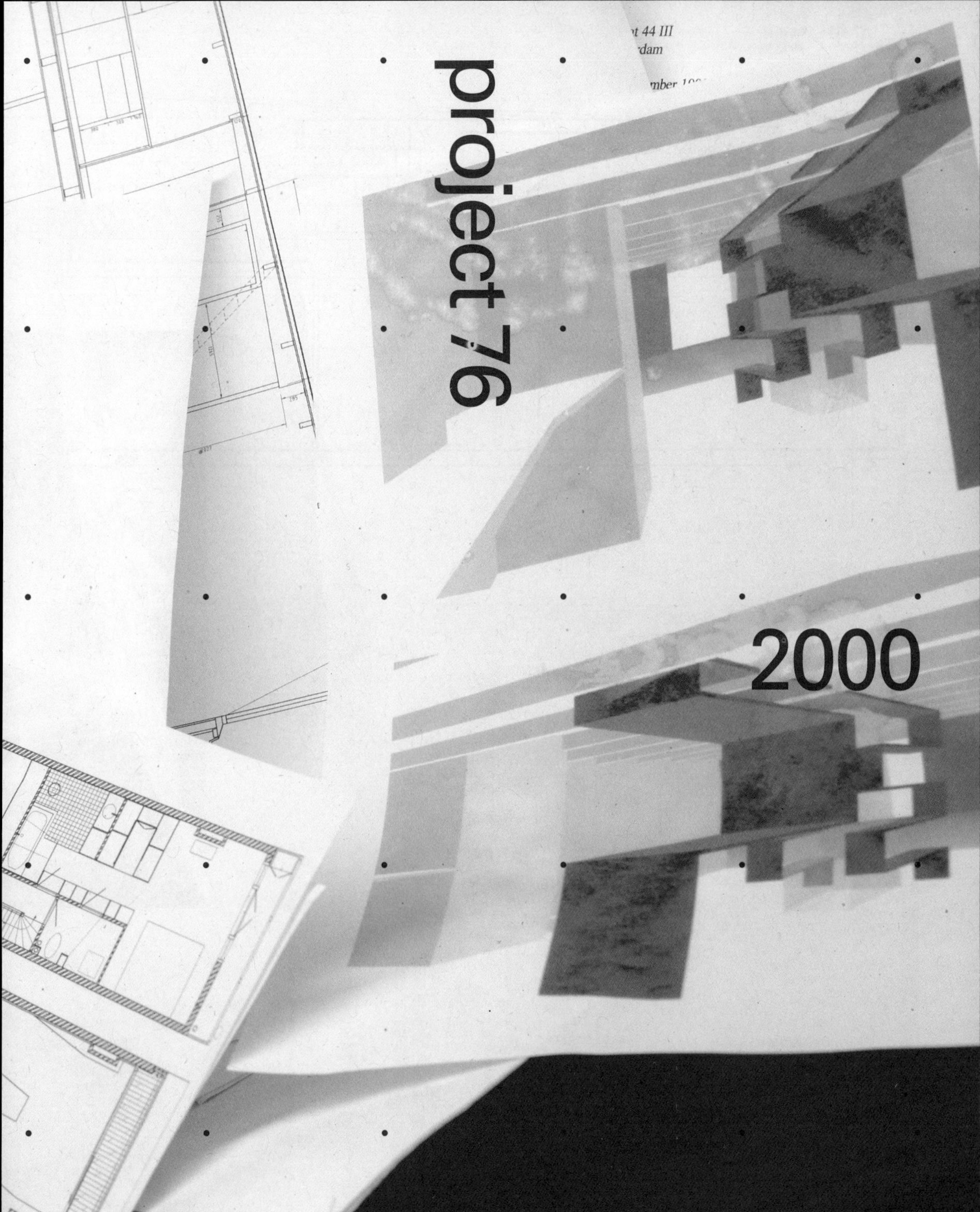

project 76

2000

Lib That Moment!
Page 193

Wilhelminastraat, Amsterdam
Project: Interior
Duration: Very long-term, 15–30 years
Year: 2000
Data: page 641

Lib That Moment!
Page 194

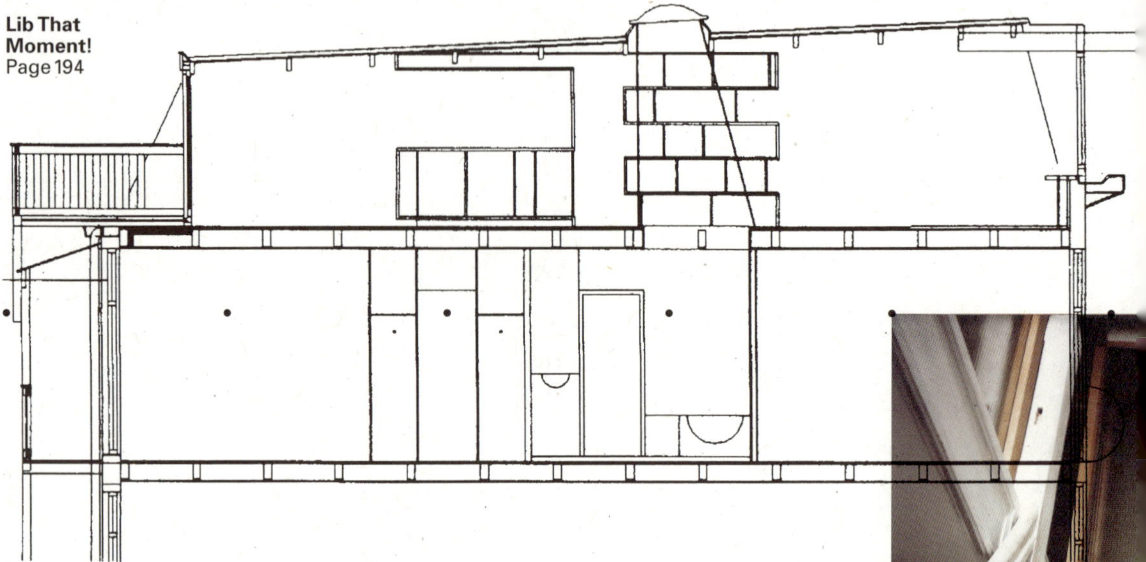

project 76

Wilhelminastraat, Amsterdam
Page 195

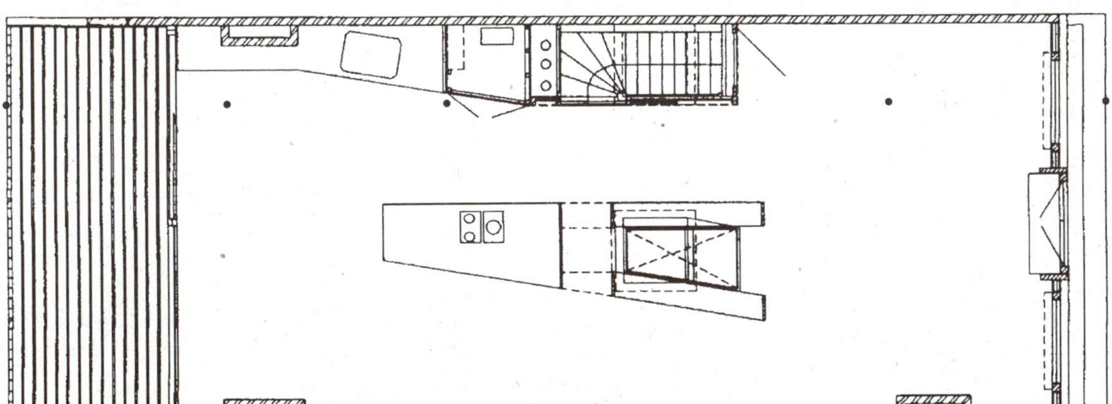

Wilhelminastraat, Amsterdam
Page 197

project 76

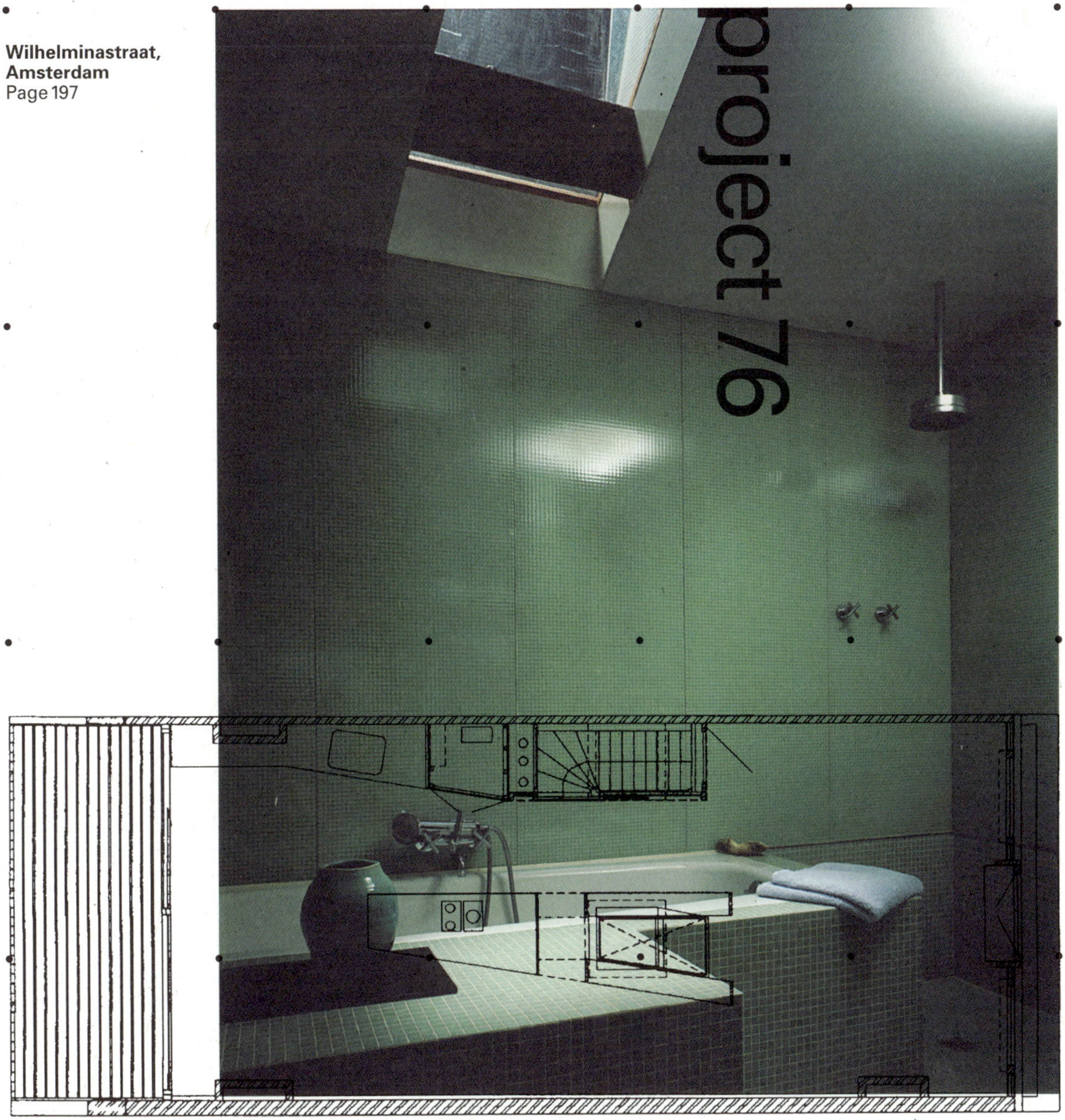

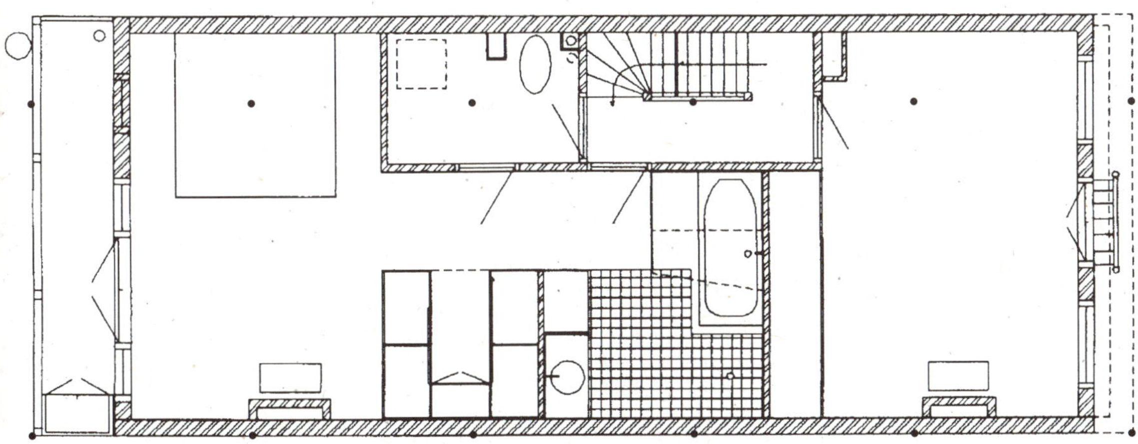

floors

Uneven floors

AB Cultural Producers

Bouwko Landstra and Alko de Vries are the principals of Landstra & De Vries in Amsterdam. They have worked together since 1997 and specialize in the preparation, construction, and installation of exhibitions. In addition, the firm, which has operated under the name Landstra & De Vries since 2002, produces artworks, prototypes, interiors, maquettes, test models, and displays. Alko de Vries has collaborated with EventArchitectuur since its inception. With only a few exceptions, Landstra & De Vries have realized all of EventArchitectuur's projects. In this conversation, Bouwko Landstra looks back over almost twenty-five years of collaborating with EventArchitectuur.

Practice

The experience of EventArchitectuur's working practice I recall most vividly was the exhibition *Start*, concerning the Koolhaas/OMA Archive, which was held in the Netherlands Architecture Institute (now Het Nieuwe Instituut) in Rotterdam in 2004. The exhibition, which Herman Verkerk designed together with Bart Guldemond, was arranged as an "open depot" containing all forty projects from the period 1978–1994, which visitors were free to delve into by themselves. The collaboration with EA was an exciting exploration of the notion of an open depot, and of how one might shed light on a design process using models, sketches, correspondence, and presentation drawings. In addition, Herman and Bart ditched the aesthetic we were used to encountering in the presentations of architectural firms. That was new for us, too, and we noticed that we felt immediately at home with this unpretentious way of working.

Synergy

In collaborations with EA, a synergy of several disciplines takes place, with Herman and Paul Kuipers, with whom Herman often works, acting as artistic linchpins. EA is a small office, the lines of communication are short, and so they are always on top of things. Our involvement starts at an early stage, in the first design phase, so that the project's development is informed not only by a design vision, but also by technical know-how. This reciprocity is crucial for the end result, with both parties keen to make something beautiful. Herman and Paul are conceptually strong, but I like to have my say about the design, because we have a better overall grasp of the technical aspects. But I'm careful not to overstep the mark. They have a wider responsibility, and also have to keep an eye on the budget. The job often involves huge surface areas, and I'm always amazed by how good they are at estimating the various scales of the spaces. When everything is in place, I'm aware of how much thought has gone into this, and how thoroughly the idea and its execution mesh. That's a quality I value greatly.

Freedom and trust

I would describe the working process at EA as trusting and agreeable. We respect one another's ideas throughout the process. Everyone involved in an EA production is given the trust and freedom to contribute to the end result on the basis of their own expertise. This generous attitude means that we all feel responsible and passionate about realizing a project through a combined effort. It is an illusion to think that you can settle everything beforehand in drawings and contracts. The process of making an exhibition is far too complex

uneven

for that. Too much has to be solved on the spot: a batten here and a batten there, simply because floors are never even. This way of working is something we understand better than anyone. And on this score, we are both exceptions. Our motto is freedom, trust, and flexibility, a trio that sums up our core values. It also meshes well with EA's work practice.

Co-creation

Our prime motivation is not commercial, but rather the idea of creating something together. That's self-evident, surely? It's about co-creation. And sure, there are constants in this collaboration with EA: Experimental Jetset for the graphic design, photographer Johannes Schwartz and fashion designer Alexander van Slobbe. All the disciplines are brought into play, that's what makes our line of work so attractive and interesting. We work in the same way: my colleagues at Landstra & De Vries come from both the visual arts field and the design profession, including the Design Academy in Eindhoven, where I myself studied. There's no exhibition design course there, or elsewhere, but I'm convinced it's a separate discipline. Designing temporary installations that are totally different from one another because of the spatial and conceptual context, and doing it on a tight budget – that's a special skill that EA has mastered to perfection. Architects who design exhibitions? Well OK, it's a discipline whose practitioners have a penchant for grandstanding. But it behooves an exhibition designer to be modest, because it is not him but the exhibited object that is the focus of attention. You have to be OK with that.

Battens and perforated board

Another constant in all the projects we've done together is the tight budget. With clients from the cultural sector, such as museums and galleries, that's scarcely surprising. Every time, it's a challenge for us to translate EA's design vision into a practically achievable plan that can be carried out within the available budget. The choice of materials always plays a key role. EA likes to use mass-produced materials with standard measurements that are used in the construction industry: pine battens, building boards or plasterboard, perforated board, strip lighting, and felt, for example. They are basic materials that are repeatedly applied in different ways, depending on the underlying concept. Take the pine batten, for instance: it's a lovely type of wood, and it's also produced in an environmentally responsible way. When you combine that with perforated board, which EA often does, you get something fantastic. You only have to look at the exhibition *Playboy Architecture* (at NAiM/Bureau Europa in Maastricht in 2012). That was a terrific presentation. That fondness for these inexpensive materials is something we share: the materials require a thorough knowledge of their vulnerabilities, such as requiring special handling to make them fire-resistant and to protect them from damage and dirt.

Way of life

Making exhibitions is a bizarre process, because they are so intensive and so brief. And there is always that looming deadline. Herman and Paul seldom deliver their drawings on time, and I can see them thinking, "It'll turn out fine." And of course it does. It's never yet not worked out. If we sense that a client is on a different wavelength and wants to nail everything down in advance, we don't even accept the commission. None of us are commercially motivated, we've no burning desire to drive around in flashy cars. That's a way of life we also share.

2

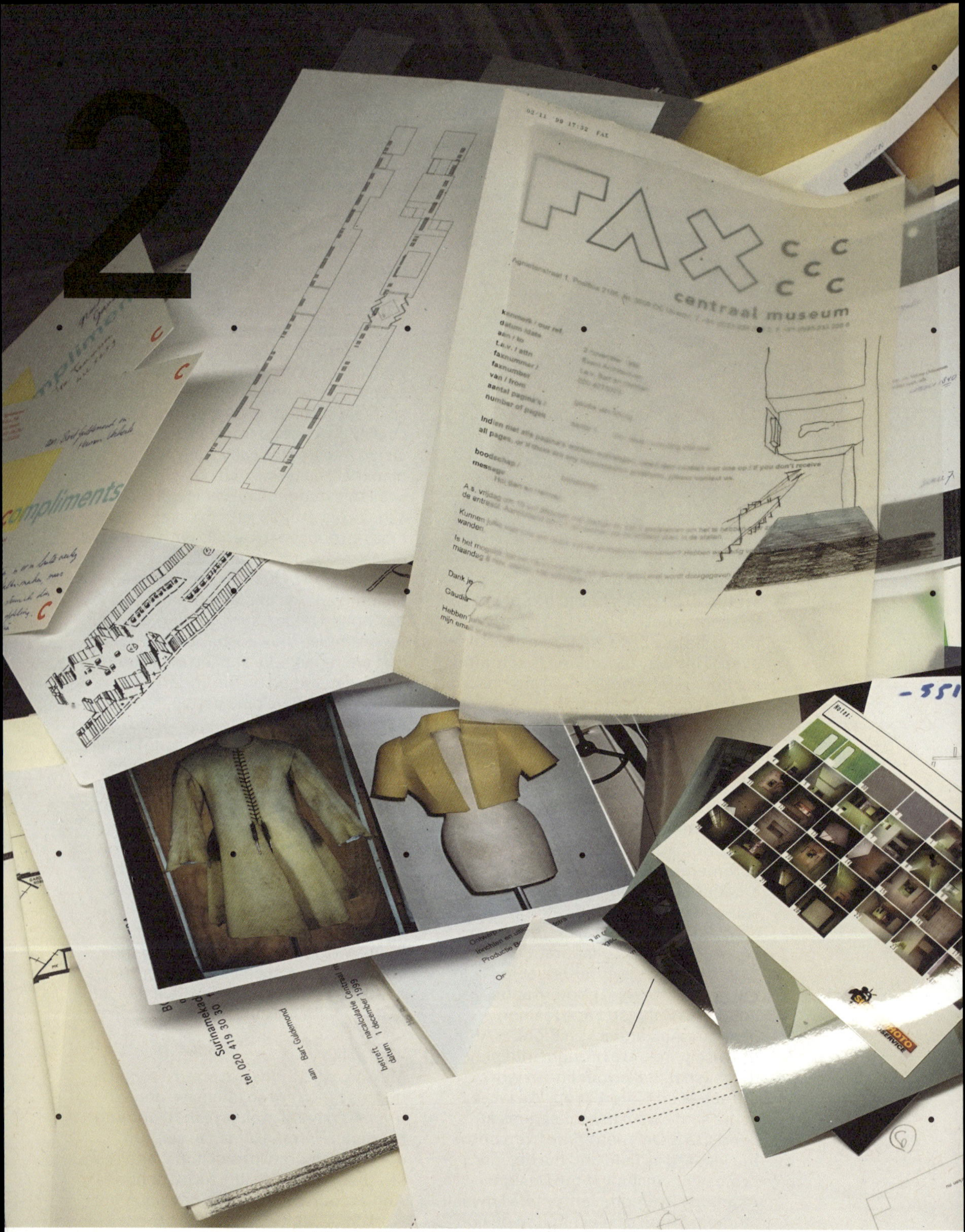

Events: Situating the Temporary
Page 200

project 68

1999

Lib That Moment!
Page 201

Styling
Project: Exhibition
Duration: Medium-term, 2 months
Year: 1999
Data: page 640

Lib That Moment!
Page 202

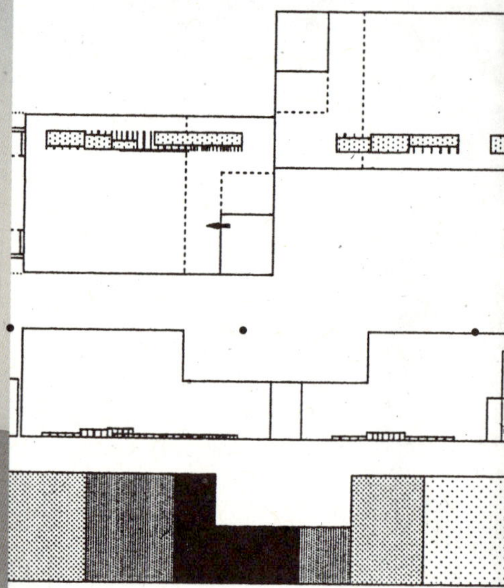

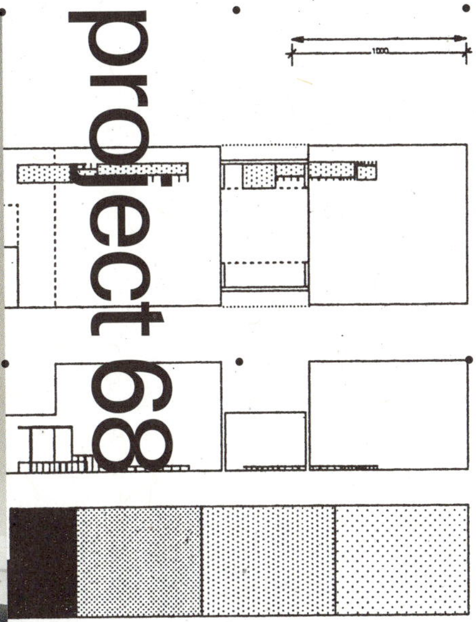
project 68
1000

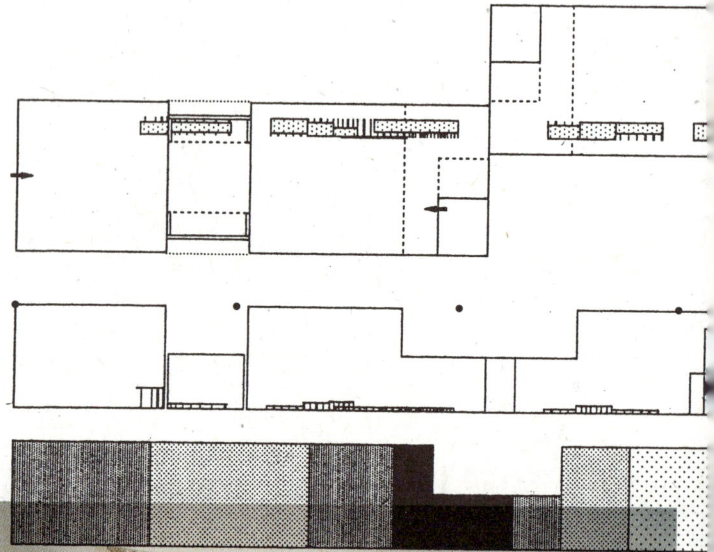

project 68

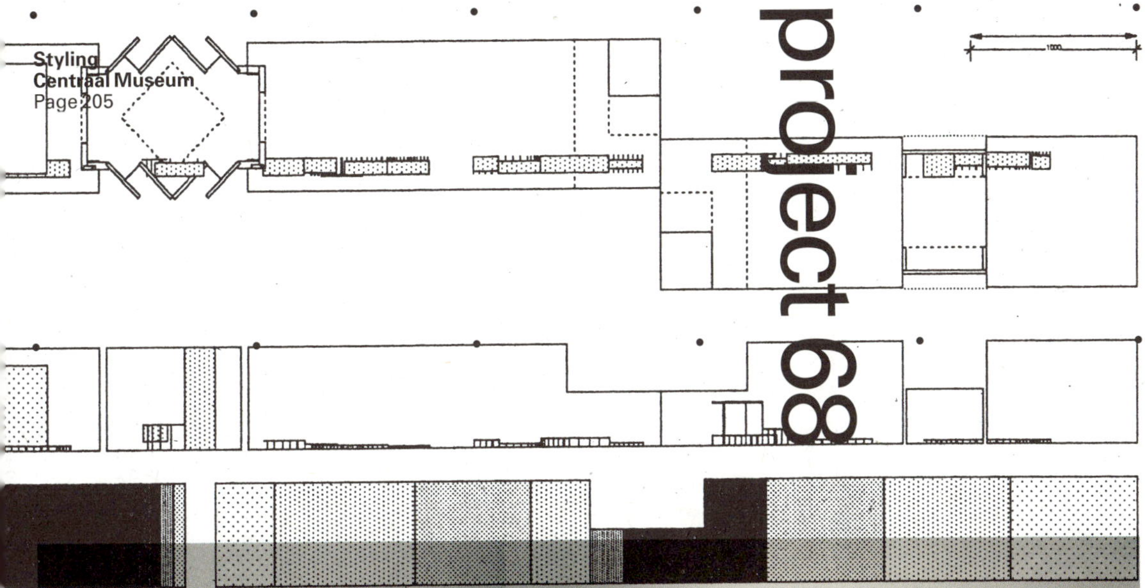

Date:
November 17, 2015

Place:
Bodega
De Posthoorn,
The Hague

People:
Tamar Shafrir &
Herman Verkerk
w/ **Bart Guldemond**

conversation 1

Design education in the '80s in NL

H: I remember in my first year of university, studying architecture, Rietveld was right and Van Ravesteyn was wrong, because he used baroque details and Rietveld was pure, was about construction. You get so indoctrinated by these good and bad examples that it takes you awhile to rethink them.
B: In the '80s, in design we didn't even have good examples! It was before the Italians came along with Memphis. I went to Milan at the end of my internship. I had a subscription to Domus magazine from my parents for my birthday. There was Studio Alchimia, Memphis, postmodernism, the architecture in which every facade has a different style. I wanted to break out, in a way, and I bought a ticket to Milano. Everyone asked me what I would do there, but I just wanted to meet the people there.
T: Did you write to them?
B: No, I thought to just go there! I went to the building of Memphis and I met Alessandro Mendini in the alley. And he sent me to meet someone else, and so on. It was totally weird, a young Dutch student without any question, I was just visiting and wondering what was going on. It was the opposite of everything I had seen in my studies. I had studied industrial design, but I didn't have any cultural background – I come from a family with an intellectual background, but I didn't see a lot of museums growing up. So, after two years studying industrial design, where do you go for an internship? You go to Curver, a Dutch factory in Tilburg that makes plastic kitchen tools.
T: How many people have their objects in their homes?
H: Millions!
T: Isn't that beautiful, then?
B: It's quite interesting, but it was very industrial. They had high-quality products for everyone. They had only one designer. When I was a student, there were design offices, but no freelance studios as there are now. There was no tradition of hiring a designer for a project. The normal way was to work for the company. There was the marketing department, and part of marketing was design. When I was studying, there was the idea that design should become a separate department and have its own responsibilities next to marketing. That was the state of industrial design in the mid-1980s. I also did an internship in Rotterdam with Industria, which was already a bit more "design." They made streetlamps, and were known for one model, very modern, by Friso Kramer. I designed a variation on that lamp using new techniques for lighting. It was a good starting point for design. At that time in the Netherlands we really still had factories. But I was hardly educated then… I had done my first year, basic and very hard work, and then in my second year the whole school collapsed. We had a strike in the old building, near the Van Abbemuseum. The older students wanted to change the system, and by the end of my studies the system did indeed change, and Jan Lucassen came. He was a visionary, together with Ulf Moritz. They had an idea about a new way to look at design (design didn't exist yet, it was called "Vormgeving"). That was the beginning of the Design Academy as it is now, with the different departments working independently, with a head that also determines the content of the education – like Gijs Bakker.
H: It became about more than the industry, you were trained as an author, interpreting the content of the company.
B: For us in Eindhoven, Arnhem was the more artistic and experimental academy.
T: You once told me about the Effenaar, that there was an interesting scene.
H: He was practically living there. Sonic Youth were playing there.
B: When I came back from my internship, in my fourth year, I started thinking. I realized that industrial design was not really my interest. Of course, first you find out what you don't want before you find out what you do want.
H: But also music – Sonic Youth as a concept or as a way of producing music, by going to these venues and having interactions with different types of creativity, it also transforms your way of thinking.
B: Before Sonic Youth came to Eindhoven, there were local bands. There was a very interesting cultural scene in Eindhoven in the mid-1980s. Especially because Eindhoven was so boring.
T: I also experienced that. The interesting thing is when you bring the techniques you learned from what you don't want to what you do want to do.
B: It's a cliché that you learn from your mistakes, and while you are making those mistakes you can't imagine you'll learn anything from them. It takes some time.
H: We talked a lot about your frustration, because you didn't graduate from the Design Academy.
T: Was it your choice, or did they not like your work?
B: When I came to my fourth year, I realized that I knew what I didn't want, but I didn't have many examples of what I did want to do. So I failed that year and had to do it again, and then I met Vincent de Rijk. We were in the same class.
H: There was also this new language that you learned, starting with your teachers, which defined a whole new culture. There was a connection to Arnhem. It's interesting to see how design culture in the Netherlands emerged from these experiments and individuals daring to challenge a commercial mentality, and starting to do labels – being so bold as to take on the major brands and factories. Arnhem was based on fine arts – and specifically fine arts in public spaces – and very different

to the approach of the Design Academy, which was connected to the industry.

Design, concept, and material

B: Eindhoven was the only school that was independent. In those years, it was developing from hardcore industrial design to a more autonomous position as a freelancer, not as part of a company. In Arnhem, they moved in the direction of self-production. Vincent and I picked up that idea from them. And at that same time, Rudi Fuchs was the director of the Van Abbemuseum; he was at the top when it came to art. He brought Sol LeWitt to the museum. It was around the corner – by that time, I did go to museums now and then – and I saw an exhibition of Allan McCollum. That really turned me – I found for the first time a focus point.
H: Can you define why?
B: In art, they were searching for the phenomenon of repetition. Allan McCollum did these great experiments; the booklet from that exhibition is well known. He used plaster molds to make random forms from industrial parts – things. And then he would connect them, make an assemblage of these forms. But the entire thing was about the repetition of this process – square tables completely loaded with all of these objects, in the famous pastel colors of the 1980s. I remember one table was all mint green, another all pink. They were also produced in Eindhoven.
I was interested in art because of its abstraction, and because it did not have to be functional. Looking at these artists, being interested in industrial processes, repetition and the variation and randomness within it, inspired me for my exam. I got over my natural shyness – I was raised to do what you had to do, and you had to follow the rules. But in that context, for the first time, I could choose for myself. I realized that was something I was interested in. I also saw that the department was a dead-end street. I realized in my last year, going for my exam, that I was standing with my back against the wall: if I tried to do what I thought they wanted me to do, I was lost, because I would never be able to do it well. And when my study was over, I was able to develop my own first steps into my design life. I was working with Vincent, and that was a very productive combination. Vincent had started to work with ceramics from the beginning. So we met each other in the ceramics department, which was a place you could be on your own. The metal department was very strict, wood was very dangerous, and you could only make furniture; but in the ceramic workshop there was nothing, because it was only there to learn mold-making in plaster. The man working there would make the copies for you in the traditional glazes. In the last year, something spectacular happened. In this very strange, old-fashioned school, all of a sudden Geert Lap popped up. There was an atmosphere of change. He was a well-known ceramic artist, a close relation of Benno Premsela, the "art pope" of those years. Geert wanted to introduce new recipes – new clays, new glazes. And who were there all day? Vincent and I! That was a lucky shot.
T: The ceramics workshop still has that character, somehow. Perhaps because you have to be calm to work with those materials; it's always quiet there, whereas in the other workshops it's very loud because of the machines, and everyone is waiting for you to finish, and you have the feeling of being watched.
B: For us it was a way to make things. For the assignments, we were always making models. But you would make a television from a block of wood, or a table from foam. The material had nothing to do with the actual product. So we were interested, of course looking at the art world – at that time *Arte Povera* was very much about a block of wood or a plate of lead – and ceramics was the place that you could make something in the real material; and it was about material itself. When you go to the wood workshop, you go to make a wooden table. You can't just go and "do" wood. But you can "do" ceramics. I learned from Geert to look at ceramic products as open and closed. In my exam, I had three ceramic products that were an open plate, a closed vase, and an in-between form, like a bowl. That was the first time I really looked at form. A plate you only see the inside, and a vase you only see the outside, but a bowl is both. The inside can be outside. We also helped Geert with his experiments with the new recipes. Normally, you use small pieces of clay to test the reactions and changes in the form during the firing. But we decided to make simple products that could be produced quickly – a little plate, which was an open mold, and a little cup. Vincent has been producing those cups for ages since then. And we started to experiment with the recipes. Starting, for instance, with putting glaze only on the inside, which was not done then, for products at least.
H: Playing with the inside and the outside, emphasizing a lesson that you learned to combine a conceptual layer with a practical layer. The glazing inside also gives some delicacy to the thing that you are storing. And from there you also went into plastics.
B: In the recipe, you have the basic color of clay, the clay slip layer, and the glaze, which is transparent. I started making experiments, for instance, a little plate where half was covered in clay slip, and a perpendicular half was glazed, so you had four different material textures. We would alternate colors as well. I realize now that Vincent and I were totally uninterested in what was happening around us, what our teachers thought. We would just talk to Geert Lap. Eventually we did our exam, which we presented as a common project.
H: That was also unique.

First job

B: Vincent was a bit calmer, I was more… you wouldn't expect it, but more of a rebel then. We each presented two other projects. And then he had the diploma and I didn't, which I didn't mind actually, because we already knew we would continue. First we went to the EKWC (Europees

Keramisch Werkcentrum). We were in the beginning of a development that was more discipline-based and experimental, but we were in this traditional arts and crafts place in a village in Brabant. In the academy, we were the arts and crafts boys, but in the EKWC, we were the industrial boys: we started to use the pressurized air, to work with plaster like industrial designers. And then we bought the kiln from the academy, and I asked Vincent to join me in Rotterdam. I didn't dare to go to Amsterdam yet, and Vincent only knew Eindhoven. At the time, there was nothing in Rotterdam, only OMA, and one of my friends knew someone there. Our first project was inspired by the first experiments in Vincent's graduation project. In Vincent's internship, he also went to a traditional Dutch factory in Maastricht, Mosa. They were doing an experiment to combine ceramic cups with plastic handles that wouldn't break. When he came back, he focused on the functional effects of the combination. Now I proposed to make a bowl, just a really nice product, a form based on originally functional archetypes. So we started to develop the product in polyester and clay; that was technically very difficult because of the different material reactions to temperature. But our career started with that bowl. Many museums bought it, it went into the MoMA.

H: And how did you start to do exhibitions?

B: I was setting up a workshop with Vincent in Rotterdam. And Vincent started to make architectural models in polyester with Frans Parthesius for OMA. I remember working once on their famous model of the library for Paris. For the competition, they had to make a model that was "colorless." I still remember working the last night on the model, with Rem Koolhaas actually in the workshop. At seven in the morning when the model was finished and about to be shipped away in a big box, everyone was dead, and we were standing on the street in front of our garage, Rem snapped his fingers, and an assistant came with a pile of A5 booklets, and he signed it, and gave it to each one of us. Over the years, I met many people who were involved on that last night and equally remembered. Eventually I realized that my atelier was turning into a workshop for architectural models for OMA. That was fine, but not for me. Then I had my first assignment to make an exhibition in Amsterdam. And in 1990 I started my own workshop there as well. I made my first exhibition for Ulf Moritz and Benno Premsela at the TextielMuseum in Tilburg. Benno divided the plan up in rooms, and Ulf wanted to test me in a way, so he asked me to come up with an idea for one little room. He asked me how I would present fabrics. I came to visit Ulf by train to present the design, and in the train I got a bit panicky, because I didn't have a proposal for a design but for an approach. I just had a material – copper tube – and I had made some little examples, how you could connect it, and how it could be a system to make an exhibition. But he accepted it and then I did the whole exhibition.

Exhibition design is not a profession

T: Was exhibition design a profession then?

B: No, that's why I still can't call myself an exhibition designer!

T: Now I think it has become more established, but how did you have the idea that you could go into that field?

B: I didn't see it as a preexisting field. I, and many others of course, including Herman, we developed the profession during that time, in a way. Before that, graphic designers did exhibitions.

H: Which is strange because especially from the nineteenth century until the 1980s, it was part of the architectural profession to do exhibition design. But somehow they got sloppy, uninterested. Maybe the architects were not interested because it seemed to lack that element of social urgency; they were no longer as concerned that much with aesthetics or display, or maybe only for their own work. Of course, OMA created this dialogue between display and content, so they played a huge role in redefining architecture and exhibiting architecture. And Bart and I started as partners at that same moment, experimenting with exhibition design as something spatial and architectural.

B: For me, making exhibitions was not a goal. It wasn't something I disliked, either, I just didn't think about it. And then Ulf Moritz asked me to do a presentation for the Dutch fashion group GILL.

H: They were four fashion brands, Gletcher, Illustrious Imps, Lawina & Lola Pagola, presenting mens- and womenswear, accessories, and shoes together.

B: I got to know the designers well, and through the organizers I came to know Nanette van der Kleyn and Alexander van Slobbe, who started orson + bodil. They needed a new tabletop for their pattern table. And I said to them, your question is clear but also complicated. It's simpler for me to just buy some beams and build you a new table. I came back with a few designs and little models, and I put the price on the back – there was a simple one and a "designed" one. Alexander wanted the second one, but it was 750 guilders, and he didn't have money. So he said, "I'll get back to you." When I left, I assumed that was the last I would hear from him, but he called me after a few months when he got the money together. So I made the table and then I started doing other jobs for them as well, and at one moment they connected me to Herman.

Meeting at Energieën

H: I remember meeting you with Lola Pagola at the *Energieën* exhibition at the Stedelijk Museum Amsterdam in 1990. In the exhibition each designer had a room... OMA was there with the model you helped make, and there was a landscape where Issey Miyake had laid down his fabrics; it was very interactive. And together with Marlie Witteveen and Marijke Bruggink from Lola Pagola we went to Bodega De Keyzer and we started talking about how to make... stuff! At the end of the 1980s, fashion was pretty alive in the Netherlands; people were starting to define themselves

as authors. Lola Pagola were maybe the least "fashionista," and they didn't have an air about them.
B: They were designers.
H: They were the most approachable of the group. They saw design as a profession, that you produce good shoes that made sense and were well made.
B: They were also self-producing.
H: That's something we started to discuss – how to produce things, and perhaps how to self-produce. And for me that was totally new, coming from Architecture in Delft, it seemed so appealingly direct.
T: Did architects pay any attention to the developments in design at the time?
H: No. At least not on the level of discourse.
T: I had that sensation, because even when I studied architecture around 2005, the Super Dutch phenomenon was strong, but design was never mentioned. It seems that there was no relationship between the two.
H: But after all architecture was very much influenced by design developments in the Netherlands. After 2000 there were a couple of exhibitions highlighting the crossover themes. The interesting thing is that when Bart started as a designer, there was still some industry, but we have hardly any left. In fashion, there was no more production. Doetinchem and those towns in the eastern Netherlands produced beautiful cotton shirts, but the industry all left the country. So fashion designers started to develop a conceptual language to be more connected to art, because they were free from the practical concerns of mass production. They would self-produce in a limited number, using their own equipment, or they would cast themselves as visionaries – Lidewij Edelkoort is a very good example of someone who said, "I am no longer designing, but I am a trend forecaster." It's something that she almost invented – if there is no possibility to produce, you find another way of connecting producers to shape what they do! And that may be fading away after her.
T: It may be coming back, but in a different way. Lidewij is very sincere.
H: She's sincere in her superficiality. She constructs. She doesn't say it's the truth, but a construction of reality. It's not about holistic thinking or spirituality.
T: Now there's K-HOLE, which is a trend forecasting group that started as artists. They have a very ambiguous position, in a way... they came up with the "normcore" idea of dressing in the basics as high fashion. I guess there was also Marshall McLuhan before Lidewij.
H: But that was much more scientific, and had much more connection to actual research. Lidewij does a lot of research, but it's to prove her instincts. She makes a statement first and then makes the argument. But I think that's beautiful; it really works as a construction and opened up many possibilities, especially for the Design Academy.
B: Before that, Jan Lucassen was the real visionary. He set up the approach of "Man and..." in all of the departments, so he divided design subjects around the center point of the human. When he left Eindhoven, he was so clever to invite Lidewij to be his successor, and she sold that idea to the world, in combination with the success of the students through Droog. The huge success of Dutch design was at its highest point, just before she left the academy, when it collapsed.
T: It's also interesting how the government support created a supportive environment for designers.
H: It was the same in architecture and fashion. All of the offices that started in the 1990s got starting grants or funding to have an international exhibition, and that really launched their careers. OMA and MVRDV and Neutelings Riedijk...
B: It was so compressed, in a way; all the names you mentioned earlier – Hella Jongerius, Jurgen Bey – they were just a few years younger than me. They were the first generation to graduate from this new system. And of course they were picked up for Droog by Gijs Bakker, who was their mentor.
H: That was maybe a new tactic, to say that it was a collective of designers.
B: And my generation was already "old school"; we didn't produce that kind of work.
H: I think you deliberately chose another path, which led you more into spatial and experimental design, where we found our connection. It's very interesting how you described giving people tools for a specific purpose, and not so much design a specific aesthetic. We were both looking for a narrative or something to communicate – not through the aesthetics of a finished product, but through dealing with a material, and how its transformation could represent something.
B: I am interested in the process and what happens in my hands. I always tell my students, "Step back, analyze, and use your own eyes to see." It's from the song "Take A Look (At Yourself)" by rapper Guru. In industrial design, you make a design without knowing how many copies will be produced. So for my graduation I made one product – a table – that was unique and made by hand; but I also made the ceramics with Vincent, which was a repeated action with an undefined outcome, using those three neutral, archetypal forms, but the way we treated it was endlessly different.
H: I recognize this trajectory of yours. I think my function in our collaboration was to counterbalance that preciousness, which by definition I hate! For instance, you've saved all of your models.
T: Because you are not precious about them.
H: Not at all. For me, the model is a tool and it's not a result.
B: I don't save them with a goal.
H: But what you've made with your hands has a sort of value to you. I was rather looking for a sort of brutality in the way things are made, but I also love the amateur – how someone constructs something like they never made anything before. Every time you start all over again. We did that a lot in the fashion shows by just going to the building shop, going through the aisles, and just picking materials at random.
B: I had to find a way out of it.
H: And you liked the open-endedness. You can be stuck in your own ability to make things perfect.

conversation 2

Fashion connections: shows & exhibitions

T: It's interesting that you have connections with the fashion industry, yet you are not so into fashion itself.

H: That's also because Guus and Alexander, Marlie and Marijke, had the more artisan approach – maybe arts and crafts is a common denominator. It's not about excess or expressing your personal imagery, but the concern for a kind of archetype or tapping into a slow development of the world not based on hype. It's more about slow transformations. If you work in fashion and you have that ability and fixation, you collect people around you with the same approach. We were part of a family of people who were critical of commercialism, of the fashion industry itself. So you would call it garments rather than clothes; you would think about how it looked on the inside. It's funny; I am wearing this knitted spencer by SO. I thought it was an industrial product – complex but still industrially made – because they had a big market in Japan. But I just talked to Alexander last weekend, and he told me that this gradient was actually sewn in by hand. So already in the early 1990s, before his 2001 collection experimenting with cutting apart and repairing garments by hand, this approach was already an extra layer of his work.

B: In our collaboration, we worked as brothers – we had a very close relationship, but only in work. It's not that we didn't like each other, but it was only practiced in the jobs we did. We got to know each other because we connected through the fashion shows. It was not a conscious choice, but it worked.

H: I think that is also still both our practice with other designers. We have affinities and start developing concepts with others.

B: We did about twenty fashion shows in Paris!

H: Yes, four a year, and you were also involved in the showrooms in Paris.

B: And you were more involved with the work in Japan. What I liked is that it was never our initiative to look for something together; we were always motivated by the job. As a working attitude, we did think about design solutions when we were apart, but we only made designs sitting together. We would come in often with a different energy, for example Herman would be totally depressed, he didn't see any way to do it, and I would come in with a solution – or the other way around.

H: What I learned from Bart is actually to be depressed. While we worked we listened to Nico and REM and Sonic Youth. I was brought up in this happy evangelical tradition of my mother, it was always, "Hallelujah, everything is beautiful, every day is a fine new day!" Of course I could relate to that emotion as well, but through Bart I learned to deal with negativity as a creative force.

B: Meanwhile, what I learned from you is to observe the responsibility, the budget, the preconceptions of the client, the competition of other designers, and just put those aside. I don't recall that we ever panicked.

H: That's a bit my anarchistic attitude. I suppose that I don't care, so that gives a sort of freedom to work without interference. It's sort of in the back of your mind, of course – even if you are a punk, you know what you're dealing with. You're not naive.

B: But we were very confident at that time. We had made our first steps, then we met, and then we took off. We were opportunistic about our success, including our individual assignments on the side. I see the fashion shows as a phenomenon and a work in progress; every time we did another trick, and there was always a bit of an expression and an invention. All of the shows together are one work; it's the accumulation that makes it valuable. But each exhibition we did together was really a highlight for me. We did *Start* for OMA, and *Styling* at the Centraal Museum in Utrecht – the museum reopened after being closed for renovations, and we did almost one-third of the whole building. We were asked by José Teunissen to connect the three disciplines of fashion, design, and painting.

H: That was good casting. I guess our thinking about expression and simple execution gave us a certain liftoff in terms of defining an environment that was readable, but also a little bit alienating. You could recognize it, but it was not the regular way to go. So there was always this tension. For instance, to show the fashion in the exhibition we made a linear showcase of fashion items, one after the other. And for the ones that were less vulnerable or old, the pedestal sufficed, while the most vulnerable and historic pieces had a glass plate in front. We played with that tension.

B: But we also had access to very precise execution. We designed aluminum joints to keep the glass plates standing. It was possible because I would just go to the workshop of my favorite metalworker and we could make it exactly as we wanted. We didn't have to rely on people from the museum or the whole procedure of looking for contractors.

H: There was one line going along four rooms with all of the furniture design, and we made a kind of timeline that played with repetition. So the pedestal height created a certain rhythm and the colors behind them changed.

B: At the moment that you have defined your concept or toolbox, then you just have to follow your line of reasoning. Using the same method we found design solutions for specific challenges.

H: So you develop a set of rules, and when you go to the venue, you have solved the generic

problems, and deal with the exceptions on-site.
T: Designing exhibitions poses such logistical challenges; it almost makes more sense to do it with the objects on the spot. It's actually a more sensible way to use your time. I wonder if you took that from the extremely short time frame of the fashion shows.
H: Absolutely.
B: For one show we used these aluminum plates.
H: The idea was that the catwalk would take up the entire space, pressing the people against the walls.
B: So it was much wider than normal, like a huge mirror.
H: The show itself was about reflection: Alexander used white fabric with fluorescent colored fabric inside, so the color would shine through.
B: We ordered ready-made podium parts in Paris and simply placed the aluminum on top. Then we took the aluminum back to NL – we had designed special cases for them – and the next time we took the plates to Paris again, we had scratched the edges to make a circle mirror floor, surrounded by a wooden border that we dusted with conté blue pigment powder. Each time a model walked on it, she would leave her shoeprint on the circle.
A fashion show is a combination of theater, a commercial and a cultural moment – the buyers and the press are seated across from each other, observing each others' reactions – and a photo opportunity. Our work was to bring them together in the *mise-en-scène*. We learned some lessons along the way – in the first show, we covered ugly walls with paper. But the moment the lights come on, no one looks at the walls anymore!
H: Our inventions for the shows were very related to art that we liked.
B: In one of the later shows, we bought only one roll of very expensive material, a kind of PVC.
H: The way it wrapped around the surface of the podium parts was very magical. The show was in the Louvre, Rue de Rivoli, Musée des Arts Décoratifs.
B: So we hired the podium, and the lighting people hired black theater curtains, and then we made the catwalk higher than usual. The idea was that when people came in the space, there would be some models standing like statues on one side of the catwalk, and the black theater curtain was blocking the view to the rest of the space. Then the public was seated in the middle of the space, and the models would move on the catwalk and disappear through another curtain to be photographed, so the audience would see only the flashes. And this PVC material was simply rolled out from the beginning to the end on the catwalk, just lying there.
H: In the same space, we also had a layout with different rooms. We used this rough gray underlay material for carpeting to make a pattern for the models to follow. We were always involved in the mise-en-scène.
B: The commercial pressure was a bit lower by that time, so we could go for more conceptual ideas. We would figure out how to produce them, and just do it on the spot. These locations are expensive, so you have very limited time.

Learning about design & architecture together

H: It was an excellent learning process. The pressure of commercial success would fluctuate, and we noticed the tension at some points.
B: There was an undefined sense of partnership, and the consequence was that we never felt individually burdened by particular aspects. We were untouchable, in a way.
H: We had such a different energy level, so we complemented each other, almost by coincidence.
B: It was not about our career, about who did what. The fashion world is far away from my approach as a designer, although I am interested in Alexander van Slobbe's work specifically. But it almost didn't matter; we explored so many ideas through the format of the fashion show. Another thing our collaboration brought out in me was a latent interest in architecture. It was always there, but it seemed far away from my starting point in ceramics. The first step was in the process of products, the second step was the spatial treatment of objects, and the third step was in the exhibition narrative.
H: Maybe you also thought, "What these architects are doing, I can do as well!" I was at that time very anti-architecture – I saw all the negative aspects of the discipline, that it was manipulative and confining, that it did not allow for improvisation or flexibility. So we were a funny match – one denying the architectural practice, the other thinking that it might be his career! What I did with Rianne [Makkink for Sloom.org], by contrast, was related to this criticism of architectural production, while Bart got very into the poetics of architecture as an art form. When I studied in Delft, there was no relation with art, except for some form studies with colors and shapes in space, but it didn't constitute an art education. We were floating between knowledge and tendencies, and we moved from a productive mode into a poetic mode, but I saw it as a form of escapism – I never thought about actually realizing my designs. I had to do it to graduate, but in fact I wanted to use the forms of architectural expression (like the cross section, the floor plan, the model), and the paraphernalia used to give an impression of the design, in order to tell a story. People could imagine it, but it might never actually materialize.
T: That's what I find magical about designers, that they just do it. It's very unusual in architecture.
B: I see that as part of my role in the design process in architecture. I have finished two building projects in the crisis period, not as an architect but as a designer, which meant I also took care of the process. My interest is in making space, manipulating it or dealing with it; I like the craft of making; and I like to learn about material skills, but what makes the project happen is the process – how to go from a very conceptual idea of building to a point where you can actually sell the outcome.
H: What I find interesting in your progress is the challenge of

producing as an architect in the same way that you produced your bowls, your ability to work with design logic and logistics.
T: It also brings up the matter of scaling up. In every process, there is a tolerance or an acceptable amount of roughness: in design, you have to transform a raw material in order to make a product, while in architecture you tend to work with an assembly of products.
H: In your design you also worked with a toolbox – the fireplace was like the core with a structure built around it, and you could add on when you have money. You could change your house according to the evolution of your family.
B: If I would typecast Herman and me in our different approaches – if I start an assignment with an empty page, I don't know what to do. If I know about the conditions and limitations, then I can react to them. Herman is the other way around: if you show him all of the limitations at the beginning, he'll say, "I can't work like this!" So I look for the restrictions or context – that's very much a designer's attitude.
T: Perhaps that's because architects have tools to deal with the unknown conditions. A building becomes a floor plan; a territory becomes a site plan. There's a systematic way to define the unknowns, whereas in design it's not as simple, because you stay involved with the process further.
H: It can be very regimented, as you say. This week you deal with the floor plan, next week with the cross section, then the detailing, and so on. You have to keep resolving the design at each scale.
B: I actually developed my interest in architecture through the books I got from Herman – like *A Pattern Language* by Christopher Alexander.
H: You loved Jean Prouvé. He and Charlotte Perriand were the bridge – they dealt as much with furniture as with space.
B: Your first questions are the deepest. Because I was almost uneducated in architecture, I could step back from what I was doing. In architecture, you still tend to "learn" how to design.
H: There is a template for work with a historical reference, but it can be objectified. It creates a system that doesn't relate well to the history.
B: In design contexts, you often talk about inspiration, whereas in architecture you speak about references.
T: I think there is a hierarchy at play. I think the need to make the reference is very much about postmodernism and the idea of historical construction.
H: I'm not so sure. Reference is also how architecture built up its own language, as in the 1920s. It was not about inventing new universes, but transforming existing elements. Even the paradigmatic change of Le Corbusier was very much about using the old to understand the new. I haven't really seen that in design.
T: I think the difference is that, in architecture, you can only acknowledge that process when the historical reference is a motif of the contemporary discourse. Since the beginning of modernism, except for a brief period of very strong postmodernism, a building is taken so seriously that it seems unjustified to use it to make a visual joke or allusion. Of course they do it – where else do you begin – but in objects, it seems there's a little bit more freedom to make such explicit references.
H: I think it's less about postmodernism than about abstraction. In design education, it's more difficult to approach – that you can deal with a subject in terms of fundamentals and not only aesthetics. Things have a certain logic and levels in themselves. A drinking glass is also similar to a building – it has a top, it has an envelope, it performs.
B: If you have a design that looks like an existing object, it seems to be a pity, while in architecture it's almost the other way around. It gets some ground that way. At a certain moment in the building process, I had a big problem – I had no education or experience at all in actually designing a house. I solved it by finding the house of a Swiss architect built in Switzerland. In its design I saw a solution that was so close to our starting point – the fireplace with the stairs – and so beautiful that I did what I usually tell my students: if you come up with a design that looks a bit like a Rietveld, for example, don't be afraid of it, don't turn away. Go look at it, because that is the only way to get over it. So I collected all of the drawings and images and copied the house exactly. Then I created my own design and worked in the detail that I envisioned. Through the process, however, it did change.
H: This learning how to structure the design process is very different in different countries. In Berlin, for example, you are asked to be original, perhaps a bit of a Dutch approach to have a connection to the profession, but find your own way and produce your own examples. In Switzerland, however, it's much more about the master and the pupil. In the course of a professor, you should do what he or she does. If you look at Swiss architecture, it has a very slow development and there is no rupture. That's how they deal with the content of their profession.
B: You can also see it as a compliment, in recognizing the beauty of a detail.
H: You talk about reference, but maybe for you it was still more about inspiration.
T: It reminds me of jazz music, which had the idea of the riff, the improvised take, and the musical quotation, which were not at all contradictory to the originality or quality of the new music. Authorship is not a problem in music in the same way, because the original score is the material through which you learn, and so it's natural to work in shared references.
H: The beautiful thing about music is that it is time-based, whereas we hate postmodern architecture because it isn't a flowing movement: it stays, and often it is very badly executed. I hosted a lecture by Marc Dubois a few weeks ago, and he spoke about "The Presence of the Past," the first Venice Architecture Biennale, and he showed the incredible excesses of postmodern architecture, which was so horrible. There was a beautiful sparkle of light in the lecture

when he showed Lucien Kroll's student housing in Leuven. Suddenly, alongside the postmodern idea of the copy and the referent, you had the notion of the unfinished. That may be the architectural translation of the jam session in jazz music – the quotes are not organized, but rather arranged in an unfinished state.

Progressive collaboration

B: You wanted to talk about the end of our collaboration, which we've never really discussed before. I had to remember what happened, which means that it wasn't a dramatic event at the time. We got to know each other through the work.
H: We had a fascination for each other's work, not that we knew so much about each other – Jorinde Seijdel called it an "affinity." If I relate to Joke Robaard or Alexander van Slobbe, I have an affinity to them. It's very vague, but also clear, relating to the choices that you take, things or people that you want to bond with. It doesn't necessarily demand a result. We didn't think about production – we're not Piet-Hein-Eek-type of people. We didn't have a strategy.
B: We didn't have a plan at all. So how did it end? When I think about that time, I think there was a specific moment with a negative association, but there was also an undefined period where it simply faded. In the period that we worked together, over ten years, we learned so much from each other, but we also had our own projects in different fields. Looking back, I could say it's a pity that we didn't have a plan, because we could have taken more from it. But at the time, it never crossed my mind – neither for the better nor for the worse. We had that in common. If you develop so intensely together towards a point, you cannot avoid aiming for your own independence at the next level. It was good for us to go our own way with the baggage of what we had learned. In every relationship, there is a moment where things don't go as you want, and that happened over an exhibition in 2005.
H: It was a very confrontational exhibition with beautiful content.
B: The working relationship was disturbed by the deal between the curator, the gallery, and us.
H: And you let me go.
B: You had already started on the idea to set up Event-Architectuur as an organization.
H: In one way, it already started in 1990. We never discussed whether the work we had done together should be Event-Architectuur or something else.
B: It could have been; I liked the term from the beginning.
H: It didn't have content yet at the time.
B: That I didn't mind. I wasn't against the idea that it could develop as an umbrella that connects people. At the same time, I could deal with the fact that you left. The next day, however, when Paul showed up – nothing against him! – but we had discussed before that I didn't work for Event-Architectuur, that was yours, but that this was something we did together. It was clear that the partnership wasn't working anymore. But the exhibition design was great!
H: We had a great time that year, because we also did Utrecht Manifest.
B: We met in the job and we split in the job, so there were no hard feelings because the friendship and the connection was sitting at a table, working together. And we were always very happy with the outcome.
H: Can there also be a risk that someone gives you too much comfort? That's part of my approach to the story. It started to be difficult for me that you comforted my anxieties. I deal with my profession through anxieties – being afraid of delivering or getting things done. I'm not the kind of person who works according to a formula; neither are you. But I also needed to work through this performance anxiety. It's as you thought just after we separated, that you had a difficulty, but it was also productive. In the collaboration, each has his part, and you get a kind of comfort from sharing, but sometimes you want to feel the anxiety again, the shock of falling in the deep end, feeling alive.
B: Our collaboration was always very progressive; it was always going somewhere. Unconsciously, I knew it couldn't last forever, so I felt at peace with it when it happened. I had a similar but opposite feeling: I was afraid that if I continued, I couldn't avoid repeating myself. You risk falling into the comfort zone of your routine.
H: We were not able to trade roles.
B: We built something that helped us to push each other forward, and we had a responsibility to do something with that. We needed to take another step. After, I set up a studio, and later I was the first one to leave. "The old has to go before the new can come."
H: Perhaps I also struggle with collaboration, and that relates to our separation. There is no rule for the division of labor, so you have to organize it anew each time with the person you work with.
B: A friend of ours predicted it, in a light way, from the very beginning. I knew that there would be a point where I was no longer part of the fashion scene, because I knew that my being there was about our working together. Independent of what was going on around us.

alexander van slobbe

Fashion designer Alexander van Slobbe, who often advises Event-Architectuur on matters of color, created fourteen collages inspired by the transformation of the use of colors during the period 1990–2015.

1989 1990

1991
1992

1993 1994

1995 1996

Alexander van Slobbe

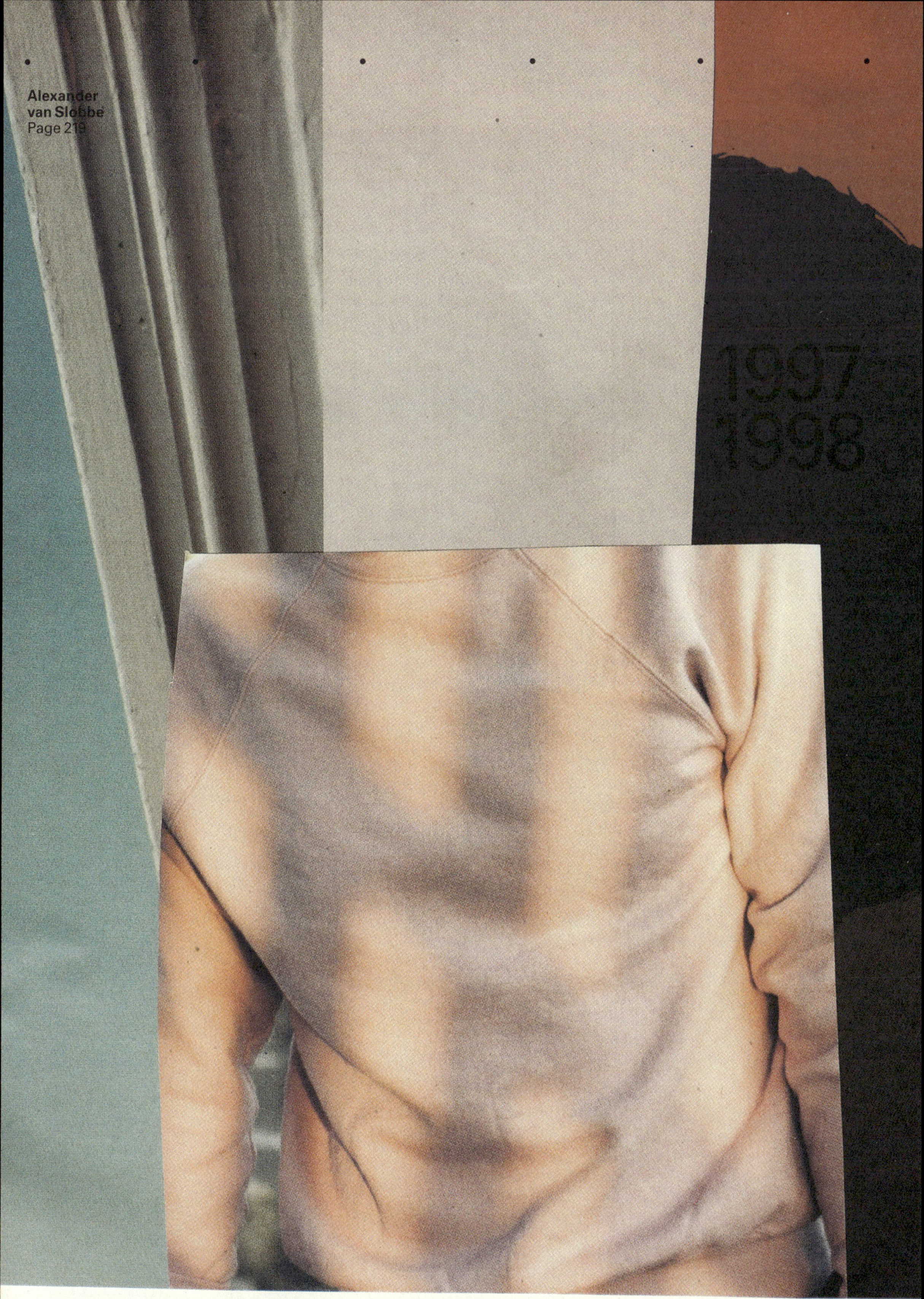

1997
1998

1999
2000

2001
2002

2003
2004

2005
2006

2007
2008

2009 2010

Events: Situating the Temporary
Page 226
2011
2012

Alexander van Slobbe
Page 227

2013
2014

Events: Situating the Temporary
Page 228

alexander

van slobbe

3

3 mirrors, models, shacks & yards 2000

the critical (1:1) model as a parallel reality 2005

3

mirrors, models, shacks & yards

3

The Critical

The experimental construction of a model reality cannot be reduced to the physical, but it can take shelter and begin to flourish in a demarcated space, however modest it may be. Radical architecture, in fact, has a long-standing relationship with the self-built structure at the edge of civilization – the architect in retreat, assembling a humble shack from the materials available then and there. While one thread of architecture was being increasingly subsumed into a market of rendered promises and real estate speculation, a second strand was rediscovering the counterculture of the 1960s and '70s, reinterpreting the primitive hut and making do in the yard. These ideas were urgent once more after the turn of the millennium, as the attack on the World Trade Center and the ensuing wars destroyed the dream of universal neoliberal progress suggested by Francis Fukuyama's essay, "The End of History?"

At the same time, the return to the city and the technological facilitation of collaborative communities also introduced a form of escapism that was decidedly urban. In cities like Berlin, communication networks and alternative economies could take root, while miniature Gardens of Eden blossomed in the cracks of the concrete landscape. Unlike the utopian idealism of the twentieth century, however, these micro-realities were candid about their improvised, contextual, and unresolved qualities. As in the work of Bertolt Brecht, their theatrical, deliberately constructed, model-like nature was not something to hide; instead, it was central to their operation.

2001: Wikipedia is launched.
2002: The idea of commons-based peer production is developed.
2003: The United States and allied forces invade Iraq.
2004: Berghain opens in Berlin.
2005: The last Xanadu house is demolished in Kissimmee, Florida.

3 dirk van den heuvel: of other spaces

Events: Situating the Temporary
Page 234

(some questions regarding

critical models in exhibition design)

dirk van den heuvel: of other spaces

Some questions regarding critical models in exhibition design

Ghosts

What is an exhibition? And more specifically, what is an architecture exhibition?

Architects and curators of architecture presentations often state that an exhibition inevitably produces an effect of alienation. An architecture exhibition always shows what is not there in the gallery spaces: the real buildings outside the museum. One might also say that this understanding of what is real and what is representation is inherent to the very proposition of the exhibition as an absence.

Following this line of thought, it can be said that architecture as building might reclaim its notion of authenticity through the medium of the exhibition; through the staging of its own absence. Exhibitions, then, are ghosts of other realities made present through resurrection and reconstruction.

The special attraction and wonder of exhibitions rests in the encounter of the visitor with these disembodied voices and images from other spaces outside that of the gallery space.

An exhibition is never an everyday space, it is always a space of dislocation. Paradoxically, this displacement opens up the possibility of critique, of imagination and rethinking ways of how to inhabit the world (or not).

A stage with actors

The exhibition proper can also be understood as another kind of architecture, thus complicating the relationship between the temporary construction of the exhibition and what is actually put on display.

Such a proposition is made by British architects Alison and Peter Smithson when they talk about exhibitions as a way of “staging the possible,” a foreshadowing of what might become real.

3

Mirrors, Models, Shacks & Yards
Page 236

A future reality is staged, or even enacted, like in their famous *House of the Future* (1956), designed for the annual Ideal Home Show in London. Live models in futuristic clothing inhabited the capsule-like house in order to demonstrate the new lifestyle and body culture, to come under the impact of new materials of the oil economy, such as plastic and space-age technologies, that would bring about an environment of control and comfort.

The house on display is the classic typology for the architecture of the modern era, to engage an audience in reimagining their own everyday domestic spaces. While lifted out of their everyday environment, the visitors inhabit the exhibition for a short while, briefly reconsidering their own home interiors, their own furniture and way of life.

Media space
Exhibiting involves techniques of communication and persuasion, from the most sophisticated avant-garde displays of the 1920s, by Lilly Reich and Charlotte Perriand, to the mainstream IKEA stores of today. Domestic interiors on display raise the question of where privacy and personal autonomy reside. Can one buy oneself into the lifestyle of the avant-garde? Can one really inhabit the ubiquitous IKEA?

The exhibition is a media space. The architecture of the exhibition constructs this media space and its specificities.

Also, our houses are not private anymore; they have become media spaces, too. Privacy is only conditional, to be renegotiated through a set of filters provided by consumer technologies.

Installations
What if the exhibition itself is already enough? What happens when the architecture of the exhibition coincides with the subject matter of the show?

Exhibition design then might become the making of installations, as we know from installation art, which in turn has overlaps with the practice of designing stage sets and scenographies.

The visitor is immersed in a situation and becomes a sensor or sensing body responding to an orchestration of stimuli. In architecture, this is an age-old technique starting with the archetype of the labyrinth in which the visitor loses her orientation. In installation design, modernist notions like critique and autonomy make way for surrealist games of association from which open-ended narratives might emerge, often polyphonic and contrapuntal.

Inspired by the work of Marcel Duchamp and Kurt Schwitters, the London-based Independent Group collective of visual artists, architects, and curators started experimenting with the creation of such temporary situations. The by now well-known *T.I.T.* show (*This Is Tomorrow*) of 1956 at the Whitechapel Art Gallery presented various group presentations displaying different approaches to interdisciplinary work and the creation of immersive environments. The installation by Richard Hamilton, John McHale, and John Voelcker entailed a distorted architecture of a folded surface for the display of then new pop art imagery, whereas the foursome of Nigel Henderson, Eduardo Paolozzi, and Alison and Peter Smithson staged a timber backyard shed in a patio of mirror-clad fences filled with fetish-like relics of a bygone age, now put on display as retrieved and "found" objects.

In both cases, the visitor was left to her own devices, trying to make sense out of the tableaux of disembodied voices and images presented to her, to find some sense of order "ideally created out of scratch."

Narrative space
An exhibition is always a narrative space. Not because an exhibition tells a story (which it usually does), but because the visitor will bring her own stories with her, and because she will relate to the exhibition by turning it into another story.

Models
The architecture exhibition might also be a model. Not only in the sense of a maquette, mock-up, or a house on display, but most radically as a conceptual reality of its own, a relational diagram which reveals a higher truth, or a deeper structure. American architect Peter Eisenman insists on such conceptual autonomy. To him, the model as a relational diagram is the real architecture which can only be accessed intellectually.

The 1:1 model is, as an exhibition device, most confusing and paradoxical. As a visitor, you enter the 1:1 model in real space and real time, but since you are dealing with a model, you are simultaneously in virtual space and time.

This alienation is made operative by Eisenman in his series of house designs, in particular in the *House VI*, which he built for Suzanne and Dick Frank in 1975. The house gained some notoriety for a few anecdotal twists, such as the column that interspersed the couple's bed or the kitchen table.

3

Mirrors, Models, Shacks & Yards
Page 238

It is not so much a disjunction that one experiences – as a visitor and as an inhabitant – but the parallel existence of two modes of understanding one's environment, two ways of inhabiting the house and the world.

One also encounters such series of dislocations in the work of artists like Gordon Matta-Clark, Dan Graham, or Thomas Demand, who famously excelled in perfecting the relational ambiguities at play between models and our constructed experience of reality.

Mirror

An exhibition is never an everyday space. An exhibition space belongs to the spaces of heterotopia, as coined by French philosopher Michel Foucault. As such the space of an exhibition is able to accommodate the juxtaposition and simultaneity of the most disparate objects, collections, cultures, histories, geographies.

One of the common explanations of the notion of heterotopia is the virtual space of the mirror behind the proper mirror, as elaborated by Foucault in the published version of his radio talk to architects, "Of Other Spaces." Foucault explains that, looking in the mirror, one sees oneself in another space; virtual and real space are both present in the space of the mirror. The reflection enables the human mind to imagine oneself in a different place, a different time, having a different life. Foucault speaks of "reconstituting oneself" and the "contestation of the space in which we live."

It is in this sense that the space of an exhibition can be such a critical space, questioning hegemonic culture while destabilizing the historiographical constructions of a disciplinary canon. The space of an exhibition is critical to the extent that it can be the space of such contestation.

3

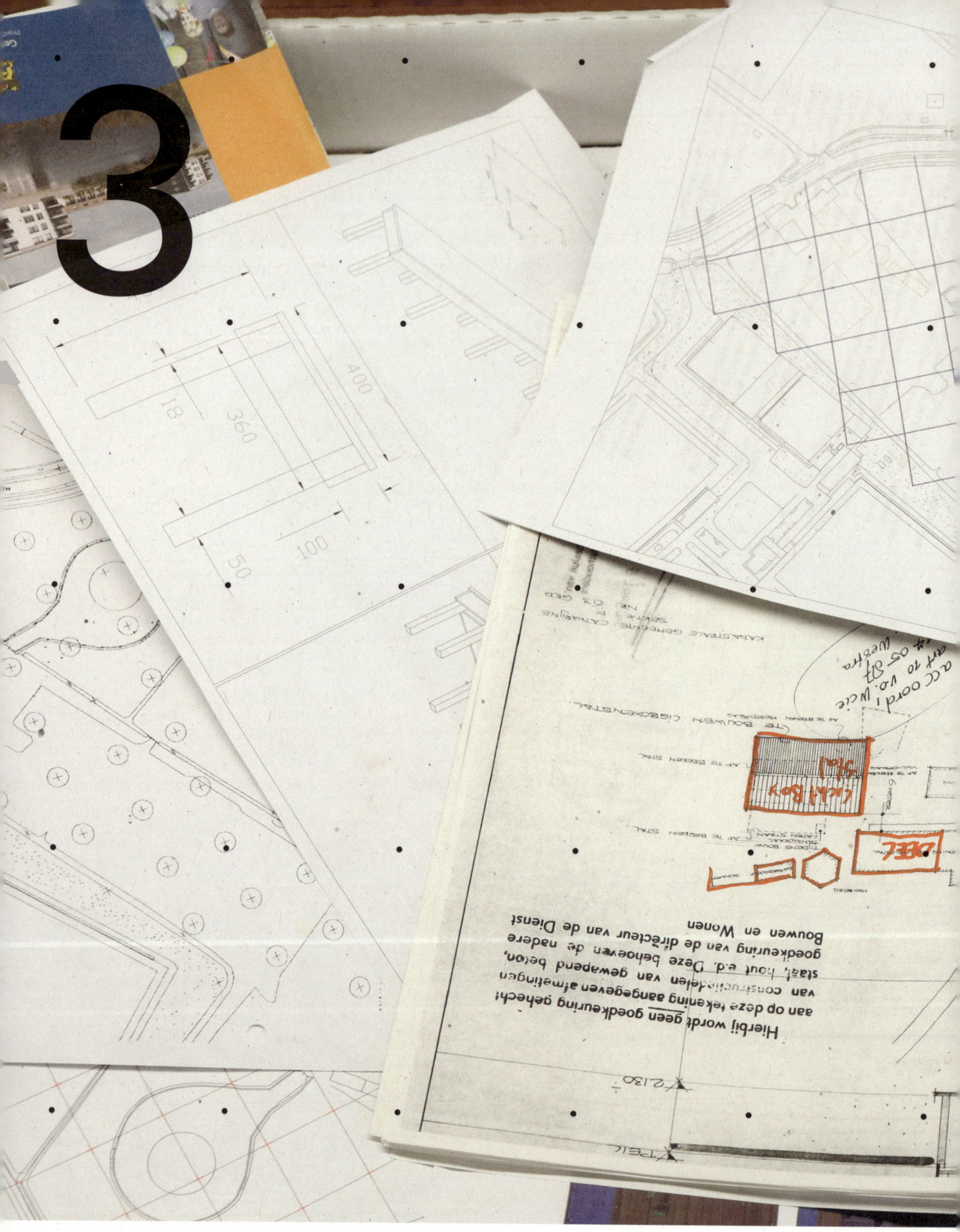

Events: Situating the Temporary

Page 240

project 113, 114

2005

Mirrors, Models, Shacks & Yards
Page 241

Pursuit of Happiness
Project: Land Art, Exhibition
Duration: Medium-term, 1 month
Year: 2005
Data: page 652

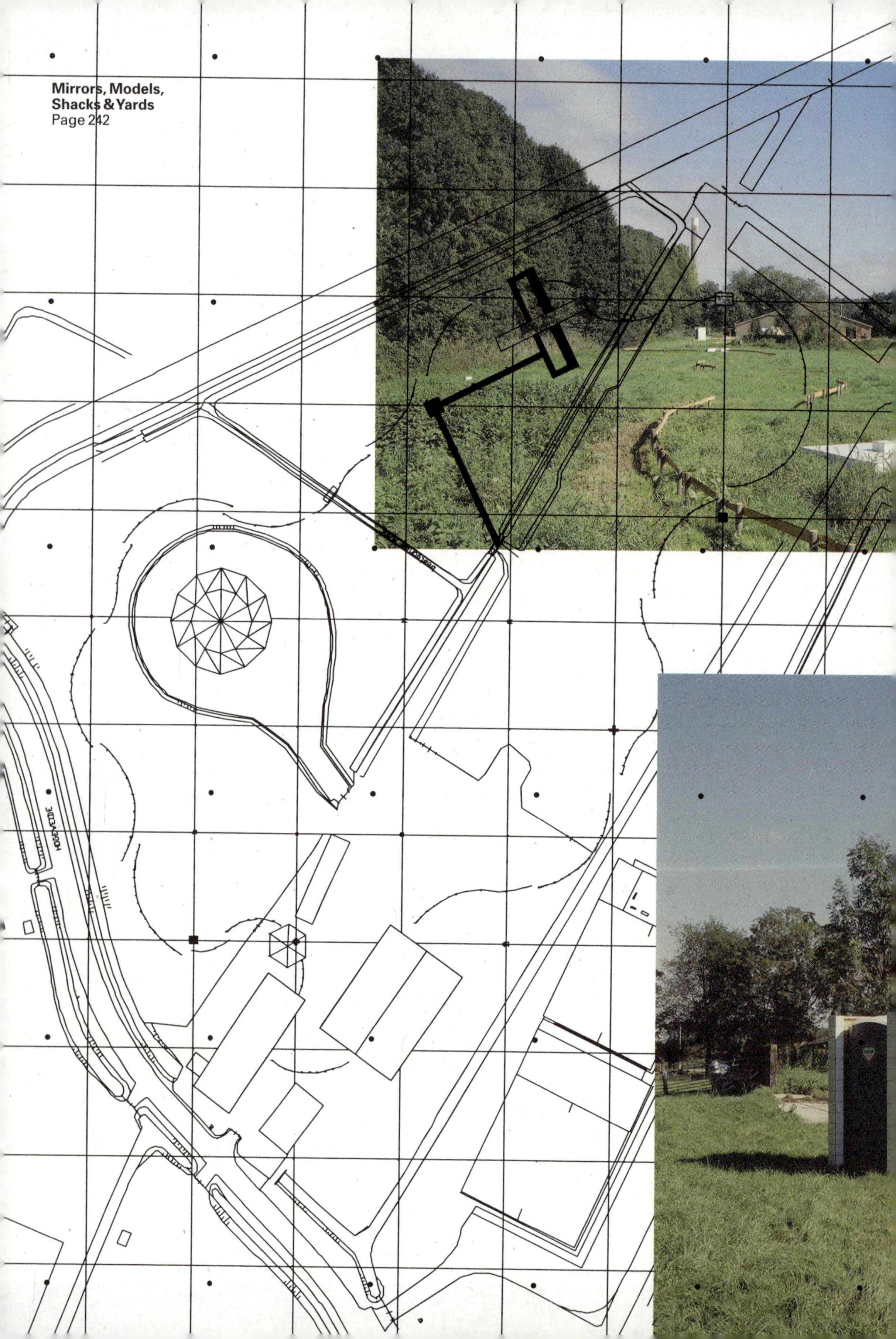
HOGEWEIDE

project 113, 114

project 113, 114

project 113, 114

3

Events: Situating the Temporary

Page 248

Mirrors, Models, Shacks & Yards
Page 249

orson + bodil
Workshop, Showroom & Store
Project: Interior
Year: 2004
Data: page 649

Models,
Yards

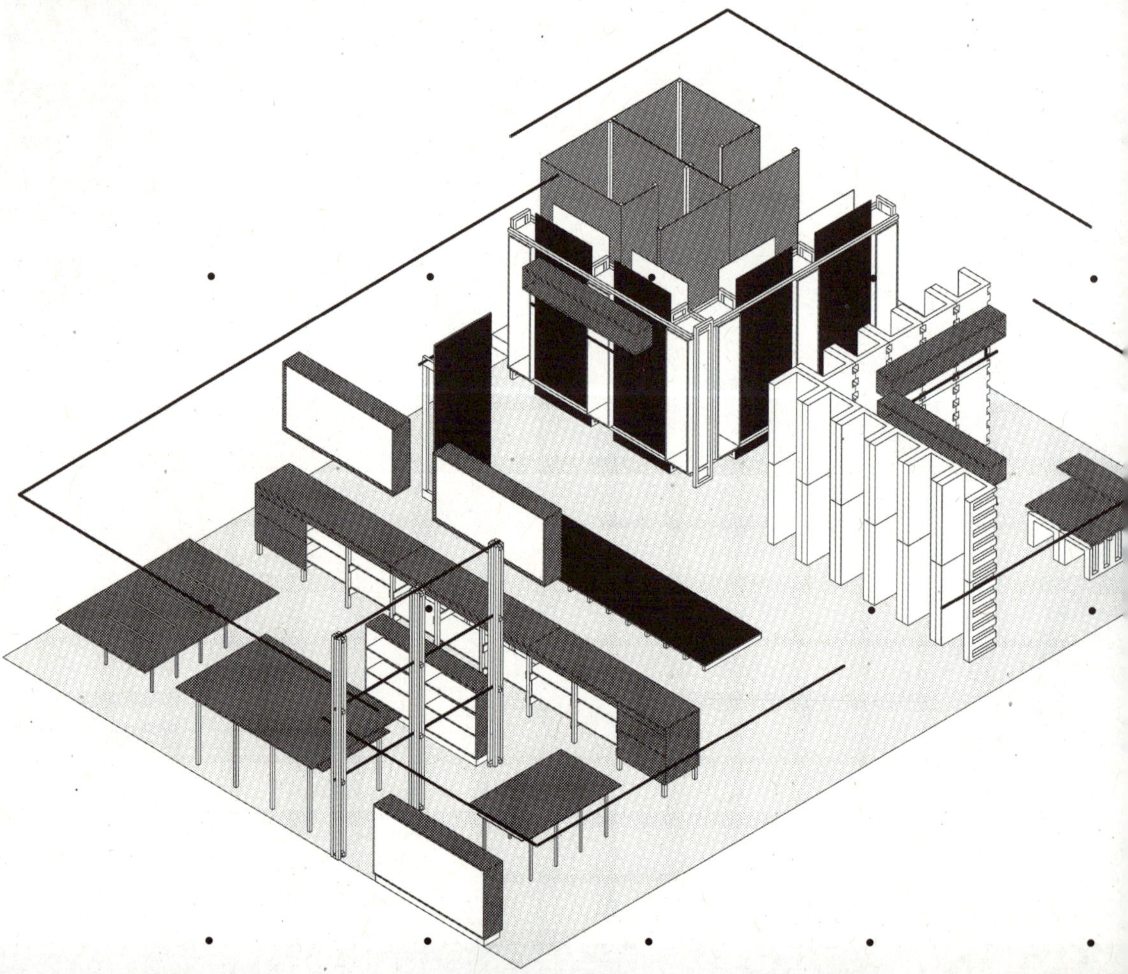

project 101

orson + bodil
Workshop,
Showroom & Store
Page 251

orson + bodil
Workshop,
Showroom & Store
Page 253

project 101

Mirrors, Models, Shacks & Yards
Page 254

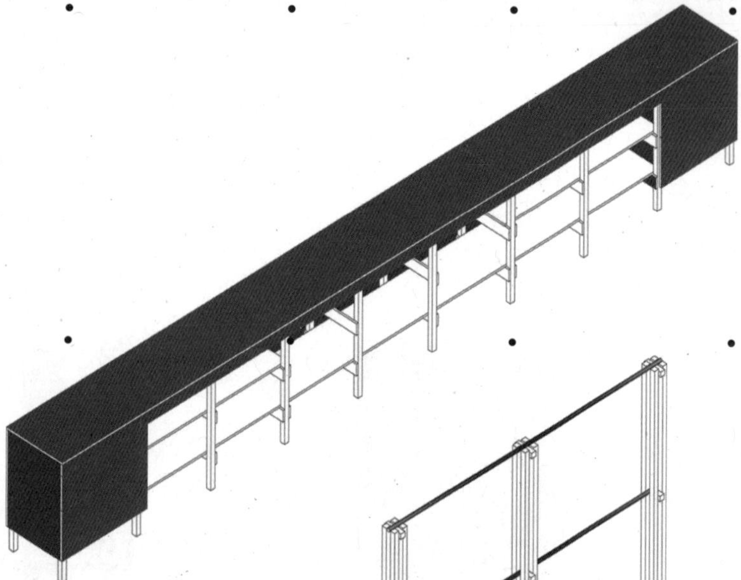

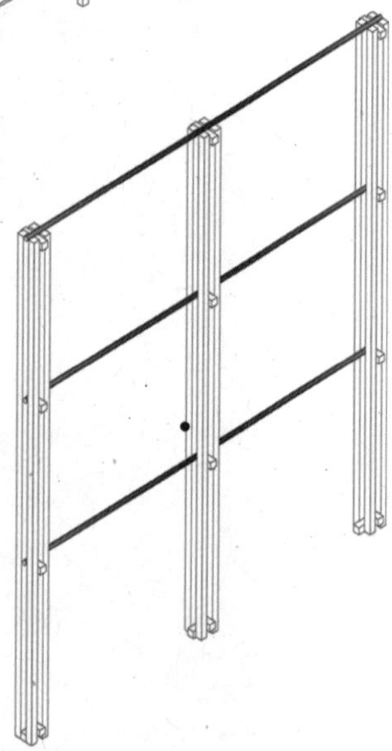

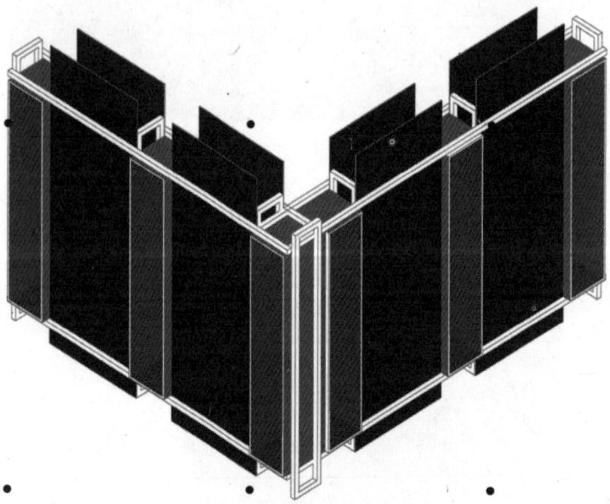

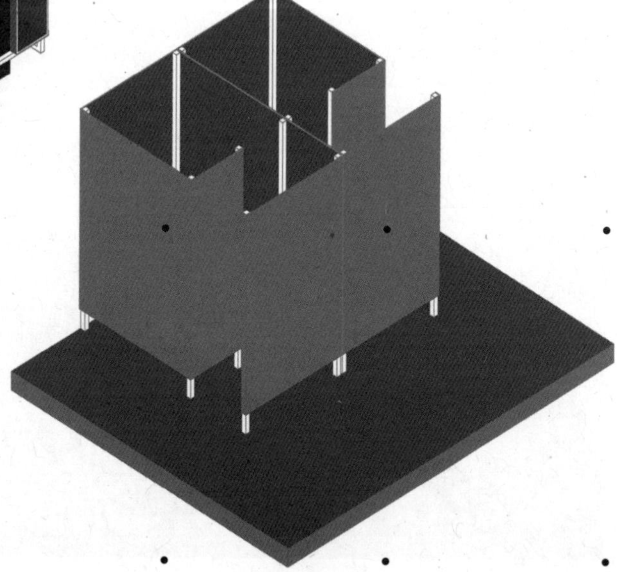

project 101

orson + bodil
Workshop,
Showroom & Store
Page 255

3

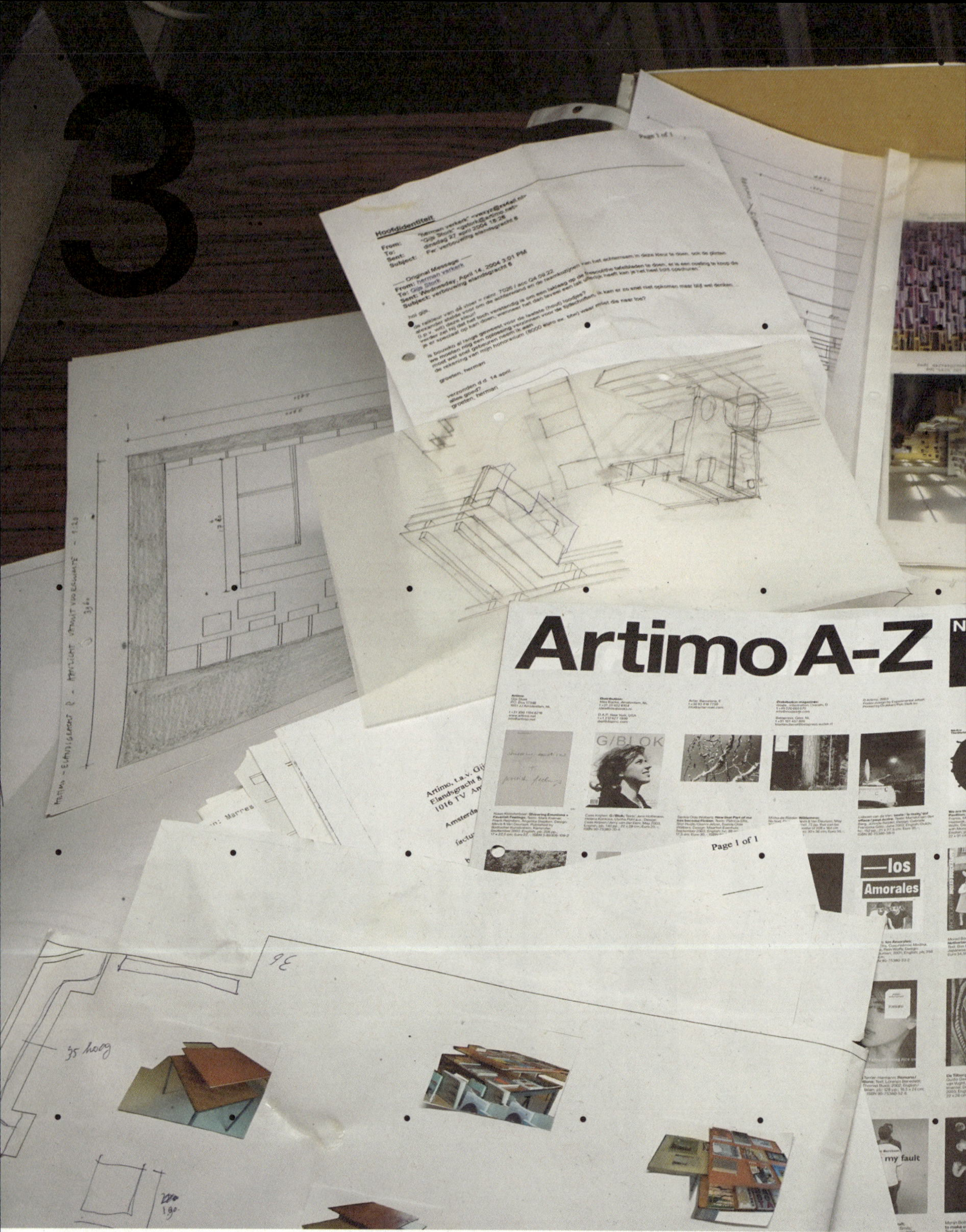

Events: Situating the Temporary
Page 256

project 103

2004

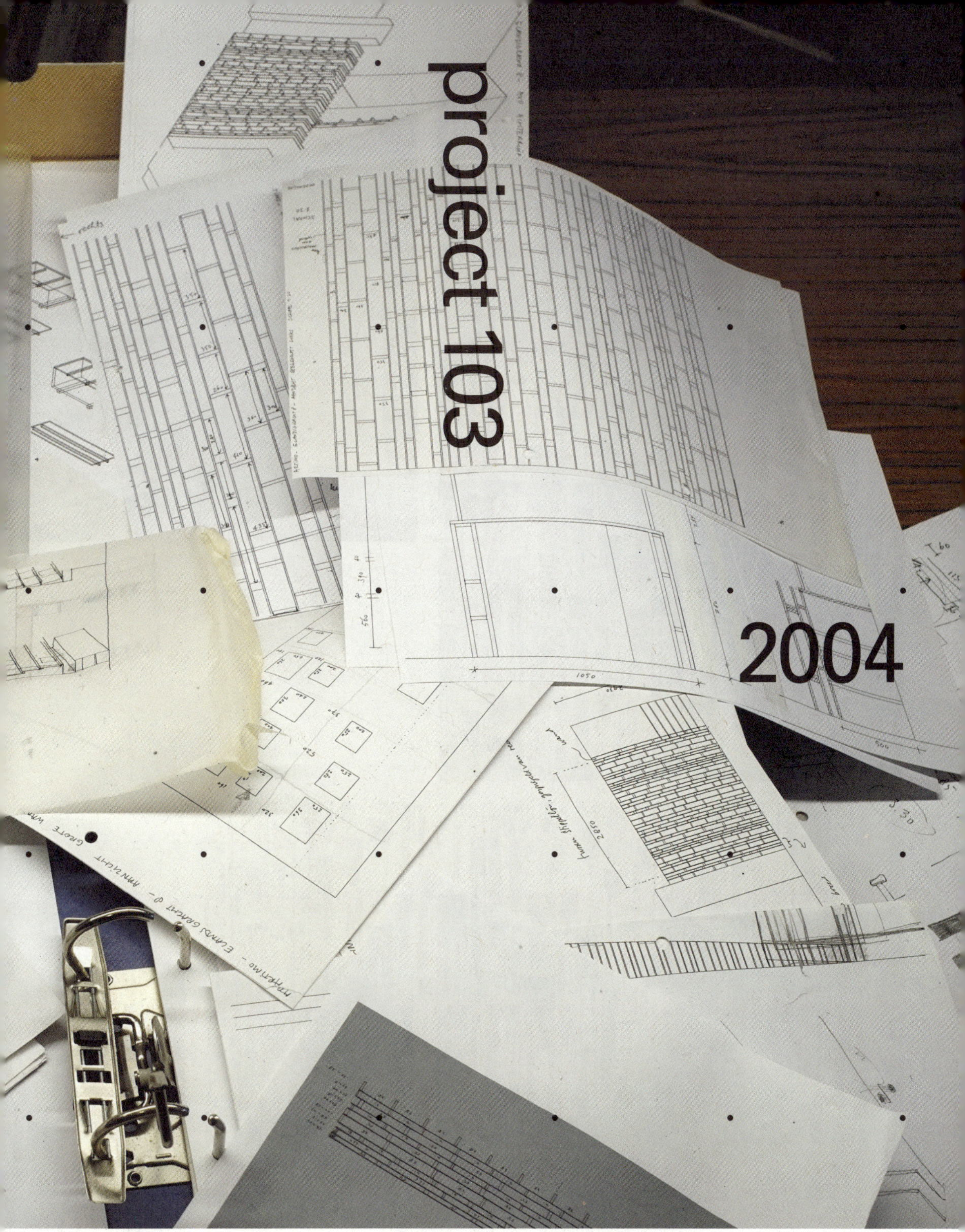

Mirrors, Models, Shacks & Yards
Page 257

Artimo A–Z
Project: Bookstore
Duration: Long-term, 3 years
Year: 2004
Data: page 650

project 103

Artimo A–Z,
Amsterdam
Page 259

Mirrors, Models, Shacks & Yards
Page 260

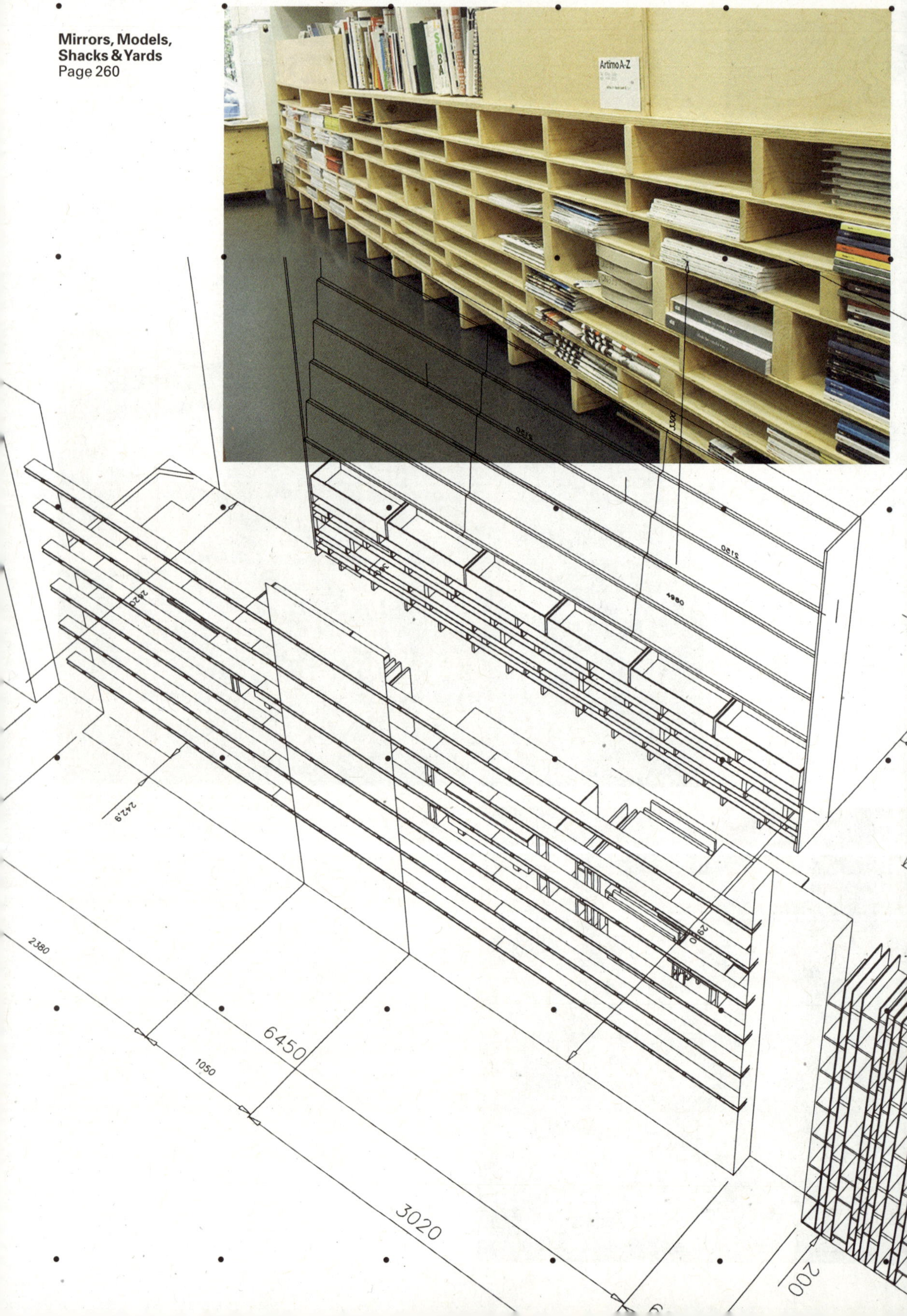

Artimo A–Z, Amsterdam
Page 261

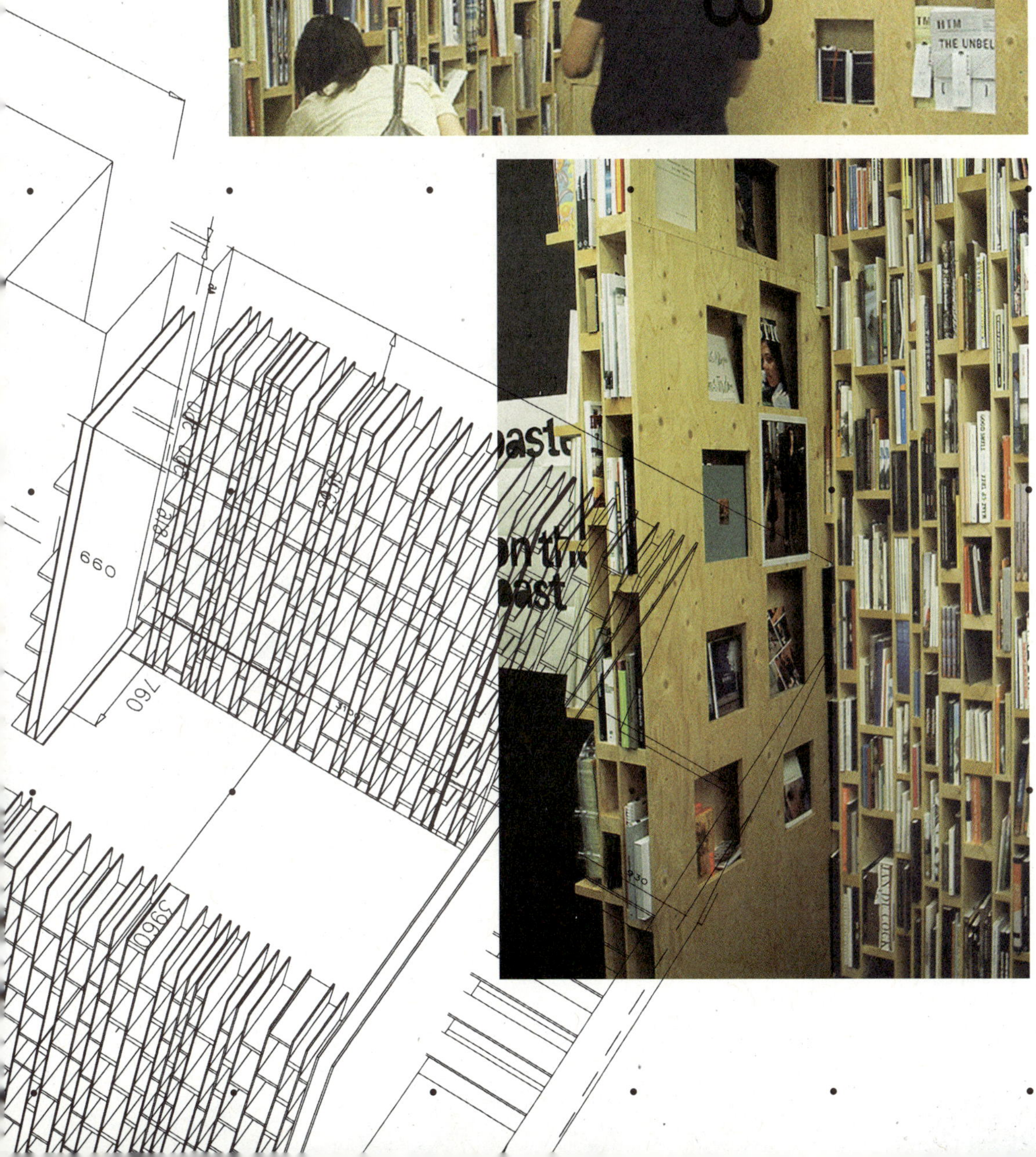

3

Events: Situating the Temporary
Page 262

project 85, 87, 88, 90, 93, 96, 104, 105, 125

2002

2005

Mirrors, Models, Shacks & Yards
Page 263

SLOOM
Project: Magazine, Activities
Duration: Short-term
Year: 2002–2005
Data: page 644

82
sloom 00:00:00
tijdschrift
ZONDAG
22 SEPT. 2002
13
SLOOM 01
dagschrift
70
sloom 02
Periodical of sloom.org
sloom 03:00:
zeitschrift

project 85, 87, 88, 90

SCHARRELEN
een onderzoek

Scharreltabellen
door Rianne Makkink
m.m.v. de familie van Veen
en de familie Meijer-Makkink

Boerenerven rond Ruinen
door Herman Verkerk
m.m.v. Heilien Tonckens

Sleuteljongens en hangmeisjes
door Rianne Makkink

Boerderijspeelgoed of
Speelgoed van de boerderij
door Toon Koehorst en Jannetje in 't Veld

Het onderzoek 'scharrelen' is een verzameling van beelden, teksten en grafieken die de grote diversiteit en het langzame groeimodel van de boerderij in het algemeen en het erf in het bijzonder laat zien.

RIANNE MAKKINK,
HERMAN VERKERK,
KOEHORST IN 'T VELD

SCHARRELEN
een onderzoek

Het onderzoek 'scharrelen' is een verzameling van beelden, teksten en grafieken die de grote diversiteit en het langzame groeimodel van de boerderij in het algemeen en het erf in het bijzonder laat zien.

RIANNE MAKKINK,
HERMAN VERKERK,
KOEHORST IN 'T VELD

1

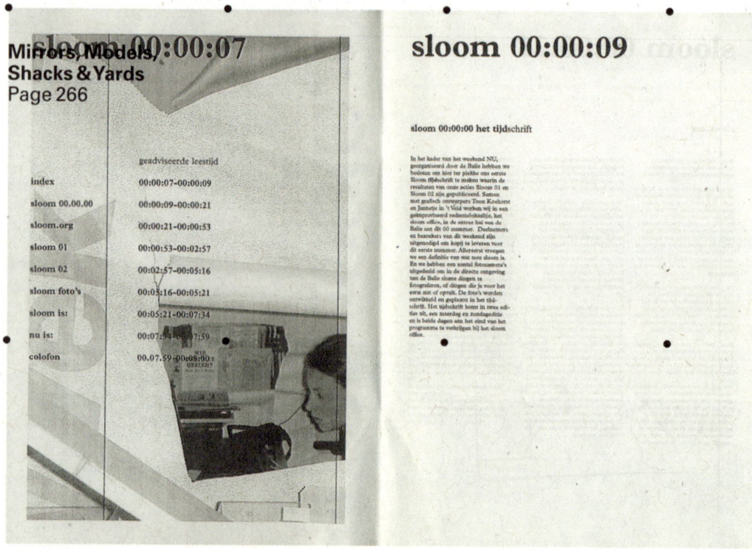
sloom 00:00:07
geadviseerde leestijd
index 00:00:07-00:00:09
sloom 00.00.00 00:00:09-00:00:21
sloom.org 00:00:21-00:00:53
sloom 01 00:00:53-00:02:57
sloom 02 00:02:57-00:05:16
sloom foto's 00:05:16-00:05:21
sloom is: 00:05:21-00:07:34
nu is:
colofon
sloom 00:00:09
sloom 00:00:00 het tijdschrift

sloom 00:05:18
foto bijdragen
Robert Vlek
Herman Verkerk
Eva Pel
Eva Pel

154 km
Dinsdag
17 september 2002
bijrijder:
Jan Hendrik Bosman
13.00-19.00 =
6 uur x 7 km =
42 km

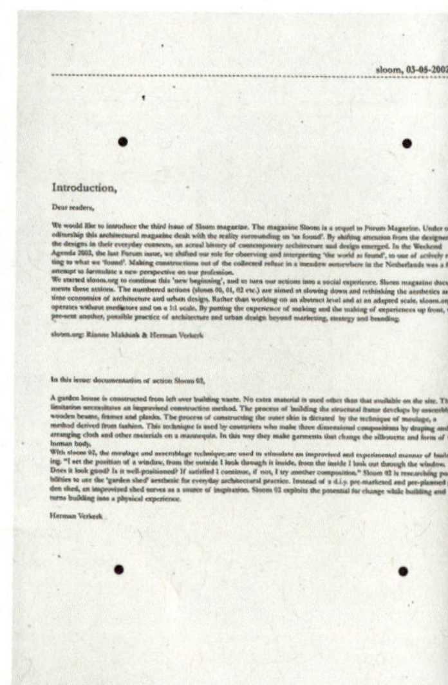
sloom, 03-05-2002
Introduction,
Dear readers,
sloom.org: Rianne Makkink & Herman Verkerk
Herman Verkerk

sloom 03:35:33
One Big Empire is:
Market
One Big Empire
(werk on page 03:35:28)
sloom 03:36:11
Shelter revisited - Kleingartenkolonie Bielefeld Berlin - type: gable

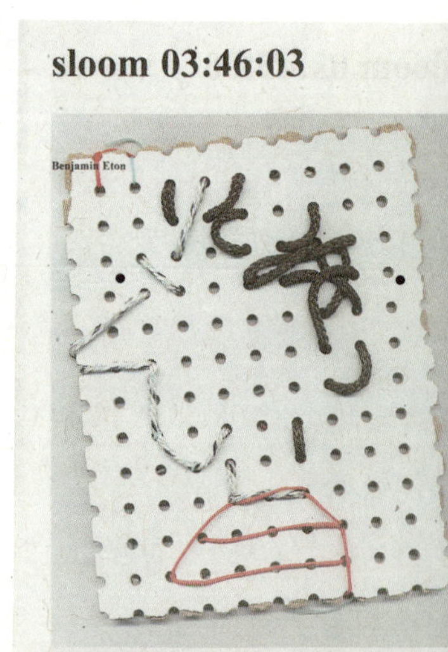
sloom 03:46:03
Benjamin Eton

SLOOM,
Magazine
Page 267

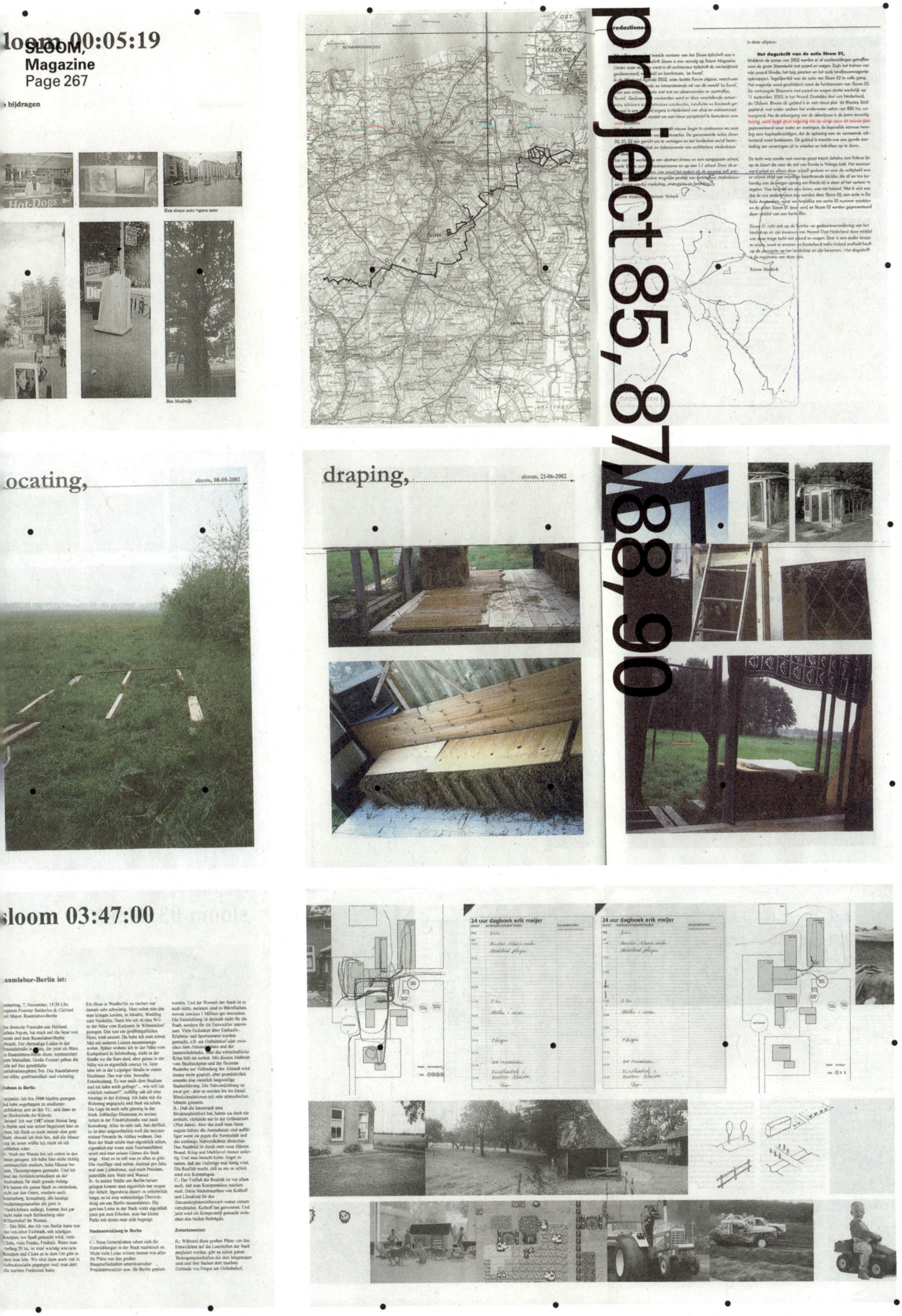

TOWMOTOR

project 93, 96, 105

topicality

Topicality

Dirk van den Heuvel

Speech given at the launch of SLOOM 4 at Artimo A–Z, Amsterdam

Dear Rianne and Herman,

Thank you for asking me to say a few words here today.

I have been privileged to be involved in some of your earlier projects, such as the *Forum* weekends, when you invited people to set to work with a collection of scrap materials in a field somewhere in Friesland. For me, that was both a disorienting and a positive experience. Friends criticized its non-committal nature – not without reason, I felt, especially when I got back home and learned that during that same weekend, while we had been puttering around with scrap, an anti-globalism demonstrator had been shot and killed in Italy. It's about topicality and its alleged necessity for our work that I wish to speak today.

I

Curators and critics are constantly confronted with that question of actuality. It's one of those cliché questions of our age, I think. Sportsmen and -women – whether they've delivered a world-class performance or failed miserably – are always asked the same old question afterwards: how are you feeling right now? Politicians can be put on the spot by quizzing them about their responsibility and whether they are finally going to step down.
The makers of magazines, or exhibitions, are constantly asked what on earth the relevance of their project is. As if it were actually possible for them to stand outside that topicality. It's my belief that no one, however unworldly, stands outside the here and now. The question as to topicality is, consequently, a misleading one. It implies involvement, engagement, a critical stance indicative of a positivist program, geared to progress and emancipation. But I think something else is going on here. It's about drawing a line, between the so-called relevant and everything that falls outside it, between who belongs and who doesn't, between winners and losers, between your friends and your foes. It's a question aimed at exclusion; a question that simultaneously covers the fields of politics and fashion. You're "in" or "out." Or, more grimly put: "either you're with us, or you're against us," without further elucidation, which has long ceased to be necessary.

II

The question as to topicality implies that there is a clear idea of what topicality is, and that this idea is shared by all. But, in my view, topicality is not unambiguous; there's no clear, linear progression from before to now, and so further along into the future. The person asking the question reveals that they still think in old-fashioned, modernist mechanical structures. The question is, moreover, often coupled with a notion of zeitgeist, and the assumption that you are only topical if your own project is grafted onto the structure of that zeitgeist – whatever that might happen to be.
In architecture, this has led to a breathtaking nihilism, a daredevil surfing on the waves of economic and social forces, which an architect or critic

is not required to judge – the waves of the zeitgeist are, after all, a sort of natural phenomenon. Now that the economic hype is over, the waves are breaking up and we are back on the beach. Even Koolhaas, until recently a vocal proponent of this notion of riding the waves, has in his most recent series of interviews embraced the end of liberalism.

III

As I see it, it's a mistake to want to graft your project onto the structure of the spirit of the age, because this attitude is exclusive (exclusionary) and one-dimensional. It is blind to the ambiguity/plurality of its own time, and it is certainly blind to what precedes the topical and the immanent. I am interested in an actuality that is inclusive, all-encompassing, and nothing less than that. Architecture and art must focus on that or, as Wolfgang Tillmans powerfully summarized it with a recent exhibition: "if one thing matters, everything matters."
As far as I'm concerned, topicality consists of all times, and all durations; it is a concentration of them. Perhaps in the sense proposed by Walter Benjamin, as a monad, a moment in which the supposed unit of time can be broken open, for that unit of time, whether it is called history, zeitgeist, or actuality, is always a construction. Consequently, I believe that a project – whether it be a magazine or an exhibition – should jolt the reader or visitor out of any supposed topicality, confront them with a different time, with different speeds, and take them along on a journey, in the time and duration of the project, positive or negative. Whether it be a Fred Astaire film or *Blow-Up*, Pierre Boulez or 2 Many DJ's, the photographs of Tillmans or of Gursky, Hertzberger's fantastic schools, or even Koolhaas's embassy in Berlin.

IV

I think the new *SLOOM* is trying to do something similar, as was the case with the *Forum* weekends. I admire the way you bring the different times and durations of rural life together in the new *SLOOM*, because it aspires to that inclusive approach, generous and open, averse to any notion of zeitgeist. If necessary, against the very grain of that zeitgeist, with cart or pickup truck against the stream. I have happily let myself slow down, opt out, opt back in.

topicality

Mirrors, Models, Shacks & Yards
Page 272

project104

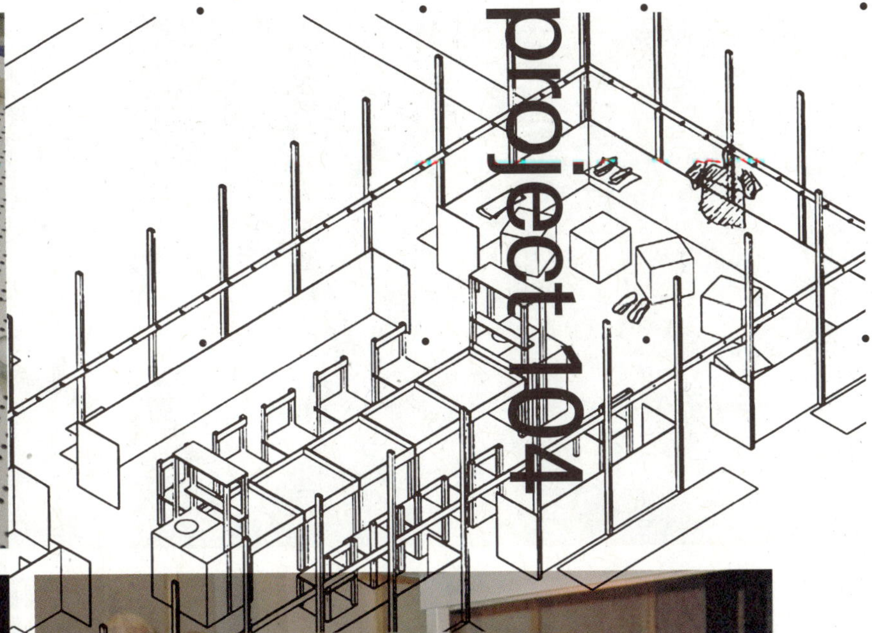

project125

johannes
schwartz

Johannes Schwartz
Allotments
[illegible] 2003

Mirrors, Models, Shacks & Yards
Page 278

Johannes Schwartz
Allotments, 2003
Allotments disappearing in Leidsche Rijn – walking on the central path, looking left and right. Published in *SLOOM 4*.

3

Events: Situating the Temporary
Page 280

project 61, 98

1998

2000
2002

Mirrors, Models, Shacks & Yards
Page 281

Forum / Weekend Agenda
Project: Magazine / Book
Duration: Long-term, 2 years
Year: 1998–2000, 2002
Data: page 638, page 645

Forum Juni 1998
25
Penitentiaire Inrichtingswerker 'Penitentiaire Inrichting Overamstel' (BijlmerBajes), Amsterdam.
Fotografie: Marie-José Jongerius/ NEL

OUT OF ORDER
BUITEN GEBRUIK
fotografie: Anuschka Blommers

31
5.BezoekUur 1998
Fotografie: Rianne Makkink en Erik Wong, vrijdag 27 maart 1998, 11:00 - 12:30 uur. Penitentiaire Inrichting Overamstel (BijlmerBajes), toren: de Schans.
Linksboven en rechtsonder: grote luchtplaats, linksonder: isoleercel, rechtsboven: kleine luchtplaats.
BijlmerBajes Revisited

DOMEINEN

Forum /
Weekend Agenda
Page 283
forum
TM
project 61
Forum Magazine
39 – Nr. 1 Juni 1998 fl. 19,50
9 789074 315111
Over het Hek
Forum Magazine Driemaandelijks tijdschrift voor architectuur – Architectural quarterly

Domesticity at war

in oorlog

een traditioneel sub-urbaan huis in ranchstijl, dat was ingegraven teneinde het te beschermen tegen de dreiging van nucleaire fall-out.[3] Het betrof een project van Jay Swayze, een voormalig militair instructeur uit Texas. Als bouwer van luxueuze villa's had deze in 1962, tijdens de Cuba-crisis, van de Plainview City Council opdracht gekregen voor de bouw van een demonstratieproject voor een schuilplaats tegen fall-out, in overeenstemming met de specificaties van het Ministerie van Burgerbescherming. Swayze veranderde het militaire project voor een schuilplaats onmiddellijk in een project voor een woonhuis. 'Het leek logischer om het hele huis en zijn onmiddellijke omgeving te veranderen in een veilige haven, waarin de familie wordt beschermd in een vertrouwde, comfortabele omgeving.... Gewapend met deze ideeën zette ik mij achter de tekentafel.... Omdat we niet in voortdurende angst voor oorlog, orkanen en extreme temperaturen kunnen leven, zal 'The Better Way' hiertegen bescherming bieden.'[4]

De gelijkstelling van oorlog en weersgesteldheid was symptomatisch. 'The Better Way' (Swayzes slogan voor het ondergrondse huis) was gebaseerd op twee 'voor de hand liggende voordelen':

Een 'constante temperatuur' en een 'bescherming tegen rampen met een natuurlijke, dan wel menselijke oorzaak'.

Het huis bood een gecontroleerde atmosfeer waarin men een eigen klimaat kon creëren door het kiezen van de juiste instellingen van temperatuur en relatieve vochtigheid. 'De bries van een bergtop en het stimulerende gevoel van opwinding van een frisse lentedag kunnen op commando worden opgeroepen.... Het rumoer van verkeer, vliegtuigen, buren.... Al dat verdwijnt met een druk op de knop....U bent vrij om te rusten in stilte, of om voor het eerst het hele spectrum aan sensaties te ervaren die door de hedendaagse stereosystemen kan worden opgeroepen.' Aangezien het in een ondergrondse schuilplaats onmogelijk leek om ramen naar de buitenwereld te maken, ontwikkelde Swayze een methode om na te gaan hoeveel waarde mensen eigenlijk hechten aan ramen. Zijn conclusie was, dat ramen dan misschien wel psychologisch

Dit essay is een ingekorte versie van een paper dat werd gepresenteerd in het Centre for Twentieth Century Studies in November 1990 en van de publicatie daarvan in Discourse 14.1, winter 1991-92, blz.3-22

noten:

1. Lyon, Peter. 'A Glorious Nightmare.' Holyday, juli 1964, p.50
2. idem
3. het ondergrondse huis werd gebouwd door de *Underground World Home Corporation* (met Jay Swayze als president), die ook voorstellen deed voor de bouw van *Underground Shopping Centers, Underground Motels,* en *Underground Restaurants and Night Clubs.* Zie Bletter, 'The Laissez-Fair (noot 14)
4. Swayze, Jay. 'Underground Gardens and Homes. The Best of Two Worlds - Above and Below' Hereford, Texas: Geobuilding Systems, 1980. p.70
5. idem
6. idem., p.10
7. Lyon, p.62
8. Virilio, Paul. *Defense Populaire et Luttes Ecologique.* Paris: Galilee, 1978. p.05-66
9. Lyon, p.57
10. idem
11. Bletter, Rosemarie Haag. 'The Laissez-Fair, Good Taste and Money Trees: Architecture at the Fair,' *Remembering the Future: The New York's World's Fair from 1939 to 1964.* New York: Queens Museum and Rizzoli International,1989. p.128
12. 'A TV View of the Fair.' *New York Sunday News* April 12 1964, World's Fair sec.. p.26
13. Phelps, Patricia C. 'Out of Order: The Public Art Machine.' *Artforum* dec. 1986. p.96

Domesticity at war

Kasbah Revisited

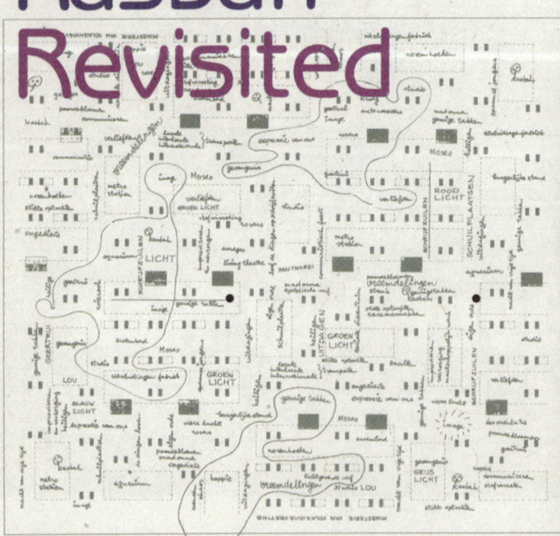

Kasbah Revisited
Samenstelling: Hester Wolters – Translation page 19
De (vak)pers besteedt doorgaans aandacht aan gebouwen op het moment dat ze worden opgeleverd.
Het verdere leven van gebouwen blijft veelal onbesproken. Over ouder worden.

Inhoudsopgave / Contents:

forum
-1°C
project 61
Forum Magazine Jaargang 39 – Nr. 2 December 1998 fl. 19,50
Round the hearth
9 789074 315111
Om de haard
Forum Magazine Driemaandelijks tijdschrift voor architectuur – Architectural quarterly

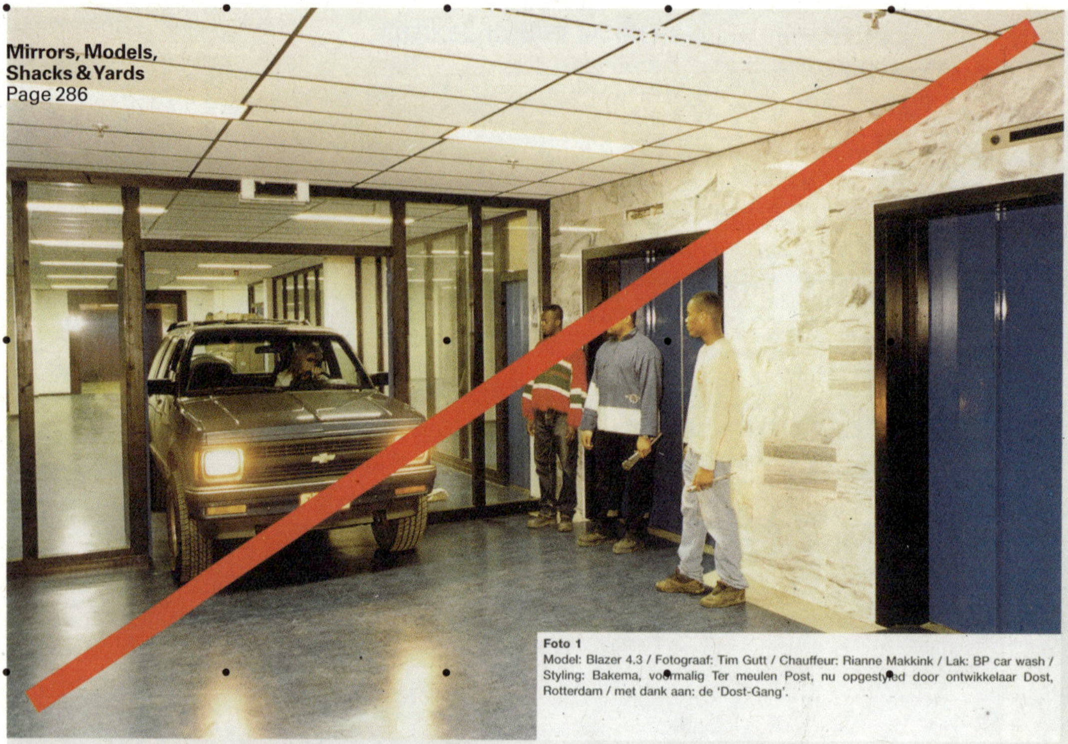

Foto 1
Model: Blazer 4.3 / Fotograaf: Tim Gutt / Chauffeur: Rianne Makkink / Lak: BP car wash / Styling: Bakema, voormalig Ter meulen Post, nu opgestyled door ontwikkelaar Dost, Rotterdam / met dank aan: de 'Dost-Gang'.

Foto 02
Model: Blazer 4.3 / Fotograaf: Tim Gutt / Chauffeur: Rianne Makkink / Lak: BP car wash / Styling: Kees Christiaanse & Partners / Borneo-Sporenburg, Amsterdam / met dank aan: vrouw met kind en bouwvakkers.

project 61

™

Forum Magazine Jaargang 40 / Nr. 3 1999 - fl. 19,50

Storage

725.35+728.99(051.2)"540.3"(492)=393+20

contains:
architecture and more

9 789074 315111

Het pad naar Room - interview II
Forum Magazine vroeg naar aanleiding van Maarten Kloos' 'Het pad naar Roem' een aantal architectuurstudenten hoe zij denken over hun carrière in het vakgebied.

Thomas Vooges (tweede jaars Bouwkunde TU Delft)
gefotografeerd door: Sannah de Zwart @Solar

Wat was je motivatie om architectuur te gaan studeren?
Tijdens mijn middelbare schooltijd was ik altijd bezig met bedenken van diezijntjes voor autootjes, bootjes en huisjes. Voor mijzelf stond vast, iets met ontwerpen te gaan doen. Industrieel ontwerpen leek me wel wat, maar bleek erg technisch te zijn. Ik voelde toen meer wat voor bouwkunde.
Hoe denk je daar nu over?
In de loop van de tijd ben ik er wel achter gekomen dat deze studie niet geheel mijn toekomst zal gaan bepalen. Vooral vorig jaar heb ik plannen gehad, om te switchen naar een kunstacademie. Toch maak ik mijn huidige studie af omdat het voor mij een stevige basis is. Misschien dat ik hierna iets met interieurarchitectuur ga doen.
Beschrijf hoe je ideale carrière eruit ziet in vier tot vijf stappen.
1. Mijn studie afronden in de richting van architectuur. 2. Part-time werken als architect op een bureau, daarnaast een extra opleiding doen, om mijn werkvlak te verbreden. 3. Met een groep mensen, met verschillende ontwerpgebieden, een bureautje starten. 4. Voor je zelf iets beginnen met de opgedane ervaringen.
Hoe denk je dit te realiseren?
Het is al moeilijk om een degelijke carrière te beschrijven laat staan dat ik weet hoe ik dit in de praktijk zal brengen. Laat ik eerst nog maar 'even' deze studie afmaken, eens kijken of ik dan nog leef.
Hoe denk jij dat een doorsnee carrière van een architect loopt?
Ik denk dat van de huidige architecten maar een klein deel gelijk via een universiteit dit geworden is. De meesten zullen via de HTS of een academie in het vak zijn gerold en later architect zijn geworden. Ook denk ik dat de meesten eerst bij enkele grote bureaus gewerkt hebben en vervolgens voor zichzelf zijn begonnen, maar dat is eigenlijk erg logisch.

[<-]

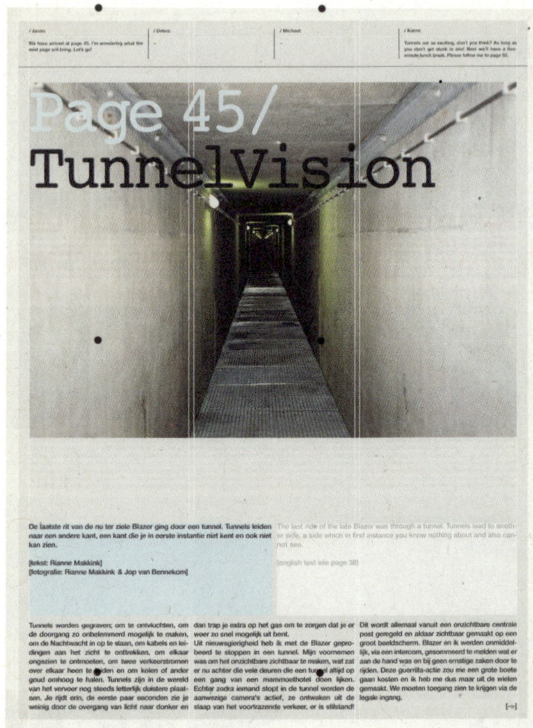

/ Jason: We have arrived at page 45. I'm wondering what the next page will bring. Let's go!
/ Debra: -
/ Michael: -
/ Karen: Tunnels are so exciting, don't you think? As long as you don't get stuck in one! Next we'll have a five-minute lunch break. Please follow me to page 55.

Page 45/ TunnelVision

De laatste rit van de nu ter ziele Blazer ging door een tunnel. Tunnels leiden naar een andere kant, een kant die je in eerste instantie niet kent en ook niet kan zien.

[tekst: Rianne Makkink]
[fotografie: Rianne Makkink & Jop van Bennekom]

The last ride of the late Blazer was through a tunnel. Tunnels lead to another side, a side which in first instance you know nothing about and also cannot see.

[english text see page 38]

Tunnels worden gegraven; om te ontvluchten, om de doorgang zo onbelemmerd mogelijk te maken, om de Nachtwacht in op te slaan, om kabels en leidingen aan het zicht te onttrekken, om elkaar ongezien te ontmoeten, om twee verkeersstromen over elkaar heen te leiden en om koien of ander goud omhoog te halen. Tunnels zijn in de wereld van het vervoer nog steeds letterlijk duistere plaatsen. Je rijdt erin, de eerste paar seconden zie je weinig door de overgang van licht naar donker en dan trap je extra op het gas om te zorgen dat je er weer zo snel mogelijk uit bent.
Uit nieuwsgierigheid heb ik met de Blazer geprobeerd te stoppen in een tunnel. Mijn voornemen was om het onzichtbare zichtbaar te maken, wat zat er nu achter die vele deuren die een tunnel altijd op een gang van een mammoethotel doen lijken. Echter zodra iemand stopt in de tunnel worden de aanwezige camera's actief, ze ontwaken uit de slaap van het voortrazende verkeer, er is stilstand! Dit wordt allemaal vanuit een onzichtbare centrale post geregeld en aldaar zichtbaar gemaakt op een groot beeldscherm. Blazer en ik werden onmiddellijk, via een intercom, gesommeerd te melden wat er aan de hand was en bij geen ernstige zaken door te rijden. Deze guerrilla-actie zou me een grote boete gaan kosten en ik heb me dus maar uit de wielen gemaakt. We moeten toegang zien te krijgen via de legale ingang.

[->]

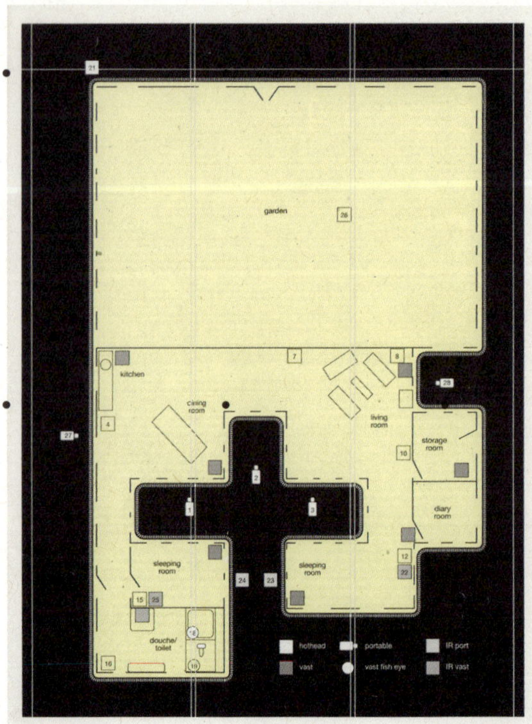

project 61
TM
Forum Magazine Jaarganc 39 / Nr. 4 1999 – fl. 19,50
9 789074 315142
de Gang/the Corridor
Hi, I'm Jason, your host for this issue of Forum Magazine. I'll take you all the way, from A to Z. Let's start right here and move on to the next page.

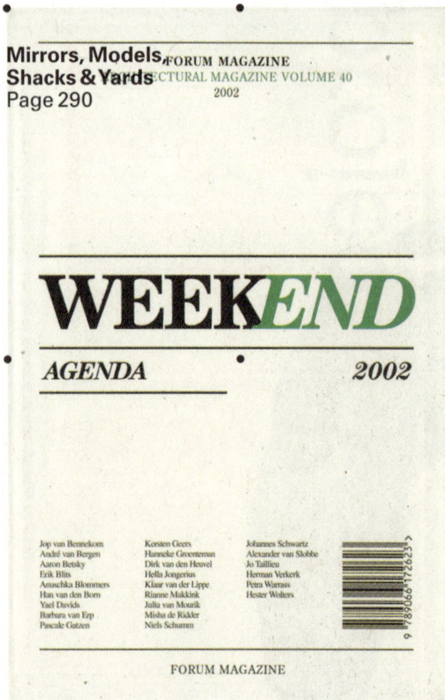

FORUM MAGAZINE
ECTURAL MAGAZINE VOLUME 40
2002

WEEK*END*

AGENDA *2002*

Jop van Bennekom
André van Bergen
Aaron Betsky
Erik Blits
Anuschka Blommers
Han van den Born
Yael Davids
Barbara van Erp
Pascale Gatzen
Kersten Geers
Hanneke Groenteman
Dirk van den Heuvel
Hella Jongerius
Klaar van der Lippe
Rianne Makkink
Julia van Mourik
Misha de Ridder
Niels Schumm
Johannes Schwartz
Alexander van Slobbe
Jo Taillieu
Herman Verkerk
Petra Warrass
Hester Wolters

FORUM MAGAZINE

WEEK 33
Saturday
2002
IT'S SUMMER
WEEK 33
Sunday
2002
IT'S SUMMER

project 86

WEEK 10
2002
IT'S WINTER

WEEK 1
Sunday January 6
2002
WINTER
IT'S WINTER
WEEK 1
Saturday January 5
2002
SUDDENLY

Date:
November 22, 2015

Place:
Farm of Rianne Makkink, Noordoostpolder

People:
Tamar Shafrir & Herman Verkerk w/ **Rianne Makkink**

conversation 3

Family

T: How did you learn how to keep this vegetable garden?
R: I grew up on a farm, so I'm used to it. We also had a lot of land, I always worked in the garden. We always had to work, every Saturday.
H: It was on very fruitful soil near the IJssel river; the river clay was very good quality. The whole family was suffused with farmer culture.
R: I'm the first one who went to university from the whole family, even the extended family. My father was one of eight children, my mother was one of four.
T: We were speaking about this, Herman's parents were both one of ten!
R: Before the war, it was quite different. More children…
T: More hands!
R: We had a similar youth; our parents are quite similar. The background, the traditions. We know exactly what to do when someone dies. The tradition is still quite strong, even now.
H: Maybe there's a slight difference with your parents, because my father came from a very Calvinist family, the orthodox Protestant Church, while my mother came from the Hallelujah church of Liberal Christianity. The reformed church.
R: My parents are both from the Dutch Protestant Church.
H: That is more the happy religion; with the orthodox there was more tension. My father went away from it all, but he still had to deal with his own father and his family, who were very strict, and my mother had a lot of problems with it. When my father's family visited, we froze; we were silent.
R: Was your father not allowed to do anything on Sundays?
H: Yes. My grandparents would walk fifteen kilometers from Breukelen to Utrecht to go to church, and they would pass my parents' house and looked in to see if they were doing things on Sunday. Can you imagine that sort of control?
T: It's strange that you go through a war and you go back to these kinds of things.
H: It's maybe because of it. You cling to the traditions.
T: Do you remember doing something with building when you were younger?
R: I always did the interiors of my room. We had a long tradition in the farm that, every spring, we took everything out of the house, cleaned and painted inside, and then brought everything back. And my mother always said that we could do the interior as we wanted it. We used to have the old coal stoves, with a lot of dust, so you had to repaint every year. My mother was very strict with it until we changed the heating system, and then we stopped. That was a shame, because the rooms became very cluttered! Before that, everything was so clean and crisp.
T: And why did you go to Delft? When did the subject of architecture make itself apparent to you?
R: I had a brother, Martin, who was working in construction. In our family, we didn't have a tradition of studying; that was a shame, because everybody could study, but they didn't know where to start. So my brothers all went to the technical school. In the 1960s, it was very disturbing – the head of the school would tell you which school you should go to. There was no discussion. But my liberation was the *brugklas* [first year, no distinction in school levels], where they allowed me to go to the highest level of education after the first year. I wanted to stay with my best friend, who was not so smart, but I was always very close to her. My parents also saw that I could go to university, but they didn't want me to go. I had two years of no communication with them. I lived above the cows for two years. I befriended a classic, highly educated family and stayed with them a lot, and they helped me to go to university. They told me about the open days, how to research the school. My parents were very afraid that I would be estranged from them. They thought it was arrogant. "It's not of our class," they always said. I had a boyfriend, Bart van Beek, and he did the middle-level of architecture and he was building, and I was completely impressed by him, but I could begin it at the university. And my parents could understand what an architect was, it was a practical job.

Friends

T: Herman said that you two met in university.
R: Almost on the first day, in fact. I was a year after Herman. I came and saw one of my old classmates from where I grew up – Esther Gramsbergen – and you were sitting with her. But we really got to know each other in a construction course.
H: I had to redo it, I think. Rianne was my excuse, because we studied at her place – I am very sensitive to spaces. She had a very nice room in Delft.
R: It was on the inner courtyard of these old houses, in the past it was a front room and a back room with sliding doors, and then the doors were fixed and I had the back room. I had a very small patio and looked into the kitchen. A beautiful room.
H: It was serene, a square. Maybe it was a cube, because it was also quite high. You had carpet.
R: Yellowish-white!
H: So we could lie on the floor and study, and she always had tea, and a nice tea set.
R: A "tea maid" on a timer, like the British ones.
H: She had boyfriends that spoiled her all the time. A couple of older guys who were infatuated with her, and so they took her for a ride, took her to Paris, gave her presents…
R: I even had one who lent me his car, a BX, and that was quite exceptional because no one had a car. A crazy guy, he already died. It's quite shocking when one of your friends dies! He was not really a lover, I kept him at a distance.
H: You did that very well! A very 1950s mentality, and this was during the '80s, when people went to bed on the first

date, and then it was over.
R: Yes, I kept them on a string for a long time.
H: So those were all the conversations we had together, and we shared some friends – Albert Jan Berman.
R: Our beautiful dandy!
H: Listening to The Smiths, David Bowie. You were a total fan.
T: Do you like the new video?
R: I saw the beginning, it's almost religious, quite freaky! He's totally back.
H: You loved his dramatic side. You also loved jiving. We went to the Eland in Delft… you wore those little suits and the hairbands.
R: The turtlenecks… I still love it!
H: And also the optimism of the 1950s is very Rianne. I would never live in the polder, and you love the construction and the positive, industrial spirit!
R: Man-made stuff. I'm not so good with nature, it freaks me out.
H: It was also the way you ran the farm – very rational, very based on figures. Of course the animals were treated well, but it was not a nostalgic project.
R: My mother was a romantic farmer. But it was all part of the reconstruction after the war; at that time you could do anything you wanted. They married after the war, had seven kids, and started this big dairy farm, with cows but also chickens and pigs. When Mansholt came to power as a minister in the 1970s, he changed the whole culture, and they had to give them up: you couldn't have all these animals together. You had to choose a monoculture. The chickens were gone, and we only had some pigs, but it was never developed like a big farm anymore. At the end, it was so funny, the pigs were still lying on straw like "natural" pigs and my father was upset. "I'm not developing anymore! I get a lot of money to treat them like in the old days! It's not logical! I want to give them a better future!" For animals, it was always seen as a better future, because in the old days pigs had a lot of diseases, and in the new farms they had much less. "They still have pneumonia!" It didn't fit with his vision. He always believed that he had to give a better future, even to the pigs: new stables, new things, not the old stuff. My brother first had the farm, because he was the oldest son. That's a very strong right in the east of the country, that the oldest son gets everything. In Brabant, below the rivers, they had to divide; that's why the plots and the farms are so small. In the east of the country, if you're not the oldest, then you have to marry or do something else. In the Protestant world, that meant being a teacher or working at a bank.
T: Herman, this reminds me of your graduation project – a circle in a triangle…
H: We went to New York. I wanted to do an internship at Steven Holl, and the interview didn't go well at all, and he mentioned, "You shouldn't do a circle in an oval." And I said, "Did you ever see an egg?"
R: Did you say that?
H: No, but I was very offended.
R: What a shame, that's beautiful. You were the only one who made a book, I was so jealous. You were so determined. Herman is very good at starting.

Studying architecture in the '80s

T: Did you present by pinning up on the wall?
H: There was a slide culture, amazingly beautiful, you could project them large-screen in the auditorium.
R: You also had the real drawings on the wall.
H: We did them by hand. I was very interested in storytelling, so from the very start of the graduation I made a slideshow of how I imagined things to be. It was an imaginary itinerary through the building with all kinds of citations. We had the opportunity that our professors were opening up to different ways of representing architecture.
T: Did you get the idea to use that approach from something you saw?
H: I think it was a combination of people who inspired us, for instance, Wim van den Bergh and Wiel Arets, of course Steven Holl, and also OMA. At that time they were very narrative. Or Alexander Brodsky.
R: Wim van den Bergh and Joost Meuwissen had a beautiful magazine, called *Wiederhall*.
H: He also designed a villa for Prince Carnival. There was a connection of a house that had certain characteristics coinciding with the person that was living there; there was an interaction between the social behavior and spatial construction. We were very interested in this psychological aspect of architecture. We thought of architecture as a cultural phenomenon, and that has quite disappeared from our contemporary culture.
R: I have been thinking about your remark that architecture is kind of lost. You hardly see it. Even the vocabulary is barely in the magazines. It's either building or nothing. When we were studying in the 1980s, there was no future for building. There was a big crisis going on. But there was a huge culture of the narrative of architecture. It was so beautiful to think about the future or non-future, or the narrative of what architecture could do. And many architects became famous because of that period. Now, if you think of a whole generation only focused on building, they are in an economically driven reality. People are stuck, also students.
T: A few years ago, when I moved to Italy, I met a lot of current architecture students. I was curious, so I asked them, "In which studio do you dream of doing your internship?" And they said, "OMA!"
H: Nothing has changed!
T: I finished architecture school in 2007, but I think you might have had the same response even before I studied.
R: It was the same in our time, all my ex-boyfriends went there. Herman even worked there!
H: I left after one project. I hated the atmosphere.
T: And after university, you stayed friends and kept collaborating?
H: We also made excursions. I did a summer semester in Berlin and Rianne visited.

Graduating TU Delft with "Ship of Fools"

R: In 1991, we went to New York.
H: We were there for a whole month.
R: That was really the glue in our friendship. I remember Herman was coming back from Switzerland for the winter in 1992 and he didn't want to go back to the ETH.

H: I was really depressed from Zürich. I didn't know how to deal with the Swiss at first. I thought in the end I was crazy! It's the only way to make sense of it, that the people around you are normal and you are crazy, because you cannot communicate.
R: But I have the attitude that once you start, you have to finish.
T: Maybe that's from the farm. In America, we have these ideas about raising the barn as a collective action, and it must be finished before it starts to rain or snow. Everything takes so much energy that you have to be committed. It doesn't matter what, but you cannot give up. So I told him he had to finish, and I am taking you back! I drove him in my old Volvo to Switzerland on my own. On my way back I was completely stripped at the border, a woman on her own!
R: I always came to visit you in Amsterdam, when you lived in the Wilhelminastraat. We would go dancing in De Trut. And being in New York together was quite beautiful. But did we work together on a project?
H: We did the 1991 Europan competition, cabins as extensions to a housing project in France. The combination of your rationalism, your efficiency and my narrative approach was very nice.
T: Do you think you often look for partners who have that quality?
H: The computer came in very handy in that sense. It's a way for me to be efficient, it forces you to become systematic, but Rianne has that naturally, which is so much better!
R: It was in Montauban, a tour de force!
H: The story was the border between an old and new town; the new town had a facade or fence of high-rise buildings.
R: This was my book to get funding. There were a lot of grants offered by the FBKVB. This one is my hammerhead shark, the first house I built. We were very much into textures, stamps, the handmade materiality. I also have my graduation project here, the "Ship of Fools." It took me two years. The idea was to design a space between a hotel and a cloister. Sometimes you want to escape your own atmosphere, but where to go? It was quite unusual in those days; when I went to a cloister then, there were no guest rooms, you were part of the religious rituals. I was between two boyfriends, and I had to choose, so I went there. My project tried to make it possible to go out of the city even inside the city.
T: It plays a bit on the idea of the medieval wall.
R: You could enter a new space or atmosphere. I first wanted to do it on the Maasvlakte – Rients, my new boyfriend, did his graduation there, so I was really into the area at the time – but luckily enough, I skipped it. This is next to the Euromast, on the old river Maas; this sketch was done by Rients, in the days of the first computer drawings, the late 1980s. This is now for housing, but then it was still an industrial area. I said, "I'll make it into an island. I'll take this land away, and I'll make it like a little ship." I wanted different possibilities for isolating yourself, you could choose different atmospheres through time, through nature, and this was a fairground. You could get there by submarine; you would have the idea of traveling a long time, but it would not be true.
T: It's like the boat in Venice to the Lido, it's only five minutes but it seems that you are going to a different country, which also feels so isolated.
R: In the 1990s, this idea of experience – tourism, free time – was not there at all.
H: It's also looking for architecture to have a role in social aspects. What Rianne did was really to have five stages from isolation to communion; it's almost like a prison, too.
R: I was very influenced by Foucault, *Madness and Civilization*, the ego and the society, what is freedom and what is confinement.
H: I think it was also inspired by the Exodus project of Rem Koolhaas. It's in London, of course, with its hidden social structure, its secret members, it never shows what's going on behind the facades. Koolhaas's criticism was that you could make a reservoir of things that went on there, so that the function would become more clear. He made this kind of grid as a bridge across the city. The city went on in the same way and you had this in-between zone where it was very clear what each section had to offer as a program.
R: Also Leonidov and the constructivists inspired me. You always layer everything. Every quarter had its own grid and circulation system.
T: Circulation? That's the shared language. It can be very insular, I think.
H: It's not at all communicable to a larger audience. And of course that's what we were looking for at that time.
R: We didn't even have the practice of going to work somewhere. We didn't go to building sites. Everything was in our head.
T: There is no ideal solution; everything is reactionary. In Italy, they have to take structures for two full years, reconstruction classes, even classes about the classical typologies. You are drowning under the weight of history, so you can be postmodern or you can work in the mainstream.
R: Delft was like that until the 1960s, and then they changed. We also had a lot of structures classes.
T: Did you see the effect of the Team X group? Like Van Eyck?
R: He was still there in my first year.
H: He went away when Koolhaas came; also Carel Weeber was a big influence in the school, and Van Eyck was so offended that he left.

MAX.1

T: Did it come very naturally, the idea to work together?
R: Yes, I started MAX.1 with my boyfriend, Rients Dijkstra. And already in the first year, Herman joined and made this very famous drawing, a section on the roof of the sunken highway, the most important thing in the project to connect Utrecht to the suburb. Now it is partly done, I think.
H: I was hired because I used the computer so much in the master's in ETH Zürich. In my graduation project, the "Swimmingpool-library," I mixed found footage of a cruise ship journey with computer animations of my design. And when I came to the office, I completely fell in love with drawing by hand, importing the drawing in the computer and working on the image in Photoshop. It was

somehow similar, but very different. I was there in the company to communicate ideas, and the task was quite free. The ingredients you use are very flexible. Rianne also did beautiful models at the time. We had these common interests, and her company was also very successful – doing urban design and architecture, also a lot of research.

R: We started with one house. MAX.1 – "maximum one." Rients also worked for Rem Koolhaas on a tunnel in The Hague, and he also had the Leidsche Rijn commission, a master plan of 30,000 houses. He was only thirty-one! The "roaring '90s," they had so much trust in young architects.

H: At the beginning of the 1980s, there was total collapse. There was social housing, and architecture almost disappeared as a discipline. Contractors could do the job without architects, and architects were no longer interested in aesthetics. They were totally into community, talking with the people, feedback and participation.

T: Like Giancarlo de Carlo.

H: Because the postmodernist dialogue, looking back at history and non-functional architecture, the communicative aspects of architecture without being pragmatic – those started to be rediscovered during our studies. It infiltrated Delft, but also Team X was still very dominant, and rationalism. Constructivism was in-between, so it had something of the postmodern – you reinvestigate the historic style and rules, but in itself it is also functional, though in a more expressive way. It was pioneering, but also had the social aspect of transforming a society. In the late 1980s, we would begin to doubt that. But after the fall of the Berlin Wall and the reunification of Germany, that gave a boost to the global economy and suddenly there was a huge amount of work. There was no reluctance about planning.

R: Vinex was the last nota – the Vierde Nota Extra – the government's last planning project, for one million houses within fifteen years. That was the government's last big spatial influence. There were many commissions related to that. And after that, they gave up. In the late 1990s, the government politics changed.

Forum magazine

H: The older generation was more used to individual styles. It was much more channeled for the younger generation. When we started *Forum* in 1998, we were commenting on the way architecture was developing. There were many advisory boards, it became much more like a business model. Being in between the team of the project developer, the client, and the contractor – the work of the architect became very marginalized as following a "build quality plan" or styling.

T: So you were the editor-in-chief of *Forum* – it's funny to look at this list of contributors, you already had Beatriz Colomina's writing, and the photographs of Viviane Sassen... which other magazines existed at the time? *Morf* and *OASE*?

H: I think *Morf* was just starting, and there was *Items* and *Archis*.

T: It's amazing how these stories come back, we are obsessed again with domestic space.

H: We wanted to confront this mentality of pushing architects into a corner.

T: And here is Philip Johnson!

R: I visited him. He was so friendly. We were in an exhibition at Storefront in New York, *Big Soft Orange*, and we had a lecture at Harvard and then went to the Glass House. We just showed up and rang. He came to the door and said, "Come in! You're from the Netherlands? Great!" I wouldn't dare to do those things anymore!

T: Now that you can find out so much information online, it seems much more difficult to actually reach them. This e-mail provider, XS4ALL, you and Guus Beumer and Louise Schouwenberg still have it!

H: They were a kind of hacker community from Amsterdam, the pioneers in 1993. This issue of the magazine is navigated by temperature (Around the Hearth). The whole idea was to approach architecture as a phenomenon, also related very much to the *Elements of Architecture* exhibition that OMA did last year at the Venice Biennale. We wanted to tell stories about the role of architecture in society by concentrating on its artifacts. We had the fence, the corridor, the storage, and the hearth – very universal elements, which told both historic and contemporary stories. Rianne's contribution was to see the social constructs that were made for the car.

R: I had a Chevrolet Blazer... I love big cars, I was one of the few women to have a big car. I went to visit unusual sites and see how I could intervene in society with the car. I had this "guerrilla" approach, I would drive into the building for the photos. I even made a "stalker" series, I went to see where architects lived. There was no gossip about architects at the time. I had a lot of trouble with this series, they were very offended. One architect didn't talk to me for ten years because I photographed his house without knowing that he had a real stalker. I had no idea how much influence such things have on personal life.

T: It seems that this information becomes less interesting nowadays. Architects are barely ever in their houses, it's only where they keep their things.

H: The idea of the house as a representation of their style or taste?

T: I wonder if they still have the desire to build their own house.

R: In design, it's quite important. The NRC featured our place on Nieuwe Binnenweg, and many people were shocked at how messy it is! They expect a big house with white walls and "design" everywhere.

T: Herman, your studio in Amsterdam is such a living archive.

R: In architecture, the idea of representation is very important. You have to look smart, new, serious. You should have good chairs and tables, and show up to meetings in an expensive car. That's what surprises people about our studio, everything is low budget. But in design, you can always play the role of the artist in the atelier.

H: *Forum* was a way to investigate

the way architecture was represented, and how it could be represented. Not to talk about star architects, which at the time was very powerful, but about architecture – sometime the architect came into view, but it was coming and going and passing, and it was a lot about creating new imagery for architecture. In each issue, artists/ photographers also had an assignment to deal with the topic.
T: It has an amazing mediatic approach – even the fact that you put URLs inside. This was also right around the time of *Big Brother* in 1998. They even invented an X-shaped corridor through the house to be able to film inside.
R: There was this new way of looking into the house. And at the same time the Internet was just starting to spread.
H: We loved the articles that transformed your reality by making another path.
R: The good thing was that you were already involved in fashion, so you had this whole other influence.
H: It was very playful. We actually won the Rotterdam Design Prize in 2001; the jury was Oliver Zahm from *Purple*, Miuccia Prada, and Bruce Mau. It was because of the graphics but also the new idea of representation. Jop van Bennekom and Erik Wong did the graphic design.
T: It reminds me that you always have to check your ego when you think you are coming up with something very radical. The cycles are so short, in fact. Now there are a few magazines, like *Dirty Furniture* or *MacGuffin*, that focus each issue on an architectural element, like you did here.
H: Also when Stephan Petermann did the lecture on "Elements of Architecture" at my school the other day, I felt it was so related.
T: Did you have any inspirations or references?
H: It was really a new way of looking. Just the idea of making a "magazine" was already such a big leap from architecture publications, so we also wanted to have it at newsstands. There was a common audience that could also take a look at architecture, not a closed community with the latest highlights.
R: That was also the problem; they didn't know where to put it. Does it go in the architecture section? Is it lifestyle?
H: It was an attempt to open up the architecture discourse.
R: We can start it again, now that narrative architecture is lost.
T: It's like in *Domus* magazine, because it has been published for so many years, that you see these cycles and resurgences of themes, you see that in some periods they featured so much contemporary art, and in other times it's so fixated on architecture as a pure discipline.
R: We won the Rotterdam Design Prize in May 2001. Everyone thought they were going to win, except us. And then we won...
H: And nobody liked it! We were the outsiders.
T: Maybe because you were not from the design scene.
H: In the evening, when we got the grant, we were sitting in Witte de Withstraat – it was a very different street – there was a snack bar.
R: And a lot of junkies...
H: And Jurgen [Bey] was also there.
R: That was the first time I met him. Guus [Beumer] introduced him to me. And then in the summer of 2001 we made this project with the prize money of 20,000 euros.

Weekend agenda

H: *Forum* was actually losing money. So it was the end of the magazine. So we did a final project to redefine for ourselves what an architecture magazine or journal could be. What would be the content of our ideal journal? That was to see how things were built up from scratch. We thought of a framework to get this information on how you start a project, how you deal with production, how you make something out of trash or out of nothing. We had this scenario that we collected old building leftovers. We put an empty wooden container in the city and it was filled up with leftovers from people. When you see a container, you always throw something in. It was filled to the brim very soon. And then we moved the trash to a place in Friesland. In 1996, we had bought a house in Friesland, and I began to renovate it; we started to live there in the summertime. It was a way to get out of the bustle of the city. In 2000, we also bought the land around it – an old farm with the garden and the fields around it.
R: The wooden container was a piece by an artist.
H: André van Bergen.
R: Also made out of scrap material.
H: So then we had a heap of trash, and we used it for building. The first weekend we built ourselves, the editorial board, we decided which place was suitable to build something. It was in the meadows, a place without too much water...
R: We approached it as, if you would start a settlement, where would you locate it? We mowed the grass to make a framed area. We had some restrictions: you had to build with scrap material and within this area. The first weekend we built ourselves, and then we had three or four weekends after that. We invited guests from all kinds of creative fields, but also from architecture. They had to build themselves, which was quite uncommon, because architects were still related to the pencil and the computer. Having conversations within the building. We also invited a writer or two, who collected the stories on the building site. All these notes are quotes of people telling stories or during dinner, because they had to stay there the whole weekend. We had a caravan and all these settlements.
T: Is that Kersten Geers? He was very young then.
R: He refused to build. It was really in his system. He was cutting grass instead. It was also raining that whole weekend.
H: Each weekend turned out very differently, also because of the weather and the collection of people; if they wanted to work together, if it was a collective. That was very interesting to see because we didn't give them a program. We just gave them the opportunity to do something on this framed land.
R: And they could start from what was left over from previous weekends, or reuse it, or continue the framework. So we were curious what kind of constellation would result at the end. One of the final ones was a playing field, we played

badminton, it was like an arena. It was also celebrating this award money with people; we had very nice weekends, nice talks, nice dinners. We had a cook, so we could enjoy each other's company. We could discuss our profession. The collection of architects and designers. These weekends were very healing, to have this new family around us.
H: We were thinking about what qualities they could have. A very powerful quality is also to be able to build a community. Pioneering in the sense that you have a new collective, and you have to take care of it and make sure that people are productive, however they define it. It was about creativity, but in a very loose or light sense, people could do what they liked. But to get them to do it...
T: It reminds me a bit of Gabriel Maher with her affinity for communication, that she prepares the field in a way.
R: It felt like starting all over, a bit Wild West, that you had to make a point somewhere to meet, we were cleaning the field, and had to make up the territory.
H: The hospitality was very beautiful, but also the nonhierarchical nature. Rianne is very approachable; maybe it has to do with relocating a specific scene to an unfamiliar environment, where they don't know how to perform.
T: You can redefine the rules.
H: Or they can open up in a different way. That was what we were after.
R: Getting them out of their own context.
T: In this period, from the outside, it appeared as this very Ayn Rand-style culture of the architect.
R: Architecture was the main focus. Design came a bit later, with Milan, Droog design was just revealed, Hella Jongerius was becoming a star. But this came before 9/11. So it was the summer before, world peace was everywhere, we were in a quite hedonistic time frame. We also wanted to get people out of their comfort zone. It was quite uncommon that we would go out into the country. No one had a garden; everyone was city-based. Thinking about land, touching material – architects never did that. It was very funny to see the difference between the architects and the designers...
H: And the artists.
R: The architects had a lot of problems with the material itself. What were they going to do with it? It was bottom-up on all levels, starting with a new community with the material.
H: Also the designer as a maker was just beginning to be more widely recognized. You don't need a company to produce.
R: You could do your own production.
H: And there we really found each other in the idea of improvisation. We were very disappointed or frustrated with the way we had to deal with architecture. We thought there was a lot of potential to improvise while building. If you see building as a process, then maybe there are different periods in this process where you could re-decide the paths you were following. You could have certain sessions where you were halfway or had the rough construction, and there you could reconsider the doors, the kitchen, the appliances, and that's really something that is still a missed opportunity. Because the building process is not instantaneous – it's not over in an hour or a day, and you can really benefit from the long duration of time to improve something that you thought of before but didn't see; or different finances. It can also be in the negative sense. Suddenly you lose money, so why spend the original sum? You could do it for cheaper, or leave something out.
T: It's like architecten de vylder vinck taillieu, the Rot-Ellen-Berg house.
R: Jo Taillieu was a student of mine. And part of the Weekend Agenda. It's almost like reinventing the actors of architecture.
T: The idea that you could live in a construction site.
R: I had this very famous book, *Starting All Over Again/Opnieuw Beginnen*, from the 1970s. With manuals, how to do things from scratch, building a house, knitting a sweater, the DIY community.
T: These manuals are very popular again, they are all scanned and put on the Internet for download. Ken Isaacs, those kinds of people, how to make the baby crib out of a cardboard box.
H: Also Alexander van Slobbe is a pioneer of that approach in fashion. He would make patterns to alter the undershirt from HEMA. He is still very much involved, and he also recognized now that there is a lot of home craft and the reestablishment of the technique. When Rianne and I were children in the 1970s, there were all these pattern magazines, like *Ariadne*; examples of how to do it yourself, also the most simple items.
R: We were from this generation that everything was still very expensive, so you had to do it yourself.
H: My mom did all the sweaters, and also my father did a lot, he decorated the whole interior. There was also the *Na Vijven* ("After Five"), a handicraft magazine.
T: It gives you a totally different vision of the world. It reminds me of the scene in *Fight Club* when they show all of the IKEA labels and price tags on the furniture, and that was a big change in the 1990s when you could suddenly buy everything. I imagine that influenced the architecture approach, it was parallel – it wasn't about doing it yourself. But now, because of the crisis, no one has money, and this approach becomes very common again. But when you did it, it was a bit more unexpected.
H: We had the criticism of Joke Robaard, Rianne's niece, who participated very briefly but didn't want her part published, because she said, "We've done this in the 1970s, get over it!" She did the exact same experiment thirty years before. You have to think in which period it is necessary to give a new incentive to approaching design and architecture.
R: She's quite particular.
H: I really love the way she deals with architecture, fashion, and the human body. She made beautiful folders for groups of people or companies. It's a format, and she numbers them. The beautiful thing is the convergence: she is an artist, and she makes it as her own project, but as a product it can also be a work of graphic design or advertising.

Events: Situating the Temporary
Page 298

Higher Truth no. 5

R: In 2001, I stopped with MAX.1.
H: We had a beautiful project together in 2001 called Higher Truth. That was a collaboration with Guus Beumer and Rutger Wolfson in De Vleeshal in Middelburg.
R: It's one of the best contemporary art venues. They gave commissions to make new work.
T: That project was an empty shop, wasn't it?
R: A shop without anything inside, only beauty, feeling good, and service.
T: You got a bag in the end?
H: Yes, but the bag was filled with articles about shopping. The exhibition space was very dominant, a medieval butcher's hall, with a Gothic ceiling, black and white tiles running diagonally through the space, brick walls painted white.
R: Fake, because it was bombed during the war.
H: It was reconstructed. To have an avant-garde fashion shop, we needed to make a space within a space. We thought that it would be nice if it were ghostlike, fata morgana, kind of unreal, that you could not focus on. Rianne came up with this beautiful material for glasshouses: shrink-plastic in an aluminum frame that you can heat to make it taut. It makes a very beautiful skin. We used that for the construction of the shop, and did the scenography of the building so you would enter De Vleeshal but still feel as if you were "outside." The shop window was a very powerful tool for the experience. We made an abstraction of the outside world. We had the shop window with a lot of mirrors. We also had a huge door with a doorkeeper.
R: You had to enter the threshold, step over it.
T: A very exclusive fashion shop.
H: Once you were inside, there was a service. Four ladies were helping you, but they were helping you with nothing. The conversation was, "What would you like?" And then you saw there was nothing. So the conversation was a bit confusing. Of course you would then be guided through the whole scenery… the main area with the counter, the clothing racks, then a more relaxed area with water dispensers, and a separate area with a changing room – with nothing to try on, but the experience of looking at yourself from another perspective. We used a delayed camera. You would see yourself going into the changing room. We were playing with the idea of the self, how the consumer looks for the transformation of the self as a shopping experience.
R: It was also a "homage" to Dan Graham, he used the technique for an installation in the 1970s – the delayed camera, seeing yourself from the back. Pointing out the origin of time.
T: It reminds me of the changing rooms in the Prada store in New York, which was done around the same time. The scripting of the shopping experience.
H: To introduce another program into the shopping experience, that was a very strong idea which never took off.
T: I think once a boy came in with a skateboard and went down the ramp, and I think that was the end of it.
H: There was this vibe with experience culture, and how to deal with it as an artist or architect – to tap into it or analyze different potentials.
T: What's interesting is that you also were doing real shops at the same time. Did you have the feeling that the commercial work and artistic work were split, that you could be ironic with one but had to be straightforward with the other?
H: No, there was no separation.
T: That's quite unusual.
H: The work with Alexander van Slobbe in Tokyo was very commercial, but it was also so liberal that we could define what we would like to do. The Japanese business contacts were completely in awe, they were totally supportive. When we arrived in Tokyo, we were treated like stars. They put us in hotels where we would look over from the breakfast table and see the Fugees or Oasis.
T: Now it's very different, but then there was a big obsession about the spectacle of fashion. In Tokyo, it was the most pronounced because the land is so expensive that, no matter what you do, the material is never the biggest cost; it's more the use of space. So to make it worth it, you need this crazy competitive edge; it can't be about functionality.
H: To have a condensed proposal, that was always very important. To combine and integrate things into a very small area. I enjoyed that challenge, but there were absolutely no concessions to the "commercial" side.

Sloom.org

R: And these are some issues of *SLOOM*… we made it from 2002 to 2004.
T: Are these the real issues or photocopies?
H: The real photocopy!
R: We didn't have money, and we liked the idea anyway.
H: We started it at this event about time in De Balie. During the seminar, we started a small editorial office and collected content for the magazine at the venue. We had Koehorst in 't Veld as graphic designers.
R: Weren't they your students in Arnhem?
H: Yes…and they could also deal with the issue of printing quickly. We asked people to document their idea of "slow" – like sluggish, slow behavior. But it also had to do with an attitude of improvisation during the building process, and how to communicate a slow process as an alternative form of architecture or urban design. We found that we could fit the magazine into our existing assignments by leaving aside a part of the fee to fund it. After we did issue zero, we developed two issues ourselves, independently – one about urban design and the landscape of the Netherlands, and one about "moulage" as a technique for building.
R: For issue1 I took a horse and carriage to De Blauwe Stad, "The Blue City," a famous urban design in the north of the country. They were creating man-made lakes in very old lands, because water sells – they were creating new housing developments in the area. But this area of the country has a rich, very left-wing history; there were huge farms there after the Second World War, with a lot of servants as well. They were so badly treated that the Communist Party became the strongest one in the area. And then it was suddenly announced that

this area would be developed almost as a luxury area, in the language of opportunistic developers. Because I come from urban design, I was used to dealing with the helicopter view and the map in order to investigate the area, but I also wanted to go through the landscape itself. At the same time, Herman was building an office for *SLOOM* in the south of Friesland. So I drove two hundred kilometers in ten days, from the north of the country to the office. I invited people to join me on the carriage to discuss what was happening to the landscape; of course only two or three people came with me… I was even sending postcards to ArchiNed, a kind of analogue footage of the journey that was posted online. We also did a video. In Dutch, "sloom" is very negative, while in German, "Langsamkeit" has a beautiful connotation of patience, development, experience, speed and non-speed. I underwent that in this trip, including the danger of driving a slow vehicle alongside very fast cars. The carriage is not of this time; you can hardly survive in it.
H: The *SLOOM* office was about how you build up a construction through a sequence, also turning it around – it's not only about what you do in what order. You could also improvise in the first stage, and then draw the outcome at the final stage.
T: It reminds me of Rietveld walking around the building site of the Schröder House carrying a window frame, and fixing the point and the vista on the spot.
H: Here I tried to make a lot of different proposals and document each of them.
T: This goes back to the conversation with Lucas [Muñoz] and Raphaël [Coutin], and the way designers approach architecture as an assembly of prefabricated elements. I've seen that also in self-made houses in Christiania in Denmark; something like the prefabricated window unit is such a convenient object that they simply build an entire wall out of them! Architects tend to think of them more as a drawing reference, they are more detached.
H: Perhaps they are also more interested in functionality; how to treat something which once had one function to perform another one.
T: I think when you look at drawings as an architect, especially plans, you develop a kind of conventional or automatic feeling of where you should place a window in a facade, for example, just by the proportion. But in fact it's a rather generic response.
H: It can be efficient, of course, or a question of units. If you actually try to see where the window fits, then you confront the "fabric" that goes in-between, which may not have a set measurement, and then you have a very different effect. It's also about how you treat surface and the elements within it.
T: Did you have any real building experience before this, or did you simply improvise?
H: No building experience.
T: And didn't the rain come in?
H: No. I actually used carpet on the roofing, and after one month it simply disintegrated! Then I had to change it or protect it with another material, so there was a combination. It was very good for learning. I made a rule to use only reused nails.
T: It reminds me of a teacher I had from Finland, who went to visit the shrine at Ise [Japan]. There is only one "clan" that is allowed to work on the construction, so you get to work on the shrine three times, every twenty years, over your lifetime. They also make the nails for the shrine by hand. My teacher asked if she could have just one, and the master builder said no, they were sacred! – but later he slipped her one! The Japanese conception of "old" architecture is quite different from the one in Europe: they consider a building to be old if the original design is old, but it can be continually rebuilt with new materials.
H: It's like a form of temporary architecture, but because it is built in the exact same way, it also remains. That was my most frustrating job, you know, fixing all those old nails! So those were the initiatives we did ourselves. I also got a grant to go to Berlin to make an issue of *SLOOM* there. I found the diary of an East German birdwatcher in a market – the time frame, the concentration. I was looking into the cultural field in Berlin in 2003, and I got some tips to interview people – from an architect working on the Reichstag to very independent designers like Bless – to document the changing landscape of Berlin over time. I asked the interviewees to make self-portraits with these pieces of perforated wood. The time frame is the time you spend reading the article. This was during the time that cultural life was first being developed; Gestalten and Quest started at the time.
T: How did you find the environment there, from a Dutch background?
H: It was so open, much more pioneering in every sense. You felt the energy of the people searching for new enterprise. I almost stayed there!
R: I really enjoyed visiting you there.
H: I lived in an apartment designed by Hans Kollhoff… and this is issue number four, on a project Rianne and I did in collaboration with a communication office and SKOR, an organization that combined artists with assignments for art in public space. It was in 2003, the year of the Dutch farm. That bottom image shows the difference between children playing in the city and in the countryside, the difference in the toys they use. We applied the principle to do the same study in each province: we would use a barn characteristic of the local vernacular to create an exhibition for a weekend – every week in two locations. It was a lot about improvisation, but also logistics! We collected a lot of information as researchers, so we wanted to talk about "scharrelen" – what goes on in a farmyard, which is as much about a rational plan as it is about doing something in the meantime – like what Jurgen has been doing today [working on the roof of the barn, mowing the grass]. So we did some research about the farmyard, using floor plans, diaries – there is a quote from John Berger on the farmer's relationship to the vicious circle of the seasons, in contrast to the factory's relationship to annual growth. I actually phoned him to ask permission to use

the quote. This is a diary about the farm from Rianne's grandfather.
R: It's interesting because we think of this document as "the" past, but he was also writing about the past – although for him that might be 1880.
H: We also mapped all of the different types of farmhouses in each province of the Netherlands.
R: Each one had to do with the way of constructing in each rural area, as well as with property and wealth.
H: In Berlin, I became interested in the theme of the cottage garden, between a farm and a household, which could produce vegetables, for example. This typology was disappearing in the connecting part between Leidsche Rijn and Utrecht, and here Johannes Schwartz made a documentary of their decline.
T: What was behind your vision to document things in this way? Did you have an idea of your audience?
H: I think it came out of our focus on the Dutch farm and the quality of life within it, and the interest in the farmyard as a model for our working environment – the ability to "scharrel." And about architectural production on an informal, improvisational level, as a way of redefining your environment in keeping with your own rhythm of life. I think that's what John Berger was referring to – the evolution of growth as an economic model has nothing to do with the cycle of human life, the biological aspects. I don't know if we really thought about our audience…
R: I think, because of our background in *Forum*, we had the confidence to continue with our own magazine and document things.
H: Some of these issues were actually quite successful!
T: The drawing of the farmyard is extremely beautiful.
H: It's by Peter Möller; I met him in Berlin when he came to show me his portfolio. He made a book about his own home farm; his drawings were like time-based X-rays of the place. Here we invited him to document a farm in Gelderland, and the owners allowed him to live there for several weeks. He slowly began to draw all of the possessions – not just an architectural layout, but also the objects of the farm, concentrated in the house. And this here is very common in the Netherlands, this construction of plastic and old tires around hay.
R: It's fermented grass, very healthy for the cows. After that, we had a photography exhibition in Rotterdam of all of the different houses. We even rebuilt some of them in the exhibition. I remember the swings in particular!

Go Slow

H: Then we had an assignment from Droog. They knew we were starting *SLOOM* as an organization, and they were also starting the project "Go Slow," a joint project with a designer from Eindhoven to find new roles in society for pensioners. She made a restaurant where they were serving. Droog transformed that into an exhibition for the Salone del Mobile, and asked us to do the spatial design. So we were involved in the design of the shop and a tea room; we worked with Hansje van Halem, who used the perforated board to make letters. The tea room had very normal square tables in white-painted wood, but we melted paraffin wax onto the tabletops. Of course it slowly hardened, but if you put something warm on it, it would melt again and create an indentation. We also had curved cups that could only stand up with the help of the wax.
R: It was an attempt to translate the slow movement into spatial design, furniture, or scenography – how you entered the space.
H: Everything was ritualized – our interest in the Shakers! – so the chairs were placed specifically for each visitor. We redid the show at Governors Island in New York in 2009, in a very nice little cottage. It was the 400th anniversary of the Dutch presence in New York, and the island was also being transformed into a park by West 8. Droog invited a Dutch artist, architect, or designer to make an installation in each cottage on the island, and visitors could see different ways of dealing with the challenge. The show was called "Pioneers of Change." We had these pensioners from New York, but they were so active – they were not slow at all! But it was a wonderful opportunity to restage the exhibition, and Hansje developed a different typography.

Wroeten

H: In 2005, Rianne and I were asked to design the grocery shop for *Wroeten*, a television program about a city guy [actor Arjan Ederveen] moving to the countryside. It also took place in Friesland. The main character was not so keen on doing things with his hands, everything was too much hassle, everything went wrong, he had an existential crisis. There was a gardener, Hans Engelbrecht, who advised him on how to grow things. It was also educational, in a way. We made a model of the farm and the farmhouse that could be transported to different locations on the grounds. Heilien Tonckens was the external advisor using the model to reenact certain problems dealing with the development of the garden. The grocery was like a saloon.
R: It was like an extension of *SLOOM* 2, a similar construction but a bit bigger.
H: It was very interesting to work on a set. Because it was on television, there was a lot of tension about when exactly things should be ripe in the time line of the show.
R: Reality and non-reality. Do you remember what we also did together? A manual for the Architecture Biennale in Venice.
H: Yes! That was for the NL Lounge in 2000, during the same period as *Forum*. It was called "De-Fence": we had a magazine on how to behave in the lounge, when it was just beginning to be a phenomenon. It demanded a new kind of interaction, because it was a public space but you could treat it as your private space. You could relax. But how to relax in public? It was a manual about appropriation.
T: It's a mode I've never understood.
H: You have it a lot in The Hague, it's part of the beach culture of letting go and relaxing… it's trying to copy the resort culture in Asia. I'm so glad you remembered it!
R: That project had a lot to do with spatial behavior, which was so important to us – what space does to you.

D-I-Y

DIY – The ape, the blue-collar worker, and the revolutionist

Tal Erez

The alpha male

Tim Taylor: "What do we want?"
Audience: "More power!"
Tim Taylor: "Arrh! Arrh! Arrh!"

Between the years 1991 and 1998, millions of Americans anxiously waited every week for the prime-time airing of *Tool Time* with Tim Taylor. *Tool Time*, sponsored by a fictional tool company, Binford Tools, was a show for the American handyman, with his garage full of power tools, screws, and wooden planks, and the pastime of repairing, re-modifying, and building things around the house. *Tool Time* was also fictional, a show within another show – *Home Improvement*, starring Tim Allen – one of the most successful sitcoms of all time. For Allen, Taylor was the stereotypical all-American male, and his portrayal of the handyman was blatantly linked to a primal stage of masculinity. Taylor portrayed the urge for DIY (Do-It-Yourself) as an ancient, macho form of ownership and providing. The independence and control over the physical environment, to be able to fix your own house and its infrastructure, to be able to provide it with the facilities it requires – without outside assistance – was akin to fighting a bear or hunting a mammoth. For Taylor, DIY was not only an obligation, but also a rush.

In *Tool Time*, it seemed, it was never about the task to be done, but about the tools that made it happen. Whether it was more horsepower, RPM, or capacity, Taylor always looked for "more power" in his tools, with a blatant disregard to whether they fit the job at hand. With his apelike war cries following every manifestation of tool power, it seemed that DIY for him was about taming a beast; about conquest and control in its purest form. In *Home Improvement*, the handyman was the desperate cry of testosterone, the last breaths of the alpha male in American suburbia.

The factory man

"We hate air at IKEA."[1]
– IKEA chief executive Peter Agnefjäll

In 2010, IKEA's EKTORP sofa was made to be packed flat, reducing its packaging size by 50 percent. This reduced the number of trucks used annually to ship it by 7,477, and the retail price of the sofa was cut by 14 percent. IKEA makes low-cost design items.

To achieve this cost reduction, they have perfected a very traditional mass-production cycle. Efficiency and control is a goal practically throughout the chain of production: from the purchase of forestlands in Romania to standardize and maximize efficiency, through a

1
Saabira Chaudhuri, "IKEA Can't Stop Obsessing About Its Packaging: Retailer increasingly designs furniture with shipping costs in mind from the start," *The Wall Street Journal*, June 17, 2015.

D-I-Y

constant effort to flatten and minimize packaging for transportation, to the very specific choice of wood for each part of the furniture, so that quality and structure appear only where necessary, and nowhere else.

Yet while cost reduction found its way into IKEA through tightening control of early production stages, it was in other parts of the production chain that cost reduction meant letting go. For assembly, IKEA's radical solution was to extend the IKEA factory into the customer's home via do-it-yourself assembly. The customer buys a flat package containing only the needed parts, and using a set of instructions, assembles and finishes the product at home. IKEA has formed a contract with us. The consumers become IKEA's assembly line workers, and in return, the company cuts the cost of the non-assembled products. The furniture provider for the white-collar middle class asks its consumers to wear a blue collar. As hard as it might be to imagine, if you own and have assembled an IKEA product, then at a certain point you have also been working on IKEA's assembly line.

The rebel

"Information wants to be free. Information also wants to be expensive. […] That tension will not go away."[2]
– Stewart Brand

2
Stewart Brand, *The Media Lab: Inventing the Future at MIT* (New York: Viking/Penguin, 1988), 202.

There was a very clear social signature on the *Whole Earth Catalog* (1968–98). Its free information and access to tools and knowledge was a form of political liberation. A product of the technologically oriented counterculture of the late '60s, the WEC offered access to makers of everything; a catalogue designed to render the tools of making accessible. Already deemed one of the Internet's most prominent predecessors, DIY meant freedom for the WEC, and for the makers community that came as a later offshoot, knowledge and the sharing thereof meant social power. It is, of course, not so simple in reality. While, in its essence, the maker counterculture leans on the notion of open-source knowledge sharing with an unmediated-as-possible access to tools, the accumulation of knowledge and tools, with a clear focus on invention, leads in itself to power, and the urge to keep it from others. The principles drafted in the '60s by the WEC – DIY is knowledge, power, and an act of resistance – are being tested by the power of business in an innovation-oriented market. Is the DIY phenomenon of the makers community a subversive counterculture revolution? Or is it an intricate, bottom-up business model?

IN HET VEEM
28 29 30 september 2001
Werkgebouw Het Veem Van Diem
INDEX PRINT 35

project 78

2001

Mirrors, Models, Shacks & Yards
Page 305

Veem 20 Years
Project: Exhibition
Duration: Very short-term, 1 day
Year: 2001
Data: page 643

RENÉ
GERRITSEN

project 78

YVONNE STRANG

project78

3

Events: Situating the Temporary

Page 310

Mirrors, Models, Shacks & Yards
Page 311

Boys '97 / Principle Junk
Project: Installation
Duration: Medium-term, 2 months
Year: 2003 / 2005
Data: page 648 / page 653

Boys '97,
Foam
Page 313

project 94

Boys '97, Foam
Page 315

project 94

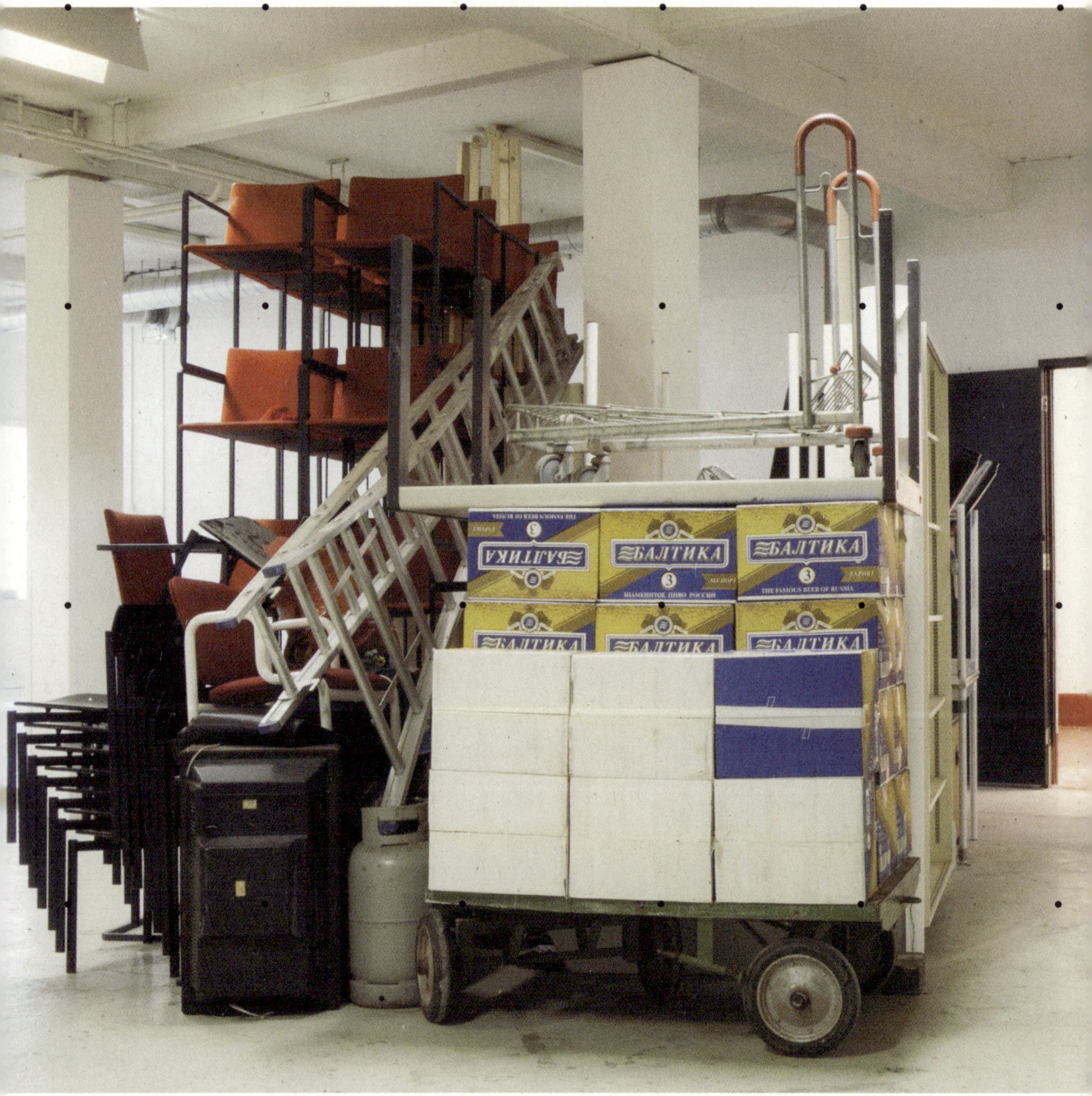
БАЛТИКА
3
THE FAMOUS BEER OF RUSSIA

project 124

Mirrors, Models, Shacks & Yards
Page 318

Principle Junk,
P/////AKT,
Page 319

project 124

3

Events: Situating the Temporary
Page 320

1
What's in a name? On the website of EventArchitectuur, theorist and curator Guus Beumer says: *The name of this design office seems at first glance to be part of a current trend.* EventArchitectuur *is, after all, one of a long line of hybrid conceptual names that characterize the modern vocabulary, like MusicFactory, PartyDesign, FoodStyling and GardenArt. The use of English supports this conjecture, because that language is virtually mandatory whenever the aim is to evoke the dynamism of the here and now. It requires a deeper acquaintance with the various projects of EventArchitectuur in order to become enthusiastic about the name of this office and the work of its founder, Herman Verkerk. Only then does it become clear that the use of the construct EventArchitectuur goes beyond image creation and is in fact a reflection of the office's ambition. EventArchitectuur's portfolio lives up to the literal meaning of the English word "event": the projects are a series of happenings.* See http://www.event-architectuur.nl.

jorinde seijdel: (un)framing the event

In this modest reflection, I will attempt to expand on the notion of "event" in relation to EventArchitectuur. However, I do not intend to come to a final interpretation of this part of EventArchitectuur's name, or how that is connected to and reflective of the office's practice.[1] Rather, I would like to try to reveal something of its inherent contradictions and potential tensions – assuming that this architectural office is as much a cultural construct as its overarching institutions and social contexts – by pointing to some of the problems and possibilities of the (concept of the) "event" today. After all, the event can be associated as much with the neoliberal market economy and creative industries as with specific branches of radical philosophical and critical thinking.[2]
As it happens, the event is a topical concept within very different realms and discourses – it is reflected upon by philosophers, but also by architects such as Aldo Rossi, Bernard Tschumi, and Rem Koolhaas.[3] Simply put, the term "event" means "something that happens." It is also described as "a public assembly for the purpose of celebration, education, marketing or reunion." Seemingly, an event is an active and public situation, action, act, or happening that operates in the present. Dance parties, demonstrations, fashion shows, exhibitions, concerts, and soccer matches are all called events. Thus, architecture as such is not exactly an event, but it can create frameworks and spaces for them. Does this imply that EventArchitectuur is principally facilitating and designing events? Or is it also participating or interfering in the events it contains and manifests? Is it perhaps even an event in itself?

1. The event as a commodity

Within the field of art, theorist and cultural critic Stephen Wright wrote an interesting publication titled *Towards a Lexicon of Usership* (Van Abbemuseum, 2013).[4] This lexicon questions the notion of autonomy within the arts – interpreted as art separated from society – by proposing perspectives of use and usership. The lexicon includes terms that Wright feels should be "retired," along with what he refers to as "emergent concepts" and "modes of usership." The event, or "eventhood," appears as a term that,

2
Philosophers Jean Baudrillard, Gilles Deleuze, Alain Badiou, Brian Massumi, and Slavoj Žižek, to name but a few, have all offered reflections on the nature of the event.

3
Graham Livesey, *Deleuze, Whitehead, the Event and the Contemporary City*, accessed September 8, 2015, https://whiteheadresearch.org/occasions/conferences/event-and-decision/papers/Graham%20Livesey_Final%20Draft.pdf.

4
Stephen Wright, *Towards a Lexicon of Usership* (Eindhoven: Van Abbemuseum, 2013). See http://www.arte-util.org/tools/lexicon.

according to Wright, should be removed from the vocabulary of art and culture:

> Eventhood is the horizon line in the spontaneous ideology of much art-historical discourse. Art historians have accustomed us to seeing art in terms of events: artworks, exhibitions, publications, movements… construing art as an irruptive event, penetrating stable appearance with novelty and all the attendant fireworks. But this is a strangely masculinist understanding of art-historical process. To focus on the epiphany of "events" – and to see art itself as event – rather than on fugitive occurrences, is to foreground particular moments when a set of material, social and imaginary ruptures come together and produce a break in the flow of history. As Dimitris Papadopoulos, Niamh Stephenson and Vassilis Tsianos have argued in *Escape Routes – Control and Subversion in the Twenty-First Century* (2008), an escapological perspective is inherently different: "An event is never in the present; it can only be designated as an event in retrospect or anticipated as a future possibility. To pin our hopes on events is a nominalist move which draws on the masculinist luxury of having the power both to name things and to wait about for salvation. Because events are never in the present, if we highlight their role in social change we do so at the expense of considering the potence of the present that is made of people's everyday practices: the practices employed to navigate daily life and to sustain relations, the practices which are at the heart of social transformation long before we are able to name it as such." In our society of the event, the event itself disappears from view. It becomes the horizon line itself.[5]

Wright evidently considers the event as the objectification and commodification of artistic and cultural practices. To launch and name things as events is to withdraw them from daily life and to value them mainly in commercial terms. His interpretation of the term seems to critically refer to the vocabulary and value system of the experience economy and the production and consumption of goods; in short, to the neoliberal event economy. In 1998, B. Joseph Pine II and James B. Gilmore published *The Experience Economy: Work is Theatre & Every Business a Stage*,[6] in which they argue that businesses must orchestrate memorable events for their customers, and that memory itself becomes the product – the "experience." *The Experience Economy* has introduced the concept of "transformation" as a system of experiences which concerns a reality in which the customer is the product.[7] Since then, this cynical business philosophy has been successfully applied by many companies, be it Walmart, Apple,

5
Ibid., 25.

6
B. Joseph Pine II and James H. Gilmore, *The Experience Economy: Work is Theatre & Every Business a Stage* (Boston: Harvard Business School Press, 1999).

7
See also Jorinde Seijdel, "Theatre and Emotion in the Supermarket," *Mediamatic Magazine*, 1999, http://www.mediamatic.net/5687/en/theatre-and-emotion-in-the-supermarket.

or Facebook. It is significant, however, that the title of Gilmore and Pine's book refers to theater – in other words, to the world of culture, illustrating once again the blending together of the categories of commerce, entertainment, and art in the course of modern capitalism.

Meanwhile, in the twenty-first century, arts and culture are fully participating in the experience economy. In this light, Wright's straightforward rejection of an event-centered conception of art is understandable. The "user" he favors in his activist evaluation of the neoliberal art system can indeed not remain a mere spectator or consumer of events, but should be an active practitioner of everyday life, a sphere that he considers endangered. One of the dilemmas in his lexicon that appears as an "emergent concept" is *Usual (the usual ≠ the event)*:

> A generation ago, the work of Henri Lefebvre and Michel de Certeau persuasively analyzed the goings-on, inventiveness and usership of what has come to be called "the everyday." Though it's hard to believe, the everyday has since become a victim of its own unforeseeable success. It has been championed, commodified and framed by spectatorship. For a long time, I considered "the everyday" to be the environment of usership – the way eventhood is to spectatorship. But it was a poor fit. I couldn't quite figure out what the right concept and the right word might be to name usership's sphere of engagement. I never did figure it out; that's not how language use works. I overheard it one day. A regular stepped up to the bar, exchanged a quick glance with the barman who asked, invitingly, as if confident in what he already knew, "the usual?"[8]

8
Wright, *Towards a Lexicon of Usership*, 65.

2. The event as agent of transformation or becoming

For Stephen Wright and his references, the event within the concrete context of "useful art" is a restraining outcome of power relationships. Again, as he quoted: "An event is never in the present; it can only be designated as an event in retrospect or anticipated as a future possibility." To designate and construct something in retrospect as an event is to execute power and to exclude or ignore everyday life.

Wright's point of view seems here to be in conflict with the philosophical thinking on the event by Gilles Deleuze and Slavoj Žižek, among others; to invoke these seminal others, such as Jean Baudrillard, Alain Badiou, or Brian Massumi, is beyond the scope of this text. In Deleuze's more abstract thinking, the event (*l'événement*) is a key concept, about which he stated: "Every event is revolutionary due to an integration of signs, acts and structures through the whole event. Events are distinguished by the intensity of this revolution, rather than the types of freedom or chance."[9]

9
James Williams, *Gilles Deleuze's Difference and Repetition: A Critical Introduction and Guide* (Edinburgh: Edinburgh University Press, 2003), 78.

For Deleuze, the event is an intervention of time, pure state, and a "becoming," a bifurcation between the actual and the virtual. Deleuze follows mathematician and philosopher Alfred North Whitehead in affirming that "the world is made of events, and nothing but events: happenings rather than things, verbs rather than nouns, processes rather than substances." In *The Fold*, in a chapter entitled "What is an Event?," Deleuze writes:

> A concert is being performed tonight. It is the event. Vibrations of sound disperse, periodic movements go through space with their harmonies or submultiples. The sounds have inner qualities of height, intensity, and timbre. The sources of the sounds, instrumental or vocal, are not content only to send the sounds out: each one perceives its own, and perceives the others while perceiving its own. These are active perceptions that are expressed among each other, or else prehensions that are prehending one another: "First the solitary piano grieved, like a bird abandoned by its mate; the violin heard its wail and responded to it like a neighboring tree. It was like the beginning of the world…"[10]

Deleuze's event is an elusive concept and "is always that which has just happened and that which is about to happen, but never that which is happening."[11] According to him, "the event is inseparably the objectification of one prehension and the subjectification of another; it is at once public and private, potential and real, participating in the becoming of another event and the subject of its own becoming."[12] The event here is not a distinctive thing or object, let alone a "product," but rather a constituent; a process and a relationship between sensations, time, space, and structures. It is not reserved for a particular domain, social field, or moment, but "affirming the complexity of life as a constantly changing condition."[13] The abstract Deleuzian event is about transformation and the production of the new – that in itself can be quite concrete. As such, it is a thing that cannot be designed or constructed in advance.

3. The event as a change of frame

Philosopher and cultural critic Slavoj Žižek recently published an exploration of the event, entitled *Event: Philosophy in Transit*.[14] "What is really happening when something happens?" he asks. Although Žižek is not exactly a follower of Deleuze, and much more involved with psychoanalysis, in this text he refers repeatedly and without too many objections to the nomadic thinking on the event of his peer. Žižek begins with confirming the event as an "amphibious" notion by stating that "an 'Event' can refer to a devastating natural catastrophe or to the latest celebrity scandal, the triumph of the people or a

10 Gilles Deleuze, *The Fold, Leibniz and the Baroque*, trans. Tom Conley (Minneapolis: University of Minnesota Press, 1992), accessed September 8, 2015, http://mysite.pratt.edu/~arch543p/readings/Deleuze.html.

11 Alain Badiou, "The Event in Deleuze," *Parrhesia*, no. 2 (2007): 38.

12 Gilles Deleuze, *The Fold: Leibniz and the Baroque* (London: Continuum, 2006), 78.

13 For Deleuze's event in the context of urbanism and architecture, see Graham Livesey, "Deleuze, Whitehead, the Event, and the Contemporary City," accessed September 8, 2015, https://whiteheadresearch.org/occasions/conferences/event-and-decision/papers/Graham%20Livesey_Final%20Draft.pdf.

14 Slavoj Žižek, *Event: Philosophy in Transit* (London: Penguin, 2014).

brutal political urge, an intense experience of a work of art or an intimate decision."[15] For Žižek, the event is an occurrence not grounded in sufficient reasons and escaping causality. He asserts that "an event is the effect that seems to exceed its causes – and the space of an event is the distance of an effect from its causes." The basic feature of an event is the "surprising emergence of something new which undermines every stable scheme," Žižek says. As a result, the event is a change of frame, or a reframing: "… event is not something that occurs within the world, but is a change of the very frame through which we perceive the world and engage in it."[16]

At the same time, as Jodi Dean puts forward in *Žižek's Politics*, the very notion of event installs a frame; to refer to something as event is to take it out of the manifold of experiences and impressions, to enframe it.[17] The question, then, is if the event is always making an interruption with our dominant frame or if it can also reinforce it. If a revolution takes place, is this event necessarily creating a new frame of perception and experience, or can it also affirm and strengthen an already existing frame? This seems to depend on where and who you are in relation to this revolution, to this event. The event is apparently not universal in its effect and affect.

15 Ibid., 3.

16 Ibid.

17 Jodi Dean, *Žižek's Politics* (London: Routledge, 2006).

4. Event as in EventArchitectuur

The event from the perspective of philosophy to a large extent eludes our grasp. With Deleuze, and also Žižek, it refers to a turning point – with the former, an event can happen in passing; with the latter, it is more explicitly regarded as an upheaval – and as such, it can be easily mystified. Within the ideology of the market and B. Joseph Pine II, however, the event is foremost a saleable and consumable material or immaterial product, and in that sense tangible and identifiable. Stephen Wright in his turn rejects thinking in terms of the event at all, be it philosophical or commercial, as he considers it bereft from the everyday here and now, and therefore without any social "agency."

What, then, about the event in terms of EventArchitectuur? The office is certainly as much a concrete, productive space as it is a conceptual edifice. According to Guus Beumer, its portfolio reflects a series of events that should not be confused with the products of contemporary phenomena, with names like MusicFactory, PartyDesign, FoodStyling, and GardenArt.[18] The volatile trendiness of these examples of the Experience Economy à la Pine is not to be compared with EventArchitectuur, he seems to suggest. But, at the same time, EventArchitectuur cannot be regarded as separate from this more mundane and commercialized sphere of life. Can it, then, be a critical design practice as well, one that questions dominant and controlling frameworks?

18 See note 1.

3

Mirrors, Models, Shacks & Yards
Page 326

The body of work of EventArchitectuur seems to reflect a structural orientation toward modernist and capitalist activities, such as storing, archiving, displaying, and exhibiting – for example, with *Start*, *Higher Truth*, *Out of Storage,* and *Temporary Fashion Museum* – that refer to corresponding habits like viewing, inspecting, shopping, and consuming. However, the aesthetics of these presentation models, installations, or structures seem to be in contradiction with this. They are functional and unpolished, looking provisional, unadorned, and rudimentary, exposing the construction and the raw material. As such, they seem to question their own content, and to critically appeal to the awareness, behavior, and perceptiveness of its public. The installations of EventArchitectuur function as frameworks, but in the sense that they reframe familiar typologies. By doing so, they can create new stories, new events that unfold at the transition or turning point of one framework into another. Exactly this transitioning can be regarded as the event. With EventArchitectuur, the reframing often takes place on a 1:1 scale (*Start*, *Higher Truth*, ArtEZ Fashion Show). This strategy is extensively considered by Wright in his *Lexicon*:

> Art and art-related practices that are oriented toward usership rather than spectatorship are characterized more than anything else by their scale of operations: they operate on the 1:1 scale. They are not scaled-down models – or art world-assisted prototypes – of potentially useful things or services (the kinds of tasks and devices that might well be useful if ever they were wrested from the neutering frames of artistic autonomy and allowed traction in the real). Though 1:1 scale initiatives make use of representation in any number of ways, they are not themselves representations of anything.[19]

Wright asserts that 1:1 practices break with modernist conceptions of scale and are "both what they are, and propositions of what they are."[20] With EventArchitectuur, this seems to reflect the movement or tactics of framing and reframing, and to constitute an activist aesthetics. However, the works of EventArchitectuur, 1:1 or not, are always encapsulated by an institution – be it a museum, an exhibition, or an arts organization. By not subjecting its scale to the institution, EventArchitectuur seems to resist appropriation and to escape being completely enframed by the institution. The event with EventArchitectuur is not really a spectacular, noisy happening, but rather a shift or change of frame that is being envisioned by the perceiver. It is truly a "process and a relationship between sensations, time, space, and structures" (Deleuze), attempting to neither become institutionalized nor become a final object.

19
Wright, *Towards a Lexicon of Usership*, 3.

20
Ibid.

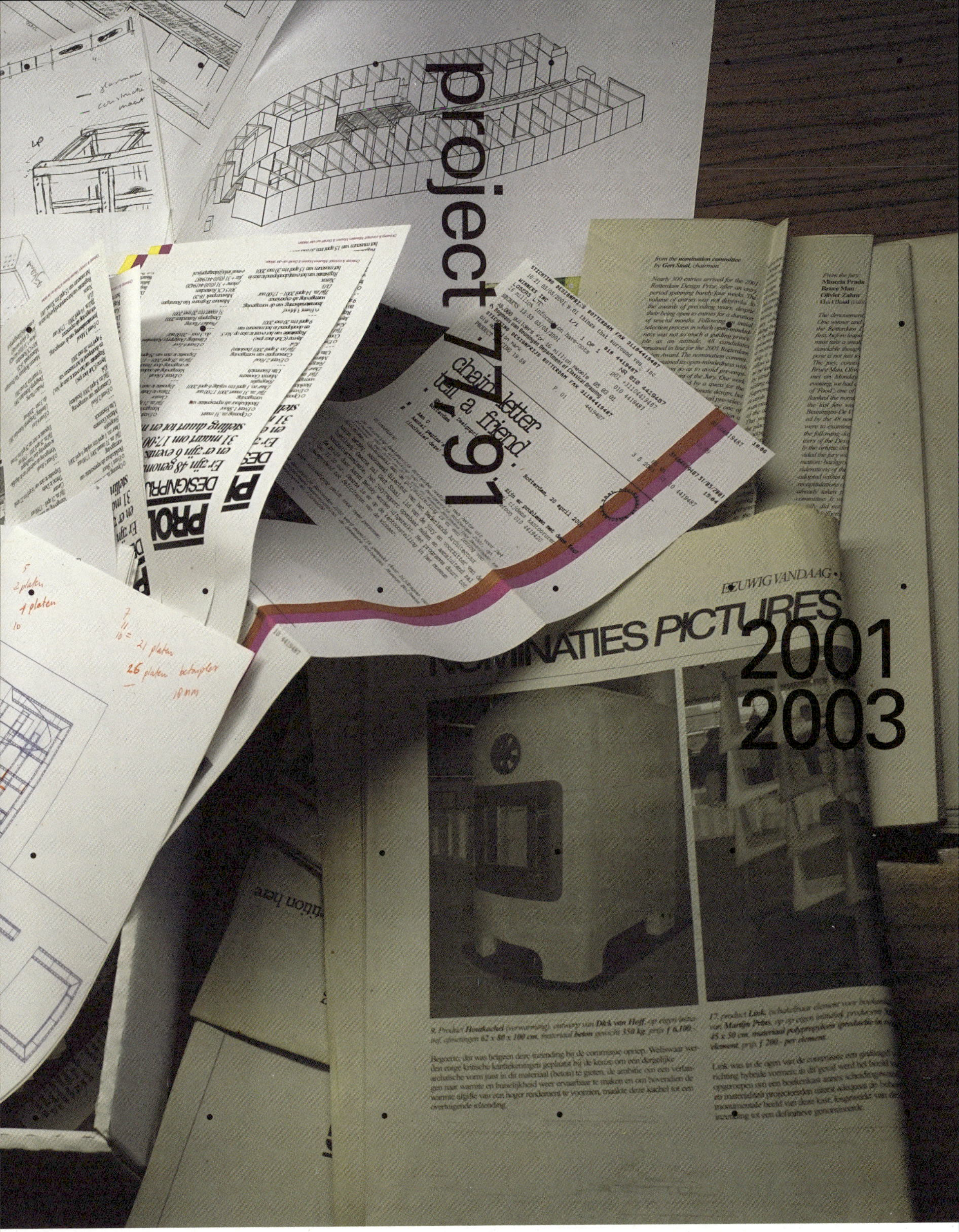

**Mirrors, Models,
Shacks & Yards**
Page 329

Rotterdam Design Prize
Project: Exhibition
Duration: Medium-term, 2 months
Year: 2001, 2003
Data: page 642 / page 647

Rotterdam Design Prize, 2001
Page 331

project 77

Designprijs Rotterdam 2003

project 91

Mirrors, Models, Shacks & Yards
Page 334

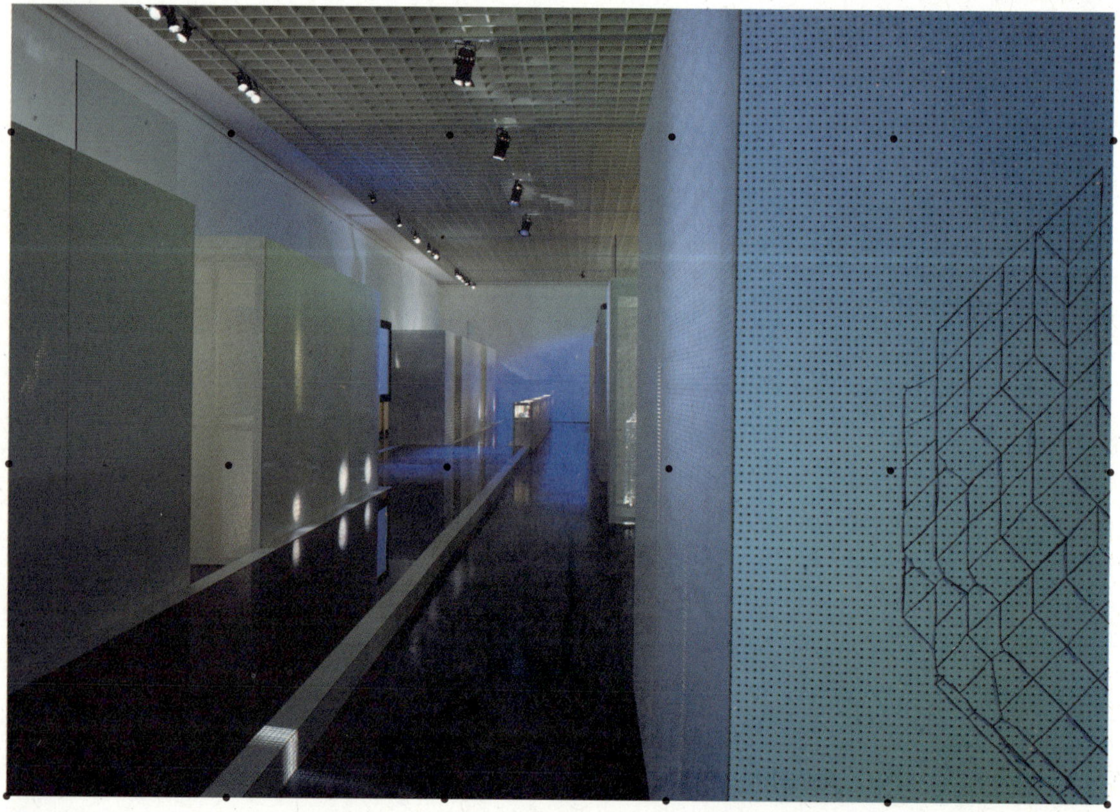

Rotterdam Design Prize, 2003
Page 335

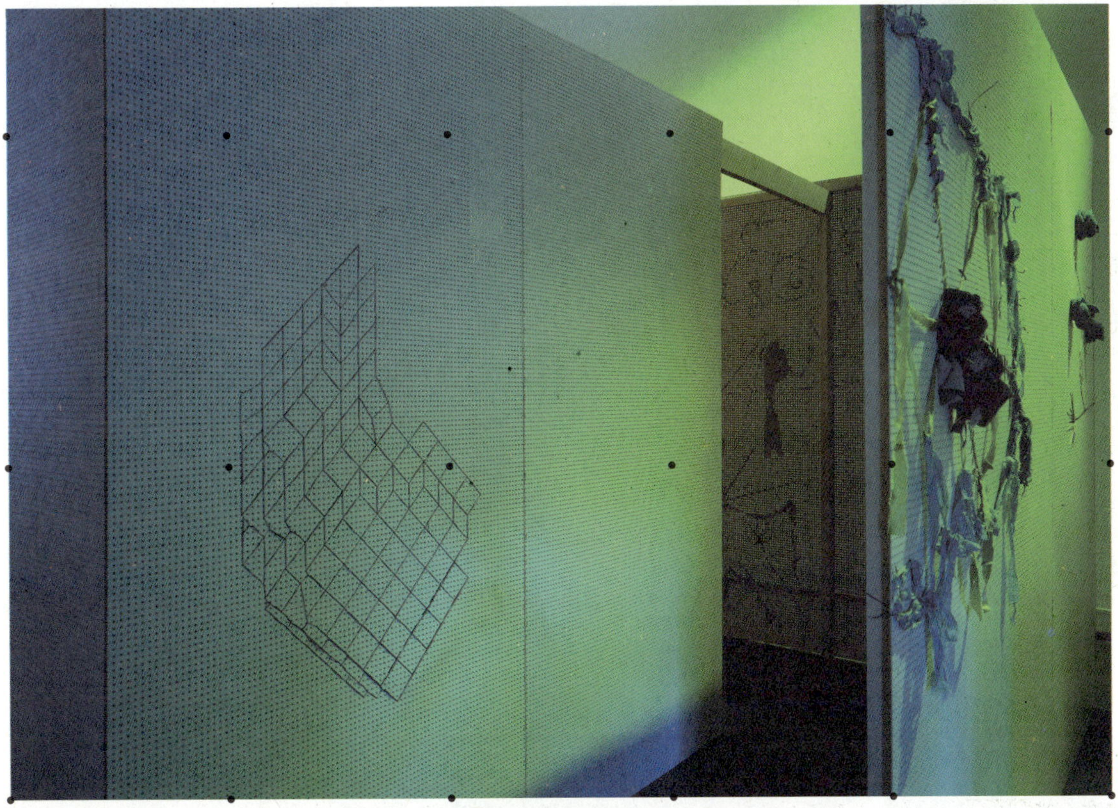

3

Events: Situating the Temporary

Page 336

project109

2005

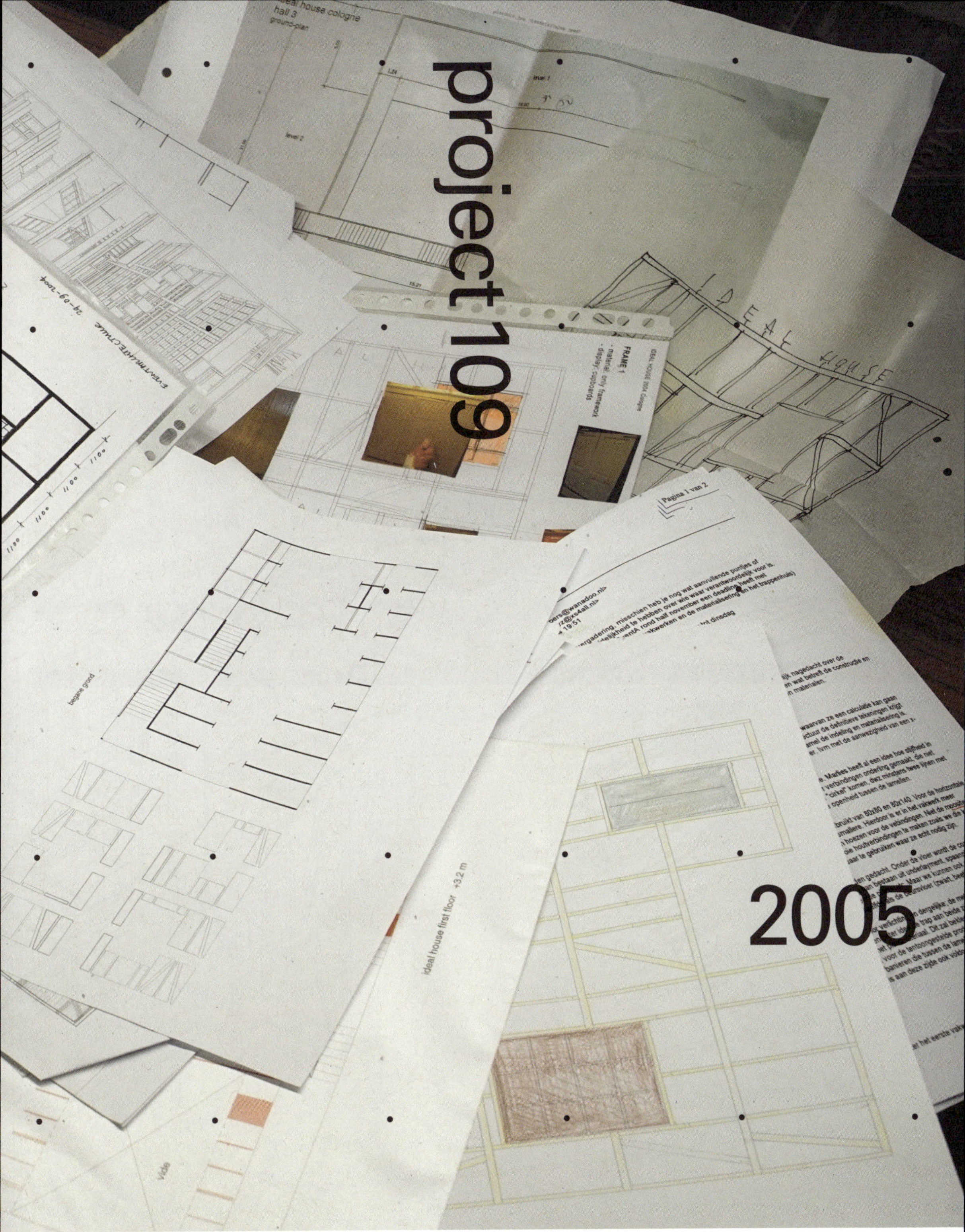

Mirrors, Models, Shacks & Yards
Page 337

Ideal House
Project: Exhibition
Duration: Short-term, 5 days
Year: 2005
Data: page 652

ideal house cologne

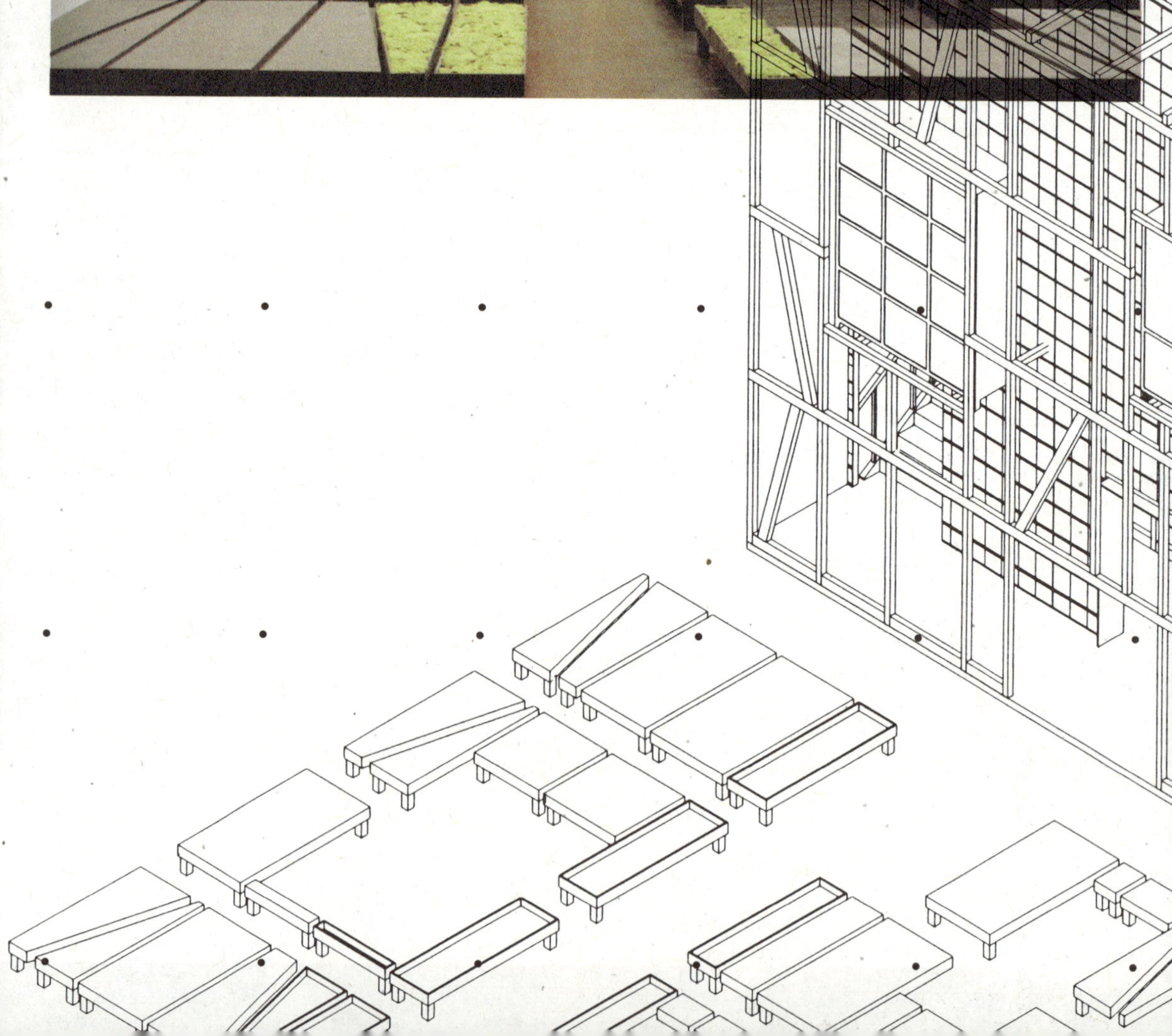

project 109

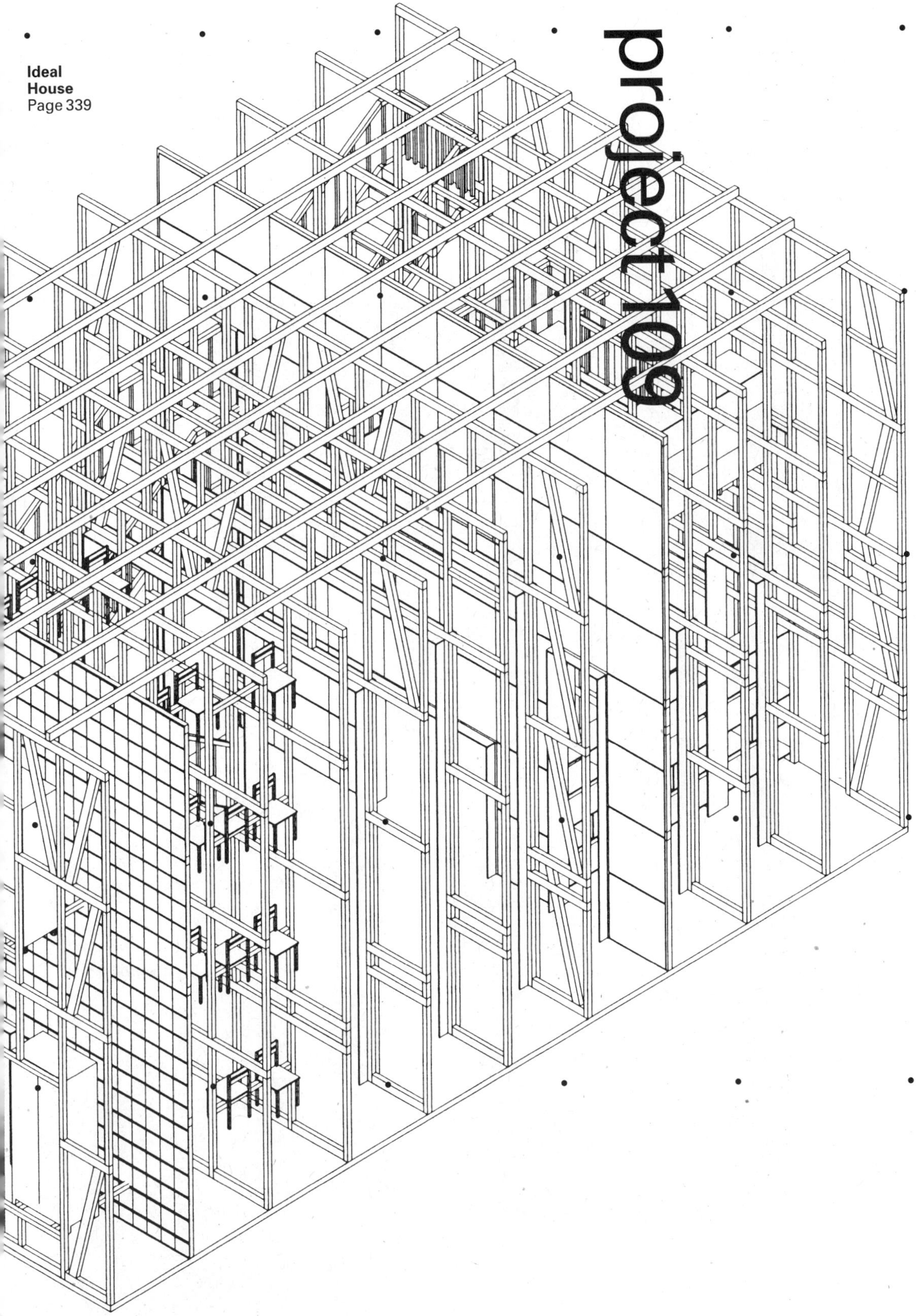

project 109

GROUND FLOOR

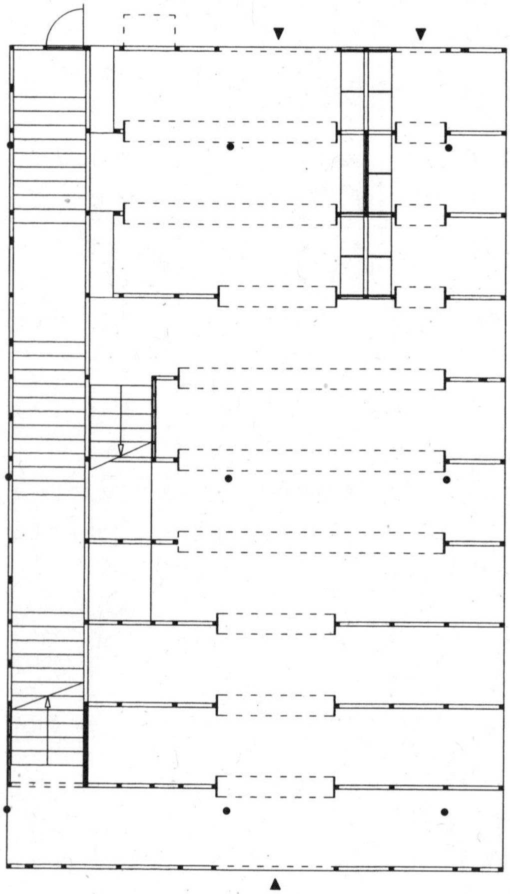

FIRST FLOOR

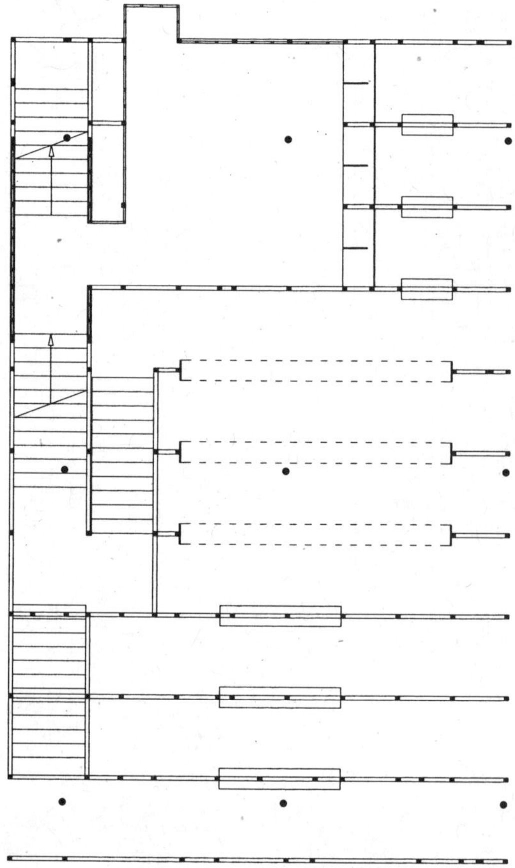

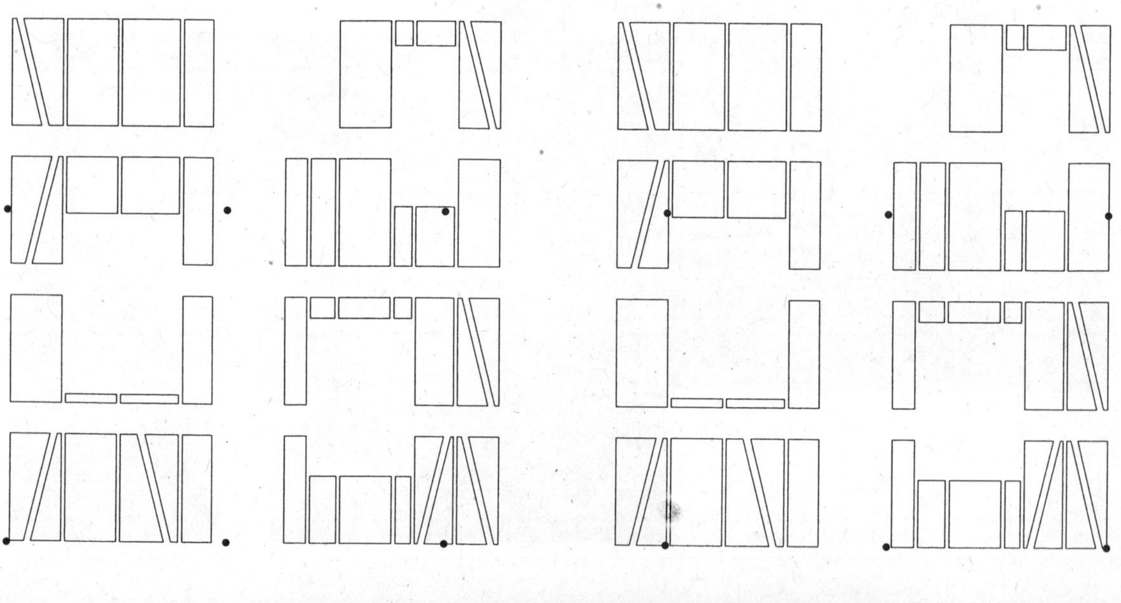

project 109

Date:
May 15, 2015

Place:
Studio of Event-Architectuur, Amsterdam

People:
Tamar Shafrir & Herman Verkerk
w/ **Paul Kuipers**

Conversation 4

The ruin

T: It's an artifact of the relationship.
H: That's a good word. There's always a relationship between the production of the design and how it got used or accepted. And maybe the ruin is this artifact. Our interest in the ruin is based on storytelling, but storytelling in a very broad sense. Most of the time the storytelling is associated with fairytales or fantasy, but it can also be used to pinpoint certain historical facts or analyses that you think could help to explain certain situations.
T: Do you know forensic architecture from Eyal Weizman? It became quite popular to use the tools of architecture for other purposes.
H: We know this example of the Israeli army who has the liberty of lessons in architecture. The reason is to walk through walls or to first have an idea about the architecture and then to relativize that the wall is a construct. It's not something permanent. So they would have another mind-set, very interesting exercises where they literally go through these walls as ruins.
T: And they are reading Deleuze! Paul, do you remember your case study?
P: Villa Müller.
T: The one that looks like a stage? I think Colomina wrote an article about it. But her pictures were in black and white, I don't recognize anything!
P: It reminds me of the movie of the capture of Osama bin Laden, this very secret team who was completely familiar with this compound, with this building and all the rooms, which was based on guessing, from reconstruction from images from satellites and drones. Because it was completely secret, they could not go inside. When they entered, they knew exactly where to go.
T: But now they said the whole movie is based on false information, the story is not exactly true. There was recently an article in the *London Review of Books*.
P: A lot of conspiracy theories. Even the Twin Towers are blown up by George W. Bush. It's the last story.
T: That's quite strange, that buildings are inspiring those theories.
P: But it doesn't matter if it's true or not true. You can rebuild something you never visited.
H: But evidence in a building, it brings you to the '90s, everything was all about the "traces," the center stage of design research – to leave traces, human interference with things, remnants, the dependence of humans on things – the things will last, while humans will disappear. It's very interesting, this evidence of life. There was a very nice master's project that a student from the Fachhochschüle Düsseldorf did on evidence in hotel rooms. She ordered the cleaning lady to interfere with the property of the hotel guests. They would be there for three or four days and the cleaning lady would have a choreography to place things differently. It was very beautiful, this idea of transforming an interior where you don't expect it. It was also unnecessary. And she recorded evidence of the decay of the hotel room, from very light to very dense things. The level to what you accept these things is very interesting. What is the limit of the ruin, where you can still live in it, or where it becomes unhealthy?
T: Maybe in one moment it becomes almost an eighteenth-century concept of ruin, it becomes so exaggerated that it is a folly.
H: And then it becomes again the stage or the theater. But I think in all of our work there is this sense of decay that is already anticipated, but we don't call it decay… we call it "patina."
P: The reference to the eighteenth-century ruins can also be about reenacting some stories. We were walking this afternoon in the Mountain Idyll park, and this reference to a castle or a bunker or a fortress came up. It's completely not a fortress, but somehow the thickness, the lenght of the wall, recalls it.
H: We reused bricks, tiles from the pavement, in the structure. We worked on this project a very long time, and the development of this wall that we constructed transformed a lot in the materiality over that period. It's sort of...
P: One of the running gags is that when we talk about things, there's a lot of "It's sort of…" My friend said, "I hate your 'sort of'!"
H: I know "Aren't you exact? You're an architect!"
P: It's never exact, it's always researching around the object, it's always "sort of," a little bit of that, a little bit of this, it's always composed, never one thing.
H: And we always leave a lot of freedom to the execution. Of course there are limits…
T: Do you mean to the fabricator?
H: In terms of architecture, the build takes place on-site. You give them the freedom to do an example, and then you correct them, but it's not that we know exactly how it should look and here is the drawing and you should do it exactly like this. There is always the feedback of their expertise and maybe some of the mistakes that can be made or potentially make it better. For instance, with the tiles, we saw that there are a lot of dented tiles, and we thought "this is perfect"– it gives a very nice little detail in the fabric, and we didn't say, "Now be careful with the dents and put them here and there," we just left it to them to do it.
P: To a certain extent…
T: There was an acceptable threshold?
P: There were "sort of" restrictions or limits, and within whose boundaries they could play.
T: Do you find it easy to document or communicate? How do you explain that in a drawing, or is it impossible and has to be explained in words or interaction?
H: I think in

interaction. The drawings are much more for the conceptual level, but we are convinced that this will never be the reality. We don't even want it to be the reality, because we don't want this airbrushed, CAD-CAM image to be real, although it's totally possible nowadays to have the cleanness of the concept, the SketchUp literally translated into the material. So we always have the abstraction, but we don't sell this, we sell the concept of what you see, and then the materiality is another world, and then we step into that world and make examples with it.
P: If you look at those shelves, it was completely produced by a computer, so it's on the millimeter, it's very strict. But the way we treat or tolerate the material, like the aluminum with the traces of the production, normally they would brush them and everything would disappear. We are also playing with the traces of the production process and the aging of the material, like wood discoloring over time. That's what we tolerate in this system, but in another case we work with wood construction that becomes very exact. The material itself is nothing, it's cheap, it's bare.
H: You have to treat the plywood really well, if you just use nails you split the wood, so we had some examples from builders that were totally insensitive to that degree of breaking the surface, so there is a sort of limit to what we can tolerate. It's also about treating the material respectfully.
T: When I looked in the portfolio I didn't see much expensive material; also expensive materials probably tolerate rough treatment better, strangely enough. If it's cheap you actually have to be more delicate.
H: But also the flexibility of the cheap material gives us freedom. So we could work with marble or steel, but never welded or HD, we tend to choose flexibility – like the wood can transform while you are doing it.
P: Steel is not so expensive.
H: No, but it's already kind of rigid, so when it goes to the builder you need to know you want a hole there, etc., it's not a process material. Or you have to make a Meccano, like a toolbox with elements that you place together.

EventArchitectuur?

T: Event-Architectuur is you and Paul?
H: It started before.
T: What does the studio or the platform or name represent?
H: To integrate architecture in events. Very simply put, there is a happening or event – which can last fifteen minutes, but it can also last three decades – it's more that you think about how it's going to be used, the daily routines, and how you can integrate architecture and more theoretical elements and things from architecture history into the design of something temporary.
T: Do you think that's another form of layering two events in one, with a historical reference?
H: The topic of this book is a challenge, similar to design, which has a very relative history. It has to create its own knowledge, also how an event has been constructed spatially. In the last twenty years there has been a lot of research on fireworks as a mode of expression, but also an architectural interpretation of an event. There are more of these examples that are getting more attention. Also Beatriz Colomina's article that we will publish on the pavilion – the pavilion is a structure where a lot of architectural history was made, but it was made in a very light version, a temporary one. As an exercise that you're not really sure of. You use it as an experiment. That was the idea that I discovered, because the first years I worked a lot for the fashion industry, and they were very interested in a spatial translation of their fashion, and I really felt that I first couldn't serve it. I thought it was very superficial and trendy and not very inspiring, and then I met Alexander van Slobbe, and he opened this whole world of fashion which was totally linked to architecture. Suddenly, I could tell stories with my architectural knowledge about fashion…
P: And about architecture itself…
H: And this triggered the name EventArchitectuur.
T: If he would speak about fashion, it would also be totally different.
H: It's more making a garment, like the old tailor.
T: What's interesting already is in the fashion show pieces there's already this sort of recombinability, not one statement but elements…
H: …that could be combined perpetually in different forms.
P: Maybe the similarity is that his fashion is also very bare. You have a big piece of cloth and one action is giving it a construction.
H: And it's showing this construction, it has no back side. If you look inside the garment, the construction is as aesthetically pleasing as the outside, and there is no hiding.
P: It's not representing something else. It's very simple, it's only referring to the thing itself, not to another world.
T: It's like the opposite of the Moschino style, which is just reference.

Storytelling

H: That's what I mean by storytelling, because people confuse the word with that kind of example – costume; a lot of the time it's very one dimensional, it's kind of an issue and you see that it's performing, but the storytelling can also be about the fabric, endurance, silhouette, so it's much more subtle to use the word storytelling in design.
P: If you construct something and deconstruct it afterwards, it also tells you the story of the object itself. It's never covered in something. That's why we like the exploded views, because you see the component, how it's made; if you see the back side you get an insight into how it's constructed. It's never covered. Also in our work, we never do it – we never make solid pedestals.
T: Do you still get the instinct to think about form, and then get rid of it and move onto something more in your language, or do you not think at all in that way?

You come in and what do you see?

H: The event really starts it off. We have this saying, "You come in, and what do you see?" It's more this question of what do you experience. There are a number of experiences

conducted by the client, who may propose a vision or some contradictory wishes, and in the conversation we get this information, digest it, and try to transform it into new experiences. But they are not really materialized yet. They are much more about spaces – bigger, smaller, narrower, higher – more an experience of an environment than the physicality or formal qualities. They come much later on. A lot of people hate this dryness of the forms – in the end the thing you have to construct, the experience, in itself doesn't have any appeal if you isolate it or put it on a pedestal. It doesn't mean anything in itself. It needs a context. That's not for every element, but about the relativity of "to make something" or to work as an ensemble, or for isolated pieces that work together to make a total. That's also our struggle, that a lot of times we go for the structure, and then the client is attacking this structure, and then of course there is a balance between, does the structure still work, is there a solution to treat it lightly and with a lot of nuance, but there is also a limit where you think the structure has been attacked so much that we need a new structure. This may be what you're talking about with formality.
I think with us it lies much more in the structure – a grid structure, a pavilion structure, a garden path structure, an urban structure – and we try it out and see if it's a solution for the very different demands, and if not we try another structure. We don't force the structure to become anything.
P: Our clients are rather tolerant to our experiments, and it's a little bit of give-and-take situation. Budgets are maybe also not high enough to do real experiments where we can prove some things, it's more trial and error, and maybe accepting the error. Now we are doing a project in Barcelona and they are asking for legal documents about the constructions, a guarantee if it will stay as it has been made, but we don't have that. If it's falling then we improvise – an extra leg.

Structure and stability

H: It's not about stability, we don't design with stability, it comes during the process, because we know that it has to stay standing, but it generates new solutions. If you think you have an environment, you want to give an experience, so you try to visualize it, you try to materialize it, then with the materials also comes, "now it's collapsing," so you have to figure out a way to make it stable, and that's also trial and error.
T: It kind of reminds me of the Renzo Piano approach; he always has some detail of the project that is very unique, but usually they are also very complex. I was curious if there's a simplicity or a range of simplicity that you aim for when you look at one piece of the module. Of course you can design a complex module in order to achieve something complex, but even this one may be the most complicated.
H: This one is already more towards a more complex design.
T: And maybe this is the least because the module is actually all made from the same material.
H: We did some research, but not a lot.
P: It's not completely true…
T: Maybe because you achieved a very convincing simplicity.
H: We changed this wedge piece that goes inside to fix it, we developed it a little bit, but also not so much.
P: That is a system that we found out, at a certain point we went with that. Then there is a distance for instance from the next material you use on the facade. It's always playing with dimensions, and we like to start with the size of the board, how it comes from the DIY store. Not only for budget concerns, but also thinking about efficiency, how you can use the material, and if there are leftovers, how we can use them to make at least a new part of the system. That's what I found when we worked in Barcelona with perforated board, it's usually one meter wide; now we have to clean it, to cut the edges, so it's not a meter, so you are constantly changing the system and the depth, it's a sort of dialogue between materials, between what's on the market.
H: It's physically clear that this… The Piano detail is definitely high-tech: it solves some pressure, movement, it integrates lighting… we don't try to make these kinds of pressure points or jewels of ingenuity.
P: On a certain scale, if you look at the Boxorama, it's clear what it is: it's referring to the old wood boxes that we played with as kids. But then you have to translate it into a certain computer program, because the idea is that you can cut it from an existing board, so maybe the complexity is more hidden, not visible in the thing itself.

Complexity in simplicity

H: That's also a clear standpoint that we don't want to communicate complexity. Of course there is a lot of complexity in making the optimal. As in the wedges, it develops through a lot of stages, but the visual of the element stays simple. You need to see how it works.
T: Sophistication also has many different aspects. For example, having the sensation of what the multiplication of these elements will be is a level of complexity that is generally not addressed in architecture. If you design an apartment or a house, you should probably have the sense of what it would be if all the houses were designed that way, but I don't think we are taught to think on that scale…
H: …and as architects we don't design the tiles, which would be a nice exercise. I will try to develop this in The Hague, to link the design of the space to the materiality of the space, and to have them influence each other, much more than that the interior architecture remains abstract and the designer comes in and makes the skins.

Gesamtkunstwerk and improvisation

T: Do you feel quite sympathetic to the *Gesamtkunstwerk* model?
H: Yes, but I also see how I make interiors for myself as a private person, it's very eclectic and not so controlled as the *Gesamtkunstwerk.* But a lot of times when I propose something for a client it is much more coherent, this interaction between the tables and the skins and the inside.
T: The historical reference for the Gesamtkunstwerk seems to be a justification for the

architect to become a decorator, the direction is to scale down the design, until you have an extremely ornate outcome. Yours is almost the opposite approach, you design a small thing and you make the big thing out of the small ones, you let the logic of the piece determine the whole. That approach is not necessarily the only one that could have emerged from the understanding of events, it's still quite unique. Was there a point where that became one of the "ten commandments" of the studio?

Five chapters

H: I think it's transforming all the time. That's why we decided for the five chapters in the EA book. In the last couple of years, because of the financial crisis, we found out that physical labor and expertise and woodworkers became so expensive that CNC and prefabrication, which were there before, were suddenly high on the priority list for how you get things into the world. That demanded another type of design. Also the structure of the office or the expertise transforms when you are dealing with these computerized approaches to making elements of the experimental environment with a computer that is kind of working against you. It wants to repeat, it wants to use one language. It's always a struggle to find a way to improvise within this structure. That may be something that characterizes the entire period of our work, one of the "ten commandments" that you have to be able to improvise with what you have been offering to clients. I remember that we did this very nice interior for Piet Paris, a fashion illustrator, and we had this in-between space between the studio and the lunch place, and there was a gap of one meter with two walls, and we designed the walls and then we came up with a sort of covered structure with lighting. It became very unclear what it became, but they liked it, and we also discovered the possibilities of our structure. Also for us it's a sort of playing with, you had first your basic layout and within that you look for detail, but the details could be very surprising. They could go wild.
T: Or emerge from a mistake or an architectural feature…
H: That's a good example of a transformation within a project. First you have one language and then you have another one added.
P: It can also take form in different ways. In the conversation with Piet Paris mentioned here we offer a system that you can reuse and easily transform into different elements or basic parts, but you are giving it more, the client sees the opportunities, you hope he sees the same ones that you see and likes the same opportunities.

Computer tales

T: Did you do a master's in ETH?
H: It was a postgraduate one year; I totally immersed myself in digital technology. We also learned programming, e-mail became in vogue in 1992, e-mail conferences and all that type of stuff. Apple was developing a lot of programs, like Vectorworks and other visual programs. That was really good to experience.
T: Did you already feel that you would look for traces or ways to exaggerate the mark of the machine?
H: At that time it was more about having the machine working for you in the design process. I was really looking for a use of the computer, which was before used for presentations or executional drawings, and I was aiming for ways to use the computer for structuring your thought process and having different stages of the design visualized by the computer. It was how to make the computer improvise. We had a small group of six persons studying, and we got a lot of attention and feedback. I had a huge development in one year of dealing with visual implications of abstract surfaces and those types of things. Representation and certain aesthetics that couldn't yet be changed at the time. My final project was a combination of found footage with animation of 3D programming. It had a kind of two parts of the brain, one with the found footage that was very physical, the movement of people through space, it was a cruise ship, where obviously people do nothing and you see them on the deck and at the bar, and I made animations of the building which I designed, which related to these scenes on the cruise ship so you would feel that there was a certain physicality, although the 3D modeling was not able to show it yet. Now of course it's completely doable. I think I started studying there on virtual reality, that was my dream at the time, to have an extra room in your apartment that could change, and I totally forgot about that and thought it was ridiculous when I left. And only now it's getting more attention again with the glasses and the idea of gaming dens that people install in their homes, the big screens that they get immersed in, this other environment. I totally lost my appetite for virtuality, and although it was very good, an idea of escapism, I really wanted to stay on the physical side.
T: Paul, how did the computer enter your vocabulary in making?
P: At the Art Academy we used Illustrator and Photoshop, InDesign not so much because we had QuarkXPress for presentations. I think you were quite at the beginning with this 3D stuff, and in some way the last generation to have a choice, because a lot of your same-age architects never touched a computer.
H: That's also why I went there, I was working in an office and had to deal with the draftsman, and he would continuously tell me, "This is not possible to draw!" so I better learn myself because I know for sure that it is possible. But, Paul, I'm also curious, did you use the computer as an expression tool? Here of course you see a kind of computer makes a certain aesthetic, you can wipe it out but you can also keep it visible. You hate my photoshopping when there are rough cut-out pieces put on top of each other.
P: How do you think we started? You were in love with these nice collages from the 1960s, but our other teachers kept saying, "The computer is the future!" They were introducing a new language, and although the computer was taking a lot of time, it was a slow process, they

were completely euphoric about it. In the meantime, our generation was not so interested in computers. We were looking at ways to copy it somehow, which is strange. Photoshop is a different thing than a 3D program. It took me a long time to learn AutoCAD. The other projects I did at the Art Academy were all by hand. It started with your lessons, with analysis lessons. Draw an existing floor plan; and although it is a very academic exercise, by doing that, you get a feeling of how it is constructed. We designed a house for each other in pairs by interviewing each other and translating that into a house.
T: I saw a really funny assignment, the teacher asked them to pick someone from Twitter and design a house for them. I thought it was really strange, that when you are studying you have a client – I had once a tattoo artist – now you don't have to have that generic category anymore. You can pick someone completely specific.
H: You can construct it around the demands, or around what he or she is saying.
T: I suppose when you look at these really incredible buildings, Rietveld Schröder House would be the best example, there is always the most interesting client relationship that produced the most unusual architecture.
P: Maybe you were interested in this idea of virtuality because it also has to do with your own position with regard to dreams, utopias, the original, all those notions about imagining a space, what an architect is doing, all of a sudden there was a technology to shape it, form it, transform it. I think it's the same for you as for me, that doing it and making it and playing with it takes a lot of time and it's a profession in itself. For me, I don't want to sit at the computer all the time and to make plans and to build these spaces. I am not a gamer, I see it around me, I know more or less what's on the market, but I am not sitting the whole day on it. I am addicted to Netflix, but other people are playing all of the time, connecting to people all over the world, with SimCities, it's amazing. But somehow it's not in my genes to do so.
H: For me there is a limit to a game that you always find out, and maybe a movie is nice because you already know that it is limited. Someone else was thinking about it, and you can consume it, and you can interpret it the way you want to, whereas with a game I always have the feeling that I'm playing someone else's life.
P: But it's improving; SimCities are quite complex and even developing towards a situation where you are completely autonomous.
H: So it's not like playing with Lego, that finally they all have these little round heads.
T: Do you find the same with your own works, that you designed a game and through each project you learn the limits or the potentials even within those systems?
H: That's the reality of it, and you want to escape it, but you come to the same thing all over again.
T: I think there is one rhythm of projects, and another of languages. For you, with this shelving system, is it the equivalent of using bricks or wood, in the sense that this is a project by itself, or is the project the adaptation of the systems or languages that you have? And how do you decide when to adapt them?

Design as a communication tool

H: It's what we started to document when we did the *SPACES* project. It was a suggestion from outside; EventArchitectuur is okay, but if you want to continue your clientele you have to do design. And because I was teaching at the Design Academy, I saw that design was working as a communication tool. And so we started to think about the language of these *SPACES* structures, and we did a summary of all the places that we used in each one, and where and how they were functioning. And with Tal (Erez), we tried to transform it into a product, so with a specific size and materiality; we tried different ways of doing it, and in the end we found out it is a good communication tool but it didn't give us any additional satisfaction. The system almost reduced in a way, whereas before, because it was site-specific or client-specific, we always gave it a kind of interpretation that triggered our energy to go further. With this, I'm sure we could make a very good product out of it, but we need a designer for that – someone who will go into the detail, into the industry, transforming the language until it is completely a product. There lies a sort of interest for us.
P: The product world is about logistics, how to produce it – that's what we like – but then there is a balance between what things cost and what people are willing to pay for them. One of the qualities of this structure is that it doesn't get its quality from a wow-factor in the material or like you see a lot of design, it's made of clay and it's hard and wow-wow-wow, this Maarten Baas effect. It's not what we are doing, inventing a material. We are not that kind of designer.
H: It's more about the complexity of using it. We installed it in one guy's working space, and for a week he was very offended because he couldn't alphabetize his books in these bookshelves. And this is extraordinarily funny, that the structure gives you a new way, you have to deal with it. He solved it by using his old encyclopedia A–Z books as markers.
T: It's strange because you go from the thing that is the most site-specific to the most generic. In that sense product is even more generic than object, you'll get some boards and pieces and it can fit anywhere. But actually it should fit perfectly. It's a strange contradiction.
H: For us it was also a riddle. What are the rules? How do they play? It's also triggering my interest, how people can deal with design in that way. I see the struggle of students more with convincing themselves that they can present a product rather than developing it. Sometimes the product is developed in the second week, and then they spend six or seven weeks doubting how to get the product into the world, how it becomes accepted, what kind of story to build around it, how to pitch it. These kinds of things are so important in design.

In architecture there is a much more fluid development of the restrictions that you're dealing with, you have always something to work on, then you do the cross section, then you work on the material, then on the surfaces, then on the logistics. It was also interesting to see the design process as something so different.
P: Some designers are more about the idea, but there are also more furniture makers.
T: Or keep interpreting a process in different ways in whatever time frame they have. But in design you have the opportunity to make a statement, but architecture you have a longer process, but there are so many opportunities for the design elements of the work to be removed because of budget constraints. There's always a pressure to go back to the most generic. What's funny for you is that you think about the duration so you plan for it, but in another sense you precede the choice by going to the most generic, for example, in terms of the material.

The temporary

H: We are the critic ahead. It's what we think about, the temporality is our escape. It doesn't last, it's a proposition, so you endure it while it lasts, and we don't guarantee that it stays forever. And you see with the interiors that we made, after five years, they are gone. That's the experience that you had, talking about it. The thing that lasts is the story.
P: It can go in both directions. You can also maintain it.
H: That it is still there but transported to a new location. There was a shop in the Warmoesstraat...
T: Between a smart shop and...
H: ...and a condom shop! It was a grocery, it didn't survive. It had a very nice inner courtyard. And when it was dismantled the owner, Piet Hekker, took the interior with him to another location on Katendrecht in Rotterdam to use it for a local "Buurt-supermarket."
T: When did you start to work in this way? I can barely compare this at all to any Dutch architecture mentality.
H: Maybe the use of data? That you start with the research in the form of data, which you go on to visualize. But it's not about the data as a result, we use it as a tool.
P: We are not simply showing it.

Unity and contrast, whole and parts

H: The '80s Russian movement of paper architecture really inspired me.
T: What about Hertzberger?
H: He taught me.
T: I remember going to this kindergarten...
H: Also Aldo van Eyck taught me. But with Hertzberger we learned about the threshold, how it can be extended so you can have a gliding trajectory from the inside to the outside. That was very valuable. His talking was great, his examples were, too; with van Eyck it was very rigid, fixed. The brutality of Hertzberger was very enlightening, the gray bricks, like the aesthetics of this wall. It's kind of funny to see that it sometimes works in structures and sometimes not at all, it gives too much detail. When a building is all made of parts, you also lose a kind of coherence and you feel it's all fragments, it's not really a building.
T: There's a quote from Zumthor where he says that my Swiss colleagues Herzog & de Meuron always work on theme of contrasts, whereas I work on unity.
H: "Harmony," perhaps?
T: And he says it's much better to work on harmony because if a visitor understands that your theme is juxtaposition, then they have figured it out, but if they understand that your theme is harmony then they have to keep searching for every sign of harmony in the building; it withholds these secrets that you have to discover yourself. You are inspired to keep looking for the work of the architect, not just admire the composition.
H: There's an element of truth there, if you exaggerate the contradictions, it becomes very one-dimensional. H&deM did very bad works with that and also very good ones. It's a little bit difficult to say either/or. This building they did in Spain with a kind of eruption or volcano, I loved it!
P: A sort of grotto...
H: ...and the materiality is sexy. But that's the boring part of Zumthor, where he says there's an interest to look further, maybe people have no clue. It's total harmony, and then...? How do you appropriate it?
T: And if you're not in harmony, then you should leave!
P: Harmony is not a word that fits here in the studio (pointing at shelf). It's more collisions. You can tell stories in different ways, but it's always an internal conversation. We love the work of Dom van der Laan but also of De Vylder Vinck Taillieu. I was so touched by what Hertzberger was saying last time in his lecture; he did these "Montessori" schools in Amsterdam, also made of the gray bricks, in its materiality it's quite simple, it's concrete, but he was explaining to a crowd of young architects who are used to prefabricated panels, how difficult it was in the 1970s to make it as it looks. Every brick is stacked by a man, by a mason, which was very expensive. It's nice to hear, we take it for granted, architecture, but there are so many positions that lead to a building or a construction.
H: A lot of times you don't see the making of a building or a product.
P: Now it's rather dictated by what's in the market. A brick is no longer a brick, it's a cladding.
H: You can also redevelop it, it's a possibility if you are Zumthor, you have a brick factory at your service.
T: It's also strange, as you said, it's not the thing itself but the conditions around it that are changing. When labor becomes expensive then a humble material becomes luxurious, like if you have a real double-wall brick house, maybe in a hundred years no one will know how to fix it.
H: Then it will be a riddle.
P: But if you look back, you also realize you are making something together. There are a lot of disciplines and professions that we no longer possess.
A carpenter makes things with wood and construction, it's physical and heavy, it asks a lot from the back, all those aspects of the work are interesting, how you make it altogether in a group of people. That's what I hate about this prefab reality, you see a lack of love and compassion about

what you are making, using kits and using foam for everything.
T: It's also erasing these other people from the process, making it look like the designer presses a button and something is made automatically for the user.

The hand of the maker

P: That's why we are always searching for people who have a certain hand, touch, you have a conversation, "How are we going to make this?"
H: And also with the detailing of the things that roll out of the computer – they are not sanded, the edges are rough, you have to treat it to translate it into the real world. These things are important. The basic elements could be standardized or prefab, but you still need to think about how to treat them when they come together. It makes a difference in the experience.
T: In Milan, we organized an exhibition, with this group Opendesk, who are totally into this myth. The point of their platform is that you get the furniture made in the nearest fabricator. You can download the drawings for free, but they have a network all over. It is kind of a perception that you get an identical product everywhere in the world.
H: That was also our assumption when we started. When we started to develop it with different manufacturers, then we found out, how do we put them together? It doesn't fit! There was always something going wrong. We noticed that you can't sell it like that, it's impossible. You still need an in-between, someone controlling the output of the computer and making it acceptable.

3

Events: Situating the Temporary

Mirrors, Models, Shacks & Yards
Page 353

Higher Truth no. 5 / "We'll slide down the surface of things..." / Safe Haven
Project: Installation
Duration: Medium-term, 1 month
Year: 2001, 2002, 2003
Data: page 643, page 646, page 647

Mirrors, Models, Shacks & Yards
Page 354

Higher Truth
no. 5
Page 355

project 82

Higher Truth
no. 5

project 82

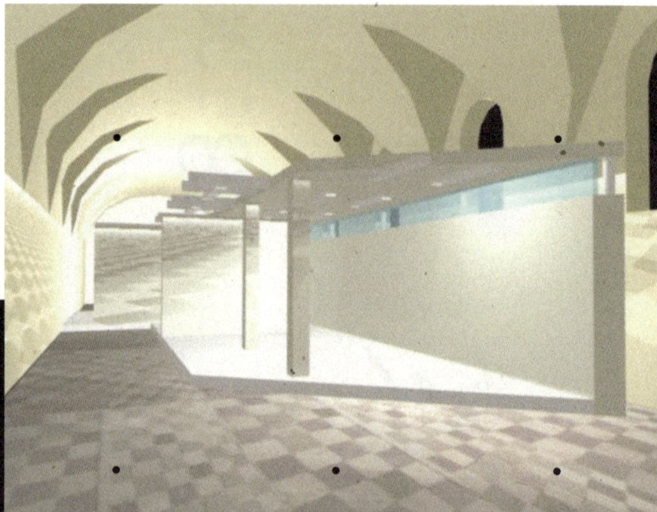

project 89

"We'll slide down the surface of …"
Page 359

project 92

Safe
Haven
Page 363

project 92

3

Events: Situating the Temporary
Page 364

project 97

2004

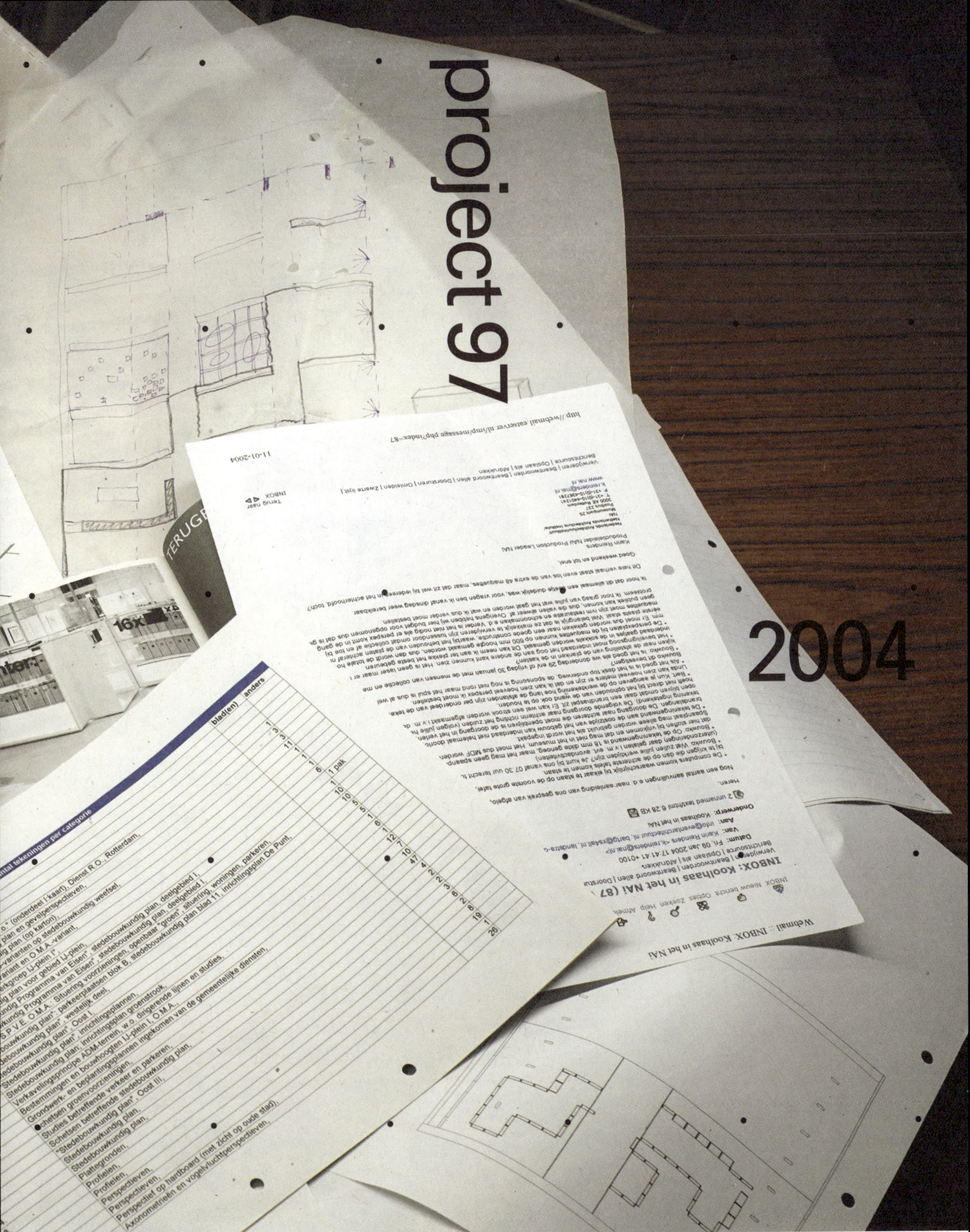

Mirrors, Models, Shacks & Yards
Page 365

Start: OMA open archive
Project: Exhibition
Duration: Medium-term, 3 months
Year: 2004
Data: page 648

Mirrors, Models, Shacks & Yards
Page 366

Start: OMA open archive
Page 367

project 97

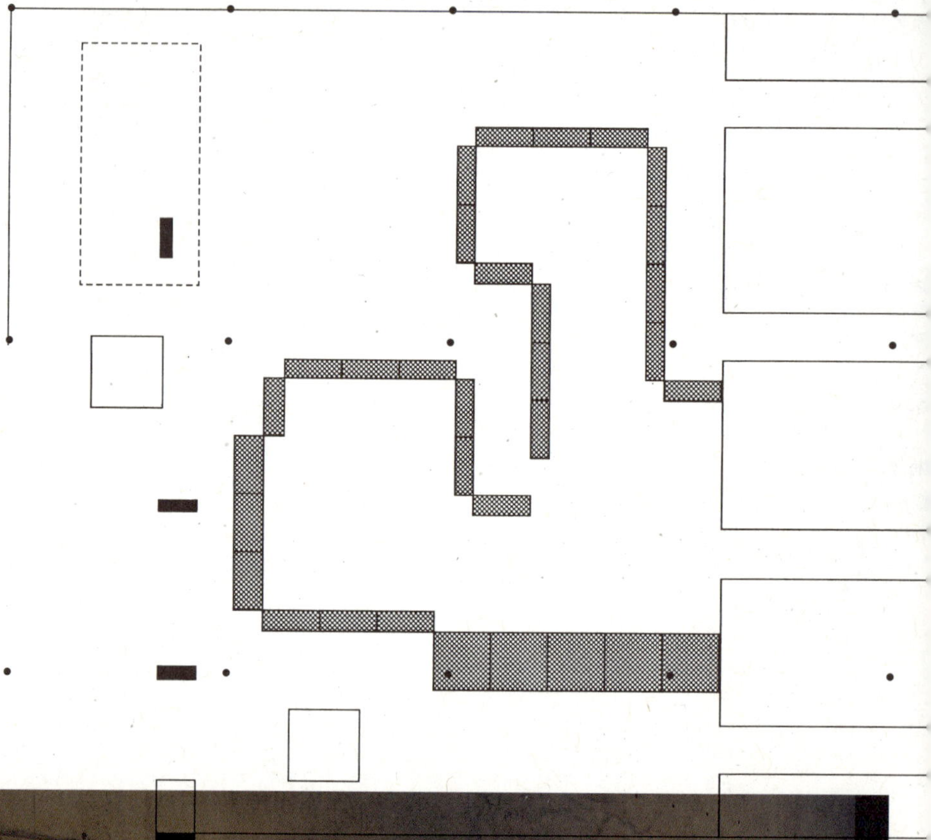

Start:
Balie:
Counter:
X

Start: OMA
open archive
Page 369

project 97

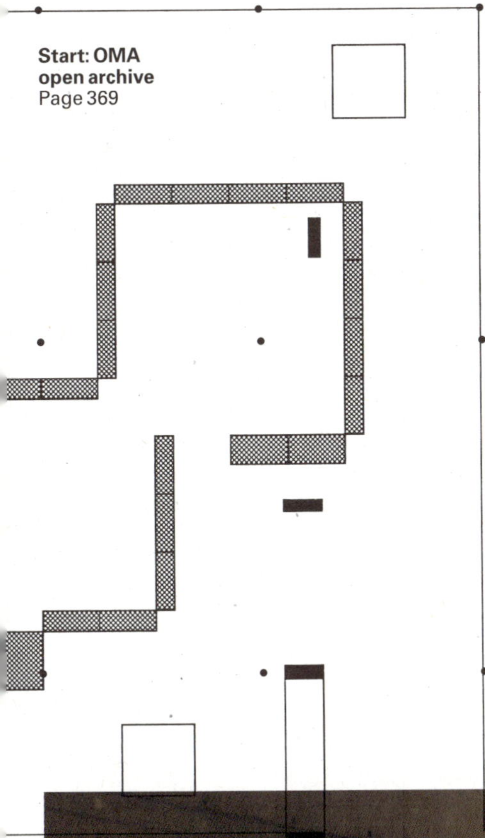

4

4 immersed in the amazing maze: experience economy, the white wall, and a safe haven for the arts

2005

2010

4

immersed in the amazing maze

The Experiential

In the second half of the first decade of the new millennium, the rise of new technological frameworks fused with the excesses of the pre-crisis global economy, introducing new demands on architecture. The intrinsic, built qualities of structure and spatial organization were given over to the production of sensory effects in the visitor. The emphasis on experience and spectacle was ubiquitous, from the high culture of an institution to the popular culture of a theme park. The museum became Disney-fied and Disneyland became "curated" in equal measure – in other words, there was no "outside" Disneyland anymore.

In this environment, the tourist became the primary position for navigating the world, its distances collapsing in the era of low-cost aviation. From airport to station to hotel to gallery to club, the crowd was channeled into seamless flows of pre-programmed experience, modeled on the competitive syntax of the game world. Yet this increasing circulation would inspire new forms of critical consumerism shaped by the dialectic of boom and crisis, of luxury and decline. Participation became a form of currency that fundamentally changed the logic of the cultural space, and the universalizing elements of allegory and theater were crucial to its success.

2006: In New York, the High Line is opened and work begins on the Freedom Tower.
2007: The Burj Khalifa becomes the tallest building in the world.
2008: The mortgage crisis in the United States sparks a global financial recession.
2009: *Avatar* is released, becoming the highest-grossing film of all time.
2010: More than 100,000 European flights are cancelled in one week due to volcanic ash from Iceland's Eyjafjallajökull.

4

4

Events: Situating the Temporary
Page 374

ellen blumenstein: experiential setup

... my problem is to construct myself, and to invite others to share an experience of what we are, not only our past but also our present, an experience of our modernity in such a way that we might come out of it transformed.
– Michel Foucault[1]

Taking two discursive art projects, *Salon Populaire* at Kunstsaele (2010–2012) and *Studiolo* at KW Institute for Contemporary Art (2013–2016), both in Berlin, as a starting point, this essay explores the fabric of these venues and conceives them as cultural spaces specifically designed to enable experiences.
An experience in this sense differs – following the late Michel Foucault – from the colloquial use of the term: firstly, in the sense that it enables the individual to create a sense of self (by the means of distancing, even wrenching the subject from itself); secondly, it allows him or her to enter a communal space within which he or she transcends individuality and becomes part of a collective. This conception appears perfectly apt for the field of visual art as well, since it is almost common courtesy these days to ascribe art with the capacity to produce transformative experiences. The core question of how such an experience might be made possible, however, usually remains unconsidered.
The implicit expectation, generally, is that an encounter with art infuses the individual with some kind of pre-existing meaning from outside: a high-quality "transcendental experience."
For Foucault, though, an *experienc*e is intrinsically linked to creative labor (in his case, writing), within which the subject exposes him- or herself to a yet unknown outcome – in the process, gaining knowledge about an object of interest and, in turn, about themselves. A completed book, then, if successful, encapsulates the experience and allows others to share that very experience, in the sense that the transformation the author has undergone by means of writing is available to the recipient when reading. This notion prioritizes the process over the creative act, and favors incessant constructions of subjectivity to stable identities. In this respect, there is no fundamental difference between creating and receiving.[2]
Within the field of art, this firstly, and contrary to prevailing

1 Michel Foucault, *Power: Essential Works of Foucault*, 1954–1984, ed. James D. Faubion, trans. Robert Hurley, et al. (New York: The New Press, 2001), 239–273, 242.

2 See Ludwig Hohl, *Die Notizen* (Frankfurt am Main: Suhrkamp Verlag, 1981), 322.

4

Immersed in the Amazing Maze
Page 376

convictions, implies that the artist and the spectator principally pursue the same goal. Secondly, the artwork is neither revealed to the artist by sheer genius, nor does it automatically enlighten the viewer through its presence. On the contrary, according to Foucault, it would be the occasion to step out of one's daily routine and review one's relation to the outside world, as well as to oneself and others.

As much as could be written about the individual experience of/with/through art, this article takes the multilayered fabric of the aforementioned venues as instances of a specific type of collective involvement with art. This type of engagement is facilitated within semi-public (both private and institutional) formats, which settle along the spectrum between jointly perceiving spatial installations and actively participating in the common production of knowledge.

Both raumlabor's spatial concept for *Salon Populaire* and EventArchitectuur's *Elegant Scaffolding* are deprived of the museum's archetypal feature, the white wall; on the other hand, they must be distinguished from a mere social location. Their common characteristic feature is the spatial setup. We will therefore expand upon Foucault's view, restricted to the relation between the labor of writing, or alternatively, the finished object (the book) and the experience of reading, to consider also the spatial and social conditions that facilitate or intermediate such occurrences, and describe the specific role of these projects against this background.

However, before introducing the specific shape of each design, we should look into historical formats and examine the intellectual and spatial-formal foundations, from which the recent interest in salons and other participation-based, social-artistic formats derive. Their development will shed light on why the broader notion of *sociability* has settled as an exclusive derivative in the arts today. Sociability playfully detaches the individual from the power structures and social hierarchies of socialization, and thus has been an effective counterbalance to the quagmire of daily business for a very long time.

While readily invoked as the last bastion against the logics of profit in our times, such unintentional, joyful human interaction and exchange was once considered a value in and of itself in most societies. Sociability has been largely studied in human sciences, among others, by the German sociologist Georg Simmel, who ascribes to it the core social function of individual and collective identity formation. Sociability, according to Simmel, is grounded on rules as tacit and as binding as any business environment. In contrast to its stable structures, however, it does not create a pre-fixed formal corset into which the individual has to fit; instead, it enables the subject to position him- or herself within society in relation to others.

Over the centuries, the manifestations of sociability in Europe emphasized different aspects of cohabitation: in antiquity, the symposium assembled aristocratic men to eat and drink well and debate philosophical questions, while during the Renaissance it was both male and female members of the court who created environments where people from different social statuses could come together to reflect on their times, share knowledge, and educate each other. Between the eighteenth and early twentieth centuries, the bourgeois culture yielded to the salon – predominantly led by women. During this period, it also exceeded the mere reproduction of existing cultural artifacts, like reciting prose or poetry, singing, or playing instruments, to emphatically support the production and introduction of new works (mostly literature and music). The salon was a place to gain attention for one's work from an informed and critical audience; to network and find – or give – social or financial support.
Despite relying on fundamentally distinct conceptions, all of these formats share particular features: they construct and represent a community and a discourse, they establish an exceptional temporary order – which is not outside, but within the ruling social conventions – and they refer to culture as a tool for the production of meaning.[3]
With the transition to democratic forms of government, the state has arguably taken responsibility for this cultural and educational ideal. Consequentially, cultural formation has become a fundamental right, as opposed to its earlier conception as a humanist responsibility by certain members of society.[4] Commissioning and enabling access to culture transitioned into a public service, available potentially to each member of society: one does not have to concern oneself with creating cultural experiences; they are laid out for everyone.
In a parallel development, the ties between sociability and culture have loosened, or to be more precise, the two engagements became separate from each other. Modernity gave rise to a differentiated system of clubs, associations, and unions on various social levels, which are either based on social commitment (i.e., Rotary or Lions Clubs), pursue collective leisure activities (sports, chess), or meet for specific cultural interests (reading circles, musical societies), at the cost of socially mixed groups and a broad knowledge base. Networking as a targeted version of sociability blurs the boundaries between labor and leisure, but also between purposeful and open-ended communication. The economic mandate of efficiency infringes on all spheres, and results in arrangements like the Bologna process, which allows international competition in education, or the continual evaluation of outreach programs in cultural institutions.

3
In France, for example, philosophers like Voltaire and Diderot frequented the salons of Paris in the late 1700s, where they contributed to preparing the ground for the French Revolution.

4
In Germany, for example, culture is a basic right, which is guaranteed in the constitution.

4

In this light, to return to art institutions from this broader perspective, the function of museums has shifted from reaffirming a stable collective identity (via cultural artifacts) to shaping contemporary worldviews, as well as to constituting ever-changing variations on prevailing self-perception/self-definition. The obsession with education accompanying this process has brought about attempts to re-emphasize the social function of art and culture – and has experimented with creating spaces for sociability, both within the institutional context and on the practitioners' side.

While museums and project spaces equally refer to the modernist conception of the white cube, thereby naturalizing conditions of presentation until this very day, there is no prerequisite spatial conception for these discursive projects. Above all else, a venue that intends to create sociability by the means of, or within, the field of art must carefully define its point of reference. Searching for a starting point, in the last few years many practitioners have made recourse to one or several of the above-mentioned historical models and adapted them for the present moment – just as I have done.

Due to firsthand experiences, which I hope will prove insightful to the reader, two of my own curatorial endeavors may now serve as examples documenting this development. The first project, *Salon Populaire*, was an independent venue conceived for events in and around visual arts, founded in Berlin (2010–2013).

The idea for the *Salon* was born from the observation that, in a city with nearly 200 museums and allegedly more than 400 independent project spaces, there was a gap between social events like exhibition openings and traditional discursive formats like lectures, book launches, or artists' talks. On the one hand, there was social interaction without generation of content; on the other, there was production of knowledge deprived of communication between the attendees – the urge to reconnect the two and revitalize the concept of sociability was in the air, and I simply picked it up and gave shape to it. My goal was to create a place with the intimacy and intensity of a bourgeois salon, but without the elitism intrinsic in its traditional setup.

Located in a 250-square-meter apartment in the district of Schöneberg, *Salon Populaire* joined Kunstsaele, a private institution run by a gallerist and two collectors, and took the spatial setup also as a starting point to develop its program.[5] Together with Markus Bader from raumlaborberlin, we conceived of six specifically designed architectural elements, formally conceived as a hybrid between theater props, furniture, and sculptural objects. Each event should develop out of a confrontation with an already charged environment – the contrary of the white cube, so to speak. Our intention was to reverse the relation between the setting and what happens in it. Not that

5
See www.kunstsaele.de.

the event requires a specific surrounding, but a situation calls for an idea to react to it…
In this sense, the six objects could be combined at will for each evening, and could create numerous spatial constellations, within which most elements could take on differing functions, depending on the value of use ascribed to them.
Our first object was, of course, a bar – *the* prime tool for generating a social atmosphere. A mixture between peephole, puppet theater, and a real bar, this item automatically took center stage in the room, and the space was usually arranged around its positioning. Another key element was a simple wooden frame, slightly taller than body height, covered with pink glitter and a golden curtain. Wherever the structure was placed, it automatically opened a stage, defining and separating the "auditorium" from the "backstage." More clear in its function, the seating element (no. 3) could either be used as a podium or for other, more intimate conversations between guests. Two stairs and a plinth, all of them multifunctional as well, completed the group. Each could become a backdrop for a presentation, but also accommodate visitors, incorporate technology, or serve as a repository for other objects.
From this point of departure, my colleagues, Tania Schomaker and Fiona Geuß, and myself either conceived an event or a format for a series of events, or we invited other artists, curators, critics, or designers to respond to the given setting. We set a twofold topic for each year that consisted of two unrelated terms (such as "love" and "space," or "labor" and "transcendence"), thus designating a field of interest that could be addressed individually or in combination, and created a content level parallel to the spatial challenge.
The programs made use of a variety of artistic genres, from philosophy to personal narration, from painting or sculpture to film and social media. The series of filmic mise-en-scènes, *Film City Berlin*, for example, was organized once a month by Berlin-based artist and curator Florian Wüst, and sought to contextualize *Salon Populaire* spatially. By showing and commenting on selected film references and excerpts, Wüst reflected on the history and the present of West Berlin from the 1960s until now through the lens of love, space, labor, or transcendence. Against the backdrop of ever-changing settings, each event conceived of the content at hand and its spatial setting as an entity, which involved the viewer as an active participant in the evening.
In a similar way, Portuguese critic Ana Pinto's project, *Pecha Cucha*, made use of the space as an actor in its own right. Based on the assumption that the average adult attention span is limited to twenty minutes, Pinto brought together several speakers, each of whom presented his or her topic of choice

4

Immersed in the Amazing Maze
Page 380

in relation to the *Salon*'s themes in only fifteen minutes, while using the furniture as props for each of their performances. Conversely, the *Bar Populaire* event format developed its conception from the furniture itself. The bar-cum-puppet show element took center stage in our own crossbreed of a social and content-based get-together, in which two guests from Berlin's cultural context, who would normally not necessarily have the opportunity, time, or occasion to meet and talk, suggested a topic and asked friends and colleagues to join them for a drink at the *Salon*'s bar. The social function of a common architectural device was purposefully enhanced, so that the often secretly worshipped byproduct of a cultural event – the chat – turned into its main act, confronting attendees with the challenge of filling the resulting gap. Through the expectation of acquiring surplus meaning (different than at a "mere" party), each and every one of the guests suddenly lost his/her comfortable consumer position and became personally responsible for the evening's gains. Finally, the most elaborate event series/format was a banquet, *Can you pass the salt, please?*, organized in collaboration with Greek architect Fotini Lazaridou-Hatzigoga. In line with Plato's idea of the symposium, we arranged several thematic dinner conversations. For each event, we invited and asked guests to subscribe to and each submit their philosophical texts, personal experiences, stories, and thoughts, while a passionate cook prepared an opulent multicourse dinner. Within this sensuous and intimate, although purposefully not private atmosphere, the conversations would go beyond the usual dining small talk, but remained more personal than a public seminar or podium discussion. In this series, the furniture took a backseat, as it served "only" as an atmospheric device to signify the space's texture. Its presence was no less important, however: it marked the in-between status of the *Salon*, from which its entire potential was derived.

A second, significantly different example, which nonetheless has important structural similarities, is the flexible display furniture, *Elegant Scaffolding*, designed by Dutch architecture studio EventArchitectuur. The furniture ensemble has provided ready-to-use working and presentation facilities for the *Studiolo* at KW Institute for Contemporary Art since I started there as its chief curator in 2013. My first move when taking up the position at this renowned Berlin institution was to analyze the building and find out how the institutional program made use of its different spaces.

For many different reasons, among them financial and infrastructural restraints, the house had been predominantly used for exhibitions, which mostly covered all floors of the rear building, plus a project space on the ground floor in the front house in recent years; other parts of the institution were not publicly accessible. In my view, however, KW had never been merely a venue for exhibitions, but also a place for artistic production, for study, for public debate, and for experiences, among many other things.

Hence, I created a structure of different spaces with varying uses, different time economies, and addressing different kinds of audiences as a result. Firstly, the four exhibition floors in the rear building were divided into two units: the ground floor and big exhibition hall became *Basis*, hosting projects for broader audiences, while the first and second floors, which are connected by an opening in the downstairs ceiling, were renamed *1+2*.[6] The third, most charismatic floor, was given a new function: it turned into the *Chora*, the newly created space for public programs. The term "chora" comes from Plato's dialogue, *Timaeus* (ca. 360 BCE), in which he refers to a space, a container, which can also be a place in between the sensual and the intelligible, between truth and necessity. *Chora* offers a space to all discourses, but has no fixed form in itself. Practically speaking, a varied program – from discussions and lectures through workshops, performances, film screenings, and concerts – is organized every Thursday by KW's staff and its long-term partners, and regularly draws a diverse audience.

As its smaller sibling, the *Studiolo* is located in the front house of KW, farther away from the exhibitions and its visitors. The term "studiolo" stems from the Renaissance (the same time period when the precursors of the salon first took shape) and designates a type of space that is equally dedicated to study and an engagement with the arts. I first heard about this kind of space from a Berlin-based artist, architect, and friend, Erik Göngrich. Erik was excited about what from today's perspective is a doubly coined spatial conception, since the studiolo both hosted (and presented) artworks, and was equipped with books and other objects of study. In contrast to the salon, which adopted any social space that was available in its respective environment, the studiolo established a new type of space – and prioritized the aspect of individual research over the social within an otherwise consistent setup.

The studiolo combined an active space for knowledge acquisition with contemplative reflection; functions that have since become strictly divided spatially. While, for Erik, the historical studiolo served as an inspiration for a public sculpture, I wanted to translate its original qualities to the needs and expectations of a contemporary art institution. In his painting, *St. Jerome in his Study* (ca. 1475), Antonello da Messina (1430–1479) depicts the studiolo as a space within a larger space, only half separated from its public surroundings, and used by only one man. Like before, its current version at KW adapts the original insofar as it intends to preserve the intimacy of the space, while conceiving of it as

6 Additional smaller and more flexible exhibition programming is conducted at KW projects, which is freely accessible from the courtyard, across from the café, and in the tiny 3 ½, comprising six square meters, diverting from the staircase between the third and fourth floors.

4

Immersed in the Amazing Maze
Page 382

common property (unlike the salon, which always needs a clearly defined host). As a semipublic space, which is both an integral part of the institution and withdrawn from its daily business, it facilitates participation-based discussions, internal workshops, and develops interpersonal performance formats, as well as ephemeral, exhibition-like presentations. The space holds a growing library for KW's team, guests and residents, and is open to the public only for events and by appointment. Bigger team meetings or juries are held here, as well as press conferences and dinners, and sometimes even parties.

Against this background, the brief for EventArchitectuur was to develop a multi-use architecture that could create a setup for any of the institution's spaces and its formats, but was neither an exhibition display nor merely functional furniture. Similar to raumlabor's conception for the non-institutional *Salon*, *Elegant Scaffolding* aimed to define a space and facilitate encounters within it, but as opposed to the previous, clearly social surrounding, its elements were in-between objects in a different way at KW: partly exhibited work in itself, partly accommodation for art and people, partly institutional CI.

Against the eccentric theatricality of the *Salon* furniture, *Elegant Scaffolding* focuses on a modest, expandable system composed of a double layer of light birch wood painted in shiny red from below as a surface, and aluminum frames providing the rack system. The completed components to date are a bar, a counter, a presentation facility, and straight and curved tables and benches. All elements can be combined at will.

The institutional surrounding of KW requires more intimacy than the *Salon*, whose configuration deliberately charged the location and infused the atmosphere with expectation, which served to distinguish it from both the bourgeois apartment surroundings and the traditional shabbiness of Berlin project spaces. The institution is a highly performative place from the outset, where practitioners and audiences are equally aware of their acting in public, and this piece of institutional identity was meant to build confidence and proximity between individuals. *Elegant Scaffolding* connects the exhibition area, where publications and other accompanying materials often complement the information counter, with *Chora*, where the bar serves as a stable point of reference throughout diverse programs, and further to the *Studiolo*, its "home base." Also a former apartment, but less atmospheric than *Salon Populaire*, EventArchitectuur's sophisticated yet simple tables, benches, and voluminous objects form the backbone of the institution's only semipublic space. Used by the team and colleagues, as well as the public, the *Studiolo* mediates between the visible and invisible structures of the institution. For the team, the space feels more representative than the offices, and thus heightens the perceived importance of a gathering; here, professionals are welcomed to enter the backstage area of the institution. Though the broader audience is not explicitly excluded from this terrain, there is definitely a threshold to cross: anyone coming to *Studiolo* makes the decision to abandon the status of a mere spectator and become a participant – someone who engages with the institution and its contents.

Elegant Scaffolding adds a layer to the complex fabric of the institution and the experiences it intends to enable. It interjects an element of unclear status towards the established variables of exhibition and social spaces, artworks and their arrangement, and visitor behavior – like a ball, which has no function as an object alone and takes on meaning only when it is tossed, marking the player in possession of it as the one driving the game forward. In his study, *The Parasite*, French philosopher Michel Serres calls materials or forms that reveal their full function only in relation to other elements "quasi-objects."[7] According to Serres, quasi-objects mark a subject in a specific way, and form a bridge to other subjects. Just like these quasi-objects, *Elegant Scaffolding* changes its function when activated in a particular constellation. It is the mutual reference to its deliberately open-ended status – both artwork and support structure, but at the same time neither – that has a significant share in forming a community and preparing the setup for experiences.

7 Michel Serres, *The Parasite*, trans. Lawrence R. Schehr (Minneapolis: University of Minnesota Press, 2007).

4

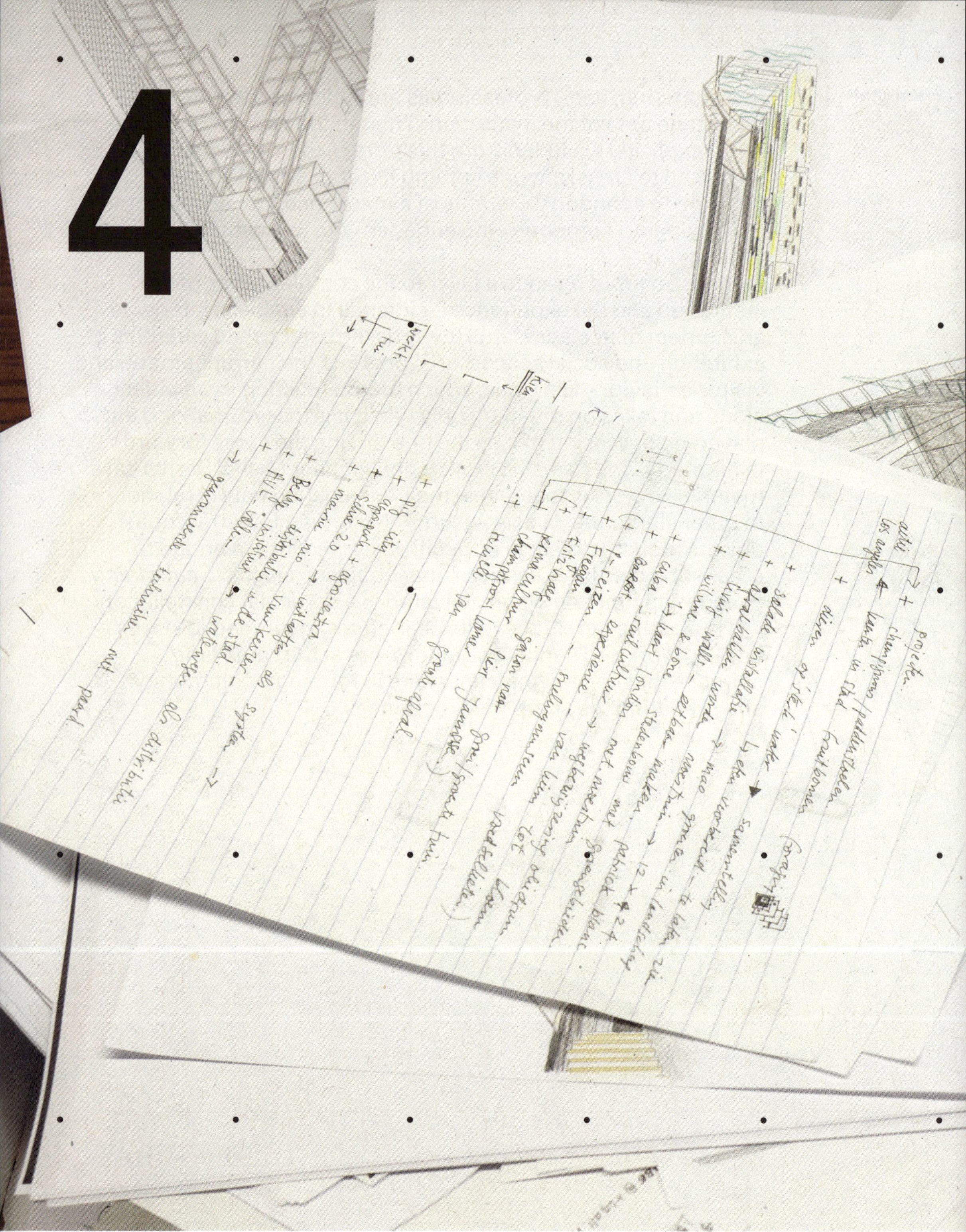

Events: Situating the Temporary
Page 384

project 149

2007

Immersed in the Amazing Maze
Page 385

The Edible City
Project: Exhibition
Duration: Medium-term, 4 months
Year: 2007
Data: page 658

Immersed in the Amazing Maze
Page 386

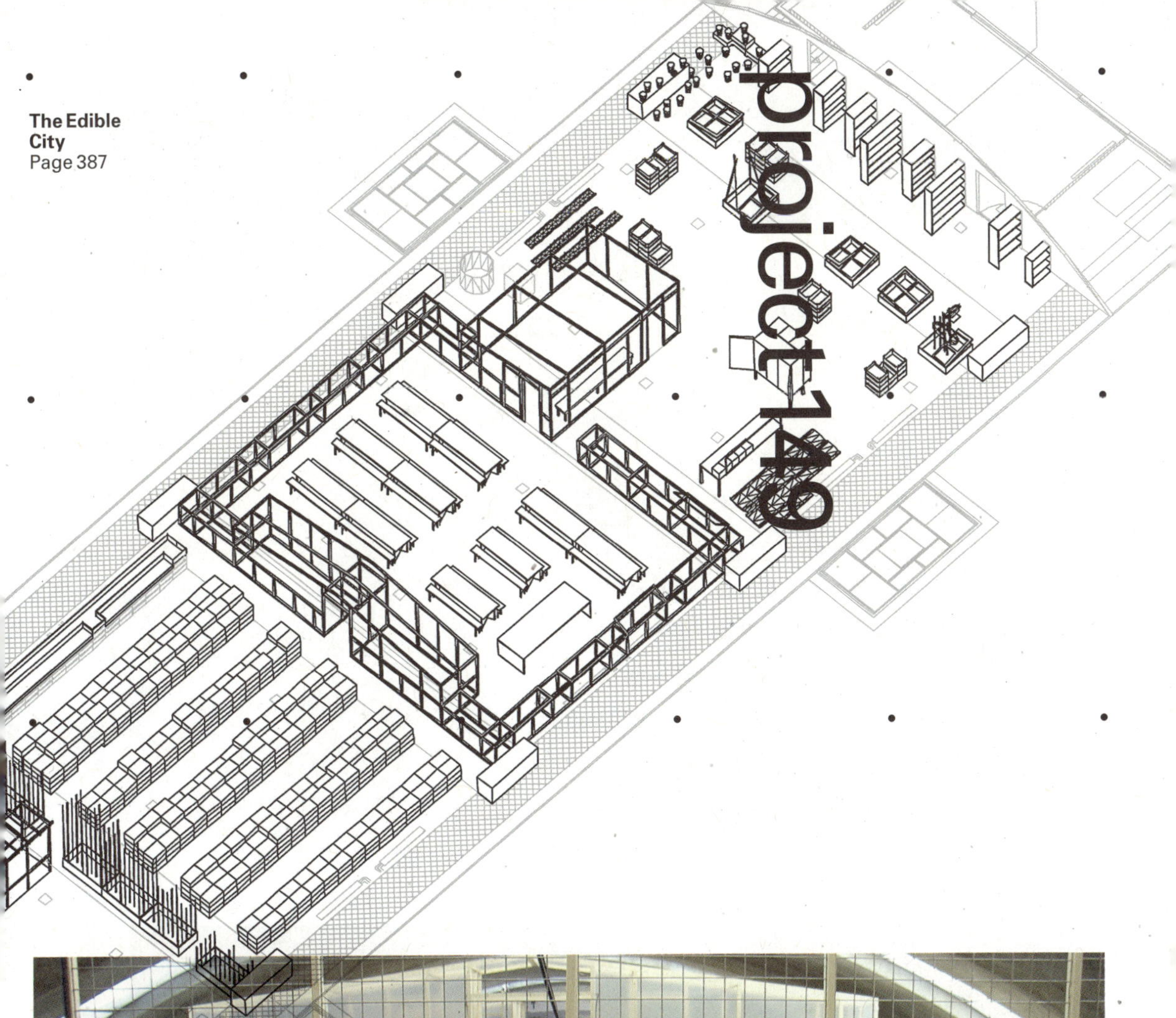
project149

THE EDIBLE CITY

Immersed in the Amazing Maze
Page 388

project 19

Immersed in the Amazing Maze
Page 390

project 149

4

Events: Situating the Temporary

Page 392

project 154

2008

Immersed in the Amazing Maze
Page 393

Warmoesmarkt
Project: Grocery Store
Duration: Long-term, 2 years
Year: 2008
Data: page 659

Immersed in the Amazing Maze
Page 394

project 154

Warmoesmarkt, Amsterdam
Page 395

Immersed in the Amazing Maze
Page 396

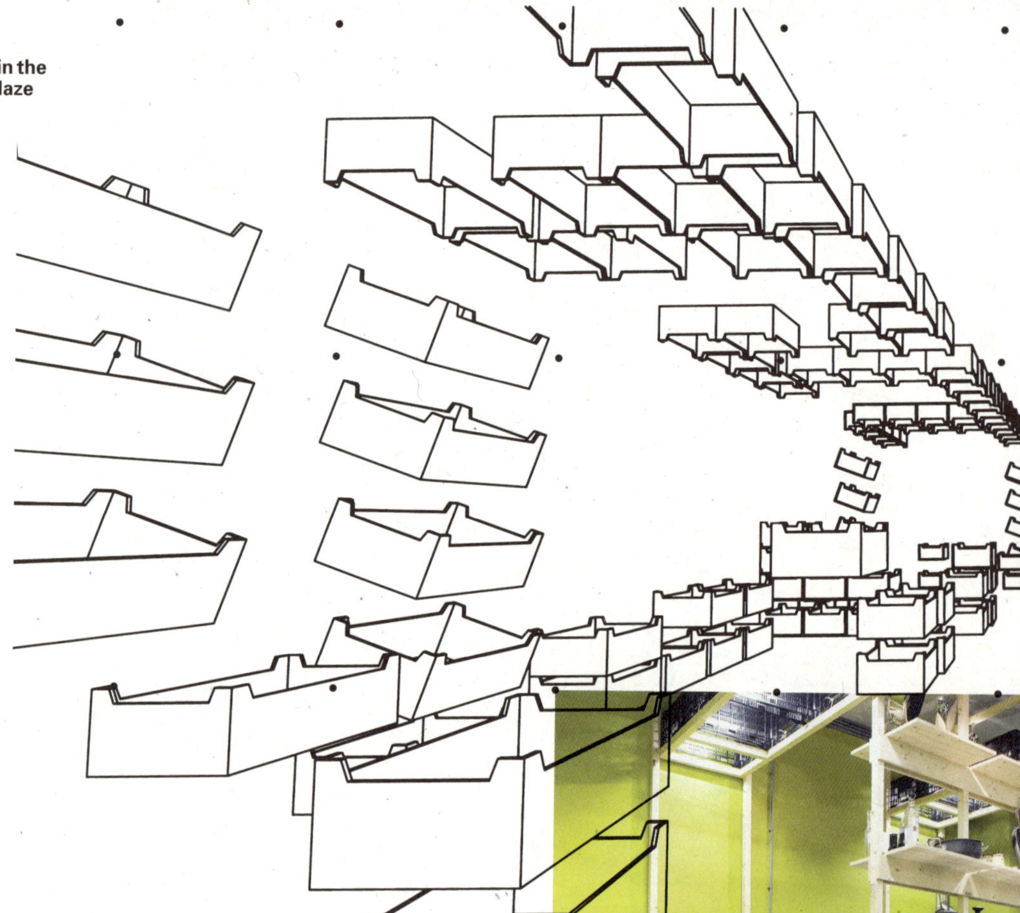

Warmoesmarkt, Amsterdam
Page 397

project 154

4

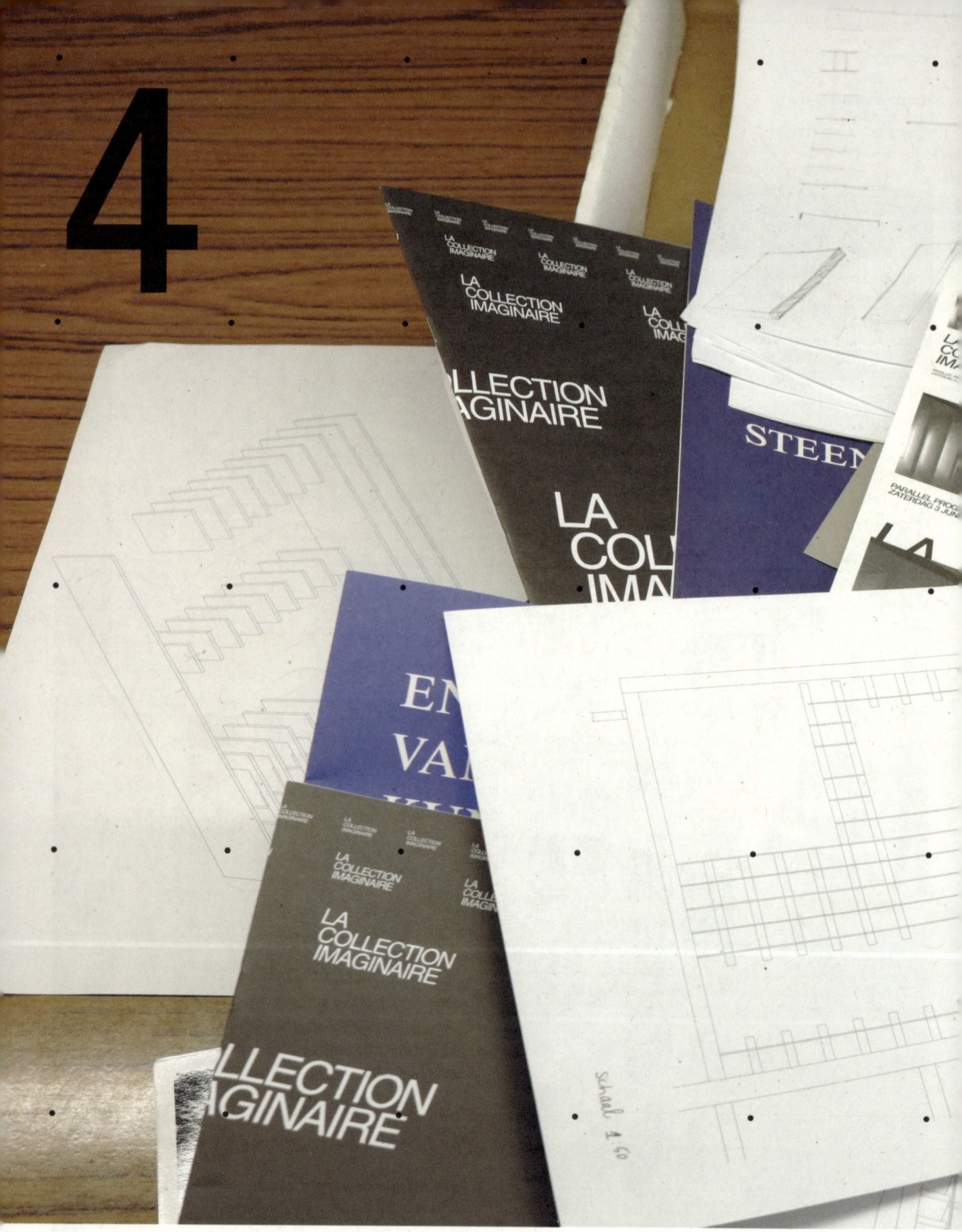

Events: Situating the Temporary

Page 398

project 130

2006

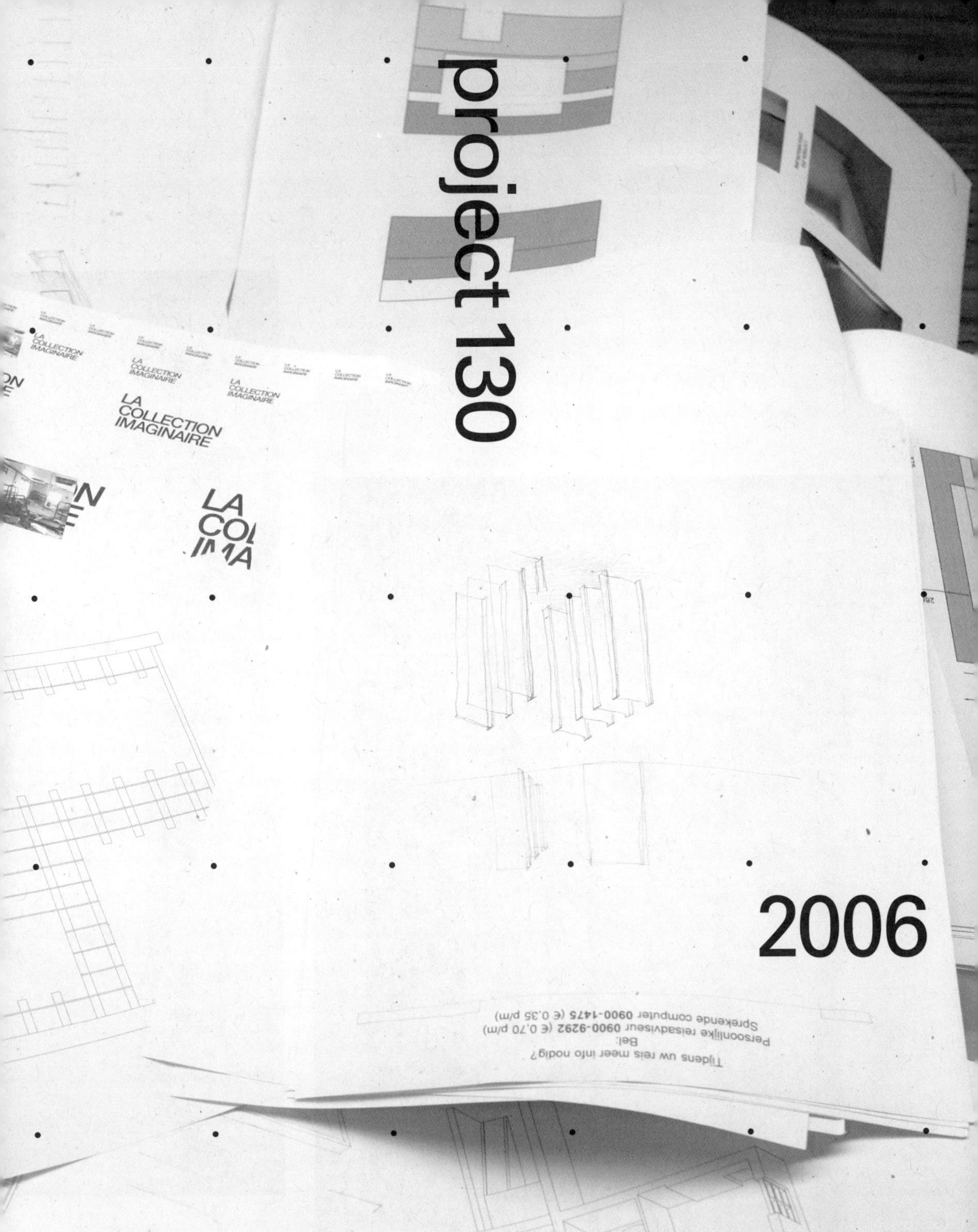

Immersed in the Amazing Maze
Page 399

La Collection Imaginaire
Project: Installation
Duration: Medium-term, 3 months
Year: 2006
Data: page 654

Immersed in the Amazing Maze
Page 400

project 130

Immersed in the Amazing Maze
Page 402

project 130

le collectionneur imaginaire

There is no such thing as a monogamous collector. The sight is a promiscuous sense. The avid gaze always wants more. [...] So the collector is a dissembler, someone whose joys are never unalloyed with anxiety. Because there is always more. Or something better.[1]
– Susan Sontag, *The Volcano Lover*

Le collectionneur imaginaire

Renée Steenbergen

Collectors entertain an equivocal relationship with the physical aspect of art. The fact that artworks are objects you can buy, own, and perhaps sell on again constitutes a major part of their appeal. Art possesses a tangibility, a material presence, that collectors desire to feel around them. But no sooner do they have it, then the hunt is on for the next object they want to appropriate, in order to bring it within their intimate circle.
The next acquisition is always the most beautiful. That is the hypnotic allure that holds the collector captive: he must always keep going, further, on the way to more, better, more complete. Yet physical substance is only one of the attractions of collecting. It is not the object that is temporary – we are, thanks to our mortality. Sooner or later, we will have to leave behind all those so zealously coveted and guarded objects, at least their physical form.
But, in our heads, we are able to carry the biggest, most massive collections around with us wherever we go. Collecting is first and last a mind game that the collector plays with himself.

There, in the mind's eye, the collection is safely ensconced, protected from deterioration, and from the incomprehension of non-collectors. For ordinary mortals, the most beautiful artworks are notional, for it is only in their imagination that they are able to access them. In his series of essays entitled *Le Musée Imaginaire*, André Malraux described this phenomenon thus: "But our knowledge covers a wider field than our museums... the assemblage of so many masterpieces – from which, nevertheless, so many are missing – conjures up in the mind's eye *all* the world's masterpieces."[2]

1
Susan Sontag, *The Volcano Lover* (New York: Farrar, Straus and Giroux, 1992), 71–72.

2
André Malraux, *The Voices of Silence*, trans. Stuart Gilbert (Garden City, New York: Doubleday & Co., Inc., 1953), 14.

An art collector collects visual impressions, sensory perceptions. A collector once admitted to me his hope of one day being able to purchase a performance: "That is ephemeral art; it's purely of the moment. To my mind, that is the ultimate possession: an exceptionally beautiful memory." He joins a long line of accumulators of immaterial, but in no way fictional, collections. Wine collectors, for example, do not lay down a collection of bottles, but of flavors. Writers and poets collect dialogues and phrases, music lovers accumulate sounds, and balletomanes fill their memory with movements. The ability to fantasize is an important aspect of the game; it gives the collection a reach it would not otherwise attain. Via this purely intellectual collecting, masterpieces can be added to the collection, great works that are, in reality, quite beyond the reach of the collector. Moreover, notionally arranged in striking juxtapositions, these trophies acquire unsuspected meanings, which lend the imaginary collection an inimitable stature.

Through these dreams of passionately coveted and mentally appropriated artworks, the collector also acquires a different status. No longer a mere mortal at the mercy of restrictions and limits, he can finally play the starring role of, say, the logical collector. He is the collector with complete self-control, who never succumbs to impulse purchases. He can afford to wait until a masterpiece comes along that satisfies his highest standards and that richly deserves a place within the imaginary collection.
Such an ideal collector may also aspire to possess fewer and fewer objects of greater and greater quality, until, in theory, only a single work of art remains. This object stands for all things; it represents the universe. At this point, the ideal collector resembles the Creator himself. In his novel, *Rituals*, Cees Nooteboom describes an eccentric collector who for years has waited and saved for one exquisite Japanese *raku* bowl, which tradition demands should be destroyed at the conclusion of the tea ceremony. Having finally procured the bowl, and having used it in the ritual, he duly smashes it, and then kills himself. His mission as collector has been accomplished, and with that, his life is fulfilled.
Literature abounds with imaginary collections and fascinating imaginary collectors. What impression emerges when we consider these fictional art lovers? What drives them, what do they dream about, what do their imaginary collections look like?
Interestingly, collectors – real and fictitious – are greatly fascinated by their collecting behavior, and are constantly reflecting upon it. For example, Susan Sontag's Cavaliere – based on the historical figure of Sir William Hamilton – is a British diplomat in eighteenth-century Italy and a collector of antiquities. Thinking about his mania for collecting, he muses, "Collecting... is a succession of desires. The true collector is in the grip not of what is collected, but of collecting."[3] He concludes, "The collector's need is precisely for excess, for surfeit, for profusion... a collection is always more than is necessary."[4]

Excess, indeed, is the hallmark of every collection. Take Kaspar Utz, a Czech baron who accumulated a peerless collection of Meissen porcelain behind the Iron Curtain. Over a thousand pieces he had hidden away from the communist regime – Bruce Chatwin's novel is set in 1967 – in a cramped, two-room apartment in Prague. Art, after all, was supposed to be for the people; it was not permitted as a decadent private pleasure. Utz is a modern-day Augustus II the Strong, suffering from *Porzellankrankheit*. He sees himself as the savior of this precious eighteenth-century art form, which time and again prevents him from fleeing to the West. How could he think of leaving his harlequin, his knave, the porcelain shepherdess behind, unprotected?
Utz is motivated by the prohibition, in a dual sense: he collects human figurines, while his Jewish faith forbids the depiction and worship of graven images (as do Islam and Protestantism, for that matter). This precious but fragile collection forms a bulwark against the world, in the same way as the huge book collection of Professor Kien does in Elias Canetti's novel, *Auto-da-Fé*. The same motive drives decadent aesthete Jean des Esseintes who, after a life of excess, has withdrawn from the vulgar everyday world in favor of a life lived in

3
Sontag, *The Volcano Lover*, 24.

4
Ibid., 72.

sublime isolation. French symbolist writer Joris Karl Huysmans portrays him in *Against the Grain* as a man who has become so hypersensitive to every sensory impression that he has obscured his windows against daylight and lives only at night. His eyes can only abide images that are infused with an immense but terrible beauty. This dream collection consists exclusively of existing masterworks, the pièce de résistance being Gustave Moreau's stunning *Salomé*, the showpiece of French Orientalism.

Impotence and jealousy seem to be the motives driving American collector Gilbert Osmond, depicted by Henry James in his novel, *Portrait of a Lady*. This expatriate American and failed artist represents the stereotype of the male collector who is capable of loving only objects. Objects do not change, they do not age, they seldom disappoint. Osmond is a misanthropist and a misogynist, and marries solely to get his hands on his unsuspecting wife's fortune, so as to use it to expand his collection of antiquities and antiques.
Revenge is the dark motivating force of the German-American brewer and collector, Hermann Raffke. The fabulous art collection imputed to him by his creator, Georges Perec, turns out, after his death – and after having been auctioned off for vast sums of money – to contain nothing but forgeries. Once upon a time, Raffke had been sold forged artworks by crooked art dealers, and when he discovered the deception, he decided to pay the art world back in kind by assembling a collection of imaginary masterpieces.

By contrast, a genuine love of art is the faithful companion of Sylvain Pons, a kindly, naive musician, but an extremely fanatical collector. He is the creation of Honoré de Balzac, himself a frenetic collector, whose pursuit of antiques and curios almost bankrupted him. In *Cousin Pons*, Balzac depicted him as a victim of his social milieu. As soon as it becomes clear that the good-natured fool, now gravely ill, has amassed a very valuable collection, his landlady and distant relations gather like vultures around his collection. The novelist may well have hoped that his own collection of bric-a-brac would someday turn out to be worth a fortune... One quite literal imaginary collection is that of Franz Kronfeld, the blind collector conjured up by Stefan Zweig in the short story, *The Invisible Collection*.
The elderly, now blind, art lover is unaware that during the course of the recession that followed the First World War, his family has gradually sold off his precious prints, filling the passe-partouts with blank sheets of paper. Every day, the unsuspecting, proud owner still fingers all the works – having assimilated them so completely while still sighted that he now has no trouble *looking at them* in his memory.[5]

This image represents the ideal that many collectors envisage: to be able, at some stage, to live without material art, purely with the visual (after) images in their mind. Anyone with a sufficiently vivid imagination, who trains their visual memory well, should be able to make do with that, according to the ideal: mental appropriation as the ultimate form of ownership that renders the more vulgar, material ownership – which can also be taken away from you – superfluous. Yet, deep in their heart, collectors know that they cannot live without the tangible, sensory experience of art. The ultimate imaginary collection has about it something of a perfect museum, arranged personally by the art lover, but one in which you are permitted to touch everything. In the words of the porcelain collector, Kaspar Utz, "An object in a museum case must suffer the de-natured existence of an animal in a zoo. In any museum, the object dies – of suffocation and the public gaze – whereas private ownership confers on the owner the right and need to touch. As a young child will reach out to handle a thing it names, so the passionate collector... restores to the object the life-giving touch of its maker."[6] And, if that object is not accessible, collectors – real *and* imaginary – bring them to life in their mind.

5
Stephan Zweig, *The Invisible Collection*, trans. Anthea Bell (London: Pushkin Press, 2015), 118.

6
Kaspar Joachim Utz, "The Private Collector," in Bruce Chatwin, *Utz* (London: Jonathan Cape, 1988), 20.

le collectionneur imaginaire

4

Events: Situating the Temporary
Page 408

project 156, 162

2008

Immersed in the Amazing Maze
Page 409

Changing Ideals / State Alpha
Project: Exhibition
Duration: Medium-term, 3 months
Year: 2008
Data: page 659, page 661

Immersed in the Amazing Maze
Page 410

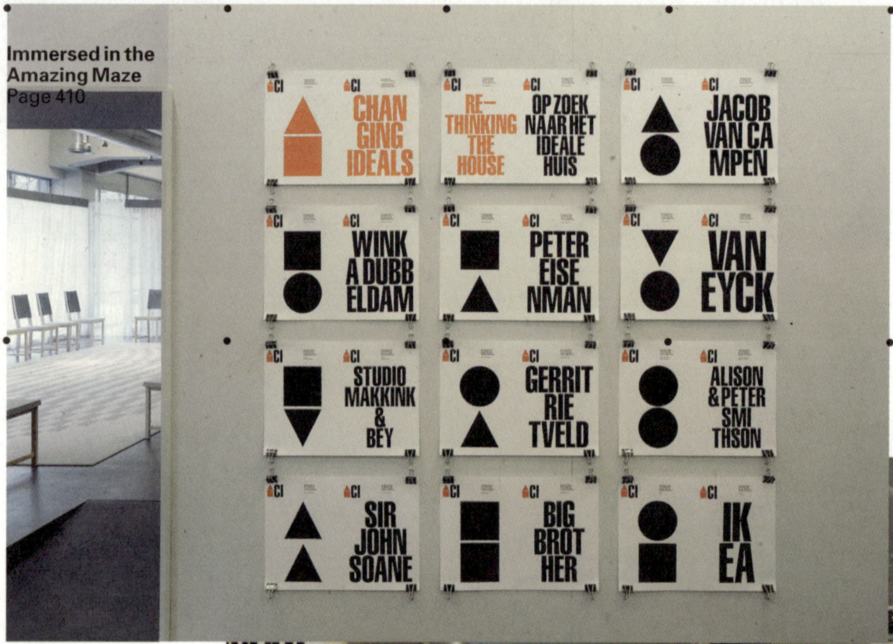

project156

VISS

project 156

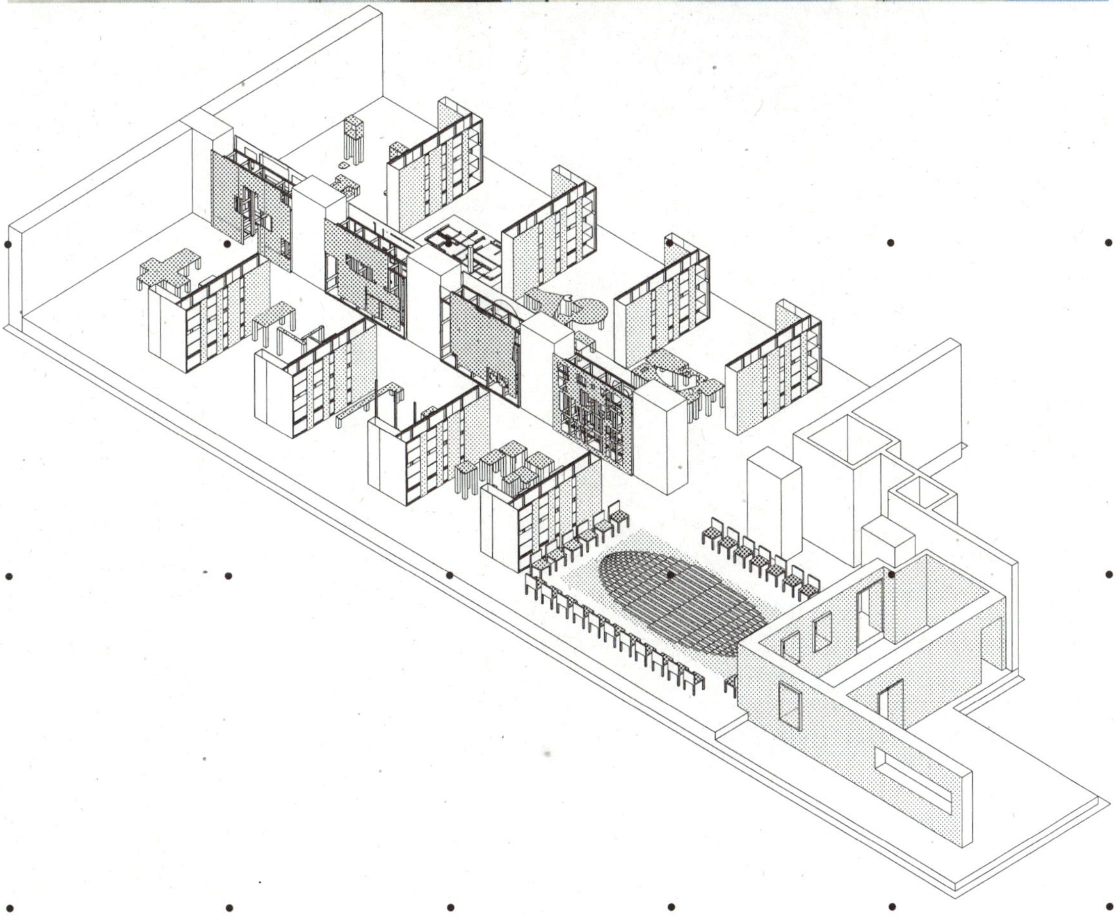

Immersed in the Amazing Maze
Page 414

project 162

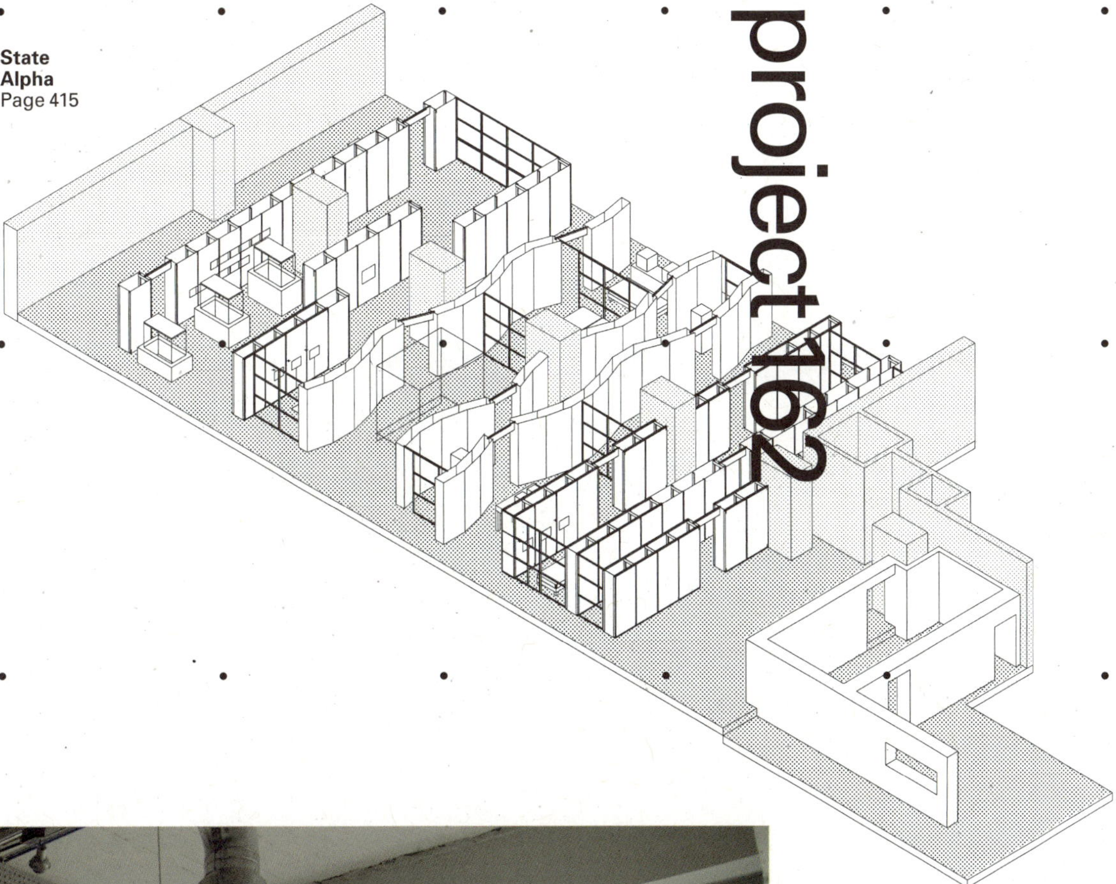

Immersed in the Amazing Maze
Page 416

project 162

4

Events: Situating the Temporary

project 159

2008

Immersed in the Amazing Maze
Page 419

NL = New Luxury
Project: Fashion Store
Duration: Long-term, 3 years
Year: 2008
Data: page 660

Immersed in the
Amazing Maze
Page 420

project 159

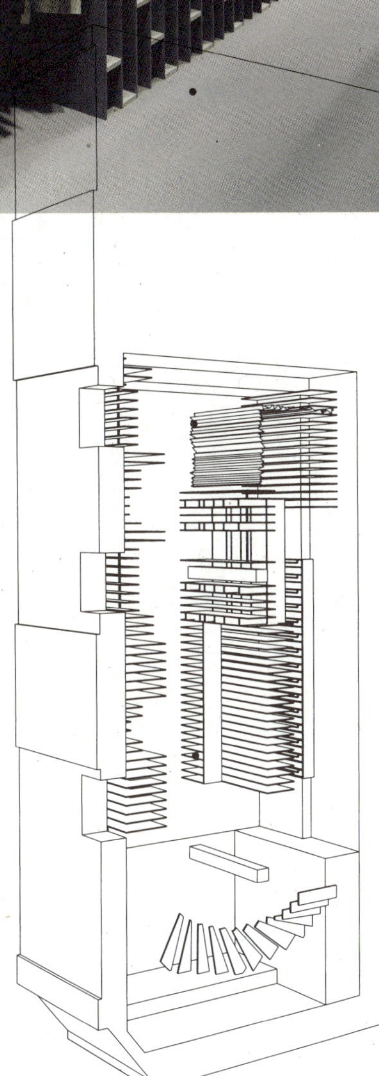

Immersed in the Amazing Maze
Page 422

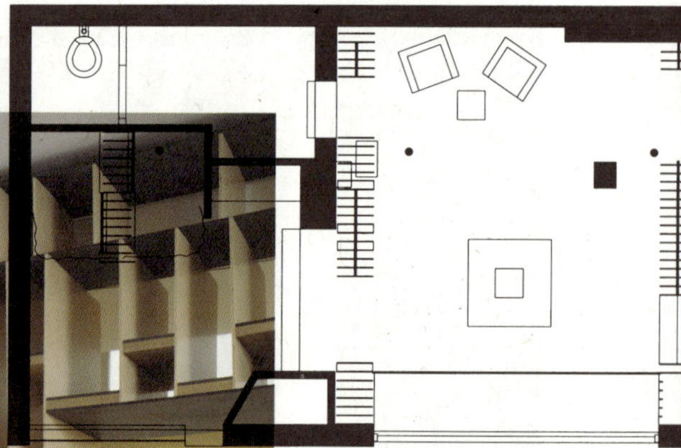

NL =
New Luxury
Page 423

project 159

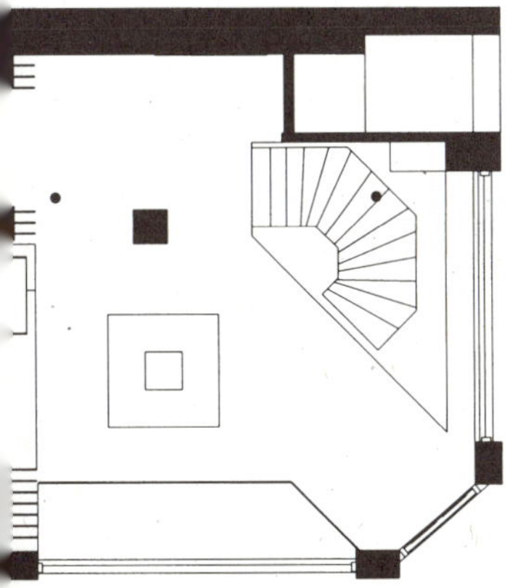

4

Events: Situating the Temporary
Page 424

project 107, 145

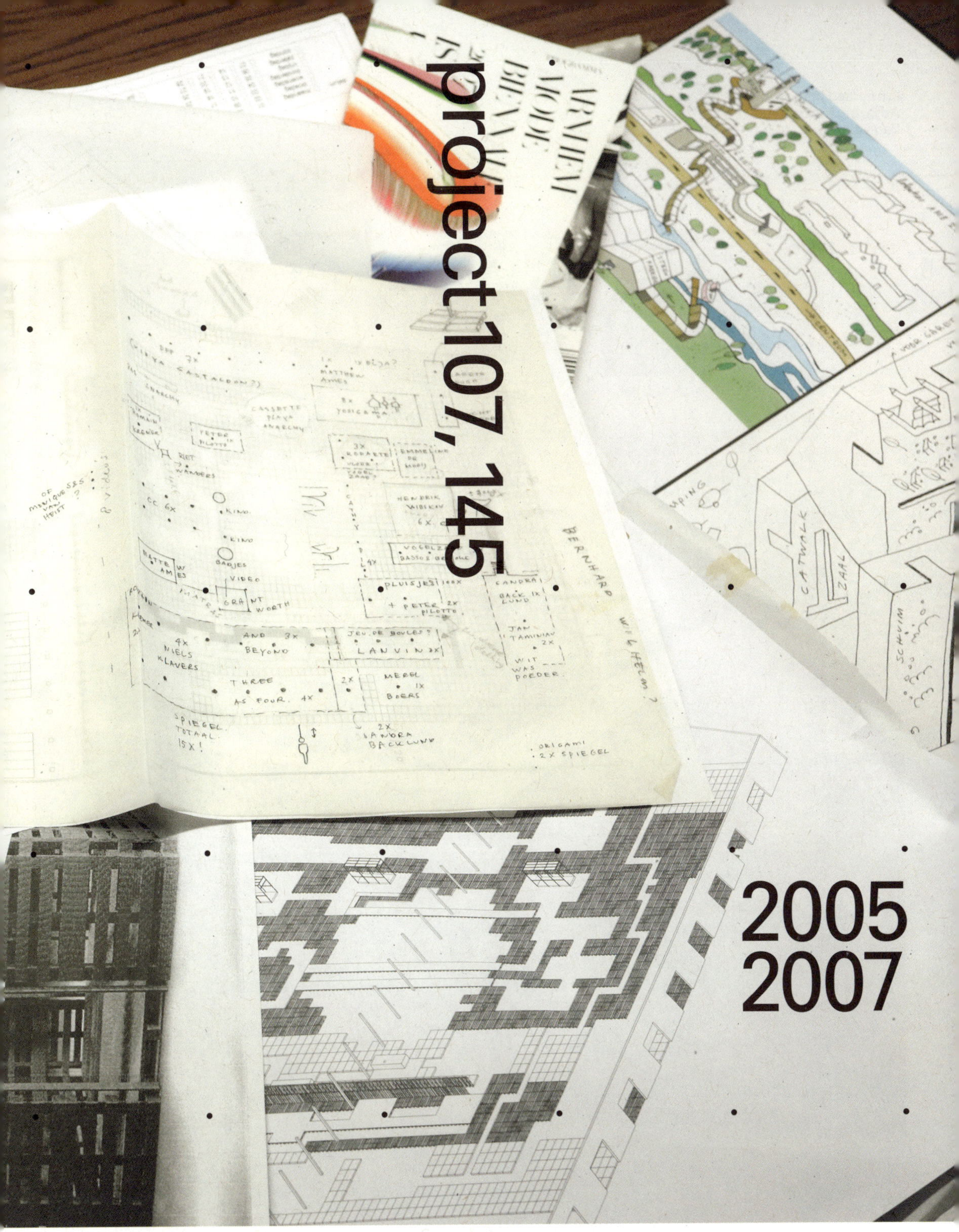

2005 2007

Immersed in the Amazing Maze
Page 425

Arnhem Fashion Biennale
Project: Exhibition
Duration: Short-term, 1 month
Year: 2005, 2007
Data: page 650, page 657

Immersed in the Amazing Maze
Page 426

project 107

Immersed in the Amazing Maze
Page 428

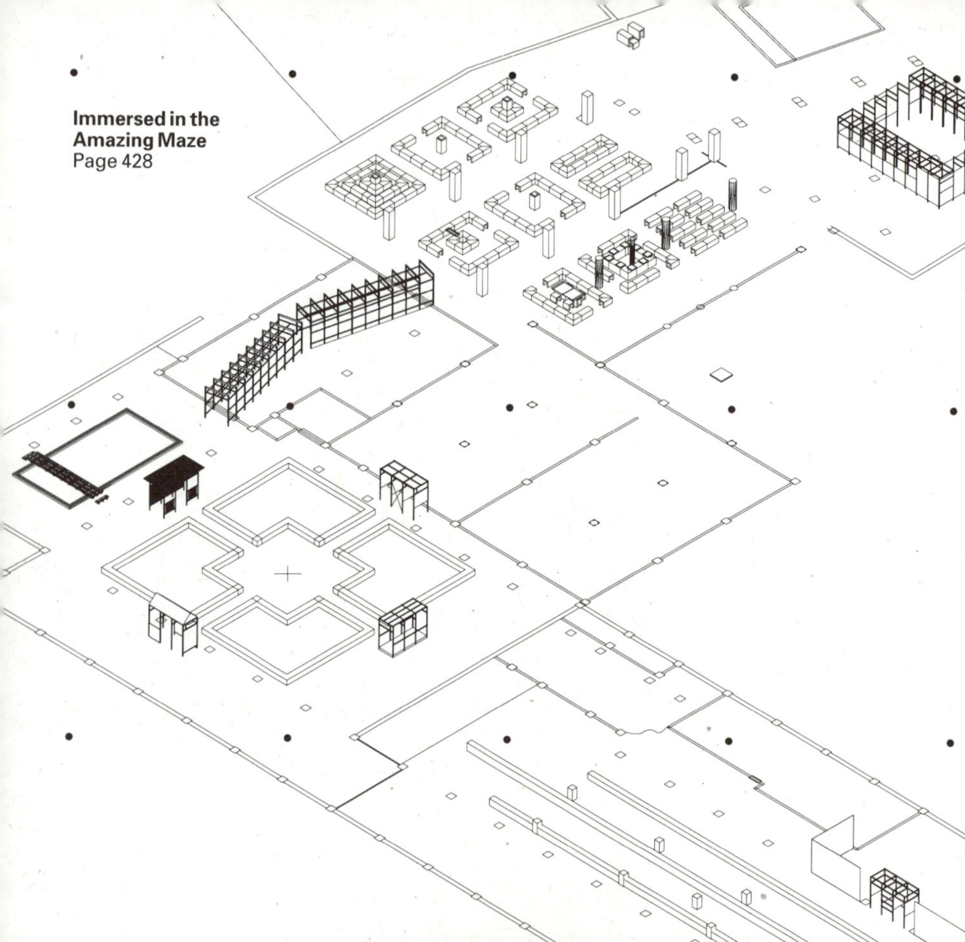

Arnhem Fashion Biennale, 2005
Page 429

project 107

Immersed in the Amazing Maze
Page 430

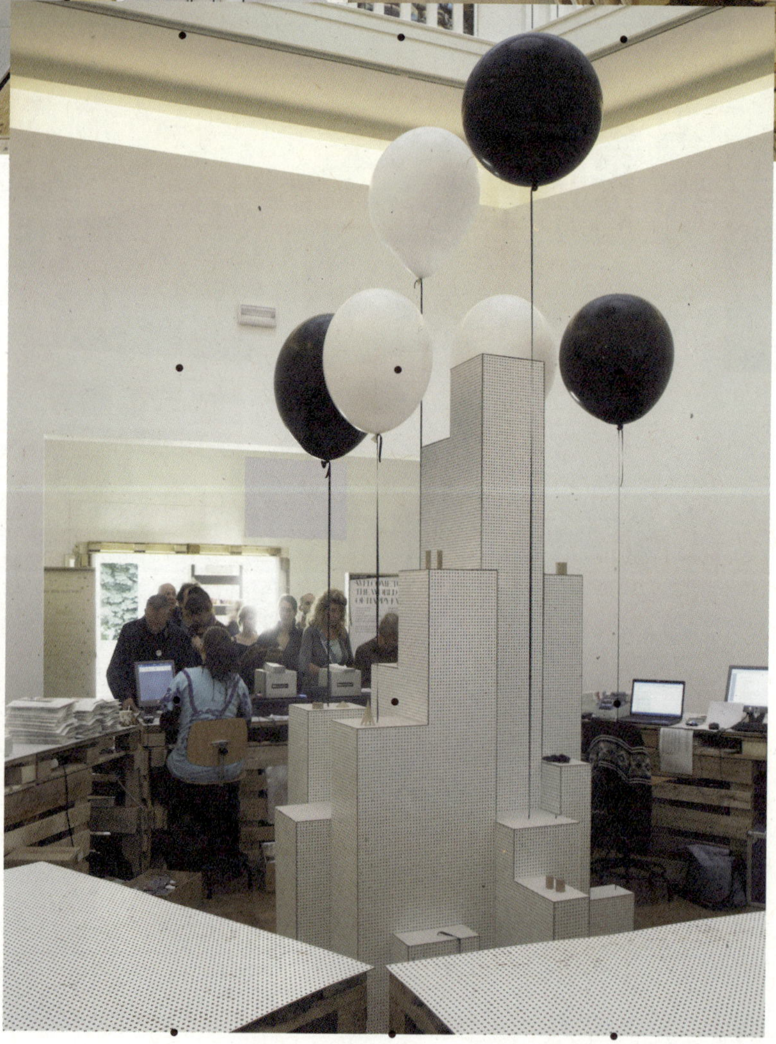

project 145

Arnhem Fashion Biennale, 2007
Page 431

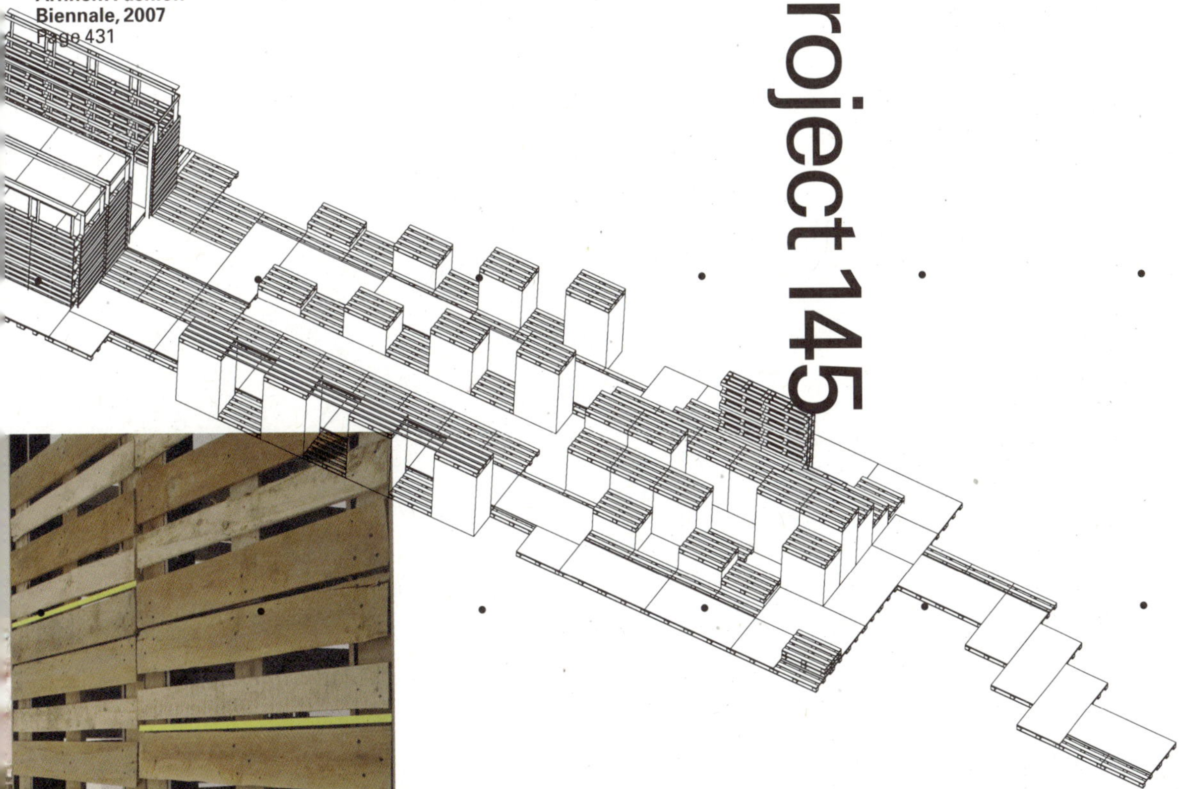

Immersed in the Amazing Maze
Page 432

Arnhem Fashion Biennale, 2007
Page 433

project 145

4 andreas angelidakis:

Events: Situating the Temporary
Page 434

collage: Andreas Angelidakis

Immersed in the Amazing Maze
Page 435

a brief moment in the history of white walls

State Museum of Contemporary Art
photo: Andreas Angelidakis

A rock and a hard place
The 3rd Thessaloniki Biennial took place in 2011, just as Greece was beginning to feel very attacked, due to its shaky economy. The Biennial's curators, Paolo Colombo, Mahita El Bacha Urieta, and Marina Fokidis, spoke of the exhibition they were planning as a temporary respite from the crisis, a party that you throw when you know it's all over. I was asked to come up with ways in which the exhibition could inhabit the Biennial's ten venues, five museums and five historical buildings. I began to think of the exhibition architecture as that device which would create a moment of calm before the storm, a way of protecting the art from the crisis.
Curiously, the city's most often used emblem is a white tower, a leftover from a set of fourteenth-century fortification infrastructure of white walls. It was built by architect Mimar Sinan on commission from Sultan Murad III, who had just captured the city and wanted to fortify his new acquisition. I began to hallucinate on the relation of this white tower and the long gone white fortification walls that surrounded the city, and the white walls that one almost always provides to an exhibition design. Could these white cube walls act as the Biennial's conceptual fortification? Did they think they could protect us from the bad times ahead? Is a gallery wall ever allowed to have such heroic ambitions? The ten Biennial venues were spread out across the city, and each one had its own micro-history, so this would have to be a story told in parts.

A room inside a room
Casa Bianca is an early twentieth-century eclectic villa, long rumored to be inhabited by the ghost of a daughter who fell in love with an Italian sergeant during World War II. Maybe the ghost could give us a hand? The Walls decide that the villa is no longer strong enough to withstand attacks, and its interior too precious to accept reinforcements. By adding a room inside a room, a second layer of wall surrounds the work of the artists and the villa becomes stronger. The Walls are painted white on the inside, but decide to leave their unseen side unpainted; this is a moment of crisis, after all, and we cannot spend money on something no one will see.

Unfortunately, the standard panel of wood that the Walls are to be made of is shorter than the glamorous four-meter-high ceiling that Dino Fernandez Diaz built for his family under the guidance of architect Pietro Arrigoni, so the original rooms are still visible once the new, shorter rooms are inside them. Moreover, the doors to the new rooms don't match the doors to the old rooms exactly, leaving the unpainted and unfinished side of the wall slightly visible. The Walls are intrigued by these mishaps, and begin to question the facilities of contemporary standardized construction versus the made-to-measure luxuries of the past. The overall effect of mismatched rooms is somewhat intriguing to the visitor, so the Walls remain undecided as to whether this was a fortification failure or an architectural triumph. In the next venue, we'll try something different, they say.

Yeni Djami
photo: Andreas Angelidakis

Double protection

Yeni Djami is a building of double identities. Everybody knows it as the Old Archaeological Museum, even though it was clearly a mosque. But even as a mosque, it had a double identity. It was built by a faction of the Jewish community that had converted to Islam, otherwise known as *dönmeh*. The *dönmeh* were in fact rumored to be crypto-Jews that had publicly converted to Islam to avoid the inferior condition of the *dhimmi* in the Ottoman Empire. So they built a mosque that ended up looking much more like a synagogue. In studying this curious history, the Walls begin to imagine ways they could tell this story, because apparently walls want to tell stories, too. The building in question seems quite strong in comparison to Casa Bianca, so no extra layer of walls is needed, let alone that the walls of the mosque are even higher than those of the villa. But the building tells the Walls that the main problem here is that the door is too big, and it leads directly to the main prayer room. The mosque that looks like a synagogue, but everybody calls a museum, feels too exposed. Also, the quick entry process makes for a boring exhibition experience, because once you've stepped in, you've seen it all.

The Walls decide to fix this by adding two fortification walls. One outside the mosque, another inside, blocking the entrance entirely. On the sides of the blocking wall they provide two small doors, which let you go inside the wall that is blocking the entrance. In fact, that wall is a crypto-corridor and, once inside, you find another door that eventually leads to the main space. The Walls are happy that the main space is protected, and the building is happy that it can provide the visitor with at least some sort of cinematic expectation.

Protect me from what I am

Looking more like a cross between a convention center

and a big pharmaceutical headquarters, the Teloglion was a curious choice of venue. Still, it is one of the municipal art centers, and the Biennial could use it for free. But how do you put works in a corporate building without making it look like tacky lobby art? The Walls decided that the real threat here was the building itself, and they took it upon themselves to protect the artworks and the visitor from the big chrome and marble extravaganza. The Walls made a set of rooms and corridors connected in a continuous path. Once you were in there, you wouldn't see the host structure anymore. To economize, they left the outside surface of the rooms unfinished, unpainted, and with exposed structural elements. From inside the atrium, these rooms ended up looking like wooden crates carelessly left inside the space, making no attempt to integrate themselves in this luxurious middle-of-the-road airport interior. Rumors spread that this was an intentional, passive-aggressive way for the Walls to express their displeasure with the banality of the host architecture.

top: **Teloglion**
bottom: **Alaca Imaret**
photos: Andreas Angelidakis

Blackout

A similar technique had to be used for the Macedonian Museum of Contemporary Art, an exhibition space almost entirely covered in white marble and unnecessary architectural aspirations. Too much architecture can be bad for an exhibition space, and this one had almost certainly overdosed, even though the 1980s PoMo vibe was amusing. Still, the Walls could not allow for works to be exhibited there, so they consulted with the curators and decided to place only screen-based works.

The space disappeared under a heavy coat of black paint. Suddenly, the space was nothing more than an enormous video room, where the visitor stumbled in the dark from projection to plasma screen, guided only by the little sunlight that the Walls allowed in.

Big plinth

Alaca Imaret is a fifteenth-century mosque that included a public charity kitchen. In Ottoman times, it was surrounded by housing for the poor, which by now had been replaced by a thick wall of poor-looking modernist blocks. The mosque stands there like an island of history inside a derelict yet vibrant neighborhood of people and cars and clotheslines. The Walls were inspired by the typology of the building as island, and decided to replicate that for the art. Inside the tall space of the mosque, the Walls laid down and made an enormous plinth. The plinth would hold up the entire exhibition, including smaller walls and the visitors themselves.

Two sets of steps allowed visitors to ascend the plinth, like a white island in a space of spiritual elevation.

4

Immersed in the Amazing Maze
Page 438

top: **Bey Hamam**
bottom: **Casa Bianca**
photos: Andreas Angelidakis

A building inside a building
Bey Hamam is a fifteenth-century bathhouse known for its opulent interior. How could a wall made of cheap composite wood ever inhabit this intricate labyrinth of carved marble and pink stucco? The Walls studied the floor plan of the labyrinthine space and realized there were just too many doors and passageways; a crisis could enter from anywhere. The Walls decided to superimpose another building on top of this building, because architects love to impose themselves and archaeologists love to analyze these kinds of superimpositions. The curators had chosen this venue as a site for all the archive-related projects of the Biennial, works that would require long periods of study by the visitors, just like the baths had offered long periods of relaxation to its bathers. The Walls began to transform themselves into a series of modules, each with a wall on one side and an added function on the other. A wall desk, a wall library, a wall vitrine, even a wall chair. The new wall modules formed an orthogonal perimeter, a kind of archive building, with the white wall side (let's call this the art side) on the interior, and all the other types of program on the outside. The archive wall was making an extra secure interior, as it passed through the pink-colored walls of the luxurious bathhouse. Looking nothing like the interior, it was to be an alien invader, an architecture of intrusion.

Breakup
The space of the State Museum of Contemporary Art was a monastery before it was an art place. The curators realized that the large communal halls were dangerous for the art, especially the arched colonnade, the red ceramic floor, and the awkward proportions of the rooms. The Walls had to provide protection from this multifaceted attack, so they just studied the solutions from all the previous venues. A platform floor like that used in Alaca Imaret would solve the problem of the floor. Placing rooms inside the rooms as they did in Casa Bianca would protect the visitor from the attention-seeking arches. And the unfinished exterior of Telloglion would provide some breathing space to the visitor, a space between entering the room and exploring the exhibition. The Walls placed a white cube space inside each of the large galleries, then preceeded to break each new object into four parts, to make the proportion more like a gallery and less like a garage. After breaking them up, they turned them around to face the white walls of the museum, and their backs to the colonnade. Each white room fragment had its own white floor, and the Walls proceeded to cut out more openings and windows. Now the visitor could step on and off the white space, get momentarily lost in the colonnade corridor, and explore the space in a meandering path. Works from

the museum's constructivist collection were placed on the museum walls, and works from the Biennial were placed on the new walls, because walls have curatorial aspirations, too.

Conclusion

It is clear that no wall can protect you from a financial crisis, but the Walls did enjoy the attempt, even as a distraction from reality. There were more venues in the Biennial, but these are not listed here, because the installations proposed for them were merely phantoms. They were designed just to use up the budget allocated to constructions in the ESPA contract for European funds. Once the budget was in place, the installations were canceled and exchanged for the production of new artworks, whose budget was significantly less compared to the construction budget. We could call these installations an architecture of sacrifice, there just to provide funding for what they meant to protect. What the Walls did provide was a narrative on how to place exhibitions inside historical venues, how to place a temporary exhibition architecture inside spaces that had existed for centuries. Instead of attempting to create perfect museum conditions in each of the venues, they focused on the distinctions between what was there and what was imported. Each shortcoming was turned into a narrative, a dialogue between different epochs of construction, generations of walls. Cheap MDF walls were placed inside opulent, sometimes ancient walls, and instead of apologizing for their lowly materiality, they decided to claim it as a conceptual approach in how to make an exhibition space in times of crisis.

State Museum of Contemporary Art
photo: Andreas Angelidakis

4

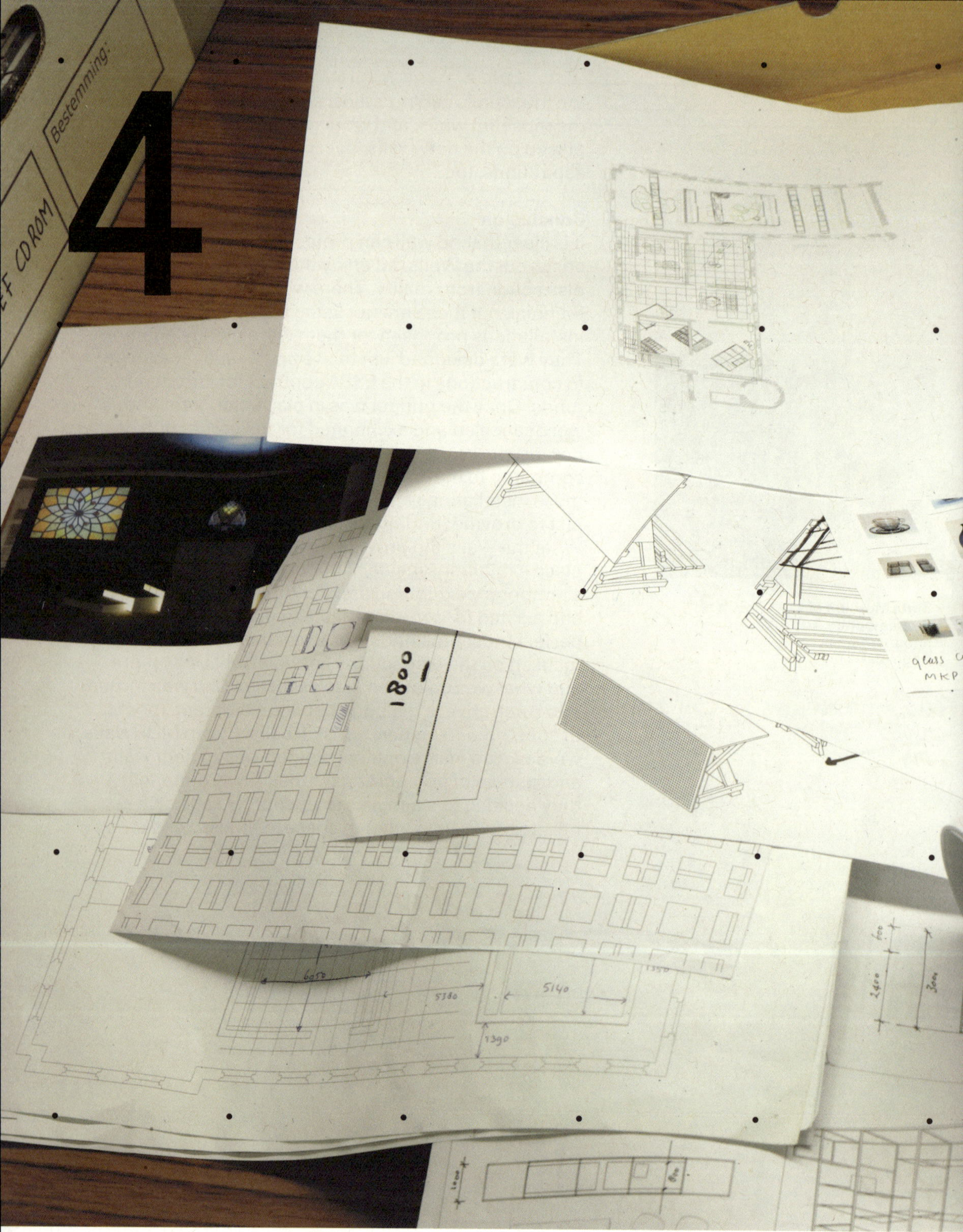

Events: Situating the Temporary
Page 440

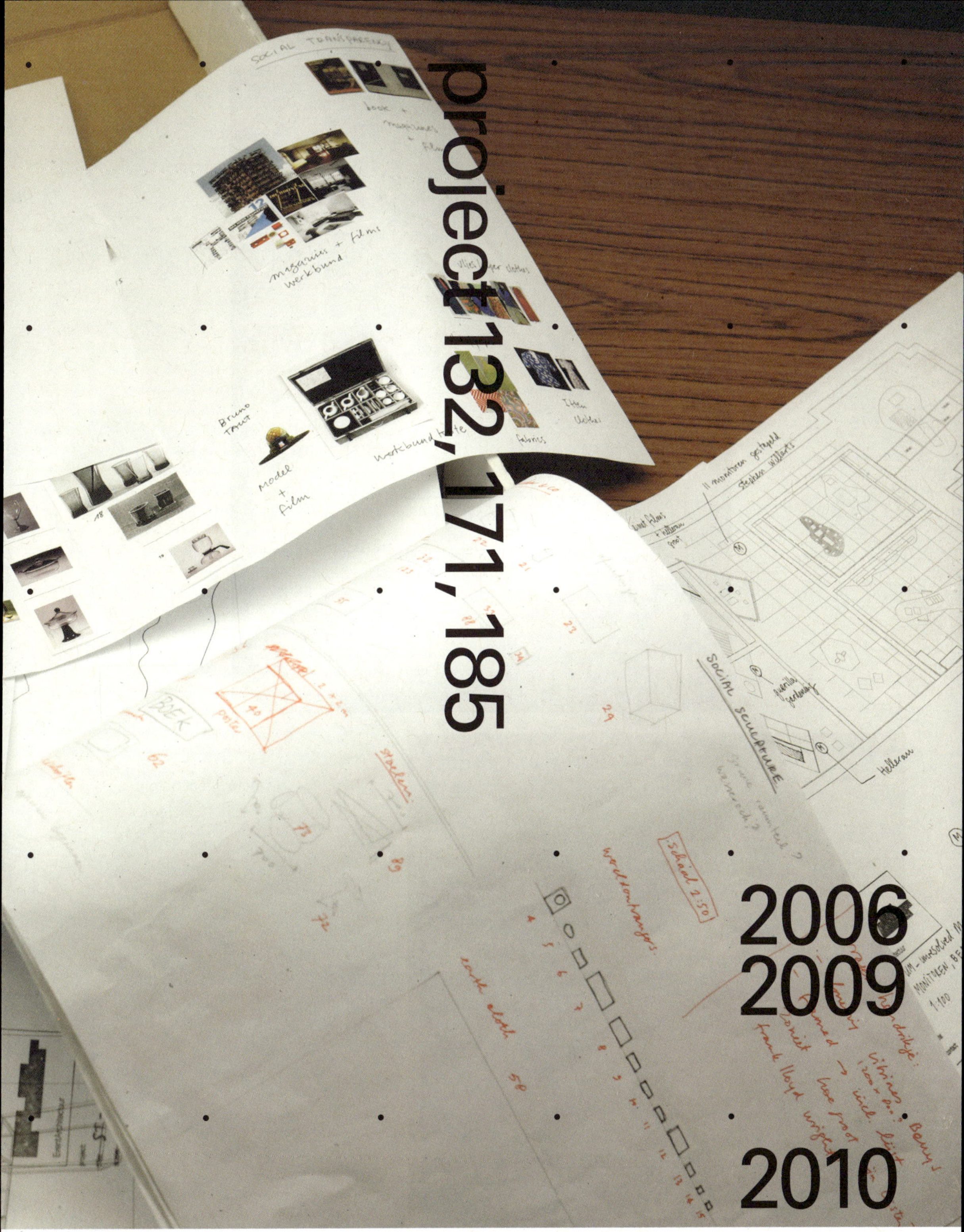

project 132, 171, 185

2006
2009
2010

Immersed in the Amazing Maze
Page 441

Die Dinge / Unresolved Matters / Hygiene – The story of a museum
Project: Exhibition
Duration: Medium-term, 3 months
Data: page 655, page 662, page 664

Immersed in the Amazing Maze
Page 442

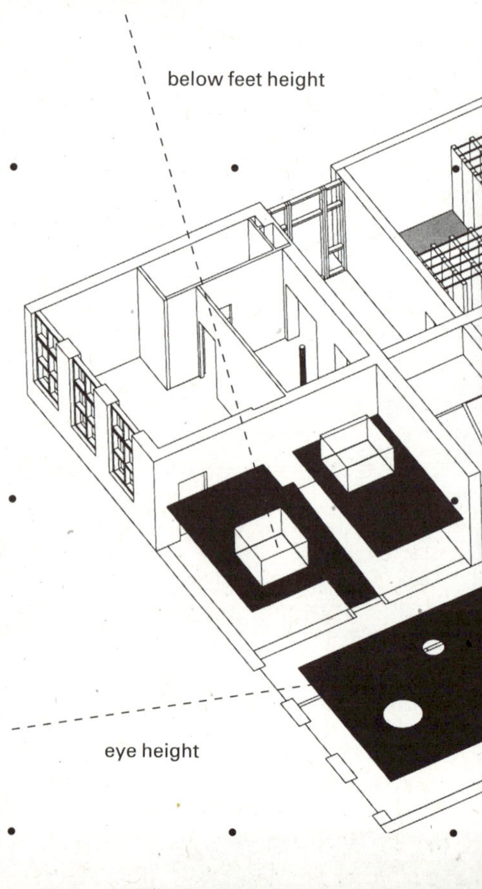

project 132

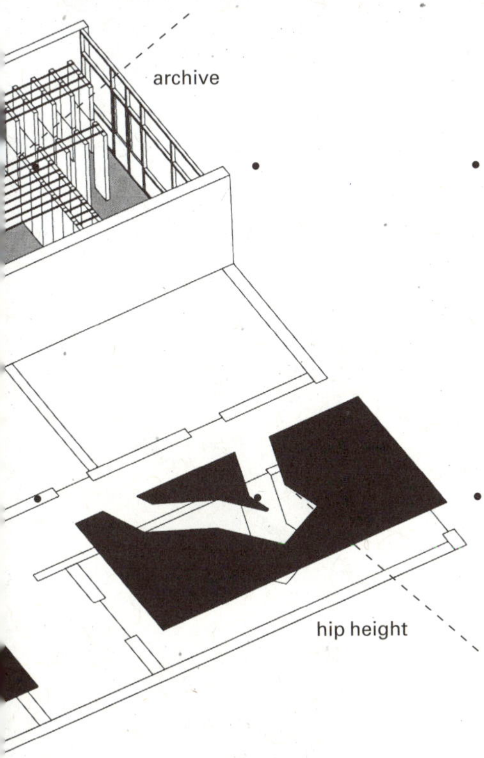

Immersed in the Amazing Maze
Page 444

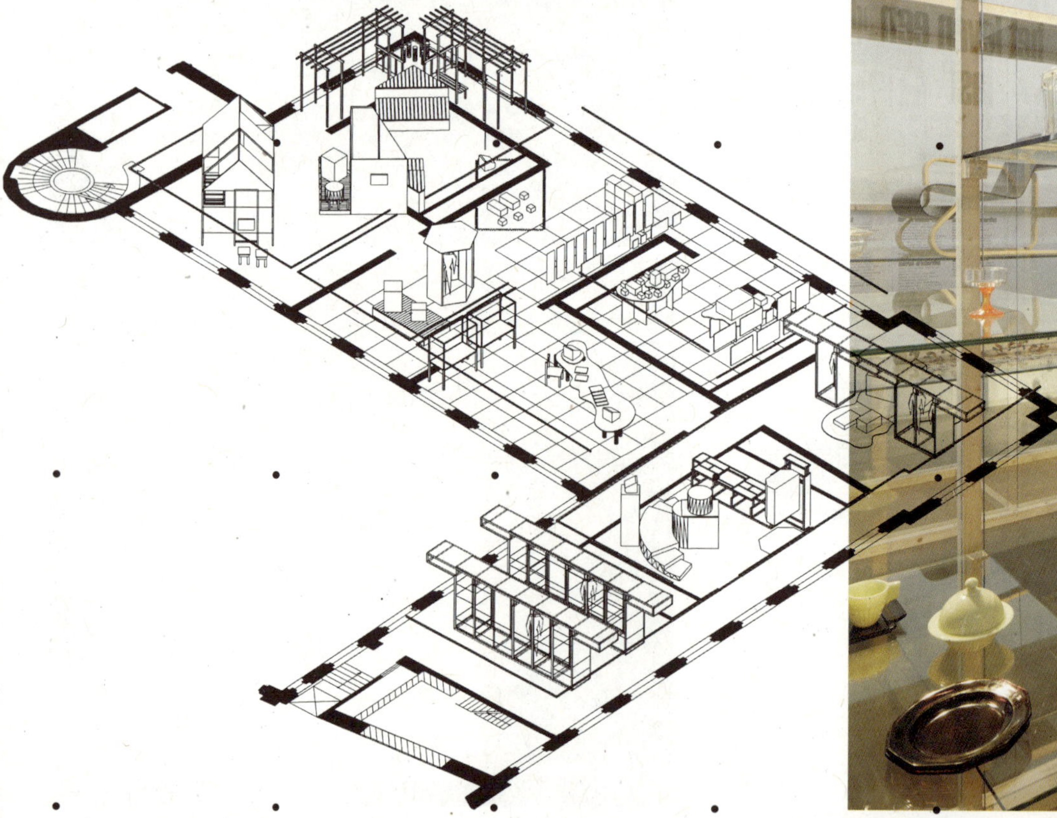

project 171

Unresolved Matters, Centraal Museum
Page 445

Immersed in the Amazing Maze
Page 446

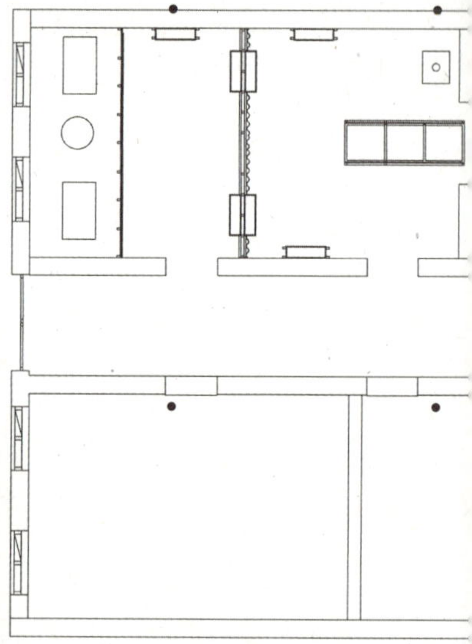

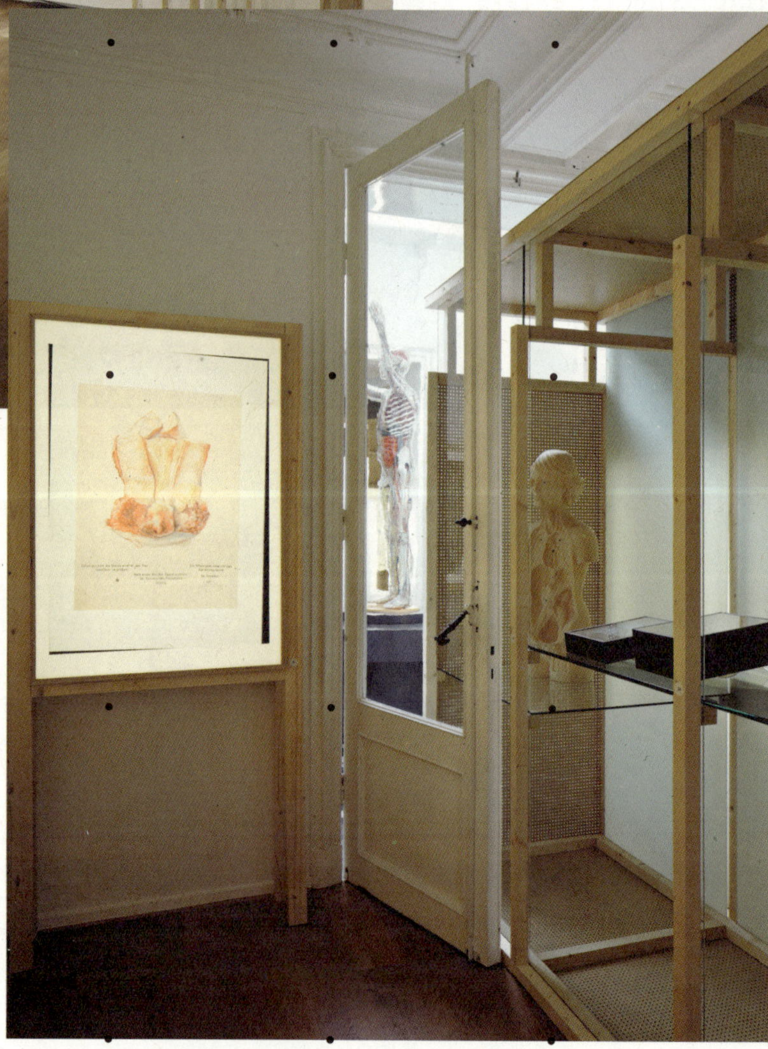

Hygiene – The story of a museum, Marres
Page 447

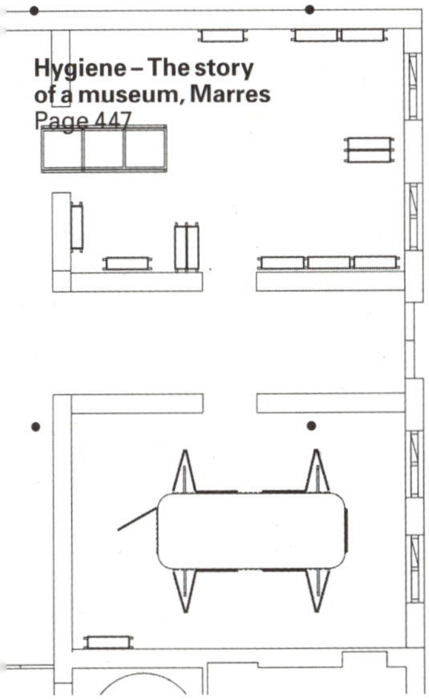

project 185

matters

1
William Drenttel and Julie Lasky, "Reasons Not to Be Pretty: Symposium on Design, Social Change and the 'Museum,'" *Change Observer*, August 3, 2010, accessed August 5, 2010, http://changeobserver.designobserver.com/entry.html?entry=14748.

Unresolved Matters: Is it possible to revisit social design? – An interview with Claudia Banz and Herman Verkerk

Joana Ozorio de Almeida Meroz

The exhibition Unresolved Matters, *held at the Centraal Museum from October 4, 2009, to February 14, 2010, was part of the 2009 edition of the Utrecht Manifest Biennial for Social Design. More than simply a showcase of social design relics, the exhibition questioned the position of the institutionalized model of the museum exhibition when dealing with the dynamism implied in social design within the broader cultural framework of the Biennial. Joana Ozorio de Almeida Meroz, PhD candidate and Teaching Assistant for Design Cultures at the VU University Amsterdam, interviewed exhibition curator Dr. Claudia Banz, together with exhibition display designer Herman Verkerk, about the role of aesthetics, the museum institution, the importance of visitor participation, and the critical agency of products in relation to the program of social design.*

Joana Ozorio de Almeida Meroz (JOAM): In the recent symposium *Reasons Not to Be Pretty: Symposium on Design, Social Change and the "Museum,"* attendees concurred that the museum should focus less on the objects of social design and place more emphasis on "systems and strategies."[1] It is possible to argue that aesthetics is not an extraneous aspect, but on the contrary, that it is a fundamental concern and component of social design. How did you approach the question of the aesthetics of social design, both in terms of the objects themselves and when designing the exhibition display?

Claudia Banz (CB): There were very few artists in *Unresolved Matters*, but the reason I chose Joseph Beuys was due to this question of how the social and the political are linked to aesthetics and form. During his performances, Beuys really interacted with society – say he would start writing on a blackboard – but the problem is that now we only have the blackboard. Beuys did not want to make art for art's sake, but for the relevance it could have on the social sphere. So the question is how to show Beuys's social engagement when we only have his objects left. I would be careful to say that social and political strategies are always linked to certain aesthetics and certain forms. Although Beuys used objects to reach his ideal, the objects that he transformed were mainly objects from everyday life.

Herman Verkerk (HV): The radio is a good example of how we approached the aesthetics of the object. By showing a sequence of how radio designs changed throughout history, it became possible to see in these physical examples the immaterial transformation of radio broadcasting practices, as well as the increase of its social relevance. Thus, the political and social aspects of the radio became very readable through its aesthetics. But our interest goes as far as to what aesthetics stands for; in other words, in the ability of aesthetics to revisit and to reinterpret a thought.

unresolved

Even though we are talking about "objects with an aura," in fact, you can also define most of them as quite normal: chairs, phones, clothes, etc. Therefore, the information texts that accompanied the objects were of key importance to the exhibition – in effect, the texts formed in themselves a complete story, so we decided to give them an independent carrier. We kept the walls free as much as possible and placed the texts on a "continuous horizon," materialized as wooden beam that ran throughout the exhibition. No information was placed on or near the displays of the objects. This literally created a space in between the object and its "official meaning," and this space was to be filled in, or finished, by the visitor – all the pieces were there, but no clear directive on how to reconstruct them into a meaningful whole. The element of choice was further elaborated by how Metahaven organized the texts in the continuous horizon. Since the information was fragmented and layered, the meaning of an object was never determined; it was never allowed to close up on itself and become hermetic, but was always in dialogue with the other elements of the exhibition. By destabilizing the semantic relationships between the elements in the exhibition, the visitor could not stay an outsider and had to interact.

JOAM: What is the role of the museum in relation to the program of social design? What is unique about the ways museums can display the artifacts of social design and communicate their value to a diverse audience? Must the visitor interact?

CB: There is no ultimate solution of how to develop an experimental exhibition within the very classical environment of the museum. Exhibition-making is also a kind of social design, so if you display the objects in such a way that they do not become hermetic, then the exhibition will not become hermetic, either. Ultimately, how can art catalyze social transformations? Although, as a curator, the aim of my work is not social work in itself, the notion of the social is always present. How can exhibitions be used to open up people's minds? Of course, we did not achieve very much in such a classical exhibition venue as *Unresolved Matters*...

CB: The question of the aesthetics of the display is also a really important point. We created a clear hierarchical exhibition narrative using three theoretical works – Ebenezer Howard, *Garden Cities of To-morrow* (1898); Sigfried Giedion, *Befreites Wohnen* (1929); Victor Papanek, *Design for the Real World* (1971) – as structure for the three exhibition "thinking rooms" (Social Green, Social Transparency, Social Sculpture), but we also undermined it by creating multiple metaphorical and physical entry points into the exhibition.

HV: We spatially translated each of the books into three distinct "visual spaces." If you compare this exhibition model with the classical display in the museum, it becomes clear that in *Unresolved Matters* the objects were not necessarily their own highlights.

HV: I think we did! It is important to realize that the exhibition in the museum was only one element of the whole Biennial for Social Design. We used the format of the Biennial to question not only what social design is, but also to investigate how its manifestation is also a form of the very production of the social. It became possible to focus on the museum model and question more specifically its role in relation to social design, rather than trying to change the museum to fit what social design should be. For me, the lesson is not to change the museum into something that is too far away from its origins, or "history." I think you should treat the museum as a permanently growing, shrinking, and changing organism, and to show the "critical" use of the power of the museum and its environment. In this sense, we did achieve something.

JOAM: With the term "human-centered design," the social is firmly back on design's agenda internationally. Social design is, in fact, nothing new, since "designers have always visualized their task as being to improve the quality of everyday life for people by creating better objects and environments."[2] What is the meaning of social design, if all objects are intrinsically social?

HV: What we did was to explore the overall theme of the social aspects of design – design as a greater construction, and not just a collection of objects. We are more interested in the *implications* of social design than in the objects themselves – or rather, in the objects insofar as they are foci in the wide network where design functions converge and become manifest, like Beuys's blackboard.

JOAM: It is possible to argue that social design, rather than being an agent for democratic change, is but a pillar of the existing social order.[3] There is great pressure on designers to make humanitarian, sustainable, or social design. In order to be recognized as a meaningful designer, you must answer this demand. How do you see the agency of design to instigate social change when the call to do so has already been normalized?

HV: Social design also uses this type of self-referential justification; in a sense, it will always be a continuation of, rather than a break with, the dominant social order. We tried to avoid falling into the political trap by steering clear of presenting the three different models of social design as the "best" agents of social change to be used here and now. Rather, we focused on how they are actually still being used today.

CB: After all, the exhibition is called *Unresolved Matters* because the same questions about how to improve the social have been asked for four hundred years, if not longer... and yet they continue being productive today. Although some of the pieces in the exhibition are romantic icons, they all refer to the same kind of movement that strives for *reform*. You could interpret this as the fossilization of the social role that design can play, and conclude that design cannot change anything anyway, since the same questions do not manage to bring about political change. But you could also read our choice in focusing on these three particular movements as a political statement as well. By juxtaposing and anchoring them in the theories put forward by the three books, we propose a new history of social design that can maybe in itself also be quite disturbing to the idea we have about the meaning of social design. We are challenging the "normalization" of social design. I guess, in the end, the main purpose of the exhibition was to show not so much how the *designs* changed, but how the *idea* of the "social" has been – and still is – changing.

2
Rick Poynor, "Design Thinking or Critical Design?," in *Now is the Time: Art & Theory in the 21st Century*, eds. Vesters, C., J. Bouwhuis, I. Commandeur, G. Frieling, M. Schavemaker, D. Ruyters (Rotterdam: NAi Publishers, 2009), 118.

3
Although there are many texts in which Jacques Rancière develops his political thought, for a thorough discussion see his major theoretical work, *Disagreement: Politics and Philosophy* (Minneapolis: University of Minnesota Press, 1995).

unresolved matters

Date:
June 1, 2015

Place:
Studio of Event-Architectuur, Amsterdam

People:
Tamar Shafrir & Herman Verkerk w/ **Paul Kuipers**

conversation 5

Digital interaction

H: I came up with a kind of installation that deliberately included people in the predecessor of Google Maps street view. Sort of the opposite you have in German cities where there is a big issue about privacy and representing facades so if you look at Google Maps you see a lot of blurred blocks. So I did the opposite. People could advertise in the street while the car with the 360-degree camera was going through. You would have all these images of people holding billboards that you could click on the website and go to the site of your neighbor. It was very nice, and very nice footage. It's also good that it triggers memories from very different kinds of projects that are connected to the work.
T: Now the whole emphasis is on integrating the Internet into daily life.
H: Of course that was the big discussion then as well. There was no imagination, just directly copying the reality into the virtual without any filter or extra quality. The "digitale stad" in Amsterdam was this organization, also at the start of the 1990s, that anticipated this virtual representation of the city, and they did make an interpretation. You could bike through the city virtually. But they had already transformed the aesthetics of the city, which made it fun. Of course now it's almost like the more real replica, the better. They have the Bijenkorf, the Dam Square, it's very modeled.
T: It's also funny when these blurred buildings become an aesthetic, a new type of architecture.
H: Well that's what you'd hope, but it's not happening! It's very detailed and very 1:1. Jan Rothuizen made this *Soft Atlas of Amsterdam*, what's good about that is that he has this cartoonish representation of the city, which makes things much more anecdotic. Things happen in different streets, so there is already a translation, and also the virtual reality could be that sort of layered reality rather than a reproduction of the physical.
T: But maybe also take the visual language of this very anecdotal…
H: … to have a new language. But that's what I found very interesting in the apps, that you could tell a story when you are walking through the city and you have this whole different approach. That's nice when it's layered, another level – the digital level – gives you other stuff than what you can experience in reality.
T: Did you ever think of integrating this layer somehow into your projects?
H: The technical aspect is keeping us out, a little bit. Most of the time these things are not working well.
P: I think it's something different, when you talk about a city with different layers; our exhibitions are more about the here and now. You are visiting a temporary environment, installation, or experience. Speaking for myself, I'm not so interested in bringing you to another world. That's what I hate, that in your personal life the iPhone is always there, and it's another world, a virtual world that is nice, but it's also disturbing the situation.
H: It can also enhance the situation if you have the right information. For instance, you were very fetishistic about the Rietveld app.
P: That's true. It's appropriate.
H: You go through the Netherlands and you get an alert when you are close to a Rietveld building.
P: It's literally like this. It's actually an architectural guide to the work of Rietveld, and it's connected to GPS. So when we were on the highway we saw this Martin Visser house close to where we were driving, I think it was in Best, and we took the exit and visited it. And an old fabrics factory he built south of Eindhoven, De Ploeg, which we never visited before. It would be nice if this virtual detour in an exhibition, for instance, would add something to the exhibition. So when you go to the Venice Biennale there are a lot of examples of things where you can add information.
T: Can you think of an example where it worked well?
H: The movie clips in the sleep exhibition (*State Alpha*), but it was video. In a way it was an extra layer. They were stories about the bed and sleep and how the bed is used for different purposes as well; it was by Eric de Kuyper, who has a huge collection of old movies and made clips of where the bed or sleeping was present. The exhibition was on the architecture of sleep, so it was about the period of the day where architects have hardly any idea about the program – how to deal with it, how to program it within the house. So you just make a square and say "bedroom."
P: We could have done it in *Die Dinge/After Cage*. Now it was done more in an analogue way, the information about the archive. The visitor was invited to pick up objects from the archive to put on display in the exhibition, and take away others, so it was constantly changing. And we did it just by webcams, that was a choice, but you can imagine that now we could do it with an app, leading to another layer of information that you could play with, and then it literally works in the exhibition. It's not only a play for the play.

Taking it from scratch

H: It literally transforms the content of the exhibition.
T: I wonder how you deal with situations when you know the purpose is an exhibition and the work you do will be a background or a frame for a series of given objects? In the projects there have been quite different approaches. Some are… not exactly oblivious, but taking on a standard logic or language of their own, while others are tailored exactly to the contents of the collection, like a snapshot of the moment.

Do you have a mentality about exhibition design as a history by itself, with the tools and techniques that it usually uses, or do you try to approach it from scratch?
H: I think from scratch, and then while we are working, we see analogies. So you think about the affinity, for instance, a curator or team has with a certain way of display, and then you research further into that aspect. For instance, to have a really specific environment for an object, clothing and products are the best or the ones that benefit the most from it, while with architecture or art we are much more reserved. To enhance their story we don't necessarily make it very specific.
T: Do you think it's because clothing and products need this formality to take them out of the very accessible status?
H: Maybe they need this alienation, and funnily enough the alienation is brought on by exaggerating their qualities.
T: A lot of the time in the works you do for exhibitions, you have the front-facing side and also the back-facing side. Some not, for example, with these white cabinets they are very perfect and totally encapsulated, while with other projects the construction of the support is much more transparent. For example, the mini-billboard (*Architecture of Consequence*), that probably does not emerge from an exhibition typology – maybe rather from a theater typology?
P: We are not so referential to existing exhibitions. In general it's more what you see on the table here, more a landscape and examples of architecture and more atmospheric. I think we don't even have books on exhibitions...
H: Well, some, but most of them are art exhibitions. On how to show art and how it transformed in the twentieth century and that type of thing, the white cube. It's all very much dealing with art, but not display in general. That's really lacking, that's why we make this book. Going a bit deeper into the qualities or the differences within the discipline of exhibition itself, how people perceive it and how people make it. How people make exhibitions is very conventional. They start with a good story, and once it's translated into an exhibition it becomes very much cliché. I see it with my students who are struggling with their graduation show, they play "exhibition"! They have this image of an exhibition in a regional museum they went to when they were sixteen. It's a very traditional and very obvious way of display. They also totally clash with retail or with shops, and this is very peculiar. We always try to see display in general – also display in your home, or display in a shop, display where you work. We love, for instance, the display of the workshop. How the worker displays his tools, how they are organized or ordered. These kinds of things fascinate us. With this in mind we design the exhibition, not with the example of "we have a box and there is a text and a showcase." So these things come during the process. We don't design a showcase.

Context and models

P: And that's very specific for EventArchitectuur. We are thinking about the context, the location, the content, the visitors, how to engage the visitor in the subject, into what is on display. That can be a workshop and not a pedestal. So we are not hunting for the effect but appealing to the collective memory, but given back in a slightly different way... not literally, but sometimes it is close, for instance an exhibition about fashion where we showed the process of fashion, where you start with the making and end in a shop. That's touching the subject of 1:1 model, where you are invited into a certain context or workshop, so it's more ambiguous, it has more layers.
T: By 1:1 model do you mean when you recreate a situation as a model within a temporary space or within a space that is not normally devoted to that function, but to the function of display – for instance, recreating some aspect of a shop environment to explain the process of clothing – or is 1:1 model also a bigger concept for you?
P: I think it's a tool to invite people to take part in whatever is on show. In *Edible City*, it was not only a carrier of the information split in three parts, but it's also inviting you to participate in different ways. Visiting an exhibition, having a dinner, giving or going to a lecture – there are more activities planned in the exhibition itself, it addresses the whole stage.
T: I thought 1:1 model could also be a working method for you towards design. I see so many models here that I thought maybe you also use models to figure out the space on-site.
H: I think we play with the scale. The 1:1 model in one way is also dealing with a recognizable formula, or something recognizable from outside the venue or museum or institute. But on the other hand it can also be scaled down, not 1:1 but exaggerated. Do you know this collection of Margiela, the doll's clothes for people? The buttons are very large, etc. That's what we try to work with, to have this alienation in the props or the things that make the exhibition work.
P: But less as a gimmick and more as a replica, or something with a function. The 1:1 models we make are often provoking something. For me the MMM could be a bit of a gimmick, or something that makes you laugh... well, we can also make things that are a little bit clumsy.
H: But people are also wondering about a certain materiality, if you enlarge or scale down certain things, it gives a question to how abstract or how detailed things are. Maybe it's more subtle than a big button, but it's similar in, for instance, the tie wraps into the perforated board, if you introduce things that have another scale into the materialization.
T: Or a flimsiness...
H: Exactly! That you feel it's a bit unstable.
T: It's like the photos of Thomas Demand. The scene is completely banal but you are fascinated because...
H: ...you know how it's made.
T: In some other way it seems the most pointless thing in the world, but very beautiful at the same time.
H: With us it's interesting to have this moment, not forever, to have this beautiful event.
P: Like the striping of the construction of the theater in Venice, you see it's sketchy, we blew it up. Scanning

it, repeating in a pattern, and printing it as wallpaper.
T: So this was really like a big model!
P: There was one guy who was just wallpapering the beams. That exhibition was for a group of artists in the Venice Biennale in 2011. (*Opera Aperta / Loose Work*)
T: Right after the Rietveld Vacancy show.
H: It was nice to reuse their stairs. People could go in the wings and from there they could see the works.
T: If we go back to the little models… the ones I see are very perfect, they are not messy, they are very representational somehow. Perhaps it's a misperception, but are they made afterwards? Or are they made in the process and then the way the model is made is affecting also the materiality of the final?
H: They are all different; this is a working model, that one was for a competition, while this model was actually playing a role in the exhibition. It was part of the exhibition, showing the three different stages – the front of the pavilion, the foyer, the proscenium arch, and then the wings.
P: This is a nice example to tell the whole story. This is also referring to the tradition in theater, we went to the theater archive (TIN) in Amsterdam and got inspired, they make for every play this kind of model at the same scale.
H: It was a very strange scale, because you started out with the prefab puppets and then in the end we used self-made puppets after all. The paper cut-outs. And this model is for a competition, so it's a finished thing. And this model is where we elaborated on the *Ideal House* with Hella Jongerius. Here it's transformed in an actual house. And this is a graduation project…
T: Is that from materials that you found?
H: Yes, this one is kind of sketchy.
T: This could be anything…!
H: It's a material that I got from Japan when I was doing the shops there for Alexander van Slobbe, and I got so many beautiful materials. I wanted to use it as a flooring with glass.
P: But it's an interesting question. A lot of models disappear. What you see here are the leftovers. A lot of time it's more like this, mimicking something, then it stays with the client and we make photos…
H: …or it goes to the builder.
T: And he throws it away!
H: Yes, sure! It's exactly like with school, you make a lot of things, and they are only to communicate, and when you finish, you don't need it anymore.
T: And is it useful for you to look at things in that scale?
H: Absolutely. It's very rarely a presentation, it's a lot of times about finding out a bit about the construction, how to hang things, etc.
T: I remember this pop-up from the Venice Biennial. That is actually a commercial product.
H: That was designed by Maureen Mooren and Veronica Ditting, graphic designers.
T: And what was the inspiration to show the architecture like that?
H: It was like a Gesamtkunstwerk. So the artwork is integrated into a three-dimensional surrounding.

The use of the (digital) drawing

T: Is there a developed process that you do as well, do you use drawing in a very different way or do you ever document also the projects in such a refined manner?
P: No, we are very sloppy!
H: We do it when there is a publication or a summary, and we have to show four projects, and then we start to translate the drawings. We hardly make definite drawings. In an architectural office you would have to deliver the definite drawings and there is a jurisdiction, and in a way we are always squeezing through, and we have only half the information when building has already begun, so we are working together with the builder to get the result, and sometimes we have just the page with a pencil sketch and it disappears, and sometimes it's even drawn on the construction itself. Sometimes I make a photo of it, but most of the time you just forget it, it's made, and there is hardly any documentation of the last stage of this development. Sometimes we don't even know how some things were made. But we have to reconstruct really, "How did it go?"
P: We have to re-measure it.
T: I've always found it super interesting the way the tool of representation is affecting also the result.
P: We draw almost always in 3D, which is very specific in the architectural field, most people are drawing in 2D, either in section or in plan. So we start always in modeling.
H: And a lot of times that is one of our saying, "Sketch is Def." Where the sketch is most of the time definite design. So once we have researched it in 3D and made a presentation that is three-dimensional rather than floor plans and facades, there is already a perspective, you can already experience a little bit about how the exhibition is going to feel, and most of the time it's like elaborating on this framework. So it's kind of definite.
T: But then do you try to purposefully look for another aspect of the project to "fuck up" the sketch somehow, for example, by using a difficult material?
H: I think that naturally happens, so when you materialize some things you see that there are also impossibilities, so we rather like this as a challenge. Just as the last time we spoke about instability, if a certain quality of the material doesn't fit, but we still have to do it because this is what we ordered or there is only half a day left, and there is also a solution which maybe you are forced to do but it is also a good solution, or it's something that surprises even yourself.
P: The computer is also correcting sometimes. When materials come together, and you draw it, and you see that it is not working.
T: You even get annoyed!
P: In the sketch it works, but you did some material research or you went to the wood supplier and got some dimensions and you agree with the carpenter, and then you are finishing your drawing and you think, "Shit! It's not working." I'm a bit more at ease with that.
H: "Laconic!" We will fix it when it's built.
T: We'll stick in a wedge!
H: Also the margins are more strict than we say now. So if you finally see a result that doesn't fit, but you have to really think of a good end, it's not enough to just

leave it.
T: But in the beginning then if you are starting quite early with the 3D model, how much context do you bring into the virtual environment, or are you able to fill it in mentally, or do you also enjoy the abstraction of the virtual environment just to think about a construction logic?
H: I think it's the construction logic. First you make a sketch and you are very optimistic, then you leave the office and you say the next day you'll do it in the computer, and then you redraw the drawing in the computer without the shifting of the transparent paper, and then you find out that it's different sizes. So it corrects a lot of the improvised situations that you had before. And once you have this computerized version, a lot of times we first elaborate much more on the system of different elements within the computer, and then we take it out again and see we have to specify certain aspects. So it's better to start again with making models to find out how the details actually work, also in terms of the sensibility and effect two different materials have together. We hardly do that on the computer.
Then afterwards, we make the drawing with the paintbucket in Photoshop, it's a beautiful tool. Paul is better in the material library or the mapping.
P: Well we are both far behind…
H: We are not far behind, we have our own aesthetics!
P: Sometimes we are lucky with the shot, and we are really satisfied with the outcome, or printing it on a certain kind of paper… some offices have a way of drawing everything, but that's not what we do.
H: I remember we had the Rotterdam Architecture Biennial, and you were not there – Paul is much better in representation – and I had to do the presentation myself. I was doing SketchUp in the perspective mode, and I saw I could add text in the perspective so I can explain the different functions in the perspective. It was great because then I had this overview, but then I had to make different slides for different perspectives, and so there were all these words in the view overlapping. Then you get into a kind of panic… first you find out you have this way of presenting, and then I had to spend the whole night taking them off and remaking the slides… but actually it was refreshing, a fresh approach to SketchUp.
I suppose it's hardly used like that. Also with the mapping, you do some kind of contradictory things and it's suddenly very expressive and it works.
P: Going back to the drawing, I think we are pretty trained in thinking in abstractions, also the drawings that are lying on the table are mostly black and white. The abstraction of the construction in 3D and floor plans, and when it comes to material we have samples, to see it, to feel it, to smell it.
H: This drawing is not for the client, it's for us.
T: It's probably more useful to have the floor plan notations right here in the drawing.
H: It's more information at the same time, different functions.
P: Ten years ago that was also for the client.
H: We would redraw this beautifully in pencil, and then it would be for the client. But a lot of times it was also to show that it's not finished, or that you have the sketch period, you also show it in the aesthetics of the presentation.

Paper architecture

T: Last time you mentioned paper architecture as an inspiration, but is it something you are interested in doing in your own work?
H: I think that we are lucky that the assignments trigger this interpretation, but we can really make it real. Maybe there will be a certain period in our career that we can pursue it. For instance, in my graduation period, I didn't really choose if it should be built or not. Although I had this technical professor who really defended my design in the graduation, more than me. There were questions about the construction, it's the Villa Karamazow, people were doubting – did you think about constructions and materials, and then this guy stood up and gave a lecture of half an hour on my project and how it could be built. But I guess it was not my main concern, the main concern was much more to use architecture as a communication tool. And I did some more for competitions that were paper architecture, more exploring how a cross section or floor plans are communication tools of architecture, are working to tell a story.
T: When I learned architecture, we would go look at *Detail* magazine and then draw these very complicated sections, but it was totally aesthetic – you had no idea what those things were.
H: I think it's about copying. I had to do that kind of thing, and I found a cross section of the Rietveld Academie, and I just copied the cross section but with insulated glass. What can you do, how much information can you digest?
P: In the pre-course of the academy of architecture, we had to do 1:5 cross section with all the layers and all the hatches and patterns.
I can do it now, but you immediately forget it. But it's just boring information that you can find in the moment you need it.
H: That's also why someone like Vito Acconci is inspiring, that it's not dealing with that, or Lacaton & Vassal, maybe they have a drawer full of details but they do it always the same. If they work with the greenhouse system, they don't need to invent that detail because it's already made as a prefabricated element.
T: But it's also a question of who the drawing is for. If you get a builder who specializes in that technology…
H: …he will do it his own way anyway.
P: And I am sure that there are a lot of drawings made afterwards to explain it, to make cross sections.
If you are in the development process…
H: It's also that we don't do it much. We don't produce it. That's why architects need a certain size, you have to make some of these drawings beforehand.
P: We also do it sometimes, it's all scaled… maybe the difference is that what we build is sort of a mock-up for us. It's the final result of the whole process, but it's also the playground where we find out if it works.
H: In that sense it's a 1:1 model, not in a concluded stage. I suppose that is our definition of the 1:1 model. It also represents that it's in the world

for the first time, and now it's ready for interpretation. That's why we also sometimes hate when the stuff gets in. Sometimes we have very little time to see the actual structure before it is filled with stuff. It's not really politically correct to say, a bit like making housing without people. As a physical representation of an idea, and you can enjoy it in the structure itself.
T: That's interesting, because there are so many parts of your work that could be categorized in the cabinet typology. What is an empty cabinet, what does it mean?
H: Could also be after the show. We had this ghost department store made for objects and drawings of Piet Paris, and you take it out and you think the installation is even more beautiful.

The container and the contained

T: It's probably the same from the perspective of exhibition design, when you can appreciate it as an empty system it can also be very beautiful, but it becomes more banal when it's full of artifacts.
H: I think we really want to have a balance between the two. It needs also the hand of the curator, in that sense. You have to be lucky for people also to see the limit of how much it can contain. Also in a shop, how you deal with the space over time. Of course the collection changes and maybe the intention changes. We had made the shop Coming Soon in Arnhem, and it was curated/owned by a woman who also initiated it, so she was on the job and she really knew how to deal with the aesthetics that we gave her. And then afterwards it was taken over by another person. And then we went back and thought we'd rather burn it down! It's also very delicate to see how to interpret the stuff. Maybe that's oversensitivity? I have to force myself to say, "No, it's very good that people interpret it..." It was the same with Piet Hekker in the Warmoesstraat, where there was a grocery market; once it was taken out he saved the elements and then he made a shop in Katendrecht, a small supermarket with the elements. And then by coincidence we walked by and recognized it! Then we walked in and there was a friendly woman and they had the same concept that you could buy the bread that they make and sit there, it was kind of like a franchise of the Warmoesstraat... I really had to say to myself, "No, it's okay...!"
T: Did you feel a little sense of betrayal?
H: No, but you see that if they put a pillow on these stools, a crate with legs, and there they put a pillow on it, and it turned it into kitsch, the whole idea was gone, it was just a construction for the pillow...
T: ...instead of a pedestal for the person.
H: To have the idea of the crate that was also in the facade, in the wall, but you could also sit on it... that idea was gone. But I always wonder if I am oversensitive...
P: What we make, and why we like it when it's empty, is that it's already telling a story. I think we can say about ourselves that we succeeded if it's okay when it's empty.
T: And if it's bad when it's empty then it was a failure?
P: Well, luckily it never happened!
H: [knocks on wood]
T: Unfortunately, that's laminate.
P: It's telling a story in itself, *Coming Soon* is a landscape like a city, you start in a sort of street, and when it's completely packed with gadgets...
H: The first owner made it delicate, everything had its own place, she made a context of different objects, and then it turned into this display of gadgets all over, if you had a mini-market it would be equally interesting. You didn't need a design for the display of the gadgets.
T: It's the same debate of the Le Corbusier project in Quartiers Frugès/ Pessac, and he says, "In the end, it is always life that is right!" It's interesting that there were different interpretations in different periods. Not just physical but also critical interpretations about the physical modifications. Philippe Boudon went in the '70s to document how people had changed the facades and added kitsch decorations like stones, or didn't maintain the original quality. So his book *Pessac de Le Corbusier* was used to demonstrate how stupid people were and pumping up the ego of the architect. But the critic from the *New York Times*, Ada Louise Huxtable, said the opposite, that his book showed that Le Corbusier's architecture was good because it was robust enough to deal with the variety of what people want. It can only be a good aspect of the project that it changes or adapts in a way.
H: I think we are in the middle of that. When you translate it into design you see that designers are really for one side or the other. The ones you really cannot mess with, because it would ruin it, and the ones that can deal with a lot of things around them, they just blend in and can be appreciated, also with the mess or the noise around them.
T: Or the ones who don't even want you to use their designs.
H: But it's totally acceptable. Today I saw the new fashion collections from fashion students in The Hague, and you see all these garments, and you immediately see that they are not day-to-day garments. But it has this tension which is also fabulously beautiful, something that is not appropriated by the user. I think we are in the middle. Sometimes we really think that it's art, and as soon as it's appropriated it loses some of its effect; with other things it's the opposite, the more people improvise with it, then it grows and the system can deal with it. So it's not always clear what comes out.

Influences

T: When I was studying, the architecture was building its own culture, that's where you took inspiration from – the culture of architecture itself. Now you see that most of the references are mixed, half architecture but also architects that are using very different techniques. Examples like the documentaries Rem Koolhaas does, or an art installation interpreting the *Peacock Room of Whistler* by Darren Waterston.
H: Or making new fabrics while building, or using prefabricated elements, we like that a lot. Or making an oversized middle, like you have one central place where nothing happens. That's something that

inspires us, as in the Rietveld Sonsbeek Pavilion, which is a construction but deals with emptiness, or spaces that could become platforms, and you make the contours for the surroundings to read the space, more than giving it content. Or with Hélio Oiticica, we found it more or less afterwards. You have a career and you do things, and then you find this person who was doing it in the 1970s, with a very similar approach and also his research into the favela and improvised architecture and design, how you could use this way of coming up with the design or making your own context within an art surrounding. That was very interesting.
T: Every time those things come up in a different contemporary period and for different reasons, even if the end result is the same, with the same mentality or materiality…
H: Yes, we see that we have a lot in common with the Italian avant-garde, and then I am shocked when I open the magazine and I see it's exactly what we did or what we were thinking about when constructing an installation or the exhibition. It's also a kind of amnesia; on the other hand maybe it's something that you are inspired by because of a culture and you have an affinity to it, and then you are drawn to it at a certain stage in your life, so it's also not a coincidence in a way. It's inevitable that you will find a common intersection. Lina Bo Bardi was kind of late for us to see and how we got to know her work only in 2008. I think the work of Kabakov was one of the earlier examples where you see the influence quite strongly in our work. A little bit of absurdism. The work is of course much more social/political, but there are some elements in our work that relate to this confrontation of the self, "what am I doing in a museum? how am I manipulated here? I have to go through this narrow corridor and now I have to go there, etc." These kinds of things we like to play with, which Kabakov does excellently. I think his greatest pieces deal with this kind of awkwardness of finding yourself in a space that demands something of you; you don't know what it is, but then you go through with it. You have to stretch…
T: Do you feel in that sense it was more an autodidactic approach to finding these influences?
H: Yes, in the sense of exhibition design it was very much a territory that still needs to be explored, that is very much… maybe kind of similar to design, in the sense that it is not so defined yet compared to architecture, where there is so much rhetoric and theory.

Landscape design as inspiration

T: But it was interesting you mentioned, for example, landscape not only as a literal reference, as it is in some of your projects, but also the concept of a landscape as a design method. The approach of landscape design has always been much more about effect and stories than about precise spaces, even to the degree that things didn't have to be real or the size they appeared to be, they could also be flat or smaller or framed in a distorting way. Did you have an influence from that era of landscape design in the eighteenth century with the classical, the picturesque?
H: I think from all the periods. We steal from the Renaissance period, the very formal gardens with maybe one or two viewpoints but very much referring to itself, and we also deal with the baroque garden which has this absolute viewpoint, while in the "boscos" it's much more labyrinthine. But the English landscape garden examples we use the most. When two layers become dislocated; when the way you move through the landscape is different from the way you look at it, where the view is different from where you are going. It's something that we work on the most, because we think it's the more relaxed way of finding yourself in an environment or an exhibition.
P: It also brings more tension. A formal garden can be more predictable.
T: Do you find it interesting to work in that way in the traditional scale of the landscape, or in the small scale of an interior space or an exhibition? Does the scale put any conditioning factors on the work?
H: Not at all. I think it's rather a new concept to use this kind of landscape ordering principles inside architecture, to see how they work in a temporary context and not in growing trees and having the physical reality. But I think we are very happy that we have this example of the reality at the scale of the landscape garden (*The Mountain Idyll, The Water Idyll*), and I think the effect is something that we really like, that we spend a lot of time adjusting heights and distances, I think we spend more time on that than on materialization, to get the right height and distance, the integration of different walking lines.

Proportion

T: I imagine that if something is smaller than your body, then you are very sensitive to a change of five centimeters, whereas if something is much bigger than you, then it's somehow less relevant. You see that it's big, either it's a building or a mountain. I think from table to low platform to a step, those subtle grades are totally changing your behavior. For example, you would never sit on one step, but you would sit on two steps, then it depends on how old you are and how big you are.
P: Well, we are pretty basic in those proportions. We don't play with them that much. A step is a step, sitting is sitting, a table is a table, a bar is a bar, a door is a door, and a ceiling is a ceiling. That's what we always mimic, and we always forget how much it was again, so you re-measure it. But I was still thinking about this landscape, it's referring to the formal garden, landscape garden, enclosed garden, etc., but it's also a part of your package in general, how you move through the world. Even if you are standing inside a building, we are the kind of designers who think about a mountain. That's what we always do automatically. Barcelona is the most recent example; if you enter a location and you want to get a grip on it and it is half-rational

and half-intuitive, having perspectives, proportions, etc., they end up somewhere in the design. In this case the Cerda grid of the city suddenly appeared in the cut-off corners of the pavilions at the Sónar Festival.
H: I think it's always this interrelation. I don't really agree with what you're saying about the smallness and the bigness. If you are walking and you have an estimation of how much time it will take you to walk a certain distance, you would have an expectation of what you expect if you look horizontally, but also in a vertical direction there's also an expectation, in the same way that you would have about things close to you in your surroundings. I think you're talking about the consequence – in the close range, the direct consequences are more fixed, with the longer range you have more variation because you have ten steps and you can alter them, while when there is just one, you can only sit that moment. It's more direct in the sense of the moment that you are using it. That's something that we still have to see if it works, this invitation to start walking in a park or environment. In an interior we have it under control, we know more or less what triggers people from A to B and back again, we hardly ever have problems with people not finding their way. Sometimes it doesn't matter, of course that's another concept.

Shortcutting the requirements

P: Though we are also good at ignoring problems… a drawer might be too low, and then you get those functional complaints. We are a little bit autistic sometimes…
H: No, ignore is a good word, because we have the information but we think it would ruin the design.
T: Do you find you come into this more in an exhibition context, or when you have to make, for example, a shop?
H: It's in every context, also the landscape. We had to do a railing, because suddenly there was a need for the railing because people might climb on a wall. But we thought, climbing on the wall is fun, but then it's 2.5 meters, and then they can fall, and above 1.2 you need a banister, etc. And it's really in your face and you have to deal with it, so you think of a way to find an answer. But it's really tough because you don't want to ruin the design, you don't want an "add-on." So we gave the edge of the wall an angle so you can't walk on it. With the IABR that was a very annoying moment. We made pedestals for the models. And suddenly there was a safety requirement, there had to be a little line drawn around the model for insurance reasons. It was a ridiculous exercise that had to be done in the last week, and it was not designed. And these things I really hate. It's like the opposite of the nice form of improvisation, it's the bad way of something coming in that's not about experience; it's not about the quality of the design, it's another reality, the reality of insurance and responsibilities and some people not wanting the responsibility. You come across those kinds of things.
T: So Peter Eisenman was a big inspiration for you!
H: Well, I think he's super with non-programming, to say I have a system that I transform, and then I transform it again, and now I'm done. And in comes the user who can interpret the thing. We are much milder, but we have this sort of attitude sometimes. Fuck it, just interpret it!
P: The work is milder, but the mentality is not.
H: It's like what I said about the man with the *SPACES* cupboard who couldn't put his books in alphabetic order. That's a good example. It's milder, it's not like he couldn't put any book inside, that the sizes are all wrong!
T: That would be architecture to drive people insane! A house for someone with obsessive-compulsive disorder!
H: You have to enhance it instead of solving it.
P: We have to admit that in this case the shelf becomes very precise for us, and we take also the medium to be stored seriously – the CD, the DVD, the pocket, the novel, etc., so that it makes sense.

The garden and the void

T: What I wanted to ask was about your list of references. I could tell a difference between standard typologies that were quite specific in terms of behavior or function, or the history of that kind of space, and then on the other hand you had very allegorical typologies like "the void" or "the garden." For me the garden, as opposed to the landscape, is less about a spatial typology and more a metaphor. And the void could be both. But what does it mean for you?
H: The void is like in this building by Artigas, the architectural faculty of São Paulo, it has this huge central square in the plan, and during the teaching period it is empty, so it is also like a school square…
T: It reminds me of Neutelings Riedijk's Minnaert building, it's very similar in a way. They said they calculate 15 percent of the building for circulation, so actually they just made a big courtyard – well, an interior courtyard full of water – and then all of the rooms go around it. But it's really similar in this kind of hulking volume.
H: Of course in Holland it can only be solved with data, to make an argument to build it, whereas here it's much more social.
T: Was it innovative in that sense, also in this project?
H: Yes, also that it's public space and the enclosures are relatively small in the whole building, so everything is public and only when it's really necessary to make a wall, he made a wall, but never reaching the ceiling. So it was always this feeling of openness, and maybe the void is also that the activities go around this center, and most of the time it stays empty, only for big assemblies it's filled. It's like a potential playground, so you make it for distribution of the elements, also to make it a center-point, but it's also made for events or things that you did not program or were not sure about yet. And this is what I think the void is. For example, for the fashion biennale in 2007, we made a huge water basin where nothing happens, and you had to walk across it on a small pier, and there was a little drip and it made rings on the surface of the water, but it was kind of a reflection pond, more or less, a quiet moment amidst the

bombardment of all the exotic fashion.
P: In the Design Prize we did a similar thing with a reflecting pond, and you could have two experiences in the exhibition. You could step inside the installation, and you would see nothing – only the pond, the skylight, and the white walls – or you took another route, and then you saw all the objects. That was quite an extreme decision that we were allowed to make.
H: And of course we ignored the opening ceremony. There was of course an expectation of three hundred people entering, and we thought, "Well there's another exhibition by Wim Crouwel next to it, and it was kind of spacious, so we thought, well it won't be a problem, people will walk around in both exhibitions…"
P: But no, they were standing on the pond, on the glass!
H: And the builder was really shitting his pants because he didn't construct it really properly for that kind of weight. But we love this, speaking of hierarchies, differences, and specificities. I just read an article on an apartment by Loos in Pilsen, Wohnung Teichner. It's one of the last apartments he did, or one of his assistants did for him, and this author (Eva Stricker) is trying to prove that actually Loos did also use the Raumplan in the apartment. Not having the ability to change the height of the ceiling in an apartment building, he worked with the height and material quality of the paneling, and also the lines on the walls. So you would have this hierarchy of heights between when you entered, in the bedroom, and for the public spaces inside this house it would be again a different height. So you would have this very subtle play of architectural language, but it immediately affects the way you would interpret the room. Interpret is already active, I think it's a much more passive experience, but emotionally or intuitively you read these kind of signs, where the wall and the ceiling meet there is a difference. Not like you have nowadays, you have the rooms that just have the wall and then the ceiling, there is no more play in the zone where they meet. These kinds of things we really like. It's something about perceiving architectural differences.
T: I once interviewed Jonathan Olivares for an article for *Apartamento* and he mentioned how everything is just plasterboard now, the interior language is so completely abstract now, there is no actual material – well, of course it's also a material – but you don't have this sense of manufacture, unless it's very rough, very exposed, where it's conscious that you didn't cover with another material. Usually the ceiling and the wall are the same.
H: The nice thing is that Loos was really thinking about public/private. You see that originally this apartment has its own logic, the logic of the mass-produced housing – equal rooms, connecting corridor, everything is functional, it's the cheapest way to do the building – and when he enters, with very small elements he completely changes the hierarchy between the rooms, the amount of privacy you have. For instance, the bedroom was originally connected to the corridor, and now he makes an extra walk-in closet in front of the bedroom, so you would have to go through the walk-in closet first, so of course it changes your way of feeling once you are in the bedroom, those kinds of things we really like. And sometimes it's also something that you are interested in and not so much the client. That's also the case of Loos, that he was concerned about these qualities…
T: …like the bedroom should be away from the street.
H: And the clients might even not have these demands. The drawing room, the dining room and the bedroom each were a separate room in the original apartment, and then after he did the refurbishment, the bedroom was pushed aside with the walk-in closet and the drawing and dining room he turned into one space, he places two central elements at the end of each room that were equal in size, so you would have this axis connecting these two and not to the outside view, and to accentuate that he even put a glass wall inside in front of the original facade, so there was a one-meter space that he called a "garden," but it was just to make this real separation, and to change from a relation with outside to an inside relation. That type of thing we really work with, that for instance we change the main axis of the space when we think it would otherwise be really one-dimensional. We try to disrupt the actual space into another structure.

Antechamber

T: Another thing you mentioned is the antechamber, which really relates to this story but also to the void; the function it has is you either wait or leave. But is it also in the sense of permanent waiting? Can you make something of only antechambers?
H: I think it's more like this bedroom walk-in closet situation, that you have this transitional space. We use the antechamber more as shutting off the outside world and entering another world, like the exhibition or the shop. People are sometimes very annoyed about that ingredient, for instance, in the *Design Prize 2003* the first thing you experienced was a fence you had to walk around; people are really not used to that anymore. When I did a lecture in The Hague, invited by architect Wim de Vos, he said afterwards, "You make it very difficult to enter your projects!" I see it more like a follow-up of different experiences.
P: That was in 2003?
T: It's not taking the mentality from this idea that architecture should be very clear and self-explanatory, or asymmetrical to communicate function clearly, whereas symmetrical architecture has a different effect – not saying exactly what function occurs in each part, but rather having more of a metaphorical or narrative effect.
H: At the same time, the antechamber does not have to be literally a room, it could also be an introductory space.
P: There's a very nice house close to the Koepelkerk on the Singel; it's on the corner, and you have these stairs to the piano nobile, and then you enter a big room that is richly decorated, there is no corridor. The door is integrated into a facade of glass, so it's very transparent, and you step into the room, it's a very

nice introduction to the rest of the house. That's how we use it also, like in the Ideal House or in *Changing Ideals*, also as an introduction…
H: There was this room that was like a salon, these seats here were from that exhibition, and each seat had the first name of an architect – Jo, Mart, Gerrit – the curator, Dirk van den Heuvel, had an idea of architects conversing over time, from the sixteenth century onwards, to discuss ideals of architecture.
P: This is sort of a mental introduction on the exhibition, it was not so literally a space that is first an antechamber and then you come into the exhibition… it was more a mental thing to prepare the stories of ideal houses throughout time, but starting with these architects thinking about what is the ideal.
T: It's like a vitrine that could be the antechamber of the shop; that you have to start the experience there.
H: I like *World of Interiors* a lot.
T: Really! Why?
H: I like it because it gives a kind of spatial quality, also with objects, often made with a personal hand, and there is never a floor plan or architectural reference, and there is hardly an owner reference.
T: And it's styled, or the objects are brought there just for the photograph.
H: They do extra effort to make a spatial quality, and I was thinking about this house that has an entrance, a door, and a courtyard – but then from the courtyard you immediately enter the house, so the courtyard is also the antechamber or the entrance. I think we always think about that type of transformation for the exhibition. So you could say there is no entrance but there is also this filter before you go into the story.

Cultural staging

T: In this example of the *Design Prize 2003*, what's interesting is, you wrote also cultural context, and I was curious what it means for you. Which elements do you prioritize as the contributing factors, or which part of the cultural context are you interested in and which are you not? Of course it might depend on the project, but it could be contemporary or time-specific, site-specific, typological, functional, or based on the personality of the client, and so on. What does the cultural context for these kinds of projects mean for you? Perhaps it's not fixed?
P: It's definitely not fixed. The client is definitely interesting for us, or the curator, or the story to be told, and there is often a social or political background in a project we are doing. And if it's not there we bring it on.
T: Do you feel that it should be readable in the end result, or is it not as important if it's apparent to a viewer?
H: It should be apparent to the viewer.
T: In which project do you think it's the most obvious to the viewer, something like a political dimension to the project?
H: For instance, with the Utrecht Manifest, we did a sort of billboards and integrated them into seats. So there was this hybrid moment where you had propaganda and display connected to an element for social interaction, to be used together. This is the kind of thing that we are looking for, giving the opportunity to change behavior and to have this kind of interaction happening. The project *Pursuit of Happiness* in Leidsche Rijn is also a good example, this idea of critically analyzing how the toolbox of the architect functions in an environment of a new town, to show that it's kind of reduced to a grid system, and it plays with this grid system and it has this other system that is connected, more the nineteenth-century stroll that would connect all elements in a different way. It's looking to find ways to communicate the complexity of a cultural situation.
T: Or behavior.
H: Yes, because it's culture you are a bit outside… you can do anything. This thing with the billboards in the street with a 360-degree view, as soon as you mentioned it was art, it was "it's okay, come in, do you want a coffee?" and before they were totally offended when we were doing stuff in the street, "what are you doing here??!" So you might need another platform to make it happen.
P: You cannot blame art, those are some traditional conventions of the location. That is also what we do with the museum, we always try to change these conventions, to react on the white cube, whether it's bad or good, it's giving some conflict. We are able to show graphic design in a sort of crumbling environment, it's unbelievable. It gives a lot of interesting discussions with curators and people from museums.
H: When we had to design the display for the last design acquisitions of the Stedelijk Museum Amsterdam, we had this huge discussion on showcases. Everything had to be in a showcase, while around the corner you have the whole contemporary design collection including the most expensive and vulnerable chair by Marcel Wanders, the knotted chair, just standing there in the open! "No, but we need to make sure…" It was just in their heads. So we thought, okay we are going to make a vitrine showcase, but we make an exploded one, one that is totally not functioning as a showcase but it looks like a showcase. So this is the fun in a way, playing with these kinds of demands or the cultural field gives its own status quo and ways of dealing with it.

Sensations

P: For me that's even a political thing, those conventions and how we treat objects in our society, it's like putting a baby in a "couveuze," it's just a chair telling a nice story, it's a good chair, but it's just a chair, so that's what we play with.
H: It's also about the service, also depending on people controlling a room – if you have enough people controlling the room, you are safe. But they don't have enough people. So they are saving on all these service qualities. Wouldn't it be super nice if there were a host who would tell something about the things on display? It's not so difficult to arrange. And you spend your money there and have no showcases that cost a fortune. Those types of decisions are not being made, because there is no connection between us and those type of assignments. The museum is so professionali-zed in itself that once they give us the assignment they already have everything detailed.

They need us for execution, but they don't invite us… for the things we do with other curators, where we are there at the start of the process, so we can also think about services and interactions, for the cultural environment we are in, which methods or ways of showing function the best. Do we need lectures, do we need a specific podium, those types of things. In the latest shows we did it has been very regulated.

P: My parents went to the Nussbaum museum in Osnabrück, and they are not frequent visitors of art museums, but they were interested in his work, and they came back impressed but complaining about the security guards. My parents are walking around and asking them things about the building, the collection, and they don't know anything, so why are these people sitting in these rooms?

H: They are totally not involved, it's a shock!

P: When she told me, I was already used to this situation; in the Stedelijk there is no connection between the guard and the collection. It was very nice in Arnhem though. We did two exhibitions in the museum for modern art there, and there was a security guard, and he showed everyone his favorite painting, I think it was a Charley Toorop, because he was sitting the whole day in front of this painting, and he knows every detail about it without art history knowledge. And sometimes we have to bring it in unofficially…

H: It's very much about the details. I was once in this show of PS1 in New York, and I just couldn't stay because the paint was not dry and the stink of the paint and the woodwork and the formaldehyde from the black MDF. We are very sensitive to those qualities.

T: It would be interesting to work on those qualities with students. Like the museum in Osnabrück, I remember it has the heaviest door I ever felt, huge and very hard to open, like a vault. Or the Kunsthal in Rotterdam, they have one room, the glass is covered in this jungle-pattern film, where all the children take off their shoes so it smells just like feet. It's terrible, but you remember very strongly these elements of the architecture, much more than the details of the actual architecture.

H: We would not accept this sort of smell in the exhibition [laughs].

4

Events: Situating the Temporary
Page 462

project 129

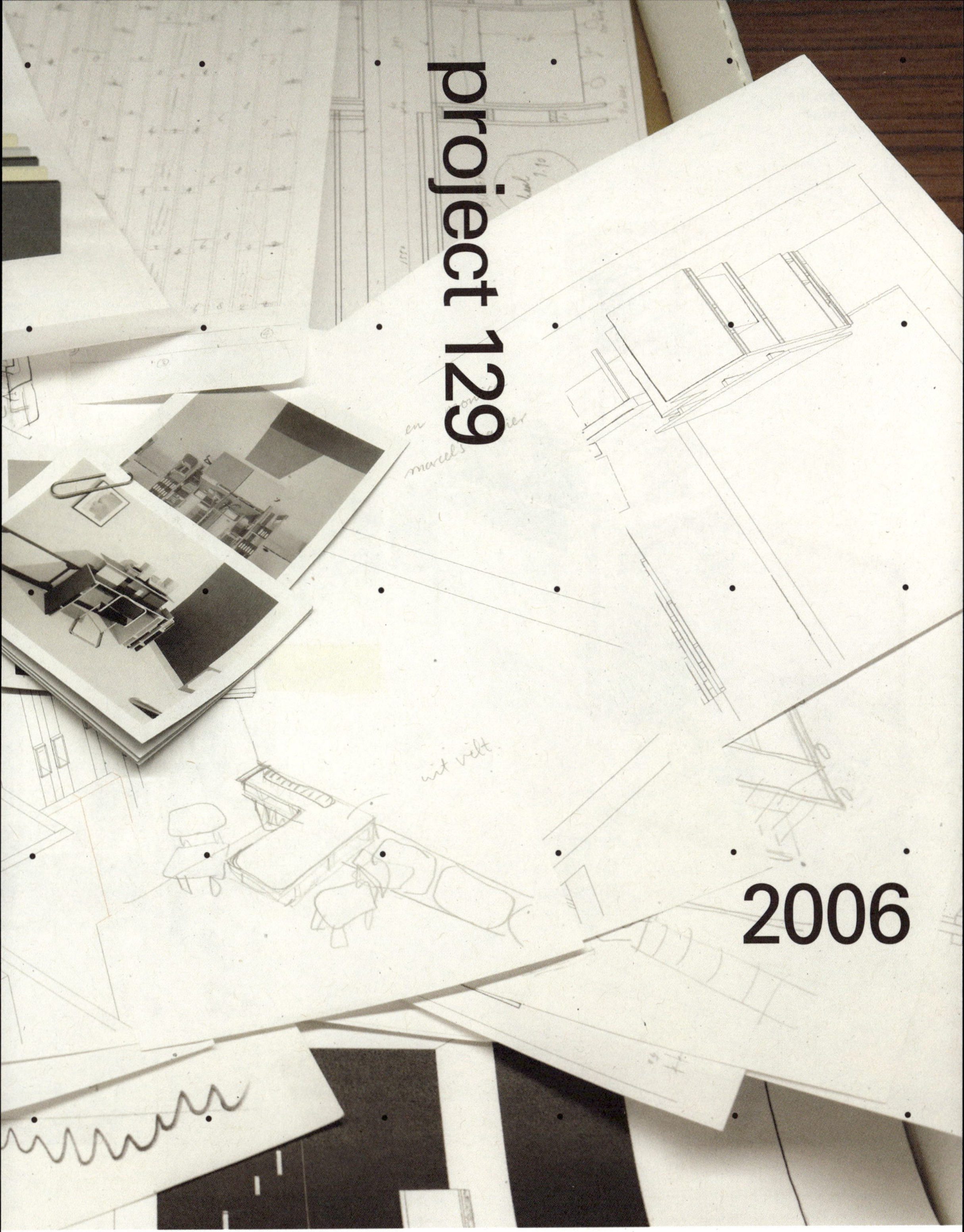

2006

Immersed in the Amazing Maze
Page 463

Office BremerDeZwaan
Project: Interior
Duration: Long-term, 5 years
Year: 2006
Data: page 653

Immersed in the Amazing Maze
Page 464

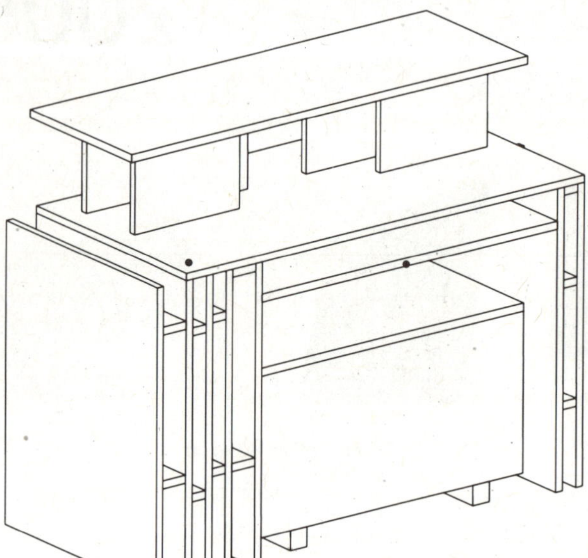

project 129

Immersed in the Amazing Maze
Page 466

project 129

JOR
NJB
Ondernemingsrecht
Mediaforum
IER
ami
BMM bulletin
VvL Bulletin
Advocatenblad

Esselte

Office
BremerDeZwaan
Page 469

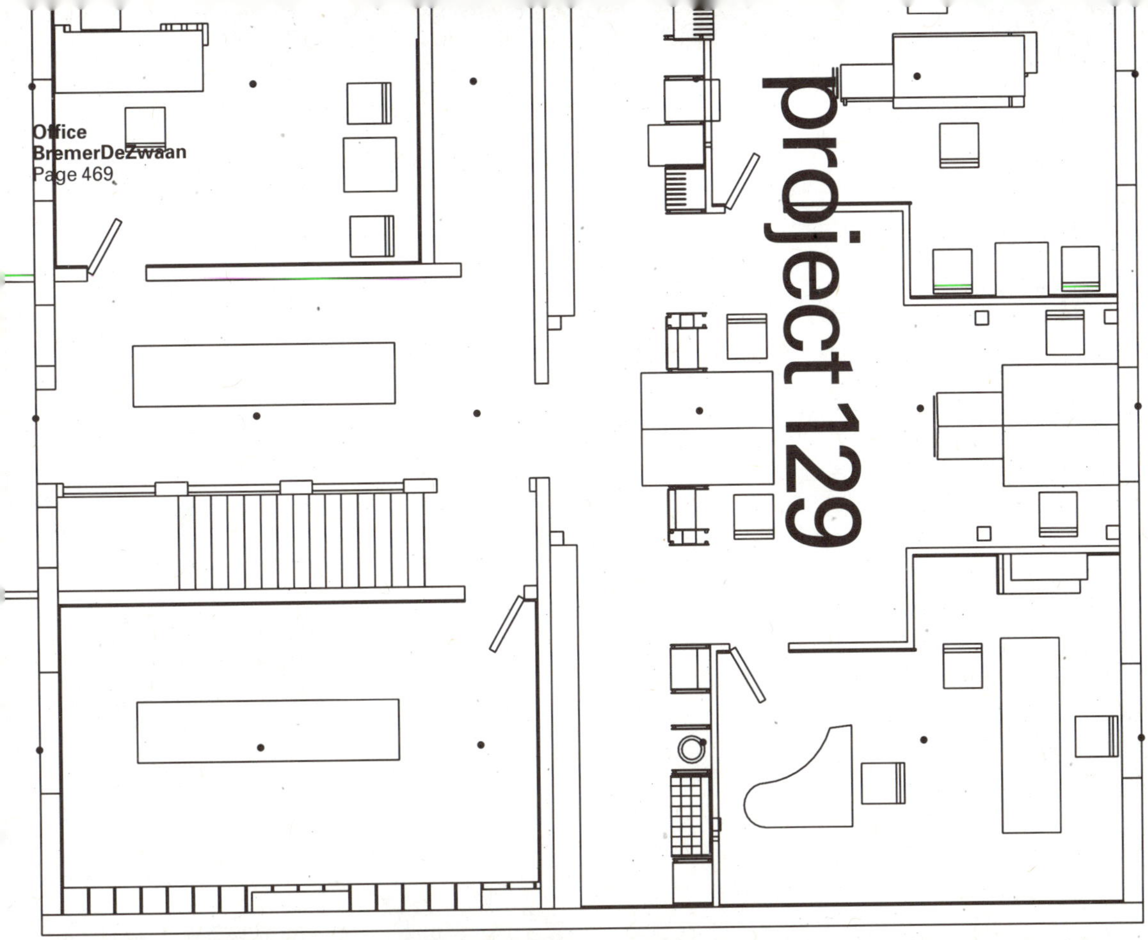

4

Events: Situating the Temporary
Page 470

project 141, 231

2006

2016

Immersed in the Amazing Maze
Page 471

Idylls for Lingezegen Park
Project: Landscape Art
Duration: Very long-term, 15–30 years
Year: 2006–2016
Data: page 655

Immersed in the Amazing Maze
Page 472

Idylls for Lingezegen Park
Page 473

project 141

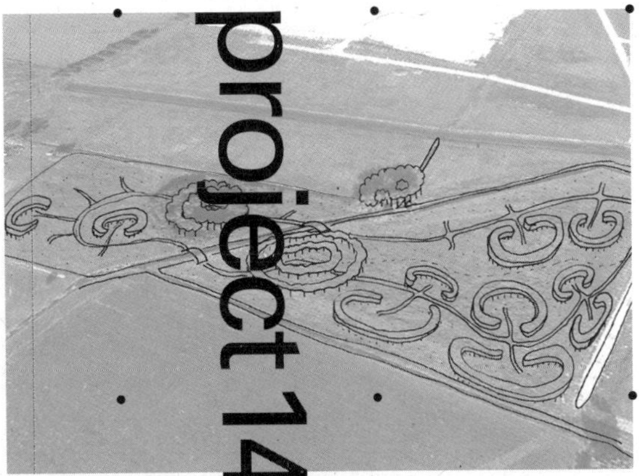

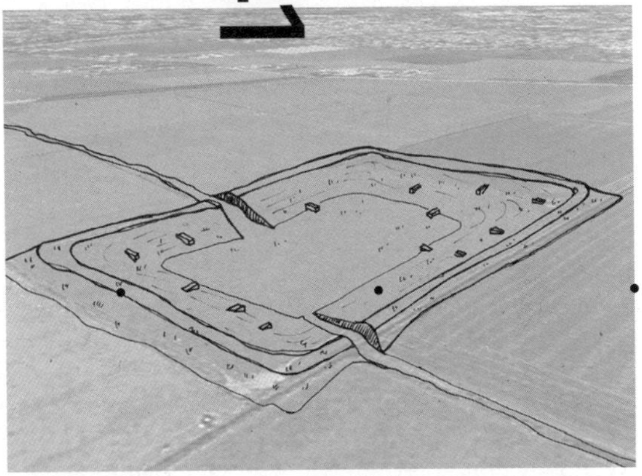

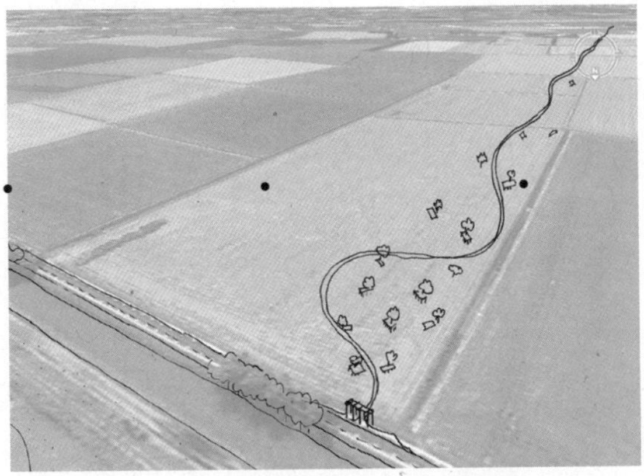

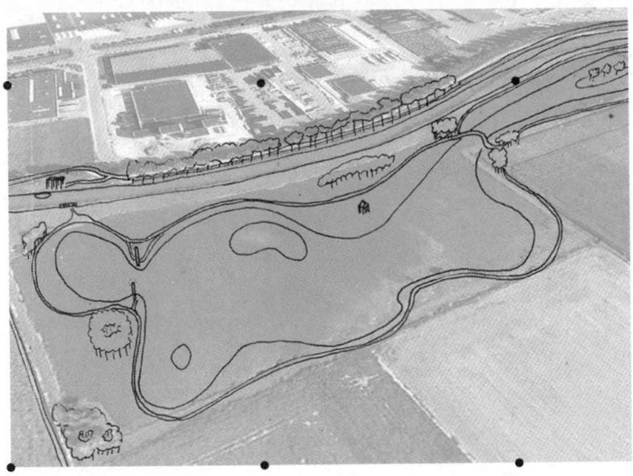

Immersed in the Amazing Maze
Page 474

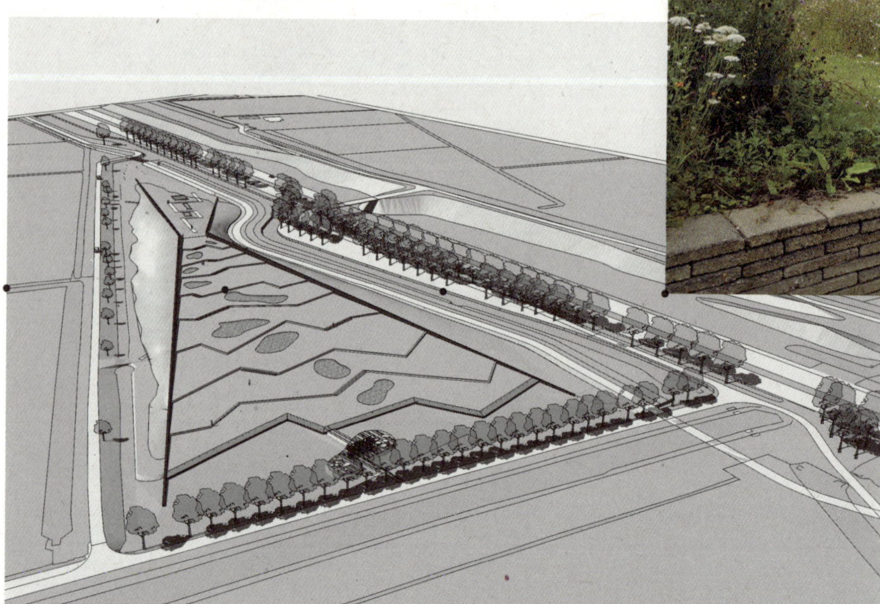

Idylls for
Lingezegen Park
Page 475

project 231

Immersed in the Amazing Maze
Page 476

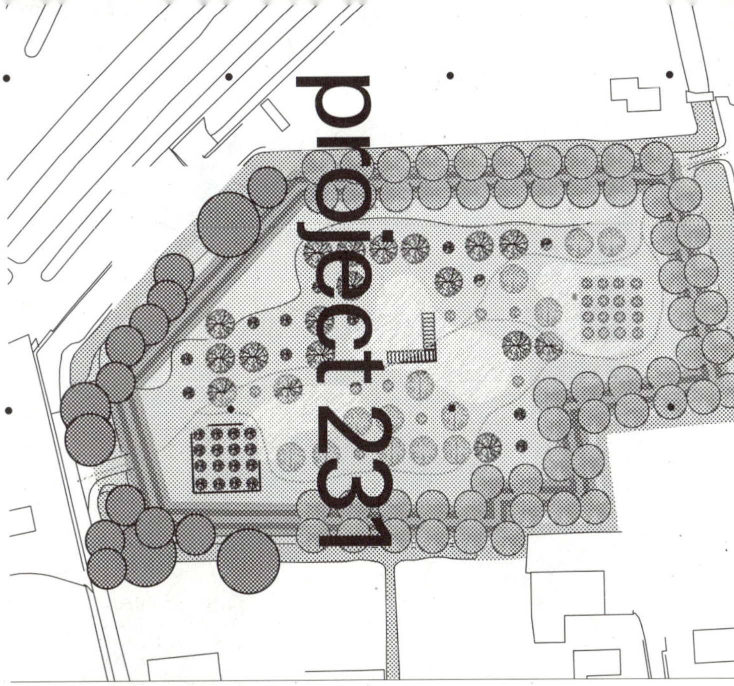
project 231

5

merging matters

5 producing art in a culture of convergence 2010 2015

5

merging matters

The Convergence

In the wake of the international financial crisis, the traditional boundaries of architecture had grown untenable. The architect evolved into a truly transdisciplinarian figure, assimilating the languages of design, landscape, and media into the structural mode. This not only diversified the potential of his/her creative output, but further allowed architecture to unfold at many different scales, each time reaching a new resolution at the level of the total scheme and the smallest detail, the design in its a priori state and its manifestation in different materials, each with their own frictions and idiosyncrasies. Architecture embraced a multiplicity of meanings and interpretations, while its fundamental provision of shelter, place, and permanence were open to question anew.

In parallel, the fields of commerce, culture, data, and politics became interconnected by dense relationships. The architect could no longer depend on a clean division between the realms of cultural preserve and retail enterprise: his/her main challenge was not to demarcate but rather to infiltrate. In practice, this brought a critical stance back into the commercial environment, a degree of contemplation to the exuberance of the spectacle, a dialogue between the generic and the specific. The impossibility of an outside has reached its peak – to search for it means to find, instead, other insides to inhabit, new niches in which to operate.

2011: The Occupy movement begins in New York and spreads to 82 countries.
2012: The Higgs particle is discovered in CERN's Large Hadron Collider.
2013: Edward Snowden reveals large-scale surveillance programs by the United States, the United Kingdom, and other international governments.
2014: Malaysia Airlines Flight 370 disappears over the Gulf of Thailand and Flight 17 is shot down by missile in eastern Ukraine.
2015: The Islamic State destroys ancient architecture and artworks deemed polytheistic in Syria and Iraq.

5

5

Events: Situating the Temporary
Page 482

project 194

2011

Merging Matters
Page 483

Opera Aperta / Loose Work
Project: Installation
Duration: Medium-term, 6 months
Year: 2011
Data: page 665

OPERA
APERTA
/LOOSE
WORK

OPERA
APERTA
/LOOSE
WORK

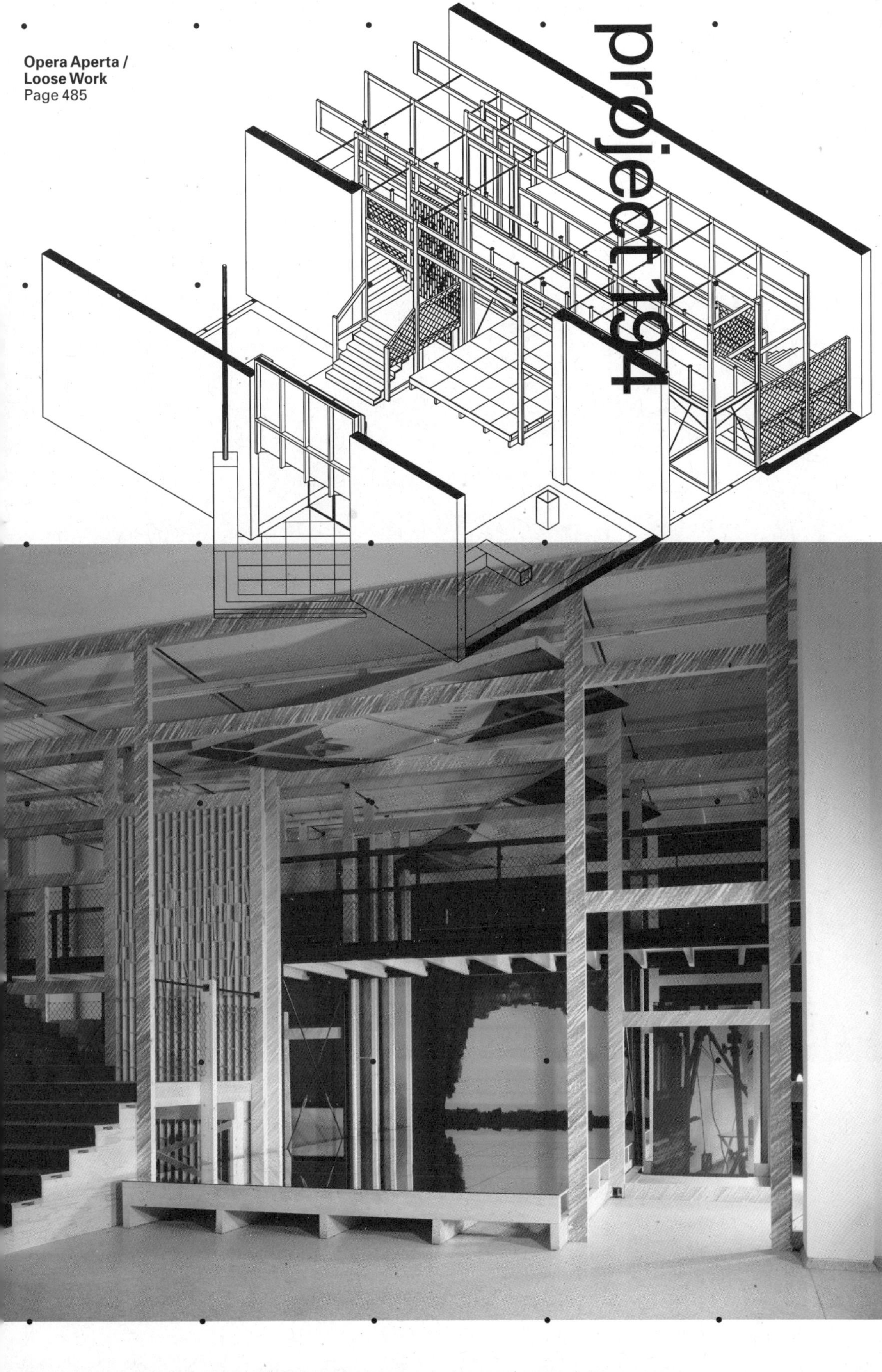
project 194

project 194

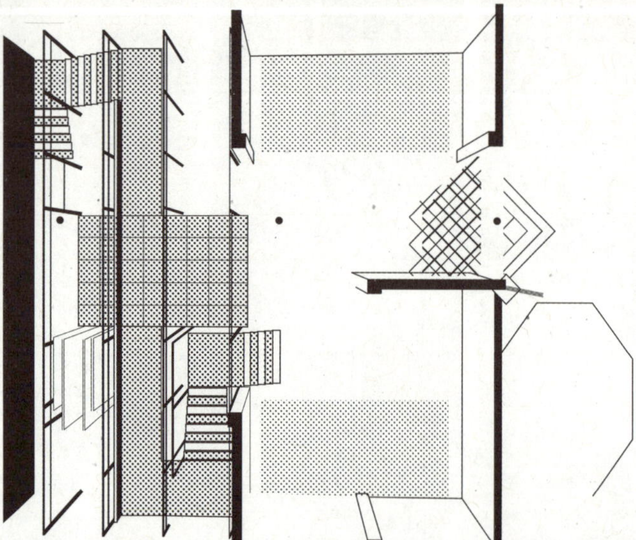

project 194

LABYRINTHS - LUCIA IMPELLUSO
DE JA-SPRONG - ANNA TILROE
HALL OF MIRRORS - BADER
THE OPEN WORK - UMBERTO ECO
IS IMPORTANT - OZERKINA & THEODOROU
THE WHOLE CREATURE - WENDY WHEELER
128 FOTOS VON EINEM BILD - RICHTER
FACHWERKHÄUSER - BECHER
PIÈCES DE CLAVECIN - JACQUES DUPHLY

Opera Aperta /
Loose Work
Page 491

project 194

5

Events: Situating the Temporary
Page 492

project 204

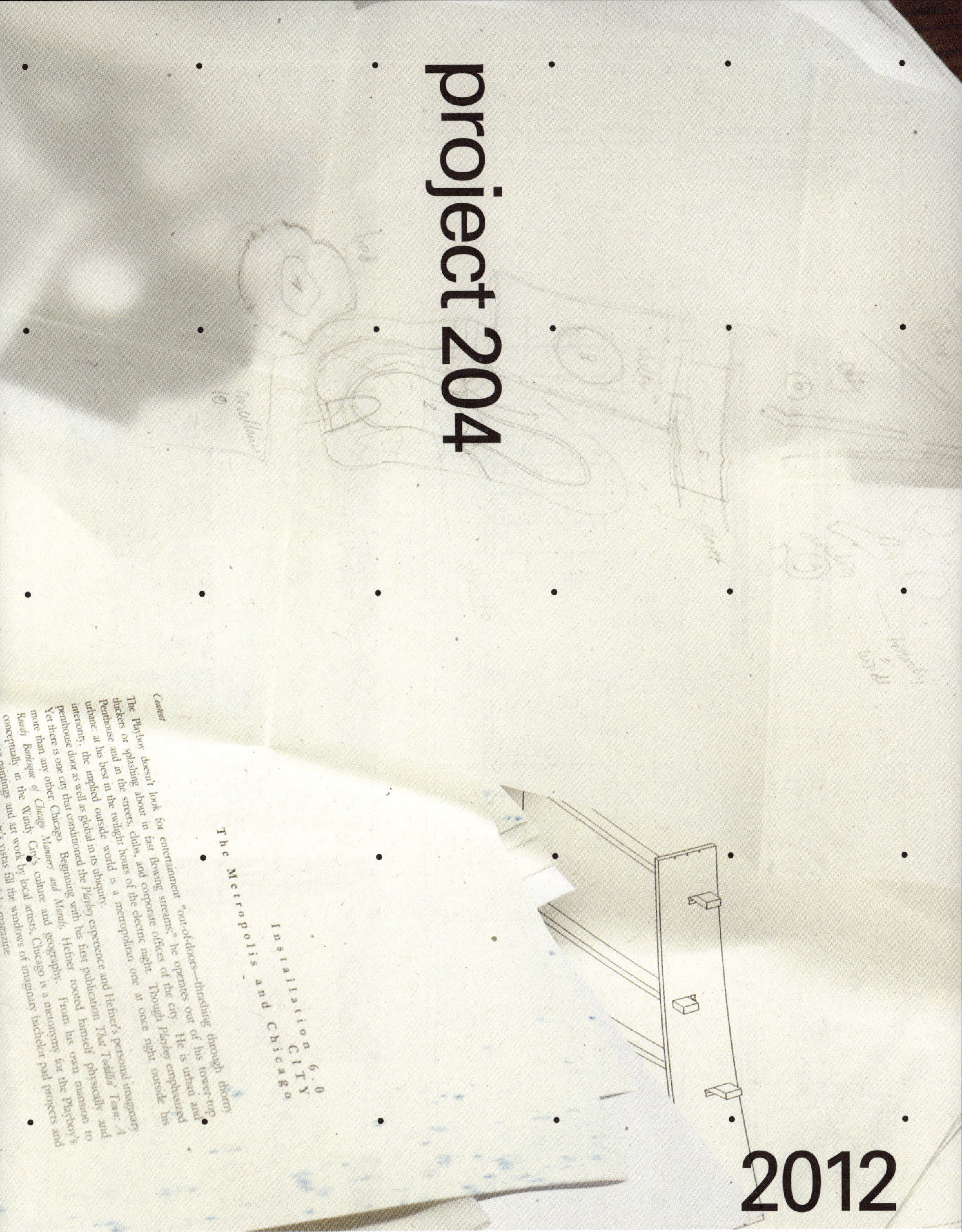

2012

Merging Matters
Page 493

Playboy Architecture 1953–1979
Project: Exhibition
Duration: Medium-term, 4 months
Year: 2012
Data: page 667

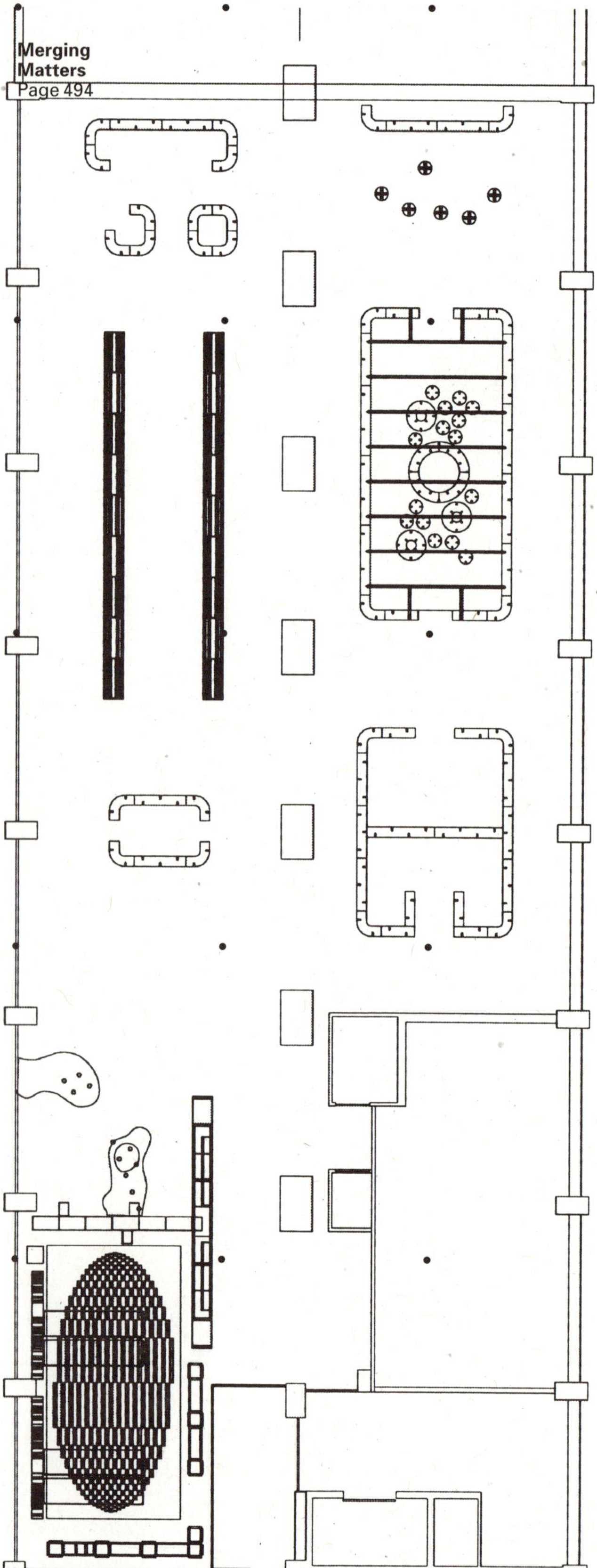

PLAYBOY
PLAYBOY
PLAYBOY

project 204
PLAYBOY

BACHELOR PAD

PLAYBOY
FIFTEENTH HOLIDAY ANNIVERSARY ISSUE

PLAYBOY AND LITERATURE
CAPTIONS:

PLAYBOY KIOSK

project 204
Sep 2012–
Feb 2013

PLAYBOY
BACHELOR PAD
INTRODUCTION:
Bache
Pad
PLAYBOY'S PENTHOUSE APARTMENT
a high, handsome haven—pre-planned and furnished for the bachelor in town.

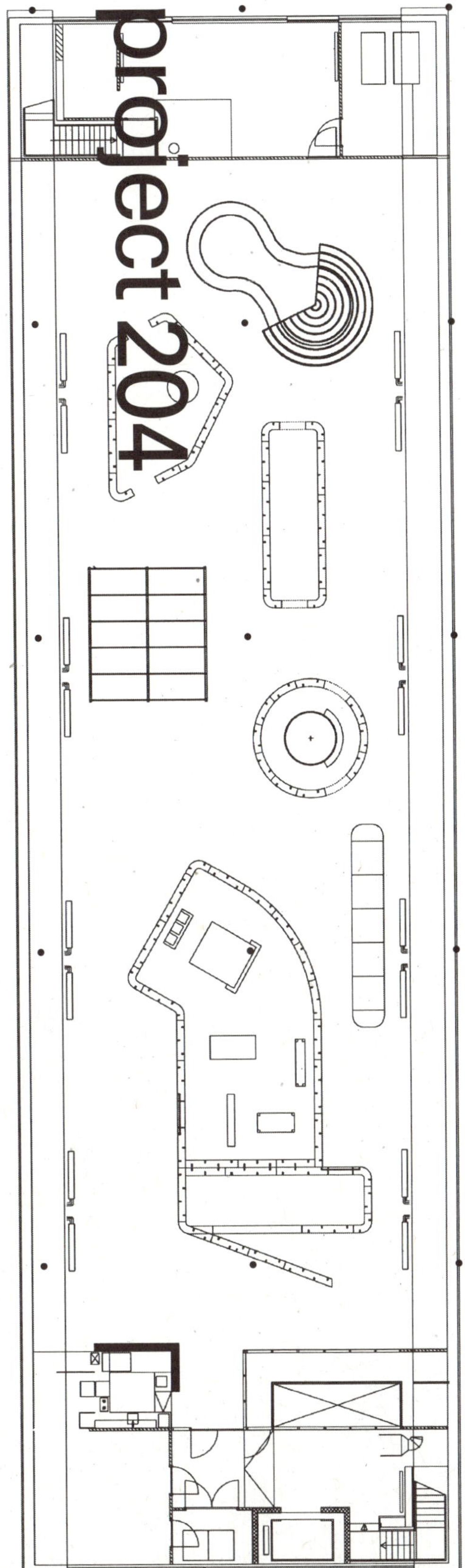
project 204

project 204

PLAYBOY
GROTTO

PLAYBO
CONTROL ROOM
CAPTIONS:
PLAYBOY'S ELECTRONIC ENTERTAINMENT WALL
PLAYBOY'S WONDER WALL
SWITCHED-ON SUPERWALL

project 204
PLAYBOY CONTROL ROOM
PLAYBOY CONTROL ROOM
INTRODUCTION:
Control Room
Controlekamer
Contro
PLAYBOY CONTROL ROOM

5

Events: Situating the Temporary
Page 504

project 193

2011

Out of Storage
Project: Temporary Museum
Duration: Medium-term, 8 months
Year: 2011
Data: page 665

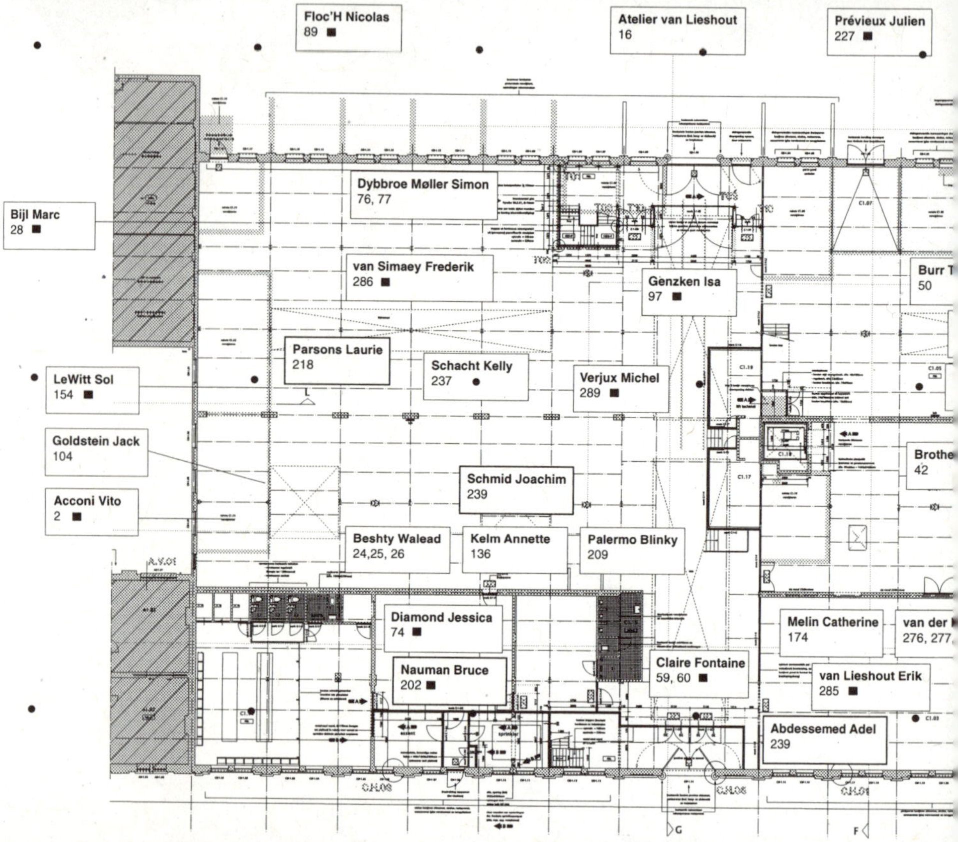
Floc'H Nicolas 89
Atelier van Lieshout 16
Prévieux Julien 227
Bijl Marc 28
Dybbroe Møller Simon 76, 77
van Simaey Frederik 286
Genzken Isa 97
Burr T 50
Parsons Laurie 218
Schacht Kelly 237
Verjux Michel 289
LeWitt Sol 154
Goldstein Jack 104
Acconi Vito 2
Schmid Joachim 239
Brothe 42
Beshty Walead 24,25, 26
Kelm Annette 136
Palermo Blinky 209
Diamond Jessica 74
Nauman Bruce 202
Claire Fontaine 59, 60
Melin Catherine 174
van der 276, 277,
van Lieshout Erik 285
Abdessemed Adel 239

corner
FRAC
COLLECTION FRAC NPDC

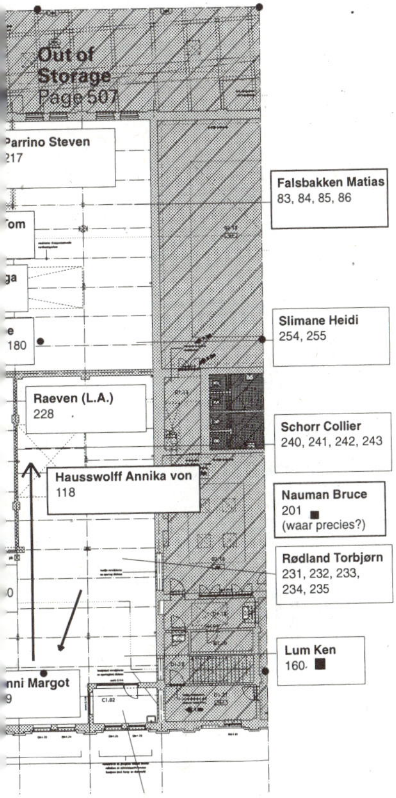

Out of Storage
Page 507
Parrino Steven
217
Falsbakken Matias
83, 84, 85, 86
Slimane Heidi
254, 255
Raeven (L.A.)
228
Schorr Collier
240, 241, 242, 243
Hausswolff Annika von
118
Nauman Bruce
201
(waar precies?)
Rødland Torbjørn
231, 232, 233,
234, 235
Lum Ken
160
nni Margot

project 193

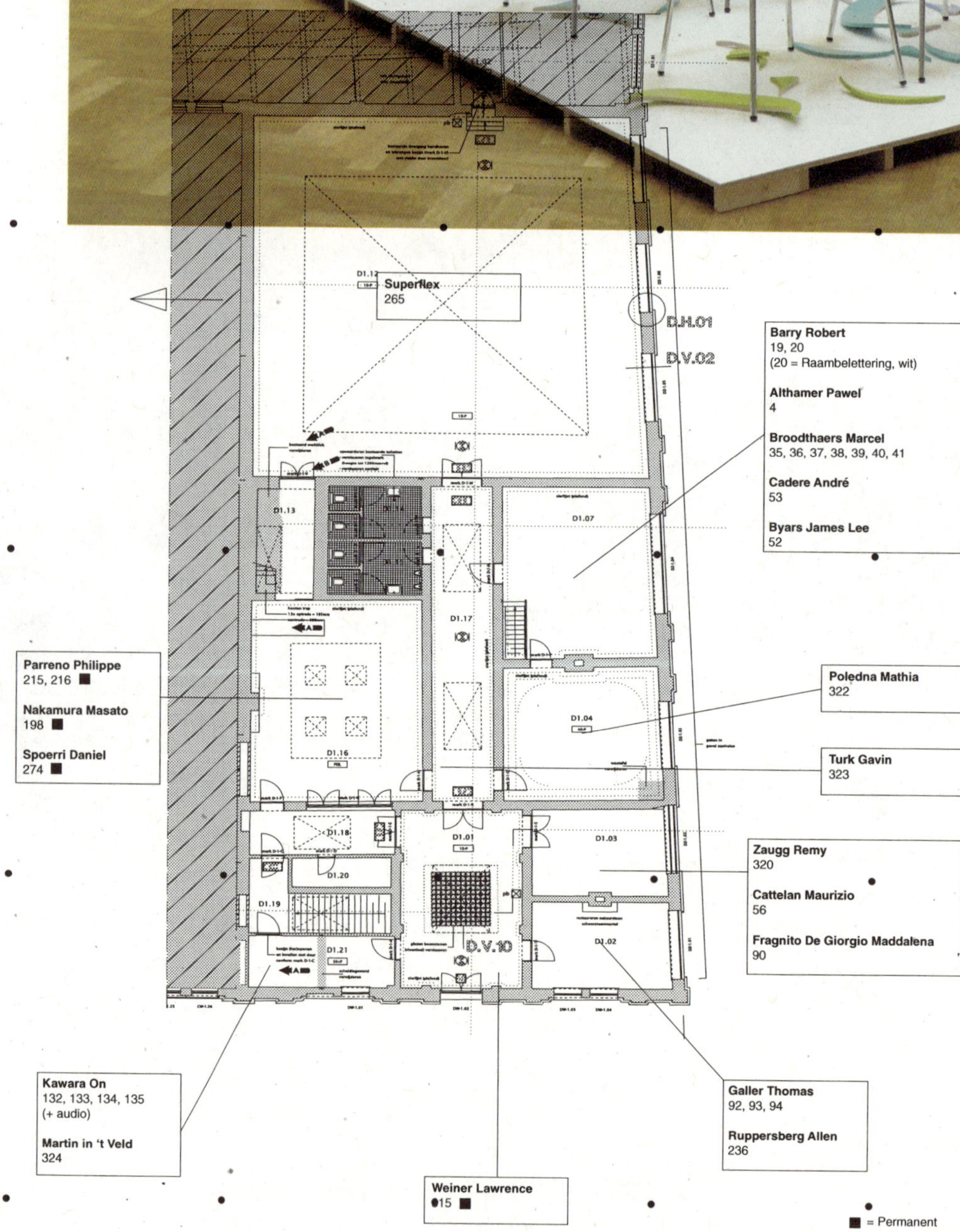
Superflex
265
D.H.01
D.V.02
Barry Robert
19, 20
(20 = Raambelettering, wit)
Althamer Pawel
4
Broodthaers Marcel
35, 36, 37, 38, 39, 40, 41
Cadere André
53
Byars James Lee
52
D1.12
D1.13
D1.07
D1.17
D1.16
D1.04
Parreno Philippe
215, 216 ■
Nakamura Masato
198 ■
Spoerri Daniel
274 ■
Poledna Mathia
322
Turk Gavin
323
D1.18
D1.01
D1.03
D1.20
D1.19
D1.21
D1.02
D.V.10
Zaugg Remy
320
Cattelan Maurizio
56
Fragnito De Giorgio Maddalena
90
Kawara On
132, 133, 134, 135
(+ audio)
Martin in 't Veld
324
Galler Thomas
92, 93, 94
Ruppersberg Allen
236
Weiner Lawrence
015 ■
■ = Permanent

Out of Storage
Page 509

project 193

project 193

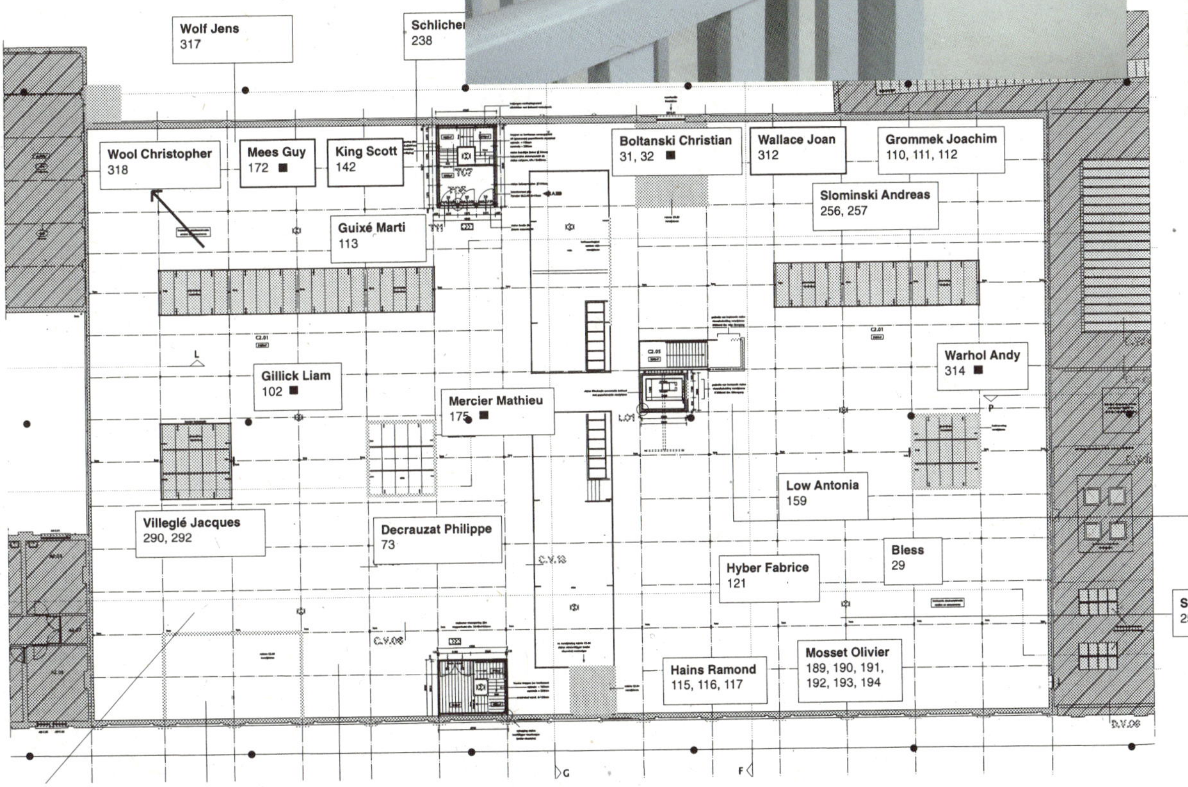
Wolf Jens
317
Schlicher
238
Wool Christopher
318
Mees Guy
172
King Scott
142
Boltanski Christian
31, 32
Wallace Joan
312
Grommek Joachim
110, 111, 112
Slominski Andreas
256, 257
Guixé Marti
113
Gillick Liam
102
Mercier Mathieu
175
Warhol Andy
314
Low Antonia
159
Villeglé Jacques
290, 292
Decrauzat Philippe
73
Bless
29
Hyber Fabrice
121
Hains Ramond
115, 116, 117
Mosset Olivier
189, 190, 191,
192, 193, 194

5

Events: Situating the Temporary
Page 512

tal erez: as systems reshuffle

1

In one of his many appearances, Nobel Prize-winning economist Milton Friedman uses the pencil to explain the global cycle of the free market. He describes a long chain of production, which interweaves wood from the United States, graphite from South America, rubber from Malaysia, which came from trees imported by the British from South America, and so on. "Literally thousands of people cooperated to make this pencil," he states. "When you go down to the store and buy this pencil, you are in effect trading a few minutes of your time, for a few seconds of the time of all those people." Friedman even goes so far as to argue that this global productive collaboration of people is one with political effects, as it fosters global harmony and peace. Friedman's example stops there, in his analysis of the participants in harvesting the raw materials of the pencil, yet there are even more people involved in the route of this pencil. Businessmen, engineers, factory workers, marketers and store owners, distributors and ship captains. All of these facets, disciplines, nationalities, and hierarchies collaborate to place this pencil on a shelf for a consumer to buy, even while making that person eager to buy it. In the midst of this massive economic machine which drives the Western world and links politics, finance, social struggles, ecology, business plans, and territories stands the industrial product. It has been designed to cooperate with these mechanisms.

The Industrial Revolution was one of scale. While, to some extent, these connections were present for centuries, it was the transition to mass production that permitted such immense interrelations to become the economic mainstream, by making them profitable and affordable, both by cutting the costs of production as well as by generating a market for products by disseminating the notion of consumption to the masses. Yet this kind of operation needed to be orchestrated, and required the capabilities of those businesses which manufactured and traded those mass-produced goods as well. To make this transition, products had to be adapted to fit these methods of mass production, not based on artisanship, but on large factories and a division of labor. It was this division that required the designer. Not exactly an evolutionary stage of the craftsman, nor of the engineer, and with only a few precursors in the Renaissance and a slowly coalescing definition in the early Industrial Revolution, the term "industrial designer" was not even coined before 1919. Contradictory, perhaps, to the way it is communicated, it is not an age-old profession like architecture, and does not carry a long theoretical and practical history. It was formed for the scaling up and systemization of the production of tangible goods. With the spread of urbanization and the middle class as a consequence of the Industrial Revolution, a growing consumer market required messages and marketing to advance to mass scale, and other practices of design were surfacing. The term "graphic design" was coined in 1922. Design was a product of the dramatic industrial outcomes of the early twentieth century, and was birthed to serve these new commercial constructs.

As consumption grew to define and drive our economy, the designer's role has been fixed as a bridge between the interests of companies, as defined by manufacturing capabilities, target costs, and business strategies, on the one hand, and the desires of consumers as defined by marketing on the other, through to the point where business and consumer meet: the product. The design discipline existed within the gap formed by the division of labor, which was, in turn, created by scaling up – the gap between those who produce, and those who plan, so that identical products could be made by different workers of generic skills. Unlike the artisan, in the vast economic system of mass production, distribution, and consumption, the designer was a key service provider, at the center of the economic system.

This is, if anything, what makes design unique: a cultural field deeply embedded in, and in direct service of, the economic mechanisms that drive society. It is a creature both of culture and of market, and it refuses to see them as standing in opposition. Therein lies its power. It is not a reflection on popular culture – it is part of popular culture. Therefore, it always partakes in the definition of the cultural zeitgeist. Industrial design – only as old as modern industry, with no real historical and theoretical bindings – is always corresponding with industry's changing face. Whether it is critical or complying, whether aimed at a large or small audience, it has never been a discipline with a parallel lifeline to the economic and social systems. It leans, serves, and reacts to them; to the businesses that fund it, the advertisements that sell it, and the policies that define its boundaries.

2

Yet the structure of industry is transforming. Digital culture and the Internet have been gradually creating alternative economic structures, rapidly breaking down the intertwined product cycle into separate core elements, while distributing these services, once almost exclusively for the orchestration of business, as platforms and tools that have become directly approachable by consumers. Gradually, in the course of the last half century, production economy has been transforming into service economy, and through the course of twenty years the Internet has dramatically increased alternative operations to key elements of the system, and introduced new ones. Financing is becoming ever more attainable for individuals through different platforms, like direct online micro-financing and micro-loans; the distribution of ideas, products, and concepts is readily available through portals, social networks, and intricate algorithms; marketing leans on individuals using ratings and reviews; business models are being challenged daily by peer-to-peer initiatives; traditional commerce is being reinvented in alternative "free" transactions.

Online, again another tectonic shift separates production and design. On the Internet and in digital media, production is no longer the junction of industry, as it is slowly transforming into yet another service for hire. On Alibaba, factories of any scale and technique take job orders from any business, large or small, at a few clicks of a button. Labor is distributed and attainable on different scales, from craftsmen to makers and designers, and up to a multitude of people who will take work starting at a single cent. These transformations find a direct connection to the physical world through new tools for digital manufacturing. They both symbolically and literally plug the Internet, its structures, and culture into personal or small-scale production facilities. The costs of 3D printers have been so dramatically reduced that some can now be bought for less than a mid-level smartphone.

Moreover, design is also sold and shared independently of products. On financing platforms such as Kickstarter, products are sold as potentials before their production feasibility has even been proven. Around the Web, digital files for production are for sale, or available for free. Instructions for making, how-to videos, and apps for adaptations and customizations of design are expanding. Tender platforms sell design files on specific briefs. Many traditional designed products are now being realized only partly before being circulated or sold as photoshopped prototypes or high-end models. For what seems to be the first time in its history, consumers pay separately for a product's design and its production.

Consumers are changing as well. Gradually redefined as users, they are urged to be creative by being given tools to voice themselves, while utilizing these new services to create new gatherings, to figure out their strength as groups. They are exposed to an immense amount of knowledge, raw and edited, as well as tools – both specific and generic – for making, adapting, and distributing. As such, users are eager to generate new content, or to adapt and recontextualize existing content. More and more, they are invited to produce themselves: images, music, photo albums, videos, and physical products, from shoes to furniture. Moreover, this user involvement exists on a huge spectrum. No longer either makers of goods or consumers of them, online users can place themselves on the scale in between. They can be highly involved in planning and producing, like in the makers community, or very mildly involved, or not at all. They can be either journalists or bloggers, talkbackers or readers. Whether willingly or not, users are now playing a triple role: as a resource for data, as manufacturers of content and goods, and as consumers of the same.

3

In the midst stands the designer. In the transformation to a service economy; in the digitization of so many once physical products; in the leveling of the production and distribution playing field, the bond between designer and product is breaking, and the product is losing its role as the center of the chain. The service of the designer – who now holds not only knowledge and skills, but also accessibility to services once out of his reach – at present has the grounds to take the lead.

No longer a peon in the economic game, he is faced with new tools and opportunities, new responsibilities and knowledge, and new competitors. The Internet has not only generated new tools, but also dramatic new social issues. Questions of privacy, data mining, regulation, control, and copyright can no longer be avoided by design. While some aspects of the economic system become increasingly exposed and distributed, others are becoming more intricate, hidden behind complicated algorithms and almost unfathomable business models. These issues are now issues of the physical world through tools of digital manufacturing. They are underlining every discussion over the "Internet of things." This time around, with a dismantled production cycle, the designer can no longer hide behind the business. With his knowledge and education in all these mechanisms now for hire – marketing, financing, production, consumer psychology, cultural trends, pricing, etc. – the designer now seems a prime candidate to be the orchestrator of product cycles, rather than service ones. He is left to stand in front of the user, and can be held responsible for the consequences of his designs.

For the product designer, the Internet is a no-man's-land of unexplored opportunities and new tools. How will products be designed peer-to-peer? How can big data be used as a tool? What kind of interfaces can be offered to users? How can products handle a dialogue with the growing power of communities and social networks? How will copyright and privacy be addressed? How will the concept of "free" adhere to products? How can one put a price on design in separation from production? These are only some of the practical questions that designers never before faced. They will inevitably generate new products, models, and social structures.

In the face of the new industrial structures and new users, the designer must redefine his position. In an endless array of knowledge and possibilities, in the midst of adaptations and recontextualization, the designer must take a step back from the narrow perspective of a physical product. In a digital world of platforms and direct interaction with consumers, a design is no longer a final product, but rather a set of boundaries in which products could happen, communities can be generated, and new ideas can emerge. To stay relevant for creative consumers, designers must open up their practice for dialogue, while maintaining their expertise in defining the boundaries of this dialogue. Yet it is not enough. In order to take a position that is valid, designers must reappropriate a larger understanding of the system they are part of, and the ways in which it operates – both in micro, with the new tools of design and communication, and in macro, with a control over new business models and production chains, social implications, and regulatory and political consequences. It requires a "RealPolitik" approach to design, one that is based on manipulation of the system in order to push for a goal. As systems get more complex, with fewer places to hide, and in his unique position as linking production with users, the designer is faced with a new power to redefine the field he is part of, those who consume it, and those whom it serves.

4

It is a unique time to do so. The system is in flux, and all futures are open to it. Big businesses, traditional organizations, social

5

movements, and radical groups all try to capitalize on this change to push for their respective goals, from monetary profit to new political orders. All are trying to apply their weight on the way the system will eventually be defined. This battle, once purely digital, is increasingly reflected in the physical world in new consumer behavior, new tools for making, and new regulatory and legal issues. As such, not only can it still be influenced, but it directly touches those who are in charge of shaping the physical world: designers. They, too, perhaps more than ever, operate on that spectrum – from the very capitalist agenda to the very socially oriented one, and all its in-betweens. Each new product introduced by and to this new system has a potential to redefine the system itself, in the way it is designed, marketed, sold, and produced, in its longevity and adaptation, and in the new ways it can be used and made.

It is an exciting time for designers and for users, as new opportunities emerge, new questions need answering; as it seems nothing is fixed and endless possibilities unfold to influence and shape culture, business, services, and day-to-day life.

Yet, among the many new fields that have been opened up for design by the Internet, it is worth remembering Friedman's final conclusion. A product is never just a product. It is always part of a larger economic, and eventually political system. In the changing of the economic system, in the new power the designer holds, hides a sociopolitical shift. The products, systems, strategies, and models designers will create will have a great influence on what will be the face of this new world.

You never change things by fighting the existing reality. To change something, build a new model that makes the existing model obsolete.
– R. Buckminster Fuller[1]

1
R. Buckminster Fuller, *Critical Path* (New York: St. Martin's Griffin, 1982).

5 joana meroz: event architecture,

Events: Situating the Temporary
Page 520

fig. 1
Dunne & Raby
Faraday Chair,
Hertzian Tales
1994–97,
photo: Lubna
Hammoud

fig. 2
Dienand Christe
Sex Table, 1998
CNC milled MDF,
spray painted brown,
automotive lacquer
and smoked glass,
80 x 30 cm

critical design in the age of convergence culture

The practice of EventArchitectuur (EA) compels yet frustrates the application of old oppositional models that contrast "spectacle" with "reality" as a means through which to contextualize its approach towards product design. Founded by architect Herman Verkerk and subsequently joined by visual artist Paul Kuipers, EA established its reputation among prominent cultural and entertainment institutions as exhibition designers, by creating a type of editorial display furniture that at once supports and critiques the shows of its clients. According to Verkerk, "Institutions use us to tip the balance in favor of what they need at that moment: at times they need to show the critical aspect and other times they need to be more careful. No institution can afford to be critical all of the time; it boils down to a question of self-preservation."[1]

Thus, when EA was asked to create the complete interior of the Arnhem Fashion Biennale in 2005, it had no qualms about designing a flawless mainstream display in perfect harmony with the conventions of fashion. And, in contrast, when the organization wanted to go more "activist" in the 2007 edition, EA had no trouble abiding, making the arbitrariness of the manufacture of the fashion spectacle abundantly clear by employing construction and packaging materials.[2] In straddling the perceived oppositions between "resistance" and "co-optation," criticality and manipulation, EA incisively exposes the fragility of hackneyed dualities in an age of rapidly advancing convergence "where old and new media collide, where grassroots and corporate media intersect, where the power of the media producer and the power of the media consumer interact in unpredictable ways."[3] But, within a framework of convergence culture in which the "spectacle" of the market is no longer discernible from the "reality" of daily life – and in which the traditional values attached to one or the other evaporate – what can the significance of the role of critical design be, and how is EA negotiating the relevance of its critical design practice?

The critical project

Willingly or not, EA is inevitably affiliated with the

1
Herman Verkerk, in discussion with the author, May 7, 2010.

2
Ibid.

3
Sven Lütticken, "Het Schilderij en de Afvalbak," in *De Witte Raaf*, accessed May 8, 2010, http://dewitteraaf.stylelabs.com/web/flash/content.asp?struct_id=8&pagetype=search&language_id=6&pagecount=1&site=DWR_site (my translation); Henry Jenkins, *Convergence Culture: Where Old and New Media Collide* (London and New York: New York University Press, 2006), 2.

project of critical design. Although, up until recently, critical design had not received much media attention, in the past couple of years it has been addressed by a number of exhibitions and publications.[4] While some commentators conflate critical and conceptual design into one project – they certainly do have some characteristics in common, among them, the reliance on speculative proposals instead of functional products, as well as the aim to make us "think about materials, processes and traditions, and also about the difference between desire and need, or comfort and excess" – I will will treat them separately here, since they descend from different lineages. While conceptual design is closely related to postmodernism and the "end of the grand narratives," critical design has its roots in the post-Marxist tradition of critical theory.[5]

At its most basic, critical theory's main purpose is to investigate modernity's notion of the fundamental dichotomy between reality and spectacle, along with many of its derivative oppositions, such as high and low culture, art and design, producer and consumer, compliance and resistance.[6] Although critical theory purports to detachedly discriminate mass culture from autonomy, it is possible to see the project of critical theory itself as one of modernity's products, alongside those phenomena it aims to critique. According to Van Winkel, if "both the autonomous work of art and the culture industry were predicated upon social, economical and technological changes that followed the Industrial Revolution," then it becomes possible to conceive of the concomitant development of post-Marxist critical theory as being likewise a product conditioned by the aforementioned parameters.[7] Thus, while critical theory's project is to separate the wheat from the chaff and to denounce "the dark, solid reality concealed behind brilliance of appearances," rather than doing so from a privileged vantage point, it instead integrally participates in the mechanism of the system it professes to denounce.[8] Jacques Rancière drove this point home in the essay "The Misadventures of Critical Thought" (2009). According to him, the basic mechanism of the critical project – and, as I propose, of critical design – can be deconstructed into two main moments. While the first is preoccupied with revealing the "reality" behind the image, the purpose of the second is to confront the viewer with this new knowledge, "in order to bolster activist energies" and prompt him to take action. "The critical procedure thus aimed to have a dual effect: an awareness of the hidden reality and a feeling of guilt about the denied reality."[9]

The speculative proposal

Thus, if critical design's aim can be summarized as

4
Among them: *Designing Critical Design* (Hasselt: Z33 Gallery, 2007); *Don't Panic: Emergent Critical Design* (London: Architecture Foundation, 2007); *Forms of Inquiry: The Architecture of Critical Graphic Design* (Architecture Foundation, London, and other venues 2007–2009); and the exhibition catalogue of *Wouldn't it be nice . . . wishful thinking in art and design* (Centre d'Art Contemporain Genève, and other venues, 2007–2009). For a thorough overview and discussion of critical design's state of the debate, see Rick Poynor, "Design Thinking or Critical Design?," in *Now is the Time: Art & Theory in the 21st Century*, eds. C. Vesters, J. Bouwhuis, I. Commandeur, G. Frieling, M. Schavemaker, D. Ruyters (Rotterdam: NAi Publishers, 2009), 119.

5
Roberta Smith, "Is It Design? Art? Or Just a Dutch Joke?," *The New York Times* (December 30, 2006), accessed May 14, 2010, http://query.nytimes.com/gst/fullpage.html?res=9A05E5DF1630F933A05751C1A9609C8B63. For a lucid account of the importance of the concept of the end of the grand narrative for conceptual design, see Renny Ramakers, "Introduction," in *Droog Design in Context: Less and More* (Rotterdam: 010 Publishers, 2002).

6
For a discussion on the dichotomies of modernism, see: Camiel van Winkel "Middle Culture: Designers, Artists, Professionals," in *Now is the Time: Art & Theory in the 21st Century*, eds. C. Vesters, J. Bouwhuis, I. Commandeur, G. Frieling, M. Schavemaker, D. Ruyters (Rotterdam: NAi Publishers, 2009).

7
Van Winkel, "Middle Culture: Designers, Artists, Professionals," 125.

"mainly to make us think [b]ut also raising awareness, exposing assumptions, provoking action, sparking debate," then its affiliation with the project of critical theory becomes immediately apparent.[10] Anthony Dunne, who coined the term "critical design" in 1999, explains it by way of simple negation: "Its opposite is affirmative design: design that reinforces the status quo."[11] Dunne, widely acknowledged as critical design's fiercest proponent, together with design partner Fiona Raby, puts this into practice by relying almost solely on the form of the aforementioned speculative proposal. Taking the form of videos, illustrations, and props, the speculative proposal can be compared to "paper architecture" in that its purpose is precisely not to be "built" so as to be able to investigate the possibilities of architecture freed from the constraints inherent in the actual building of a project.[12] The design collective known as Speculative Design explains this emerging practice as led by a research methodology that promotes designed objects as tools for critical reflection.

"It serves as an alternative to existing research strategies by channelling findings through symbolic material objects. The interaction and experience one has with speculative objects are used to initiate further design. Developing an iterative design practice that reflects upon cultural realities."[13]

Dunne and Raby's *Faraday Chair* (1994–1997) is one such speculative proposal. Conceived as a "shelter in specially constructed non-radio spaces or negative radios," it exists in fact only as an *image* of a translucent orange Plexiglas display case mounted on a metal structure encasing a woman lying down and breathing through a mask (fig.1).[14] The point is not for it to actually *function* as a shelter but to make the viewer aware of the negative consequences of the rapid technological changes in his/her environment. Thus, in its most basic sense, critical design can be taken as a project "to make viewers aware of the ways they are being manipulated by design."[15]

Critical objecthood

In contrast to the logic of the speculative proposal, but in keeping with the critical project, EA's main goal is to develop a criticality that emanates from the *objecthood* of design rather than simply from its representations, linguistic or otherwise. Thus, departing from the premise that display furniture is never just a neutral support, EA investigates how its aesthetics – material, shape, color – contribute to directing a viewer's preferred interpretation of the object on show. For the *NL = New Luxury* exhibition (2009), whose explicit purpose was to promote the newest batch of star designers produced by Design Academy Eindhoven during the International Furniture

8
Jacques Rancière, "The Misadventures of Critical Thought," trans. Gregory Elliott, in *The Emancipated Spectator* (London and New York: Verso, 2009), 25.

9
Ibid., 27.

10
Anthony Dunne and Fiona Raby, "Critical Design FAQ," accessed May 13, 2010, http://www.dunneandraby.co.uk/content/bydandr/13/0. For discussions on the relevance of modernism to design history, theory, and practice, see Kjetil Fallan, *Design History: Understanding Theory and Method* (Oxford: Berg Publishers, 2010), especially the chapter "Epistemology"; Alastair Fuad-Luke, *Design Activism: Beautiful Strangeness for a Sustainable World* (London: Earthscan, 2009), particularly the chapter "Past Lessons: A Short History of Design in Activist Mode, 1750–2000"; Vera Bühlmann, "Pseudopodia: Prolegomena to a Discourse on Design," in Vera Bühlmann and Martin Wiedmer, eds., *Pre-Specifics. Some Comparativistic Investigations on Research in Design and Art* (Zürich: JRP-Ringier, 2008).

11
Dunne and Raby, "Critical Design FAQ."

12
Poynor, "Design Thinking or Critical Design?," 121.

13
Speculative Design, accessed May 24, 2010, http://speculativedesign.com.

14
Dunne and Raby, "Critical Design FAQ."

15
Poynor, "Design Thinking or Critical Design?," 121.

5

fig. 3

Fair in Milan, EA designed a display entirely composed of IKEA's iconic plain wood dining table, *Björkudden*, covered by square mirror tiles (fig. 3). The table was transformed into a unit in a modular system and was unceremoniously "elongated, stacked, sawed up, covered [and] turned over," depending on the specificity of each product displayed.[16] As a result, although the total effect of the exhibition was indeed one of luxury, the contrast between the brand of modernistic ideology embodied by the "democratically" priced seventy-nine-euro IKEA table and the spectacular fanfare surrounding the launch of the latest author-designers destined for stardom (symbolized by the mirrors, which, incidentally, cost more than the tables) did not fail to register as a critique of the compromised position of product designers wedged between the utopia of an autonomous practice and the reality of the marketplace. Insofar as EA relies on its objects to build the world in which a script can be staged, EA develops a physical rather than a speculative discursive practice.

But how can intrinsically spatial media, such as architecture and product design, communicate a story simply by virtue of its material properties, without resorting to the kind of linguistic and other illustrative reinforcements developed by the speculative practice of critical design? EA's conceptualization of the discursiveness of design has its roots in architectural narrative discourse, particularly in the work of architect and theorist Bernard Tschumi.[17] Tschumi's work can be characterized as following the critical tradition, in that its program is to question and revise the social conditions as they are represented – and thus, perpetuated – by architecture.[18] EA appropriates this agenda and summarizes it into its own key question: "How far can design program a specific experience?"[19] Thus, instead of purely instrumentalizing design towards a specific type of manipulation of experience as advocated throughout modernism, or wallowing in postmodernism's absolute relativism that warned us of the impossibility of predetermining meaning, since it all boils down to interpretation, EA's practice can be understood as a continuous negotiation with the ability of material constructions to articulate the range between those two positions. Arguably, in its beginnings, discursive architecture was "superficial and formalistic," in that it largely resorted to language as a means of creating a narrative. This can be compared to product design's literal use of language, as can be seen in, for example, Dienand Christe and Rob Veelenturf's *Sex Table*, in which the word "sex" serves as the table's legs (fig. 2).[20] However, by the 1970s, architects such as Tschumi turned to the chronology inherent in film as another means of creating narrative architecture:

16
Utrecht Manifest website, accessed May 24, 2010, http://www.utrechtmanifest.nl/node/257.

17
Herman Verkerk, in discussion with the author, May 7, 2010.

18
Bernard Tschumi Architects website, accessed May 24, 2010, http://www.tschumi.com/projects/18.

19
Herman Verkerk, in discussion with the author, May 7, 2010.

20
Ibid.

since one experiences a building sequentially – first the corridor, then the stairs, a room, another room – it becomes possible to appropriate this method to tell a story as a "sequence of events" experienced by walking through the building.[21] This is the basic discursive principle EA applies, whether in designing buildings, interiors, exhibition displays, or furniture. Since, according to Verkerk, "life is also but a performance," EA first scripts the scene that should play out in a space (whether fictional or real), and subsequently designs the props of that scene to support it.

Such is the case with EA's *Social Billboards* (2009), constructed for the third edition of the Utrecht Manifest Biennial for Social Design. The brief EA received specified that the communication trajectory of the biennial should offer a perspective on how the social can emerge from the model of communication itself.[22] In response, EA designed three distinct but related billboards, each of which addresses the problematic of acting socially versus representing the social. The starting point was juxtaposing social action and representation in the same site. Thus, a public bench (where the act of the social could take place) had its back extended upwards to form a support on which two posters containing information about the event hang side by side (where the representation of the social could take place) (fig. 4). The purpose of the second billboard was to question the relation between the "real" social and its representation, which EA did by creating a poster-size hole in place of one of the posters, which literally framed the "real" social in place of its representation, but whose image was, of course, relative to the point of view of the subject, thus succinctly illustrating the point that representation (of the social) is always a matter of perspective (fig. 5). The third billboard was not a billboard at all, in fact, but just a chair; a reduced format of the benches used in the previous two. Here, EA ups the ante by stripping the social of any representation and creating instead the place where activism can actually happen. Through the use of "activist aesthetics" – the employment of untreated, cheap wood, the sandbags reminiscent of trenches, the exposure of the construction method – EA reveals the inherent contradiction of representing the social and creates an open invitation for action. Thus, in one moment, EA discloses the ineffectuality of representation, and in the next, prompts the viewer into questioning his/her own responsibility and implication in the reality of the situation.

fig. 4, 5

Spectacular criticality?

However, as has been drilled into us over and again, the procedure of this simple mechanism of revelation and

21 Ibid.

22 Utrecht Manifest website, accessed May 24, 2010, http://www.utrechtmanifest.nl/node/257.

ensuing activism is ineffective: knowing unfortunately does not lead to change. EA is not only well of aware of this, but also exploits this knowledge, which complicates a straightforward reading of their practice as a form of "uncritical" critical design. They had no qualms transforming their critical display furniture from *NL = New Luxury* into a spectacular, glinting, sprawling, autonomous design piece in its own right for the exhibition *Unforeseen Magic*, also part of Utrecht Manifest 2009 (fig. 6). As EA explains:

> This complex stacking is empty, stripped from every project, and seems by its emptiness to be a metaphor of the demand for a new luxury and the position that the designer can still assume vis-à-vis the industry and the consumer. Is this a choice for a more autonomous position and consequently an escape from the current democratization of designing? Do they see this democratization of designing as the last form of populism as the umpteenth ideology of the market? Or does EventArchitectuur attempt to fuse the designing with equally democratic forms of appropriation as autonomous forms of artistry in an attempt to maximize the critical potential of the designer?[23]

fig. 6

The implication here is that the display of protest itself has become one more spectacular image in a system of capitalist production. And yet, EA offers up its own images of denunciation as glossy display design – as one more commodity to be consumed. Consequently, the critical project continues, presenting "itself as a luxury commodity pertaining to the very logic it denounces," and "show[ing] us absorbed into the belly of the beast, where even our capacities for autonomous, subversive practices, and the networks of interaction that we might utilize against it, serve the new power of the beast – that of immaterial production."[24] Indeed, according to Sven Lütticken, "For the contemporary art world... self-criticism and complexity have become unique selling points that have turned art into a successful up-market branch of the culture industry at large, and therefore part of the present society of the spectacle."[25] But, as Rancière reminds us, rather than following to the logical conclusion that if everything is nothing but spectacular exhibition, then there is no opposition between reality and spectacle – and therefore no necessity for the critical project any longer – the critical project remains caught in its own opposition between image and reality. Thereby its theories and practices are reduced to an unproductive merry-go-round between denunciation of the spectacle and compliance with, and reproduction of, the very structure of the dichotomy of this system.

23
Ibid.

24
Rancière, "The Misadventures of Critical Thought," 30, 33.

25
Sven Lütticken, "Art, Consumption, Criticism," in *Secret Publicity: Essays on Contemporary Art* (Rotterdam: NAi Publishers, 2005), 7.

As a means of escaping this catch-22, Rancière approaches the issue of the critical project as actually being a question of intellectual equality and emancipation, rather than of reality and images. Rancière fully elaborates this proposition in *The Emancipated Spectator* (2009), where he compares the relation between artist and spectator to the one between teacher and student.[26] Rancière refers to Joseph Jacotot's pedagogical theory, which observes that the teacher, rather than bridging the gap between student and himself, instead maintains that distance by implicitly making the object of learning *knowledge* rather than *ability to learn*. Regardless of how much the student can come to know, the teacher, being the one who explicates and transmits knowledge, will always remain one step ahead. The critical project functions in an analogous way: as long as the position of the critical artist is one of revealing the illusion in which the poor spectator finds himself, the result is the perpetuation of the circle between image and reality ad infinitum. The pressing question then becomes: how to critique criticality without participating in its mechanism of denunciation and revelation? Rather than focusing on the position of the artist, Rancière concentrates instead on the agency already present in the very act of spectatorship. Skeptical of the orthodox Marxist fixation with the importance of production as generative and controlling of meaning, Rancière opposes this view, advocating instead the importance of the divergent ways objects can be consumed, or in other words, interpreted: "An emancipated community is a community of narrators and translators," he says, requiring "spectators who play the role of active interpreters, who develop their own translation in order to appropriate the 'story' and make it their own story."[27] It is precisely this concept that emancipation is based on interpretation and appropriation, rather than on explication and revelation, that forges the link to how EA approaches the critical project in today's convergence culture.

26 For an in-depth discussion of his thought on emancipation, see Rancière, *The Ignorant Schoolmaster* (1991).

27 Rancière, "The Misadventures of Critical Thought," 22.

Convergence culture

"Convergence" technically signifies the process by which "content" (a story, an image, an object) is presented throughout different media platforms (cinema, mobile phones, blogs, galleries), and how this specific type of flow inherently effects the behavior of production, distribution, and consumption. However, as Henry Jenkins argues, more significantly than simply referring to a multitude of media technologies coming together in a multifunctional "black box" of television-cum-Internet-cum-game-cum-telephone, convergence culture indicates instead the politico-socio-cultural effects of recent technological developments supported by digitalization:

> [Convergence] is both a top-down corporate-driven process and a bottom-up consumer-driven process. Corporate convergence coexists with grassroots convergence. Media companies are learning how to accelerate the flow of media content across delivery channels to expand revenue opportunities, broaden markets, and reinforce viewer commitments. Consumers are learning how to use these different media technologies to bring the flow of media more fully under their control and to interact with other consumers. The promises of this new media environment raise expectations of a freer flow of ideas and content. Inspired by those ideals, consumers are fighting for the right to participate more fully in their culture.[28]

Jenkins proposes that one of the effects of this rearrangement of positions between producers and consumers, corporate and grassroots initiatives, is the rise of a new discursive form, frequently referred to as "transmedia storytelling."[29] According to Jenkins, this is a "new aesthetic... that places new demands on consumers and depends on the active participation of knowledge communities... [it] is the art of world making."[30] Basically, in transmedia storytelling, a story is told across different media platforms, each of which adds to the whole according to its own medium specificities. Up until now, it has mostly been consciously employed by multinational media conglomerates producing content with several points of entry, and is situated at the crossroads between movies, games, and Internet platforms such as blogs. Although this is obviously in keeping with a capitalist logic of selling the same content in as many different ways and to as many different customers as possible, the distinctiveness of transmedia stories is that they do not function without an active participatory culture willing to build the story by sharing its collective intelligence.

Although new digital technologies have been essential to the proliferation of this new type of cultural production, it is important to realize that, by now, the paradigm of convergence culture has qualitatively moved beyond them. As such, its logic has infiltrated in other sites of cultural production that, in principle, do not necessarily utilize digital, virtual, or social media. The way this can be understood is by comparison with the Industrial Revolution:

> When Marx proposed the dominance of industrial capital... in the mid-nineteenth century most workers... were not in the factories but in the fields. Industrial production was dominant instead in qualitative terms, that is, insofar as its qualities were

28
Jenkins, *Convergence Culture*, 18.

29
Although there are different terms for this narrative form, such as "cross-media storytelling," I use here the term "transmedia storytelling," since it is that used by Jenkins, and since I base my own definition largely on his.

30
Jenkins, *Convergence Culture*, 20–21.

> imposed over other forms of production. Mining and agriculture, for instance, had to industrialize by adopting industry's methods of mechanization, its divisions of labour, its wage relations, its discipline, its time precision, its working day, and so forth. All forms of production throughout the world and social relations themselves gradually were forced to adopt the characteristic qualities of industrial production.[31]

In an analogous way, it is possible to say that the logic of convergence culture is infiltrating into all sorts of places that at first sight may seem to have nothing to do with the idea of "new media," such as humble tables, bookshelves, and chairs.[32]

EA deploys both the aesthetics of transmedia storytelling and its wider sociopolitical implications in its first furniture line, SPACES (2010). Ambiguous as to whether he is promoting a new form of social and democratic design as a means of formulating a new critical position vis-à-vis the problematic situation of critical design as sketched above, or whether he is simply earnestly capitalizing on transmedia storytelling's multiple entry point device – or indeed, both simultaneously – Verkerk calls this indefinite situation "the aesthetic problem of the unfinished." A significant aspect of SPACES is that it is EA's first "real" furniture functioning in "real" life rather than as prop furniture functioning within the institutional setting of an exhibition. Verkerk explains that, although continuing to design with the method of scripting events and subsequently attempting to influence the materiality of the object, so as to facilitate that script and thereby avoiding any sort of speculative proposal, the main difficulty with real furniture is that EA has less control over how its pieces will ultimately be used and therefore also to what the predicted outcome of that interaction can lead.

However, the truly innovative aspect of SPACES, in terms of EA's practice, is not so much the transposition of its discursiveness into the real, but the rearrangement of positions between consumer and designer as brought about by its *distribution* system. During its first launch at the 2010 International Furniture Fair in Milan, the furniture was presented in very accessible and informal circumstances, in which the viewer was welcome to try it out. With this in mind, the pieces presented in Milan were made of cheap wood, reminiscent of recycled material. For the more adventurous and interactive souls, EA supplied scaled-down three-dimensional cardboard models of the modules, which more engaged viewers were free to play with, cutting, rotating, and constructing. For those with more modest interest, EA provided stickers of the scaled-down modules, which

31
Michael Hardt, "Production and Distribution of the Common," in *Being an Artist in Times*, eds. Pascal Gielen and Paul De Bruyne (Rotterdam: NAi Publishers, 2009), 48.

32
See Vera Bühlmann's discussion on how the paradigm of the digital has infiltrated every aspect of design in her "Pseudopodia: Prolegomena to a Discourse on Design," in *Pre-Specifics: Some Comparativistic Investigations on Research in Design and Art*, eds. Vera Bühlmann and Martin Wiedmer (Zürich: JRP-Ringier, 2008).

viewers could cut up and paste, thereby creating their own version of the furniture. Based on those drawings, EA created a promotional video of SPACES launched on YouTube. A week later, SPACES was launched in Vivid Gallery in Rotterdam (fig. 7, 8), but this time in a transformed fashion, clearly aiming towards the high-end, more exclusive audience. The models previously used as promotional eye-catchers were presented in Plexiglas boxes – no longer a gadget, they had become collector's items. The furniture itself was made of expensive birch, and the gallery offered the possibility for the customer to select from a range of different tabletop colors and furnishings as a step towards further customization.

Still in the development phase is a fully interactive website, which, similar to the 3D models and the 2D stickers, would enable viewers to virtually cut, rotate, paste, and also directly place an order for the furniture, as well as allowing clients to effectively try out the pieces in their homes by creating virtual collages.

Conclusion
Clearly, SPACES possesses several characteristics of transmedia storytelling. Its transmedia aspect is developed in its use of different media platforms, such as the fair, gallery, home, models, stickers, and videos. The fact that it gives consumers the freedom as well as the responsibility to produce the pieces is a form of participatory culture, and if consumption is indeed a new form of collective intelligence – according to Jenkins, "consumption has become a collective process," and that is what he means by collective intelligence – then SPACES also touches on this aspect.[33] However, it is also possible to argue that SPACES is still only a precarious form of transmedia storytelling in comparison to other more fully developed examples, such as the franchise of *The Matrix* (1999). Perhaps the strongest objection would be not to how it relates to transmediality, but how it relates to the concept of storytelling. In this respect, the format of speculative critical design could more easily be understood as a form of storytelling given its reliance on text, illustrations, videos, and models. By concentrating on EA's practice, which consciously eschews illustration in favor of discursive materiality, the debate on design as a form storytelling indeed remains less articulated. Although it would be possible to continue contemplating these issues in an attempt to prove that product design is a perfect example of transmedia storytelling, that would be missing the real point of thinking about product design in terms of the paradigm of convergence culture, which is what this essay set out to do in the first place. The point of so doing lies elsewhere. Firstly, an increasing number of designers,

33 Jenkins, *Convergence Culture*, 4.

fig. 7, 8

such as EA, are intentionally adopting the aesthetic formats being developed within the paradigm of convergence culture, and unless their practices are examined from the perspective of convergence, the understanding of what they are doing, or attempting to do, will remain incomplete. Secondly, as mentioned before, the paradigm of convergence culture is by no means restricted to those media that are "natural" to it; arguably, its qualitative impact affects the entire system of cultural production and consumption, so that even projects that do not intentionally associate themselves with it nevertheless remain under its spell. Thirdly, and most significantly for the purpose of this essay, convergence eloquently sketches from a technocultural perspective the challenges and opportunities facing the critical project today, thereby allowing for reflection on the subject from a fresh perspective.

To return to the problem posed at the beginning of this essay: does critical design still have relevance in today's paradigm of convergence culture, where the fundamental dichotomy between spectacle and reality proposed by the critical project is severely put into question? As the investigation into the translation of critical theory into critical design has shown, while the effectiveness of the speculative practice has largely worn off, the investigation into the criticality of materiality, as EA researches, can still provide opportunities for a continuation in thinking about the relevance of a critical practice. And while, on the one hand, the paradigm of convergence culture blurs entrenched positions, on the other, it can serve as means to highlight the possibilities of redistributing them. Even if Jenkins and other commentators seem at times overtly optimistic about the unproblematic effect of convergence into the political and social spheres, it is important that designers continue questioning the relevance of their role within this new paradigm of convergence. Further research into other designers' practices is necessary to form a broader understanding of the impact of convergence in the culture of design.

5

project 181, 182, 187, 197, 223

2010

2012

SPACES / Design for Download
Project: Furniture
Year: 2010, 2012
Data: page 663, page 666

Merging Matters

project 181, 182, 187

Merging
Matters
Page 536

project 181, 182, 187

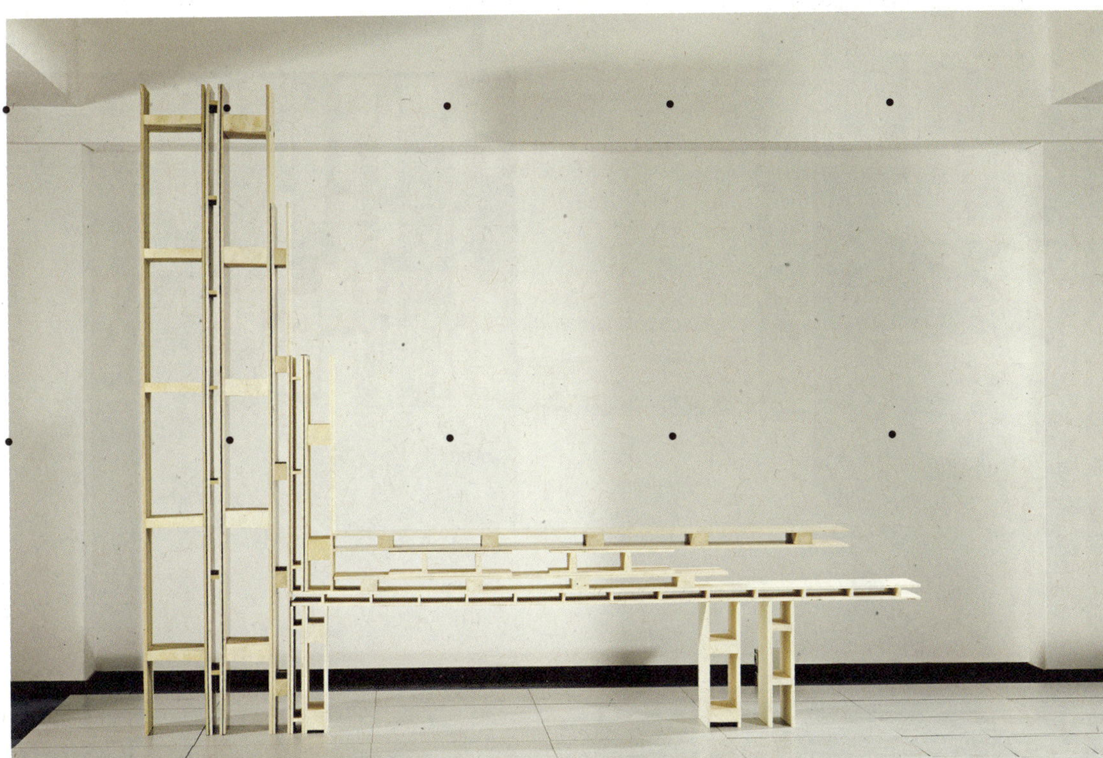

project 181, 182, 187

Merging

SPACES

Voids

EA

SPACES

2003
In 2003 EventArchitectuur introduced a series of libraries, desks and shelves, all based on the idea of the cross-section. These designs immediately caught the imagination thanks to its surprising visual quality based on the irregular rhythm of voids.
The international media created a growing interest for these unique designs, which questioned the classic relationship between an object and the surrounding space. It was not for long that the first interpretations of this idea could be recognized in the market. After several years however, it has become obvious that the full potential of this design idea has not been touched by the industry. EventArchitectuur decided to introduce SPACES, which can be seen as a tool to create a variety of designs as well as a limited series of unique products.

2010
SPACES not only breaks the classic boundaries between objects and spaces, but also between designer and user, offering a system of building blocks. These blocks contain the genetic code of the design, while supplying tools for the user to create his own interpretation. These building blocks are under development and will be presented in the coming year.

February 2010 EventArchitectuur presents a limited series of their own interpretation of SPACES in order to show the full potential of their genetic code. This first series of unique prototypes is handmade from birch wood multiplex and oak wood and will be signed and numbered.

www.eventarchitectuur.nl

project 18, 182, 187

SPACES

Modules

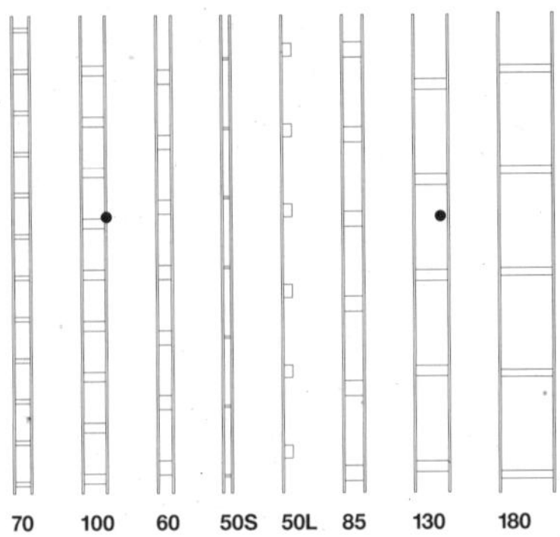

SPACES

Shelves / Desks
Vertical & Horizontal Libraries

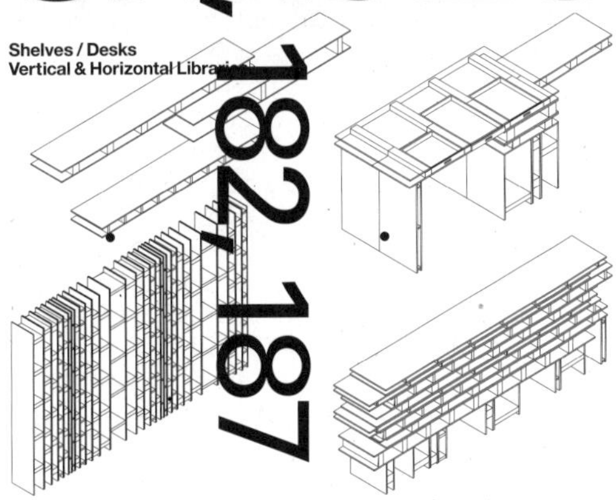

SPACES

Drawers / Chairs
Tabletops / Lamps

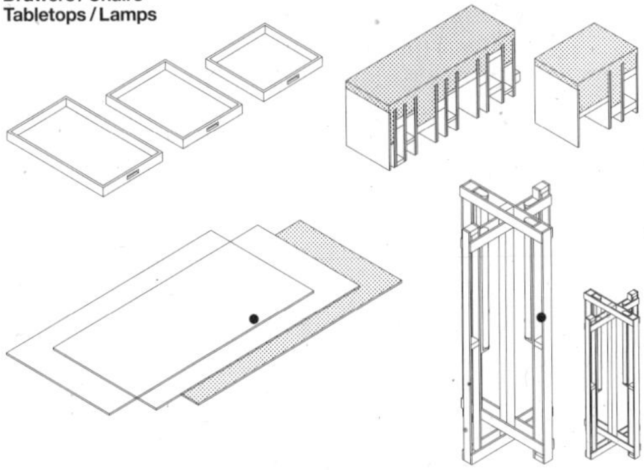

SPACES

Home Office

EA

SPACES

Tal Erez

About fifteen pages of variations lay on the table, a decade on the concept of a rhythmic library, a three-dimensional curtain, explored again and again in different projects – as a kitchen, as a bookstore, as a law firm interior. As a first step of the newly founded EventFurnituur, we aimed to systemize them, creating a modular storage system. An endless array of configurations were already present in those pages, which now needed to be consolidated into a coherent and workable system. And so SPACES came to be: rethinking the concept as a series of continuing dashed lines of different proportions, which could be cut at any height and used as building blocks for different furniture systems. The modules were carefully selected to offer versatility and usability, based on traditional paper and media sizes. They could be joined as shelves, vertical and horizontal libraries, as desks, benches, and all the spectrum in between.

We explored them in scale and in real size, experimented with the possibilities of this new system, and finally showed them in Milan. To further explore the versatility of this system, we made sticker pages, a separate sticker for each module, and alongside scissors and A4 pages marking floor and wall, we created a physical interface where visitors could use these modules in scale and offer new configurations. We were surprised with the results, and the unknown potentials discovered through this dialogue with users. One of our own configurations, a desk made with the system, was presented at OBJECT Rotterdam, where it was picked up by Renny Ramakers of Droog. Seeing the system, she invited EventArchitectuur to submit proposals for a new project they were working on, design for download, a concept in which users would buy designs – production plans – online and produce, separately, worldwide.

In two of our proposals for Droog, eventually realized, we used the same principles again: storage, interface, dialogue, and a two-dimensional composition which translates into a three-dimensional one. We learned from SPACES while adding to it what we felt design can be, in a time of a shift in how we see the users. Boxorama turned the endless dashed lines into a series of scalable boxes which could be stacked together. On a digital interface, it was a two-dimensional composition laid down by the user, to which structure had been algorithmically added and extruded into a three-dimensional storage unit. Facades & Functions reversed the process and offered the external composition fixed – a desk, a cabinet, a bench – while the cavities were open for configuration. We again offered an interface for user interpretation (this time digital), and again we were surprised with the results, later putting them back to work for us.

But SPACES was not left out.
We reintroduced the system, this time as a design tool for EA, in a project we called the Digital One-Off. A digital competition was to be held, where we would invite users to be critical about their space and their need for order in a specific context. EA would choose the winners, those with the most fascinating interiors to work with, who would win a unique SPACES composition by EA, designed specifically for their space, needs, and context.

Boxorama was further developed and fixed in three configurations now sold by Droog. Facades & Functions has been left out. SPACES is still an evolving, living product. In the span of a two years, this ever-developing concept has become a platform to explore ideas on space, design, context, functionality, and users. The ideas developed in this series of projects are still being explored by us, years later. So are the projects themselves.

Events: Situating the Temporary
Page 543

It was on a car ride to one of the old Rotterdam harbor hangers, in an old, yet beloved Saab, that a sense of what EventArchitecuur was became clear. Herman and I were going to see the constructed elements of an exhibition EA designed before these boarded a ship to São Paulo. I was on my second, perhaps third day of work with EA, working on an adaptation for a design sparked by this São Paulo exhibition – a hybrid of a bench and a billboard – which, in the project I was working on for Utrecht Manifest Biennial, turned into a series of "social billboards," each calling for a different social activity.

On our way there, I asked Herman something about the process of his work. I think I was then curious how he felt about working again with the same element he has just shipped to São Paulo – so uniquely present in that show – in a new project. This idea, of developing or reusing an element again and again, had then almost seemed blasphemous to me. Each project has a context, I thought, each one requires complete originality. "We work the elements from exhibition to exhibition," Herman explained. "Some exhibitions I am more happy with than others. But once every few exhibitions, there is one exhibition in which you feel it all clicks. Around these moments we sometimes leave old elements out and introduce new ones."

This notion, seeing the office's oeuvre as one continuous project, clarified at once the scope of EA's work. As a project, it is constantly being researched. As a project of twenty years, it absorbs new ideas, yet is not confined by fashion but by the boundaries and thematic explorations it has set itself. Sketches and prototypes are financed and realized through commissions, leaving a trail of experimentation and byproducts, tested in reality. Yet the project that is EA is ongoing, and it is bigger than the sum of its parts.

That Saab was a great car.

spaces

spaces

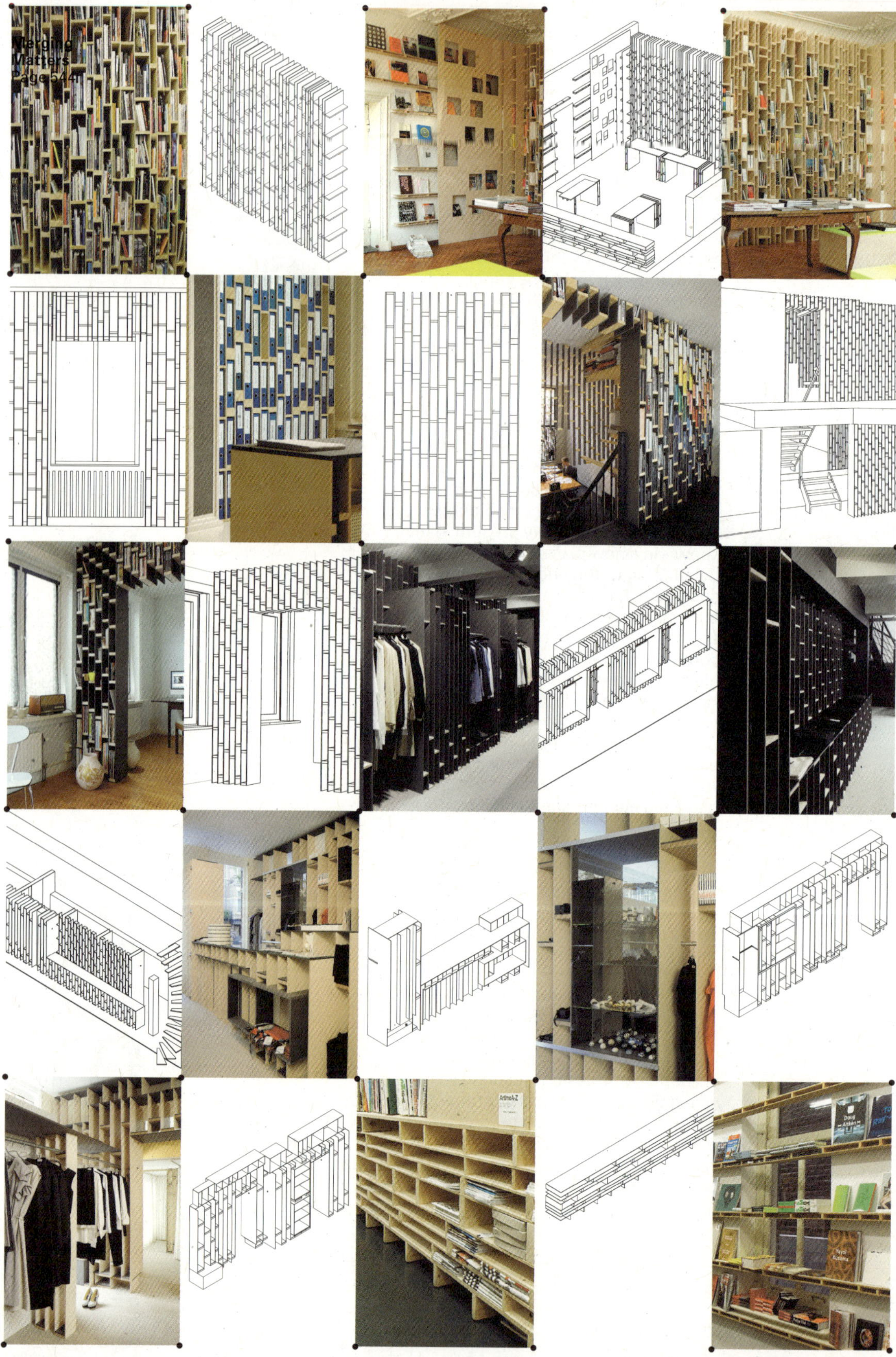

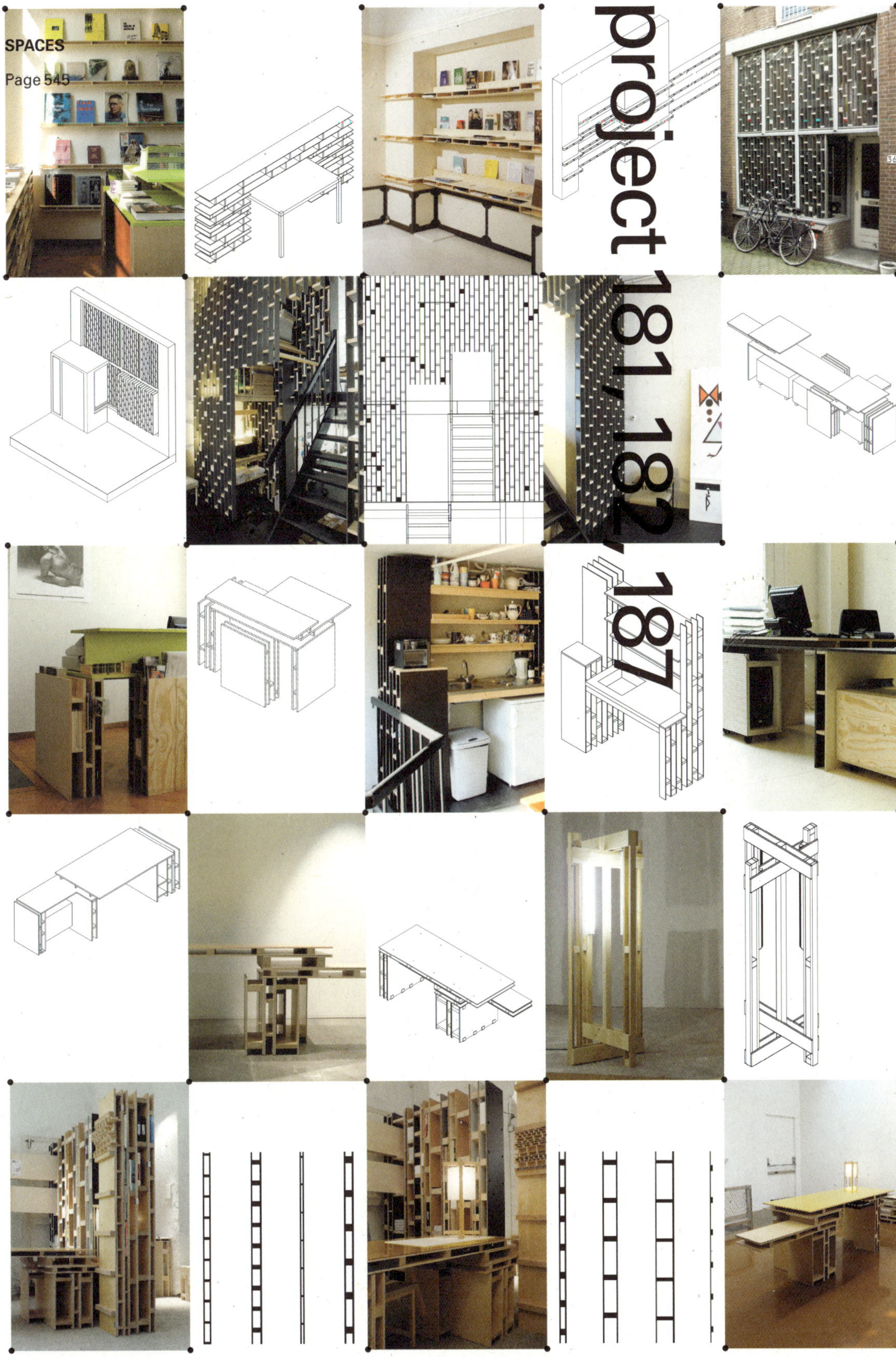
project 181, 182, 187

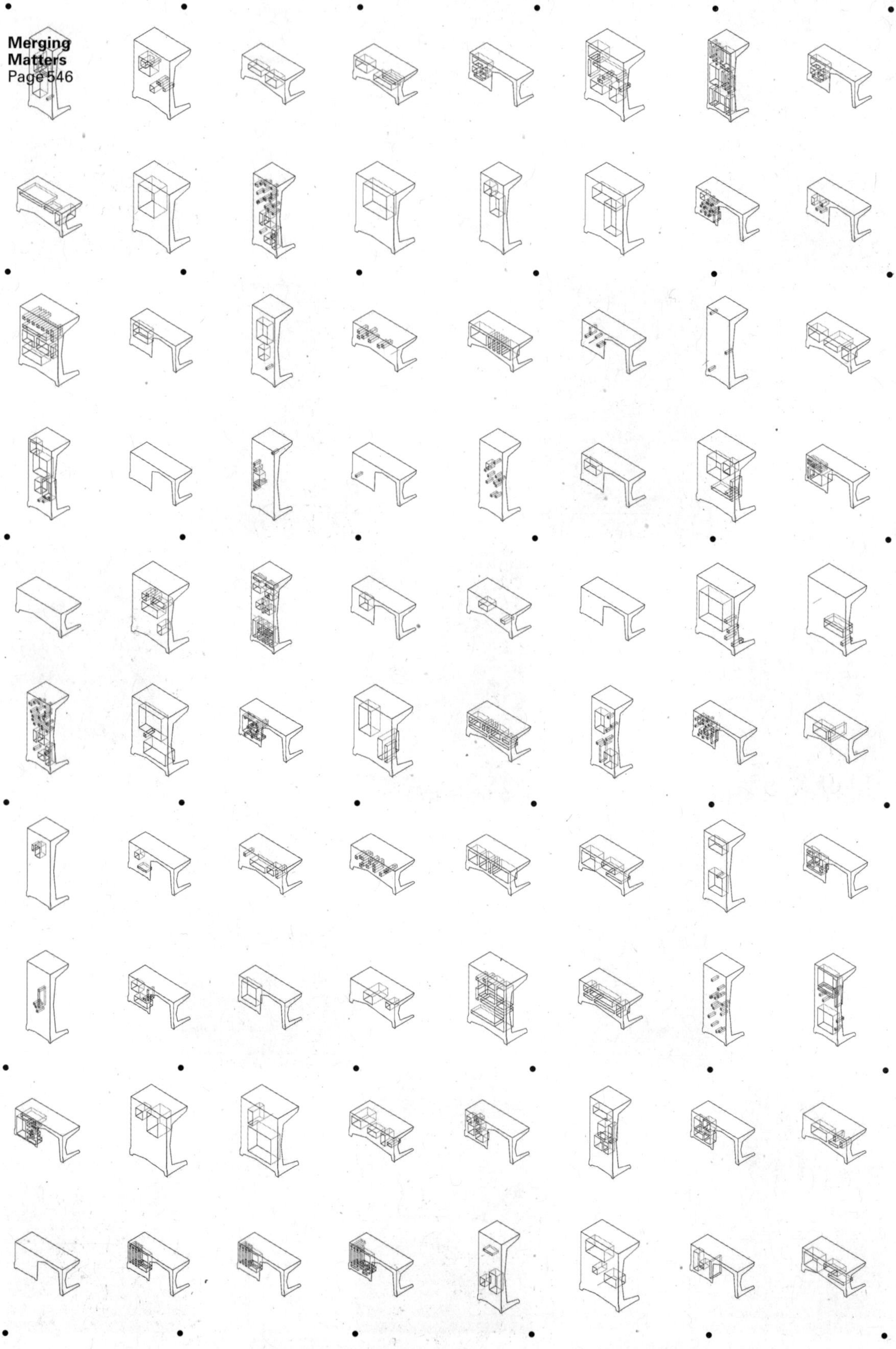

project 197, 223

project 197, 223

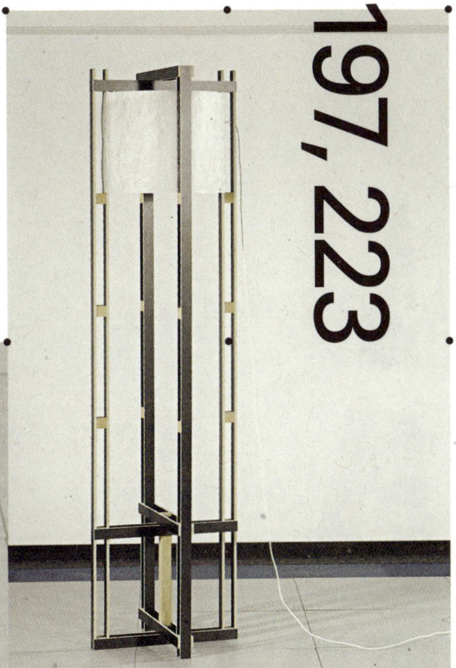

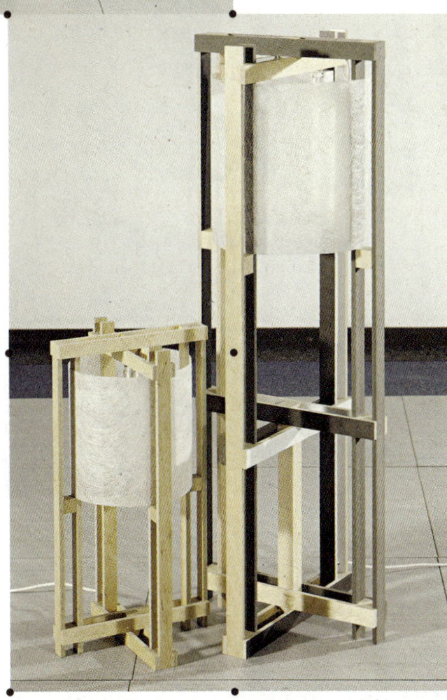

5

Events: Situating the Temporary

Page 550

project 224

2014

Merging Matters
Page 551

IABR 2014 – Urban by Nature
Project: Exhibition
Duration: Medium-term, 3 months
Year: 2014
Data: page 669

IABR–2014–
International Architecture
Biennale Rotterdam
IABR–URBAN
2014 –BY
NATURE
Introduction/ Introductie
Introduction/ Introductie
Introduction/ Introductie

AP
C–
A PLANET CULTIVATED/ DE AARDE EEN TUIN
A Planet Cultivated/ De Aarde een Tuin
Introduction/ Introductie
G–
Subtheme/ Subthema
GARDENS/ TUINEN

B-
Subtheme/
Subthema
BUILDING WITH NATURE/
BOUWEN MET DE NATUUR
G-
Subtheme/
Subthema
GAR
TUIN

project 224

17

Encyclopédie
Denis Diderot and Jean le Rond d'Alembert
Blenheim
Naturism
Systema Naturae
Carl Linnaeus
Carl Linnaeus
1707–1778
Georges Cuvier
1800
Essay on the Principle of Population
Thomas Malthus
The Sublime and the Beautiful
Edmund Burke
Philosophy
Jean-Jacques Rousseau
1712–1778
Essays on the Picturesque
Du contrat social
Jean-Jacques Rousseau
Salines de Chaux
Claude Nicolas Ledoux
Gulliver's Travels
Jonathan Swift
Die Leiden des Jungen Werthers
Johann Wolfgang von Goethe
Painting

Merging Matters
Page 554

IABR 2014 –
Urban by Nature
Page 555

project 24

Seth Denizen
EN
Agronomy has always considered urban areas immaterial, but that is about to change. New York has been mapping the impact of urban processes on the urban underground. A cross section of the city was examined to a depth of 1.8 m to find out how soil develops while exposed to, for instance, construction, garbage dumping, and urban agriculture. On the basis of origin, age, and exposure, 18 types of soil have been identified.
Seth Denizen
NL
De stedelijke ondergrond is altijd een witte vlek geweest voor de bodemkunde. Daar komt verandering in. Voor New York is een onderzoek gestart naar hoe urbane processen de stadsbodem beinvloeden. Tot op 1,8 m diepte is gekeken hoe bodemlagen zich ontwikkeld hebben onder invloed van onder andere bebouwing, vuilstort en tuinbouw. Op basis van ontstaanswijze, ouderdom en bewerking zijn 18 bodemtypen onderscheiden.
26
Title/Titel
SOIL NOT
DIRT
/SOIL
NOT DIR

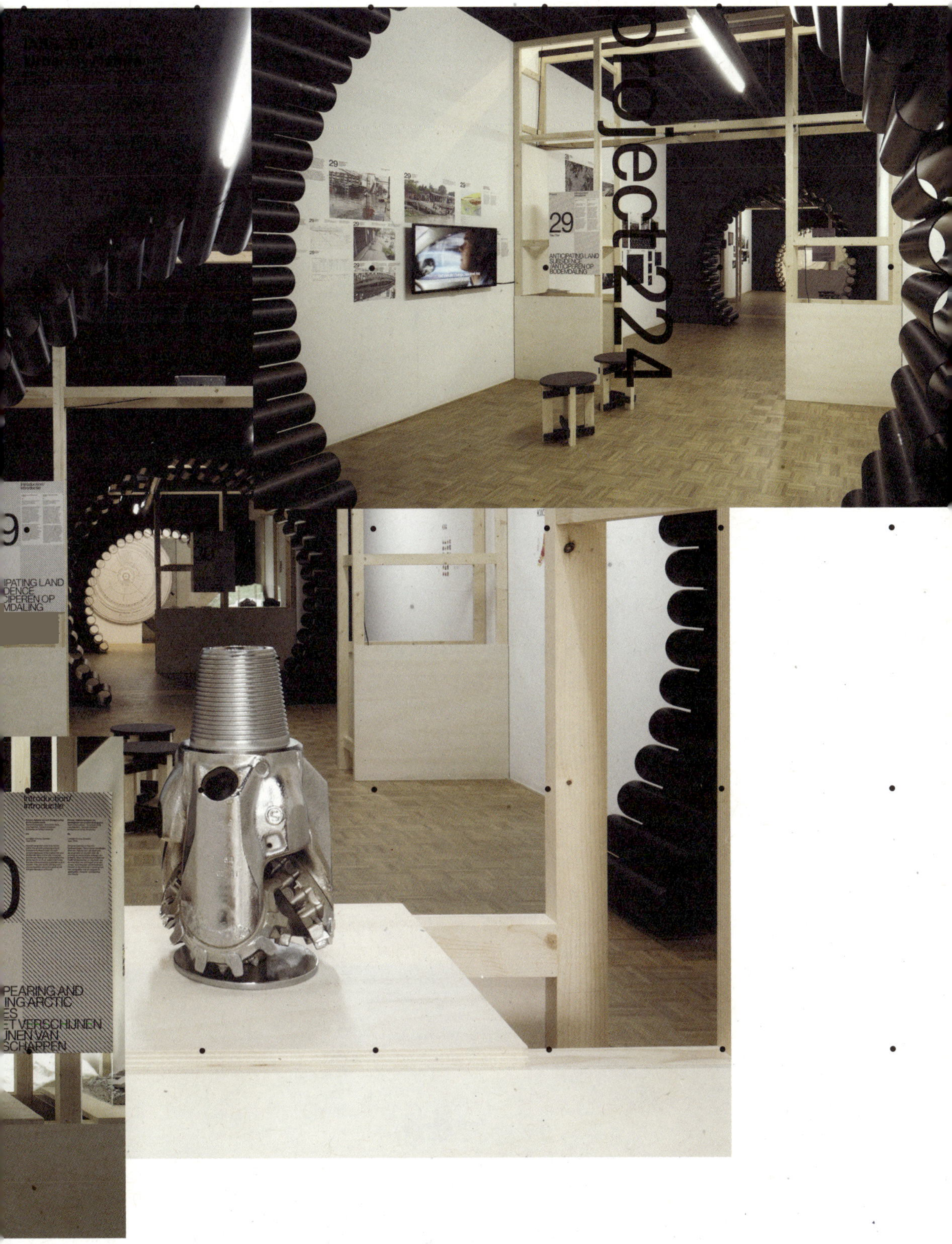
oject224
29
ANTICIPATING LAND
SUBSIDENCE
ANTICIPEREN OP
BODEMDALING
Introduction/
introductie

The Urban Metabolism–
Het Stedelijk Metabolisme–
AIR/
LUCHT
SAND/
ZAND
37
97

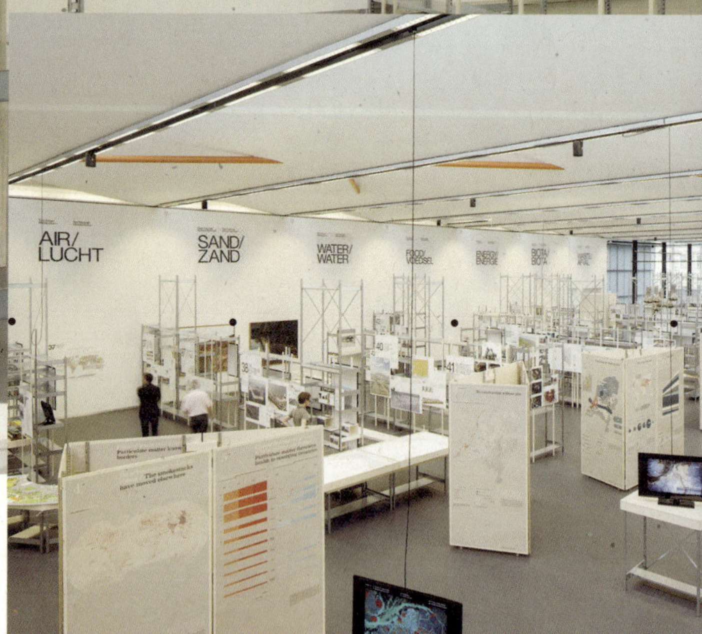
AIR/
LUCHT
SAND/
ZAND
WATER/
WATER

project 224

73
UNCONSCIOUS
METROPOLIS
/UNCONSCIOUS
METROPOLIS
PRAWL OR
ONCENTRATION/
PREIDING OF
ONCENTRATIE

1
2
3
LOLA LANDSCAPE ARCHITECTS

project 224

bewildering bricolage

Bewildering bricolage

Dirk Sijmons

One of the reasons for my accepting the invitation to curate the sixth edition of the International Architecture Biennale Rotterdam, the IABR – 2014, is the exciting thought that it could involve an exhibition. There's no ironclad rule dictating that an architecture biennial must make use of the exhibition medium. Film, guided walks, or even an entirely digital display of what the designers' world has to offer are other possibilities. Not such strange ideas, because the exhibition of architecture is notoriously tricky. Only if it succeeds at the communicative level can visitors – from the perspective of their own house or living environment – relate to it. Conveying urban planning ideas and designs to the general public, the IABR's task, on this occasion and with the theme of *Urban by Nature*, is perhaps doubly difficult. These kinds of plans are often highly cerebral. The local and regional plans of landscape architects likewise run the risk of passing over the heads of everyone but colleagues. The IABR is, of course, more than just an exhibition. It is one of the rare opportunities to engage in an in-depth exchange of ideas with the international design community around a chosen theme, to compare design solutions, and to highlight advances in research. Nonetheless, the exhibition is the centerpiece. So the question becomes: what kind of exhibition are you going to make? As curator, your job is to give the lead.

Swirling around in my head are memories of exhibitions that for a variety of reasons made an impression on me and that might offer useful pointers. The first exhibition I recall is *The Atom*, at Schiphol in 1957; an exhibition featuring a working miniature nuclear reactor. The unbridled optimism about the future was infectious. In "The Future," not only would everything be better, but electricity would be virtually free, thanks to the exploitation of the nuclear forces we humans had succeeded in taming. I was eight years old, and with my father, and came home with an indelible impression of what my electrified life would look like. It no doubt radiated the same faith in progress as an exhibition I never saw, but which, owing to the surviving pictures, has gradually assumed mythical proportions in my own image bank: the General Motors Pavilion by Norman Bel Geddes at the New York World's Fair in 1939 (ten years before I was born). Sixty people at a time were allowed in to sit around a gigantic model and goggle at the imaginary future city of stunning high-rises and a tantalizing traffic structure: sixteen-lane motorways outside the city and eight-lane expressways to the city center, crisscrossing one another in traffic interchanges the like of which the world had never seen. A bit over the top as a comparison with the IABR, but Geddes set a standard in visualizing the future, and also showed just how important the staging of an exhibition

Events: Situating the Temporary
Page 563

is. Exhibitions can act as a catalyst. Still, number one on my list of exhibitions is the 1961 *Bewogen Beweging* (Moved Movement) exhibition at the Stedelijk Museum in Amsterdam, which drew me into the lively world of kinetic artists. I realize that the building, the Stedelijk, played a major role, and seemed to determine which Tinguelys, De Saint Phalles, Spoerris, etc., were placed where (naturally, very carefully considered by the curators, but still). A perfect symbiosis between building and art was one I saw at the Dia Art Foundation, which had turned the old Nabisco box-printing plant in the city of Beacon (NY) into the headquarters of the American Minimalists. The gigantic works – often made especially for the location – are shown in a way that borders on the sublime. The building informs the exhibition, something that we should also try to achieve in the Kunsthal in Rotterdam, where the IABR is held. Actually, a surprising number of Stedelijk exhibitions seem to haunt my memory when I enter the search term "exhibition." The ingenious simplicity of the Dutch architect Aldo van Eyck, who, with two large cylinders of rice paper, managed to organize the – difficult – room in the new wing, and within the circles provided a perfectly lit intimate setting for the impressive steel samurai by the Japanese-American sculptor Shinkichi Tajiri. Could we manage to keep it that simple? With the Biennale, we have to show a great quantity of very diverse material. Something like a map exhibition? I don't really recall much of the layout of the *Cartes et Figures de la Terre* exhibition in Centre Pompidou in 1979. But I do remember it being one big cartographic feast; in effect, you wandered around in the map room of the world. If the material is sufficiently rich, does that make the layout less important? A rigorous selection, in that case. The equally evocative and poignant layout of the "Dolhuis" (madhouse) in Haarlem, by Amsterdam-based office Kossmann. dejong, suggests other ideas. Rather than wandering around at will, a choreographed route through this former mental hospital makes the visitor increasingly uncertain about just what is normal and what not, and aware of how dramatically those

bricolage
bewildering

definitions have shifted over time and in the history of psychiatry. For me, this is where the power of the narrative resides. The exhibition in the Arsenale at the 2010 Venice Biennale, designed by the Japanese firm SANAA, where all our senses (sight, hearing, taste, smell, touch) were represented in every room, demonstrated that an exhibition can be an intense sensory experience. Is looking at other media an option? The glowing memory of the (2004/2005) exhibition in the Groninger Museum, *Working for Diaghilev*, which I walked through with all senses wide open, deeply moved and in a state of love, makes it abundantly clear that beauty also lies in "the eye of the beholder." You can choreograph for all you are worth, but receptivity on the other side is a precondition for a positive click.

Then I recall an issue of *OASE* (#88, 2012) devoted entirely to the exhibition of architecture. It provided a good overview of the history of famous architecture exhibitions, but it also contained an interview with Herman Verkerk and Paul Kuipers of EventArchitectuur, which suddenly attaches a name to an exhibition I had seen and liked. Exhibition architect is an ancillary and sometimes almost anonymous profession. To be honest, I hadn't noticed who had made the *Edible City* at Bureau Europa in Maastricht, and now I saw it: EventArchitectuur. The odd bilingualism of the office name already seems to hint at the bricolage character of the work.

An initial conversation takes place in Herman and Paul's studio in Amsterdam, surrounded by and made out of their favorite materials: wood, perforated hardboard, shelving units, corrugated cardboard. Small displays, posters, and details of previous exhibitions almost filled the small space. They show work and speak intensively about the way they work: not just drawing, but also making and adjusting *in situ*. I find it all enormously appealing.

Urban by Nature is about a new way of looking at cities. It is not about a clearly defined city, but vast urban landscapes, patchwork metropolises comprising not just buildings, but also intensive farming, airports, industrial estates, open-pit mines, nature reserves, leisure areas, harbors, all tied together by infrastructure. Many global environmental problems are related to urbanization, or are rooted in this gigantic artifact, and the solutions must also be sought in that sprawling urban landscape. In 2013, we issued a call for proposals, from which plans and projects would be selected from around the world, aimed at elucidating the changing relationship between man and nature, suggesting ways of adjusting the metabolism of the city, or providing strategies for the patchwork metropolis. An abstract subject matter that had to be rendered communicable in the exhibition.

The most important decision we make together is to structure the exhibition as a narrative. A narrative in which the words and sentences would be formed by projects from all corners of the world. The narrative is about an optimistic plan of action with which to tackle intimidating environmental problems. The chapters of the narrative are formed by the themes, each of which will be allocated its own room in the Kunsthal. The route through this landscape-building designed by OMA/ Rem Koolhaas will be conceived as a "promenade architecturale." The deceptively simple idiom employed by EventArchitectuur (EA) makes for a lighter presentation of the indigestible material, and ensures that the exhibition as a whole will radiate the sought-after optimism. EA's cheerful associations invest the various sub-themes in each room of the Kunsthal with their own distinctive character through the use of the same material, but with slightly different visual means.

The logical casting for the room that looks out on the beautiful Museumpark and is supported by those tree-columns is, of course, the sub-theme "A Planet Cultivated," which EA conceptualizes using abstract planters and flowerbeds as exhibition supports, to which projects are attached. A view of the Museumpark with the history of the representation of nature in the Western park tradition, as a tribute to the park's late designer, Yves Brunier. And a beach pavilion with panoramic digital projection as the glowing focal point. These sorts of things are not pre-planned, but gradually take shape through an interaction between the participating designers, the exhibition designers, the curator, and the IABR planners – with EA's initial sketches as the starting point of every discussion.

The main room, where the projects about "The Urban Metabolism" are shown, acquires a more industrial feel, with large shelving units that are in keeping with the room's north-facing light roof. Unlike many exhibitions in the Kunsthal, EA chose not to do battle with the light, but rather made full use of it. Water, Energy, Food, Heat, Building Materials, Biota, People, and Cargo: in short, all the flows that make up the urban metabolism are each given their own pavilion, and at right angles to that is the gigantic folding partition where Project Atelier Rotterdam displays its results. Everything bathed in overhead light. The two zones are demarcated by five man-sized infographics for each flow, designed by CatalogTree, an office based in Arnhem, on which data from the Netherlands Environmental Assessment Agency is displayed.

The Kunsthal's Upper Room has to make do without daylight, for it is the most suitable location for the "Strategies for the Urban Landscape" sub-theme. It is laid out as a map room, with a gigantic planning chart from the Atelier Brabant project, in the form of an actual wall tapestry, as its centerpiece.

Skirting the upper and lower exhibition halls of the Kunsthal are two more smaller, corridor-like spaces. The dark, lower corridor is used to choreograph an exploration of the underground: six subterranean projects arranged according to depth. EA sets the scene for this journey by having visitors enter the dimly lit domain via a perpendicular, abstract portal. The upper, light-filled corridor houses all the projects dealing with climate change. The plans are hung from wobbly stacks of pasting tables. It is typical of EA's working method that it deliberately aims for this kind of ludic instability, and the much-needed bracing is only applied *in situ*.

The graphic design is much more than a "layer"; rather, it is more a symbiosis with EA's work. Experimental Jetset, the graphic designers that often team up with EA, suggests giving all the projects a number, and marking every project component, whether maps, photographs, drawings, explanations, or models, with the same number. No names, just numbers, and no distinction between the work of star architects and that of students. In addition, all projects are cut up into A-format sections, ranging from A4 to A0. This strictly enforced typology, together with the material unity of the supports, lends the exhibition as a whole a certain tranquility, especially in the "metabolism room," where some fifty projects and presentations by Project Atelier Rotterdam vie for the visitor's attention – an inspired decision!

I love it when a plan comes together. Before my eyes, I see the fragile structures coalesce to form an exhibition. One by one, the bits and pieces of the projects are fixed to their supports. It is exactly as I had hoped. EA's work makes no secret of the fact that this is a temporary event. I'm delighted by this. The magic of an exhibition may well lie in that temporariness. After the closing date, it quickly disappears. It's gone forever. All you have are your memories. The profession of exhibition designer occupies a specific position between the transience of graphic design and – wrestling with weighty claims to eternity – architecture. The name says it all: EventArchitectuur.

bewildering
bricolage

5

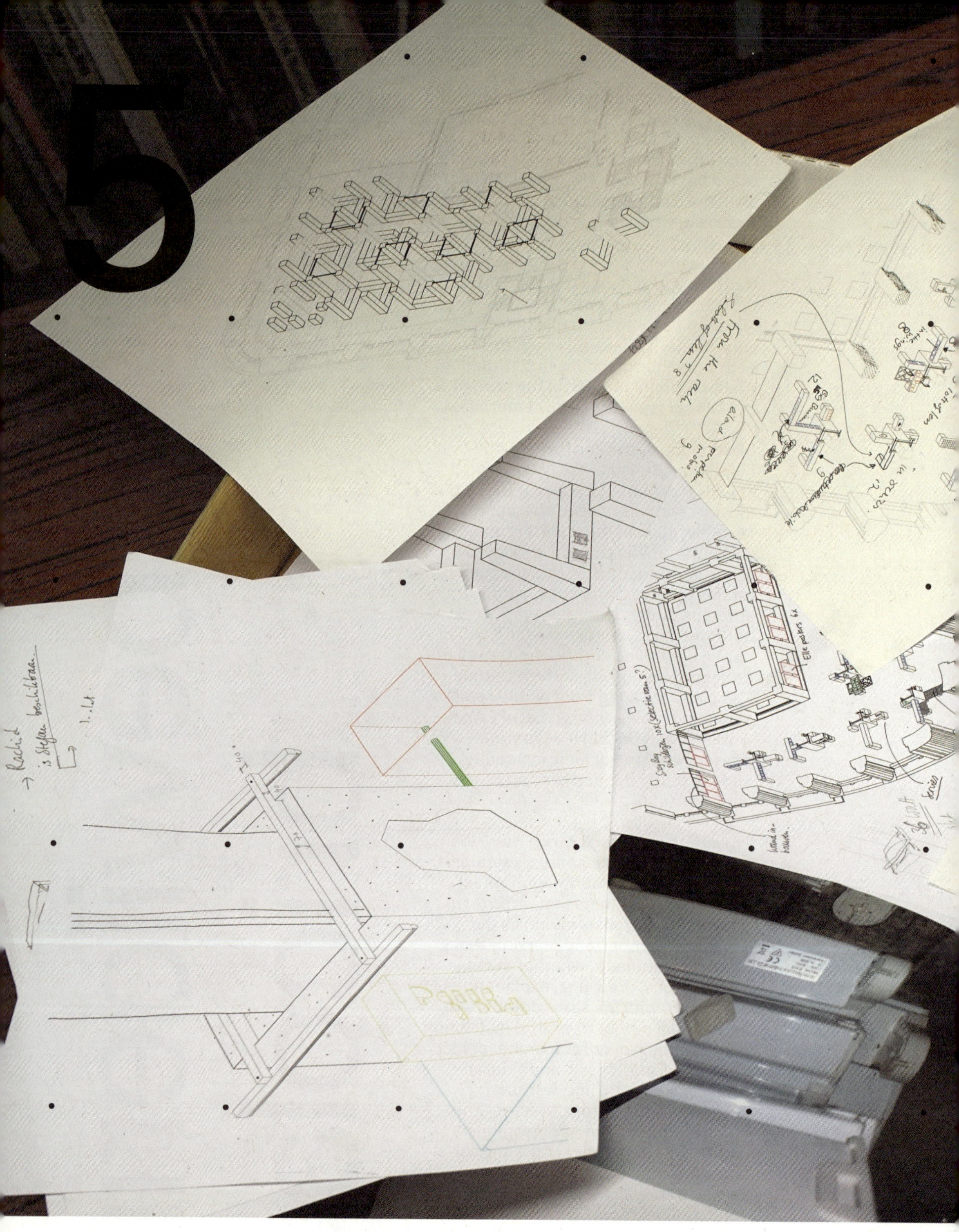

Events: Situating the Temporary
Page 566

project 189,190

2010

Ghost Department Store
Project: Presentation, Installation
Duration: Short-term, 10 days
Year: 2010
Data: page 664

project 189, 190
Kassa

5

Events: Situating the Temporary
Page 570

project 216

2013

Elegant Scaffolding
Project: Installation
Year: 2013
Data: page 668

Merging Matters
Page 572

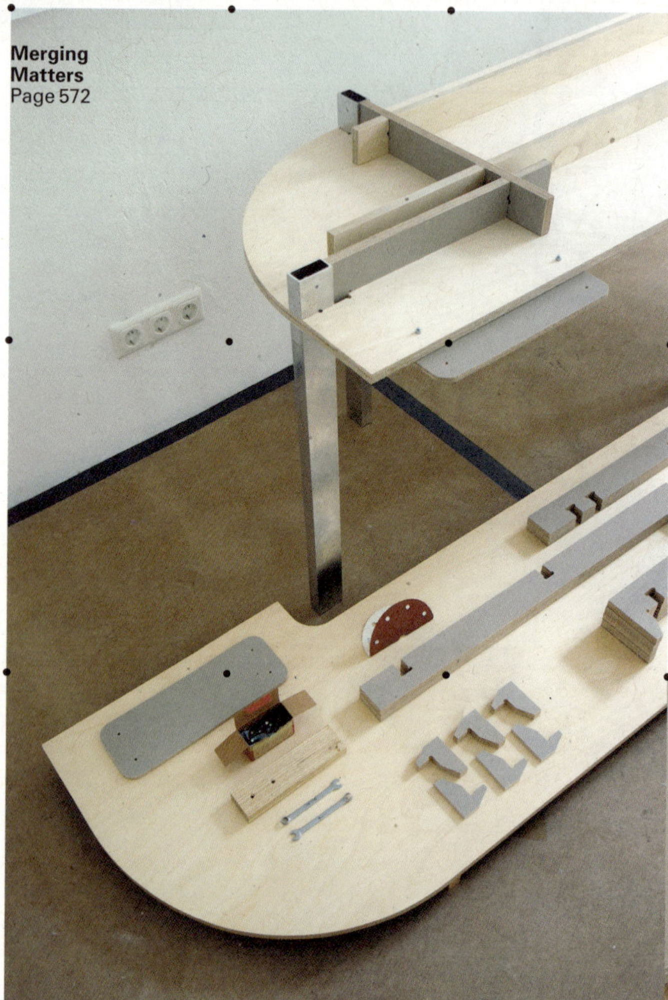

project 216

Jacques Derrida
Das Problem der Genese in Husserls Philosophie
diaphanes
Alain Badiou
Platons ›Staat‹
diaphanes
diaphanes

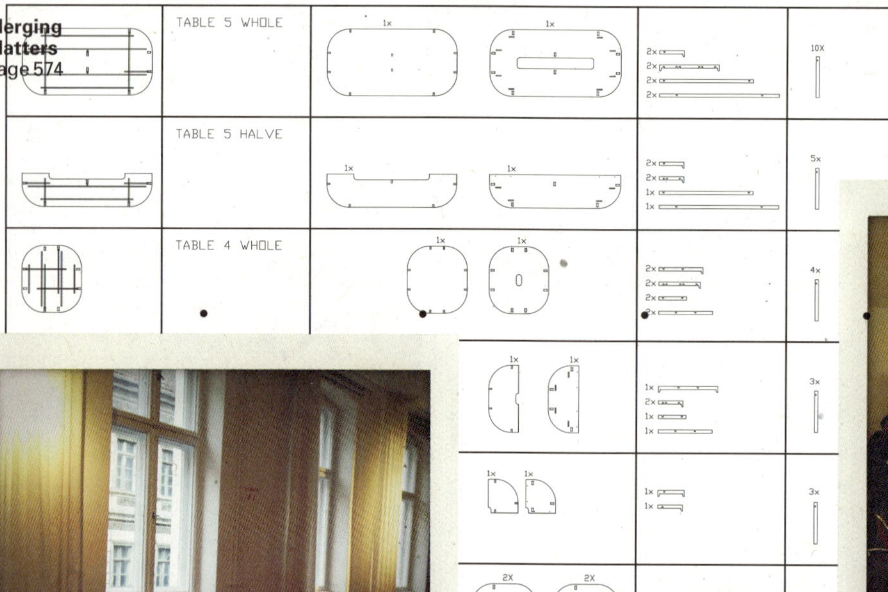
TABLE 5 WHOLE
1x
1x
2x
2x
2x
2x
10X
TABLE 5 HALVE
1x
1x
2x
2x
1x
1x
5x
TABLE 4 WHOLE
1x
1x
2x
2x
2x
2x
4x
1x
1x
1x
2x
1x
1x
3x
1x
1x
1x
1x
3x
2X
2X

BAR
1x
9x
2x
51x
9x
27X
9x
51x

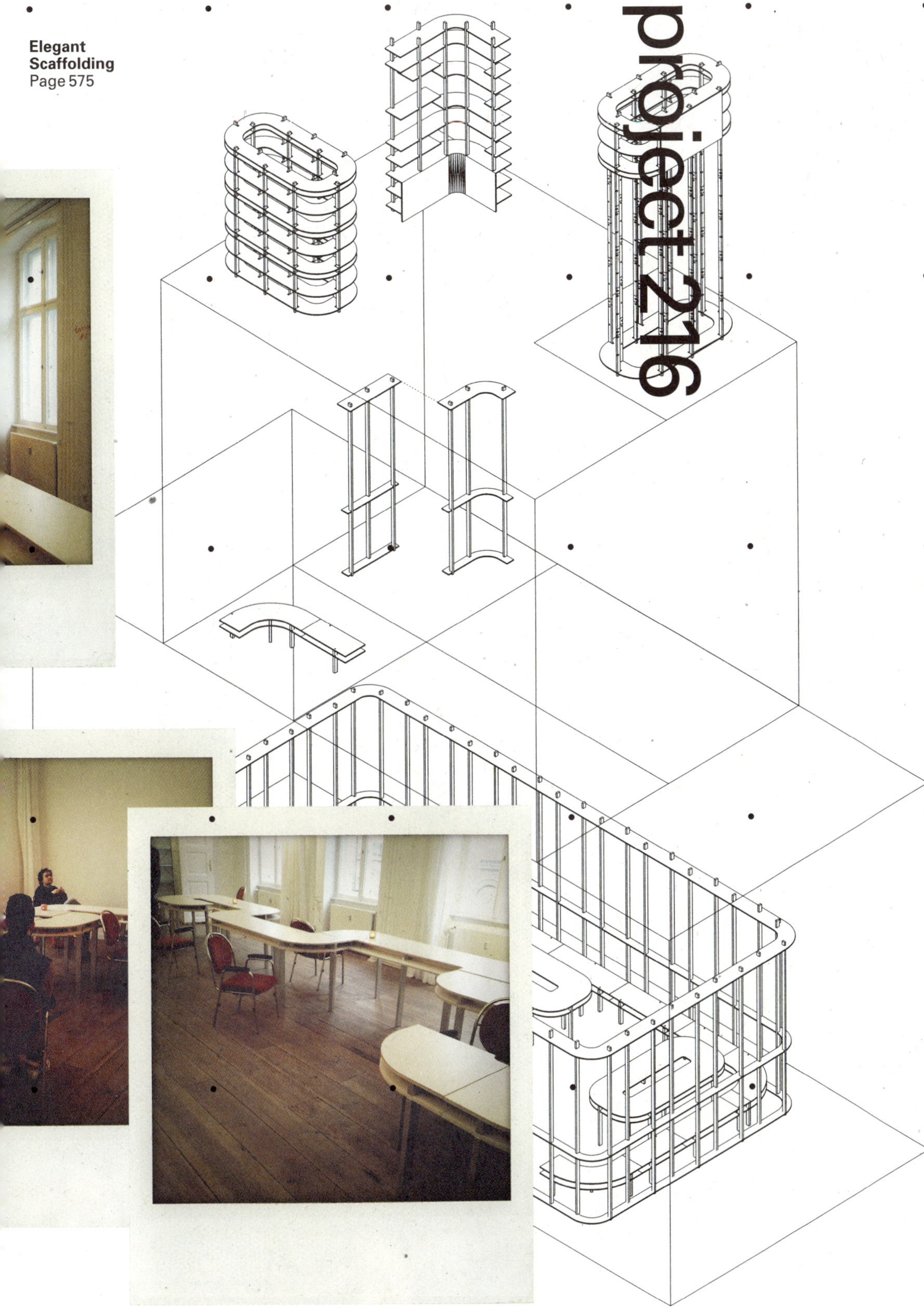
project 216

5

Events: Situating the Temporary
Page 576

project 167, 196

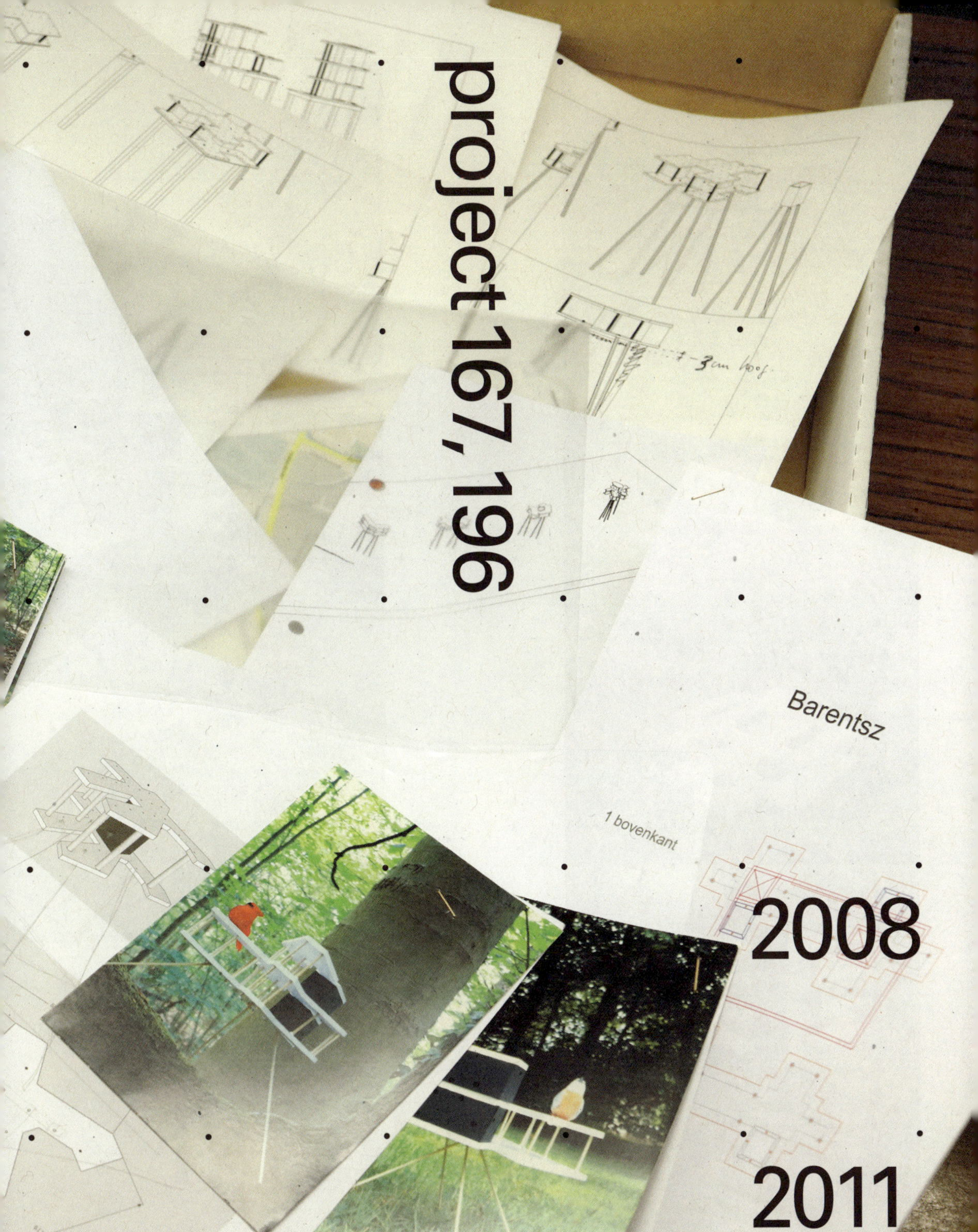

2008

2011

Feeding Platforms for Birds
Project: Installation
Year: 2008, 2011
Data: page 662

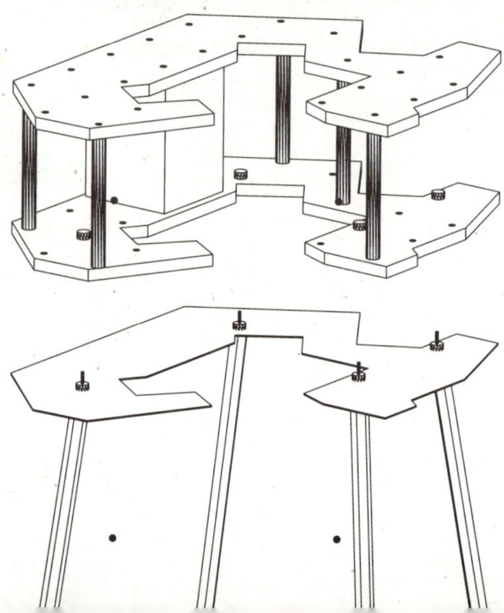

Feeding Platforms for Birds
Page 579

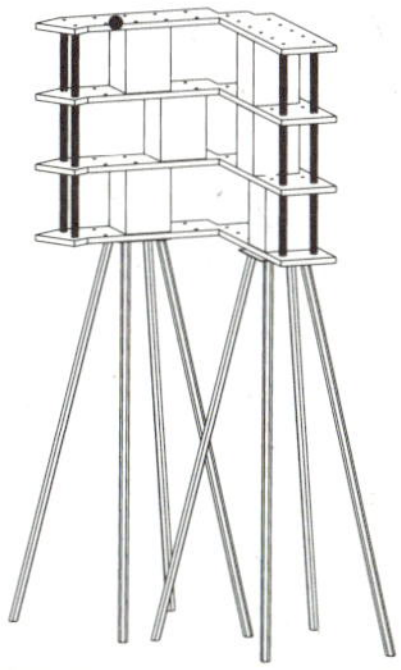

project 167, 196

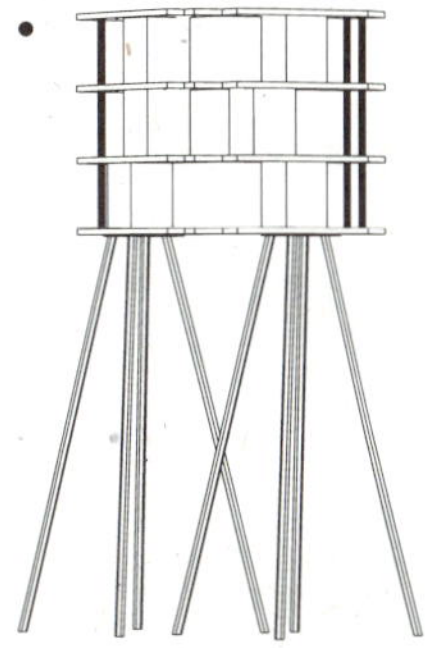

5

Events: Situating the Temporary

Page 580

project 236

2015
2016

Merging Matters
Page 581

Temporary Fashion Museum
Project: Temporary Museum
Duration: Medium-term, 8 months
Year: 2015–2016
Data: page 670

PARFUMERIE DU PARC

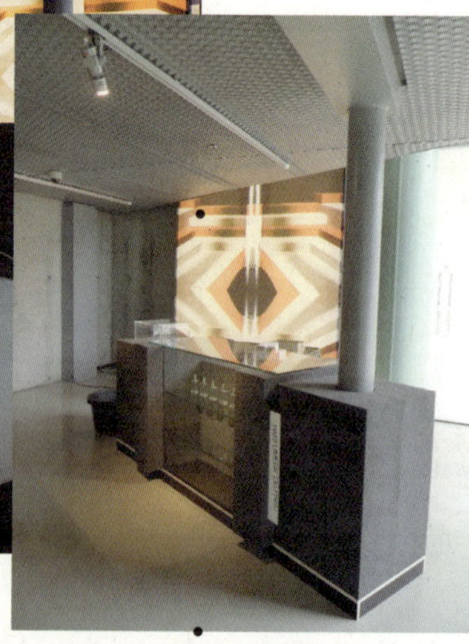

project 236

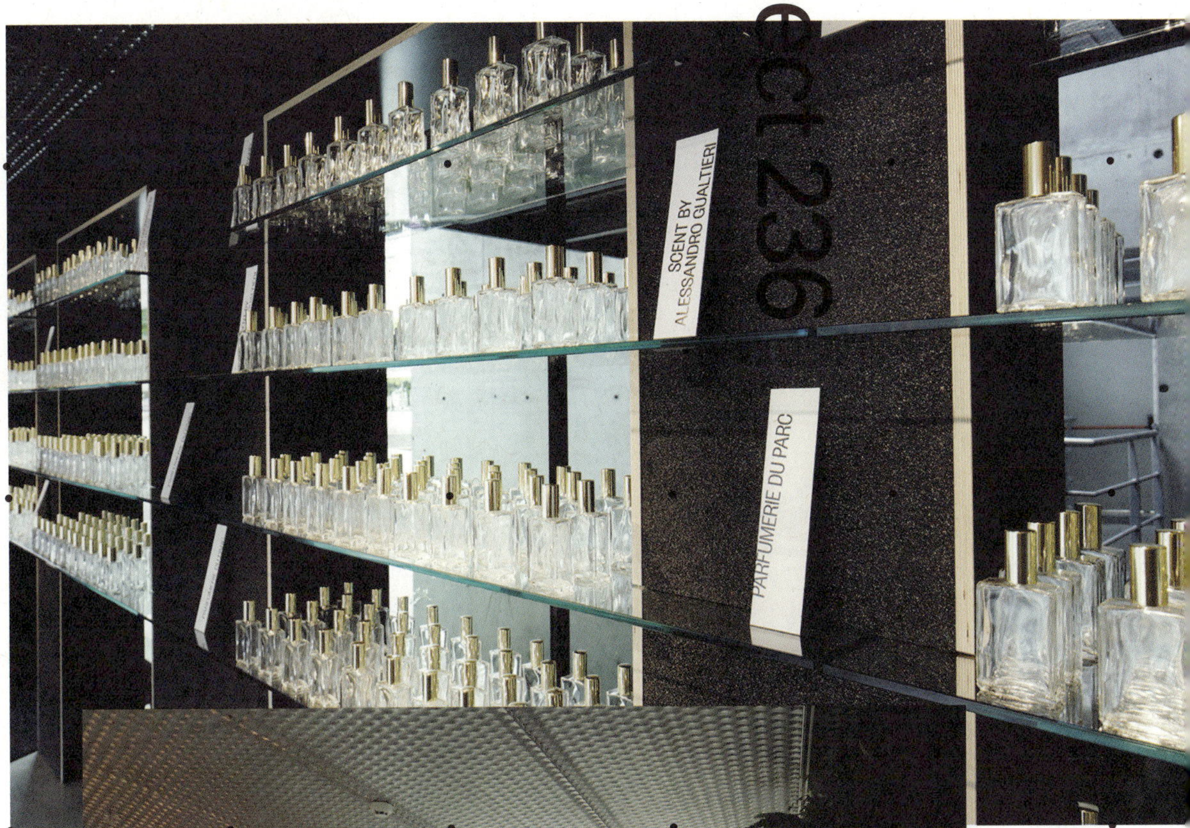

project 236

AJ
BI
CH
KR
MP
STUDY
FITTING ROOM
DG

STUDY
STU

project 236
PRECIOUS

HACKED
STORE

Temporary Fashion Museum
Page 589

Date:
October 25, 2015

Place:
Eindhoven, Sectie C, the studio of Lucas, Raphaël and Gabriel

People:
Tamar Shafrir & Herman Verkerk w/ **Lucas Muñoz** and **Raphaël Coutin**

conversation 6

Network and transformation

T: Herman, what is the goal of this talk? As I understand, it's to see EventArchitectuur as a network.
H: I never plan these things, but they happen as I go along. It was very funny that having some distance from Paul gave me the opportunity to fulfill a dream of the collaborative part of EventArchitectuur.
L: Did it happen before?
H: Not so much, actually, although from the 1990s on, I envisioned it as an umbrella. That's also why I don't call the office Herman Verkerk, I call it EventArchitectuur. There is this duality between "Is it a style?" or "Is it a company?" I love that duality, and it also gives you the freedom to reinvent yourself all the time. Of course, I did reinvent EventArchitectuur, or EventArchitectuur reinvented itself; that's why I also introduce Bart Guldemond and Rianne Makkink in the book, because the story is longer and more diverse than just the last ten years. But it is only positive that it's taking a lot of different guises. In this specific situation, the collaborative part was very interesting because it started out with asking Gabriel Maher to assist me on quite a large project for the *Temporary Fashion Museum*, which was supposed to be executed within a framework of three months. Simultaneously, there was also research going on for the exhibitions of the museum; participants were not really clear yet, signing up and going away again, so it was kind of an unclear situation. What I liked about Gabriel's work [read the interview with Gabriel on page 600] is that it deals a lot with social interaction – it's about design, but it has a lot to do with gestures, gender, but in an almost normative sense, in that it is a fact, you have to deal with it and confront it: it's not something that you play, it's rather something that is part of society. I thought that fashion as an institute or topic would be very interesting to relate to her. Personally, I am immersed in it: I'm not an objective bystander, I was part of the fashion system, and of course I know a lot about how things work, analyzing different kinds of retail environments and how media plays a specific role in fashion. The dialogue with Gabriel was good to reflect on what we were doing and how we were doing it. But this particular project also allowed me to experiment more in finding new modes of expression, letting go a little bit of the normal way of doing things. It sounds very funny for EventArchitectuur, but of course there is a certain way of doing things. For instance, we would have the computer: the computer is a sort of holy thing, when you start the assignment, the first thing you do is recreate the situation that is there, digitize it, so you can work with the 3D computer model. So I asked Gabriel to do that, and she said, "Yes, yes, I can totally do it, I will learn AutoCAD, I've done it before, I worked in an architecture office in Australia, I will do it." So she did all kinds of courses on her own, and she was really stomping and stumbling into this new world. She was not necessarily interested in the thing itself – neither am I; I'm just interested in it as a tool. It makes your work easier and allows you to communicate on very different levels.
T: But for you it was clear it was a necessary step.
H: But when you are stumbling, the hiccups or the difficulty translating a normal way of working into a different mode that you have to adapt to towards what someone can offer, it makes you also change your way of working. You have to go through this process and you deal with it together, and that was interesting for me to see how Gabriel went down different paths, making models or making details or doing a very different research into the whole idea of making an exhibition. That was very good as an experience for me.

Diversify

H: We really soon found out that it would be impossible for us to clearly cover all the details of the show. You can envision it in abstraction, but when you have to deal with all of the details, it becomes very difficult. Time-wise, together with the builders from Landstra & De Vries, we made the decision quite early on that we were not going to use the computer to have things prefabricated. It gave us the liberty to experiment on-site and to introduce other people to design on the project without having the deadline for the CNC mill or other kinds of preproduction. Then Gabriel said, "I also work together with two people, maybe you know them; we share a studio space together and they could help us on the project." By coincidence, I knew them both from the Design Academy, so it was also easy for me to "cast" them in the role they would play in the whole adventure.
T: Was the scope of the project also set from the beginning, so that it should be taking over the whole building?
H: That was clear, and that the temporary could become permanent – that was also a strategy. So we knew how to deal with that. It might be my basic instinct to just jump into it and see how it fares, and then you adapt to different situations. You feel a potential in this brief, and if you would do it in a linear structure, it wouldn't be as diverse as the project should be. So it was also a matter of choosing different voices to accommodate this idea of museum instead of an exhibition. It should really become multiple exhibitions, multiple experiences, and by collaborating you can develop these different voices and different takes on the same material – the same basic materials of which of course EventArchitectuur has made a sort of language – but we also found out that it could be interpreted and also invaded by a very

different approach to the limits of a new understanding of material.

Lucas & Raphaël, Foam & Hack

T: For you, what was the relationship with the subject? Did you have a conception of what fashion was in terms of this exhibition? Was fashion relevant for the way you worked?
L: Not at all, for me. Of course, I look at fashion itself and find it inspiring, but in my case, it was fun because, to be completely frank, the content was not defined, so we almost had to define a container without content. We could imagine, we knew abstractly that it would be fashion, but we didn't know exactly what materials and what colors; we also knew that it would be a very long-term exhibition and it would shift during the course of the exhibition, so whatever we did should not be just for the first two months but also flexible enough to host different contents. So we knew that there would be an area for pumps, an area for the mannequins inside – we knew some constants, but also the curators were taking their time. When Herman approached us, we heard from Gabriel a lot of stories about her struggles with the computer and AutoCAD, and we helped her with all of those crazy little hiccup things like printing.
T: That's always the catastrophe of AutoCAD, when you have to get something out of the computer… that's why the Swiss knew better, in Vectorworks it's very easy!
H: You start by choosing the page for printing, not with the drawing.
L: So, we don't have a studio together, but we do share this space. We kept seeing Gabriel coming back and forth – "I was in Amsterdam working with Herman" – and at some point she said, "We realized that to get as deep as we want in the project, we need to open up to new voices and get some experts in different areas," and they thought of us. Gabriel said that I was a foam expert – I might be a foam expert now, but before this project I knew nothing about foam, I had only made some experiments and things. But it seemed that everything came together like planets aligning. For example, we found this warehouse full of foam that was being sold off unit by unit, so we bought the foam at 10 percent of the normal market price. Finding that was crazy – needing it in that scale of a museum and then finding a warehouse that is a ten-minute drive from here that is completely on sale – that was a blessing somehow.
T: And some of it is still around here!
H: The foam story is also where EventArchitectuur was put to the test. Foam is not really something that I would choose…
T: You don't like it?
H: I think that any kind of plastic is difficult for me to work with. The reason why I chose it is that it's so solid and vulnerable at the same time. For me it was the essence of a fashion "thing," it's kind of structured but you can also fold it in different ways, and I thought it would also be nice to be confronted yourself with a new sort of expression, to go away from the perforated board and the things that were commonly used.
T: But the *Hacked* shop was not with foam?
R: I was a bit apart from the foam story. But I was also not related to fashion at all. I never worked in that field. For me what was really interesting was the fact that we wanted to hack the exhibition, to make new use of an existing thing, and that's a bit the theme I'd already been working on for a few years, so I found a new way to interpret what I wanted to do in my own practice and put it into a totally different context as a store and as a fashion museum. I actually never thought of it as a store. I really realized that at the very end, when everything was built up: "This is a store." But in the plan, in the way we designed it, it was not really in our minds; it was more about trying to hack the previous exhibition on glass with other pieces of furniture, trying to make this dialogue between the previous exhibition and the new one. And then it became a store. It's very black and white, a bit severe.
T: Do you think that's also because, in the nature of a fashion store, most of them have to elevate the objects – not through the objects themselves, but in the setting?
R: There is something very particular in this work, which gives me the feeling that I cheated. I was talking with Experimental Jetset, who made all of the graphic design of the space, and they had the same feeling. They said, "We didn't struggle at any moment of the process," and that's very strange as a designer, because normally something doesn't work, and you need to find another way, and this time it went so smoothly, the idea just popped up, and we also shared the vision from the very beginning to reuse the previous exhibition, and then we came up with the first hacked furniture with the open corner, and then it was obvious that it needed to be there. But there were no struggles; it was very strange. Experimental Jetset arrived and put up the stickers and everything made sense immediately. That was unbelievable.
T: Did you feel the same with the other parts of the exhibition?
H: We definitely had some struggles… That's very interesting about the way the curator approaches the expertise of the designer, and also with Experimental Jetset, because I worked with them a lot already: you have a natural understanding, you have one or two words, then they do their production work, so it's not your final responsibility; they do the paper or the stickers or the little tags and that's taken care of, so it's really great to have them. I think also, in your case, you were treated as an expert in the detailing and also you did a very nice lighting schedule for the whole project, which is a very different layer in the whole system. I like the way you talk about not knowing that it would be a store, because of course the whole temporary museum is about this confusion: "Does a retail environment actually cater much more to the needs of a temporary fashion museum than a normal museum could ever do?" There is always this dialectic within this museum between retail and museum. That's also the tension of the design itself, which makes it very fun to experience.
T: Another interesting question is, if it works better as a museum than

as an exhibition. In my opinion, it does – the exhibition language doesn't work on you only in the gallery – it's not isolated, but you see it in different manifestations all around the building, in the café or in the bookstore. Or you are assaulted by the smell when you walk in.
H: That's the essence of fashion, the intangible.
R: But also the cheating part. Experimental Jetset said, "What we made worked so perfectly that it was also kind of scary." They made these leaflets that they put on top of each other, and they were happy that they turned out to be transparent; that was at least something they didn't anticipate.
H: What Event-Architectuur does usually is to improvise, so we have a certain defect or detail that we thought about but that works out differently. In this case, it was much more fluid, which suited perfectly. Maybe it had to do with the use of the existing structure, where you add stuff– it could also be giving you a certain freedom, as the hacking idea ought to do.

Cleaning and maintenance

T: As you said before, you don't know how this foam withstands the passage of time – in a few projects you leave open this window of instability or unpredictability.
H: The moment of enjoyment can be very temporary. Lucas was much more the guy who was talking about sustainability. If it has to stand for eight months, it's good to take this into account. Like cleaning and maintaining a certain image of the work. I am not really the person who is patient enough to design in that way.
T: What is the concept of sustainability there?
H: Sustainable is maybe a big word.
R: The foam is not sustainable anyway...
H: We can eat it afterwards!
L: It was more about how it ages and works in the long run, how the installation needed to be used over the course of eight months. Perhaps it had to be more "sustainable" in the sense that it needs to sustain within the microenvironment of the museum. For example, the foam should not touch the floor because the cleaners will wipe the floor, and then it would stain the edge over time. There are details that were conditioned by this specific temporality. It's not an ephemeral exhibition: eight months is a long time. In a pop-up show, you could have a lot of freedom and be more "sketchy," but in this case it is a museum and a lot of people are passing by. You cannot make a three-meter structure and be unsure if it will fall.
T: The aspect of the floor is beautiful, because in clothing you have the same concern: wherever it makes contact it has to be more durable. Although Alexander van Slobbe is not taking that into account...
H: And you can play with it – we did it on certain elements, while on other ones, we just said, "Fuck it, that's the concept!" and we will see how it ages. That's part of EventArchitectuur's strategy. It is always meant to be light, never heavy or overconstructed, it's not about the clever solution. That's also what we discussed, that we need to maintain this clarity and simplicity.
L: One day, I suggested to Herman to use a forty-five-degree cut in wood and he said, "No, Event-Architectuur doesn't do forty-five-degree cuts."
H: Just put two plates together!
T: Don't overthink it!
H: This comment is related to the front side and back side idea. Alexander van Slobbe says, "There is no back side to the clothes I design, and what I wear on the inside is as important as what I wear on the outside." That gives you a lot more to think about as a designer, because the inside is often the hiding part, where you put together all of the things that make it stand, and then you have the decoration, the decorated shed, let's say. So that's a fundamental ground rule for EventArchitectuur, that it's not about having a structure and an outside that communicates the concept, but rather the whole thing is what it is.
T: What's interesting is that when you make the design in the scale of small architecture, you start to get to this tension. Look at this room: most architecture is about layers. The problem is where do you glue the layer, where do you seal it?
H: And which one do you bring to the front? That was also the struggle with the hacked exhibition – what do you leave, what do you transform? And maybe, Lucas, you can elaborate on the foam story – I don't think it's necessarily the foam, but more your eagerness to go into material as a very physical relationship.
L: I don't think you only chose us because we share a studio with Gabriel. You had other options, but Raphaël seemed perfect for the hacking and, as you said, I work with the material I have around. So if you put me in a warehouse full of foam, suddenly we pass from wooden structures and cages with some foam inside to the other way around: we have tons of foam, but how to connect it? We had an extraordinary provision of foam, there was even a lot left over.
R: As you can see here...
T: And in MU [art center, Eindhoven] there's the blue foam!
L: The Syrian refugees also had some extra beds... we had a lot of foam to share around.

1:1 tests

L: We got a lot of foam samples here and I built a huge cutting wire, and it was really terrible, cutting just about one centimeter every five minutes.
T: The wire is totally not straight...
L: And then all of a sudden it snaps, and it's in the middle of the piece! I spent almost two days cutting foam – very badly – just to see how it worked structurally.
H: But then we had 1:1 models, and that was incredible for the exhibition design development.
L: And it was the only way, we didn't know how it would behave. You cannot make a scale model in foam and say it will behave the same as a two-meter construction. Foam is a filler, it's not a finished material, so that was the challenge. But it's also vulnerable, and almost sweet.
H: It needs a lot of attention.
L: You can make things like this [shows an abstract shape of a woman] which is awesome; you just bend it twice with two clips.
T: It's the Venus of Willendorf!
L: Through these kinds of things we discovered that foam is a very true material, it has the same cells in every direction and they

all answer in the same way. It has no nerves, it has no preconditions, it doesn't get sharp, it doesn't cut, it doesn't weigh much. It is a very weird material. Normally it is used as a filler or for its specific properties – for acoustics, for softness – and normally it is conditioned by the fabric that is on top and the structure around it, but it is never conditioning. Our foam is just cut in the necessary shape and plugged in. We started building up prototypes and then the whole design changed. When I began to collaborate with EventArchitectuur, there was a design for some cages, and then we made a prototype for those cages, and then we were asked, "No, flip it around." The brief changed in the middle of the project and we had to start from zero. We knew that we had this huge warehouse, and we went for the big challenge – a fun challenge, too. We got some prototypes here, it started to fill up with foam blocks, and eventually we knew what we wanted: we had some designs and we wanted to make these shelves, but we had to cut it. We had an infrastructural problem. We couldn't find anyone to cut it professionally – no foam seller will cut foam from another manufacturer. Everyone said, "No, you have to buy the foam from us." Even if we were bringing a hundred blocks of two meters by one meter and offering a lot of money, they refused. How could we do it? We were working with Bouwko Landstra, and he assembled an amazing construction team, and in that case the ease Raphaël mentioned was also present in the construction part. He made a team of designers and artists, and during the construction period you saw that people were solving problems by themselves or coming to you with a problem as well as options.

R: We also spoke the same language as them, which helped a lot.

L: They were finishing things with the same love that you would do it yourself.

H: Most of them are artists, so they have a relationship to material, and they think twice when they hammer a nail into a piece of wood.

Foam to pieces

L: For the foam, we ended up finding a woodcutter called Hes...

T: Hans the woodcutter? It sounds like a fairytale.

L: No, Hes. He's a huge guy, completely zen; there was no problem about anything, even if he was annoyed, he would say, "Shall we cut another one?" Even when he wants to go home and his wife is calling. He cut some really thin slices, three millimeters thick, really skins. He was kind of enjoying it, because he usually cuts trees. Whenever you cut down a forest, he comes with his trolley – twenty meters long on four wheels – and you put the whole trunk on it and then it slices the trunk in twenty-meter-long slices. That's the machine we used for the foam.

T: So for him they were like baby toys!

L: For him it was like cutting butter! Sometimes the foam would shoot off in different directions, and we had to wear masks constantly, we were covered in foam dust, it was really raining color.

H: I discovered some in Gabriel's hair days later.

L: We found this guy and put him into the warehouse, and we had only two days to cut everything into shape. And he said, "But how many blocks?" And since we had to be flexible and decide on site, we decided to cut chorizos – long narrow pieces – and cut them into smaller blocks on-site, at the dimensions we wanted, so we could be flexible until the very last minute. So when we arrived at the site at the New Institute with the chorizos, we told Basil, from the Landstra & De Vries team, "Start cutting. Fifty centimeters."

R: He was cutting for two days.

L: Once he was cutting a very tough one, because they were different densities, and we were hanging around, checking everything, and we said something like, "No, let's not put that 45 x 45 centimeterblock...," and then he stopped cutting and came to us saying, "Sorry, I don't want to disturb, 45 x 45 – we are not doing it?" "No, I don't think so." "Good, then I'm not cutting it, because I have blisters on my hands!"

H: Making decisions while working... but it's a luxury, it's something I really love to do together. And also the colors, we didn't choose them, they were in the warehouse. We just said, "The café is colorful, and we do black for the rest," and the only thing we chose was the glamorous pink.

T: I think the space is very difficult to approach from a CAD mentality. Maybe for you it was more clear, but in this huge mixture of bookshelf, desk, Pumporama, coatrack...

H: Also to change it from a system, because we thought it was very much structured. The difference of atmosphere should be in the foyer itself. So there would be different compartments with different feelings of the foam, used in a different way. That's what gave it the spatial complexity.

L: It's a very capricious building; it goes up and down, different finishes, water sprinklers at one height here and another height there.

R: It's very badly designed for exhibition spaces.

H: But the foyer of course was not an exhibition space at all, so it was also a challenge to get out of the modernist ideal of emptiness. Before the emptiness gave you an overview, with the bar on the left and the bookstore on the right, and that was your experience, and now we really wanted to thicken it, to increase the density.

T: I remember the first time I was in that building was in 2006, so it was completely different! The bookstore was on the left when you entered, and back then it was very much about presenting the NAi as a book publisher and seller. Speaking of architecture, did you have the blue foam/ Dutch architecture connection in the back of your mind?

H: No.

T: As designers, you might not know: fifteen years ago, because of OMA and MVRDV and those kinds of foams, there arose this obsession with cutting blue foam for architectural models. There was always this strange reduction to shape... I think now people care more about the materiality or the content because it almost became ridiculous, this approach – you should have fifty different models, and some of them might be

the random leftover pieces.
H: Also Jurgen Bey and Rianne Makkink of Studio Makkink & Bey really love the blue foam, and they really made a project out of it. *The blue house*, and then the material was more like clay. We didn't use the foam like that – we do have the art piece by Niek Pulles, which is like a sculpture made of the pieces of the foam. There was also the grotto, but that was really about showing the elementary part of the foam.
L: I think we explored the foam in every way, apart from treating it with chemicals. We didn't melt it, we respected it as a pure mass of color – and you can cut it, shape it, and it always keeps that color. That was the beauty of it. And even in the warehouse, we didn't know the color or the texture, because the foam was full of dust. The outer two or three centimeters was like a crust, it had to be thrown away. All of a sudden a blue would come out, then a yellow, then a strange spongy material, while the black one was like a mineral, like a stone.

Work on site

H: The rooms on the third floor were given to the artist Conny Groenewegen to respond to the waste of fashion. I had an apocalyptic vision of an overgrown jungle that would suffocate you once you came inside, that would grow from the top down, and when she got the assignment, she said, "No, I'm not going to be negative, I want a positive story." She started to work on the fleece jacket as an item that is very bad for reselling or reusing, so she gathered a number of students and volunteers to work with her on the project to tear apart the jackets into stripes with a cutting technique. She made huge nets out of this material by knitting as a collective effort. To have this whole factory there also transforms that space as an active part of the whole fashion trajectory.
R: I think what also created the specific atmosphere is that, for two weeks, everybody was there working. No one worked in the workshop to prefabricate the pieces, except a bit for the hacked furniture. On the third floor, all the volunteers were there knitting; on the ground floor, people were working with foam; on the second floor, the building up of the store. That made everything much better: you go every morning and there are twenty builders working together.
L: We had an Airbnb next door and it was just fabulous for two weeks to go every day and make decisions on the spot. One night you leave with a problem but the next morning you come with a solution, but someone already thought of another solution.
H: It sounds medieval!
T: Almost like a cathedral.
H: I was more involved in what was going to be on show, and it's not that deliberately leaving you out, but a different trajectory, which is very interesting for me, that there is a certain autonomy in designing exhibitions and creating an environment for the experience of fashion or the topic you address. Not necessarily displaying objects or artifacts chosen by a curator. That makes it also a much more flexible situation, that you could have an environment that can transform into a very different thing. That's why I also like that Lucas and Raphaël designed some chairs on-site, and they turned out to be nice things in themselves, a spin-off that started there, so it was almost like a workshop.
L: It was my birthday, actually. I said, "I'll take a chair from the cafeteria and rip out the leather, and then I'll take some leftover foam from the exhibition, and later I showed it in Dutch Design Week, and there is now a gallery in Milan that wants to showcase them in December in a solo exhibition. That spontaneous action came out of having the workshop there, all the materials and possibilities; as Herman was saying, my approach to design is, if you put me in the middle of the material, then something will happen. On the other hand, I studied product design and exhibition design and management, and coming back to the computer and AutoCAD and all the things I can do. It was nice to face that because, since I arrived in the Netherlands, I never used the computer as a designer. Coming back to the professionalism of the A3 drawing package.
H: It's a communication tool, so it's not about the computer.

Archetype and functionality

H: And maybe that's what Raphaël found about the retail environment – maybe you don't like it as a professional, but in the autonomy of creating an environment that coincidentally people sell in. You have this idea of what you want to be as a designer, you are confronted with an assignment, and then you adapt or find out a new layer.
R: It's really about the approach – you can design a store without thinking of it as a store and tackle more in their content, which was about hacking clothes. The furniture and storage was a tool to communicate that concept. But if the store format had been more present, I would have put pressure on myself to design a "store" – it would have changed everything.
T: It's always dangerous to exhibit fashion, and in this exhibition there is a very ambiguous attitude towards fashion, so it's not promoting it. Even in the store, it's clarifying the concept behind those clothes, but it's not choosing to put them in an attractive way – you have this group of mannequins facing away, they are not on a catwalk.
R: The hacked area has two parts – the shop and the "back side" of fashion. When you go there the lights are very bluish, the coldest temperature of color, and you don't want to stay there. You have all the statements and the moments where they show the process of hacking the leftovers, but the idea was not feeling too comfortable. That was interesting to contrast this comforting feeling of the shop and the uncomfortable feeling of the work behind it.
T: You also have that feeling in a shop when you go into the back room and all of a sudden you see boxes and coffee machines…
H: That's also about storage, about front side and back side. I like that in the archive there was a space that was unused, and they immediately used it for storage. It's a natural thing to do.
L: We also stored some foam behind the disco, in the

gap between the structure and the wall, and immediately it was labeled as a storage space. So backstage becomes messy and temporary…
T: But very functional.

Collaboration

H: I want to go back to the way of collaboration, which was very specific. We worked here on Sunday afternoons where we collected information, discussed different things, and then everyone went again on their project. For me that was a very new way of working. I'm a very basic physical environment person, that's why I don't like electronic communication that much, and in that way our method was really excellent. It could have been a great risk for me, giving part away and people develop it and you don't know what's going to happen; you don't work together every day and see what you are developing or what are you doing, and this was actually very good for my conscience, because I also don't like to control literally in that sense. I think the collaboration simply succeeded. Maybe you didn't even want to do it any other way. Collaboration needs an individual approach, and not working for Event-Architectuur as an assistant, let's say.
R: There was a lot of trust as well. Sometimes you would have meetings with the builders at 10 a.m., and at midnight the day before, we thought, "We should send Herman a file for tomorrow…" You didn't e-mail us, you knew that we would send the file by the morning. There was no panic, and maybe we were even more efficient because of that. But it was a risk because you never worked with us before.
H: That's also the way to get to an optimum, through my experience. I don't work with pressure, at least not for the product that I am looking for. I am looking for people to get attached to the things that they are doing, and then it needs their own time. That was a very good experience, that even having to dislocate the office actually benefited from the more theoretical aspect of giving room for development that you don't predict before.
R: That was the amazing part of working with Gabriel, that she was managing all of the communication, and she would keep you updated about everything, which meant that we never worked double. There are really few people that can manage to keep you informed all of the time, so you don't get worried and start to do things that someone else is already working on.
H: Also her interest lies in this communication, and it was really fun to see how this was sort of an art form in itself, how to make a list of things or how to get the network figured out, who gets the information, who gives it, who wants it.
T: Do you think there is something from your way of collaborating that helped in this case?
L: I think friendship and trust. We went through the master's program together and we have seen each other struggling, so we were already a group in that sense, with these two masters of ceremonies – Gabriel with the order and Herman in control but also not controlling.
H: But also exploring, I think – you hadn't worked together on a project but you had organized exhibitions together?
T: Such as *Fictional Collective*.
H: And this studio space.
L: It's very improvised. We are standing on something that we built up together. Raphaël is the kind of person who you can count on to be there, and I know we were here together until 3 a.m. for many days, so in that sense there is a total trust.
R: It was also the creation of specific tasks in the exhibition, which made it much easier when you know exactly what you need to do. The way you work with the other people, the atmosphere is very different.
H: If you have something to solve, we wait for you to solve it. We don't all go with the pencil giving our opinions because it doesn't work, it has to come from you. If it finally needs to change, then we can discuss it, but I don't really believe in interfering in each other's design process.
T: Did you also have the feeling of knowing that you would work on something that the public would perceive as one project?
R: The first idea was a very common thing, but the specific way to approach it was personal, but we never tried to bring our personalities out in the actual product, but our process and methodology is definitely personal. The design was somehow more or less there, so it was also a common thing.
L: It was like jumping onto a train that is already moving.
H: That's also the challenge, and now you know that you are also able to do this kind of project.
L: Do you think that being a mentor also influences your approach?
H: Totally. The reason that we have this working relationship really depends on at least having contact before. We worked together on your projects as students, and you explained to me your work, and there was an understanding that really helped develop the collaboration. If we had met for the first time at the start of the project, it would have been much more difficult. Also with Gabriel – I was not her mentor, but I mentored her a little bit and did a project with her in her first year, and that helped a lot in understanding people. Also in the respect for me, that helped, in all honesty. When you know each other, you see that there is respect on both sides, it gives you freedom to develop things together. If that were not there, it would be more difficult. Also in the clashes of our characters, they are very different, although we might end up making the same things.
R: You are not an Aries.
H: Now we come to the star signs… we also have the evangelical trio of Lucas, Raphaël, and Gabriel.
L: Two angels and one apostle.
T: I was also going to ask from your perspective, I think there is something very interesting about continuing this relationship with a mentor when you are no longer a student, when you are somehow "in the real world" – even if the Netherlands is not exactly "the real world…" Did that change your perspective as former students?
L: Suddenly we were colleagues. At some point, we recognized this huge responsibility

in the middle of the summer – five thousand people will pass by every day, kids will jump on it, expensive things will be inside – this isn't a hypothetical project in an academic sense. It was the first project I did in the Netherlands, and I was a professional before for ten years, I had my studio in Madrid, so this was a reentry into the "real world." There is a flip where there are no longer mentors and students, but colleagues – of course there is a hierarchy, but it is a flip.

Designers and architects

R: I never really thought about it. Also in the Academy, I never really perceived people as mentors, also colleague is kind of a strange word. You just work one moment together and then you continue.
H: That's also something I have to accept, the diaspora. You disappear again. You have concentration points where you collaborate, and then everyone goes their own way. That's very now. Of course you think about the continuation, but it's very related to other offers. It's a little bit tough for me, but also understandable; I can see that you have to develop and I'm not able to give this framework.
R: But that will also make us stronger, now the work can come from four different parties; if we have another project like that, then the team will come back, because it worked well.
T: I have this feeling after working on a few projects of a similar scale: you have these two weeks where you are like a tiny village where you know everybody and you understand the social network, and in this one hundred people, as a social phenomenon, it's very strange and very enjoyable.
H: It's like a theater group. We always had it with the fashion shows. Of course that was more compressed, it was night building, day show, and night destroying, and then go back home again. Those two weeks were compressed into a day, but you still had these hundred people – the models, the lighting and sound people – it's very interesting to have this connection and then to go your own way. I have to get to grips with it in terms of the office, but I like it a lot, so I'm hoping I can find a way to continue this way of working. If I think about projects in terms of the next five years, I would really love to build. The non-trained architect is very interesting, and my experience with Gabriel and with you two is that you think in structures. In general, my position as an architect engaged with Design Academy students is that they are very connected to architecture but they approach it in a very different way. It gives a light approach to the heaviness that my education brought, and also the environment of architects; it's very loaded with "things you should know" before you can start working. This notion of freely gliding over the information, taking what you like, not going too deep – you are more a collector of information. It's very nice to think how you would implement that attitude in more permanent structures.
T: I always have the feeling that when designers think at an architectural scale, they see it from eye-level. Architects are always seeing it from the bird's-eye view… and in architecture you are often surprised by what comes out in terms of scale.
H: There are always blind spots, you can't imagine all of the details from all angles, whereas the designer is much more focused on the points where it comes together.
T: Even the containers you used in Plug-in City, you can relate those to your body size in almost every dimension.
R: Because it's a buildup of elements, it's not something bigger that you design in abstraction. It's like the difference between Vectorworks and AutoCAD. It starts with the size and you multiply the size… but AutoCAD starts in space, and you start to shape without a real sense of scale. The designer learns much more by working within structures.
T: Or with physical elements. I think you get very nice outcomes – even this studio here is built up of elements – and architects would never think to do it in that way. You get very interesting features.
H: Like going up and going down again. There are all these things that as an architect you are told you should not do.
L: It's the distinction between planning and improvising.
R: All the architects I know, especially in France, start projects by considering all the regulations and problems. If you start from that point of view, then of course you'll end up building corridors with two exits, and that's it. Designers approach it in a different sense, so it's good that we collaborate because sometimes we do things that can of course benefit from some rules.
T: Where is the fire exit here?
R: Jump out of the window!
T: The structure of the industry is also affecting the situation. In design, you are rarely selling just a concept, it has been realized in a material prototype; in architecture you are just selling the idea, so the improvisation is difficult. That's what's interesting about using 1:1 models. What is a 1:1 model, actually? In a way, it's already real.
H: My period of collaboration with Rianne was very much about the struggle for informality and improvisation in the building industry. It's so difficult to tap into that, almost that nobody really likes it in the end to have so much flexibility or to introduce instability into the "safe environment" of the house or the office.

pumporama

haberdashery

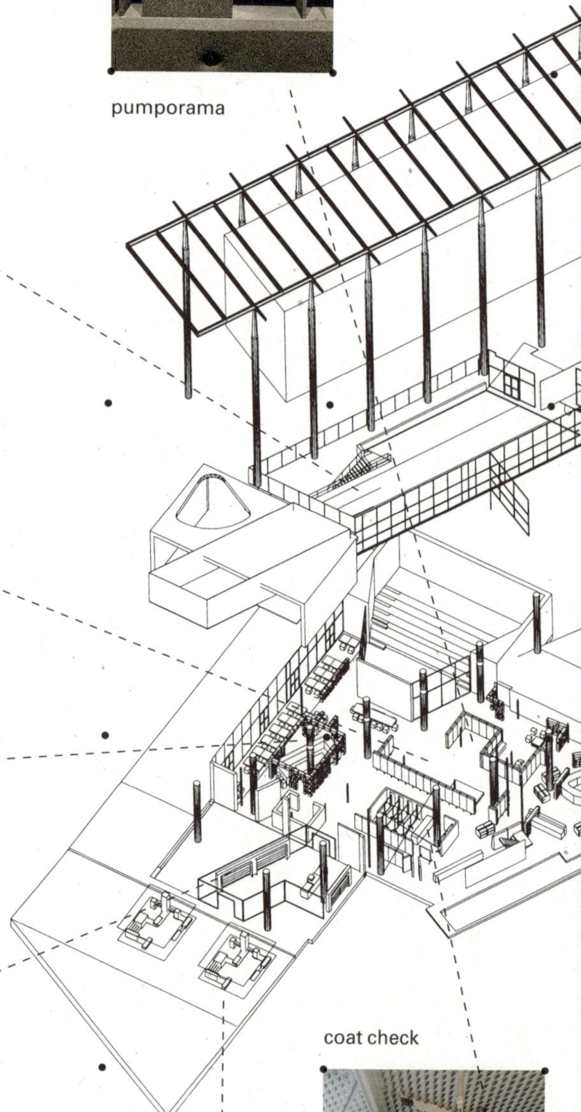

now

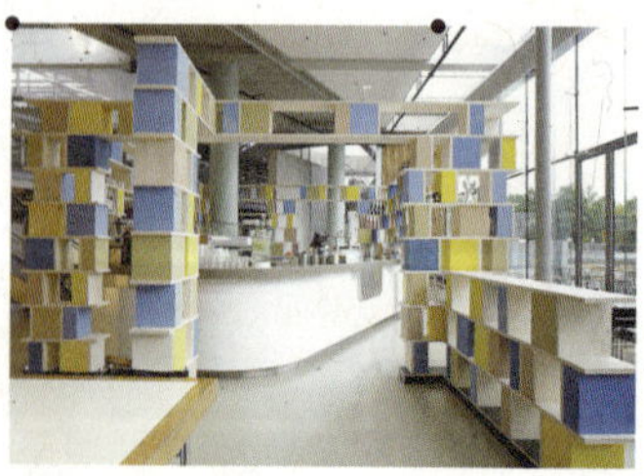

café

perfumery

coat check

entrance

project 236

book shop

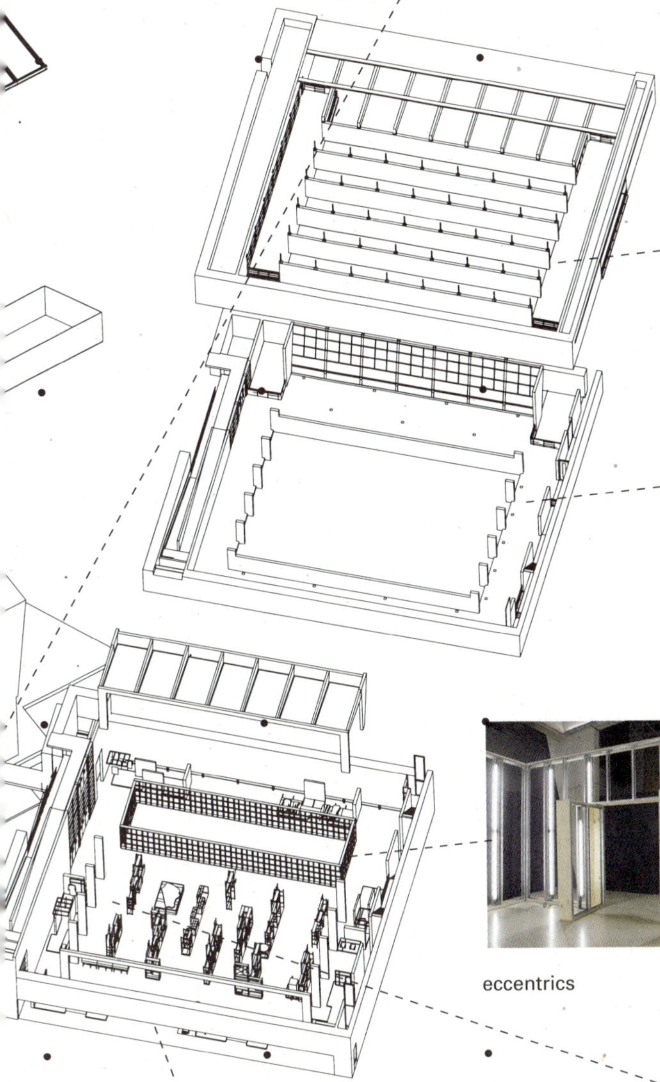

fashion reality check

hacked

eccentrics

speculative history

archive

conversation 7

Queer space

G: I'll start from the beginning. I met Herman in the Design Academy – not as my main mentor but as a mentor on a particular project, which was *Scarcity*. You were working with Rianne Makkink and we were working in groups, with Zeno and Aya. That was really challenging for me, working with people who worked in a completely different way to me, and the results were very different. But what I remember is Herman's approach that always showed a sense of delight in the idea, and finding this strange abstract way to throw a curveball in or a completely different way of thinking about an idea, but you would say it as if we had come up with the idea ourselves. When I started the graduation project, I was really trying to come from a queer position. In design, that word was unuttered, whereas in art it was very present. Queer theory was really moving up in the ranks of academia and we started very casually to talk about this idea together.

T: Does it mean a specific thing to you, in the sense of design?

G: When you think about design, it's incredibly commercially oriented, so it depicts and reinforces very traditional or nostalgic conservative visions of lifestyle, and if you look through the media and the way things are structured in design in general, even speculative design, it is always from a white, middle-class, heteronormative position, almost ad nauseam. For design, the lived experience of queer or deviation from the normal is very intriguing to look at in terms of space, objects, positions, and media. That's where we really got talking. I sent two texts – an architectural text by a poet called Caroline Bergvall, and it was called "Eclat," it was a stitching of body and space through text that was flying off the page.

H: Graphically also.

T: Like concrete poetry?

G: It worked on the premise that even the A4 page is conventionalized: the way a book or text is structured, you always have standards or conventions, and it locks you into these modes of behavior, and it repeats over and over. This text for me was my favorite architecturally queer text because of the idea of the body inseparable from the space, spreading itself over surfaces, becoming part of the architecture, but in a very forceful and sexual way. It was also breaking apart this idea of the normal way of structuring something. And Herman, you said, "I want to be a disciple!"

H: I wanted to learn to be sensitive to this subject, and I think you have to learn to see things from a different perspective. It doesn't come from one day to the next, but you need guidance, someone to pinpoint how things work, and how they exclude a lot of things. We talked about artists like La Roux, who has this beautiful video where she is part of the geometrical figures, she dissolves into a Bauhaus square circle triangle; the interesting thing is that when you objectify these gender issues it's also a lot of fun, it gives you a new way to approach each other. That clip made it very clear. Then you started to analyze *FRAME* magazine, which I thought was very clever, to see how gender was represented in the magazine through the protagonist designer, and you came to some harsh conclusions.

G: That study was using methods of cultural analysis like montage, and a seductive criticism. How can the aesthetics of something be used to critique? If it is beautiful or easy to look at, or has a pleasing arrangement, can you also appreciate the information even if it is very critical? We had really nice conversations about ways of doing things, different methodologies and positions. You also have very strong positions on architecture, the event, the exhibition…

H: About how it deals with the body, in the end. That's what I am always interested in: if you make propositions that it really gives you an experience, even if the experience is intellectual or sets your mind on a path that has a narrative and maybe also a challenge in the way the object or the proposal is displayed. You were really struggling with how to capture that as an action, it was not just a research where you make a point. The point you reached was very powerful, and you could have ended there. It would have been a good graduation. Talking to [*FRAME* editor] Robert Thiemann, going into the world, applying it to other media, that would have been a very nice and relatively easy end. But you chose to translate it into a physical experience: "Now I want a sort of machine that will let people experience this manipulation of the body in order to change the gender or to specify certain gendered gestures."

G: It was really to question the construction of gender and how architecture or objects or design contribute to this convention and shape your body in terms of how you turn towards it. We now sit towards the table, sitting on the seats with these horizontal and vertical surfaces framing us that we call "architecture" or "objects." After the study on *FRAME*, I went further to look at mechanisms of design, like clothing, objects, and space. I had a bit of naivety, but in that there was a strength that I could work with the cliché.

T: Did you ever consider making just those objects rather than something that was incorporated into the body and worn as clothing or apparatus?

G: In the end, I wanted to create a scenario or scene that the body would act within. They became more like behavioral tools or experience-based things, not pieces of fashion that you would wear or objects that you would use, but demonstrative.

First, I did everything myself, but I was too personal about it, and when I asked other people to "perform" the object or garment, it was from their intuitive position, so the garment would move you in particular ways or ask for particular gestures. To maybe make a different vocabulary of movement for the body, one that was sort of uncomfortable, there's slippage, ambiguity, confusion…

All hands

G: When I started to work with Herman on architectural ideas for the temporary fashion museum, I would say we had to make it really clear and smooth, and I really admired the way you said, "No, why would we want to do that? It's much more interesting to have a confrontation," because that is where the head pops a bit.
H: That is of course why I "casted" her, for some head popping, and then this old-school architectural training emerged! It was really interesting, something that you thought you would leave behind, but it comes back as this surface-minded approach that is at the core of architectural practice and education. The client, comfort, it was really interesting, because in a way you need this counter-position to create a definite statement. You need this dialogue.
G: I remember one moment where I had a CAD question on how to make a mitered edge, and Herman just looked shocked! "There are no miterd edges at Event-Architectuur!" That was something I really wanted to put down, because it was also kind of a rebellion, a "punk" vibe that I admire. A lot of designers and architects create beautiful things, but they are not interesting. I'm not well versed in academic architecture but it's just the feeling of space and how that either excludes you on the basis of how…
H: …how perfect it is.
G: There were a few moments where I also had to question the previous training or what you think you should do in an architectural practice. I was taught technical subjects like drawing, and I was all hands. I felt a bit mute when the hands went away on CAD, because I was so slow, and the confidence was very difficult because I couldn't access all of the experimentation and play that were there in my hands. That was an interesting move, but in the practice I had to often question myself about my assumptions of the discipline that I thought you wanted. It was always refreshingly unconventional – if we had to make a presentation, I would try to make it very precise and consistent, and you would say, "Why would we do that?" I was thinking, "For all my queer approaches, I'm being very conventional!" You were probably surprised!
H: I appreciated it a lot because I was so into the computer, and I see it as part of my body. Really communicating through the computer, because when I do sketches, the computer saves me from measuring mistakes. I'm a little bit sloppy, and I even use the computer sloppily, but it already gives me a framework. When I saw Gabriel working manually and having so much fun, she really enjoys having the whole table organized, almost like a ritual of the design, the line becomes important as a communication tool, whereas in the computer there are always multiple lines, there is never one line that starts here and stops there, and in your drawings you see when you do a grid or transfer, you make the transfer first with the grid, then you put the alternative on top; it was also in the model-making… I'm very sketchy with the model-making, and this was a similar way of doing experiments in the model instead of just making the model for a presentation. Using the model for yourself.
G: I'd never been in an architectural practice that was so patient with the way you actually did things and encouraged your methodology rather than pushed their methodology onto you. That was surprising, and also something I had to get used to. It was only when I stopped questioning what I thought you wanted that things worked well. In that sense, it was a very nice learning curve to unlearn a lot of the stuff I was used to.
H: It was maybe more in your social behavior than in the way your mind works. For me it was also interesting to see how you grew up in a polite society. We talked a lot about it; for instance, you abhor the service in Holland, you think it's very horrible. I'm very used to it and also to being assertive and taking a different role, and I asked her when in Australia do you learn that service works like that, that you can be demanding, that when you give the service you take all of the crap?
G: It's very interesting because the Dutch culture was very fascinating on that level, because of the directness to say, "I don't agree," with no fluff, and as an Australian that takes some getting used to. We're always saying we're sorry, that's one of the main words. It's a very apologetic society.
H: In a collaboration, of course it depends on the way you do things, and I was sometimes really offending Gabriel. It comes as a shock, or "You can't say that!" and politically incorrect.
T: Well, that's a very problematic issue here…
G: Certain aspects of the way people frame people, genders, races, it's crazy. It's not even questioned, these expressions are so normal, but it seemed so not okay to me. In the Design Academy, the question was always what is your position and what is your privilege; I was studying with a lot of people with different privileges. I know mine, but I'm also very working class, so it was so bizarre to be in an environment that was so different and assumes that everyone lives like that. Especially as a designer you have to be incredibly sensitive to context and different levels of living. In the Design Academy, many of the projects assume that everyone lives in the way that generates the problem the project is trying to solve… that is not even a problem, it's a luxury.
I find it frustrating that people don't acknowledge that they are taking a certain position in that. I don't care if someone's designing a luxury good, but own it – "I'm designing a luxury good for the upper echelon of society and I'm aware of it!" I found an alignment with

Herman's way of thinking; a lot of the mentors had a totally different perception of what I was talking about. With Herman and with Rianne I could extend what I was talking about because the language was there.

Beauty as seductive criticism

H: Also maybe the unsettling or frustration, I always like that development a lot. A lot of the things that you showed were a kind of rejection, and then what next? I could relate to that, that you more or less digest your proposals and give an evaluation to the collaborator or the listener and then you can reevaluate. It's more interesting than simply leaving the interpretation to the viewer.
G: That's the scary part, because then you can have a flat interpretation. I prefer to have a provocation, and then you can leave it to the audience.
H: But provocations can also go into educational methods.
T: The "seductive criticism" you mentioned is perhaps more interesting. Strangely enough some of the most interesting questioning of gender and sexuality actually come from the fashion world, but they do it through a guise of beauty. The interesting thing is how beauty can sanction a lot of discussions as open – it can be used to make things palatable. On one hand you have the argument that anything can be made beautiful, that standards of beauty can morph to encompass different behaviors and appearances and structures, but there's also a question about those standards of beauty being enforced in the first place.
H: I just invited Marc Dubois for a lecture on the beginning of postmodernism in architecture and design, and you see that the facade or the surface becomes so predominant and strangely perfect in its dimensions, but because the scales are very different between buildings, it becomes a laughable exercise, especially when you look forty years after. The beauty is not there anymore. It's scary when you project the beauty of yesterday or today onto something that has to be beautiful tomorrow, that has to be rewarded for its specificity. For instance, the old Mini car is small, it's almost on the ground, it's very noisy, you have contact with the earth. Now you have the imitation, the Mini "form" is like a bodybuilder – why is this the answer to the new Mini? Is it for comfort or safety? The iconic form has "survived," but it didn't really survive. It was "pumped up" and lost its essence. That's common to the formulation of beauty – if you copy it, it's very risky.
G: I think we are really trained in beauty. I love the films of John Waters for their depictions of something we would usually see as very ugly. In *Cry-Baby*, Hatchet Face is this terrifying-looking woman, but Johnny Depp, who is very characteristically beautiful, says, "You're beautiful, baby!" He says it so seriously, and you believe it. Waters finds this way of bringing forward the periphery of the current vision of beauty in this very filmic, cinematic way, with seductive characters and repositions beauty in that way. It puts anybody who is a little bit at the outskirts to the foreground, gives them such a strong place, and it's very empowering. It's not a meek take on beauty, it's like, "Bodies are crazy!"

Fashion and the body – The Temporary Fashion Museum

H: And you have the combination of the strong character and the appearance, that communicates beyond the shallow image. We discussed a lot of those things in the office in relation to fashion as well, and what happens when you put fashion in the forefront of an exhibition. What is it about, what is the question you want to ask? We had excellent curators who were quite straightforward in saying that in an exhibition you need to feel that fashion concerns you and your body, rather than sex appeal, commercial appeal, role models, trendiness, etc. Of course they are part of it, but how fashion defines your body in a society and how the fashion industry manipulates but also solves different social tensions. The main physical question for the exhibition designer was this dialectic between retail and museum. Of course we had to agree that retail has so much more money to spend on display!
T: Even to the extent that fashion houses like Prada or Louis Vuitton become art foundations.
H: Of course art is the proof of being a museum, but also the modern way we think of the museum as an archive where our collective memory is in store and can be shown once in a while, fashion brands also have their own version of that. For instance, with G-Star, we tried to get their archive and couldn't because it is their resource. They have mariner suits and a lot of military suits that they use as a pattern for their clothes. They would like to show their denim couture, but it's of course a very different sort of archive, much more promotional. We were interested in the type of information that they buy in order to regenerate. That's what we hope the museum does for our society, that we feel regenerated through what is on show and we can analyze it and appropriate it temporarily as citizens, have a dialogue with it. You see that fashion has privatized this aspect already, so they also buy magazines from the 1970s and '80s, they have a huge collection, also fashion photography; in the house they have very analytical R&D departments that are not designing but going through the history of the brand.

Speculative history of Dutch fashion

T: There's a thread of Dutch fashion in the exhibition, which I understood is also semi-fictional in the sense of the *Speculative History* – for example, in the toiles?
H: And also in the citation by Maison Martin Margiela of the white suits of the Provo. I think that the exhibition that we made was also about shop windows, pavements, the nightclub, the idea that it had a location and was taking place somewhere in the world. That connection to the garment was very important. The garments were made for the exhibition. There were no originals in the *Speculative History*, they were all "props," remakes.
T: I was very drawn to the piece of

Pascale Gatzen. I found out about her through the book of Alexander van Slobbe. I like her work because it's not really about the fashion body; it doesn't matter if you are not tall, for example. Perhaps it's a selfish reason!
H: The garment of Pascale has nothing to do with sex per se, it doesn't sell the body. But the garment in itself has a certain logic, it connects to the body.
G: That was another first meeting. I met her in New York because I had a piece in a show there. The curator said, "You have to meet Pascale and tell her I want her to be involved in the exhibition, this is your first assignment." She was actually attending the exhibition anyway, and she was a complete delight, very down-to-earth, soft in the way she spoke. That was a very nice introduction to the network of people around Event Architectuur.
T: Did you feel you had to build your own understanding of Dutch fashion in order to work on the exhibition?
G: In the beginning, before I started working with Herman, my first understanding was that it was a small community of designers, not like Paris, but very precise, clear, well-finished, incredible tailoring, but not en masse, not in-your-face in the vein of Dutch design. When I started to work on this project, through the work of Alexander van Slobbe, I wasn't familiar with it, and it really blew me away because there was almost eccentric classicism there, but details which were really messing with things or commenting on things. That was a bit of a starstruck kind of moment. I very much appreciated his work. I didn't know about Provo or all these movements, and that was a big jump because Herman has an incredible reference library. I have lists and lists of notes of people I should look up.
H: It's also interesting to see how different generations work with references. This speculative history of Dutch design was something that the curator wanted to tell, because if you have a temporary fashion museum in the Netherlands, maybe it's nice to have a Dutch aspect, but not an emphasis on star designers – apart from the fact that we don't have many, we have a lot working in the fashion field for huge companies, that would have been an option and still may happen, but he was much more seduced by the idea of a speculative take on the fashion world. It's Dutch but it's also global, you see that most of the time it's the tribe that transforms the habit of clothing, either if you let it be made, if you make it yourself, if you really have to buy it, and then again an anti-movement. That's also nice in the tour through the decades, that you feel this tension of different times where it's nice to go to the Waterlooplein to have the secondhand clothing and appropriating shitty garments and making them luxurious.
G: The way fashion was interpreted was very unexpected for a viewer. You take a little bit of a turn. With the perfumery, I liked it for the comment on fashion. I didn't know before, but fashion labels actually make their profit on their perfume. To have that confusion as a viewer – to come in and wonder, "Am I in a museum?" – that sort of confusion is really nice. I like these subtle comments exploring the fashion industry not always in a positive light, or you could make your own conclusion from that.
H: It wasn't presented as a simple success story.
T: It's also not promotional, but it does seem to resonate more than the typical architecture exhibition.
H: It's a crowd-pleaser in that sense.
T: It doesn't have this forced attempt to be relevant to everyday life. But at the same time, fashion is much easier to make yourself than architecture.
H: But you are also much more conscious of that fact, so it has to be pretty good; the standard is higher.

Immersed in the exhibition spaces

T: What about the design of the exhibition?
H: Two times we really failed. First time we thought we would take a systematic approach. There was so much content that we thought to systemize it.
G: But the content was still being decided at the time.
H: So it was not determined, which is great. I always work like that.
G: It's a strength, actually.
H: It means that as a designer you can still influence the research and explore the gaps. But we totally missed the idea of the physicality of the shows. Experiencing fashion by playing with the surfaces of the spaces and with the follow-up of spaces with different atmospheres.
T: I found it one of the strongest aspects of the exhibition, this experiential course, and there were some systems, but they were not dogmatic. In the main hall, sometimes it is unclear – in a good way – where you should stand, and sometimes you feel you almost enter the exhibition yourself, you are on display.
H: That's something that we worked on. Guus Beumer, the head curator and initiator of the Temporary Fashion Museum, insisted that it should not be a voyeuristic experience. The first briefing was about the body, and the body and architecture: there is a relationship where you cannot stand outside and see the things on display, but you are actually inside a maze or a labyrinth, it's an inside in which you are part of things and also on display; you have a relationship with the things you are looking at. In the speculative fashion history you see a systematic layout with the floors, which are similar but have different surfaces, the foyer has a zoning system, etc.
G: It becomes very embodied and immersive. Especially when you walk into the foyer area, it completely transformed the building. You usually walked into this huge open space.
H: A very modernist experience.
T: I love seeing the hangers with the cut-outs, you see it and wonder, is this a garment, is it a garderobe, is it an exhibition piece? It's almost like a fitting room.
H: You feel it as an interior, but you also ask, am I supposed to be here, or is this a back room? But once we started this trajectory of diversity, we knew that we couldn't

design it alone, that is, just the two of us. Gabriel would do the perfumery, I would do the Now, but it was only one-tenth of the exhibition!
G: That's where Lucas and Raphaël came in. That was great, because you really went with your instincts with that. You gave them so much independence right away. Raphaël was off immediately with the curator. Lucas thinks super quick; on-site he was coming up with solutions left, right, and center. We were working with foam, which was also a very different material to work with. It was great exploring all of its possibilities – the transparency, the glowing pink womb wall, or the big structural blocks. In the perfumery, I wanted the foam to "bite" the other material, like it was pushing in the glass. The foyer was a real challenge, actually, to figure out all of the different elements: the bookshop, the bar…
H: There were different clients.
G: When you brought in the grid, it really started to work. In the beginning, we were looking at it being quite open with little pods…
H: …little temples, like the booths in the department store. But they were just a collection of booths, where the inside and the outside were too clear. A thing with corners. We looked instead for a zoning system, where you weren't really sure if you were inside or outside, if it was a facade or an inner wall, and that's the structure that emerged.
G: And in that grid there are still some really nice alignments, but you don't really notice them on-site, or you do in certain lines of sight when you see yourself in the mirror. That was great, because it really blocked off the space but made these meandering paths, but also allowed people to disperse. There was no forced single path. You just had to explore to try to figure it out. Parts of the architecture make you think, "Maybe I can just step over that!" It's like desire lines… and I like that it's called desire, "I want to go here!" I like the looseness.
H: The temple of the old-time favorites with the neon tubes, The Eccentrics, is also an enclosed space but you can actually walk through it. It's up to the people to go in different ways.
G: It gives an openness to the viewer. It's not exploiting, it makes you feel comfortable to be there. You are sometimes on display, but sometimes you feel like you can own it. Not that it's there and you have to inhabit it, but you can own parts of it. You can participate. It's also in the materials, which are not excluding, they are simple in the way they are put together. It's ply and foam.
T: How did you find working on-site, how was your relationship to the original design?
G: For Raphaël's part, he could control it quite well. But in the foyer, because we were using these random kinds of foam – high density, low density, different colors – from the warehouse, there were a lot of things that had to be done on-site. Foam is such a strange material that we couldn't really anticipate everything that it would do, and the builders hadn't worked with it either.
H: We let them choose freely where to put the different colors in the bar. Can you imagine that you would have to pinpoint every block? If you give that freedom, it also saves you unnecessary headaches.

Process manager

H: I also would like to elaborate on your management and communication skills. Raphaël mentioned it in one sentence in the last interview, but I think you really have a talent or automatism. You are a social designer in the sense that you want to know the construction of the social situation, which people have what information and where it needs to transform and end up. These questions about coherence and presentation were very helpful. You make a lot of lists. Could you elaborate?
G: There are two parts – the people and the tangible communication. I was in between Herman, Raphaël, and Lucas, the curators, the graphic designers, the builders, and the clients. That was a really nice position, but also one in which, if I was asking a lot of Lucas or Raphaël, there has to be a real appreciation for their skill. It's generally part of how I am, but it has to be done in this motivated and encouraging way, even if it was a very big problem to solve. I tried to keep the balance of how that person was feeling or coping with the task, but with the presentations to people who are not designers but other kinds of stakeholders, like the bookshop or the bar, they were nervous because their business was at stake. We were going to transform the way their business would work, the storage, the display. That's where the seduction had to come in, because you had to make it exciting for them. We would put together these drawing packages that looked like you could be in them. That's where the hand drawing or presentation skills came in.
H: You know that you have to design a communication tool. But you also know how to address certain people in a certain way. You have a natural knowledge for not offending people!
G: That's actually true, though I find it hard to say it myself. If you are really malleable in your own persona, you can switch into different modes with different individuals. When there are so many people involved, you don't maintain your consistent persona; I can't speak to everyone in the same way. That was nice to realize – how do you get the most out of each collaborator?
T: We talked last time about the village-like, theater group traditional way of living during the exhibition, with these maximum one hundred people that you spend all your time with. In that sense the emotional strategy cannot be detached from the exhibition. If I think of exhibitions I've worked on, I always remember the social situation more than the particular design solutions we made. Just to reach that solution would mean convincing a guy who has already changed something once for you to do it again… that's always a jigsaw of opinions.
G: There was a very cool team of builders, and especially considering that not everything was solved when we began… I was used to working with architects who would put notes on

the drawing that were so legal and terrifying, that if the builder made a mistake, you would not be liable.
T: It's a very antagonistic relationship.
G: "Who is the person who I can blame?" And these builders almost expected there to be a discussion and flexibility on-site. That was a new experience for me. I think it required a different way of working.

Improvisation as a strategy

H: For a designer, it is. With *SLOOM* with Rianne Makkink, we invented a way of introducing the informal aspect of building, to not be too strict in the preparation, rules and regulations. If a door doesn't fit, we can use another door, or trade places with that sink, and those things happen, but they only happen as financial arguments. That's so ridiculous, but we started to communicate how much flexibility and possibility for improvisation there is in a building, because it takes awhile to build. You can still push the plates to the left, to the right, do something with the cladding or the finishes, and it's never done. That was so nice with the builders, that you stay responsible when it's getting built up and you see the details and you are there until the last minute to see how the effect is – not how perfect it is, but another way of perfection; you feel that it has to work the way we envisioned it, you stay on the job until it's what you want – not to say, this was the design, you figure it out! And this could happen in building as well. I just saw this image of a beautiful building by Lucien Kroll in Leuven, a student housing, a fantastic '70s building, a structure that looks unfinished because it is improvised with each student home. It was very nice because on the right side of the photo there was a hospital built in the same period, a modernist structure; on the left there were the student buildings that looked like stacked shacks. And it looked so contemporary because it didn't have a style, it was very fresh.
It was such a strong statement about how things that are defined age so quickly, and things that are undefined or ambiguous can last much longer.
T: You see that, strangely, also in the structuralist architecture before everything became industrial or resolved.
H: It's become so overstructured, this structuralism, they couldn't help themselves, poor things! If you go from the small unit and you multiply it, you have the freedom to change the units according to your needs and changing the structure. They started out like that, but then they thought, "Why make it different? Let's just do them all the same!"
T: Is it the first time you worked on an exhibition of this size?
G: Of this size, yes. In Eindhoven, I worked on four or five exhibitions, nowhere near this size. I had some experience in exhibitions, the manner of making them, making an experience, and that was also part of the training. I always had this communication role, overseeing other exhibitions, and the other tasks were very divided, the CAD work especially was done by someone else! But this time it was more integrated.
H: It was a lot to ask. I remember you attacking the foam to say, what can we do with it? We just mixed all of the things that we traditionally use at Event-Architectuur with the foam, like the tie wraps, the perforated board, the gray carton, slicing, the way we treat the material. I think you finished in a day. We digested this physical, one-day research over three months. Parts of it popped up in other solutions. First, I was a little bit worried that we do this exercise and it stays in a closet. But it kept emerging.
T: I always find that negotiation difficult, when the design phase ends and the construction phase begins; of course they overlap, personally I find it very difficult to have this overview. Once construction begins, my tendency is to become very preoccupied with the social and logistical situation. For example, you don't have an infinite number of tools, then in one moment, people in the project are competing because one needs the tools to finish. There is a strange economy popping up. In the end, you also should think about, "Is this following the original concept, should we change it?" It can be quite overwhelming!
G: Having Linde Dorenbosch, the production leader, as one of the primary bounce-offs, she's a dynamo. She has a really fantastic manner and has a bird's-eye view over everything.

Blurring retail and museum space

T: What about the display, working with the conventions of fashion? For example, there are quite a lot of different mannequins, hangers, different languages.
G: Because of the blur between the museum and retail, a lot of those aspects used retail archetypes. It was definitely not about having the traditional fashion exhibition model, all about the clothes. This wasn't only about the clothes as the primary thing.
H: Maybe you're referring to the idea that if you have a contemporary fashion exhibition, you often use the latest trends or the state-of-the-art in mannequins. Working with Rianne Makkink of Studio Makkink & Bey, it was very nice to see that she chose the mannequin or bust that displays the idea of the clothing – in the archive.
T: Every time I pass by the punk mannequin lying on the ground, I have a little shock – also because he has a head. Without the head, it would be totally different.
G: I like the ones where they are real enough, but you know they are fake. The Edward Kienholz thing, a bit grotesque.
H: We started with the idea of the Kienholz bar in the Stedelijk, the enclosure, as the setting for the speculative history. It works with the texture that you are familiar with, and alienates you because of the slightly off quality.
T: I saw his installation in the Stedelijk Museum, you have a claustrophobic feeling there.
G: They are always slightly smaller or bigger than human scale, but hardly noticeable. It has an awkward aspect, and the materials are very strange, but also like a still life.

Events: Situating the Temporary
Page 606

johannes schwartz

Johannes Schwartz
Kinderhütten, 1998
Page 609

Johannes Schwartz
Kinderhütten, 1998

projects 1990–2016

1990

1
Book – *De Villa Karamazow*, Graduation project, TU Delft, w/ Christine Rothuizen, graphic designer

2
Competition – *Three Sisters*, Experimental theater, Moscow (RU)

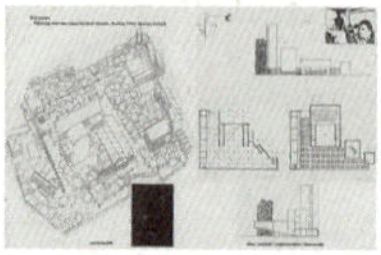

3
Proposal – *Datsja*, Moscow outskirts (RU), client: Svetlana Kunitsina

4
Fashion Show – *Petit Pouf* by orson + bodil and Lilian Driessen, Amsterdam RAI, w/ Joke Robaard, artist, sound by Eddy de Clercq

5
Workshop – *Museum for sculptor Carel Visser*, Berlage Institute Amsterdam

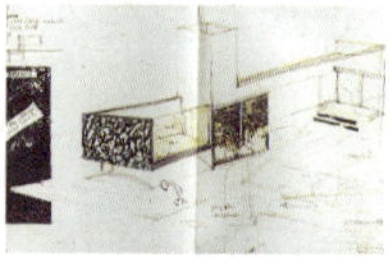

6
Grant – *Talent development*, Fonds BKVB Amsterdam

91

7
Exhibition – *Zaal der Goede Intenties*, Centraal Museum, Utrecht, curator: Guus Beumer, w/ Frans Ankoné, stylist, Vinoodh Matadin, Alexander van Slobbe, fashion designers

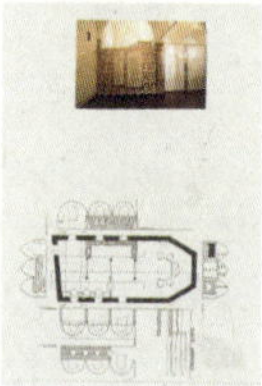

8
Competition – *Tours de Force*, Europan 2, Montauban (FR), w/ Rianne Makkink, architect

92

9
Booth – *TiPi*, orson + bodil, w/ Joke Robaard, artist, Pascale Gatzen, designer

10
Grant – *Work development*, Fonds BKVB Amsterdam

11
Competition – *Spreebogen Areal*, Berlin (DE), w/ DC23 Collective: Jurjen Zijnstra, Michiel Riedijk, Diederik Nortier, Bart Goldhoorn, Juliette Bekkering, architects

12
Animation – *Four Stages of Life*, project for Architecture and CAAD, ETH Zürich (CH)

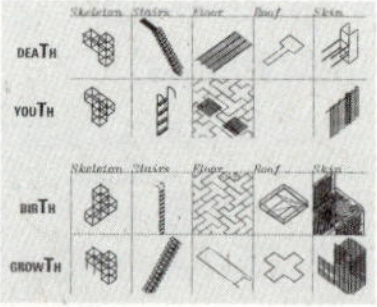

93

13
Proposal – *Fischiff*, postgraduate project for Architecture and CAAD, ETH Zürich (CH)

14
Video – *Swimming poollibrary*, graduation project, ETH Zürich (CH)

94

15/16
Fashion Shows – orson + bodil, ws 1994/95, ss 1995, Paris (FR), w/ Bart Guldemond, designer, sound by Eddy de Clercq, lighting by Ruud Pouwels

17
Fashion Show – SO, ss 1995, Paris (FR), w/ Bart Guldemond, designer, sound by Eddy de Clercq, lighting by Ruud Pouwels

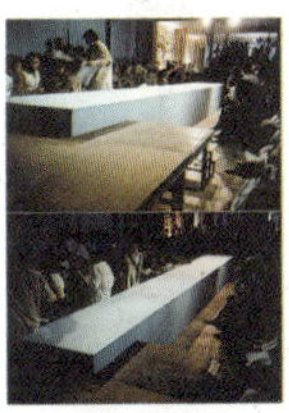

18
Concept Development – ArtEZ Fashion Show, Arnhem, w/ Joke Robaard, artist, Guus Beumer, publicist, sound by Fred Kolman

19
Proposal – Poster Museum for OMA + Exhibition Leidsche Rijn for Maxwan Rotterdam

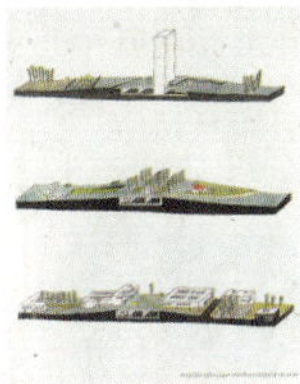

20
Screening – *Swimming poollibrary*, Ars Electronica, Linz (AT)

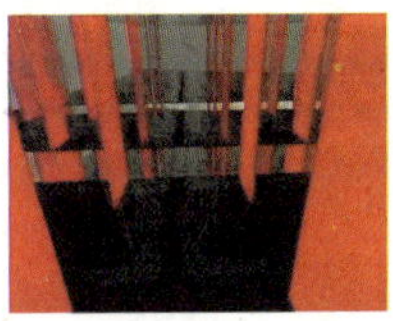

21
Proposal – *WorldCondom installation*, W139, Amsterdam, w/ Hermen Maat, artist

1995

22
Exhibition – *Junichi Arai*, Vormgevingsinstituut, Amsterdam, w/ Bart Guldemond, designer

23
Presentation – Limpergprijs for orson + bodil, Vormgevingsinstituut, Amsterdam, w/ Bart Guldemond, designer

24
Competition – *Prix de Rome*, entrance building for the Netherlands Open Air Museum, Arnhem

25
Fashion Show – orson + bodil, 1995/96, Paris (FR), w/ Bart Guldemond, designer, sound by Eddy de Clercq, lighting by Ruud Pouwels

26/27
Fashion Shows – SO, ws 1995/96, ss 1996, Paris (FR), w/ Bart Guldemond, designer, sound by Eddy de Clercq, lighting by Ruud Pouwels

28
Concept Development – ArtEZ Fashion Show, Arnhem, w/ Bob Verheyden & Team, sound by Mr. & Mrs. Cameron

29
Competition – *The Juice*, design for a square, Los Angeles (US), w/ Maarten Theuwkens, artist

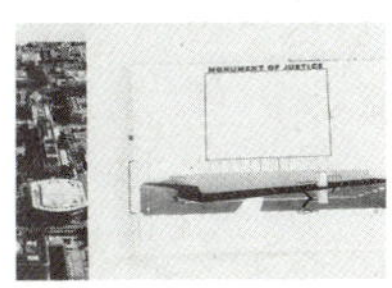

30
Competition – *The Glass House*, 2nd prize, Leerdam, w/ Laura Weeber, architect

96

31
Viewing – *Swimming poollibrary*, Long Beach Museum of Art (US)

32
Interior – Keizersgracht 682/1, Amsterdam, client: Theo van Adrichem, w/ Laura Weeber, architect

33/34
Fashion Shows – SO, ws 1996/97, ss 1997, Paris (FR), w/ Bart Guldemond, designer, sound by Mr. & Mrs. Cameron, lighting by Ruud Pouwels

35
Fashion Store & Showroom – *Marui Shibuya*, SO by alexander van slobbe, Tokyo (JP)

36
Proposal – St. Agnietenstraat 20, Amsterdam, renovation and penthouse, client: Cor Dubuy, w/ Laura Weeber and Floris van der Kleij (executed by Floris van der Kleij, 2005)

37
Script – *Got to get up*, video for Plattel

38
Performance – Breitnerstraat, Rotterdam, *Google Street View*, 360-degree camera, curators: Jouke Kleerebezem, Maarten Sprenger, w/ Rianne Makkink, Klaar Plattel

39
Exhibition – Kunstvereniging Diepenheim, installation of works by Joke Robaard, artist

97

40
Exhibition – *The Drinking Glass*, Fort Asperen, Leerdam, curator: Brigitte van der Sande, w/ Bart Guldemond, designer

41
Renovation – Hoeve Gabardine, Noordwolde, clients: Guus Beumer, Arjan Ederveen

42/43
Fashion Shows – SO, ws 1997/98, ss 1998, Paris (FR), w/ Bart Guldemond, designer, sound by Mr. & Mrs. Cameron, lighting by Ruud Pouwels

44
Concept Development – ArtEZ Fashion Show, Arnhem, w/ Bob Verheyden, designer and team, sound by Mr. & Mrs. Cameron

45
Interior – Bureau Amsterdam, counter and workspace, client: Leontine Coelewij, w/ Maarten Theuwkens, artist

46
Presentation – *Park 4D-TV, Park-TV CD-ROM*, Paradiso, Amsterdam, client: Maarten Sprenger

47
Proposal – *Quality Assessment of Research*, exhibition at TU Delft

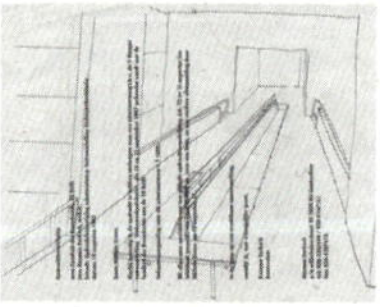

48
Competition – *The Snake*, Europan, Bern (CH), w/ Laura Weeber

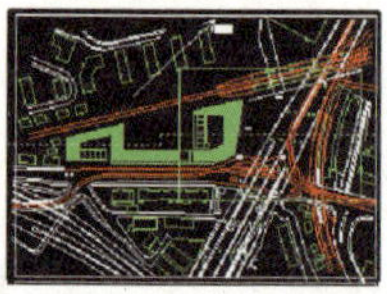

98

49/50/51/52
Exhibitions (4) – *Sports in the City, Double/Use, Oosterdok, Green City*, ARCAM, Amsterdam, curator: Marina van den Bergen

53
Fashion Store – Harajuku, SO by alexander van slobbe flagship store, Tokyo (JP)

54
Concept Development – Fashion Show Amfi, Bagagehal 6, Amsterdam, w/ Michiel Zegers

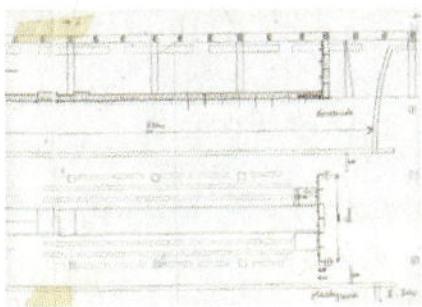

55/56
Fashion Shows – SO, ws 1998/99, ss 1999, Paris (FR), w/ Bart Guldemond, designer, sound by Mr. & Mrs. Cameron, lighting by Ruud Pouwels

57
Proposal – Nieuwe Keizersgracht 53, renovation, Amsterdam, clients: Roos Theuws, Marien Schouten, w/ Gerrit Schilder, architect

58
Presentation – Flyers EventArchitectuur, w/ Jop van Bennekom, graphic designer

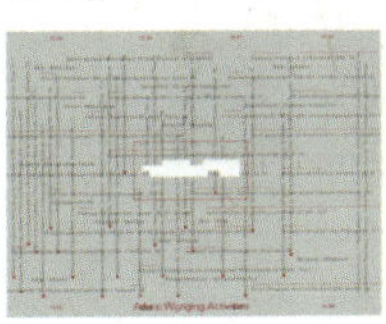

99

59
Fashion Shoot – *Balloon*, Amsterdam, client: Mario Testino, inflatable by Rens Bouma

60
Temporary Interior – *Doors of Perception 5: Play*, symposium in Beurs van Berlage, Amsterdam, inflatables by Rens Bouma, photo installation by Hermen Maat, graphic design by Joseph Plateau, production by Landstra & De Vries

61
Magazine – *Forum* magazine, architectural biannual, w/ Jop van Bennekom, graphic designer, Dick van Gameren, Bart Goldhoorn, Rianne Makkink, architects, Hester Wolters, art historian, Erik Wong, graphic designer

62
Presentation – SO droog design, Harajuku, Tokyo (JP), graphic design by Experimental Jetset

63
Exhibition – *AEX*, design and photography purchase, Stedelijk Museum, Amsterdam, graphic design by Vanessa van Dam, production by Landstra & De Vries

64
Concept Development – Fashion Show Amfi, Bagagehal 6, Amsterdam, w/ Michiel Zegers, artist

65
Presentation – SO Women, Paris (FR), inflatable by Rens Bouma

66/67
Fashion Shows – SO, ws 1999/2000, ss 2000, Paris (FR), w/ Bart Guldemond, designer, sound by Mr. & Mrs. Cameron, lighting by Ruud Pouwels

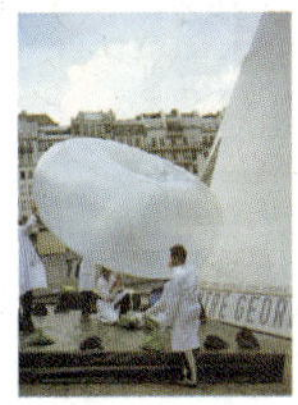

68
Exhibition – *Styling, Fashion, Art & Design*, Centraal Museum, Utrecht, production by Landstra & De Vries, w/ Bart Guldemond, designer

2000

69
Proposal – *Perfume Store Concept* for Sephora, w/ Bart Guldemond, designer

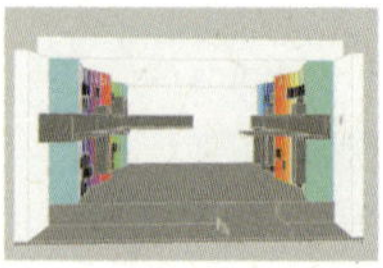

70
Fashion Store – Daikanyama, Dutch design shop for SO by alexander van slobbe, Tokyo (JP)

71
Exhibition – *orson + bodil 10 years*, Centraal Museum, Utrecht

72
Catalogue – *De-Fence*, for the installation NL Lounge by NL Architects, Venice Biennale of Architecture (IT), w/ Rianne Makkink, architect, Jop van Bennekom, graphic designer

73/74
Fashion Shows – SO by alexander van slobbe, ws 2000/2001, ss 2001, Paris (FR), w/ Bart Guldemond, designer, sound by Mr. & Mrs. Cameron, lighting by Ruud Pouwels

75
Exhibition – *Neuro Fuzzy World*, Da Vinci Techno Activity Center, Enschede, w/ Bart Guldemond, designer

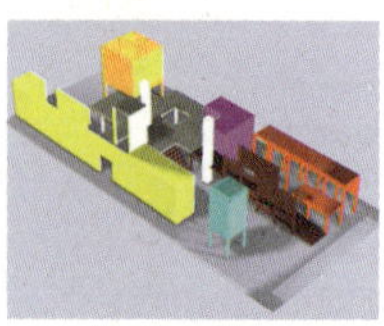

76
Interior – Wilhelminastraat 44, Amsterdam, production by Landstra & De Vries

01

77
Exhibition – Rotterdam Design Prize 2001, Museum Boijmans Van Beuningen, Rotterdam, w/ Michiel Zegers, artist, graphic design by Mooren VanderVelden, production by Landstra & De Vries

78
Exhibition – *Veem 20 Years*, Veem Building, Amsterdam, w/ Gerrit Oorthuys

79
Installations – *Anti Prophet & Hortus Non Conclusus*, Marres, Maastricht

80/81
Fashion Shows – SO by alexander van slobbe, ws 2001/2002, ss 2002, Paris (FR), w/ Bart Guldemond, designer, sound by Mr. & Mrs. Cameron, lighting by Ruud Pouwels

82
Installation – *Higher Truth no.5*, Vleeshal, Middelburg, curators: Guus Beumer, Rutger Wolfson, w/ Rianne Makkink, architect, Alexander van Slobbe, fashion designer, Project_ Jordan, graphic design, production by Kees Wijker & Team

83
Exhibition – *Waterproof*, Fort Asperen, Leerdam, curator: Brigitte van der Sande, production by Landstra & De Vries, w/ Bart Guldemond, designer

84
Proposal – Tichelstraat 38, refurbishment, Amsterdam, clients: Annelies Dop, François Bouchez (executed by the client, 2012)

02

85
Workshop – *SLOOM 0*, Saturday & Sunday issue at NU Seminar, De Balie, Amsterdam, curator: Pim Ox, w/ KoehorstIn'tVeld, graphic designers, Rianne Makkink, architect

86
Book – *Weekend Agenda* by *Forum* magazine, w/ Julia van Mourik, art producer, Hester Wolters, art historian, Rianne Makkink, architect, Jop van Bennekom, graphic designer, Johannes Schwartz, photography

87/88
Magazines – *SLOOM 1 & SLOOM 2*, self-initiated publications of sloom.org, founded with Rianne Makkink

89
Exhibition – *We'll Slide down the Surface of Things*, Vleeshal, Middelburg, curator: Rutger Wolfson, production by Kees Wijker & Team

03

90
Magazine – *SLOOM 3*, living and working in Berlin, artist in residence of Fonds BKVB

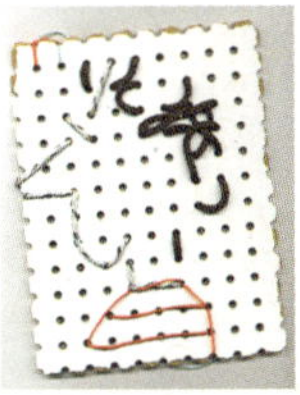

91
Exhibition – *Rotterdam Design Prize 2003*, Museum Boijmans Van Beuningen, Rotterdam, production by Landstra & De Vries, w/ Paul Kuipers, artist, "Freshly Mown Grass" fragrance by Alessandro Gualtieri, textile overgrowth by Conny Groenewegen & Team, graphic design by Mooren VanderVelden

92
Installation – *Safe Haven*, Vleeshal, Middelburg, curator: Guus Beumer, graphic design by Goodwill, styling by Marjo Kranenborg, production by Kees Wijker & Team

93
Exhibition Series – *Year of the Farm*, one in each province of the Netherlands, w/ Rianne Makkink, architect, production by Kees Wijker, Erik Vijn

94
Installation – *Boys '97*, Foam, Amsterdam, w/ Johannes Schwartz, photographer/artist

95
Installation – *Higher Truth 2*, Büro Friedrich, Berlin, w/ Rianne Makkink architect, production Kees Wijker & Team

96
Exhibition – *Mixed Farming*, Foto Museum Rotterdam, w/ Rianne Makkink architect, artwork by Peter Moeller, production by Kees Wijker & Team

04

97
Exhibition – *Start: OMA open archive*, NAi, Rotterdam, curator: Linda Vlassenrood, w/ Bart Guldemond, designer, graphic design by Experimental Jetset, production by Landstra & De Vries

98
Exhibition – *Mode 50DE*, Museum of Contemporary Art, Arnhem, curator: Piet Paris, w/ Paul Kuipers, artist

99
Exhibition – *Mark*, graphic design purchases, SMCS Amsterdam, curator: Marten Jongema, w/ Paul Kuipers, artist

100
Exhibition – *Geest & Grond*, Bulb Museum Lisse, curator: Hans Venhuizen, w/ Paul Kuipers, artist

101
Fashion Store – *orson + bodil, workshop, showroom and store*, Polonceaukade, Westerpark, Amsterdam, production by Wouter de Baat

102
Proposal – *Willem Arntsz Hoeve urban design plan for oldest part*, Den Dolder

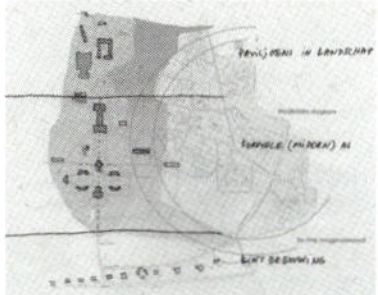

103
Bookstore – *Artimo A–Z*, Amsterdam, client: Gijs Stork, production by Landstra & De Vries, graphic design by Experimental Jetset

104
Installation – *Go Slow*, Milan (IT), curator: Droog, food design by Marije Vogelzang, graphic design by Hansje van Halem, production by Kees Wijker & Team

2005

105
Presentation – *SLOOM 4* in Artimo A–Z, w/ Rianne Makkink, architect, speech by Dirk van den Heuvel, architect, and Joke Robaard, artist, graphic design by KoehorstIn'tVeld

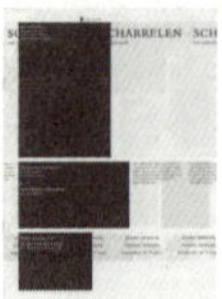

106
Proposal – *WonderHolland*, exhibition on Dutch design and fashion, Rome (IT), curator: Angelique Westerhof

107
Exhibition – *Arnhem Fashion Biennale 2005*, former Coberco Milk Factory, Arnhem, curator: Piet Paris, production by Landstra & De Vries, w/ Paul Kuipers, artist

108
Exhibition – *Fashion Cabinets*, part of AFB 2005, Arnhem, w/ Paul Kuipers, Mark Mantingh, artists

109
Installation – *Ideal House* Hella Jongerius at the IMM fair, Cologne (DE), w/ Hella Jongerius, Arian Brekveld, designers, Louise Schouwenberg, publicist, Paul Kuipers, artist

110
Exhibition – *Best Designed Books 2004*, SMCS Amsterdam, curators: Esther Hemmes, Marten Jongema, production by Kees Wijker & Team, w/ Paul Kuipers, artist

111
Fashion Store – Kiki 2, outlet store for Kiki Niesten, Stokstraat, Maastricht, production by Kees Wijker & Team, w/ Paul Kuipers, artist

112
Bookstore – *ArtiMarres*, collaboration with Artimo A-Z and Marres Books, Marres, Maastricht, production by Guus van den Akker & Team

113
Land Art – *Pursuit of Happiness*, art exhibition at an old farmyard, Leidsche Rijn, Utrecht, curator: Mariette Dölle, production by Landstra & De Vries, w/ Paul Kuipers, Pieter Wackers, artists

114
Exhibition – *Pursuit of Happiness*, video art exhibition at an old farmyard, Leidsche Rijn, Utrecht, curator: Mariette Dölle, production by Landstra & De Vries, AV by Ruud Pouwels, w/ Paul Kuipers, Pieter Wackers, artists

115/116
Exhibitions – *Soft Target: Concerning War*, art exhibitions at Hoog Catharijne and BAK, Utrecht, curator: Brigitte van der Sande, graphic design by KummerHerrman, w/ Bart Guldemond, designer

117–121
Exhibitions (5) – *Utrecht Manifest*, design biennial at different locations in Utrecht, w/ Bart Guldemond, designer; Now and Again, curator: Lisette Smits, and Choice, curator: Ed van Hinte, both in the Pastoe Factory and showroom; Now and Again Black House, in a housing project of G. Rietveld, concept by Guus Beumer, styling by Marjo Kranenborg; Campana and Uithof, Centraal Museum, Utrecht, curator: Ida van Zijl, graphics Solar Collective, production by Landstra & De Vries

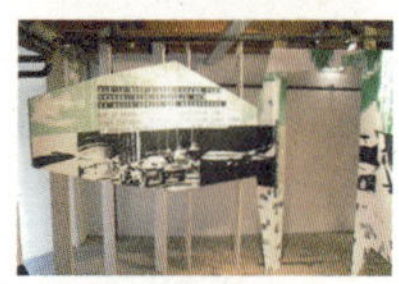

06

122
Installation – *Just In*, ultimate interiors, NAi, Rotterdam, curator: Saskia van Stein, w/ Idan Hayosh, artist

123
Installation – *Just In 2*, ultimate interiors, Zuiderkerk, Amsterdam, curator: Saskia van Stein, w/ Idan Hayosh, artist

124
Installation – *Principle Junk*, P///AKT, Amsterdam, w/ Johannes Schwartz, photographer/artist

125
Installation – *Wroeten*, set for TV series in the Friesian countryside, director: Lernert Engelberts, main character: Arjan Ederveen, w/ Rianne Makkink, architect

126
Presentation – Oilily, children's clothes at the Pitti Bambini fair, Florence (IT), curator: Liam Maher, production by Erik Vijn, w/ Jurgen Bey, designer, Rianne Makkink, architect, Guus Beumer, publicist

127
Concept Design – *Graduation Show Furniture*, working drawings for the Graphic Design Department of Gerrit Rietveld Academie, Amsterdam, curator: Linda van Deursen (executed by students)

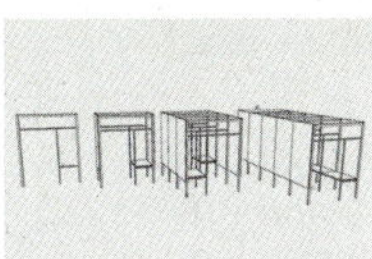

128
Exhibition – *Seeing is Knowing*, architectural drawings of NAi, Venice Biennale of Architecture (IT), curators: Martien de Vletter, Aaron Betski, graphic design by Hansje van Halem, production by Stylos, Herman Pols & Team

129
Interior – Office BremerDeZwaan, Keizersgracht 604, Amsterdam, clients: Monica Bremer & Marcel de Zwaan, production by Landstra & De Vries, w/ Paul Kuipers, artist

130
Installation – *La Collection Imaginaire*, Marres, Maastricht, curator: Renée Steenbergen, production by Guus van den Akker & Team, w/ Paul Kuipers, artist

131
Exhibition – *Best Designed Books 2005*, SMCS Amsterdam, curators: Esther Hemmes, Marten Jongema, w/ Paul Kuipers, artist

132
Exhibition – *Die Dinge*, random presentation of objects from regional museums, Marres, Maastricht, curator: Claudia Banz, graphic design by MoorenVanderVelden, production by Guus van den Akker & Team, w/ Paul Kuipers, artist

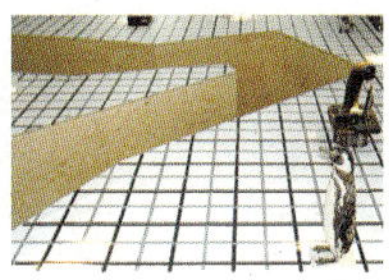

133
Interior – Goudsbloemdwarsstraat, Amsterdam, client: Wendel ten Arve, production by Landstra & De Vries, Kees Wijker, w/ Paul Kuipers, artist

134
Proposal – Beethovenstraat interior, Amsterdam, client: Alexander van Slobbe, w/ Paul Kuipers, artist

135
Interior – *SPACES*, Heerenstraat, Geulle, first private interior with the SPACES concept, client: Joop Schermerhorn, production by Andre van Bergen, w/ Paul Kuipers, artist

136
Competition – *Simplicity*, 100,000 euro House, Almere, w/ Paul Kuipers, artist

137
Proposal – Baker's Attic, Westerpark, client: Piet Hekker

138
Exhibition – *Pierre Bernard*, Museum for Communication, The Hague, graphic design by Hansje van Halem, w/ Paul Kuipers, artist

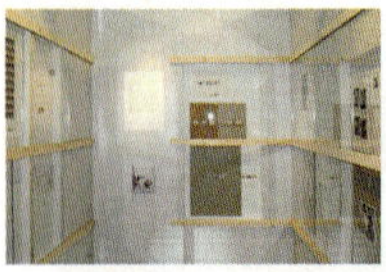

139
Exhibition – *WunderKammer*, routing, Z33, Hasselt, curator: Jan Boelen, graphic design by Julie Peeters, w/ Paul Kuipers, artist

140
Installation – *WunderKammer*, collection of leftovers from regional museums, Z33, Hasselt, curator: Jan Boelen, w/ Paul Kuipers

141
Proposal – Idylls for Lingezegen Park, landscape art, client: SKOR and Province of Gelderland, w/ Paul Kuipers, Pieter Wackers, artists (executed from 2015)

142
Proposal – Holistic Center New Old Kraggenburg, Northeast Polder, client: Fam. Wolters, w/ Rianne Makkink

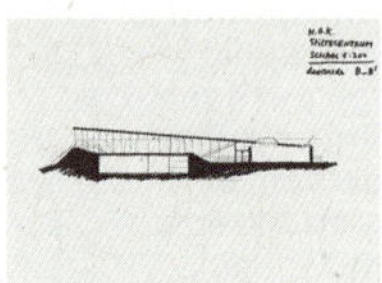

143
Re-Use – *Artimo A–Z*, Hertenweg, Kraggenburg, client: Rianne Makkink

144
Exhibition – *Best Designed Books 2006*, SMCS Amsterdam, curators: Esther Hemmes, Marten Jongema, w/ Paul Kuipers, artist

145
Exhibition – *Arnhem Fashion Biennale 2007*, Museum of Contemporary Art, ArtEZ, boat across the river Rhine, former Brick Factory, Arnhem, curator: Piet Paris & Joff, graphic design by Maureen Mooren, production by Landstra & De Vries, w/ Paul Kuipers, artist, Gent Vranovci, designer

146
Exhibition – *Jan, Jans & de Mode*, CODA, Apeldoorn, curator: Piet Paris, production by Landstra & De Vries, w/ Paul Kuipers, artist

147
Exhibition – *Seeing is Knowing 2*, Zuiderkerk, Amsterdam, curators: Martien de Vletter, Aaron Betski, w/ Paul Kuipers, artist

148
Fashion Store – *Coming Soon* Arnhem, client: Judith ter Haar, graphic design by Experimental Jetset, production by Landstra & De Vries, KLIEF, w/ Paul Kuipers, artist

149
Exhibition – *The Edible City*, producing food in the city, client: NAiM, Maastricht, curator: Guus Beumer, Hans Ibelings, Debra Solomon, Anneke Moors, planting by De Groene Stap, graphic design by Experimental Jetset, production by Guus van den Akker & Team, w/ Paul Kuipers, artist

150
Temporary Interior – *The Great Indoors 2007*, seminar and award show on interior design, NAiM, Maatricht, clients: *FRAME*, NAiM, Marres, sound by Mr. & Mrs. Cameron, graphic design by KoehorstIn'tVeld, production by Guus van den Akker & Team, w/ Paul Kuipers, artist

151
Installation – *Stairs*, Lego intervention at art show of Johannes Schwartz and Experimental Jetset, Marres CCC, Maastricht

08

152
Interior – Studio Piet Paris, Palmdwarstraat 36, Amsterdam, client: Piet Paris, production by Landstra & De Vries, w/ Paul Kuipers, artist

153
Competition – *Temple for the Spirit*, Dordrecht, w/ Paul Kuipers, artist

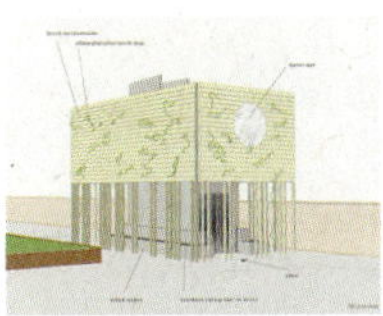

154
Grocery Store – Warmoesmarkt, Warmoesstraat, Amsterdam, organic and regional food, initiator: Piet Hekker, graphic design by Lesley Moore, artwork by Peter Moeller, production by Landstra & De Vries, w/ Paul Kuipers, artist

155
Exhibition – *Best Designed Books 2007*, SMCS Amsterdam, curators: Esther Hemmes, Marten Jongema, w/ Paul Kuipers, artist

156
Exhibition – *Changing Ideals*, changing ideals for living, NAiM, Maastricht, curator: Dirk van den Heuvel, graphic design by Experimental Jetset, production by Guus van den Akker & Team, w/ Paul Kuipers, artist

157
Exhibition – *Come to My Place*, interiors made by international designers, Westerhuis, Amsterdam, client: Experimenta Lisboa & Droog, graphic design by Hansje van Halem, production by Landstra & De Vries, w/ Paul Kuipers, artist

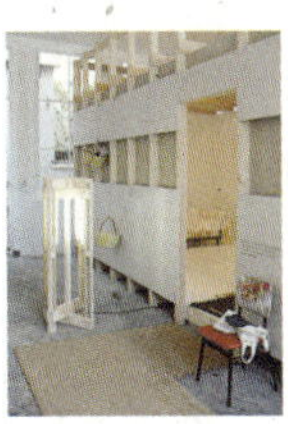

158
Exhibition – *At Home in My Mind*, personal interiors for three clients, Het Dolhuys, Haarlem, curator: Floris Mulder, production by Landstra & De Vries, w/ Paul Kuipers, artist, Gent Vranovci, designer

159
Fashion Store – orson + bodil / Francisco van Benthum, Jacob Obrechtstraat, Amsterdam, production by Guus van den Akker & Team, w/ Paul Kuipers, artist

160
Fashion Show – orson + bodil / Francisco van Benthum, Stadsarchief Amsterdam, production by Landstra & De Vries, w/ Paul Kuipers, artist

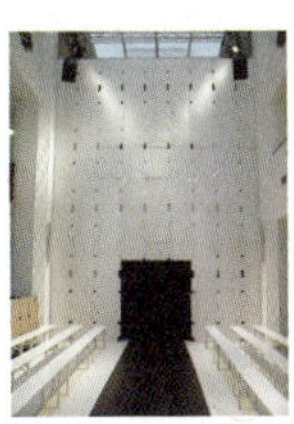

161
Proposal – Fashion Showroom Wolf, Herengracht, Amsterdam, fashion by Francisco van Benthum, w/ Paul Kuipers, artist

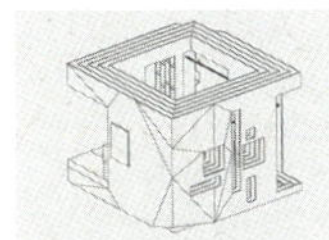

162
Exhibition – *State Alpha, on the architecture of sleep*, NAiM, Maastricht, curator: Liquid Frontiers, graphic design by Experimental Jetset, production by Guus van den Akker & Team, w/ Paul Kuipers, artist

163
Interior – *SPACES*, Marco Polostraat, Amsterdam, w/ Paul Kuipers, artist

164
Proposal – Glashütte, design collective in a community building, Stralau, Berlin (DE), w/ Jurgen Bey, Rianne Makkink, Guus Beumer, Hella Jongerius, Lucas Verwey

165
Proposal – Sphinx, old factory in Maastricht, first location for the exhibition *Out of Storage* (executed in 2011), w/ Paul Kuipers, artist

166
Proposal – *Gone with the Wind*, wind installation, Zuiderzee Museum, Enkhuizen, curators: Alexander van Slobbe, Francisco van Benthum

167
Proposal – *Feeding Platforms for Birds*, Altrecht Den Dolder, Artist in Residence at Het Vijfde Seizoen (executed in 2011)

09 2010

168
Exhibition – *Architecture of Consequence*, presentation of Dutch architectural offices, International Architecture Biennale São Paulo (BR), curator Saskia van Stein, Ole Bouman, graphic design Koehorst In'tVeld, production by Landstra & De Vries, w/ Paul Kuipers, artist

169
Presentation – *NL=New Luxury*, Design Academy Eindhoven at the Salone del Mobile Milan (IT) and NAiM/Bureau Europa, Maastricht, curator: Alexander van Slobbe, w/ Paul Kuipers, artist

170
Temporary Interior – *The Great Indoors 2009*, seminar and award show on interior design, NAiM/Bureau Europa, Maastricht, clients: *FRAME*, NAiM, Marres, sound by Mr. & Mrs. Cameron, graphic design by KoehorstIn'tVeld, production by Guus van den Akker & Team, w/ Paul Kuipers, artist

171
Exhibition – *Unresolved Matters*, social utopias revisited, Centraal Museum, Utrecht, curator: Claudia Banz, part of Utrecht Manifest, graphic design by Metahaven, production by Landstra & De Vries, w/ Paul Kuipers

172
Installation – *Billboard Seats*, Utrecht Manifest, graphic design by Metahaven, production by Landstra & De Vries, w/ Tal Erez

173
Proposal – Vitrahaus Presentations for JongeriusLab, w/ Hella Jongerius, Arian Brekveld

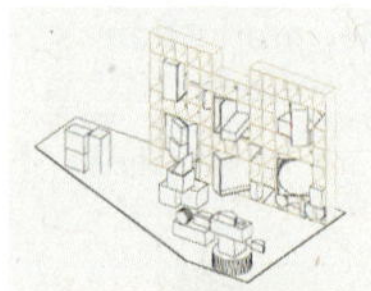

174
Project – Book, *Space*, Show, contribution to a research project by Jenny Eneqvist, graphic designer at Gerrit Rietveld Academie

175
Exhibition – *Best Designed Books 2008*, Bijzondere Collecties, Allard Pierson Museum, Amsterdam, curators: Marten Jongema, Mathieu Lommen, Just Enschede, Garrelt Verhoeven, graphic design by Lesley Moore, w/ Paul Kuipers, artist

176
Proposal – *Dressed*, exhibition on fashion, KunstPalast, Düsseldorf (DE), curator: Claudia Banz, w/ Paul Kuipers

177
Installation – *Go Slow New York*, Governors Island, New York (US), part of Pioneers of Change, curator: Droog, food design by Marije Vogelzang, graphic design by Hansje van Halem, w/ Rianne Makkink

178
Exhibition – *Beyond the Amateur*, exhibition on photography, Marres CCC, Maastricht, curator: Yvon Schoenmakers, Arjan de Nooy, artist, graphic design by Maureen Mooren, production by Guus van den Akker & Team, w/ Paul Kuipers, artist

179
Exhibition – *Architecture of Consequence*, presentation of Dutch architectural offices, Rotterdam / ACN Moscow (RU), curators: Saskia van Stein, Ole Bouman, graphic design by Koehorst In'tVeld, production by Landstra & De Vries, w/ Paul Kuipers, artist

180
Exhibition – *Best Designed Books 2009*, Stedelijk Museum, Amsterdam, curators: Esther Hemmes, Carolien Glazenburg, production by KLIEF, w/ Paul Kuipers, artist

181
Grant – EventFurnituur R&D, FBKVB, transforming displays into furniture, production by Landstra & De Vries, w/ Tal Erez, Itay Ohaly, designers, Paul Kuipers, artist

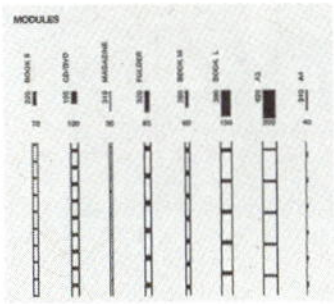

182
Presentation – *SPACES*, first EventFurnituur product at Tutto Bene Fair, Via Savona, Salone del Mobile Milan (IT), production by Landstra & De Vries, w/ Paul Kuipers, artist, Tal Erez, designer

183
Exhibition – *Clip Stamp Fold*, independent architecture magazines, Bureau Europa, Maastricht, curator: Beatriz Colomina, graphic design by Experimental Jetset, production by Guus van den Akker & Team, w/ Paul Kuipers, artist

184
Exhibition – *Club Ceramique*, social events on Ceramique district in Maastricht, Bureau Europa, Maastricht, graphic design by Experimental Jetset, production by Guus van den Akker & Team, w/ Paul Kuipers, artist, Bram Burger, designer

185
Exhibition – *Hygiene, the story of a museum*, Marres, Maastricht, curator: Claudia Banz, graphic design by Maureen Mooren, production by Landstra & De Vries, w/ Paul Kuipers, artist

186
Re-Use – Billboard Seats, entrance and garden, Marres, Maastricht, graphic design by Maureen Mooren

187
Presentation – *SPACES*, Gallery Vivid, Rotterdam, w/ Paul Kuipers, artist, Tal Erez, designer

188
Interior – Bureau Europa Office, partly of recycled elements from exhibitions and stores, Maastricht, production by Landstra & De Vries, w/ Paul Kuipers

189
Presentation – Piet Paris, book launch and shop, Hirsch Building, Amsterdam, graphic design by CoppensAlberts, w/ Paul Kuipers, Michiel Zegers, artists, Bram Burger, designer

190
Installation – *Ghost Department Store*, Hirsch Building, Amsterdam, photography by Johannes Schwartz, w/ Paul Kuipers, Michiel Zegers, artists, Bram Burger, designer

191
Proposal – *Wunder*, art exhibition on miracles, Deichtorhallen, Hamburg (DE), curator: Huerlimann + Lepp, w/ Paul Kuipers, artist

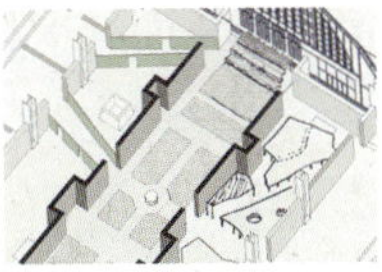

192
Proposal – Hella Jongerius, oeuvre exhibition, Museum Boijmans Van Beuningen, Rotterdam, w/ Paul Kuipers, artist

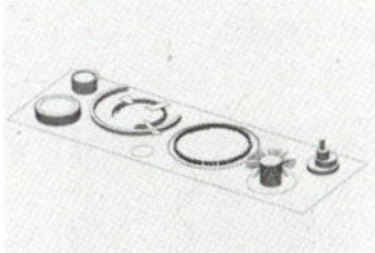

193
Exhibition – *Out of Storage*, art collection of FRAC Duinkerken, curators: Hilde Teerlinck, Erich Weiss, graphic design by Maureen Mooren, production by Guus van den Akker & Team, KLIEF, w/ Paul Kuipers, artist, Bram Burger, designer

194
Installation – *Opera Aperta / Loose Work*, Dutch Pavilion (in the Giardini), 54th International Art Exhibition of the Venice Biennale (IT), curator: Guus Beumer, production by Landstra & De Vries, artist collaboration: Johannes Schwartz, Barbara Visser, Yannis Kyriakides, Maureen Mooren, Joke Robaard, Herman Verkerk, Paul Kuipers, Sanneke van Hassel, Ernst van der Hoeven, Alexander van Slobbe

195
Temporary Interior – The Great Indoors 2011, seminar and award show on interior design, Timmerfabriek, Maastricht, clients: *FRAME*, NAiM, Marres, graphic design by Team Tuesday, production by Guus van den Akker & Team, w/ Paul Kuipers, artist

196
Installation – *Feeding Platforms for Birds*, executed work from an Artist in Residence proposal at Het Vijfde Seizoen, Altrecht, Den Dolder, w/ Paul Kuipers, artist

197
Presentation – Design for Download, Boxorama launch, Facades and Functions, Playing with Electricity and Digital One-Off by EventFurnituur at Salone del Mobile Milan (IT), curator: Droog, w/ Tal Erez, designer

198
Exhibition – *Alison & Peter Smithson, the art of inhabitation*, Bureau Europa, Maastricht, curator: Max Risselada, production by Guus van den Akker & Team, w/ Paul Kuipers, artist

199
Exhibition – *New Harloheim*, urban design competition on Haarlem, NAi, Rotterdam, graphic design by Job Wouters, production by Landstra & De Vries, w/ Paul Kuipers, artist

200
Re-Use – Warmoesmarket in Local Supermarket, Katendrecht, Rotterdam

201
Exhibition – *Best Designed Books 2010*, Stedelijk Museum, Amsterdam, curators: Esther Hemmes, Carolien Glazenburg, w/ Paul Kuipers, artist

202
Installation – *Close to Home*, Torstrasse, Berlin (DE), curators: Mr. & Mrs. Cameron, w/ Paul Kuipers, artist

203
Fashion Store – orson + bodil, Herenstraat, Amsterdam, w/ Paul Kuipers, artist, Gent Vranovci, designer

204
Exhibition – *Playboy Architecture*, Bureau Europa, Maastricht, curator: Beatriz Colomina, graphic design by Experimental Jetset, production by Brand, Broek & Erkens, Landstra & De Vries, w/ Paul Kuipers, artist

205
Interior – *SPACESRoom*, library room for Mr. Hunting, w/ Paul Kuipers, artist

206
Presentation – Showroom, overview of furniture by EventFurnituur, Duintjer CS, Amsterdam, w/ Itay Ohaly, Anke Weiss, designers, Paul Kuipers, artist

207
Presentation – *SPACES & Facades+Functions & Boxorama*, Hotel Droog, Amsterdam, w/ Itay Ohaly, designer, Paul Kuipers, artist

208
Re-Use – *Hygiene*, garden shed, Marres, Maastricht

209
Proposal – *Newtopia, the State of Human Rights*, set of exhibitions in Mechelen (BE), curator: Katerina Gregos, w/ Paul Kuipers, artist

210
Presentation – *Out of Storage*, display furniture of exhibition, Gallery VIVID, Rotterdam, w/ Paul Kuipers, artist

211
Re-Use – *Couleur Radicaal*, actuality and history of the city of Heerlen, Bureau Europa, Maastricht, curator: Lene ter Haar, graphic design by Maureen Mooren & Sandra Kassenaar

212
Presentation – *Out of Storage + Piet Paris*, illustrations of Piet Paris on Out of Storage displays, Gallery VIVID, Rotterdam, w/ Paul Kuipers, artist

213
Exhibition – *Best Designed Books 2011*, Stedelijk Museum, Amsterdam, curators: Esther Hemmes, Carolien Glazenburg, w/ Paul Kuipers, artist, Gent Vranovci, designer

13

214
Temporary Interior – IFFR 2013, lounge for the International Film Festival, De Doelen, Rotterdam, production by Landstra & De Vries, KLIEF, w/ Paul Kuipers, artist, Gent Vranovci, designer

215
Exhibition – *Best Designed Books 2012*, Stedelijk Museum, Amsterdam, curator: Esther Hemmes, w/ Paul Kuipers, artist

216
Installation – *Elegant Scaffolding*, series of flexible furniture, KunstWerke, Berlin (DE), client: Ellen Blumenstein, production by Landstra & De Vries, w/ Paul Kuipers, artist

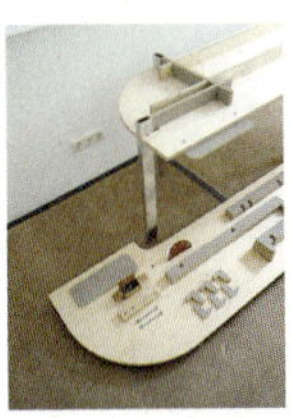

217
Temporary Interior- *The Great Indoors 2013*, seminar and award show on interior design, Timmerfabriek, Maastricht, clients: *FRAME*, NAiM, Marres, plants by Frank Bruggeman, w/ Paul Kuipers, artist

218
Interior – *(Out of) Storage*, cabinet for the home of Schwartz/Hemmes, Singel, Amsterdam, production by KLIEF

219
Re-Use – Marres Books, new front room, Marres, Maastricht

14

220
Temporary Interior – IFFR 2014, lounge for the International Film Festival, De Doelen, Rotterdam, plants by Frank Bruggeman, production by Landstra & De Vries, KLIEF, w/ Paul Kuipers, artist

221
Interior – IFFR Office, Schouwburgplein, Rotterdam, production by KLIEF w/ Paul Kuipers, artist

222
Proposal – *Urban Shade*, providing shades in the city of Tel Aviv (IL), curators: Tal Erez & Dan Handel, w/ Paul Kuipers, artist, Malkit Shoshan, architect

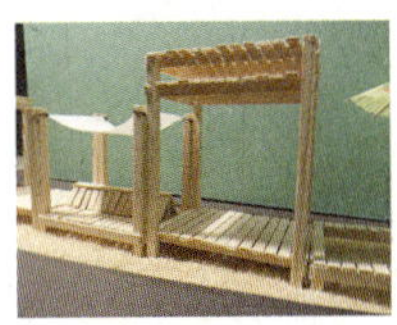

223
Presentation – *Boxorama S-M-L*, for sale at Droog. com webshop

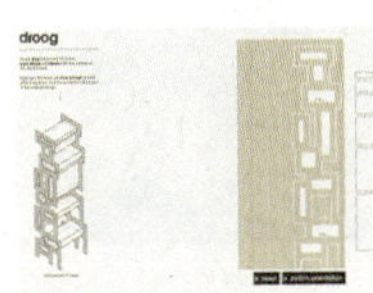

224
Exhibition – IABR 2014 – *Urban by Nature*, Kunsthal, Rotterdam, curator: Dirk Sijmons, graphic design by Experimental Jetset, production by Landstra & De Vries, KLIEF w/ Paul Kuipers, Michiel Zegers, artists

225
Exhibition – *Best Designed Books 2013*, Stedelijk Museum, Amsterdam, curators: Esther Hemmes, Carolien Glazenburg, production by KLIEF, w/ Paul Kuipers, artist

226
Exhibition – *Superbox*, design acquisitions, Stedelijk Museum, Amsterdam, curators: Ingeborg de Roode, Carolien Glazenburg, Victoria Anastasyadis, production by KLIEF, w/ Paul Kuipers, artist

2015

227
Exhibition – *Playboy Architecture* Frankfurt, DAM, Frankfurt (DE), curator: Beatriz Colomina, graphic design by Experimental Jetset, w/ Paul Kuipers, artist

228
Proposal – IBA Thüringen, VAH Weimar, curator: IBA, graphic design by HauserLacour, w/ Paul Kuipers, artist

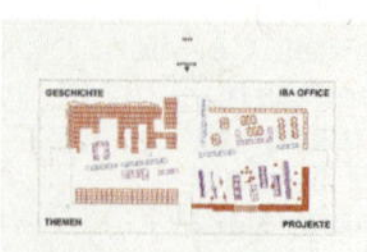

229
Interior – *SPACES*, De Pijp, Amsterdam, client: Yvon Schoenmakers, production by KLIEF

230
Proposal – Soesterberg, new use for the former US Military Airport, curator: Malkit Shoshan

231
Land Art – *idylls for Lingezegen*, three Idylls with burial gardens included: Mountain Idyll, Water Idyll in Elst, and Forest Idyll in Ressen, client: Foundation Park Lingezegen, landscape architecture by Feddes/Olthof, Veenenbos en Bosch, Astrid Harsveld, production by SmitsRinsma, DonkerGroen, w/ Paul Kuipers, artist

232
Publication – *Events, Situating the Temporary* edited by Event Architectuur, graphic design by Experimental Jetset

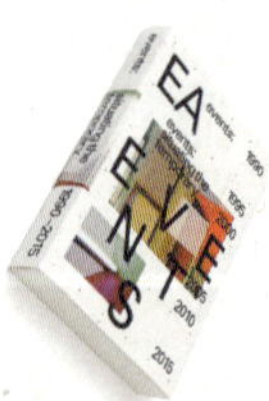

233
Temporary Interior – IFFR 2016, lounge for the International Film Festival, De Doelen, Rotterdam, production by Landstra & De Vries, KLIEF, w/ Paul Kuipers, artist

234
Exhibition – *Best Designed Books 2014*, Stedelijk Museum, Amsterdam, curators: Esther Hemmes, Carolien Glazenburg, production by KLIEF, w/ Paul Kuipers, artist

235
Temporary Interior – Sónar Festival, Barcelona (ES), w/ Paul Kuipers, artist

236
Proposal – *Prelude Kennis-As Ede Wageningen, information beacons for the "Knowledge Route" between Ede and Wageningen*, w/ Paul Kuipers, artist

237
Temporary Interior & Exhibitions – Temporary Fashion Museum, a number of exhibitions on fashion and a transformation of the existing services, Het Nieuwe Instituut, Rotterdam, graphic design by Maureen Mooren, Sandra Kassenaar, Experimental Jetset, Rudy Guedj, fragrance by Alessandro Gualtieri, installation by Conny Groenewegen, "Dressed by Architects" & "Fashion Archives" by Studio Makkink & Bey, curators: Jop van Bennekom, Penny Martin, Georgette Koning, Ferry van der Nat, Alfred Marks, Alexander van Slobbe, Francisco van Benthum, production by Landstra & De Vries, w/ Gabriel Maher, Raphaël Coutin, Lucas Muñoz, designers

16

238
Temporary Interior – IFFR 2016, lounge for the International Film Festival, De Doelen, Rotterdam, production by Landstra & De Vries, KLIEF, w/ Paul Kuipers, artist

239
Exhibition – *Precious*, Het Nieuwe Instituut, Rotterdam, part of TFM, curator: Angelique Westerhof, production by Landstra & De Vries, w/ Raphaël Coutin

project data

Project 1 / Page 94
Villa Karamazow

The project was an investigation into the possible use of literary data in architecture. Appalled by boxes without identity shooting out from the earth like mushrooms indifferent to their existing location, Herman Verkerk looked for an opportunity to restore the link between a building, its environment, and its program. To provide a constructed identity would give meaning to a building or part of a building for both the users and the context.

A comparison with literature presented itself: a full treasure chamber of constructed identities that take on meaning by the story. It seemed interesting to put such a story with constructed identities into an architectural structure and to examine whether a story could be the connecting link between the programs of building and environment. In the story Verkerk chose, *The Brothers Karamazov* by Fyodor Dostoyevsky, the characters seem larger than life in the first part. Fascinating in precisely this book is that the carefully constructed characters undergo a transformation. In the second part, they no longer have recognizable and fixed features. The question of identity is made very clear here. Although the characters in the first part follow the nineteenth-century conception of the subject, in the second they coincide more with the fragmentation of man that is typical of our times.

The architectural transformation of these data is accomplished by designing two villas, with the three brothers as the fictional clients. The first villa, a countryside villa, makes clear statements about the identity of the residents. There is continuity. The second villa, an urban villa, supposes residents without a clear identity – continuity has given way to anonymity and fragmentation.

The Landscape Villa is situated in a forested area, on a sand-drift; a bare, fruitless spot. In this void stands a lone pine, the "family" tree. The villa consists of several buildings grouped around the tree. Each of the buildings is inhabited by one of the brothers. The eldest inhabits the Bath House, the middle one the Work House, and the youngest the Prayer House. The fourth house, the Whale House, is their meeting place. The buildings have been designed by defining the characters of the three brothers on the basis of analogies, personal interpretations, associations, and secondary literature. These characteristics are in turn transformed into architectural structures, in which the characters are reflected in the absurd and contradictions are being expressed between the characters.

The Bath House, the building of the eldest, hedonist brother, Dmitri, is placed on a hill covered with moss and sheltered between oak trees. Sources of inspiration are the Maritime Theater of Hadrian's Villa in Tivoli and the books of the Marquis de Sade. With abrupt twists, one descends over a small bridge, past the sauna and swimming pool for physical cleaning, down to the more intimate parts of the building. The curving walls of the damp, dim room lead you through columns filled with personal belongings of Dmitri, to the hearth room.

The buildings of the oldest and youngest brothers are connected by flowing water. Together these components form the Water Cycle. The water vapor from the sauna condenses against the glass blocks, dropping in a concrete gutter, and then flows to the rectangular pond. From there the water flows to a basin outside the building. A water wheel is thereby put into operation. In the water basin, the water evaporates again.

The Prayer House is placed against a dune with some grass and heather. In this building, which belongs to the youngest, religious brother, Alyosha, a pilgrimage is staged, inspired by Bunyan's Christian allegory, *The Pilgrim's Progress*, the "Danteum" memorial building by Terragni, the traditional Stations of the Cross, and tours of spiritual pilgrimage that recount the Via Dolorosa of Jesus, depicted by a chain of chapels placed on a hillside, for instance, in Italy and Spain. The building consists of a closed cloister in which architectural elements are carriers of meaning. Following the route on the stairs with twelve steps, past the alcoves with stained glass windows with the signs of the zodiac, the reflecting water surface, the ten columns, and meditation cells with walls shaped like numbers, you reach a tower covered with blue, diamond-shaped tiles. Within this tower, on every floor, an act of daily life can be carried out, traditionally taking place when the sun is at a particular position. Sleep, eat, work, and clean. The relationship between the actions and the solstice is accentuated by the placement and shape of the windows. Once on top of the tower, at the "fifth" window, you are offered a panoramic view over the forest.

Across from the Bath House and the Prayer House on a bare, elongated sand hill stands the Work House, the building of the middle, scientist brother, Ivan. The analytical thinking and linear accumulation of knowledge of the philosopher arises from the fixation of life by placing himself as it were outside of life. But as knowledge increases, so does the ineffable increase in size. The Work House consists of three studios that increase in length and are linked in series to a library corridor that suggests an unlimited extension. The black boxes inside these studios contain the following work areas: first, a dark room, where images are fixed; secondly, a bat observatory, where night and day are exchanged; and thirdly, a celestial observatory.

The library corridor links the Work House to the Whale House. The Whale House has two parts, the library and the living rooms. In the library, the characters can descend to feed themselves spiritually. Like being swallowed by a whale, they feel protected here in the bowels of the building. From the labyrinth of books run shortcuts to the apartments of the oldest and youngest brothers, and also to the kitchen. The ground floor consists of a large, empty space that invites contemplation.

The dining room and the kitchen are situated as an extension of the library. It is the focal point of the villa. The room for dinner and relaxation is placed away from the (family) tree, overlooking a small green meadow. The breakfast room, with French doors to the porch, is facing east. From here is a view over the sand-drift.

In the second villa, the Urban Villa, designed for the brothers after their characterological transformation that was achieved by the murder of their father, anonymity prevails. Where in the Landscape Villa architectonic constructions were linked to specific residents, the Urban Villa contains architectural structures for residents with unspoken properties. The villa consists of a stack of three identical houses, sandwiched between collective rooms in the basement, the ground floor, and on the roof. The facade keeps the urban alignment along the waterfront intact. The cylinder that, on the outside, visually binds together the facade, also plays a role in defining the floor plans at all levels on the inside as well. The cylinder does not touch the ground, but is supported by four columns that dissolve slowly in the cylinder form. Between these four columns, a monumental staircase refers in width and placement to an alley that once cut through the block. This staircase leads to a plateau with the actual connection between the houses inside the urban villa, the elevator. On the roof level the cylinder is filled in part with water. Above this water is a swivel bridge. When the bridge arrives at the opening in the cylinder on the side of the elevator, you can either cross to a private rooftop terrace, a niche floating outside the villa, or a niche that gives access to an open roof terrace.

Villa Karamazow
Project: Book
Year: 1990
Client/Publisher: TU Delft
Graphic design: Christine Rothuizen
Photography: Hermen Maat, Herman Verkerk, Barbara Visser

—

Project 2 / Page 102
Three Sisters

Three Sisters was the name of the proposal for an experimental theater in Moscow, complementing an existing, traditional one. Three locations were given in the Hermitage Garden. As a structuring concept to the complicated program for the new theater, Herman Verkerk introduced the play, *The Three Sisters*, by Anton Chekhov. Averse to a so-called multifunctional building, which the given program more or less encouraged, this gave him the ability to create three different theaters surrounding the existing theater, each with its own program. In doing so, he chose three possible locations instead of just one. With this plan, as the characters within the play, none of the buildings would be assigned a dominant role. Each building would bear a specific atmosphere that contributed to theater production.

Olga / The Columns – This theater was organized as a training center for actors and stage designers, including a high tower for rehearsing interior monologues. This tower consisted of a number of rooms with a mirror wall as the only companion for the actor, and rooms with different sound resonances. The lower tower was called the dialogue membrane tower; two actors could choose a wall out of either concrete or glass, or an open wooden frame that separated them in the room. They could specifically practice their dialogues, respectively, with only words, with only gestures, and with gestures and words. The building also included a "traditional" auditorium and workrooms for the set designers and administration.

Masha / The Cross – This theater was designed as a modern experimental theater. The audience and the actors shared one big space where the traditional proscenium arch was gone. The tall, narrow, oblong hall made the confrontation between the actors and the audience very physical. The spectators smelled the greasepaint and felt the drops of sweat and the breath of the players. Actors and musicians could reach the theater hall by means of a train from The Columns. This train could also be used as decorative machinery. The two arms of the cross-shaped building, which are perpendicular to the hall, contained the workspaces for set designers and dressing rooms for the actors, respectively, and the public areas like the lobby and cloakroom.

Irina / The Circus – This building consisted of a steel circus tent and a hotel for traveling theater companies. The circus tent served as a restaurant for hotel guests and the restaurant / café / vaudeville / burlesque and meeting place for theater audiences. With the atmosphere of a nightclub, this theatre invoked improvised performances by performers from different fields.

Three Sisters
Project: Competition
Year: 1990
Client: Hermitage Theatre
Location: Hermitage Garden, Moscow

—

Fashion shows, Amsterdam, 1989, 2008
Project 4, 160 / Page 151

Project 4 / Page 151
orson + bodil, Amsterdam, 1989
The audience was placed in a relatively small circle looking outwards into the huge, empty hall of the fair. The rows of seats of this circle increased in height to the center point of the circle, based on their type. Starting with benches, chairs, stools, and pedestals, all the way up to barstools, it formed a pyramidal stand. The models arrived from far away in the distance of the hall. When they approached the audience, they circled around a couple of times and then disappeared behind a segment of a circle made of folding screens.

Petit Pouf
Project: Fashion Show
Year: 1989
Duration: Very short-term, 30 minutes
Team: Joke Robaard, Herman Verkerk
Client: Lilian Driessen and orson + bodil (Nanette van der Kleyn and Alexander van Slobbe)
Location: Amsterdam RAI Exhibition and Convention Centre
Graphic design: Jaap van Triest
Light design: Ruud Pouwels
Sound design: Eddy de Clercq
Photography: Jodokus Driessen
Materials: Car inner tubes, wooden billboard construction, tea lights, benches, chairs, stools, pedestals, barstools, floor painting, ready-made ingredients from the venue (red and blue runners, folding screens)

Project 160 / Page 151
orson + bodil, Amsterdam, 2008
On one side of the spacious entrance hall of the Amsterdam City Archives, a double row of benches was placed to form an improvised catwalk on the

marble flooring. A backdrop was made from unfolded archive boxes, leaving a small opening. Through a darkened corridor, the models appeared from this opening in the curtain of boxes, which were stapled together in a repetitive pattern.

Archive
Project: Fashion Show
Year: 2008
Duration: Very short-term, 30 minutes
Team: Paul Kuipers, Herman Verkerk
Client: Francisco van Benthum and orson + bodil
Location: Amsterdam City Archives
Graphic design: Hansje van Halem
Light design: Ruud Pouwels
Sound design: Mr. and Mrs. Cameron
Photography: Joke Robaard, EventArchitectuur
Materials: Unfolded Amsterdam Stadsarchief (city archives), white cardboard boxes perforated with the name of the archives, staples, Betonplex sheets

—

Fashion stores & showrooms
Project 9, 35, 53, 62, 70, 71 / Page 170

Project 9 / Page 172
TiPi
For the design of a booth for fashion company orson + bodil, Joke Robaard and Herman Verkerk put together some interpretations of the company's work – pure, timeless, archetypical. Three volumes were designed that did not demarcate the stall, but were placed loosely in the space to form a small routing. The volumes each had their own setup according to their function – fitting room and clothes hanging, cabinet and table – but they structurally and visually formed a family. The detailing of the volumes reflected the subdued luxury and the manual, tactile quality of the garments of orson + bodil.

The volumes could be mounted and dismantled by one person. First, a hexagon was made from metal strips with spikes standing out on the corners. On top of these spikes, six wooden poles were placed and fixed with a smaller metal hexagon strip on top to form a tipi shape. Between the poles, small spars were clasped that ensured stability. Pascale Gatzen, then an intern at orson + bodil, made a tent inside one of the volumes to serve as a fitting room. For the lighting, fluorescent tubes were used at the bottom of the volumes and to make a freestanding imitation of a campfire.

TiPi
Project: Booth
Year: 1992
Duration: Short-term, 3 days
Team: Joke Robaard, Pascale Gatzen, Herman Verkerk
Client: orson + bodil
Location: Hôtel Saint James, Paris
Photography: Joke Robaard
Materials: Painted wooden beams with diamond-shaped profile, cotton fabric, metal strips, butterfly nuts, piano hinges, varnished wooden plates

Project 35 / Page 176
Marui Shibuya
This first shop-in-shop design for Dutch fashion brand SO by alexander van slobbe is inspired by the sophisticated luxury of the archives and walk-in closets and boudoir spaces of the Maison de Verre by architect Pierre Chareau. By showing the cross sections of the specifically made material (aluminum sandwich with black corrugated cardboard) as the finishing of the cabinets and display units, one has the feeling that the linear paths throughout the shop are carved out from the storage space.

Marui Shibuya
Project: Fashion Store
Year: 1996
Duration: Long-term, 5–15 years
Client: SO by alexander van slobbe
Location: Marui Department Store, Shibuya, Tokyo
Production: Mode Center Tokyo
Photography: EventArchitectuur
Materials: Sandwich constructions of aluminum with black corrugated cardboard

Project 53 / Page 176
Harajuku
This flagship store of SO by alexander van slobbe consists of three different reflection walls. The first is a light brown Formica wall with extending shelves and drawers for display and storage. The second is an underlayment wall stained dark brown. Inserted in it are the

fitting room and toilet. The counter is also placed "inside" the wall, and the hollowed-out form is covered in lilac glass. The third is a shell-shaped acrylic canopy, underneath which the latest collection of the brand is shown. In the middle of the room, two wooden cabinets covered in concrete polyester are used for the display of folded clothes.

Harajuku
Project: Fashion Store
Year: 1998
Duration: Long-term, 5–15 years
Client: SO by alexander van slobbe
Location: Meji Dori, Harajuku, Tokyo
Production: Mode Center Tokyo
Photography: EventArchitectuur
Materials: Fluorescent tube lighting, stained underlayment, concrete polyester, acrylic, aluminum racks, Formica, glass

Project 62 / Page 178
SO–Droog, Tokyo
Between February 20 and 28, 1999, SO by alexander van slobbe staged the exhibition *Dutch Droog Design* at its flagship store in Harajuku, Tokyo. As part of its marketing strategy, SO's backer, Japanese fashion marketing group Joi'x Corporation, asked designer Alexander van Slobbe to brand the collection as typical of the Netherlands. To position SO in the Dutch context while avoiding cultural stereotypes, Van Slobbe and his business partner, Guus Beumer, organized a series of exhibitions in SO's stores in Tokyo showcasing other contemporary Dutch cultural manifestations that, according to them, had affinities with SO. Van Slobbe and Beumer specifically focused on those aspects that, like SO, were characterized by minimalist aesthetics and self-reflexivity – what they called, "neomodernist" works. The first such exhibition was Droog Dutch Design, where a selection of Droog's products was displayed alongside SO's collections. The paired-down graphic design by Experimental Jetset, which reduced the Droog collection to silhouettes projected over a grid, clearly reinforced the reading of Droog as neomodernist – and of SO by proxy. In its turn, the minimalist and meandering display design by EventArchitectuur staged SO and Droog as intrinsically interconnected: the single, long, thin, lightweight, and reflective platform on which the Droog artifacts were displayed circled around the shop, thereby visually and spatially incorporating them with SO's garments.

SO–Droog
Project: Exhibition
Year: 1999
Duration: Short-term, one week
Client: SO by alexander van slobbe
Location: Meji Dori, Harajuku, Tokyo
Production: Mode Center Tokyo
Photography: EventArchitectuur
Materials: Sandwich constructions of aluminum with black corrugated cardboard, metal wire, glass plates

Project 70 / Page 178
Daikanyama
The project is a fashion store for clothes and accessories of SO by alexander van slobbe, including a choice of products designed by Dutch designers chosen by the brand. The sketch design collects all the functions of the store under a big wave, forming a roof. The customer plunges into the wave to end up at a secret corridor containing showcases with jewelry and other luxury accessories. The final design is flexible and modular, and consists of stackable tables of whitewashed wood with different tabletops: glass, rubber, and lino. A back wall made of strips of black glass alternating with strips of black rubber contains black-painted wooden clothes racks and shelves.

Daikanyama
Project: Proposal
Materials: Perforated aluminum sheets, aluminum racks and shelves, dark green stone floor, glass showcases
Daikanyama
Project: Fashion store
Year: 2000
Duration: Long-term, 5–15 years
Client: SO by alexander van slobbe
Location: Luxury shopping center Dix Sept, Daikanyama, Tokyo
Production: Mode Center Tokyo
Photography: EventArchitectuur
Materials: Whitewashed pinewood, black glass, black and light brown rubber, gray lino, green canvas, black-painted wood

Project 71 / Page 174
orson + bodil 10 years
The exhibition showed highlights of the collections of Dutch fashion label

orson + bodil from their first decade of practice. The spatial design consisted of two rows of back-to-back cubicles set up as changing rooms. These cubicles were all closed off to form an archive. To be able to look at and touch the garments, each in one of the changing rooms, the visitor had to kick a hole in the exterior walls of the cubicle. Once the cubicles were made accessible in this way, visitors could also follow a route from one side of the exhibition space to the other through the various holes.

orson + bodil 10 years
Project: Exhibition
Year: 2000
Duration: Medium-term, 2 months
Client: Centraal Museum, orson + bodil
Location: Centraal Museum, Utrecht
Photography: EventArchitectuur, Centraal Museum
Materials: Pinewood construction boards, white perforated sheets

—

Project 14 / Page 112
Swimming poollibrary

Swimming poollibrary is a hybrid project, in the sense that it is at the same time a quite realistic building proposal for a site in Zürich (a transferium, or park and ride facility) and a spatial and narrative video adaptation of the cult gay novel, *The Swimming-Pool Library*, by Alan Hollinghurst.

The building proposal itself is also a hybrid, as it houses a parking garage, a swimming pool, a library, a restaurant, and a hotel. The hybrid program makes it possible at any time to have a relative view on the world, and turns the building into a little society. Or, in other words, it brings the confusing outside world inside the building as a social condenser. As the Homo Ludens in Constant's New Babylon was condemned to play and relax all day, in the Swimming poollibrary the visitors are in a world in-between; in between other, perhaps more "productive" activities.

The video *Swimming poollibrary* shows the voyage to and through the building in twenty-four hours. It uses a deliberately simple model of the proposed building structure for the computer animations to capture the potential of computer graphics, without trying to make the graphics as real as possible. The complementary images are video shots from the surroundings of the site and Super 8 film rushes; found footage from a cruise ship journey from Genoa to New York. They make the model inhabitable and add atmosphere.

The Swimming poollibrary project was made in 1993 as part of the thesis proposal for the postgraduate course C.A.A.D. at the ETH Department of Architecture in Zürich. The thesis investigates the possibilities of merging new digital media to be used for architectural design process developments. The video was shown at the Ars Electronica 1993 in Linz and at the Long Beach Museum of Art in Los Angeles.

Swimming poollibrary
Project: Video
Year: 1993
Duration: Very short-term, 30 minutes
Image: Diderot, Encyclopédie (1751–72)

—

Fashion shows, Paris, 1994–2001
Project 15, 16, 17, 25, 26, 27, 33, 34, 42, 43, 55, 56, 66, 67, 73, 74, 80, 81 / Page 140

Every three to six months, the new collections of orson + bodil (fashion design women) and SO by alexander van slobbe (fashion design men) were shown during the fashion weeks in Paris. After expounding the conceptual principles of a collection by fashion designer Alexander van Slobbe and art director Guus Beumer, together with the team we extensively discussed a spatial interpretation of these data. Materials were sought to provide input for a preliminary design. We contacted a light and sound rental company, a light designer, and sound designers. Together with them, we went through the scenario for the show. Not only to discuss the logistics of transportation, assembly, and disassembly, but also how the audience would enter the venue, how the show would start, and the highlights, plus the atmospheres during and after the show.

The first two shows had a fixed location. After these, we also went looking for the most suitable location to shape our ideas for the show. Light, sound, and location formed an integrated part of the *mise-en-scène*. What fascinated us in the design for every new show was to work with modest means to produce a sense of understated luxury (glamour) that reflects the designs of Van Slobbe. The high level of detail and the sense of materiality of the design in the finishing and making should be reflected in the spatial layout. We achieved this by selectively choosing the necessary elements needed for a show (ready-made rentals, like podium parts, lighting and sound equipment, and chairs) and manufacturing specific components, sometimes even on site. Characteristic of our design is that we redefined the chosen location:
1. Through the arrangement of the show elements (light, sound, stage, chairs). With this, we determined the routing of the models, their appearance and disappearance, and the interaction with the audience.
2. By manually finishing the self-manufactured decor elements on the spot, we achieved a high degree of tactility and detailing.

Fashion Shows
Project: Fashion Show
Year: 1994–2001
Duration: Very short-term, average of 20 minutes
Team: Bart Guldemond, Herman Verkerk
Graphic design: Jaap van Triest, Erik Wong, Jop van Bennekom
Light design: Ruud Pouwels
Sound design: Eddy de Clercq, Mr. & Mrs. Cameron

Project 15 / Page 142
1994 March: orson + bodil, winter season 1994/1995
Location: SO Showroom, Passage Sainte-Avoye
Description: A new silhouette, a low podium, emphasizing the silhouette through depth of the decor and the reflection of the steel sheets on the catwalk. The red light coming from the back makes the models emerge from a fire.
Materials: Semitransparent corrugated polyester sheets, galvanized steel sheets

Project 16 / Page 143
1994 October: orson + bodil, summer season 1995
Location: Avenue Montaigne
Description: The space is bathed in green light at the audience's arrival, in white light during the show, complemented with a yellow shine by the reflection on fluorescent paper sheets hanging along the walls. The catwalk is very wide, reflecting like a mirror and crushing the audience to the sides. The models set foot on the catwalk midway, which results in two turning points and therefore also photographers on both ends of the runway.
Materials: Aluminum sheets, painted paper sheets (fluorescent yellow)

Project 17 / Page 144
1994 July: SO by alexander van slobbe, summer season 1995
Location: SO Showroom, Passage Sainte-Avoye
Description: Three light atmospheres, amber, cool blue and industrial, podium parts in three different heights are slightly shifted in axis to make three fontal looks for the models in space. The middle podium is the highest and decorated as a block of ice. With blowing wind machines and blue-papered walls, a cool atmosphere is created.
Materials: Blue paper, sanded semitransparent acrylic sheets, projection screens

Project 25 / Page 143
1995 March: orson + bodil, winter season 1995/1996
Location: Gallery Yvon Lambert
Description: A box ring layout with a circle in a square. Models appear from a separate room, stepping out of blue light. There is no highlight (beginning and end) of the catwalk, which creates a concentrated and calm atmosphere, the models walk round, and because the outer edge of the square is loosely covered with blue Conté crayons, footsteps start to appear on the aluminum circle.
Materials: MDF sheets (coated on the borders with peacock blue Conté crayons), aluminum sheets partly sanded to create a shiny circle and misty edges

Project 26 / Page 145
1995 January: SO by alexander van slobbe, winter season 1995/1996
Location: SO Showroom, Passage Sainte-Avoye
Description: A race car track with artificial ramps made of little plank bridges; underneath the ramps, a red glow is visible. The show is held in the daylight coming from the skylights of the showroom. The models walk their track through the audience and slightly rise in height because of the little platforms.
Materials: Underlayment platforms painted silver-gray, halogen construction lights with red filter underneath little plank bridges

Project 27 / Page 145
1995 July: SO by alexander van slobbe, summer season 1996
Location: Cirque d'Hiver
Description: A meandering white catwalk, "floating" high above a more regular yellow catwalk. Lights imitated the break of dawn for the start of the show, showing the models and the sculptured decor pieces as silhouettes; during the show, the sculptured decor pieces are lighted from within.
Materials: White perforated sheets and yellow paper for the catwalks, bended white perforated sheets to make the decor pieces

Project 33 / Page 144
1996 January: SO by alexander van slobbe, winter season 1996/1997
Location: SO Showroom, Passage Sainte-Avoye
Description: Two catwalks are placed next to each other along the complete length of the long wall in the showroom. The catwalks are divided along this whole length by a slight difference in height and a black silhouette fabric. The actual appearance of the models is tantalizingly postponed because of the linear route they first follow behind the black fabric. Color changes in the lighting define the different parts of the collection.
Materials: Black rubberized silhouette fabric, wooden frame painted black, and rolls of bitumen with slate gravel

Project 34 / Page 145
1996 July: SO by alexander van slobbe, summer season 1997
Location: Galerie Nikki Diana Marquardt
Description: A sportswear-inspired collection. A catwalk made of simple podium parts is shaped into a cross; on the wooden tops of the catwalk, slightly narrower white perforated sheets are laid out, bordered by silver tape. To accentuate the entrance of the models, the white perforated sheet is lifted into a wave; the models appear and disappear on the sides of the wave. For the show, the natural daylight coming from the skylights of the gallery is used.
Materials: White perforated sheets and silver tape

Project 42 / Page 146
1997 January: SO by alexander van slobbe, winter season 1997/1998
Location: Galerie Nikki Diana Marquardt
Description: Cowboy theme. The stage set suggests a saloon with an entrance ramp under which a fire is smoldering; the side doors of the saloon seem to be riddled by bullets.
Materials: Pallets, pinewood boards, birch triplex sheets with black felt circles, woodprint vinyl flooring

Project 43 / Page 147
1997 July: SO by alexander van slobbe, summer season 1998
Location: Galerie Carole de Bona
Description: Marine theme. Around an enclosed inner courtyard the models walk along the four sides of the building following a continuous, curving line drawn on the concrete floor with white chalk. The line is regularly interrupted with written names of the main rivers and oceans of the world. Enormous horizontal cardboard rolls covered in cling film accentuate the entrance. Previous fashion shows of SO are projected on the rolls in rewind mode. The windows to the inner courtyard are covered with blue filter. The daylight entering the space from the courtyard is filtered light blue.
Materials: White drawing chalk, cardboard rolls, cling film, blue light filters

Project 55 / Page 146
1998 January: SO by alexander van slobbe, winter season 1998/1999
Location: IRCAM Centre Pompidou
Description: SO genes, the jeans collection of SO, is presented in this huge sound studio. All of the chairs are put to the side to make a skating rink;

on the floor the letters H, O, M & E are placed like signage from a game. Models are skating around on inline skates.
Materials: Large letter stickers on the floor

Project 56 / Page 147
1998 July: SO by alexander van slobbe, summer season 1999
Location: Carrousel du Louvre, Jardin des Tuileries
Description: Inside this huge space, a rectangle bordered by softly waving lace curtains is laid out to make an intimate space. Inside this rectangle, a number of wooden benches for the audience are covered in cotton fabric and placed in such a way to form a snake-like path for the models to walk through. The entrance to this breathing space inside a space is a long corridor made of the same lace curtains getting slightly narrower towards the end. On these waving curtains a video of artist Joke Robaard filming her back garden is projected.
Materials: White lace, white cotton, steel tubes, round steel parasol bases

Project 66 / Page 148
1999 January: SO by alexander van slobbe, winter season 1999/2000
Location: The Louvre, Decorative Arts Museum, Rue de Rivoli
Description: A linear corridor connects a collection of eight little rooms, four each on the left and right sides, all with an open end towards the corridor. The audience is divided among these rooms and the seats form little niches for the models to stroll into and out again. A carpet of gray felt underflooring is laid out to define the walking areas of the models. They appear in each room as a specific surprise.
Materials: Gray felt underflooring

Project 67 / Page 149
1999 July: SO by alexander van slobbe, summer season 2000
Location: Tipi on the square in front of Centre Pompidou
Description: The event starts with the ascending of the donut-shaped inflatable. The space inside the tipi is divided in two parts by a convex screen made of wooden frames covered by semitransparent Stucanet sheets. It describes a protruding curve along which the models are walking from and to their changing rooms, which are behind the curve. The space is infused with a fragrance by Alessandro Gualtieri with the smell of freshly cut grass.
Materials: Stucanet sheets, wooden portals painted gray, inflatable latex donut (by Rens Bouma)

Project 73 / Page 150
2000 January: SO by alexander van slobbe, winter season 2000/2001
Location: Hôtel Saint James, Rue de Rivoli
Description: Fashion Show “and, and, and, no.1.” The phenomenon of a fashion show is spatially articulated into three different parts. The first part is the storage room, a small room where the garments, shoes, and accessories for the show are stored on clothing racks and in cabinets; the second part is the changing room, where models are standing on little pedestals waiting to be dressed and photographed; the third part is the media room, which contains a catwalk to be stepped on by the models, one by one, to be photographed and filmed.
The changing room and the storage room are open to the public, and while they can only take a peek in the media room, the audience takes an active role in experiencing these different parts of the fashion show. They are allowed first into the storage room, which feels like a small shop or showroom. Then they enter the changing room, with the models standing like statues on the little pedestals, numbered one to twenty-four. The audience can touch the garments while the models are being dressed. The models are shifting from one pedestal to the next in order to end up at pedestal number twenty-four, ready to enter the media room and step on the mini-catwalk. After their photo shoot, the models return, one by one, to the changing room, to be dressed again in a new outfit.
Materials: Untreated underlayment, white latex paint for circles simulating spotlights, clothing racks on wheels

Project 74 / Page 148
2000 July: SO by alexander van slobbe, summer season 2001
Location: Courtyard garden of the École des Beaux-Arts, Rue Bonaparte
Description: Fashion Show “and, and, and no.2.” Models are positioned on a number of podium parts placed on

different heights to form a "tableau vivant." One by one, the models leave this fixed setting and walk around the fountain into the arcade, where they are photographed and filmed. Once they have been filmed, they return to the setting in the courtyard, and shift places with other models. The audience can observe an ongoing configuration of the models in the tableau vivant, are served a drink and a snack, and are free to walk around the courtyard garden.
Materials: Podium parts, boards cut out of various wooden sheets of MDF, HPL-coated Betonplex, underlayment

Project 80 / Page 149
2001 January: SO by alexander van slobbe, winter season 2001/2002
Location: The Louvre, Decorative Arts Museum, Rue de Rivoli
Description: Theater theme. An elongated and quite elevated catwalk is placed between two large black sets of curtains. The models step on the catwalk behind the first set of curtains and make a grand entrance through these drapes. They walk along the narrow, high catwalk, which is covered by projection sheet to give it an oily shine when illuminated. They disappear behind the other set of curtains and are then photographed. The audience is aware of this last action by the flashes of the cameras entering the space.
Photography: Sibylle Hoegger
Materials: Black felt fabric, dark brown projection fabric, podium parts

Project 81 / Page 150
2001 July: SO by alexander van slobbe, summer season 2002
Location: The Louvre, Decorative Arts Museum, Rue de Rivoli
Description: The catwalk is designed like a little corridor. The models enter the corridor from the side, along a low balustrade made of cardboard boxes. When the models get closer to the audience, their shoes and the lower part of their legs disappear. When the models meet each other in the narrow corridor, they have to decide in which way to pass.
Photography: Roma Pas
Materials: Cardboard, aluminum tubes, podium parts, white projection fabric

—

Project 38 / Page 188
Breitnerstraat

The municipal service Optitheek produced and offered 360-degree photographs, which could be consulted digitally. It was a forerunner of the Google Street View option on Google Maps. A 360-degree camera was mounted on a Morris Mini to document all the streets in the city of Rotterdam. By connecting the photographs with the plan of Rotterdam, a virtual shadow city emerged that could be used, for instance, by real estate agents. The Center for the Arts in Rotterdam invited artists to investigate more possible uses for the system.

The proposal was to make a kind of "yellow pages" application by adding information to the photographs at the moment they were taken. The inhabitants living along the photographed streets could add their own messages and invitations. The Breitnerstraat, which was not yet photographed, was chosen as a testing ground. Inhabitants were invited to participate in an action simultaneous to the shooting of the 360-degree photographs. A kind of demo was organized, and tools were given to allow the inhabitants to communicate with the camera. In this way, they also became part of the shadow city, adding to the quality of diversity so vibrant in the "real" city. By digitally clicking on one of the demo billboards or banners within the Optitheek online service, the virtual visitors of the shadow city could read the personal information and messages of the inhabitants of the photographed apartment blocks.

Breitnerstraat
Project: Performance
Year: 1996
Duration: Very short-term, 2 hours
Client: Rotterdam Festivals, in cooperation with Centrum Beeldende Kunst Rotterdam (CBK)
Curator: Jouke Kleerebezem, Maarten Sprenger
Location: Breitnerstraat and CBK Nieuwe Binnenweg, Rotterdam
Production: EventArchitectuur
Performance guidance: Rianne Makkink, Klaar Plattel
Photography: Optitheek
Materials: Gray board and spray mount,

A0 photocopies of paintings by George Hendrik Breitner, A4 billboards, paper clips, photocopies of messages like "click me" and "exit," and blank text balloons, etc.

—

Project 60 / Page 134
Doors of Perception 5: Play

Doors of Perception 5: Play was a three-day seminar on learning through play, organized by the Netherlands Design Institute in the main halls of the famous Beurs van Berlage building on the Damrak in Amsterdam. The design consisted of a choreography for existing and new inflatable shapes made by artist Rens Bouma that floated like clouds above your head in the spacious hall. They took on a different configuration every hour. The stage podium sections formed the letters P, L, A, and Y, and could be transformed for different purposes during the conference lectures, computer presentations, dance performances, group discussions, interviews, etc.

The temporary seating in the hall was organized like a maze consisting of meandering aisles between 1,000 simple gray chairs. There were a few islands in the maze: some were defined with carpets that had luxury designer chairs and couches on them, others were defined by gaps where the inflatable shapes could land on the ground. A small cushion with the word "Play" on it was placed on each chair to provide a little comfort. A pillow fight broke loose during the very first coffee break of the seminar, with everybody joining in by throwing the pillows into the crowd.

Doors or Perception 5: Play
Project: Temporary Interior
Year: 1999
Duration: Short-term, 3 days
Client: Design Institute Amsterdam
Curator: John Thackara
Location: Beurs van Berlage, Amsterdam
Production: Landstra & De Vries
Graphic design: Joseph Plateau
Inflatable shapes: Rens Bouma
Visual guest list installation: Hermen Maat
Photography: Hermen Maat, Herman Verkerk
Materials: Color-stained underlayment, stage parts, net curtains (8 x 6 m), latex inflatables, designer chairs and benches, 1,000 small cushions with glow-in-the-dark print

—

Project 61 / Page 280
Forum Magazine

Forum was a Dutch architectural magazine, which from 1946 was published by the Amsterdam society Architectura et Amicitia (A et A). A et A is a group of befriended practicing architects, historians, and urban designers. Being the publisher of a magazine, A et A had two aims. One was to give the possibility for an independent contribution to Dutch architectural discourse, and the other to produce documents that represented a very personalized history of Dutch architecture. The editorial board for this magazine changed completely every two or three years, and was given guaranteed independence from the publishers for the content and look of the magazine. The board was recruited from the youngest generation of architects, who were able to show the world their view on architecture and their fascinations through this medium. In the mid-1960s, this even resulted in an actual movement, called the Forum Group, which consisted of Dutch architects Aldo van Eyck, Herman Hertzberger, and Piet Blom.

In general, one could say that Dutch architectural discourse at the end of the twentieth century was very rich. There were two large universities of architecture and several architecture academies. Each had successful lecture programs and good documentation of its research. Numerous publications and architecture galleries, partly made possible by governmental subsidies and grants, further stimulated architectural discourse. There were also publications on individual architects and the history of architecture, and magazines like *De Architect*, *Archis*, *Bouw*, etc.

These architectural magazines were all trying to encompass the actual status of building in the Netherlands and abroad every month or two. Made mostly by architectural critics and architectural historians, they comprised information about new buildings, urban plans, and architects. Seen in this field, *Forum* had always been a more reflective kind of magazine. From the beginning of its existence, *Forum* would give more attention to the actual inspiration of the architects and artists rather than the architectural production of the time. Also, the interaction of the (visual) applied arts and architecture had been a recurring issue in *Forum* from the start. In the last two decades of the twentieth century, only *Archis* had been giving attention to the connection between these disciplines.

Forum Magazine 1998–2000
The editors responsible for the magazine from 1998 to 2000 were interested in the functioning of architecture in society. They preferred not to show the actual architectural products as ends in themselves, but to investigate the processes that define these products. As independent editors, it seemed more interesting to overlook the heroic component of the architectural profession and instead to examine what was really happening in the Netherlands at the end of one century and the beginning of another.The way this society had been shaped was not a result of a well-executed philosophy, but was an accidental coexisting of constellations of automatic processes for which nobody could really be held responsible. It was a structure of specialists, commerce, technology, personal wishes, political interests, and rules. Besides architects, there were many more disciplines responsible for the built environment. The editors wanted to show this conglomerate in all its nuances. Their working method was to distill information from the ever-growing and existing mass of information, and to bring these pieces of information into a new context. Quite literally: the magazine. It was in itself a new example of this information society. The term "magazine" stands for a ''light'' content with a fresh view. Therefore, the name of the journal changed slightly from *Forum* to *Forum Magazine*. The magazine format helped the editors to be reporters of the surface. The role of the reporter was more that of a witness and bystander than a judge or lawyer.

Interaction of design and content of the magazine
Because the graphic designers of the magazine were part of the editorial board, architectural themes merged with graphic ones. Issue "Fence" had the bars as filtering device, issue "Hearth" had a "heating up" of the pages from start to finish, issue "Storage" the layering and hiding of material, issue "Corridor" a guide and flow, so that the graphic design directly referred back to the theme. But besides this formal connection, the editors also tried to introduce an interaction of form and content by a layering of the information. The theme (object) was introduced in the first pages and given its first context. Then a report was published on a round table discussion organized by the editors, with the object as a subject. They invited specialists on the subject of the object, ranging from website designers and architects, to cultural philosophers and stockbrokers, to inform the reader of the different directions the object could take them in the magazine. The magazine was organized around reoccurring columns. The images that were used were especially made for the magazine and told their own story. In this way, the editors made sure that the images were never an illustration of the text, and vice versa.

The Fence, the Hearth, Storage, and the Corridor
Elements that are crucial to the way we look at reality, but are traditionally overlooked by the architectural history of our environment, were the main characters in the magazine: the fence, the hearth, storage, and the corridor. These banal concrete objects were interpreted by the editors as amorphous concepts with various manifestations. Seen in this way, a fence, for instance, could be a railing, ring road, or a national border. By using these simple objects as themes, it was possible to address a wealth of more abstract subjects that are inextricably linked to the objects. Subjects that uncovered ideas about the function of the objects and revealed radical shifts.

"Over the fence" dealt with the way the

fence has imperceptibly transformed and grown with architecture, and by doing so, formed a tangible witness of our changing ideas about public and private, private and collective property, accessibility, protection defense, and availability.

"Round the hearth" dealt with the shift from the single heating place being the center point of the house in the nineteenth century to an overall agreeable climate that permeates the entire modern house now. How does this new way of heating affect our perception of the home? The manifestation of an individualization of houses and interiors in the Netherlands was investigated, as well as the shift from the collective "look" of housing that used to be common.

"Storage" attempted to analyze the meaning of storage in society and the physical place it takes. The way we store our goods and information tells us a lot about how we want to reuse these goods and information in the future. Do we want to get rid of things, make them disappear, or do we want to show them right in the open, always available at any given time?

"The corridor", we learned in architecture school, is a sign of bad architecture. If you can make the organization and distribution of your floor plan flexible, corridors would be redundant. The editors saw that corridors were more alive then ever these days, in all kinds of disciplines, and served a variety of purposes like guiding lines, distribution, and accelerators. The corridor changed its look completely during the last century.

Forum Magazine
Project: Magazine
Year: 1998–2000
Team: Hester Wolters, Bart Goldhoorn, Dick van Gameren, Rianne Makkink, Jop van Bennekom, Erik Wong, Tamira Tummers, Tony Goossens, Herman Verkerk
Client: Architectura et Amicitia
Photography: Blommers & Schumm, Bas Princen, and others

—

Project 63 / Page 182
AEX Amsterdam EXposé
The exhibition showed proposals for purchases of design and photography by Stedelijk Museum Amsterdam. Objects and photographs of various scale, value, and use were exhibited in an enfilade of rooms culminating in a spacious hall. As part of the exhibition, visitors could vote to determine the final selection of purchases. Graphic designer Marjolijn Ruyg introduced a system to vote digitally. The first room (where visitors also return) was turned into a polling station.

A showcase cabinet was placed in each room in such a way that visitors had to interact with these cabinets and thus engaged with the objects on display. The visitors themselves became part of the exhibition. The showcase cabinets as well as an inflatable igloo, placed in the large hall, consisted of cavities enveloped by semitransparent material. On three sides of the igloo, video recordings were projected of fashion shows from three shortlisted designers, Alexander van Slobbe, Viktor & Rolf, and Aziz. When the visitors entered the igloo, models came walking towards them from three different perspectives.

AEX Amsterdam EXposé
Project: Exhibition
Year: 1999
Duration: Medium-term, 2 months
Client: Stedelijk Museum Amsterdam
Curator: Leontine Coelewij
Location: Stedelijk Museum Amsterdam
Production: Landstra & De Vries
Inflatable igloo: Rens Bouma
Sound: Eddy de Clercq
Photography: Anoushka Blommers & Niels Schumm, Maarten Theuwkens
Materials: Semitransparent polycarbonate channel plate (16 mm), black MDF treated with wax, transparent acrylic sheets, inflatable latex igloo

—

Project 68 / Page 200
Styling

For the reopening of the renovated Centraal Museum in Utrecht, the four big, rectangular halls called "The Stables" were the venue for an exhibition on Dutch art, fashion, and design. All the exhibited pieces – curated by Marja Bosma (art), José Teunissen (fashion), and Ida van Zijl (design) – were part of the museum's collection.

Without historical and chronological hierarchies, a number of atmospheric clusters were made containing objects and paintings of extremely contrasting expressions: rigid sobriety versus exorbitant baroque, both eminent in Dutch culture over time. The different disciplines each had their own linear display carriers that slid alongside each other, overlapping front and back sides. In this way, by walking through the exhibition the view of the visitor continually captures the three layers of the exhibition (fashion, art, design) in different combinations and shifts simultaneously.

Styling, Fashion, Art & Design
Project: Exhibition
Year: 1999
Duration: Medium-term, 2 months
Team: Bart Guldemond, Herman Verkerk
Client: Centraal Museum
Curators: Marja Bosma, José Teunissen, Ida van Zijl
Location: Centraal Museum, Utrecht
Production: Landstra & De Vries
Graphic design: Thonik
Photography: Hermen Maat
Materials: Hardened glass, aluminum placeholders, painted multiplex display units, tables and pedestals

—

Project 76 / Page 192
Wilhelminastraat

The Inhabitant
The house I have lived in since the beginning of the 1970s is the same house I live in now (2016). It consists of the two top floors of a standard apartment block from the early twentieth century in Amsterdam. The house is built from bricks (front and back side, chimneys) and wood (floors, interior walls, doors). Originally, two families would live on each floor. I bought the house in 1975 together with my friends, and we broke down all the in-between walls. The attic was turned into an apartment as well. The result of this first action was not a design but a "cleanup." The ambition was to introduce "loft living" in the apartments, but because of their specific sizes the empty apartments became corridors around the stairwell; loft spaces that were actually leftover spaces. For a long time, however, I enjoyed this emptiness. After its refurbishment, the house has a number of equally sizedspaces, each of which has a different quality, from sunny and enclosed, to dark and open spaces.

The house I live in now has a bathroom in open connection to my bedroom. Daylight pours into the room from a glass column connected to a roof light placed above the bath. Lying in the bath looking up, I can see the clouds pass by during the day and the stars shining on some nights.

The house I live in now has a terrace that catches the sun throughout the day, and from where I can look at the birds and airplanes flying over. The size makes it an outdoor room. The balustrade is fairly high, and the connection to the apartment is wide because of a sliding glass door across the complete width. My terrace enlarges the house visually, is directly accessible from the kitchen, and easily used for summer night dinners. The house I live in now has a kitchen that is part of the living area.

The house I live in now is no longer a loft. An object – not a room divider, but a room regulator – is now organizing my way of living. The object gives me extra daylight, gives me warmth and fire, stores my books, stores my kitchen utensils and crockery, and creates different views within the apartment. I can walk through it as well, making the apartment an interior as well as an exterior.

In the house I live in now, the enveloping colors are light green. The built-in and loose elements are dark green and brown. In the house I live in now, the materials are aging with me. The skin and surfaces of the forms are non-treated; stains of fat, water, wax, and sunlight bleaching transform the surfaces and make them lived.

The Architect
A big cabinet in the form of a wedge is jammed between floor and ceiling of an empty attic space. The wedge

contains a library on the wide side and a kitchen counter on the narrow side. A meandering plank embraces books, creates a doorway, envelopes the cooking island, and contains the kitchen cabinets. The wedge separates and connects a dining area and a reading area. By the angularity of the wedge in three dimensions, the parts of the spaces that are defined by it seem larger or smaller depending on the way you move through the space. Because of the sideways transparency of the object, created by the triple-folding of the linear plank, the spaces surrounding the object are never closed, and relate to each other.

The library is built around a glass column directing daylight from a roof light through a hole in the floor to a bathroom on the floor below. The walls of this bathroom are covered with wired glass, on the back sides of which light green paint is mounted.

Wilhelminastraat
Project: Interior
Year: 2000
Duration: Very long-term, 30 years
Client: Guus Beumer
Location: Wilhelminastraat, Amsterdam
Production: Landstra & De Vries
Color advice: Alexander van Slobbe
Photography: Johannes Schwartz, Paul Kuipers
Materials: Treated and untreated green MDF, wired glass panels, red cedar wooden frames for sliding doors and windows, Czech old oak flooring, certified tropical wooden parts for the terrace, recycled railing, polyester roof light

—

Project 77 / Page 328
Rotterdam Design Prize 2001

A selection of designs were nominated for the Rotterdam Design Prize 2001. To choose a winner for this competition, the nominated designs were exhibited in order to be judged by an international jury and the public. The exhibition showed the state-of-the-art design in the Netherlands in 2001. The designs were designated to a temporary "stockroom," where they were sorted by category: a. print/communication, b. not physically present (video and scale models), c. jewelry, d. on the table, e. furniture, f. garments, g. big, h. movement.

The layout for the exhibition was based on a traditional urban block principle. By downscaling the typology of the urban block, the streets became the passageways for the exhibition and the courtyards became the "thematic stockrooms" for the designs. The "urban blocks" were made from prefab Styrofoam illuminated from within by fluorescent tube lights. They served as borders to safeguard the designs, as well as comfortable seating elements. The designs were placed loosely in the "courtyards."

In the middle of the exhibition space, the biggest courtyard was left empty and designated as a workplace. This workplace became the epicenter for six events that ensured the designs were given a different context every week, for the duration of the show. Each weekend a new event would start. The organizers of the event could choose any of the designs to be part of the weekly show in the workspace. During the first week, different designs were photographed and documented (shoot). In the second week, the designs were backdrop and inspiration for the cuisine of a VIP dinner (food). The third week, a DJ paid musical homage to some of the designs (mood). The fourth week, the designs were confronted with some highlights from the permanent design collection of the museum (good). The fifth week, the designs became part of a showroom for Trendhopper, an interior design shop (booth). The final event took place in the sixth week (loot), and was the award show for the prize. Because of this, the designs could again be seen in a different light.

Rotterdam Design Prize 2001
Project: Exhibition
Year: 2001
Duration: Medium-term, two months
Team: Marnix Goossens, Goodwill, Jaymz, Uta Eisenreich, Thimo te Duits, Marjo Kranenborg (Trendhopper), Michiel Zegers, Herman Verkerk
Client: Rotterdam Design Prize
Curator: Guus Beumer
Location: Museum Boijmans Van Beuningen, Rotterdam
Graphic design: Maureen Mooren

and Daniel van der Velden
Production: Museum Boijmans van Beuningen
Photography: Marnix Goossens, Maarten Theuwkens
Materials: Betonplex purple (22 mm), foundation formworks of white Styrofoam, fluorescent tube lights, gray cardboard, yellow archive cards

—

Project 78 / Page 304
Veem 20 Years

This was an exhibition for the twenty-year jubilee anniversary of Werkgebouw Het Veem, a collective building for studios, workshops, and offices in Amsterdam. Since the office of EventArchitectuur is situated in "Het Veem," Herman Verkerk was asked if he would help organize an exhibition on the work of all the artists and designers who have studios in the building. Together with architect and historian Gerrit Oorthuys (also working in the building), the task was to think about how to present the works and projects in the public areas, like corridors and hallways.
After a little hesitation, they decided it would be better if the artists themselves looked for a place in the building to exhibit, and also which of their works they would like to show. Verkerk and Oorthuys would then respond to these choices and placements. Their goal was to overcome the idea of a regular business complex, where art would be hanging in the corridors for decorative purposes. They developed the idea of shadow art, imitating, interpreting, and commenting on the artworks and collaborating with the artists. The shadow art pieces were all made of (leftover) materials that were lying around in the corridors and hallways of the building, and from some small remnants from old exhibitions. In this way, the shadow art pieces connected the real artworks by creating a context for all of them. They also articulated the routing through the building. Using crepe masking tape, the names of the artists were written on the floors and walls, and some wayfinding devices were also designed.

Veem 20 Years
Project: Exhibition
Year: 2001
Duration: Very short-term, 1 day
Team: Gerrit Oorthuys, Herman Verkerk
Client: Werkgebouw Het Veem
Location: Van Diemenstraat, Amsterdam
Production: EventArchitectuur
Photography: EventArchitectuur
Materials: Leftover materials like old wooden frames, sheets, rope, aluminum tubes, plastic bags, glass, cardboard, fabrics, tires, lamps, computers, monitors, tables, chairs, paint, spray cans, crepe masking tape

—

Project 82 / Page 352
Higher Truth no. 5

Higher Truth no. 5 was a fashion store without products. We made the experience of a fashion store open for discussion by imitating the layout of a generic fashion store – the entrance with a porter exclusively opening the door for you, the greeting and packing rituals of the friendly staff, the route to the relaxation room and the changing room – and by leaving out the physical products. The exhibition model itself became the displayed product. By omitting physical products, the store became a critical model where visitors could concentrate on the phenomenon itself, and what impact these surroundings and rituals had on them.

The spaces were designed in such a way that the visitor followed a calculated route. Entering the Vleeshal, one was still "outside"; a "forest" of columns obstructed the view towards the shop windows and entrance of the store. This store facade shimmered and glittered, and was made from opaque fabric framed by shiny aluminum and covered with mirrors. When approaching the facade a gigantic door would slide open and a porter would welcome you into the store. Inside, one recognized all the elements of a regular store – the clothing racks, the counter, the seats –but all of them were slightly bigger and abstract, made from the same materials as the facade.

The staff welcomed you, asking, "Are you being served?" and invited you for a glass of water at the water coolers in the relaxation room. From this room you were guided to the changing room, passing a dark tunnel. In the changing room, you would see yourself entering the room through a delayed video on a screen. The video camera would permanently film you from the back. Going back through the tunnel, you were picked up again by one of the staff members who had prepared and packed a collection of written articles on the fashion experience and atmosphere, the highest form of spiritual materialism. You were relieved when the porter closed the door behind you and you were part of the embracing forest of columns.

Higher Truth no. 5
Project: Installation
Year: 2001
Duration: Medium-term, 1 month
Team: Rianne Makkink, Herman Verkerk
Client: De Vleeshal Center for Contemporary Art
Curators: Rutger Wolfson, Guus Beumer
Location: De Vleeshal, Middelburg
Production: Kees Wijker & Team
Photography: Johannes Schwartz
Materials: Greenhouse structural system (aluminum profiles with opaque shrinking foil), mirrored glass window displays, polyester tubes of varying diameter: 0.4, 0.6, and 2 m

—

SLOOM: About
Project 85, 88, 90, 93, 96, 104, 105, 125 / Page 262

Sloom.org initiates activities that express a reconsideration of architecture and urban and landscape design, no longer from a critical distance but with a direct method of intervention. Since the discussion of "high" and "low" culture has been taken over by the discussion about "fast" and "slow," sloom.org embraces the potential of "slowness." Sloom.org would like to start over by showing the importance of moderation rather than acceleration. Locality and diversity are more important than globalization and standardization. The activities of sloom.org are documented through a magazine and website.
Sloom.org was founded in 2002 by Rianne Makkink (Studio Makkink & Bey) and Herman Verkerk (EventArchitectuur).

Project 85 / Page 264–267
SLOOM 0: Local Magazine on Time
During a two-day seminar on time at De Balie in Amsterdam, we asked visitors to photograph "slow things" in the neighborhood and to give a definition of the term *sloom* ("sluggish" in Dutch). The results were collected by graphic designers Koehorst In 't Veld in an improvised editors' office on the spot, and made into a Magazine of the Day.

Project 87 / Page 264–267
SLOOM 1: Travel with One Horsepower
This issue documents a tour with horse and carriage through the northeast of the Netherlands on the normal provincial roads for cars. Guests from the architecture and urban design fields, as well as politicians and leisure experts, joined us for a ride. We questioned our guests about what they saw from the carriage and what they thought of the (im)possibility of slowness in this part of the country.

Project 88 / Page 264–267
SLOOM 2: Building Improvisations
Building Improvisations hopes to give a positive impulse to the relation between client and architect. We looked for new design and production methods for houses, to make them more personal. We built a garden house from refuse and unusual materials in which the design process coincides with the building process. Through the moulage technique of draping materials on improvised structures, we worked with trial and error, a process in which the client could also intervene. The 1:1 mock-up became the actual building.

Project 90 / Page 264–267
SLOOM 3: Berlin Insiders
Berlin Insiders deals with the experience of time and change in the reunified Berlins. We got into contact with colleagues from the city's cultural sector and had informal talks with them about their profession and how they dealt with the new market economy that invaded the city after the Wende. We asked them to make a knitted self-portrait.

Project 93, 96, 105 / Page 268
SLOOM 4: The Farmyard Model
A photography exhibition concerning Dutch farms and their contemporary use was held in "The Year of the Farm

2003." The exhibition, called *Faces of Farming*, was designed and installed by us inside and outside characteristic farms in each of the twelve provinces in the Netherlands. After completion of the twelve exhibitions, we showed the results as a single exhibition in 2004, *Mixed Farming*, at the Nederlands Fotomuseum in Rotterdam.

During the assignment, we researched the quality of the farmyard and found it perfectly suited the idea of slow growth. In addition, the old-fashioned way of moving about the farm without apparent purpose (*scharrelen* in Dutch), and seeing what is to be done by this constant walking around, somehow still existed, even in the most industrialized farms. Together with Koehorst In 't Veld we made a publication of the research and the exhibition.

Project 104 / Page 272
SLOOM 5: Go Slow Restaurant in Milan
The Go Slow restaurant was an interactive installation we made for a Droog design presentation in Milan during the Salone del Mobile 2004. All the elements of the restaurant, from entering, waiting, seating, and setting the table, to preparing and serving the food, were ritualized. Slogans like eat slowly, drink slowly, and swallow slowly encouraged you to slow down your eating and drinking behavior. Marije Vogelzang designed the menu and instructed the elderly waiters and waitresses on how to produce and serve the different courses with a lot of attention and patience. The "tablecloths" were made out of candle wax, in which the warm bowls made their own little depressions to stay upright. After a couple of meals, the wax could be melted and poured over the tabletops again. Inserted in this "tablecloth" were little tea lights.

Project 125 / Page 274
SLOOM 8: Grocery Shop & Model Table
For the Dutch TV series *Wroeten* (VPRO, 2005), directed by Lernert Engelbrecht – about a city slacker (actor Arjan Ederveen) who goes to live in the countryside – we built a grocery shop that also functioned as a little restaurant and beauty salon. The grocery shop sold homegrown vegetables. The table, with a scale model of the *Wroeten* house and garden, served as explanatory device to give advice on the different difficulties that occur while growing vegetables and regional plants and trees in your garden.

—

Project 86 / Page 290
Weekend Agenda 2002

What motivated a group of artists, architects, and designers to build a collection of structures from trash on a deserted meadow somewhere in the north of the Netherlands? They were invited to participate in this experimental project by its initiators, the editors of *Forum Magazine*.

"We decided to just go ahead and start building. Somewhere on a meadow in Friesland." These were the first lines of the publication *Weekend Agenda 2002*. The activist tone was deliberate, and emphasized the attitude of us, the editors. "Weekend" was the title of the issue as well as the project that *Forum Magazine* started in the summer of 2001. We invited a number of colleagues to be our guests for a weekend and to start building structures from trash together with us. We invited them to go outside, to work in a new and strange context. We wanted to create energy through performance. We enjoyed activating our critical stance by not concentrating on the works of others. We renounced the reflexive and descriptive role typical for a regular architectural magazine. The content of the magazine was now created and formulated on the spot. Participants were asked to define their attitude towards designing and creating things and spaces, not through plans, but by way of acting. During this acting, they would be asked to make the essence of their work explicit: how they had formulated their brief, and which resources they were using.

As editors, we wanted to function as catalysts in this process. A way to present to participants the question of how to start anew, and not to search for propositions individually but also collectively, was to give a number of shared conditions: the location (a mowed square in the meadow), the tools (no electric tools), the material (waste and nature), the duration

(one weekend), and the number of participants for each weekend (four). We became part of the project, and together worked on the patchwork of ideas. With this, Forum became the first architectural magazine to create its own building structures.
To communicate the energy that evolved by having so much talent working on a similar assignment, the publication emphasized the collectivity of the project. Each separate contribution was of great value for the project, but perhaps not so much for the individual body of work of the participant. The products were improvised, temporary structures that mainly functioned as models for thinking. To capture the act of building them resulted in characteristic imagery. These images had a special *raison d'être*. Snapshots were not seen as part of a process – like frames in a film –but were treated as temporary objectives.

The written personal statements were not treated as theoretical descriptions, but notated as diary entries, as their meaning was often cryptic and formulated between the lines. They were also detached from the personal, in order to stress the continuity of the actions.

The project was called *Weekend* to clarify its existence next to the regular practice. It was a parallel world of simultaneous reflection and relaxation. All the weekends together could also form an image of participants' lives, just as the working week does. Moreover, a weekend is not bounded by time, but by a cyclical return of retreating and refueling.

Weekend Agenda 2002
Project: Book
Year: 2002
Team: Jop van Bennekom, Rianne Makkink Julia van Mourik, Hester Wolters, Herman Verkerk
Client: Architectura et Amicitia
Funding: Rotterdam Design Prize
Production: Forum Magazine
Photography: Micha de Ridder, Johannes Schwartz, Petra Warrass
Participants: Jop van Bennekom, Andre van Bergen, Erik Blits, Anoushka Blommers, Han van den Born, Yael Davids, Barbara van Erp, Pascale Gatzen, Kersten Geers, Hanneke Groenteman, Dirk van den Heuvel, Hella Jongerius, Klaar van der Lippe, Rianne Makkink, Julia van Mourik, Micha de Ridder, Niels Schumm, Johannes Schwartz, Alexander van Slobbe, Jo Taillieu, Herman Verkerk, Petra Warrass, Hester Wolters

—

Project 89 / Page 358
"We'll slide down the surface of things..."

WSDTSOT was an installation for the artworks of Arnout Kilian, Glen Rubsamen, and Frank Bauer. According to the curator, "We live in an artificial reality. Our inner life is permeated with images of better worlds the mass media bombards us with. These images color our longings as well as our experiences. For male supermodel Victor Ward, the main character in *Glamorama*, a novel written by Bret Easton Ellis, any circumstance or emotion is only real if it reminds him of an image from a magazine, video clip, or movie. Not only in our inner lives, also in the physical world artificiality is accepted as part of reality. In the design of our everyday surroundings – landscapes, stores, public spaces and the home – spectacle and experience are more important than concepts like authenticity and reality.

How do we deal with a reality that is becoming increasingly artificial? For Ward, this reminds him of the quasi-philosophical line from a song by the band U2: 'We'll slide down the surface of things...' Generally, however, this development is condemned, as it would lead to a dangerous loss of meaning. Because of this, hardly any insights were developed on how to go about it. Hyper-realistic, (figurative) painting could contribute to this. Painting, after all, has a rich tradition of intensifying reality. Each of the three painters participating in 'We'll slide down the surface of things' researched the artificial world in which we live."

To experience these hyper-realistic artworks, it was necessary to build a "neutral" environment. The works could not be left to their own devices in the Gothic expressionism of De Vleeshal. The artworks were placed within a

1:1 model of a modernist museum or gallery, including white walls, a "floating" ceiling with fluorescent tube lighting, and a polished epoxy floor. Although on the inside the 1:1 model seemed to be perfectly hyper-realistic as well, on the edges and outside the model was crumbling into a ruin of modernism.

"We'll slide down the surface of things..."
Project: Installation
Year: 2002
Duration: Medium-term, 2 months
Client: De Vleeshal Center for Contemporary Art
Curator: Rutger Wolfson
Location: De Vleeshal, Middelburg
Production: Kees Wijker & Team
Photography: EventArchitectuur
Materials: Recycled glass and wood construction, wood panels, plasterboard, epoxy flooring, fluorescent tube lights, chrome detailing, white paint

—

Project 91 / Page 332
Rotterdam Design Prize 2003

For the 2003 Rotterdam Design Prize, each nominated design to be judged by an international jury and the public was placed in its own niche. The emphasis of the exhibition lay in experiencing each design individually, while not attempting to suggest a common denominator. This reluctance to show an "overview" was physically staged as a walled "garden" in which the walls were transformed into pergolas with a number of niches, each containing the designs. At the center of this enclosed garden, a long rectangular mirror pond reflected the empty space within the garden walls. Only by going around the garden wall and stepping inside the enclosed pergola could one encounter the designs.

Otherwise, visitors were confronted with a closed structure overgrown with "plants," a contemplative but empty center for reflection, and the scent of freshly cut grass.

Rotterdam Design Prize 2003
Project: Exhibition
Year: 2003
Duration: Medium-term, 2 months
Team: Paul Kuipers, Herman Verkerk
Client: Rotterdam Design Prize
Curator: Guus Beumer
Location: Museum Boijmans Van Beuningen, Rotterdam
Graphic design: Maureen Mooren and Daniel van der Velden
Embroidery Installation: Conny Groenewegen
Fragrance: Alessandro Gualtieri
Production: Landstra & De Vries
Photography: Johannes Schwartz
Materials: Recycled glass panels, white perforated board, pinewood beams, secondhand clothes, audio cassette tape

—

Project 92 / Page 360
Safe Haven

Safety has an aesthetic of its own. The project "Safe Haven... or the aesthetic of safety" was an attempt to illuminate our desires and fears with regard to safety by examining the aesthetic employed. The first part of the installation provided a historical context for the present aesthetic of safety by means of a number of "settings." The focus of these settings was not so much on any one style or designer, but rather on the development of the aesthetic aspect, and the use of materials in particular.

The installation layout started with a model of the velour-covered nineteenth-century interior, where touching and leaving traces were the evidence of safety and ways to feel safe. Moving on to the interior of steel, glass, and white tiled walls, visually and practically safeguarding physical hygiene, one sensed the essential aspect of feeling safe at the beginning of the last century.

The second part of the installation was a 1:1 model of a patio house. The model formed an illustration of how the aesthetics of safety has led to a radical transparency of materials, resulting in the increasing blending of inside and outside spaces. The inhabitants could constantly observe themselves, whether inside or outside, because the walls of the inner court were completely made of transparent glass. The furniture was either transparent or mirroring the space. On each end of the U-shaped patio house, extensions were built that looked like wooden shacks. Here one could escape the permanent inward-looking gaze. From here one could also enter the second half of the exhibition hall. This part of the hall was deliberately left empty to enable looking at the 1:1 model from another perspective, and to have space for debates and lectures on the aesthetics of safety in the (near) future.

Safe Haven
Project: Installation
Year: 2003
Duration: Medium-term, 2 months
Client: De Vleeshal Center for Contemporary Art
Curator: Guus Beumer
Location: De Vleeshal, Middelburg
Production: Kees Wijker & Team
Photography: Johannes Schwartz
Materials: Glass sponsored by Pilkington, wooden construction, shrinking foil, white bathroom tiles, wood panels, epoxy flooring with slate gravel, fluorescent blacklight tubes, wallpaper with relief, furniture (transparent plastic, stainless steel)

—

Project 94 / Page 310
Boys '97

With *Boys '97*, Johannes Schwartz and Herman Verkerk delved deeper into issues such as original, copy, representation, and reproduction. These have to do with the circumstances of how an image is displayed, viewed, and understood. What happens to the character of a picture or photograph as it is transferred to another medium, for example, by including (and reproducing) it in print, which is subsequently made part of the exhibition? And what happens with an exhibition space as the conditions in which the works are displayed are changed?

Schwartz and Verkerk did not provide answers; they mainly asked questions – about part versus whole, original versus copy, nature versus culture. The exhibition was therefore not a finished whole, but a project with an open end. It was up to each visitor to combine the various facets of *Boys '97* into some kind of unity.

The old motto, *natura artis magistra*, indicates that nature had previously been seen by many as a great instructor for the arts. For centuries, a true representation of visible reality was of great importance in the visual arts. To this end, examples formerly known as study sheets were in circulation: loose-leaf sheets on which one could see examples of a particular subject, such as facial expressions, hands, clouds, or trees. On the basis of such a study, the painter could compose his final work. Often there was no actual realism, but a carefully constructed entity from different parts. But this is not only a work of art; our individual concept of reality is always a (mental) structure in which many aspects play a decisive role. With the archaic study sheets as a visual starting point, Boys '97 discussed in a creative way the conditioning of our perception and the value of the components that together define our image of reality.

Boys '97
Project: Installation
Year: 2003
Duration: Medium-term, 2 months
Team: Johannes Schwartz, Herman Verkerk
Client: Foam Photography Museum
Location: Keizersgracht, Amsterdam
Production: EventArchitectuur, Johannes Schwartz
Photography: Johannes Schwartz, Herman Verkerk
Materials: Photocopies, original photo prints, untreated pinewood sheets and beams, white latex paint

—

Project 97 / Page 364
Start: OMA open archive

The exhibition *Start* was set up as an open depot in which visitors could consult material from the Rem Koolhaas and OMA/AMO archives of the Netherlands Architecture Institute. An archival database with background articles was created especially for the exhibition. The Rem Koolhaas/OMA archive is undoubtedly one of the most important in the collection of the institute. As early as 1984, the institute acquired several project files from the then relatively new practice. The collection was added to in 1988 and 1994, and at the time of the exhibition it was supplemented with sketches, drawings, and models relating to projects already in the archive, but that until then had remained with the practice. During the exhibition, this material was unpacked, cleaned, and inventoried in the workspace.

OMAR
With the aid of a specially designed digital database (OMAR), visitors could search the archive and request and inspect items. The visitor would first select a project from the list, then select a category and note the OMAR code of the desired item on a request card. The card could then be given to one of the staff members of the archive, who worked within the counter area of the exhibition space during its opening hours. The archivist would then locate the material, and the visitor could then inspect the item(s) in the workspace.

Layout
The layout of the open depot consisted of a meandering counter going through the entire exhibition space and defining the area for the staff to work while unpacking the archive and helping to present visitors with what they were looking for. Outside this counter/working area, visitors could follow a route that led them along a long pin board with original exhibition pieces, into a centrally placed archive filled with scale models displayed like exotic plants in a botanical greenhouse. After going through this greenhouse, they could continue following the pin board, turn back into the model archive again, and return to the starting point, where the digital database was at their disposal on workstations. Along the route were a couple of large, low pedestals on which projections were shown of the hands of researchers wearing white gloves and going through the archive of drawings. At the entrance of the open depot was a wooden cage with a huge stack of boxes and crates containing the new acquisitions of the OMA/AMO archive.

Start: OMA open archive
Project: Exhibition
Year: 2004
Duration: Medium-term, 3 months
Team: Bart Guldemond, Herman Verkerk
Client: Netherlands Architecture Institute
Curator: Linda Vlassenrood
Location: Museumpark, Rotterdam
Production: Landstra & De Vries
Graphic design: Experimental Jetset
Photography: Johannes Schwartz, EventArchitectuur
Materials: Yellow acrylic sheets, birch wood sheets, desk top lino, pinewood beams, underlayment sheets, white paint

—

Project 101 / Page 248
orson + bodil Workshop, Showroom & Store

Fashion label orson + bodil opened their headquarters in 2004, in one of the buildings of the former Westergasfabriek in Amsterdam. The headquarters were unique in the sense that they combined three distinct functions of the fashion label into one venue. The showroom and archive, the workshop, and the fashion store each had their own zone in the overall layout, but cross-pollination and interaction was encouraged through their proximity.

"Parallels between the Bauhaus and the philosophy of orson + bodil are remarkable. Ideological zeal for a utopian future is not part of Van Slobbe's mind-set, but the same cannot be said of the modernist terms generally associated with architecture and design [he uses to describe his work –Ed.]. His designs fuse function, structure, skin, and silhouette in eye-pleasing garments assembled with ingenuity. Every aspect has functional motivation. Decoration, for example, is added only in the form of detachable jewelry. Another similarity between the two can be seen in orson + bodil's retail interior, which dovetails seamlessly with the clothes, creating a *Gesamtkunstwerk*.

Architect Herman Verkerk stripped the existing interior of all superfluous elements to reveal the bare skin and structure of the space. With inexpensive materials like plywood and felt, and anonymous products like wooden pallets and polystyrene formwork, he created cupboards, partitions, systems

for hanging garments, and a black glass catwalk for lifeless mannequins. 'Shabby glamour' is Verkerk's definition of the space. 'Frugal materials and minimal design put the glamour of the industrial product, usually aimed at perfection, into perspective.
I much prefer working with industrial materials, which are generally invisible. Using them to build temporary configurations gives my work a fresh narrative quality.'

The use of budget materials also corresponded to the expected life span of the shop: a mere two years. At the end of that time, Beumer and Van Slobbe will examine the feasibility of their project. Do modernist values and stylistic features have any bearing on the social developments of the 21st century? Or is 'contemporary Bauhaus' an anachronism? Verkerk, who refers to his work as 'beyond modernism,' agrees that an exact duplication of such methods is not advisable. 'You can take modernist principles as a point of departure,' he says. 'After all, they have certainly proved their worth within and even beyond the field of architecture.' Verkerk's layout for the shop is based on a precise, and thus very modernist, grid. Within this grid, however, he plays with elements that veer away from modernism, such as imperfection and recycled materials. 'The idea of transience, which is linked by definition to retail environments, has never occupied a mental place or assumed a material form with modernism,' says Verkerk. 'As a style, modernism can be unmasked. As an ideology, it's unproductive. But as a body of thought, it still has an incredible amount of potential.'"[1]

1 Louise Schouwenberg, "Beyond Bauhaus," *Frame*, no. 41 (November/December 2004): 86–87.

orson + bodil Workshop, Showroom & Store
Project: Fashion Store
Year: 2004
Duration: Long-term, 2 years
Client: orson + bodil (Guus Beumer and Alexander van Slobbe)
Location: Westerpark, Amsterdam
Production: Wouter de Baat
Lighting design: Airlight Holland, Ruud Pouwels
Photography: Johannes Schwartz
Materials: Glass painted black, wooden beams, wooden panels, Styrofoam blocks, central heating steel pipes, black MDF panels, white perforated board, felt

—

Project 103 / Page 256
Artimo A–Z

Artimo A–Z was an art bookstore and publishing house founded by Gijs Stork and located on the Elandsgracht in Amsterdam. The design consisted of a system of sandwiches made out of untreated poplar wood sheets with little pinewood blocks in different sizes. The sandwiches formed bookshelves, cupboards, display units, and tables. The intermediary blocks in the sandwich were placed within different distances from one another, in order to present each art book in a case especially customized to its size. Because the linearity of the regular bookshelves was broken, the meandering bookshelves became a favorite browsing tool for surprises and finds. The display units were made from recycled wooden sheets, leftovers from the workshop of Landstra & De Vries. The structure of these units made it possible to change the surface area on different levels, according to the supply of books in different sizes.

Artimo A–Z
Project: Bookstore
Year: 2004
Duration: Long-term, 3 years

Client: Gijs Stork
Location: Elandsgracht, Amsterdam
Production: Landstra & De Vries
Graphic design: Experimental Jetset
Photography: Artimo A–Z
Materials: Untreated poplar wood sheets, pinewood beams, recycled wooden sheets from the Landstra & De Vries workshop, painted birch plywood sheets, fluorescent lights, acrylic sheets

—

Project 107 / Page 424
Arnhem Fashion Biennale 2005

The Arnhem Fashion Biennale was initiated by the city of Arnhem together with the ArtEZ Institute of the Arts. Because the school delivers very good designers (most of them starting to work internationally), the city thought it wise to try to make Arnhem synonymous with fashion: a fashion city. This is a very sympathetic idea, because the city is not at all glamorous or big; it has its own special flavor. We tried to translate this flavor into the exhibition.

The biennale exhibition was the center, but only one part, of a total experience of the Arnhem Fashion Biennale. EventArchitectuur also designed thirty-six clothes closets/cupboards for the display of projects from fashion designers and students that were placed in the shopping area of the town, forming the walking route from the train station to the site of the main exhibition. The dimensions of the exhibition spaces were huge. The location was a former factory on the banks of the Rhine where milk was pasteurized and bottled. There was a large outdoor space and big halls of different sizes and atmospheres. We used these atmospheres for the design of the particular displays. The total floor area was about 1,500 square meters, and some of the spaces were more than ten meters high. The wonderful potency of the factory is that you have a big space were you can make your own routing and have people experience a new world that is a combination of new and old. A museum or school would be much more official and less experimental. Because the factory was so big and had such different atmospheres, it immediately inspired the theme of the exhibition to be a landscape or a garden park where you could experience "outdoor" weather conditions like rain, sun, wind, and cold under one large roof.

First, you entered the site of the factory through a Gate. You turned a corner and saw a central lane made of two rows of conifers in large black plastic pots. This monumental lane led you to the entrance, which looked like a summer pavilion in a park. After buying your ticket, you were handed an umbrella to enter the Rain space. Because there was a sizable open construction in the ceiling, we could easily situate the installation for the rain machines there. The long, narrow space was ideal for a linear setup, with clothes especially made by the designers for this exhibition that could withstand the rain. After rain comes sunshine, so you returned the umbrella and entered the formal garden of the Sun. This layout was entirely a baroque/enclosed garden type: symmetrical squares with neat hedges and four pavilions for each cardinal direction. The models stood on pedestals like statues. The pavilions were all different for display purposes, and to give opportunities for strolling and excitement. Next to the sun display were two rooms. One room was entirely dark, as a contrast to the soft and light atmosphere of the sun display room. The other was a reflecting pool that formed a large Mirror. You could walk over this pool to the next attraction, a tunnel with Wind gushing at you from afar. Walking against the wind is very common in the Netherlands.

After overcoming this obstruction, you entered a formal garden that looked like a plant nursery with flowerbeds for more delicate designs. Here were located the other important representational aspects of fashion, like videos, books, and runway shows.

After this, you entered the Ice hall, where the temperature was below zero and the pedestals for the models were frozen over. You could skate in between the displays. Finally, there was a restaurant and a shop especially designed by EventArchitectuur for the event. It was an enclosed monastery garden made out of white-painted pine wood and white perforated board.

For the exhibition we used cheap materials, not only for cost purposes, but also to show the visual richness of these ready-made materials; they have that shabby glamour that we were seeking. All the materials were white or painted white. For instance, we used white Styrofoam blocks normally used on building sites for foundation mullets as ready-mades to build the hedges and display pedestals of the entire exhibition. The pine wood we used as columns for the pavilions was painted white, and so became more abstract and graphic. The white perforated board was also used throughout the exhibition as screens for display and covering at the same time. The lighting was used as a support for the different atmospheres. It was not too delicate, because the spaces were rather rough and not clean.

The fashion designers shown in the space were orson + bodil, Claudy Jongstra, Kind, Melanie Rozema, Viktor & Rolf, Spijkers & Spijkers, Keupr/van Bentm, Bas Kosters, and others. All of them are Dutch designers who were working with fashion on a conceptual level. Keupr/van Bentm did a collective work with students of the academy, to translate some of their famous work into garments that could stand in the Rain space.

Arnhem Fashion Biennale 2005
Project: Exhibition
Year: 2005
Duration: Medium-term, 1 month
Team: Paul Kuipers, Herman Verkerk
Client: Stichting Arnhem Mode Biënnale
Curator: Piet Paris
Location: Former Coberco Milk Factory, Arnhem
Production: Landstra & De Vries
Graphic design: CoppensAlberts
Photography: Johannes Schwartz, EventArchitectuur
Materials: Styrofoam blocks, whitewashed pinewood, white perforated board

—

Project 109 / Page 336
Ideal House

This installation was a 1:1 model of an ideal house according to designer Hella Jongerius and EventArchitectuur, presented at the IMM Furniture Fair in Cologne. As Jongerius is not an architect, she called upon EventArchitectuur to assist in creating her ideal house. Their collaboration resulted in a sturdy, layered structure with partitions and platforms, grids and shelving systems. Eleven skeletal wooden walls held the contents of a life together "like an ever-evolving filing cabinet," in the words of the designer, who also speaks of "the inventory of your life, where you constantly potter around. Things come and things go" (Caroline Goossens, "Amongst Women," *FRAME* 44, May/June 2005).

As a complementary gesture, the Ideal House had an Ideal Garden, counterpointing the frame construction of the facade. This garden with elevated planting beds became a focal point for the visitors of the fair. It was a place for relaxation and for informal encounters, because it had no commercial program. Visitors could sit on the planting beds, some of which had a soft moss growing on top.

Ideal House
Project: Installation
Year: 2005
Duration: Short-term, 5 days
Team: JongeriusLab (Hella Jongerius & Arian Brekveld), EventArchitectuur (Herman Verkerk & Paul Kuipers), Louise Schouwenberg, publicist
Client: Rat für Formgebung, German Design Council
Location: Hall 3, Koelnmesse, Cologne
Production: IMM, parts by JongeriusLab & EventArchitectuur
Photography: JongeriusLab, EventArchitectuur

Materials: Pinewood frames (some painted black or gray, others untreated), wooden paneling from underlayment (some panels painted red), reused wooden staircase, added mezzanine of pinewood sheets and beams, flooring of wooden sheets painted black
There was no furniture on the floor; only on and within the storage walls.
Furniture in the storage:
Between frames one and two: three vintage cabinets
Frame two: A4 textile color samples Pantone
Between frames two, three, and four: modern, classic, and vintage chairs
Between frames five, six, seven, and eight: lamps
Underneath the staircase: cleaning equipment and liquids
Frame eight: dinner plates, tie-wraps, plastic sheets with prefab holes
Between frames eight, nine, ten, and eleven: the porcelain collection for Rosenthal
Between frames nine and ten: a rolled-up Danskina carpet on the mezzanine floor, candles, folded linen sheets
Between frames ten and eleven: vases by Hella Jongerius
Frame eleven: vintage door and window
Between frames four and eleven: banners with JongeriusLab print and banners with "Repeat," the upholstery designed by Hella Jongerius for Maharam

—

Project 113, 114 / Page 240
Pursuit of Happiness

Inspiration for this project came from two architectural concepts: the super grids proposed by Superstudio to cover the surface of the Earth and Bernard Tschumi's plan for Parc de la Villette in Paris. The design was for a temporary sculpture park for a visual art festival in Leidsche Rijn, Utrecht. The starting point for the festival was how happiness is being perceived in suburban places like Leidsche Rijn, where 30,000 houses are built at once. The program of the festival contained two elements: a number of new, site-specific art pieces and several art videos. The location of the festival was an old farm consisting of a number of outbuildings and a huge piece of neglected farmland. We proposed to use methods for designing urban areas from tabula rasa to design the temporary park. First, we proposed a grid of 30 x 30 meters to give the neglected land a neutral basis. On the intersecting lines of the grid, we projected service points. Secondly, we introduced a meandering path that connected all the different art pieces and buildings like a spatial necklace. Thirdly, we built a number of parallel walls into the barn that formed the zoning for the different viewing rooms.

Pursuit of Happiness
Project: Land Art, Exhibition
Year: 2005
Duration: Medium-term, one month
Team: Paul Kuipers, Pieter Wackers, Herman Verkerk
Client: Beyond Leidsche Rijn Utrecht, Mariette Dölle
Location: Farmyard in Leidsche Rijn, Utrecht
Production: Landstra & De Vries, Gemeentedienst Publieke Werken
Photography: Micha de Ridder, EventArchitectuur
Materials: White bathroom tiles, underlayment sheets, wooden poles, wooden beams, corrugated polyester sheets, B2 concrete blocks, carpet, projection fabric, wooden frames

—

Project 124 / Page 316
Principle Junk

Photographic images in *objet trouvé* surroundings. Johannes Schwartz and Herman Verkerk investigated the aesthetics of waste temporarily placed on the streets of Amsterdam. They photographed different "compositions" made by builders, demolishers, inhabitants, and passersby of old books, wood paneling, metal stud, hardboard. They took these heaps, stacks, and bundles to the gallery space of P///AKT to exactly reconstruct the compositions, or even recreate the original shapes when the pieces became broken. Photographic images of the waste *in situ* accompanied the installations.

Somewhere on the side of the gallery there was a huge storage space of 6 x 6 x 3 meters that was filled with all kinds of gallery "waste," an array of leftover tables and chairs, ladders, and paint. Johannes and Herman took these objects out of that space and placed them in the center of the gallery, exactly as they had been positioned within the storage space. The empty storage space and the stack of objects defining its contents complemented each other.

Principle Junk
Project: Installation
Year: 2005
Duration: Medium-term, 2 months
Team: Johannes Schwartz, Herman Verkerk
Client: P///AKT
Location: Zeeburgerpad, Amsterdam
Production: EventArchitectuur, Johannes Schwartz
Photography: Johannes Schwartz, Herman Verkerk
Materials: Photocopies, original photo prints, untreated pinewood sheets and beams, white latex paint, assorted found materials

—

Project 129 / Page 462
Office BremerDeZwaan

Established in a monumental building at Keizersgracht 604 in Amsterdam is the law firm Bremer & De Zwaan, the working environment of both partners, Monica Bremer and Marcel De Zwaan. Their clientele is found mainly in the cultural sector, and their expertise focuses primarily on copyright matters. In addition to the independent practice of both partners, a so-called contract lawyer's office is part of the firm, with clients in the fields of publishing, theater, and television.

A rudimentary refurbishment of the historic property in the recent past for the benefit of an office accommodation withdrew some specific and unique characteristics of the architecture from view. EventArchitectuur was asked to create a new definition of the space and to provide the specific program requirements for the office. A personal affinity of all employees with the workplace should play a major role. Because a number of sustainable investments in furniture and infrastructure were already done, these had to be overturned in the existing situation within a limited budget.

The program included two separate rooms for the two partners, a space for the contract office, a room for the joint secretary, a prominent place for the archive, a library (which also has space for an intern), and a place for a small kitchen.

We made no profound changes to the existing plan. The workspaces of Bremer & De Zwaan adjoin a central area that is ambiguous in shape. A separating wall cabinet was placed across this room, which creates an intimate workspace and a corridor zone. The contract office and the secretary use this workspace. In the corridor zone, the cabinet takes on the total archive and other practical matters, such as a reception desk, a copier, and a small pantry and storage space for office supplies.

The two separate workspaces of the partners have been improved with an acoustic wall lined with different color bands of felt. To the already existing and sustainable furniture, new seating and a dresser were added. For the contract office, we made specific desks and filing cabinets. For the library, sandwich wallboards have been made and the white-painted wooden floor has been given a (sound-insulating) definition by means of black surfaces of lino.

Finally, throughout the office the faces of the existing paneling were filled with felt, and where the paneling has been removed during previous renovations was again made with felt in the negative of the planes. Simple materials such as pinewood, perforated board, MDF, and black felt are used as a device intended for a more tactile experience in an office environment with rudimentary metal stud walls and ducts.

Office BremerDeZwaan
Project: Interior
Year: 2006
Duration: Long-term, 5 years
Team: Paul Kuipers, Herman Verkerk
Client: Bremer & De Zwaan
Location: Keizersgracht 604, Amsterdam
Production: Landstra & De Vries
Photography: Juriaan Langstraat
Materials: Pinewood, felt, black MDF, white perforated board, white tiles, lino

—

Project 130 / Page 398
La Collection Imaginaire

The motivation behind this presentation lies in the growing importance of the private collector who, in this time of retreating government, will play a vital role in cultural infrastructure. The guest curator of this presentation was Renée Steenbergen, whose PhD research, "Iets wat zoveel kost, is alles waard" ("Something that costs so much, is worth everything," 2002), shed new light on the position of the collector of modern art in the Netherlands.

The presentation in Marres occurred in parallel with the international art and antiques fair, TEFAF Maastricht, which takes place in early March each year. Many TEFAF visitors can only dream of the works offered for sale, and they experience the exhibition as an "imaginary collection." This also holds true for the everyday practice of collecting, where not everything that the collector desires can actually be added to his/her collection. Out of necessity, the collector takes refuge in imaginary additions; collecting thus becomes a mental game with fictional artworks.

In addition to the collection, the collector was centrally positioned in the presentation. The two were inextricably linked, one as a mirror of the other, the other as a shadow of the first. The collector's gaze, choices, thoughts, and dreams connected the individual works into a meaningful whole. This imaginary quality of every collection – and thereby of any expression of art and design – constituted the background of the project *La Collection Imaginaire*.

EventArchitectuur was asked to design a system that offered a spatial interpretation of an imaginary collection. The final design was not only a carrier of the imagination, but also an idealized vision of the "white box" as the ultimate presentation space. In this, the visitor experienced a transition from the level of the ideal museum to the contemplative, personal inner space; from materiality to imagination. The installation was accompanied by a small, free catalogue, through which the visitor was invited to relate to both the spatial installation and imaginary collection.

La Collection Imaginaire
Project: Installation
Year: 2006
Duration: Medium-term, 3 months
Team: Paul Kuipers, Herman Verkerk
Client: Marres, House for Contemporary Culture
Curator: Renée Steenbergen
Location: Marres, Maastricht
Production: Guus van den Akker & Team
Photography: Guus van den Akker, Paul Kuipers
Materials: Painted hardboard, fluorescent tube lights

—

Project 132 / Page 440
Die Dinge (After Cage)

Objects from different regional museums, ranging from a beer tap and an oil painting, to African voodoo masks and a stuffed penguin, were placed at random on platforms that totally filled the exhibition spaces of Marres, Centre for Contemporary Culture in Maastricht. In each room, the platform was placed at a different height. The public could walk through the first one, which was at hip height, put their heads through the next, which was at shoulder height, and walk over the third, which was at knee height. The effect resulted in three different "panoramas" with objects. The fourth room was called Archive. The visitor was allowed – under the guidance of an "archivist" – to enter the archive and choose an object to replace one of the objects on display on one of the three platforms. Real-time images of the archive and the action of replacing the objects were made visible on monitors in the central room of the exhibition space.

Die Dinge
Project: Exhibition
Year: 2006
Duration: Medium-term, one month
Team: Paul Kuipers, Herman Verkerk
Client: Marres, House for Contemporary Culture
Curator: Claudia Banz
Location: Marres Maastricht
Production: Guus van den Akker
Graphic design: Metahaven
Photography: Johannes Schwartz
Materials: Underlayment, pinewood, nettings, printed paper

—

Project 141, 231 / Page 470
Idylls for Lingezegen Park

Situated in Lingezegen Park, between Arnhem and Nijmegen, lies the land art work *Mountain Idyll. Mountain Idyll* was designed in collaboration with Berdie Olthof and Nanne Bouma of Feddes/Olthof landscape architects. It is one of three idylls that will eventually be part of the landscape park. The idylls are part of the art program of Lingezegen Park. EventArchitectuur was invited by SKOR and the province of Gelderland to contribute to the development of a park between Nijmegen and Arnhem. This initiative was to disclose the development to the (future) residents surrounding the park. This park, named Lingezegen Park, has a size of 1,200 hectares and must form a green buffer between the advancing developments of both cities. The province, however, does not own much territory in the park, and the land that they already own is scattered throughout the park.

EventArchitectuur ultimately proposed a project to build idylls on seven of these parcels of land, where a heightened experience of the existing nature would be possible. We assign to the idylls a different function than the rest of the pre-designed park, which will be focused mainly on outdoor physical recreation. Mental activities like musing and reflecting should be stimulated in the idylls. Moreover, we propose to enhance the awareness of the residents with the surrounding land by giving them the opportunity to have natural burial grounds in these areas. "Returning" their deceased loved ones to the soil will add a new character to the experience of the landscape. This can be achieved by intensifying the existing features of the seven locations and the establishment of a set of rules for their furnishing. It is intended that the locations will slowly "grow."

The various council committees substantially adopted this plan. In addition to a practical study on the technical and legal provisions surrounding natural burial grounds, an examination by Gerda Zijlstra of the cultural aspects of dealing with death in an urbanized area proved a valuable contribution for the further design and realization of this project.

Context

EventArchitectuur proposed three idylls for Lingezegen Park with the themes Mountain, Water, and Forest. These are the three basic landforms that define our experience of the landscape. According to EventArchitectuur, an agricultural landscape park like Lingezegen could benefit from a stronger landscape experience. The idylls all entail a private, contemplative inner world where the visitor can escape the daily hustle and bustle in the landscape. They are places where the visitor can feel connected to the earth, life, and the transience of it. The Mountain Idyll, along the A325 between Arnhem and Nijmegen, has a columbarium wall intended to put urns in. The Water Idyll, east of Rijkerswoerdse Lake, offers memorial plaques for deceased loved ones. The Forest Idyll, near Ressen, is designed as a collection of burial places in an orchard.

Mountain Idyll (Berg Idylle)

Mountain Idyll is a special composition of landscapes and architectural elements that together stage the experience of a hike on a small hill. The idyll consists of a number of slowly ascending terraces, with a long columbarium on one side. Along the border, a varied forest functions as an ecological stepping stone. From the hill are several vistas to the landscape.

Design

The basis of the Mountain Idyll design is a new shape for the terrain. The middle part is raised and forms a hill. Around the hill lies an edge of wooded islands that form an ecological stepping stone. The forestation has a dense character. The water in between the islands provides views over the surrounding area. One of the islands, closest to the river Linge, is the entrance to the site. At the entrance, a pergola gate is overgrown with wild honeysuckle. The gate marks the entry of the idyll and also serves as a picnic spot. Glacial stones with a smooth upper surface invite you to sit down. A wooden bridge connects the entrance island with the hill island.

Taking the route to the hilly main island gives the experience of a delay of time. The constriction of the perspective emphasizes the reflective, introverted character of the place. Once atop the hill, one can look over the scenery. Along the route there is a long ascending wall composed of stacked, recycled pavement tiles. In the wall are niches created for the placement of urns. These are covered with plates of natural stone. Mosses and plants can grow in the crevices and holes in the wall. The north side of the hill offers four rising terraces. Walls of stacked pavement stones absorb the height between the terraces. The height of the walls is forty-five centimeters, so they lend themselves to sitting upon.

Herbal vegetation grows on the terraces. Thin layers of shells increase the lime content of the soil in a number of places, which stimulates the growth of more diverse species. The multi-stemmed birch trees contribute to the refinement of the place in contrast with the vast landscape. A winding path through the herbal garden forms a possible tour of the grounds together with the path along the columbarium.

The vegetation on the south side of the hill is rougher, with currant trees scattered across the hillside. For butterflies, the vegetation is particularly attractive. An oblong water basin, which reflects the air, is included in the slope. The edge of the basin consists of stacked paving stones.

Ecological stepping stone
Mountain Idyll is a stepping stone in the ecological corridor connecting the floodplain of the Waal to that of the Rhine. The composition of the forestation/vegetation is focused on the target species, the White Admiral (*Limenitis camilla*). The vegetation consists of alder, elm, ash, blackthorn, and dewberry in different densities, which provides ecological variation and the picture of a natural forest. The advantage of this is that little management is needed. Natural processes determine the forest's development.

Idylls for Park Lingezegen
Project: Landscape Art
Year: 2006–
Duration: Very long-term, 15–30 years
Team: Paul Kuipers, Herman Verkerk, Gerda Zijlstra, Pieter Wackers, Heilien Tonckens, Feddes Olthof/Berdie Olthof, Nanne Bouma, Veenenbos en Bosch/ Jeroen Bosch, Tim de Weerd, DLG/ Astrid Harsveld
Client: SKOR and the Province of Gelderland
Location: Mountain Idyll in Elst Overbetuwe, Water Idyll in Waterrijk Overbetuwe, Forest Idyll in Ressen
Production: Joop Eilander, Smits Rinsma/Ritso Sikma, DonkerGroen/ Jacko Manse
Photography: EventArchitectuur, Jeroen Bosch
Materials: Recycled paving stones, Belgian blue limestone, gray-painted metal frames, redwood trellis, wooden beams, glacial stones, multi-stemmed birch trees, field flowers, herbal blend vegetation, grass, amelanchier

—

Project 145 / Page 430
Arnhem Fashion Biennale 2007

The Arnhem Fashion Biennale 2007 shows that you can make your own ideal world using fashion. Designers and artists are able to give form to a utopian longing through fashion. We show artists that make use of fashion as a visual arts form. The show was envisaged as a long journey where fantasy worlds and real worlds get mixed up in one continuous promenade. The promenade starts from the top of a hill at the Museum Arnhem. In the monumental halls of the museum, heaps of wooden pallets were stacked to build an artificial and arbitrarily formed landscape. After each hall, the pallet "hills and valleys" transform slowly into pavilions and formal garden layouts with a fountain and a butterfly house, all connected to the fashion on display. In these landscapes, paths for the promenade were cut out and covered with cement flooring on one layer of pallets. The entire installation was kept loose from the existing walls and floors. Continuing the promenade through the sculpture garden of the museum, a steep path led you down the hill towards the ArtEZ Academy of Art & Design, where video presentations of the students of the fashion department could be viewed while relaxing on "soft" pallets, cushions with actual-size pallet print.

From the academy, a path led to a pier on the banks of the Rhine. Here a boat specially designed for the Fashion Biennale took you to the other side of the river, to an abandoned brick factory. In this factory, the floors of the immense industrial halls were totally covered with a single layer of the same wooden pallets. Into this new platform paths and squares were cut out for the promenade and displays of fashion and art installations on the existing floor. The path zigzagged its way through the space, connecting all the squares, and changed its flooring substance with each installation. Walking on mirrors, washing powder, "water," "air," and birdseed enhanced the experience of entering different worlds without losing the overall view of the installations.

Finally, the promenade ended at the Fashion Biennale catwalk hall, the Fashion Biennale shop and restaurant, and a stunning view over the river, the academy, the museum, and the city of Arnhem.

Arnhem Fashion Biennale 2007
Project: Exhibition
Year: 2007
Duration: Medium Term, 1 month
Team: Paul Kuipers, Gent Vranovci, Herman Verkerk

Client: Stichting Arnhem Mode Biënnale
Curator: Piet Paris, Joff
Location: Museum Arnhem, ArtEZ, and a former brick factory
Production: Landstra & De Vries
Graphic design: Maureen Mooren
Photography: Juriaan Langstraat
Materials: Pallets, cement fiberboard, pinewood bars, washing powder, foam, sand, water, plants, non-woven fiber sheets, aluminum scaffolding, mirror

—

Project 149 / Page 384
The Edible City

The exhibition *The Edible City* at the Netherlands Architecture Institute Maastricht showed examples of urban agriculture, self-sustaining cities, food miles, and closed food chains. The exhibition reflected upon the awareness that architecture and design go far beyond mere visual styling, and relate not only to concrete products but also to a wide variety of practically invisible services. The exhibition considered how we have given shape to the production, distribution, and consumption of food.

Practically everything to do with the production and processing of food takes place out of sight of the city-dweller. Most of us do not see our food until it is offered for sale in shops or heaped on a plate. This whole chain of actions is virtually invisible to us. The chain is often thousands of kilometers in length: green beans from Kenya, wine from Chile, lamb from New Zealand, and honey from Central America. Like so many other parts of our lives, our daily food supply has become a globalized affair.

The exhibition presented a cross section of pragmatic proposals and utopian schemes that enable cities and city-dwellers to meet their own food requirements. They ranged from MVRDV's Pig City and Agroparks, to the urban agriculture Cuba found it necessary to develop after the collapse of the Soviet Union. As befits the subject, much of the exhibition was itself edible.

Layout
EventArchitectuur often uses urban design schemes for the layout of (large) exhibitions. The scale factor introduced by this principle turns the exhibitions into a kind of microcosm, in the sense of a replica of the world outside the exhibition. Just like for the 2005 Arnhem Fashion Biennale, EventArchitectuur turned to the principle models of garden layouts as a starting point to design *The Edible City*. This time, however, not the formal and hierarchical layout of baroque gardens were used, but layouts from gardens and agriculture landscapes for food production. Moreover, the exhibition in itself was an example of the way food production can be reintroduced in the city, and even inside a building. The exhibition literally grew food that could be consumed while listening to lectures, reading books, etc., and for special dinners prepared by top chefs. The exhibition also grew in content by inviting different organizations to present themselves to an audience (from freegans to agropark owners), and in this way contribute up-to-date material to the exhibition.

The exhibition space was on the top floor of a linear industrial building with a curved concrete shell roof. This concrete was kept raw on the inside, and divided with linear rooflights from side wall to side wall. The space had some similarity to a greenhouse. Natural light divided the space into compartments. Connecting these compartments to the requirements of the content of the exhibition, we came up with a scheme of three consecutive garden/yards. In the first yard (the Front Yard) food production projects for the city were presented which are technological, optimistic, and large-scale. The second yard (the Court Yard) served as a restaurant/lecture hall/film viewing room with reading tables for interactive use. The third yard (the Back Yard) showed the food production projects for the city that are DIY, small-scale, improvised, and critical. We called them Front Yard, Court Yard and Back Yard in relation to the sequence of formal, social, and informal aspects of the subjects that coincide with the sequence of outside spaces of a building in a city.

Routing
One entered the exhibition space through a pinewood pergola overgrown

by a raspberry bush and with little fig trees on the sides. This pergola ended at a living wall (a wooden structure filled in with a steel maze) full of tomato and cucumber plants placed in the first rooflight zone. Through this wall you entered the first section of the exhibition, the Front Yard. Here the projects were placed horizontally at table height, in between serial growing zones with onions, leeks, etc., similar to big garden centres or fields with crops. The zones were built of neat rows of stackable black plastic crates that made narrow streets to follow to the next compartment, the Court Yard. This yard was surrounded by low greenhouse boxes made of pinewood and transparant plastic, in which vegetables and sprouts grew. You could observe how the vegetables were growing by opening the top of the greenhouse boxes. The space was entered through a normal height greenhouse placed under the second rooflight. Tables were placed in the square for the restaurant and other scheduled activities. After the Court Yard, you entered the Back Yard, where the display of the projects was placed on wooden instead of plastic crates. The layout of this yard was more chaotic and improvised, with different one-on-one models of home growing and kitchen appliances. A row of mini-vegetable gardens (1.5 x 1.5 meters) were placed under the last roof light. After this experience, you retraced your route through the Court Yard and Front Yard on your way back.

The Edible City
Project: Exhibition
Year: 2007
Duration: Medium-term, 4 months
Team: Paul Kuipers, Herman Verkerk
Client: NAi Maastricht
Concept: Guus Beumer
Curators: Debra Solomon (culiblog.org), Anneke Moors, Hans Ibelings
Location: Wiebengahal, Maastricht
Graphic design: Experimental Jetset
Production: Guus van den Akker & Team
Gardening: De Groene Stap, Hans Engelbrecht, Margriet Visser
Photography: Debra Solomon
Materials: Soil, wooden and plastic crates, underlayment, pinewood bars and beams, corrugated polyester sheets, shrink wrap

—

Project 154 / Page 392
Warmoesmarkt

In the notorious Warmoesstraat in Amsterdam, we designed a grocery store complementing Piet Hekker's Bakkerswinkel. The store sold local and regional products. It had a cooking workshop and a special courtyard room with caged birds and greenhouse boxes for cultivated herbs. The black plastic crate became the measuring instrument for the layout of the shop. A little manipulation of the perspective occurred towards the back of the store, emphasizing the little courtyard room slightly elevated from the ground floor.

Warmoesmarkt
Project: Grocery Store
Year: 2008
Duration: Long-term, 2 years
Team: Paul Kuipers, Herman Verkerk
Client: Piet Hekker
Location: Warmoesstraat 135, Amsterdam
Production: Landstra & De Vries
Graphic design: Lesley Moore
Wall drawings: Peter Moeller
Photography: Vincent Zedelius, Paul Kuipers
Materials: Wooden and plastic crates, white tiles, pink lino, perforated underlayment, pinewood bars, metal sheets, shrink wrap, tube lights, nettings, water, paint, pencils

—

Project 156 / Page 408
Changing Ideals

The exhibition was conceived as an architectural study on living and the different planning models this entails. Its starting point was the idea that a renewal of the architecture of living is based on the interaction between "container" and "contained," between architectural invention and changes in the ideals of living. Aspects of mass culture, the avant-garde, modern media, lifestyle, consumption culture, privacy, and appropriation thereby guided the rethinking of the modern house.
The exhibition was conceived in two parts. In the lower hall, the "Salon Imaginaire" was shown, as well as eight positions of ideal houses in a setting for a fair. For the upstairs gallery, Jurgen Bey and Rianne Makkink were

asked to build an installation based on the industrial building that Bey and Makkink inhabited until recently. This hall functioned as their home, office, garage, storage space, production shed, gallery, barnyard, guesthouse, country cottage, school, garden, and laboratory.

The different forms of the house and changing ideals in architecture and modern society were made visible by combining the typology of the salon and that of the fair. The salon was utilized for various meetings and lectures, and consisted of a large carpet surrounded by chairs. The space was encompassed by drapes. The fair was made up of eight booths in which both the *Domus Cosmografica* of the Mauritshuis and the television culture of the Big Brother house were represented, partly with help from typography by Experimental Jetset and photography by Johannes Schwartz.

The rear walls, which consisted of a cast of each plan of the ideal houses, were placed with the mass of the counter-mold in front, allowing for a spatial comparison of the different models. Through such a positioning of L-shaped volumes relative to the cast walls, eight areas emerged in which photographs by Johannes Schwartz evoked an almost life-size, realistic experience of the rooms in the houses. Besides their historical significance, these houses served as timeless models in actuality. Within the exhibition context, each house represented not only a formal language, but was also given a speculative quality. For example, the Mauritshuis stood for representation, Soane's Museum for the collection, and the *Big Brother* house for voyeurism. The selected houses were:
Mauritshuis – Jacob van Campen (representation)
GWS 497 – Winka Dubbeldam (fashion)
House VI – Peter Eisenman (autonomy)
House Visser – Gerrit Rietveld, Aldo van Eyck (meeting)
House of the Future – Alison and Peter Smithson (lifestyle)
Soane's Museum – Sir John Soane (collection)
Big Brother house – Endemol (voyeurism)
BoKlok – IKEA (kit)

Changing Ideals
Project: Exhibition
Year: 2008
Duration: Medium-term, 3 months
Team: Paul Kuipers, Herman Verkerk
Client: NAi Maastricht
Curator: Dirk van den Heuvel
Location: Columns Hall, NAi Maastricht
Graphic design: Experimental Jetset
Production: Guus van den Akker & Team
Photography: Johannes Schwartz
Materials: Pinewood frames, gray colored poplar plates, lace, nettings, IKEA chairs ("Stefan" model customized with gray felt and cardboard), gray custom-made rug from Tretfort goat hair carpeting.

—

Project 159 / Page 418
NL = New Luxury

The brief for the design of this store was to give a new impulse informing regular and potential customers of the excellent designs by Francisco van Benthum and orson + bodil, and give more people the opportunity to try out the products. Besides clothes, they also design accessories that are for sale in limited editions.

The store needed to be something in between a showroom and a shop; more like a salon, although this sounds somewhat "stuffy." The attention that has been given to each garment by the designers and producers should be experienced in the displays and interior of the shop. Moreover, personal attention, often given by the designers themselves, should be a crucial ingredient in this retail concept. The result should be that the customer understands that the clothes of FvB and orson + bodil are not only creating a new look, but also give a new sensitivity and sensation by wearing them.

The concept EventArchitectuur developed concentrates on this "intimate" relation between the garments and the wearer. We closed the shop windows and introduced a self-referential spatial system that served as a container for the garments, and at the same time organized the spaces. The structure treated every single garment as a unique piece.

The shop was situated on a corner and had two floors: a ground floor and basement. The menswear of FvB was located in the basement, while the womens wear of orson + bodil was on the ground floor. They shared the entrance and counter on the ground floor, where customers were welcomed. In the basement, we accentuated the "darkness" of the space by constructing the spatial system out of black MDF, and its length by using repetition, mirrors, and reflecting black glass. On one side of the linear display space was the storage room, and at the end a fitting room. It had a more masculine and industrial feel.

Upstairs, on the ground floor, the spatial system was made out of whitewashed, very thin slices of plywood, to give a more feminine and handcrafted quality. Three spatial containers with an almost identical cross section were placed perpendicular to the length of the store and divided the space in three parts: first, the entrance and counter; second, the "salon" which you entered through an opening in the container and where you were immersed in the "world of orson + bodil"; third, the spacious fitting rooms, which you entered through an opening in the last container.

NL = New Luxury
Project: Fashion Store
Year: 2008
Duration: Long-term, 3 years
Team: Paul Kuipers, Herman Verkerk
Client: orson + bodil, Francisco van Benthum
Location: Jacob Obrechtstraat 20, Amsterdam
Production: Guus van den Akker & Team
Photography: Johannes Schwartz, Guus van den Akker
Materials: Whitewash color ply, black MDF, beige MDF, glass, white perforated board, cotton fabric

—

Project 162 / Page 414
State Alpha

Sigmund Freud considered the dream to be the "guardian of sleep." The exhibition *State Alpha, on the architecture of sleep* examines to what extent the same could be said about architecture. NAi Maastricht presented the exhibition, in which the architecture of sleep was approached in an encyclopedic manner from different perspectives. The exhibition aimed to encourage visitors to reflect upon how architecture organizes our sleep. The subject of sleep was explored as a more psychological inner world, and an examination of how architecture relates to this was made. The exhibition drew upon film and product design to visualize this relationship.

Various aspects of sleep were investigated in six chapters. In "Phenomenology of Sleep," the act of slumber, still an enigma, was highlighted using film clips. Film expert Eric de Kuyper compiled a selection of excerpts that situate the rituals of sleep and waking within their architectural context. The term "Architecture of Sleep" is used by medical science to describe the structure of the sleeping process. In cooperation with the sleep laboratory of the Charité Clinic in Berlin, this chapter showed different modes of observation by researchers. Moreover, "Science of Sleep" compared how other types of (pseudo-scientific) expertise, such as feng shui, deal with sleep and its physical impact on the arrangement of our bedrooms.

The "Dream House" chapter provided a picture of how commercial interests use the concept of the dream house as a means of seduction. Besides examining the dream home within the housing market, the chapter also looked at the house as a symbol within the subconscious. In "Economy of Sleep," the exhibition focused on the opposition between sleep as a gift and revitalizing power, and sleep as a product around which a huge market has developed: consider not just beds, smells, masks, creams, and herbs, but also therapies and medicines.

The final chapter, "Sleep without Architects," presented several examples that break free from the confines of architecture. By exposing the position of the homeless, among others, the chapter questioned the role of architecture and the ways in which it organizes sleep.

Spatial design
While wandering through the exhibition, you felt different kinds of enclosure and your pace was slowed down by the rhythm of the walls and different possibilities to sit, or even lie down. Sometimes the walls stood close to each other and formed a rather narrow corridor; other times the corridor was blocked half way and changed into a room. In this way, the clear zoning system slowly turned into a labyrinth.

The exhibition layout was mainly comprised of thick, wall-like wooden frames that were fully covered with white perforated board. The walls divided the space in a number of corridors with different widths; some walls were straight, some were curved. Both ends of the corridors had windows. You entered these corridors through carved-out openings perpendicular to the walls. A soft curtain made of felt strips hanging in the openings obstructed the view to the next corridor. Dayside (light) and a nightside (dark) manifested throughout the exhibition. These sides were emphasized with different color combinations of the curtains on either side of the corridor and the 98 percent filtering of daylight from one side.

The curtains were made of bedsheets that were silkscreened with an enlargement of the diagram of a sleeping curve (designed by Experimental Jetset) and then stretched around wooden frames. The thick, wall-like wooden frames were fully covered with white perforated board. Information printed on A4 pages was hung from metal pegs specifically made for the perforated board. *State Alpha, on the architecture of sleep* is the first part of a diptych. The second part, in collaboration with TU Delft and Vesteda, was curated by Dirk van den Heuvel under the title *Changing Ideals.*

State Alpha
Project: Exhibition
Year: 2008
Duration: Medium-term, 3 months
Team: Paul Kuipers, Herman Verkerk
Client: NAi Maastricht
Curator: Liquid Frontiers, Sabine Dreher, Christian Muhr
Location: Columns Hall, NAi Maastricht
Graphic design: Experimental Jetset
Production: Guus van den Akker & Team
Photography: Johannes Schwartz
Materials: White perforated board, pinewood beams, silkscreened sheets, metal pegs, ivory-colored felt curtains

—

Project 167, 196 / Page 576
Feeding Platforms for Birds

In the woods of Den Dolder sits a psychiatric institute (formerly named the Willem Arntsz Hoeve) composed of various pavilions dating from 1911 to the present. A history of different agendas in treating patients is physically revealed through these buildings. Herman Verkerk participated in an artist-in-residence program in "Het Vijfde Seizoen," one of the pavilions on the grounds, to investigate this phenomenon. Verkerk found that the pavilions that made direct contact with the surrounding woods were the most inspiring. He decided to give each of the pavilions a feeding platform for birds, in order to enhance this interaction with the trees. He placed the platforms within the gardens; each platform took the shape of the pavilion to which the garden belonged. The aesthetics, the modernist reference, points to the desire for a direct and open relationship with the surrounding woods.

Feeding Platforms for Birds
Project: Installation
Year: 2008, 2011
Clients: Suzanne Oxenaar, Boudewijn van Grunsven (a gift for the clients and staff of Altrecht, Den Dolder)
Location: Altrecht, Den Dolder
Production: Altrecht & Monica de Vries, Paul Kuipers
Photography: Johannes Schwartz, Paul Kuipers
Materials: Multiplex, Betonplex, untreated steel tubes, wooden sticks

—

Project 171 / Page 444
Unresolved Matters

Social Utopias Revisited. Three books on distinctive reform movements were chosen by the curator as a starting point for research on social utopias:

Garden Cities of To-morrow by Ebenezer Howard (1898)
Befreites Wohnen (Liberated Living) by Sigfried Giedion (1929)
Design for the Real World by Victor Papanek (1971)

These three "statements" in the form of books led to three different chapters of the exhibition: Social Green, Social Sculpture, and Social Transparency. By analyzing different urban design schemes from the three periods when the books were published, we came up with the following organization.

In Social Green, following the analogy with the urban design schemes of garden towns and allotments, we made a collection of smaller units where you would be able to experience inside and outside, and which would be distributed in such a way (diagonally, for instance) as enhance the informal character. The basic material would be wood.

In Social Transparency, in analogy to the urban design schemes for high-rises in parks, we envisioned compact transparent forms in which the objects were stacked on top of each other, and where the surroundings remained empty, free space. The main materials would be glass, lightweights, and metal.

In Social Sculpture, we made a grid in analogy with the urban designs by Superstudio for a grid that would encompass the world. In this grid, we projected islands of irregular shape that would be the surviving spaces to escape the grid. In terms of the color of the materials, there would only be one dominant contrast: black and white.

Unresolved Matters
Project: Exhibition
Year: 2009
Duration: Medium-term, 1 month
Team: Paul Kuipers, Herman Verkerk
Client: Utrecht Manifest
Curator: Claudia Banz
Location: Centraal Museum Utrecht
Production: Landstra & De Vries
Graphic design: Metahaven, Vinca Kruk, Daniel van der Velden
Photography: Johannes Schwartz
Materials: Black plastic tubes, black MDF, pinewood, poplar wood, white board, black tape, white perforated board, reinforced glass

—

Project 181, 182, 187 / Page 532
SPACES

In 2003, EventArchitectuur introduced a series of libraries, desks, and shelves, all based on the idea of the cross-section. These designs immediately caught the imagination of a wider public, thanks to their surprising visual quality based on the irregular rhythm of voids. The international media was also intrigued, seeing the designs as questioning the classic relationship between an object and the surrounding space. It seemed that it would not be long before the first interpretations of this idea would be recognized in the market.

After several years, however, it was obvious that the full potential of the design idea would not be picked up by the industry. In response, EventArchitectuur decided to introduce SPACES, a tool to create a variety of designs, as well as a limited series of unique products. SPACES not only breaks the classic boundaries between objects and SPACES, but also between designer and user, offering a system of building blocks. These blocks contain the genetic code of the design, while supplying tools for the user to create his or her own interpretation.

We made three distinctly different cabinets with a fixed size (30 ×80 ×220 centimeters) that allows for three ways of organizing the modules.
The configuration is dictated by the specific content:
1. A cabinet for books, magazines, and compact discs
2. A cabinet for folders
3. A cabinet for books of different sizes, ranging from pocket books to coffee table books
In the construction of the cabinets, the emphasis lies in the possibility to transport and rearrange the individual modules. The cabinets can all be extended and transformed.

SPACES
Project: EventFurnituur
Year: 2010
Team: Paul Kuipers, Tal Erez,

Herman Verkerk
Client: EventArchitectuur
Location: Amsterdam, Milan
Production: Landstra & De Vries
Photography: Johannes Schwartz
Materials: Birch wood, poplar wood, Betonplex, tulipwood, oak wood, Velcro dots, dowels

—

Project 185 / Page 446
Hygiene – The story of a museum

The exhibition told the story of the German Hygiene Museum in Dresden through different chapters: Museum as Discourse, Museum as Practice, and Museum as Ideology, or how a private initiative of the inventor of Odol mouthwash becomes a huge factor in informing the public on health issues. The chapters highlighted the role the museum played in society in different periods.

The first chapter was called Museum as Discourse. Here the emphasis was on the development of technical equipment to make the invisible inside of man visible. The exhibition route ran from the nineteenth-century Jaarmarkt examples showing the exterior effects of illnesses on skin resulting from bad hygiene, to the microscope, Röntgen and Spalteholz, and the "pièce de résistance," the Gläserner Mensch, in which the inside of the body of a man could be viewed in all transparency for the first time. The scenography for this chapter was the development towards transparency.

The second chapter was the Museum as Practice, displaying different products made by the museum for distributing its knowledge and education on hygiene, ranging from models and drawings to traveling exhibitions and posters. The scenography of this part copied the look and feel of the exhibitions produced by the museum in that period.

The third chapter, Museum as Ideology, dealt with the different political periods the museum has coped with, from the Weimar Republic, when unemployment and alcoholism were addressed as influences on hygiene, and the racial issues of the Third Reich period, to the dangers of sexual liberty in the German Democratic Republic. The scenography of this third chapter was basically a play with points of view of the public.

Hygiene – The story of a museum
Project: Exhibition
Year: 2010
Duration: Medium-term, 3 months
Team: Paul Kuipers, Herman Verkerk
Client: Marres, House for Contemporary Culture
Curator: Claudia Banz
Location: Marres Maastricht
Production: Landstra & De Vries
Graphic design: Maureen Mooren
Photography: Johannes Schwartz, EventArchitectuur
Materials: Pinewood beams and bars, corrugated polyester sheets, glass, transparent acrylic sheets, white perforated board, black felt

—

Project 189, 190 / Page 566
Piet Paris, book launch and pop-up store / Ghost Department Store

EventArchitectuur designed a presentation of the work of fashion illustrator Piet Paris for the occasion of the launch of his new book, *Piet Paris Fashion Illustrations*. This was to be a hybrid presentation: a gallery as well as a pop-up store for products designed by Piet Paris, and a short overview of his published illustrations.

For this project, we had the opportunity to use the Hirsch Building, one of the first nineteenth-century department stores in Amsterdam, famous for luxurious tailor-made fashion, located on the Leidseplein. After the closing of the Hirsch department store in 1976, the spaces were converted into a standard office building, where the richly decorated interiors were destroyed, ornamentation was removed, and only traces of its lavish past remained on the ceilings and columns. Out of this emptiness, we sought to evoke the aura of a commercial space that would function as a carrier for the works of Piet Paris, recalling the fashion history of the Hirsch department store. The so-called Ghost Department Store functioned as an abstract reference to the classic routing system through department stores whereby corridors frame a series of islands representing different brands. These islands were themed following the chapters of Piet Paris's book, with each island representing a chapter. On the vertical panes of the islands we displayed illustrations, and on the horizontal panes the magazines in which the illustrations were published.

As an extra, we added islands that presented Piet Paris products, such as tiles manufactured by Koninklijke Tichelaar Makkum, a new collection of tableware, a T-shirt collection, and a book corner featuring the latest Piet Paris publication.

Piet Paris, Ghost Department Store
Project: Presentation, Installation
Year: 2010
Duration: Short-term, 10 days
Team: Paul Kuipers, Michiel Zegers, Bram Burger, Herman Verkerk
Client: Studio Piet Paris
Location: Hirsch Building, Amsterdam
Production: Landstra & De Vries + EventArchitectuur
Graphic design: Coppens Alberts
Photography: Johannes Schwartz
Materials: White perforated board, tie-wraps, templates for signage

—

Project 193 / Page 504
Out of Storage

Out of Storage offers a glimpse into the dynamics within a collecting art institute and reveals functions that usually take place behind closed doors. The project consisted of a temporary museum showing hundreds of artworks from the collection of FRAC Nord-Pas de Calais. Some of the works were on display during the whole exhibition period, while others were replaced over the course of time. The visitor could take several different routes through the exhibition, each route providing insight from diverse experts about the different functions of FRAC Nord-Pas de Calais, such as restoration, education, research, and presentation. The architecture of the exhibition venue De Timmerfabriek in Maastricht was used to create three distinctive typologies of museum interiors.

The first type is the so-called "salon" style with cabinets, filtered light, and clearly defined spaces commonly used in the nineteenth century. The second type is the twentieth-century gallery space, the so-called "white cube," flooded with light and an open floor plan. The third type is the "viewing depot," where display and storage of artworks are combined. This type is being tested by several institutions (including Schaulager Basel and Collectiegebouw Rotterdam) in the twenty-first century as a new model for display. The accompanying catalogue, designed by Maureen Mooren, was based on the compilation of separate A4 leaflets, a file sheet for each art object in the collection. Starting with simple A4-sized pinewood frames, we built structures for display and other uses for the museum. The frames and surfaces of the structures adapted themselves to the typology of the museum interior.

Out of Storage
Project: Temporary Museum
Year: 2011
Duration: Medium-term, 8 months
Team: Paul Kuipers, Bram Burger, Herman Verkerk
Client: Marres Projects, FRAC Nord-Pas de Calais
Location: Timmerfabriek, Maastricht
Production: KLIEF
Graphic design: Maureen Mooren, Corine Datema
Photography: Johannes Schwartz
Materials: Poplar wood (untreated and painted), white perforated board, pinewood bars, birch wood, aluminum scaffolding

—

Project 194 / Page 482
Opera Aperta / Loose Work

In the Dutch Pavilion, 54th International Art Exhibition, Venice Biennale (IT), curator Guus Beumer presented artists Joke Robaard, Johannes Schwartz, and Barbara Visser, designer Maureen Mooren, architects Herman Verkerk and Paul Kuipers (EventArchitectuur), landscape architect Ernst van der Hoeven, author Sanneke van Hassel, and composer Yannis Kyriakides. At his invitation, they all worked on a collaborative project, entitled *Opera Aperta / Loose Work*.

Opera Aperta / Loose Work has its origins in a linking of the notions "national identity" and "community." In the Netherlands, the concept of community has been uniquely embodied in the nation's cultural infrastructure. This intricate infrastructure has been developed by the Dutch government since the 1960s. The result is a public system of production, distribution, and reflection on art and culture in which the position of the artist in society is firmly embedded. However, this cultural infrastructure has begun to lose public support, and has become a subject of major debate. Consequently, the public space, the social position of art and the artist, as well as the notion "community," need to be redefined in the Netherlands.

Opera Aperta / Loose Work implicitly revealed the potential of this cultural infrastructure. From the outset, a decision was made to use a multidisciplinary group of participants. Despite their backgrounds in various disciplines, they share a fascination with the issue of representation. In addition, the Mondriaan Foundation and the curator forged alliances with the Dutch Foundation for Literature and the Performing Arts Fund. These have resulted in commissions for the author Sanneke van Hassel and the composer Yannis Kyriakides.

In addition to this collaborative working methodology, *Opera Aperta / Loose Work* also referred to the opera model and the idea of a succession in time involving different scenes, an intermission, a powerful composition, an accompanying libretto, voices, a stage set, lighting, and costumes. This model offers both a conflicting and seductive point of departure for the blending of different disciplines and commissions. The title refers to a 1962 publication by Umberto Eco.

Three distinctive backdrops

By taking the given venue as a literal starting point, we searched for a way to redefine the way art is perceived; not as a series of individual contributions, but to blend or integrate the works into the spatial design of the pavilion designed by Gerrit Rietveld in 1954, his take on the "white cube." We interpreted his design as a theater for the arts by (re-)defining the three parallel walls perpendicular to the entrance as backdrops, staging the artworks and the visitors as active participants in the production of art.

The first backdrop was the "Outside Wall" of the pavilion, in front of which the garden scene took place, shaped by an étagère by Ernst van den Hoeven. The étagère was filled with plants that show their beauty by an inherited illness. The actual entrance of the pavilion was transformed into a movie theater entrance with ticket booth and ceiling lights.

The second backdrop was the "Stage Wall," the proscenium arch made by two of the interior walls of the pavilion enhanced by an outline of the wings of the theater. In front of this backdrop, the foyer and auditorium merged. The public was also merged into one by listening to Yannis Kyriakides's composition, *Covertures*. Visitors could read the critiques of the show collected by Maureen Mooren and listen to neglected members of the audience who have been given a voice by Sanneke van Hassel.

The mirroring stage was empty, and the public was able to go backstage. Here, placed before the third backdrop, the "Back Wall" of the pavilion in the wings of the theater, the artworks of Joke Robaard, Barbara Visser, and Johannes Schwartz told stories about loss, prompting, absence, and national (political) identity.

The story of the empty wall behind Rembrandt's *The Night Watch* at the Rijksmuseum, the story of the painting *Who's Afraid of Red, Yellow and Blue* by Barnett Newman, eternally waiting in the wings of the Stedelijk Museum, the whispering echoes of the title of this painting that linger on like a prompt. How or if a hole in the social fabric can be mended like mending a weaving error was the question asked to a group of experts from different fields, and then documented in a video and images. An abstract painting photographed in the House of Commons in The Hague addressed the difficulty of representation in the political arena.

The image was accompanied by a pianola playing *The Statesman*, a composition by Kyriakides. Dummy book props with titles that are an inspiration for the artists were placed in the huge cabinet. On the bridge, or at the backdrop in the theater wings, the public suddenly became part of the scene.

Opera Aperta / Loose Work
Project: Installation
Year: 2011
Duration: Medium-term, 6 months
Team: Paul Kuipers, Herman Verkerk
Client: Mondriaan Foundation
Curator: Guus Beumer
Location: Dutch Pavilion (in the Giardini), Venice Biennale (IT)
Artists' collective: Barbara Visser, Ernst van der Hoeven, Herman Verkerk, Johannes Schwartz, Joke Robaard, Maureen Mooren, Paul Kuipers, Sanneke van Hassel, Yannis Kyriakides
Production: Landstra & De Vries
Graphic design: Maureen Mooren
Photography: Johannes Schwartz
Materials: Pine wood, metal frames, reused stairs, carpet, mirrors, tube lights, veneer, foam, linen, paper

—

Project 197, 223 / Page 546
Design for Download

By invitation from Droog design, based on their appreciation for the SPACES project and to further examine the potential of what the online environment can offer design, EventArchitectuur reached the conclusion that merging the simplicity of online interfaces with new manufacturing possibilities allows for a dialogue to grow between the designer and the user about their objects and their surroundings. We therefore offer a platform that challenges the market for custom-made objects and stimulates an exchange of ideas about different products and services.

As designers, we offer interfaces and design communication tools with which, within certain parameters, users can choose, create, or finish their own optimal design products. They will be able to execute certain designs themselves, bid on different digital design proposals, bring or send the execution files to a carpenter, or communicate and exchange design proposals on an open-source platform.

The Design for Download platform has two different departments. A different approach is taken towards interactivity and customization in each. The first deals with programmable furniture (1.a & 1.b). The second experiments with the digital one-off (2).

1.a Facades & Functions
Facades & Functions uses a simple interface and standardized wood sheets cut into interlocking pieces to create a growing, almost limitless collection of furniture.
By providing a toolbox of archetypal furniture, pieces like the cabinet, closet, or desk, the user can choose his or her customized model, as well as the level of involvement in the manufacturing process. Knowledge and examples are offered and compiled, helping the user with the choice of materials and other tips, while the Make Me network (similar to the FabLab network) creates the link to manufacturing possibilities.

1.b Boxorama
Boxorama allows the user to create furniture by arranging boxes of different proportions and scales on a standard cut of twelve-millimeter wood. While the boxes are pre-determined, the composition is left open. When the user is satisfied, the program calculates a construction envelope.
This leads to 3D furniture that maintains the playfulness and openness of building blocks on the one hand, while transforming it into a functional fixed piece on the other.

2. Digital One-Offs
The digital environment and downloadable designs challenged us to reexamine the notion of the one-off. What does it mean to create files that are one-offs? EventArchitectuur has launched a series of time-based events that explore this notion, as well as the effects of the Internet on our perception of the interior. The first online event offered a public sphere for our most intimate environment: our interior. It provides a place to debate, explore, and see real interiors of potential clients. In the form of a competition,

EventArchitectuur presented five of the uploaded client interiors with a unique design, made specifically for their space using the SPACES furniture system.

Design for Download
Project: EventFurnituur
Year: 2012
Team: Tal Erez, Herman Verkerk
Client: Droog Design
Location: Milan, Amsterdam
Production: Landstra & De Vries, CNC Milling De Waal
Photography: Johannes Schwartz
Materials: HPL, plywood, varnish, plastics, software
www.studioludens.com/www/droog/FacadesAndFunctions.swf
www.studioludens.com/www/droog/BoxORama.swf
http://www.droog.com/webshop/product/box-o-rama-l-custom

—

Project 204 / Page 492
Playboy Architecture, 1953–1979
The exhibition *Playboy Architecture, 1953–1979* explored the crucial roles modern architecture and design played in constructing the Playboy lifestyle. This relationship between branding, image-making, and identity creation had been thoroughly researched by Prof. Beatriz Colomina and her PhD students at Princeton University for several years. Princeton joined forces with Bureau Europa, an architecture and design platform in the south of the Netherlands, to turn the research content into an exhibition.
The exhibition was shown at Bureau Europa from September 2012 until February 2013.

Playboy Architecture addressed several sub-themes around the notion of constructing *Playboy* and its use of design and modern architecture. For the exhibition, different pavilions each represented a specific sub-theme showing the relation of *Playboy* to design and architecture. Although the structure and system of elements in the pavilions were identical – prefab wooden poles and planks partly covered with white perforated boards, bubble wrap, and non-woven fibers – the shape and cladding of each pavilion adapted to its particular theme.

All pictorial content was processed by graphic design studio Experimental Jetset, who attempted to reproduce all material as it appeared in its original printed context. Immediately recognizable as blown-up fragments, clearly underlining the physical dimension of print, these images were then printed on long strips of paper, functioning as a "skin" (or wallpaper) for the pavilions, creating a collage-like tapestry of photographic and typographic material.

All the materials used for cladding the individual pavilions corresponded with the exhibition's topics or sub-themes. In addition to the pavilions and the banners, the exhibition showed a collection of *Playboy* magazines from 1953 through 1979, two models (the Playboy Townhouse and the Playboy Bunny Jet), several video clips relating to the content of *Playboy*, three soundscapes, and a selection of five design chairs.

Playboy Architecture, 1953–1979
Project: Exhibition
Year: 2012
Duration: Medium-term, 4 months
Team: Paul Kuipers, Herman Verkerk
Client: Bureau Europa, Princeton University
Curator: Beatriz Colomina
Graphic design: Experimental Jetset
Location: Bureau Europa, Maastricht
Production: Brand, Broek & Erkens with Landstra & De Vries
Soundscape: Femke Dekker
Photography: Johannes Schwartz
Materials: Prefab untreated pinewood poles and planks, custom-made white perforated boards (holes of different diameters), bubble wrap and non-woven fibers, corrugated metal sheets, water, plastic sheet, cameras, monitors, carpet, mirrors, cushions, blankets, and sheets

—

Project 216 / Page 570
Elegant Scaffolding

When Ellen Blumenstein was appointed creative director of the KunstWerke Berlin in 2013 – which has been located on Auguststrasse 69 for more than twenty years – she aimed to make the institute's activities more visible and tangible. She wanted to show that the content as well as the venue are permanently being transformed, and that both public and private events can take place there. Most importantly she wanted to use the former function of the factory building as a metaphor for production – in this case, for the making of art, design, and publications, but also to make a community. Having an affinity with our work, she asked EventArchitectuur to join the team to develop these ideas.

This state of permanent transformation is very close to our own way of working. We often refer to our works as having the qualities of a Brechtian theater piece. They are constructed realities and are shown as propositions, not as reality itself. Of course, they eventually become a reality, but we hope it is not in a fixed way. For each project, we try to communicate a story that the client would like to tell. We believe that architecture and spaces can tell stories: an *architecture parlante*.

For this assignment, we tried to emphasize the "always under construction" condition of the institute. We came up with the idea of the scaffold to symbolize this condition. We tried to think of what a more permanent scaffold could look like, and what kind of functional and aesthetic qualities scaffolding could have, besides making facades, walls, floors, and ceilings accessible for repair. We developed a structure made of vertical aluminum parts and horizontal wooden parts.

This structure can be assembled from prefabricated units and can grow in different directions. The structures have various scales that correspond to different functions or uses. They can be used as seats, benches, tables, displays, cupboards, desks, bookshelves, facades, billboards, and pavilions according to the scenario for each of the spaces, either inside or outside of KunstWerke. Because the program for the institute is forever in development, we think the flow of possibilities will be kept open by introducing this structural approach, while at the same time giving an identity to this state of flux.

Elegant Scaffolding
Project: Installation
Year: 2013
Team: Paul Kuipers, Herman Verkerk
Client: Ellen Blumenstein
Location: KunstWerke Berlin
Production: Landstra & De Vries, EventArchitectuur
Photography: Paul Kuipers
Materials: Birch multiplex, aluminum rectangular tube, color ply, rubber hammer

—

Project 224 / Page 550
IABR 2014 – Urban by Nature

Landscape architect Dirk Sijmons, curator of the 2014 International Architecture Biennale Rotterdam (IABR), claims that we can only solve the world's environmental problems if we solve the problems of the city. Looking through the lens of landscape architecture, the 2014 edition of the IABR, entitled *Urban by Nature*, redefines the way we deal with urban challenges by analyzing the relationship between urban society and nature, and between city and landscape.

Taking place at the Kunsthal Rotterdam, the exhibition addressed these issues by showcasing ninety-six projects divided into five chapters. To achieve a certain aesthetic coherence amidst the abundance of projects, we asked graphic design office Experimental Jetset to work only with DIN sizes and to request that each participating project detach the text from the images. In doing so, it was possible to clarify the position the project took in the context of the exhibition.

The five chapters of the exhibition each had their own identity, relating their content as well as their aesthetics to the distinct different spaces of the Kunsthal. For instance, the theme of "A Planet Cultivated" fitted perfectly with Hall 1, which looks out over the beautiful park designed by Yves Brunier and has a wooden floor, five huge columns covered in tree bark, and a black ceiling with neon lights that look like an abstract starry sky with comets.

Moreover, the Kunsthal was the perfect venue to design a "route architecturale" that guided the visitor along each of the different stages of the themes addressed by *Urban by Nature*. This inspired us to use the design for the Danteum by

Giuseppe Terragni as a comparative tool to define the route. While the Danteum stages the voyage of a pilgrim traveling to "Heaven," we staged the different moments in our relationship towards our planet.

1. "A Planet Cultivated" dealt with our lasting connection to the earth and was organized like a productive garden. Five tree trunks functioned as columns in this large hall, around which some projects were mounted. Two specific structures within the garden layout stood out. One was a tent construction that contained the results of the Planet Texel project, displayed like a panorama. The other was a "street" between two pavilions, in which the story of nature conservation by the World Wildlife Fund was told.

2. "Exploring the Underground" began with a hole in the pavement. Going through the hole, one delved deeply into the earth. The long, narrow, windowless corridor contained projects that dealt with going progressively deeper underground towards the end. At the end the route continued, going up a "life-saving" stairway to reach the next chapters.

3. "Urban Landscape" and "Climate Change" were where the results of the "Post Sandy" competition were "floating" on structures (folding tables) that balanced on an open metal floor grille. Light flooded in from the glass plank facade from floor to ceiling. Turning a corner, one reached the next chapter.

4. "The Urban Metabolism" consisted of a complex skyline of a ready-made metal shelving system, forming a number of corridors that each showed projects that dealt with elements that the city is transporting and transforming, like water, sand, air, cargo, people, biota, etc. Most global environmental problems are due to the malfunctioning of urban metabolism. By improving and/or combining different flows through the city, one can improve living conditions and reduce waste. On the way back through this spacious "factory hall," without columns and compartmented through shed lights on the roof, Project Atelier Rotterdam showed its models and
huge graphics for the implementation of each of the metabolism "streams" into the urban fabric of Rotterdam.

5. The layout for the final chapter, "Strategies for the Urban Landscape," was built around the existing structure and walls of a windowless space on the top floor of the Kunsthal. Like a network web spun over the existing fabric, it showed the layering and intertwining of functions and artifacts that form the new urban landscape. Urbanization is becoming a challenge for landscape architecture; urban planning difficulties are arising in the countryside. Is it possible to plan on the scale of the urban landscape? Next to the hanging structures showing the relevant projects, light boxes placed in a curving wall displayed images of the new urban landscape that can be found in all corners of the world, whether planned or unplanned. Project Atelier Brabantstad showed research results on a huge map woven on a tapestry (the urban tapestry of the metropolitan province of Brabant), with explanations on a slightly tilted desk in front of it. Here, the "route architecturale" ended with a top view of the metabolism hall.

IABR 2014 – Urban by Nature
Project: Exhibition
Year: 2014
Duration: Medium-term, 3 months
Team: Paul Kuipers, Michiel Zegers, Herman Verkerk
Client: IABR
Curator: Dirk Sijmons
Location: Kunsthal, Rotterdam
Graphic design: Experimental Jetset
Production: Bart Cuppens, Landstra & De Vries, KLIEF, Koert Verberne, Leendert Jan Brand, Arjan Broek
Photography: Johannes Schwartz
Materials: Ecoplex 38 mm, black MDF, white perforated board, birch and poplar plywood, pinewood bars, pine logs, sand, moss, stones, woodchips, gravel, black plastic tubes, black foam board, paper, corrugated polyester sheets

—

Project 236 / Page 580
Temporary Fashion Museum

While some Dutch museums include

fashion in their collections, there has never been a national fashion museum. The New Institute decided to investigate the possibilities of a fashion museum by transforming itself into one for eight months.

With the Temporary Fashion Museum, the New Institute focused not on the unique quality of a designer or clothing, but on the underlying structures and strategies of fashion as a system. One by one, the various manifestations of fashion are reviewed, from seductive to dire, from conservative to innovative, and from critical to wasteful.

What is the state of fashion in the years 2015/16?
What do designers think of their discipline?
How do they feel about the future?
What issues determine the current trends in fashion?
And above all, what role do we as users play within the global fashion system?

A tour through the temporary fashion museum
The assignment was to stage a temporary fashion museum using the complete public area of the New Institute in Rotterdam; that is, including the exhibition spaces as well as other facilities such as the bookshop, the café, and the lobby spaces. The spatial presentation of the most commercialized art form – fashion – is usually extravagant and realized with huge budgets. Nowadays, the garment collections and (fashion) magazine archives are mostly privatized by the fashion houses themselves. Because of the different experiences with both retail and museum environments in showing and selling fashion, we thought it would be a good idea to mix the two. It also made sense not to imitate, but rather to produce a new environment where the two can meet.

From the outside, the message was clear. The museum would not compete with retail, but rather start a dialogue with it. First, through the "shop window" displays seen floating above the water in the main hall and the visual campaign of Maureen Mooren, which combined a professionally glamorous female body with design for garments made of confetti and Post-its. In front of the entrance stood an abstract fragment of the department store perfume booth. Once inside, the visitor was overwhelmed by a new perfume, "Du Parc," made for the museum by Alessandro Gualtieri. Racks and counters with empty bottles emphasized that the fragrance is the main element on show here. It simultaneously symbolized the ephemeral quality of fashion and the financial cork on which the fashion system floats.

A hostess welcomed visitors to the museum; she would be the first of the guides, helpers, and shop assistants that one encountered while roaming through the exhibitions, displays, and shops. After this, the visitor entered the lobby, which was packed with different experiences, all defined by surfaces and claddings showing various uses of foam. The cloakroom was an experience in itself, and was placed in the center of the space. Here, the garments visitors donated could temporarily end up on display on one of the models by Niek Pulles, which were placed in the shop window. The counter, the bookshop, and the café each received a new look through a combination of foam and wood constructions.

Pumporama
Specially for the Pumporama (an improvised shoe showroom) Peterson + Stoop made their signature pump in sizes 28 to 48 so that visitors big and small could experience how fashion forms our bodies and postures and influences our movements.

The Now
Each season the fashion industry produces thousands of designs, from which the fashion press almost magically selects the most characteristic silhouettes. For the Temporary Fashion Museum, Jop van Bennekom of the magazine Fantastic Man and Penny Martin of The Gentlewoman chose the most iconic pieces of the spring/summer 2016 season.

The first exhibition hall was divided into three distinct spatial areas, each containing an exhibition: The Cloister, The Temple, and The Archive.

1. The Cloister contained a speculative history of Dutch fashion, told in eight

different stages, each representing a decade in the Dutch collective history, emphasizing that fashion statements were defined more by groups than by a singular designer.

2. The Temple, the area under the entresol, was transformed into a temporary temple celebrating four all-time fashion favorites: the white shirt, the red lipstick, the color black, and the high heel.

3. The Archive, at the center of the hall, was dedicated to the collecting of fashion in two guises; the collector for individual use, where visitors could ask to browse further in the archive of the collector with the help of an assistant, and the vintage shop, where one could actually buy an item from the ever-changing collection.

In the basement of the exhibition hall, visitors found a humorous collection of architectural drawings from the archive of Het Nieuwe Instituut, dating from the end of the nineteenth century to the 1990s, with renderings of people like extras walking around in the latest fashion of their day.

The corridor of the second exhibition hall was completely dedicated to "Hacked," a project by label VSB. Mainly reacting to the overproduction of ready-to-wear clothes, VSB bought the overproduction of the latest collections of H&M and hacked the designs to enable them to (re-)enter the market. The exhibition itself hacked the spatial installation left over from the previous exhibition that occupied the space (dedicated to glass), and new displays were thrown over the old ones. One first encountered the retail environment for the newly hacked clothes, including changing rooms, staff, and hip music; from there one could walk through a corridor explaining the campaign, followed by some showcases featuring the process of transforming the garments and sneakers into new fashion items. After passing a pile of the newly collected overproduction, one entered the storage space, where the total range of the new products could be seen, touched, and purchased.

On the third floor, an installation by artist/fashion designer Connie Groenewegen confronted visitors with the harsh reality of fashion data, giving a glimpse of ways out of the polluting and discriminatory industry. She formed a sweatshop together with a group of students and shredded a huge number of leftover fleece garments (the most polluting fiber), making them into one large, unending thread with which new fabrics can be woven. From here, visitors went down again to the first floor where a haberdashery was installed that sells beautiful new fabrics on the roll, offering patterns to actually make a dress or a pair of trousers on the spot, with the help of a few sewing machines and experienced seamstresses and dressmakers.

Temporary Fashion Museum
Project: Temporary Museum
Year: 2015/16
Duration: Medium-term, 8 months
Team: Gabriel Maher, Raphaël Coutin, Lucas Muñoz, Studio Makkink & Bey (Rianne Makkink), Herman Verkerk
Client: Het Nieuwe Instituut
Location: Het Nieuwe Instituut, Rotterdam
Production: Landstra & De Vries
Graphic design: Maureen Mooren
Photography: Johannes Schwartz
Materials: Betonplex (18 mm), foam (in different densities, sizes, and colors), poplar wood, metal stud, prefab aluminum racks, carpet, paving stones, pavers, glass, mirrors, marble, roof bitumen, underlayment, aluminum diamond plate, black MDF with white HPL coatings, steel rectangular tubes, printed wallpaper, white tiles, black flannel

project index

Underlined page numbers refer to the visual archive of EA projects in this book and to the corresponding entries for each in the project data section.

index a–z

Unless otherwise indicated, all cities and other locations are in the Netherlands.

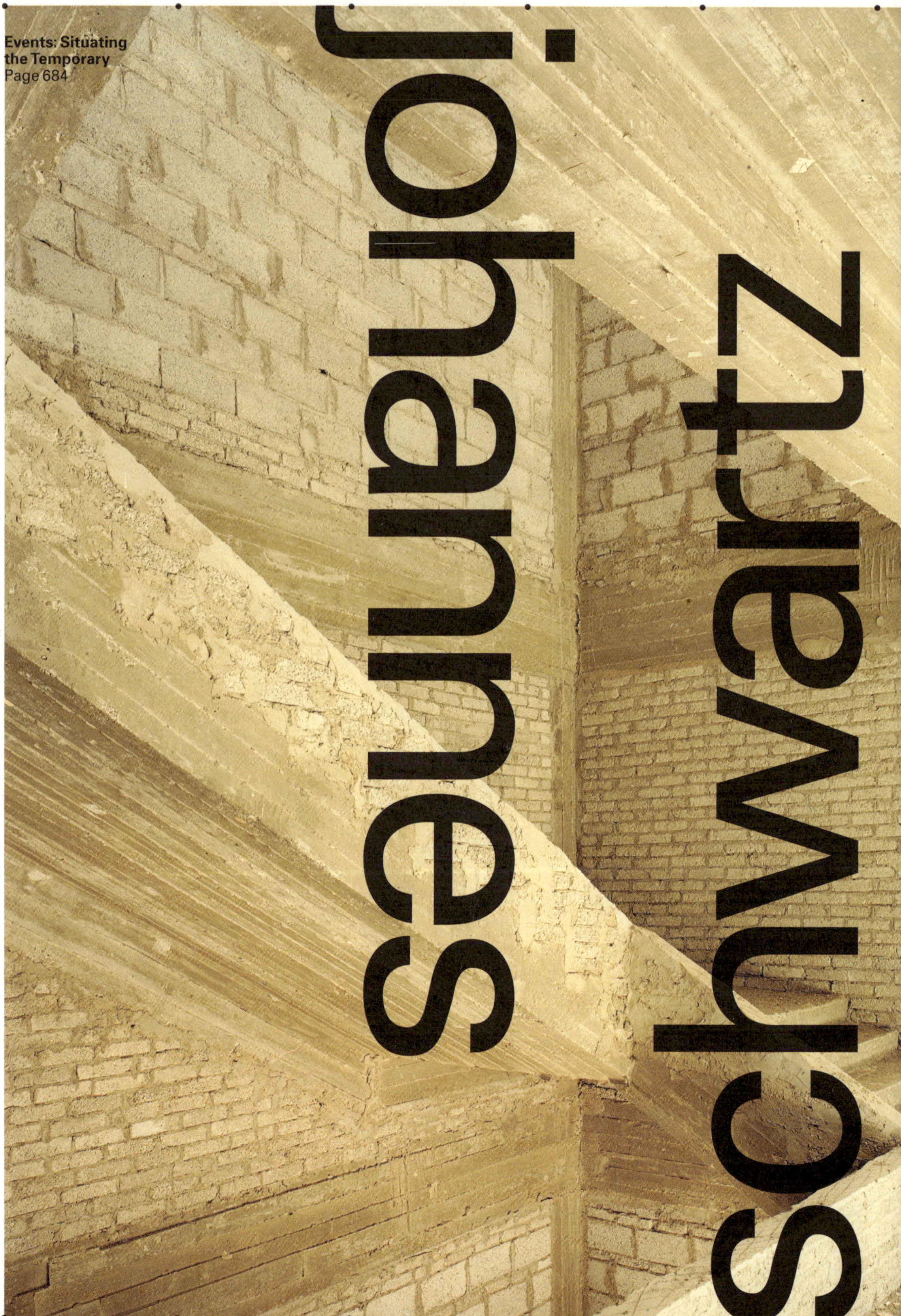
johannes
schwartz

Johannes Schwartz
Treppen, 2006
Page 685

Johannes Schwartz
Treppen, 2006
Page 687

Johannes Schwartz
Treppen, 2006
Page 689

Johannes Schwartz
Treppen, 2006
Page 691

Johannes Schwartz
Treppen, 2006
Page 693

biographies

AB Cultural Producers
AB Cultural Producers are Anne Hoogewoning and Bonnie Dumanaw. Together they share fifteen years of work experience within the cultural sector, including involvement with the Foundation for Visual Arts, Design, and Architecture (now the Mondriaan Fund) in Amsterdam. The two joined forces in 2014 to support visual artists, designers, and architects in the development and visibility of their own work. Depending on the type of project – whether it is a concept, book, website, exhibition, or manifestation – they take on different roles in fundraising, advice, guidance, and research.

Angelidakis, Andreas
Andreas Angelidakis describes himself as "an architect who doesn't build." Instead, he has developed an artistic voice that switches between the languages of architecture, curating, writing, and the Internet. He often speaks about spaces, buildings, and the society that inhabits them, with the exhibition format acting as both a vehicle for ideas and the medium for his artistic practice. Among the exhibitions Angelidakis has worked on are *The System of Objects* (co-curator and architect); *Heaven*, 2nd Athens Biennale, 2009 (architect); the 3rd Thessaloniki Biennale of Contemporary Art, 2011 (architect); Deste Foundation, Athens, 2013; *Fin de Siècle* at the Swiss Institute, New York, 2014 (curator and architect); XII Baltic Triennial at CAC Vilnius, 2015 (architect and participant).

Banz, Claudia
Claudia Banz is an art historian, curator, researcher, and head of the Department of Art and Design at the Museum für Kunst und Gewerbe (MKG) in Hamburg. She also teaches history of art, fashion, and design at several universities and academies of art. She has curated various international and interdisciplinary exhibitions, among them *Unresolved Matters: Social Utopias Revisited* in 2009 at Centraal Museum, Utrecht, and *Fast Fashion: The Dark Sides of Fashion* (2015/16) at the MKG. Banz is co-editor and author of *Dressed: Art en Vogue* and editor of *Social Design: Gestalten für die Transformation von Gesellschaft*.

Blumenstein, Ellen
Ellen Blumenstein holds a master's in literature, musicology, and media studies. Living in Berlin, she currently works as a curator and author for contemporary art. From 2013 to 2016 she was chief curator at KW Institute for Contemporary Art in Berlin. Her curatorial practice is international in scope and often involves collaborating with visual artists and other curators to develop monographic and thematic exhibitions that explore the possibilities and limitations of contemporary art.

Colomina, Beatriz
Beatriz Colomina is an architectural historian and theorist who has written extensively on questions of architecture and media, and whose work has been published in over twenty-five languages. She is a professor of Architecture and Founding Director of the interdisciplinary Program in Media and Modernity at Princeton University. Her books include *Manifesto Architecture: The Ghost of Mies* (2014), *Clip/Stamp/Fold: The Radical Architecture of Little Magazines 196X–197X* (2010), *Domesticity at War* (2007), *Privacy and Publicity: Modern Architecture as Mass Media* (1994), and *Sexuality and Space* (1992).

Coutin, Raphaël
Raphaël Coutin is a social designer and researcher. He graduated from the Design Academy Eindhoven in 2014, and now works as an independent design studio. Fascinated by abandoned buildings and observing the life cycle of building material, he sees design intervention as the new way forward. This entails reassembling of the elements at hand, readdressing previous design solutions, and repurposing. Coutin is a member of Fictional Collective, an international body of designers, researchers, artists, and writers. The collective works as a strategic agency to engage and confront design implications in specific geographical contexts. It generates new perspectives, critical dialogues, and tangible outcomes, from publications to installations.

Dalziel, Robyn
Robyn Dalziel has translated numerous Dutch books on art and architecture over the years, including the last

nineteen editions of the *Architecture in the Netherlands Yearbook* (nai010 publishers). She has translated website content for Dutch architects and numerous articles on art and architecture for a wide variety of clients. Robyn is also an experienced copy editor, having worked in that capacity for the magazines *Archis* and *A10 new European architecture*, as well as on books such as *Skins for Buildings: The Architect's Materials Sample Book* (BIS Publishers), *Reclaiming (the Urbanism of) Mumbai* (SUN), and *Workplaces Today* by Juriaan van Meel.

Erez, Tal
Tal Erez is a designer and researcher who explores issues of political change, institutional critique, and contemporary forms of resistance. He has exhibited internationally with the Israeli Pavilion exhibition at the Venice Architecture Biennale in 2012, Droog Design, and Z33 House for Contemporary Art in Hasselt, among others. He is a research fellow at Het Nieuwe Instituut, Rotterdam, where he curated the exhibition *Plastic, Promises of a Home-made Future*. In addition, he is curator of the Jerusalem Design Week. Erez holds degrees from the Holon Institute of Technology, Israel, and the Design Academy Eindhoven. He teaches Design and Architecture at the Bezalel Academy of Arts and Design in Jerusalem.

Experimental Jetset
Experimental Jetset is a small, independent and Amsterdam-based graphic design studio, founded in 1997 by (and still comprising) Marieke Stolk, Erwin Brinkers, and Danny van den Dungen. Focusing on printed matter and site-specific installations, and describing their methodology as "turning language into objects," Experimental Jetset have worked on projects for a wide variety of institutes. Their work has also been featured in group exhibitions such as *Graphic Design: Now in Production* (Walker Art Center, 2011) and *Ecstatic Alphabets / Heaps of Language* (MoMA, 2012). In 2007, a large selection of work by Experimental Jetset was acquired by the Museum of Modern Art in New York, for inclusion in its permanent collection.

EventArchitectuur
EventArchitectuur is an architecture/design office that tries not to define its style. It deliberately aims to make the outcome of its projects a result of the interactions of the different participants in the design process. The office recognizes its dependence on the know-how of so many experts (clients, designers, advisers, and builders), and endeavors to include these within the design team.

It attempts to do this by starting from scratch with every new assignment, addressing things that are new for the office. With every assignment it looks for the right form of organization and realization. Being connected with different (design) disciplines makes it easy for EventArchitectuur to form the appropriate team.

One could say that EventArchitectuur is an empty shell, to be filled with the necessary knowledge to make the right product or project. The office name serves as a focal point for clients and participants alike. EventArchitectuur communicates not through style or a personal signature from a master designer, but with the way it thinks about space.

It defines space as a three-dimensional organization of light, sound, and movement. Architecture in this definition becomes the temporary stopping of certain processes (matter) to organize other processes (time). Designing, then, is to make this snapshot of space that can last five minutes, but also fifteen years, depending on the assignment.

It is no wonder that, especially in the cultural sector, EventArchitectuur has found very interesting clients who dared to long for the new, the not-yet-existing. From day one, it designed the *mise-en-scène* for the Paris fashion shows of SO by alexander van slobbe, and eventually came to design the shops for SO in Japan. Different museums have commissioned it for exhibitions on design, fashion, and art (Stedelijk Museum Amsterdam, Centraal Museum Utrecht, Vormgevingsinstituut Amsterdam, etc.). Artists and actors have requested the restyling or reshaping of their newly bought properties and the design of their new houses. Both small and large events, as well as self-initiated projects, have been exposed to a crowd of culture lovers and beyond.

Guldemond, Bart
Bart Guldemond founded his practice in 1987. The spatial context plays a crucial role in his work, both in the fields of exhibition and furniture design, as well as, for example, in the *mise-en-scène* of the fashion shows for SO by alexander van slobbe in Paris. Between 1996 and 2006 Guldemond was a design teacher at the Design Academy Eindhoven. In 2009, he founded B29 Studio's with a group of his first students. In recent years, his work has developed towards architectural projects, such as the realization of the RSVP house, a prize-winning design concept for self builders, which he developed in collaboration with Joost Grootens. Together with artist Papa Adama, he is working on the Artist House, an artists' residency and children's education center in Ouagadougou, Burkina Faso.

Hauhart, Dutton R.
Dutton R. Hauhart is known under the name Reitz Ink. He graduated *cum laude* from the University of Amsterdam with a master's in art history, Dutch Art in European Context, with a thesis on identity in architectural and cultural theory. Reitz Ink is specialized in editing, proofreading, (copy)writing, and criticism in the English language. Reitz Ink works for clients and projects primarily in the areas of architecture, art, design, music, academia, and culture, and has become a household name for the Stedelijk Museum Amsterdam and Roma Publications, among others.

Havik, Klaske
Klaske Havik is associate professor of architecture, Methods & Analysis, at TU Delft and visiting professor at Tampere University of Technology, Finland. She has developed a distinct research approach relating architectural and urban questions to literary language. Her book, *Urban Literacy: Reading and Writing Architecture* (2014), based upon her PhD research, proposes a literary approach to architecture and urbanism. Other publications include *Writingplace, Investigations in Architecture and Literature* (2016). Havik is editor of *OASE Journal for Architecture* and her literary work has appeared in Dutch poetry collections and literary magazines. For her contributions to the architectural debate, Havik received the Dutch Architect of the Year Award in 2014.

Heuvel, Dirk van den
Dirk van den Heuvel graduated as an architect from TU Delft, where he is currently associate professor with an expertise in the field of postwar modern architecture. He is also head of the Jaap Bakema Study Centre at Het Nieuwe Instituut, Rotterdam, editor of *DASH* (nai010 publishers), and editor of the online journal *Footprint*. In 2014, he was curator of the Dutch Pavilion at the Venice Architecture Biennale.

Kleijn, Koen
Koen Kleijn is an art historian, journalist, documentary filmmaker, and writer. He regularly publishes articles on art and architecture in *De Groene Amsterdammer, Art in America, Museumtijdschrift*, and *AVRO Kunst and Cultuur*. Kleijn teaches at the Design Academy Eindhoven and the Gerrit Rietveld Academie, Amsterdam.

Kuipers, Paul
Paul Kuipers graduated in 2001 from the department OK5 / Visual Arts and Public Space at ArtEZ University of the Arts in Arnhem. From 2001 to 2003 he was part of the threesome mark&mark&paul, undertaking research-related art projects within urban planning. Subsequently, in 2003, he started working at EventArchitectuur. Kuipers will graduate from the Academy of Architecture in Amsterdam in 2017. Meanwhile, he collaborates with artist Jonas Staal on his art-politics projects, like *Allegories of Good and Bad Government* and the *New World Summits*.

Landstra & De Vries
Landstra & De Vries is Bouwko Landstra and Alko de Vries, who have been working together since 1997. Since 2002, they have operated under the company name Landstra & De Vries. They specialize in the planning, building, and arrangement of exhibitions. The firm focuses on creating artworks, prototypes, interiors, models, mock-ups, and displays, and does work for

the Stedelijk Museum Amsterdam, Het Nieuwe Instituut, Eye Film Institute, and the Centraal Museum in Utrecht, among others. From its very beginnings, Landstra & De Vries has collaborated with EventArchitectuur.

Maher, Gabriel A.
Gabriel A. Maher graduated in 2014 from the Design Academy Eindhoven with a master's in Social Design. Maher's graduation project was awarded with the Gijs Bakker Award and a Keep an Eye Foundation Grant. Maher's practice is essentially focused on relationships between body and structure, with an interest in objects and systems. Questioning design practices through queer and feminist frameworks has become a core position and approach for Maher. Until 2012, Maher practiced and taught interior architecture and design in Sydney and Melbourne, Australia. Now living in Eindhoven, last year Maher became a recipient of a Creative Industries Fund Development Grant for the Netherlands.

Makkink, Rianne
Rianne Makkink graduated as an architect from TU Delft in 1990. A year later she founded MAX.1 (currently MAXWAN architects and urbanists), where she was director for ten years. Together with designer Jurgen Bey she founded Studio Makkink & Bey, in 2002. The studio works in various domains of applied art and includes public space projects, product design, architecture, exhibition design, and applied arts. Their ambition is to push the role of the designer, expanding it to the most strategic function possible. With Studio Makkink & Bey, she has been awarded, among other things, the Prins Bernhard Cultuurfonds Award in 2005, and Iconic Awards 2015, "Best of the Best" in category interior for the project Dexter & Sinister Orléans. Since 2011, Makkink has been a tutor at the Master Social Design at Design Academy Eindhoven.

Mellegers, Ernie
Ernie Mellegers studied History of Art at Leiden University. He wrote his thesis on the influence of the car on the French architect Le Corbusier. He lectures at a variety of universities, academies, and other institutions on a wide range of subjects related to architecture and urbanism, both historical and theoretical. The focus of his research and publications has remained the influence of the machine, especially the car, on modern architecture and urbanism. Passionate about the subject, he is known for his intensive lectures that explore a vast area of knowledge, and which are not necessarily meant to be remembered in detail, but instead intend to paint a picture and "spark your thoughts."

Meroz, Joana
Joana Meroz is a Design Cultures PhD candidate at the Vrije Universiteit Amsterdam. Her doctoral research focuses on the intersection of international cultural politics, new materialism, and museology. She has published in *The Journal of Design History, The Design Journal, Dutch Crossing: Journal of Low Countries Studies, Kunstforum*, and *Design History Netherlands*, has contributed chapters to the *Routledge Companion to Design Studies* (2016) and various exhibition catalogues, and is guest co-editor of the *Journal of Design History* special issue, "Beyond Dutch Design: Material Culture in the Netherlands in an Age of Globalization, Migration and Multiculturalism" (2016).

Mik, Edzard
Edzard Mik has written nine novels, including *De Bouwmeester* (1995), *Schaduwdagen* (1998), *Laatste adem* (2001), *De Wachters* (2004) and *Bleke Hemel* (2007). His most recent novels, *Goede tijden* (2011) and *Mont Blanc* (2013) were longlisted for the Libris Literature Prize. Mik has written reflections on art, architecture, literature, and theater for the newspapers *Vrij Nederland* and *NRC Handelsblad*. In 2010, he was commissioned by the Foundation for Visual Arts, Design, and Architecture (now the Mondriaan Fund) to write an essay on the CCTV Headquarters in Beijing by OMA. Since 2015, Mik is the editor of *De Gids*, the oldest and most widely read literary magazine in the Netherlands.

Muñoz, Lucas
Lucas Muñoz graduated in 2005 as a product designer from Istituto Europeo di Design, Madrid, and Central Saint

Martins, London. A year later, together with his friend David Tamame, he founded enPieza! eStudio in Madrid. In 2011, he was acknowledged for the design career category of Spain's national creativity youth awards. Since 2012, Muñoz has worked on his own in the Netherlands, using humor and rawness as tools. His body of work includes a wide range of typologies that span from boats, skateboards, and speakers, to chairs and lamps. In 2014, he graduated from the Design Academy Eindhoven with a master's in Contextual Design.

Patteeuw, Véronique
Véronique Patteeuw is an engineer architect, critic, and editor. She is an associate professor at the Ecole Nationale Supérieure d'Architecture et du Paysage Lille and lectures at the FRAC Orléans, among others. From 2001 to 2010 she directed architectural publications for NAi Publishers (now nai010 publishers) in Rotterdam, and has been one of the editors of *OASE Journal for Architecture* since 2005. Patteeuw recently finalized a doctoral research project entitled "Architects without architecture" at ENSA Paris-Malaquais and is currently co-editing a volume on the role of the architectural media in shaping postmodern architecture (Routledge, 2017). She develops architectural projects at Studio SNCDA together with Sara Noel Costa de Araujo.

Schwartz, Johannes
Johannes Schwartz studied photography at Gerrit Rietveld Academie in Amsterdam. From 2004 until 2010 he was head of the photography department of the Rietveld Academie, at which he still currently teaches. Schwartz initiated an ongoing succession of publications in collaboration with graphic designers Experimental Jetset. The series launched in 2003, published on the occasion of a group exhibition that took place at Centraal Museum, Utrecht. Schwartz was one of the participating artists in *Opera Aperta/ Loose Work*, the official Dutch entry at the Venice Biennale in 2011. His awards include the Esther Kroon Award (1998) and the Cobra Kunstprijs Amstelveen (2007).

Seijdel, Jorinde
Jorinde Seijdel is an independent writer, editor, lecturer, adviser, and art theorist. She is editor-in-chief of *Open! Platform on Art, Culture & the Public Domain* (www.onlineopen.org) and has contributed articles to many different publications, mostly on subjects concerned with the topic of art and media in the developing society and its public sphere. Currently, Seijdel is theory mentor and head of the Studium Generale at the Gerrit Rietveld Academie in Amsterdam. With *Open!* she is a partner of the Dutch Art Institute MA Art Praxis (DAI) at ArtEZ University of the Arts in Arnhem.

Sloom.org
Sloom.org was founded in 2002 by Rianne Makkink and Herman Verkerk with the aim to initiate activities that express a reconsideration of architecture and urban and landscape design, no longer from a critical distance but with a direct method of intervention. Since the discussion of "high" and "low" culture has been taken over by the discussion about "fast" and "slow," sloom.org embraces the potential of "slowness." Sloom.org would like to start over by showing the importance of moderation rather than acceleration, and how locality and diversity are more important than globalization and standardization. The activities of sloom.org are documented through a magazine and website of the same name.

Shafrir, Tamar
Tamar Shafrir is a writer and designer. She researches design as part of the R&D team at Het Nieuwe Instituut and teaches at the Design Academy Eindhoven and Sandberg Institute in Amsterdam. Her writing has been published in magazines such as *Domus, Abitare, Volume, Disegno, Dirty Furniture,* and *MacGuffin*, and in books such as *Adhocracy* (Istanbul Design Biennial), *Designing Everyday Life* (BIO 50), *Konstantin Grcic – Panorama, Printing Things*, and *Symbolic Exchange*. In addition, she is one of the co-founders of Space Caviar, a design research studio in Genoa, Italy.

Sijmons, Dirk
Dirk Sijmons studied architecture at TU Delft. He was one of three founders of H+N+S Landscape Architects in 1990,

with which he remains associated as a consultant. Sijmons was awarded the Rotterdam Maaskant Prize in 2002; the book *Landkaartmos en andere beschouwingen over het landschap* was published on this occasion. In addition, Sijmons has numerous other titles to his name. He was appointed the first Rijksadviseur (Government Advisor) on Landscape in 2004, and in 2007 he received the prestigious Edgar Doncker Prize for his contribution to "authentic Dutch culture." Sijmons also curated IABR 2014 – *Urban by Nature* at the Kunsthal in Rotterdam. Until 2015 he was professor of landscape architecture at TU Delft.

Slobbe, Alexander van
Alexander van Slobbe studied fashion design at ArtEZ University of the Arts in Arnhem. There he became interested in the minimalist school of Dutch architecture and design, and began applying these principles to his fashion design. In 1989, he introduced his women's line, orson + bodil. The men's label SO by alexander van slobbe was developed in 1993. In 2003, SO was sold and Van Slobbe was able to concentrate again on orson + bodil, as well as on ongoing collaborations with companies like Royal Tichelaar Makkum. In recent years, Van Slobbe has been involved as guest curator of different design exhibitions in the Netherlands and abroad, including at Het Nieuwe Instituut, Rotterdam. Van Slobbe has received numerous awards, such as the Theo Limperg Prize for Best Industrial Design and the Prins Bernhard Cultuurfonds Award.

Steenbergen, Renée
Renée Steenbergen is an independent advisor, researcher, journalist, and curator on private collecting and arts philanthropy. She is a senior research fellow for Arts Philanthropy at Utrecht University. Parallel to this, she is the owner of a consultancy office, bureau Renée Steenbergen, that advises arts organizations about strategies to stimulate individual giving. Renée is also a consultant to private collectors and donors who intend to support the arts. She has organized several exhibitions about private collections of modern and Asian art and published extensively on the subject. Her PhD thesis focused on modern art collectors. In 2008, her book *The New Patron: Culture and the Return of Private Money* was published by Business Contact, Amsterdam, as a result of her continuing research on Arts Philanthropy.

Stricker, Eva
Eva Stricker studied architecture at TU Berlin and ETH Zürich. Since her graduation, she has worked for von Ballmoos Krucker Architekten, Zürich, and started her own architectural projects. Since 2009, she has worked for Staufer & Hasler Architekten, Frauenfeld, as project manager on two cinema projects, as well as on several competitions and urban studies. Stricker has contributed to several journalistic publications, such as the magazine *Werk, Bauen und Wohnen*.

Teufel, Philipp
Philipp Teufel studied visual communications at the HfG Schwäbisch Gmünd. Since 1994, he has been working as a professor for Communication Design at the Design Faculty of the Düsseldorf University of Applied Sciences and Arts, focusing on exhibiting and media-specific visualization. He is co-head of edi, the Exhibition Design Institute. Philipp was a member of the nowakteufelknyrim studio association in Düsseldorf from 1995 until 2007. Since 2008, he has been sharing the malsyteufel studio with Victor Malsy in Willich. Philip curates, plans, and designs exhibitions and museums, as well as guidance and orientation systems.

Tschumi, Bernard
Bernard Tschumi is an architect based in New York and Paris. First known as a theorist, he exhibited and published *The Manhattan Transcripts* and wrote *Architecture and Disjunction*, a series of theoretical essays. Major built works include the Parc de la Villette, the New Acropolis Museum, Le Fresnoy Center for the Contemporary Arts, and MuséoParc Alésia. Tschumi has been awarded France's Grand Prix National d'Architecture in 1996, as well as numerous awards from the American Institute of Architects. He was Dean of the Graduate School of Architecture, Planning, and Preservations of Columbia University in New York from 1988–2003, where he is currently a professor.

His drawings and models are in the collections of several major museums, including MoMA in New York and the Centre Pompidou in Paris.

Verkerk, Herman
Herman Verkerk trained as an architect at TU Delft and ETH Zürich, and in 1990 formed EventArchitectuur, a design firm for time- and experience-based architecture. Since then, he has collaborated with different partners on projects ranging from fashion shows, public and private interiors, cultural events, and festivals, to exhibitions and installations on contemporary culture and a series of landscape parks. Verkerk has taught design and architecture at TU Delft, ArtEZ University of the Arts in Arnhem, Design Academy Eindhoven, and Fachhochschule Düsseldorf. Currently he is head of the department for Interior Architecture and Furniture Design at the Royal Academy of Art in The Hague and co-head of the temporary master Materialization in Art and Design at the Sandberg Institute in Amsterdam.

colophon

Events:
Situating the Temporary,
by Herman Verkerk/
EventArchitectuur

Contributors:
Andreas Angelidakis, Claudia Banz, Ellen Blumenstein, Beatriz Colomina, Brendan Cormier, Raphaël Coutin, Robyn Dalziel (translations), Bonnie Dumanaw, Tal Erez, Bart Guldemond, Klaske Havik, Dirk van den Heuvel, Anne Hoogewoning, Koen Kleijn, Paul Kuipers, Landstra & De Vries, Gabriel A. Maher, Rianne Makkink, Ernie Mellegers, Joana Meroz, Edzard Mik, Lucas Muñoz, Ingrid Oosterheerd (credits), Véronique Patteeuw, Johannes Schwartz, Jorinde Seijdel, Tamar Shafrir, Alexander van Slobbe, Renée Steenbergen, Eva Stricker, Dirk Sijmons, Philipp Teufel, Bernard Tschumi, Sonja Wesseler (index)

Graphic design:
Experimental Jetset, Amsterdam
Photography:
Cover, EA Archive Boxes, and EA Materials by Johannes Schwartz
Image editor:
Experimental Jetset
Editor for EventArchitectuur:
Dutton R. Hauhart, Reitz Ink, Amsterdam
Editor for the publisher:
Andreas Müller, Berlin
Production:
EventArchitectuur with AB Cultural Producers
Printing:
drukkerij Tienkamp, Groningen
Paper:
Cyclus, 80 gram
Duplex, 300 gram

This publication was made possible thanks to the generous support of the Creative Industries Fund NL.

creative industries fund NL

Library of Congress Cataloging-in-Publication data /
A CIP catalog record for this book has been applied for at the Library of Congress /

Bibliographic information published by the German National Library /
The German National Library lists this publication in the Deutsche Nationalbibliografie; detailed bibliographic data are available on the Internet at http://dnb.dnb.de.

EventArchitectuur
Van Diemenstraat 412, 1013 CR
Amsterdam, the Netherlands

1st edition, 1,500 copies

P.O. Box 44, 4009 Basel, Switzerland
Part of Walter de Gruyter GmbH, Berlin/Boston

Printed on acid-free paper produced from chlorine-free pulp.

Printed in the Netherlands.

ISBN 978-3-0356-1020-8

9 8 7 6 5 4 3 2 1
www.birkhauser.com

1990

1995

2000

2005

2010

1

2

3

4

5

events: situating the temporary – table of contents

1990

1995

2000

2005

2010

1 2 3 4 5

1990

1995

2000

2005

2010

1

2

3

4

5

E V
E N
T S
EA

EA

E V

E N

T S

EA

EVENTS

E

V E

N T S

EA

E V E
N T
S
EA